SPORTS AND PASTIMES

Artist's Illustrators. 89.

Joseph Strutt, 1749-1802.
From the Portrait in the National Portrait Gallery.

THE SPORTS AND PASTIMES OF THE PEOPLE OF ENGLAND

FROM THE EARLIEST PERIOD, INCLUDING THE
RURAL AND DOMESTIC RECREATIONS, MAY
GAMES, MUMMERIES, PAGEANTS, PROCES-
SIONS AND POMPOUS SPECTACLES,
ILLUSTRATED BY REPRODUCTIONS
FROM ANCIENT PAINTINGS IN
WHICH ARE REPRESENTED
MOST OF THE POPULAR
DIVERSIONS

BY

JOSEPH STRUTT

1801

A NEW EDITION, MUCH ENLARGED AND CORRECTED BY
J. CHARLES COX, LL.D., F.S.A.

WITH A PREFACE TO THE 1969 EDITION BY
NORRIS McWHIRTER M.A.(Oxon)

ROSS McWHIRTER M.A.(Oxon)

" One should make a serious study of a pastime."—*Alexander the Great*

AUGUSTUS M. KELLEY · PUBLISHERS
NEW YORK 1970

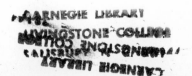

Previously published 1903
Published in the United States by

Augustus M. Kelley · Publishers

New York, New York 10001

SBN 678 08014 3

LC 76 111201

Printed by Redwood Press Limited
Trowbridge & London
Printed in Great Britain

PREFACE TO 1969 EDITION

Joseph Strutt's *Sports and Pastimes of the People of England*, first published in 1801, is a classic reference work which can be relied upon as an excellent starting point for all but the most minute investigations into many of the sports that the world plays today.

This remarkable Englishman who lived in Essex, London and Hertfordshire from 1749 to 1802 was artistic, scholarly and industrious.

This book pioneered the study of popular recreations and amusements as a whole. Strutt mined his information the hard way from the books, manuscripts and illustrations housed in his beloved British Museum in London.

Joseph Strutt was that comparative rarity of the 18th century – the social historian. In his youth however his interests centred on the high and the mighty, as witness his *The Regal and Ecclesiastical Antiquities of England (1773)* but gradually his interests turned towards ordinary people and their customs, their behaviour, and their dress; and so, quite logically, to what they did with their leisure.

In these days when the practice and teaching of sport is a major part of school life the world over and about one page in five of the world's newspapers are given over to the reporting of contests in at least 100 international sports or games, the possession and the study of a copy of Strutt's great work is highly rewarding.

England is fairly and rightly regarded as the "cradle of sport". Joseph Strutt showed how the very egg of play was fertilized by the spirit of competition. Organized, sport only came into its own sixty years after his death with the advent of the half working day on Saturdays.

Sports and Pastimes was an immediate publishing success. It was republished thrice during the 19th century and in 1903 J. Charles Fox revised and added with a skilled touch to Strutt's original work to produce this best and most valuable edition of them all.

London 1969   NORRIS & ROSS McWHIRTER

PREFACE TO 1903 EDITION

IN bringing out a new edition of "Sports and Pastimes," it will probably be of interest to put on record a few facts with regard to the author, who has a fair claim to be ranked among the distinguished literary men of the close of the eighteenth century.

Joseph Strutt, engraver, artist, antiquary and author, was born at Chelmsford in 1749.[1] His father, a wealthy miller, died the year after his birth. He was educated at the Chelmsford Grammar School, and apprenticed at the age of fourteen to the engraver, William Wynne Ryland. In 1770 he became a student of the Royal Academy, and in the following year secured both the gold and silver medals, the former for oil painting and the latter "for the best Academy figure." In the summer of 1771 he was employed by a gentleman to make some drawings for him from British Museum MSS. This gave the direction to his subsequent life's work, and he resolved to devote himself to the study of mediæval social England. In 1773 Joseph Strutt produced his first work, "The Regal and Ecclesiastical Antiquities of England," drawing and engraving the whole of the plates, and at the same time producing letter-press that bore witness to the breadth and accuracy of his reading. This is also true of all his subsequent works; considering the almost entire absence of genuine works of reference at that period, his books are marvels of careful research. Between 1774 and 1746 he published the three volumes of "Manners, Customs, Arms, Habits, etc., of the People of England," and in 1777-8 two volumes of "Chronicle of England," all of them being in large 4to and profusely illustrated. From this date he for some years gave his attention to painting, and exhibited nine pictures in the Royal Academy, which were chiefly classical subjects. In 1785 Mr Strutt published the first volume of his "Dictionary of Engravers"; the second volume appeared in the following year. Continued asthma caused him to leave London in 1790, and whilst residing in a county village of Hertfordshire, he produced a series of engravings for Bradford's edition of the Pilgrim's Progress. With the improvement of his health in 1795 Strutt returned to London, and resumed his favourite researches at the British Museum. In 1796-1799 he brought out his valuable work on "Dresses and Habits of the English People." This was followed in 1801 by the most popular of all his books, "Sports and Pastimes of the People of England," "a performance," says his son, "which, from the novelty of the subject, attracted the notice and admiration of readers of almost every class." In 1802 he died, when he had nearly com-

---

[1] This brief sketch of the literary life of Joseph Strutt is taken, in the main, from a short biography contributed by his elder son to Nichols' *Literary Anecdotes*.

pleted "a legendary romance," intended to illustrate the usages and domestic manners of the fifteenth century, to which he gave the name of "Queenhoo Hall." A very special interest attaches to this posthumous work. After Strutt's death the incomplete manuscript was placed by John Murray in the hands of Walter Scott, who added the concluding chapter. It was published in four small volumes in 1808. In the general preface to the Waverley notes, written by Sir Walter Scott in 1829, acknowledgment is made by the great romance writer of his indebtedness to Joseph Strutt. Although "Queenhoo Hall" was not a success, in consequence of its appealing only to antiquaries through being overloaded with details, Scott acknowledges that Waverley would never have been completed, and his initial triumph won, had he not been called upon to edit Strutt's tale. Even if Strutt had no special merit of his own, he is well deserving of a niche in the temple of literary fame as the foster-parent of the immortal series of Waverley novels.

When, however, any reflective person, more particularly the English mediæval antiquary or historian, studies the writings and illustrations of Joseph Strutt, he cannot fail to realise that he was a laborious and conscientious worker in a hitherto unexplored vein of literary research, and possessed a remarkable power of assimilating a vast store of material. Somewhat shallow or inconsiderate folk from time to time indulge in sneers at the mistakes or inaccuracies in certain points of a writer who toiled a century ago ; they do not reflect on the remarkable accumulation of valuable works of reference during the nineteenth century, absolutely unknown in the days when Joseph Strutt was a British Museum reader, or on the present far greater accessibility of public records and similar documents. Strutt was the pioneer in almost every branch of English mediæval archæology, and as such is entitled to the respect of every antiquary.

With regard to "Sports and Pastimes," this, the most popular of all his works, was originally published in quarto in 1801. The numerous plates were hand coloured in the majority of the issues ; but were evidently drawn by the author with sufficient care to be produced without any colouring adjunct. Indeed, from the style of the drawings it is debatable whether the colouring was not an afterthought of the publisher. It may safely be asserted that Joseph Strutt had nothing whatever to do with the colouring. He was ill at the time the work was produced, and died shortly afterwards. Though in the main an engraver, it will be recollected that Strutt was himself a colourist and won his first Academy medal by an oil painting. His son states of his first work, "The Regal and Ecclesiastical Antiquities of England," that the plates of part of the impression were coloured in order to make them more nearly resemble the originals. But whoever was responsible for treating a large number of the copies of "Sports and Pastimes" in a like fashion never took the trouble to even glance at the originals, but simply dipped the brush into whatever colour caprice suggested, with a result that is sometimes comical in its extravagance and sometimes false in its facts. An ape painted brilliant green is an example of the one, whilst the same coat of arms appearing twice on the same plate in quite different tinctures is an example of the other. After collating five coloured copies of the first edition, with the more important MSS. of the British Museum which furnished Strutt with his illustrations, it was found that each one differed absolutely in colours from the actual pictures. The primary intention of giving coloured plates in this edition was therefore abandoned, more particularly as the drawings from some of the most frequently used manuscripts are not definitely coloured in the originals, but merely tinted here and there with a delicate wash.

The decision to take this course was confirmed, when it was found that the work was reissued in 1810, with the plates printed in a uniform terra-cotta shade as reproduced in the current volume. The 1810 edition was in slightly larger and much superior type to that of 1801, and it is thought that the type now used will favourably compare with it.

"A Set of Humorous and Descriptive Illustrations in Twenty-one Engravings, by Stephenhoff and others, of the Sports and Pastimes of the People of England, from Paintings of the XVII. and XVIII. Century, in continuation of Joseph Strutt's," was issued in 1816; but they are vulgar in subject, poor in style, and quite unworthy to be associated with any work of Strutt's.

That enterprising cheap publisher, William Hone, reprinted "Sports and Pastimes" in octavo, in 1830, with rough cuts in the letterpress in lieu of the plates. This octavo edition, nearly identical in letterpress with the original, was reproduced in 1837, in 1841, and again in 1875.

This is, however, the first time that any endeavour has been made to bring out a new edition of Mr Strutt's great and entertaining work. In producing this largely revised edition, Mr Strutt has been left for the most part to speak in his own characteristic fashion and out of his own store of learning. A few obvious mistakes and rash conclusions have been corrected, whilst now and again certain unimportant omissions have been made. It is peculiarly difficult in a work of this kind to decide on the best plan and arrangement; but Mr Strutt's scheme of dividing sports and pastimes into four books descriptive of "Rural Exercises practised by Persons of Rank," "Rural Exercises generally practised," "Pastimes usually exercised in Towns and Cities," and "Domestic Amusements"—each book being sub-divided into chapters—has been followed. In one or two cases a slight rearrangement has taken place; such, for instance, as bringing together the descriptions of bear and bull baiting, and the scattered references to dancing.

Nearly a third of the book is new. To the paragraphs for which the Editor is responsible a small asterisk is prefixed.

It was found necessary to rewrite almost the whole of the chapter dealing with cricket, golf, tennis, football, and other ball games. There is also much that is new with regard to archery, wrestling, and the hunting of wolves and boars.

No attempt has been made to bring the book generally up to date, or to turn it into an encyclopædia of sports, ancient and modern. Many volumes would be required for such a purpose, and they are already to be found in the admirable Badminton series. At the same time, brief indications are given of the growth and change in sports and pastimes during the nineteenth century, together with references to the best modern sources as to their respective methods.

It is interesting to reflect upon the simply astounding change that has come over all classes of the community with regard to games during the hundred years that have elapsed since Joseph Strutt first wrote upon the subject. Whether the extraordinary devotion of the English of the present generation to every conceivable kind of sport and pastime is a sign of national decay or of national progress is not a matter for discussion in these pages, which merely aim at being a true chronicle of the past.

J. CHARLES COX

CLYDE LODGE,
SYDENHAM, *May* 1903

CONTENTS

INTRODUCTION

A GENERAL ARRANGEMENT OF THE POPULAR SPORTS, PASTIMES, AND MILITARY GAMES, TOGETHER WITH THE VARIOUS SPECTACLES OF MIRTH OR SPLENDOUR, EXHIBITED PUBLICLY OR PRIVATELY, FOR THE SAKE OF AMUSEMENT, AT DIFFERENT PERIODS IN ENGLAND.

BOOK I

RURAL EXERCISES PRACTISED BY PERSONS OF RANK

CHAPTER I

CHAPTER II

CHAPTER III

ix

BOOK II

RURAL EXERCISES GENERALLY PRACTISED

CHAPTER I

BOOK III

PASTIMES USUALLY EXERCISED IN TOWNS AND CITIES, OR PLACES ADJOINING TO THEM

CHAPTER I

CONTENTS

The British Bards—The Northern Scalds—The Anglo-Saxon Gleemen—The Nature of their Performances—A Royal Player with three Darts—Bravery of a Minstrel in the Conqueror's Army—Other Performances by Gleemen—The Harp an Instrument of Music much used by the Saxons—Harpers at Durham—The Norman Minstrels, and their different Denominations and Professions—Troubadours—Jestours—Tales and Manners of the Jesters—Further Illustration of their Practices—Patronage, Privileges, and Excesses of the Minstrels —A Guild of Minstrels—Abuses and Decline of Minstrelsy—Minstrels were Satirists and Flatterers—Anecdotes of offending Minstrels, Women Minstrels—The Dress of the Minstrels—The King of the Minstrels, why so called—Rewards given to Minstrels—Payments to Minstrels—Durham Minstrels and Players—Minstrels at Parish Festivals 148-166

CHAPTER IV

The Joculator—His different Denominations and extraordinary Deceptions—His Performances ascribed to Magic —Asiatic Jugglers—Remarkable Story from Froissart—Tricks of the Jugglers ascribed to the Agency of the Devil; but more reasonably accounted for—John Rykell, a celebrated Tregetour—Their various Perform-ances—Privileges of the Joculators at Paris—The King's Joculator an officer of Rank—The great Disrepute of modern Jugglers 167-173

CHAPTER V

Dancing, Tumbling, and Balancing, part of the Joculator's Profession—Performed by Women—Dancing connected with Tumbling—Antiquity of Tumbling—Various Dances described—The Gleemen's Dances—Exemplifica-tion of Gleemen's Dances—The Sword Dance—Rope-Dancing and wonderful Performances on the Rope—Rope-Dancing from the Battlements of St Paul's—Rope-Dancing from St Paul's Steeple—Rope-Dancing from All Saint's Church, Hertford—Rope-Dancing from All Saint's, Derby—A Dutchman's Feats on St Paul's Weathercock—Jacob Hall the Rope-Dancer—Modern celebrated Rope-Dancing—Rope-Dancing at Sadler's Wells—Fool's Dance—Morris Dance—Egg Dance—Ladder Dance—Jocular Dances—Wire-Dancing—Ballette Dances—Leaping and Vaulting—Balancing—Remarkable Feats—The Posture-Master's Tricks—The Mountebank—Domestic Dancing—The Pavone—Antiquity of Dancing—The Carole Dance . 174-194

CHAPTER VI

Animals, how tutored by the Jugglers—Tricks performed by Bears—Tricks performed by Apes and Monkeys—Bears in Britain—Tricks by Horses in the thirteenth Century—In Queen Anne's Reign—Origin of the Exhibitions at Astley's, the Circus, etc.—Dancing Dogs—The Hare beating a Tabor, and learned Pig—A Dancing Cock—The Deserter Bird—Imitations of Animals—Mummings and Masquerades—Mumming to Royal Personages—Partial Imitations of Animals—The Horse in the Morris-dance—Counterfeit Voices of Animals—Animals trained for Baiting—Paris Garden—Bull and Bear-baiting patronised by Royalty—How performed—Bears and Bear-wards—Baiting in Queen Anne's time—Recent Bull-baiting—Bull-running at Tutbury and Stamford—The Masters of Defence—Pepys on Prize-play—Public Sword-play—Quarter-staff 195-215

CHAPTER VII

Ancient Specimens of Bowling—Poem on Bowling—Bowling-greens first made by the English—Bowling-alleys—Long-bowling—Gaming at Bowls—Charles I. and Charles II. fond of Bowls—Supposed Origin of Billiards —Kayles — Closh — Loggats — Nine-pins — Skittles — Dutch-pins—Four-corners—Half-bowl—Nine-holes—Troul in Madame—John Bull—Pitch and Hustle—Cock-fighting—Cock-fighting in nineteenth Century—Throwing at Cocks—Duck-hunting—Squirrel-hunting 216-228

BOOK IV

DOMESTIC AMUSEMENTS OF VARIOUS KINDS; AND PASTIMES APPROPRIATED TO PARTICULAR SEASONS

CHAPTER I

Secular Music fashionable—Ballad-singers encouraged by the Populace—Music Houses—Introduction of the Harpsichord—Origin of Vauxhall—Ranelagh—Sadler's Wells—Marybone Gardens—Operas—Oratorios—Bell-ringing—Its Antiquity—Hand-bells—Burlesque Music—Shovel-board—Billiards—French Billiards—Trucks—Mississipi—The Rocks of Scilly—Shove-groat—Swinging—Tetter-totter—Shuttle-cock . . 229-244

CONTENTS

CHAPTER II

CHAPTER III

CHAPTER IV

LIST OF ILLUSTRATIONS

Plates XIII., XXXVII., XXXVIII., XXXIX. of the original edition are omitted; the first of these is a large picture of a tilting toy copied from a German engraving, the subject of which had been already illustrated on the previous plate; the three last are merely additional examples of "Games Unknown," and are copies of capricious illustrations out of the Bodleian MS. 264, of which no reasonable explanation can be given.

Plates III., IX., X., XI., XXXVI., together with the Frontispiece of this edition, are new, and have been specially prepared for this work.

[An asterisk is prefixed to all the newly written paragraphs throughout the work.]

INTRODUCTION

A GENERAL ARRANGEMENT OF THE POPULAR SPORTS, PASTIMES, AND MILITARY GAMES, TOGETHER WITH THE VARIOUS SPECTACLES OF MIRTH OR SPLENDOUR, EXHIBITED PUBLICLY OR PRIVATELY, FOR THE SAKE OF AMUSEMENT, AT DIFFERENT PERIODS IN ENGLAND.

Object of the Work, to describe the Pastimes and trace their Origin—The Romans in Britain—The Saxons—The Normans—Tournaments and Jousts—Other Sports of the Nobility, and the Citizens and Yeomen—Knightly Accomplishments—Esquireship—Military Sports patronised by the Ladies—Decline of such Exercises and of Chivalry—Military Exercises under Henry the Seventh and under Henry the Eighth—Princely Exercises under James the First—Revival of Learning—Recreations of the Sixteenth Century—Old Sports of the Citizens of London—Modern Pastimes of the Londoners—Cotswold and Cornish Games—Splendour of the ancient Kings and Nobility—Royal and noble Entertainments—Civic Shows—" Merry England "—Setting out of Pageants— Processions of Queen Mary and King Philip of Spain in London—Chester Pageants—Public Shows of the Sixteenth Century—Queen Elizabeth at Kenelworth Castle—The Master of the Revels—Rope-dancing, tutored Animals, and Puppet-shows—Minstrelsy, Bell-ringing, etc.—Baiting of Animals—Pastimes formerly on Sundays—Royal Interference with them—Dice and Cards—Regulation of Gaming for Money by Richard Cœur de Lion, etc.— Statutes against Cards, Ball-play, etc.—Archery succeeded by Bowling—Modern Gambling—Ladies' Pastimes Needle-work—Dancing and Chess-play—Ladies' Recreations in the Fourteenth Century—The Author's Labours —Character of the Engravings.

OBJECT OF THE WORK.—In order to form a just estimation of the character of any particular people, it is absolutely necessary to investigate the Sports and Pastimes most generally prevalent among them. War, policy, and other contingent circumstances, may effectually place men, at different times, in different points of view, but, when we follow them into their retirements, where no disguise is necessary, we are most likely to see them in their true state, and may best judge of their natural dispositions. Unfortunately, all the information that remains respecting the ancient inhabitants of this island is derived from foreign writers partially acquainted with them as a people, and totally ignorant of their domestic customs and amusements ; the silence, therefore, of the contemporary historians on these important subjects leaves us without the power of tracing them with the least degree of certainty ; and as it is my intention, in the following pages, to confine myself as much as possible to positive intelligence, I shall studiously endeavour to avoid all controversial and conjectural arguments. I mean also to treat upon such pastimes only as have been practised in this country ; but as many of them originated on the continent, certain digressions, by way of illustration, must necessarily occur ; these, however, I shall make it my business to render as concise as the nature of the subject will permit them to be.

THE ROMANS IN BRITAIN.—We learn, from the imperfect hints of ancient history, that, when the Romans first invaded Britain, her inhabitants were a bold, active, and warlike people, tenacious of their native liberty, and capable of bearing great fatigue; to which they were probably inured by an early education, and constant pursuit of such amusements as best suited the profession of a soldier; including hunting, running, leaping, swimming, and other exertions requiring strength and agility of body. Perhaps the skill which the natives of Devonshire and Cornwall retain to the present day, in hurling and wrestling, may properly be considered as a vestige of British activity. After the Romans had conquered Britain, they impressed such of the young men as were able to bear arms for foreign service, and enervated the spirit of the people by the importation of their own luxurious manners and habits; so that the latter part of the British history exhibits to our view a slothful and effeminate race of men, totally divested of that martial disposition, and love of freedom, which so strongly marked the character of their progenitors; and their amusements, no doubt, partook of the same weakness and puerility.[1]

THE SAXONS.—The arrival of the Saxons forms a new epoch in the annals of this country. These military mercenaries came professedly to assist the Britons against their incessant tormentors the Picts and the Caledonians; but no sooner had they established their footing in the land, than they invited more of their countrymen to join them, and turning their arms against their wretched employers, became their most dangerous and most inexorable enemies, and in process of time obtained full possession of the largest and best part of the island; whence arose a great change in the form of government, laws, manners, customs, and habits of the people.

The sportive exercises and pastimes practised by the Saxons appear to have been such as were common among the ancient northern nations; and most of them consisted of robust exercises. In an old Chronicle of Norway,[2] we find it recorded of Olaf Tryggeson, a king of that country, that he was stronger and more nimble than any man in his dominions. He could climb up the rock Smalserhorn, and fix his shield upon the top of it; he could walk round the outside of a boat upon the oars, while the men were rowing; he could play with three darts, alternately throwing them in the air, and always kept two of them up, while he held the third in one of his hands; he was ambidexter, and could

[1] *These remarks require some qualification, as the knowledge of the long period of the Roman occupation, as well as of the times immediately preceding their first invasion, have become more accurately known in the last half of the nineteenth century, through careful archæological investigation. The later Celts used gold coinage, cultivated four sorts of grain, practised the crafts of spinning and weaving, melted iron and wrought cunning ornamented work in both iron and bronze; used the flesh of the red deer and the roe for food, and their horns for many a useful purpose; and domesticated the horse, ox, goat and dog. Such a people, as shown by the investigations at Hunsbury Camp, Northampton, and elsewhere, would certainly have some acquaintance with genuine sports and pastimes, little as we may know of their nature. The excavations at Silchester, and more particularly those conducted by the late General Pitt Rivers among the Romanised British villages of Dorset and Wilts, also afford evidence of a superior race, with higher acquirements than was supposed to be the case at the time when these pages were first written, and of their acquaintance with various breeds of dogs.

[2] Pontoppidan's *History of Norway*, p. 248.

cast two darts at once; he excelled all the men of his time in shooting with the bow; and he had no equal in swimming. In one achievement this monarch was outdone by the Anglo-Saxon gleeman, represented on the twenty-first plate, who adds an equal number of balls to those knives or daggers. The Norman minstrel Tallefer, before the commencement of the battle at Hastings, cast his lance into the air three times, and caught it by the head in such a surprising manner, that the English thought it was done by the power of enchantment. Another northern hero, whose name was Kolson, boasts of nine accomplishments in which he was well skilled: "I know," says he, "how to play at chess; I can engrave Runic letters; I am expert at my book; I know how to handle the tools of the smith; I can traverse the snow on skates of wood; I excel in shooting with the bow; I use the oar with facility; I can sing to the harp; and I compose verses."[1] The reader will, I doubt not, anticipate me in my observation, that the acquirements of Kolson indicate a much more liberal education than those of the Norwegian monarch; it must, however, be observed, that Kolson lived in an age posterior to him; and also, that he made a pilgrimage to the Holy Land, which may probably account in great measure for his literary qualifications. Yet, we are well assured that learning did not form any prominent feature in the education of a young nobleman during the Saxon government: it is notorious, that Alfred the Great was twelve years of age before he learned to read; and that he owed his knowledge of letters to accident, rather than to the intention of his tutors. A book adorned with paintings in the hands of his mother attracted his notice, and he expressed his desire to have it; she promised to comply with his request on condition that he learned to read it, which it seems he did; and this trifling incident laid the groundwork of his future scholarship.[2]

Indeed, it is not by any means surprising, under the Saxon government, when the times were generally very turbulent, and the existence of peace exceedingly precarious, and when the personal exertions of the opulent were so often necessary for the preservation of their lives and property, that such exercises as inured the body to fatigue, and biassed the mind to military pursuits, should have constituted the chief part of a young nobleman's education: accordingly, we find that hunting, hawking, leaping, running, wrestling, casting of darts, and other pastimes which necessarily required great exertions of bodily strength, were taught them in their adolescence. These amusements engrossed the whole of their attention, every one striving to excel his fellow; for hardiness, strength, and valour, out-balanced, in the public estimation, the accomplishments of the mind; and therefore literature, which flourishes best in tranquillity and retirement, was considered as a pursuit unworthy the notice of a soldier, and only requisite in the gloomy recesses of the cloister.

Among the vices of the Anglo-Saxons may be reckoned their propensity to

---

[1] Oläi. Worm. Lit. Run. p. 129; Bartholin. p. 420.   [2] Asser. in Vit. Ælfredi.

gaming, and especially with the dice, which they derived from their ancestors; for Tacitus[1] assures us that the ancient Germans would not only hazard all their wealth, but even stake their liberty, upon the turn of the dice; "and he who loses," says the author, "submits to servitude, though younger and stronger than his antagonist, and patiently permits himself to be bound, and sold in the market; and this madness they dignify by the name of honour." Chess was also a favourite game with the Saxons; and likewise backgammon, said to have been invented about the tenth century. It appears moreover, that a large portion of the night was appropriated to the pursuit of these sedentary amusements. In the reign of Canute the Dane, this practice was sanctioned by the example of royalty, and followed by the nobility. Bishop Ætheric, having obtained admission to Canute about midnight upon some urgent business, found the king engaged with his courtiers at play, some at dice, and some at chess.[2] The clergy, however, were prohibited from playing at games of chance, by the ecclesiastical canons established in the reign of Edgar.

THE NORMANS.—The popular sports and pastimes, prevalent at the close of the Saxon era, do not appear to have been subjected to any material change by the coming of the Normans: it is true, indeed, that the elder William and his immediate successors restricted the privileges of the chase, and imposed great penalties on those who presumed to destroy the game in the royal forests, without a proper licence. By these restrictions the general practice of hunting was much confined, but by no means prohibited in certain districts, and especially to persons of opulence who possessed extensive territories of their own.

TOURNAMENTS AND JOUSTS.—Among the pastimes introduced by the Norman nobility, none engaged the general attention more than the tournaments and the jousts. The tournament, in its original institution, was a martial conflict, in which the combatants engaged without any animosity, merely to exhibit their strength and dexterity; but, at the same time, engaged in great numbers to represent a battle. The joust was when two knights, and no more, were opposed to each other at one time. These amusements, in the middle ages, which may properly enough be dominated the ages of chivalry, were in high repute among the nobility of Europe, and produced in reality much of the pomp and gallantry that we find recorded with poetical exaggeration in the legends of knight-errantry. I met with a passage in a satirical poem among the Harleian MSS. of the thirteenth century,[3] which strongly marks the prevalence of this taste in the times alluded to. It may be thus rendered in English:

> "If wealth, sir knight, perchance be thine,
> In tournaments you're bound to shine:
> Refuse—and all the world will swear
> You are not worth a rotten pear."

---

[1] De Moribus Germ.   [2] Hist. Ramsien. apud Gale, vol. i. an. 85.   [3] No. 2253, fol. 108.

OTHER SPORTS OF THE NOBILITY, AND THE CITIZENS AND YEOMEN.—While the principles of chivalry continued in fashion, the education of a nobleman was confined to those principles, and every regulation necessary to produce an accomplished knight was put into practice. In order fully to investigate these particulars, we may refer to the romances of the middle ages; and, generally speaking, dependence may be placed upon their information. The authors of these fictitious histories never looked beyond the customs of their own country; and whenever the subject called for a representation of remote magnificence, they depicted such scenes of splendour as were familiar to them: hence it is, that Alexander the Great, in his legendary life, receives the education of a Norman baron, and becomes expert in hawking, hunting, and other amusements coincident with the time in which the writer lived. Our early poets have fallen into the same kind of anachronism; and Chaucer himself, in the Knight's Tale, speaking of the rich array and furniture of the palace of Theseus, forgets that he was a Grecian prince of great antiquity, and describes the large hall belonging to an English nobleman, with the guests seated at table, probably as he had frequently seen them, entertained with singing, dancing, and other acts of minstrelsy, their hawks being placed upon perches over their heads, and their hounds lying round about upon the pavement below. The two last lines of the poem just referred to are peculiarly applicable to the manners of the time in which the poet lived, when no man of consequence travelled abroad without his hawk and his hounds. In the early delineations, the nobility are frequently represented seated at table, with their hawks upon their heads. Chaucer says,

> " Ne what hawkes sytten on perchen above,
> Ne what houndes lyggen on the flour adoun."

The picture is perfect, when referred to his own time; but bears not the least analogy to Athenian grandeur. In the romance called *The Knight of the Swan*, it is said of Ydain, Duchess of Roulyon, that she caused her three sons to be brought up in " all maner of good operacyons, vertues, and maners; and when in their adolescence they were somwhat comen to the age of strengthe, they," their tutors, " began to practyse them in shootinge with their bow and arbelstre,[1] to playe with the sword and buckeler, to runne, to just, to playe with a poll-axe, and to wrestle; and they began to bear harneys, to runne horses, and to approve them, as desyringe to be good and faythful knightes to susteyne the faith of God." We are not, however, to conceive that martial exercises in general were confined to the education of young noblemen: the sons of citizens and yeomen had also their sports resembling military combats. Those practised at an early period by the young Londoners seem to have been

---

[1] The cross-bow.

derived from the Romans; they consisted of various attacks and evolutions performed on horseback, the youth being armed with shields and pointless lances, resembling the ludus Trojæ, or Troy game, described by Virgil. These amusements, according to Fitz Stephen, who lived in the reign of Henry II., were appropriated to the season of Lent; but at other times they exercised themselves with archery, fighting with clubs and bucklers, and running at the quintain; and in the winter, when the frost set in, they would go upon the ice, and run against each other with poles, in imitation of lances, in a joust; and frequently one or both were beaten down, "not always without hurt; for some break their arms, and some their legs; but youth," says my author, "emulous of glory, seeks these exercises preparatory against the time that war shall demand their presence." The like kind of pastimes, no doubt, were practised by the young men in other parts of the kingdom.

KNIGHTLY ACCOMPLISHMENTS.—The mere management of arms, though essentially requisite, was not sufficient of itself to form an accomplished knight in the times of chivalry; it was necessary for him to be endowed with beauty, as well as with strength and agility of body; he ought to be skilled in music, to dance gracefully, to run with swiftness, to excel in wrestling, to ride well, and to perform every other exercise befitting his situation. To these were to be added urbanity of manners, strict adherence to the truth, and invincible courage. Hunting and hawking skilfully were also acquirements that he was obliged to possess, and which were usually taught him as soon as he was able to endure the fatigue that they required. Hence it is said of Sir Tristram, a fictitious character held forth as the mirror of chivalry in the romance entitled *The Death of Arthur*, that "he learned to be an harper, passing all other, that there was none such called in any countrey: and so in harping and on instruments of musike he applied himself in his youth for to learne, and after as he growed in might and strength he laboured ever in hunting and hawking, so that we read of no gentlemen who more, or so, used himself therein; and he began good measures of blowing blasts of venery, and chase, and of all manner of vermains; and all these terms have we yet of hunting and hawking; and therefore the book of venery, and of hawking and hunting, is called the Boke of Sir Tristram." In a succeeding part of the same romance, King Arthur thus addresses the knight: "For all manner of hunting thou bearest the prize; and of all measures of blowing thou art the beginner, and of all the termes of hunting and hawking thou art the beginner."[1] We are also informed that Sir Tristram had previously learned the language of France, knew all the principles of courtly behaviour, and was skilful in the various requisites of knighthood.

[1] *Morte Arthur*, translated from the French by Sir Thomas Malory, knight, and first printed by Caxton, A.D. 1481. "The English," says a writer of our own country, "are so naturally inclined to pleasure, that there is no countrie wherein gentlemen and lords have so many and so large parkes, only reserved for the purpose of hunting." And again, "Our progenitors were so delighted with hunting, that the parkes are nowe growne infinite in number, and are thought to containe more fallow deere than all the Christian world besides." *Itinerary of Fynes Moryson*, published in 1617, part iii. book iii. cap. 3.

Another ancient romance says of its hero, " He every day was provyd in dauncyng and in songs that the ladies coulde think were convenable for a nobleman to conne; but in every thinge he passed all them that were there. The king for to assaie him, made justes and turnies; and no man did so well as he, in runnyng, playing at the pame,[1] shotyng, and castyng of the barre, ne found he his maister."[2]

ESQUIRESHIP.—The laws of chivalry required that every knight should pass through two offices : the first was a page ; and, at the age of fourteen he was admitted an esquire. The office of the esquire consisted of several departments ; the esquire for the body, the esquire of the chamber, the esquire of the stable, and the carving esquire ; the latter stood in the hall at dinner, carved the different dishes, and distributed them to the guests. Several of the inferior officers had also their respective esquires.[3] Ipomydon, a king's son and heir, in the romance that bears his name, written probably at the commence-ment of the fourteenth century, is regularly taught the duties of an esquire, previous to his receiving the honours of knighthood ; and for this purpose his father committed him to the care of a " learned and courteous knight called Sir 'Tholomew." Our author speaks on this subject in the following manner :

> "'Tholomew a clerke he toke,
>   That taught the child uppon the boke
>   Bothe to synge and to rede ;
>   And after he taught hym other dede.
>   Afterward, to serve in halle
>   Both to grete and to smalle ;
>   Before the kynge mete to kerve ;
>   Hye and low fayre to serve.
>   Both of howndes and hawkis game,
>   After, he taught hym all ; and same,
>   In sea, in feld, and eke in ryvere ;
>   In woode to chase the wild dere,
>   And in feld to ryde a stede ;
>   That all men had joy of his dede."[4]

Here we find reading mentioned ; which, however, does not appear to have been of any great importance in the middle ages, and is left out in the *Geste of King Horne*, another metrical romance,[5] which seems to be rather more ancient than the former. Young Horne is placed under the tuition of Athelbrus, the king's steward, who is commanded to teach him the mysteries of hawking and hunting, to play upon the harp,

> " Ant toggen o' the harpe
>   With his nayles sharpe,"

---

[1] Written also paume ; that is, hand-tennis.

[2] *Romance of Three Kings' Sons and the King of Sicily*, Harl. MS. 326.

[3] *Mem. Anc. Cheval.* tom. i. p. 16.

[4] Harl. MS. 2252, p. 54b. It is a long poem, extending from p. 54 to p. 84, entitled *The Lyfe of Ipomydone, Son to Ermones, King of Toyle* (Apulia).   [5] *Ibid.*

to carve at the royal table, and to present the cup to the king when he sat at meat, with every other service fitting for him to know. The monarch concludes his injunctions with a repetition of the charge to instruct him in singing and music :

" Tech him of harp and of song."

And the manner in which the king's carver performed the duties of his office is well described in the poem denominated " The Squyer of Lowe Degree." [1]

" There he araied him in scarlet red,
And set a chaplet upon his hedde ;
A belte about his sydes two,
With brode barres to and fro ;
A horne about his necke he caste ;
And forth he went at the laste,
To do his office in the halle
Among the lordes both greate and small.
He toke a white yeard in his hand ;
Before the kynge than gan he stande ;
And sone he set hym on his knee,
And served the kynge ryght royally
With deynty meates that were dere.—
—And, when the squyer had done so,
He served them all to and fro.
Eche man hym loved in honeste,
Hye and lowe in their degre ;
So dyd the kyng "—etc.

MILITARY SPORTS PATRONISED BY LADIES.—Tournaments and jousts were usually exhibited at coronations, royal marriages, and other occasions of solemnity where pomp and pageantry were thought to be requisite. Our historians abound with details of these celebrated pastimes. The reader is referred to Froissart, Hall, Holinshed, Stow, Grafton, etc., who are all of them very diffuse upon this subject; and in the second volume of the *Manners and Customs of the English* are several curious representations of these military combats both on horseback and on foot.

One great reason, and perhaps the most cogent of any, why the nobility of the middle ages, nay, and even princes and kings, delighted so much in the practice of tilting with each other, is, that on such occasions they made their appearance with prodigious splendour, and had the opportunity of displaying their accomplishments to the greatest advantage. The ladies also were proud of seeing their professed champions engaged in these arduous conflicts; and, perhaps, a glove or riband from the hand of a favourite female might have inspired the receiver with as zealous a wish for conquest, as the abstracted love of glory; though in general, I presume, both these ideas were united; for a knight divested of gallantry would have been considered as a recreant, and unworthy of his profession.

DECLINE OF MILITARY EXERCISES.—When the military enthusiasm which

---

[1] Printed by Copeland ; black letter, without date ; Garrick's Collection, K. vol. ix.

so strongly characterised the middle ages had subsided, and chivalry was on the decline, a prodigious change took place in the nurture and manners of the nobility. Violent exercises requiring the exertions of muscular strength grew out of fashion with persons of rank, and of course were consigned to the amusement of the vulgar; and the education of the former became proportionably more soft and delicate. This example of the nobility was soon followed by persons of less consequence; and the neglect of military exercises prevailed so generally, that the interference of the legislature was thought necessary, to prevent its influence from being universally diffused, and to correct the bias of the common mind; for, the vulgar readily acquiesced with the relaxation of meritorious exertions, and fell into the vices of the times, resorting to such games and recreations as promoted idleness and dissipation.

DECLINE OF CHIVALRY.—The romantic notions of chivalry appear to have lost their vigour towards the conclusion of the fifteenth century, especially in this country, where a continued series of intestine commotions employed the exertions of every man of property, and real battles afforded but little leisure to exercise the mockery of war. It is true, indeed, that tilts and tournaments with other splendid exhibitions of military skill, were occasionally exercised, and with great brilliancy, so far as pomp and finery contribute to make them attractive, till the end of the succeeding century. These splendid pastimes were encouraged by the sanction of royalty, and this sanction was perfectly political; on the one hand, it gratified the vanity of the nobility, and, on the other, it amused the populace, who, being delighted with such shows of grandeur, were thereby diverted from reflecting too deeply upon the grievances they sustained. It is, however, certain that the jousts and tournaments of the latter ages, with all their pomp, possessed but little of the primitive spirit of chivalry.

MILITARY EXERCISES UNDER HENRY VII.—Henry VII. patronised the gentlemen and officers of his court in the practice of military exercises. The following extract may serve as a specimen of the manner in which they were appointed to be performed: "Whereas it ever hath bene of old antiquitie used in this realme of most noble fame, for all lustye gentlemen to passe the delectable season of summer after divers manner and sondry fashions of disports, as in hunting the red and fallowe deer with houndes, greyhoundes, and the bowe; also in hawking with hawkes of the Tower; and other pastimes right convenyent which were to long here to rehearse. And bycause it is well knowen, that in the months of Maie and June, all such disports be not conveniently prest and redye to be executed; wherefore, in eschewing of idleness, the ground of all vice," and to promote such exercises as "shall be honourable, and also healthfull and profitable to the body," we "beseech your most noble highness to permit two gentlemen, assosyatying to them two other gentlemen to be their aides," by "your gracious licence, to furnish certain articles concerning the feates of armes hereafter ensuinge":—"In the first place; On the xxijth daye of Maie, there shall be a grene tree sett up in the lawnde of Grenwich parke; whereuppon shall hange, by a grene lace, a Vergescu[1] Blanke, in which white shield it shalbe lawfull for any gentleman that will annswear this chalenge ensewing to subscribe his name.—Secondly; The said two gentlemen, with their two aides, shalbe redye on the xxiijth daie of Maie, being Thursdaye, and on Mondaye thence next ensewinge, and so everye Thursday and Monday untill the xxth daye of June, armed for the foote, to annswear all gentlemen commers, at the feate called the Barriers, with the Casting-speare, and the Targett, and with the bastard-sword,[2] after the manner following, that is to saie, from vj of the clocke in the forenoone till sixt of the clocke in the afternoone during the tyme.—Thirdly; And the said two gentlemen, with their two aiders, or one of them, shall be there redye at the said place, the daye and dayes before rehearsed, to deliver any of the gentlemen answeares of one cast with the speare hedded with the morne,[3] and seven strokes with the sword, point and edge rebated, without close, or griping one another with handes, upon paine of punishment as the judges for the time being shall thinke requisite.—Fourthly; And it shall not be lawfull to the challengers, nor to the answearers, with the bastard sword to give or offer any foyne[4] to his match, upon paine of like punishment.—Fifthly; The challengers shall bringe into the fielde, the said daies and tymes, all manner of weapons concerning the said feates, that is to saie, casting speares hedded with mornes, and bastard swords poynt and edge rebated, and the answerers to have the first choice."[5]

*The Harleian MS. just cited contains accounts of the proclamation and articles of a tilting to be held at the palace of Richmond on the birth of the Princess Mary, daughter of Henry VIII.; of a joust at Grenwich in 1516; and of a "Justinge, Tournay, and Fightinge at Barrier holden at the Palace of Westminster," in 1540.[6]

MILITARY EXERCISES UNDER HENRY VIII.—Henry VIII. not only countenanced the practice of military pastimes by permitting them to be exercised without restraint, but also endeavoured to make them fashionable by his own example. Hall assures us, that, even after his accession to the throne, he continued daily to amuse himself in archery, casting of the bar, wrestling or dancing, and frequently in tilting, tournaying, fighting at the barriers with swords, and battle-axes, and such like martial recreations, in most of which there were few that could excel him. His leisure time he spent in playing at the recorders, flute, and virginals, in setting of songs, singing and making of ballads.[7] He was also exceedingly fond of hunting, hawking, and other sports of the field; and indeed his example so far prevailed, that hunting, hawking, riding the

---

[1] For *vierge escu*, a virgin shield, or a white shield, without any devices, such as was borne by the tyros in chivalry who had not performed any memorable action.

[2] A sword without edge or point.

[3] That is, with heads without points, or blunted so that they could do no hurt.

[4] Foyne, or foin, signifies to push or thrust with the sword, instead of striking.

[5] Harl. MS. 69, f. 56.

[6] *Ibid.* ff. 4b, 16b, 18.   [7] Hall, *Life of Henry VIII.*

great horse, charging dexterously with the lance at the tilt, leaping, and running, were necessary accomplishments of a man of fashion.[1] The pursuits and amusements of a nobleman are placed in a different point of view by an author of the succeeding century;[2] who, describing the person and manners of Charles, Lord Mountjoy, regent of Ireland, in 1599, says, "He delighted in study, in gardens, in riding on a pad to take the aire, in playing at shovelboard, at cardes, and in reading of play-bookes for recreation, and especially in fishing and fish-ponds, seldome using any other exercises, and using these rightly as pastimes, only for a short and convenient time, and with great variety of change from one to the other." The game of shovelboard, though now considered as exceedingly vulgar, and practised by the lower classes of the people, was formerly in great repute among the nobility and gentry; and few of their mansions were without a shovelboard, which was a fashionable piece of furniture. The great hall was usually the place for its reception.

PRINCELY EXERCISES UNDER JAMES I.—We are by no means in the dark respecting the education of the nobility in the reign of James I.; we have, from that monarch's own hand, a set of rules for the nurture and conduct of an heir apparent to the throne, addressed to his eldest son Henry, prince of Wales. From the third book of this remarkable publication, entitled "ΒΑΣΙΛΙΚΟΝ ΔΩΡΟΝ, or, a Kinge's Christian Dutie towards God," I shall select such parts as respect the recreations said to be proper for the pursuit of a nobleman, without presuming to make any alteration in the diction of the royal author.

"Certainly," he says, "bodily exercises and games are very commendable, as well for bannishing of idleness, the mother of all vice; as for making the body able and durable for travell, which is very necessarie for a king. But from this court I debarre all rough and violent exercises; as the foote-ball, meeter for lameing, than making able, the users thereof; as likewise such tumbling trickes as only serve for comœdians and balladines to win their bread with: but the exercises that I would have you to use, although but moderately, not making a craft of them, are, running, leaping, wrestling, fencing, dancing, and playing at the caitch, or tennise, archerie, palle-malle, and such like other fair and pleasant field-games. And the honourablest and most recommendable games that yee can use on horseback; for, it becometh a prince best of any man to be a faire and good horseman: use, therefore, to ride and danton great and courageous horses;—and especially use such games on horseback as may teach you to handle your arms thereon, such as the tilt, the ring, and low-riding for handling of your sword.

"I cannot omit heere the hunting, namely, with running houndes, which is the most honourable and noblest sort thereof; for it is a theivish forme of hunting to shoote with gunnes and bowes; and greyhound hunting is not so martial a game.

"As for hawkinge, I condemn it not; but I must praise it more sparingly,

---

[1] *Arte of Rhetorike* by Tho. Wilson, fol. 67.   [2] Fynes Moryson's *Itinerary*, published A.D. 1617.

c

because it neither resembleth the warres so neere as hunting doeth in making a man hardie and skilfully ridden in all grounds, and is more uncertain and subject to mischances; and, which is worst of all, is there through an extreme stirrer up of the passions.

"As for sitting, or house pastimes—since they may at times supply the roome which, being emptie, would be patent to pernicious idleness—I will not therefore agree with the curiositie of some learned men of our age in forbidding cardes, dice, and such like games of hazard: when it is foule and stormie weather, then I say, may ye lawfully play at the cardes or tables; for, as to diceing, I think it becometh best deboshed souldiers to play at on the heads of their drums, being only ruled by hazard, and subject to knavish cogging; and as for the chesse, I think it over-fond, because it is over-wise and philosophicke a folly."

His majesty concludes this subject with the following good advice to his son: "Beware in making your sporters your councellors, and delight not to keepe ordinarily in your companie comœdians or balladines."

Revival of Learning.—The discontinuation of bodily exercises afforded a proportionable quantity of leisure time for the cultivation of the mind; so that the manners of mankind were softened by degrees, and learning, which had been so long neglected, became fashionable, and was esteemed an indispensable mark of a polite education.   Yet some of the nobility maintained for a long time the old prejudices in favour of the ancient mode of nurture, and preferred exercise of the body to mental endowments; such was the opinion of a person of high rank, who said to Richard Pace, secretary to King Henry VIII., "It is enough for the sons of noblemen to wind their horn and carry their hawke fair, and leave study and learning to the children of meaner people."[1]   Many of the pastimes that had been countenanced by the nobility, and sanctioned by their example, in the middle ages, grew into disrepute in modern times, and were condemned as vulgar and unbecoming the notice of a gentleman.   "Throwing the hammer and wrestling," says Peacham, in his *Complete Gentleman*, published in 1622, "I hold them exercises not so well beseeming nobility, but rather the soldiers in the camp and the prince's guard."   On the contrary, Sir William Forest, in his *Poesye of Princelye Practice*, a MS. in the Royal Library,[2] written in the year 1548, laying down the rules for the education of an heir apparent to the crown, or prince of the blood royal, writes thus:

> "So must a prince, at some convenient brayde,
> In featis of maistries bestowe some diligence:
> Too ryde, runne, leape, or caste by violence
> Stone, barre, or plummett, or suche other thinge,
> It not refusethe any prince or kynge."

However, I doubt not both these authors spoke agreeably to the taste of the times in which they lived.   Barclay, a more early poetic writer, in his *Eclogues*

---

[1] *Biograph. Brit.* p. 1236.   [2] No. 17 D. iii.

first published in 1508, has made a shepherd boast of his skill in archery; to which he adds,

> "I can dance the raye; I can both pipe and sing,
> If I were mery; I can both hurle and sling;
> I runne, I wrestle, I can well throwe the barre,
> No shepherd throweth the axeltree so farre;
> If I were mery, I could well leape and spring;
> I were a man mete to serve a prince or king."

RECREATIONS OF THE SEVENTEENTH CENTURY.—Burton, in his *Anatomy of Melancholy*, published in 1660, gives us a general view of the sports most prevalent in the seventeenth century. "Cards, dice, hawkes, and hounds," says he, "are rocks upon which men lose themselves, when they are imprudently handled, and beyond their fortunes." And again, "Hunting and hawking are honest recreations, and fit for some great men, but not for every base inferior person, who, while they maintain their faulkoner, and dogs, and hunting nags, their wealth runs away with their hounds, and their fortunes fly away with their hawks." In another place he speaks thus: "Ringing, bowling, shooting, playing with keel-pins, tronks, coits, pitching of bars, hurling, wrestling, leaping, running, fencing, mustering, swimming, playing with wasters, foils, foot-balls, balowns, running at the quintain, and the like, are common recreations of country folks; riding of great horses, running at rings, tilts and tournaments, horse-races, and wild-goose chases, which are disports of greater men, and good in themselves, though many gentlemen by such means gallop quite out of their fortunes." Speaking of the Londoners, he says, "They take pleasure to see some pageant or sight go by, as at a coronation, wedding, and such like solemn niceties; to see an ambassador or a prince received and entertained with masks, shows, and fireworks. The country hath also his recreations, as May-games, feasts, fairs, and wakes." The following pastimes he considers as common both in town and country, namely, "bull-baitings and bear-baitings, in which our countrymen and citizens greatly delight, and frequently use; dancers on ropes, jugglers, comedies, tragedies, artillery gardens, and cock-fighting." He then goes on: "Ordinary recreations we have in winter, as cards, tables, dice, shovelboard, chess-play, the philosopher's game, small trunks, shuttlecock, billiards, music, masks, singing, dancing, ulegames, frolicks, jests, riddles, catches, cross purposes, questions and commands, merry tales of errant knights, queens, lovers, lords, ladies, giants, dwarfs, thieves, cheaters, witches, fairies, goblins, and friars." To this catalogue he adds: "Dancing, singing, masking, mumming, and stage-plays, are reasonable recreations, if in season; as are May-games, wakes, and Whitson-ales, if not at unseasonable hours, are justly permitted. Let them," that is, the common people, "freely feast, sing, dance, have puppet-plays, hobby-horses, tabers, crowds,[1] and bag-pipes": let them "play at ball and barley-brakes"; and afterwards, "Plays, masks, jesters, gladiators, tumblers, and jugglers, are to be winked at, lest the people should do worse than attend them."

---

[1] Crowd is an ancient name for the violin.

A character in the *Cornish Comedy*, written by George Powell, and acted at Dorset Garden in 1696, says, "What is a gentleman without his recreations? With these we endeavour to pass away that time which otherwise would lie heavily upon our hands. Hawks, hounds, setting-dogs, and cocks, with their appurtenances, are the true marks of a country gentleman." This character is supposed to be a young heir just come to his estate. "My cocks," says he, "are true cocks of the game—I make a match of cock-fighting, and then an hundred or two pounds are soon won, for I never fight a battle under."

OLD SPORTS OF THE CITIZENS OF LONDON.—In addition to the May-games, morris-dancings, pageants and processions, which were commonly exhibited throughout the kingdom in all great towns and cities, the Londoners had peculiar and extensive privileges of hunting, hawking, and fishing; they had also large portions of ground allotted to them in the vicinity of the city for the practice of such pastimes as were not prohibited by the government, and for those especially that were best calculated to render them strong and healthy. We are told by Fitz Stephen, in the twelfth century, that on the holidays during the summer season, the young men of London exercised themselves in the fields with "leaping, shooting with the bow, wrestling, casting the stone, playing with the ball, and fighting with their shields." The last species of pastime, I believe, is the same that Stow, in his *Survey of London*, calls "practising with their wasters and bucklers"; which in his day was exercised by the apprentices before the doors of their masters. The city damsels had also their recreations on the celebration of these festivals, according to the testimony of both the authors just mentioned. The first tells us that they played upon citherns,[1] and danced to the music; and as this amusement probably did not take place before the close of the day, they were, it seems, occasionally permitted to continue it by moonlight. We learn from the other, who wrote at the distance of more than four centuries, that it was then customary for the maidens, after evening prayers, to dance in the presence of their masters and mistresses, while one of their companions played the measure upon a timbrel; and, in order to stimulate them to pursue this exercise with alacrity, the best dancers were rewarded with garlands, the prizes being exposed to public view, "hanged athwart the street," says Stow, during the whole of the performance. This recital calls to my mind a passage in Spenser's "Epithalamium," wherein it appears that the dance was sometimes accompanied with singing. It runs thus:

> "——The damsels they delight,
> When they their timbrels smite,
> And thereunto dance and carol sweet."

LATER PASTIMES OF THE LONDONERS.—A general view of the pastimes practised by the Londoners soon after the commencement of the eighteenth century

---

[1] The words of Fitz Stephen are, *Puellarum cithara ducit choros, et pede libero pulsatur tellus, usque imminente lunâ*. The word *cithara*, Stow renders, but I think not justly, timbrels.

occurs in Strype's edition of Stow's *Survey of London*, published in 1720.[1]
"The modern sports of the citizens," says the editor, "besides drinking, are
cock-fighting, bowling upon greens, playing at tables, or backgammon, cards,
dice, and billiards; also musical entertainments, dancing, masks, balls, stage-
plays, and club-meetings, in the evenings; they sometimes ride out on horseback, and hunt with the lord-mayor's pack of dogs when the common hunt goes
out. The lower classes divert themselves at football, wrestling, cudgels, nine-
pins, shovelboard, cricket, stowball, ringing of bells, quoits, pitching the bar,
bull and bear baitings, throwing at cocks," and, what is worst of all, "lying at
ale-houses." To these are added, by an author of later date, Maitland, in
his *History of London*, published in 1739, "Sailing, rowing, swimming and
fishing, in the river Thames, horse and foot races, leaping, archery, bowling in
allies, and skittles, tennice, chess, and draughts; and in the winter scating,
sliding, and shooting." Duck-hunting was also a favourite amusement, but
generally practised in the summer. The pastimes here enumerated were by no
means confined to the city of London, or its environs : the larger part of them
were in general practice throughout the kingdom.

COTSWOLD AND CORNISH GAMES.—Before I quit this division of my subject,
I shall mention the annual celebration of games upon Cotswold Hills, in Gloucestershire, to which prodigious multitudes constantly resorted. Robert Dover,
an attorney, of Barton on the Heath, in the county of Warwick, was forty years
the chief director of these pastimes. They consisted of wrestling, cudgel-
playing, leaping, pitching the bar, throwing the sledge, tossing the pike, with
various other feats of strength and activity; many of the country gentlemen
hunted or coursed the hare; and the women danced. A castle of boards was
erected on this occasion, from which guns were frequently discharged. "Captain
Dover received permission from James I. to hold these sports; and he appeared
at their celebration in the very clothes which that monarch had formerly worn,
but with much more dignity in his air and aspect."[2] I do not mean to say that
the Cotswold games were invented, or even first established, by Captain Dover;
on the contrary, they seem to be of much higher origin, and are evidently
alluded to in the following lines by John Heywood the epigrammatist :[3]

> "He fometh like a bore, the beaste should seeme bolde,
> For he is as fierce as a lyon of Cotswolde."

Something of the same sort, I presume, was the Carnival, kept every year, about
the middle of July, upon Halgaver-moor, near Bodmin in Cornwall; "resorted
to by thousands of people," says Heath, in his description of Cornwall, published
in 1750. "The sports and pastimes here held were so well liked by Charles II.
when he touched here in his way to Sicily, that he became a brother of the

---

[1] Vol. i. p. 257.
[2] *Athen. Oxon.* ii. col. 812; and see Grainger's *Biographical History*, vol. ii. p. 398.   8vo.   *There is a good
illustrated account of these Cotswold Games in Chambers' *Book of Days*, i. 712-714.
[3] In his *Proverbs*, part i. chap. 11.

jovial society. The custom of keeping this carnival is said to be as old as the Saxons."

SPLENDOUR OF THE ANCIENT KINGS AND NOBILITY.—Paul Hentzner, a foreign writer, who visited this country at the close of the sixteenth century, says of the English, in his *Itinerary*, written in 1598, that they are " serious like the Germans, lovers of show, liking to be followed wherever they go by whole troops of servants, who wear their master's arms in silver." This was no new propensity: the English nobility at all times affected great parade, seldom appearing abroad without large trains of servitors and retainers; and the lower classes of the people delighted in gaudy shows, pageants, and processions.

If we go back to the times of the Saxons, we shall find that, soon after their establishment in Britain, their monarchs assumed great state. Bede tells us that Edwin, king of Northumberland, lived in much splendour, never travelling without a numerous retinue; and when he walked in the streets of his own capital, even in the times of peace, he had a standard borne before him. This standard was of the kind called by the Romans tufa, and by the English tuuf: it was made with feathers of various colours in the form of a globe, and fastened upon a pole.[1] It is unnecessary to multiply citations; for which reason I shall only add another. Canute the Dane, who is said to have been the richest and most magnificent prince of his time in Europe, rarely appeared in public without being followed by a train of three thousand horsemen, well mounted and completely armed. These attendants, who were called house carls, formed a corps of body guards or household troops, and were appointed for the honour and safety of that prince's person.[2] The examples of royalty were followed by the nobility and persons of opulence.

In the middle ages, the love of show was carried to an extravagant length; and as a man of fashion was nothing less than a man of letters, those studies that were best calculated to improve the mind were held in little estimation.

ROYAL AND NOBLE ENTERTAINMENTS.—The courts of princes and the castles of the great barons were daily crowded with numerous retainers, who were always welcome to their masters' tables. The noblemen had their privy counsellors, treasurers, marshals, constables, stewards, secretaries, chaplains, heralds, pursuivants, pages, henchmen or guards, trumpeters, and all the other officers of the royal court.[3] To these may be added whole companies of minstrels, mimics, jugglers, tumblers, rope-dancers, and players; and especially on days of public festivity, when, in every one of the apartments opened for the reception of the guests, were exhibited variety of entertainments, according to the taste of the times, but in which propriety had very little share; the whole forming a scene of pompous confusion, where feasting, drinking, music, dancing, tumbling, singing, and buffoonery, were jumbled together, and mirth excited too often at the expense of common decency.[4] If we turn to the third *Book of*

---

[1] Bede, *Eccl. Hist.* lib. ii. cap. 16.
[3] See the *Northumberland Family-Book.*
[2] Henry's *Hist.* vol. ii. lib. v. cap. 7.
[4] Johan. Sarisburiensis, lib. i. c. viii. p. 34.

Fame, a poem written by our own countryman Chaucer, we shall find a perfect picture of these tumultuous court entertainments, drawn, I doubt not, from reality, and perhaps without any exaggeration. It may be thus expressed in modern language : Minstrels of every kind were stationed in the receptacles for the guests ; among them were jesters, that related tales of mirth and of sorrow ; excellent players upon the harp, with others of inferior merit seated on various seats below them, who mimicked their performances like apes to excite laughter ; behind them, at a great distance, was a prodigious number of other minstrels, making a great sound with cornets, shaulms, flutes, horns, pipes of various kinds, and some of them made with green corn,[1] such as are used by shepherds' boys ; there were also Dutch pipers to assist those who chose to dance either "love-dances, springs, or rayes," or any other new-devised measures. Apart from these were stationed the trumpeters and players on the clarion ; and other seats were occupied by different musicians playing variety of mirthful tunes. There were also present large companies of jugglers, magicians, and tregetors, who exhibited surprising tricks by the assistance of natural magic.

Vast sums of money were expended in support of these spectacles, by which the estates of the nobility were consumed, and the public treasuries often exhausted. But we shall have occasion to speak more fully on this subject hereafter.

CIVIC SHOWS.—In London, pageants and displays, or triumphs, were frequently required at the reception of foreign monarchs, or at the processions of our own kings and queens through the city to Westminster previous to their coronation, or at their return from abroad, and on various other occasions ; besides such as occurred at stated times, as the lord mayor's show, the setting of the midsummer watch, and the like. A considerable number of different artificers were kept, at the city's expense, to furnish the machinery for the pageants, and to decorate them. Stow tells us that, in his memory, great part of Leaden Hall was appropriated to the purpose of painting and depositing the pageants for the use of the city.

The want of elegance and propriety, so glaringly evident in these temporary exhibitions, was supplied, or attempted to be supplied, by a tawdry resemblance of splendour. The fronts of the houses in the streets through which the processions passed were covered with rich adornments of tapestry, arras, and cloth of gold ; the chief magistrates and most opulent citizens usually appeared on horseback in sumptuous habits and joined the cavalcade ; while the ringing of bells, the sound of music from various quarters, and the shouts of the populace, nearly stunned the ears of the spectators. At certain distances, in places appointed for the purpose, the pageants were erected, which were temporary buildings representing castles, palaces, gardens, rocks, or forests, as the occasion required, where nymphs, fawns, satyrs, gods, goddesses, angels, and

---

[1] Pypes made of greene corne are also mentioned in the *Romance of the Rose*.

devils, appeared in company with giants, savages, dragons, saints, knights, buffoons, and dwarfs, surrounded by minstrels and choristers; the heathen mythology, the legends of chivalry and Christian divinity, were ridiculously jumbled together, without meaning; and the exhibition usually concluded with dull pedantic harangues, exceedingly tedious, and replete with the grossest adulation. The giants especially were favourite performers in the pageants; they also figured away with great applause in the pages of romance; and, together with dragons and necromancers, were created by the authors for the sole purpose of displaying the prowess of their heroes, whose business it was to destroy them.

Some faint traces of the processional parts of these exhibitions were retained at London in the lord mayor's show about twenty or thirty years ago;[1] but the pageants and orations have been long discontinued, and the show itself is so much contracted that it is in reality altogether unworthy of such an appellation.

*MERRY ENGLAND.—Outside military pastimes, and the sports of princes, or of noblemen, and gentlefolk at large, it must not be forgotten that the townsmen had many an opportunity of amusement and enjoyment after their own heart. In pre-Reformation days their feasts and frolics and plays were usually associated with, or at all events somewhat slightly allied to the observances of religion. In his chapter on "Gilds and Misteries," Mr J. A. Wylie, the historian of Henry IV., gives a vivid and faithful picture of this side of town gild life of the fifteenth century:—

"England was then 'Merry England,' and sad and sober pleasure was not the people's creed. The brethren did not put in their weekly shot merely to dole groats to pittancers, or help the bedrid and brokelegged, or find poor scholars to school, or dower poor girls, or burn their soul-candles round the corpse of a dead brother, or follow at his forthbringing and 'terment. Such duties were soon relegated to chaplains, who were paid and lodged at the cost of the gild. The gildsmen lived for mirth, joy, sweetness, courtesy and merry disports. Once every year came the Gild-day, usually on a Sunday or one of the greater feasts, when the brethren, fairly and honestly arrayed in their new hoods, gowns, and cloaks, in livery suit of murrey, crimson, white, or green, would assemble at daybreak, and form up in the house or hall of their craft. In front rode the beadle or crier, in scarlet tabard or demigown. Next came the pipers, trumpers, corners, clarioners, cornemusers, shalmusers, and other minstrelsy, clad in verdulet, rayed plunket, or russet motley; and then the craftsmen, mounted or a-foot, moving in procession through the streets to the church where their chantry was appointed. They carried with them a huge wax serge, sometimes weighing fifty pounds, to burn before the shrine of their saint. Then began the morn-speech, communion, or speaking together, which was usually held in the church while the mass was proceeding, where the year's accounts were squared, the gild

[1] [Before 1801.]

chattels were laid on the checker, points were promulgated, defaulters announced, new members enrolled, and the Master, Skevins, Proctors, Dean, Clerk, Summoner, and other officers elected for the coming year. Thence they returned to the hall for the general feast, otherwise known as the drink, the meat, or the mangery. The walls would be hung with hallings of stained worsted, and dight with birch boughs, and the floor over-strawed with mats, or a litter of sedge and rushes, that swarmed with the quick beasts that tickle men o' nights. The benches were fit with gay bankers, before tables set on trestle-trees spread with board-cloths of clean nap. On these was laid a garnish of pewter or treen, together with the masers and silver spoons bequeathed by brethren since dead. Men and women alike brought their beaker of ale, and the poor received their share of the good things by the custom of the day. Each member was required to bring his wife or his lass, and the sick brother or sister had still to pay his score, though he might have his bottle of ale and his mess of kitchen stuff sent to his own house if he wished. If any disturbed the fellowship with brabbling or high language, the Dean delivered him the yard [of scourging], or fined him in two pounds of wax, to be paid in to the light-silver. The cook was often a brother of the gild, and skilled waferers were always to be had for a price. When all had washed and wiped, the Graceman placed them in a row with his silver wand, and the Clerk stood up and called ' Peace,' while prayers were said for England and the Church.

* " The feast began with good bread and brown ale. Then came the bruets, joints, worts, gruel aillies and other pottage, the big meat, the lamb tarts and capon pasties, the cockentrice or double roast (*i.e.* griskin and pullet stitched with thread, or great and small birds stewed together), and served in a silver posnet or pottinger, the charlets, chewets, collops, mammenies, mortreus, and other such toothsome entremets of meat served in gobbets and sod in ale, wine, milk, eggs, sugar, honey, marrow, spices, and verjuice made from grapes or crabs. Then came the subtleties, daintily worked like pigeons, curlews, or popinjays in sugar and paste, painted in gold and silver, with mottoes coming out of their bills ; and after them the spiced cake-bread, the Frenchbread, the pastelades, doucets, dariols, flauns, pain-puffs, rastons, and blancmanges, with cherries, drajes, blandrells, and cheese, and a standing cup of good wine left by some former brother to drink him every year to mind.

* "When the cloth was up and the boards were drawn, came the merrymaking and the hoy-trolly-lolly. They laughed and cried at the jester's bourds, or the gitener's glee ; they watched the tregetoners sleight, or they diced and raffled, while the sautryours and other minstrels harped, piped, gitterned, flutted, and fitheled a merry fit aloft. As they left the hall they gathered about the leapers and tumblers, or thronged the bearward and the apeward to enjoy the grins, mous, and gambols of their darlings, or formed a ring about the bearstake to see the baiting with the dogs. Or the summer afternoon would be spent in running a bull, when the poor brute's skin was daubed with smear, its tail cut, and its horns sawn off, the sport being to goad it with dogs and sticks and see who could get near enough to cut a few hairs from its greased back.

* " But the great diversion of our forefathers was mumming. Give them but free air and an antic guise, and they would mask and mime with all the seriousness of children at play. Every mistery must have its riding, and every gild its procession. At Beverley, on St Helen's Day, the gildsmen dressed up a boy as a queen to represent the saint. One old man marched before her with a cross, and another with a spade; the music played up, and the brethren and sistern followed the parade to church. At Candelmas, a man in woman's dress represented the Virgin Mary, and carried 'what might seem' a baby in his arms, Joseph and Simeon walked behind him, and two angels carrying a heavy candlestick, with twenty-four wax lights. At York they showed the Vices and Virtues by means of the petitions in the Lord's Prayer, or they acted out the articles of the Creed, while the gildsmen in their livery rode with the players on the route. At Leicester the images of St Martin and the Virgin were borne through the streets with music and singing, twelve of the gildsmen making up as the Apostles, each with his name stuck in his cap. At Norwich, on St George's Day, they chose their George and a man to bear his sword and be his carver; two of the brethren bore the banner and two 'the wax,' and the rest rode with them in their livery round the town. The Norwich peltyers (skinners) dressed up 'a knave-child innocent,' with a large candle in his hand, and led him through the city to the minster, 'betwyxen two good men,' in memory of St William, the boy martyr, to foster hatred against the Jews. At Canterbury, every 6th of July, at the city march, a cart was drawn about the streets, showing a boy vested as 'Bishop Becket' struck down before an altar by four other children, who played the knights; and as the martyr fell beneath their blows, real blood was spurted on his forehead from a leather bag, which was carried in reserve for use at a given signal. At Cambridge, the scholars of Michaelhouse played a comedy in masks, beards, and embroidered cloaks. In London, the brethren of the fraternity of SS. Fabian and Sebastian carried 'the Branch' springing from the root of Jesse, dressed out with lighted candles, to the church of St Bololph, Aldersgate. On St Nicholas Eve (Dec. 5th), the chorister boys in every cathedral, and probably in every collegiate and parish church where singing boys were found, elected one of their number to be their 'Barne-Bishop,' or 'St Nicholas Bishop,' and to rule the services of the church, in mitre, ring, gloves, cope, surplice, rochet, and full pontificals. He rode or strutted about the streets with his crozier borne before him, blessing the crowd, and collecting their pennies in a glove, with his canons, chaplains, clerks, vergers, and candle-bearers till Childermas.

* " Each season brought its ales, its mayings-round-the-shaft, its Piffany mummings, its Candelmas, Hochtide, and Yule; but Corpus Christi was the feast of feasts, when the gildsmen carried torches, candles, and banners around the

Blessed Sacrament as it passed through the streets, and all the town turned out at sunrise to watch the annual play.

* " They could play you gracious mysteries grounded in Scripture, such as the story of the Children of Israel, or of Moses in Egypt, or legends of the martyrdom of Saints Salenia and Feliciana, or of St Catherine of Alexandria and the angels feeding her in her torture house, and smashing the wheel like bruchel glass, or the miracles of St Nicholas, the hearer of prayer, who sent the handsome suitors in the very nick of time to the poor but virtuous gentleman with the pretty penniless daughters, and brought the little boys back to life after they had been cut up in the pickle-butt by the naughty taverner. . . . Such exhibitions were usually known in England as 'the miracles,' or 'the marvels,' and occasionally 'the mysteries'; we trace them wherever town records are preserved, and they penetrated even to the remotest manor-house and the most secluded village."[1]

SETTING OUT OF PAGEANTS.—In an old play, *The Historie of Promos and Cassandra*, by George Whetstone, printed in 1578,[2] a carpenter, and others, employed in preparing the pageants for a royal procession, are introduced. In one part of the city the artificer is ordered "to set up the frames, and to space out the rooms, that the Nine Worthies may be so instauled as best to please the eye." The "Worthies" are thus named in an heraldical MS. in the Harleian Library:[3] "Duke Jossua; Hector of Troy; kyng David; emperour Alexander; Judas Machabyes; emperour Julyus Cæsar; kyng Arthur; emperour Charlemagne; and syr Guy of Warwycke"; but the place of the latter was frequently, and I believe originally, supplied by Godefroy, earl of Bologne: it appears, however, that any of them might be changed at pleasure. Henry VIII. was made a "Worthy" to please his daughter Mary, as we shall find a little further on. In another part of the same play the carpenter is commanded to "errect a stage, that the wayghtes[4] in sight may stand"; one of the city gates was to be occupied by the fowre Virtues, together with "a consort of music"; and one of the pageants is thus whimsically described :

> " They have Hercules of monsters conquering ;
> Huge great giants, in a forrest, fighting
> With lions, bears, wolves, apes, foxes, and grayes,
> Baiards and brockes ————
> ———— Oh, these be wondrous frayes ! "

The stage direction then requires the entry of " Two men apparelled lyke greene men at the mayor's feast, with clubbs of fyreworks"; whose office, we are told, was to keep a clear passage in the street, "that the kyng and his trayne might pass with ease." In another dramatic performance of later date, Green's *Tu Quoque, or the City Gallant*, published in 1614, a city apprentice says, " By this light, I doe not thinke but to be lord mayor of London before I die ; and have

---

[1] Wylie's *History of England under Henry IV.*, vol. iii. ch. 75.   [2] Garrick's Collection of Old Plays, H. vol. iii.
[3] No. 2220, fol. 7.   [4] Or waits, the band of city minstrels.

three pageants carried before me, besides a ship and an unicorn." The following passage occurs in Selden's *Table Talk*, under the article Judge, "We see the pageants in Cheapside, the lions and the elephants ; but we do not see the men that carry them ; we see the Judges look big like lions ; but we do not see who moves them."

PROCESSIONS OF QUEEN MARY AND KING PHILIP OF SPAIN IN LONDON.— In the foregoing quotations, we have not the least necessity to make an allowance for poetical licence : the historians of the time will justify the poets, and perfectly clear them from any charge of exaggeration ; and especially Hall, Grafton, and Holinshed, who are exceedingly diffuse on this and such like popular subjects. The latter has recorded a very curious piece of pantomimical trickery exhibited at the time that the Princess Mary went in procession through the city of London, the day before her coronation :—At the upper end of Grace-church Street there was a pageant made by the Florentines ; it was very high ; and "on the top thereof there stood foure pictures ; and in the midst of them, and the highest, there stood an angell, all in greene, with a trumpet in his hand ; and when the trumpetter who stood secretlie within the pageant, did sound his trumpet, the angell did put his trumpet to his mouth, as though it had been the same that had sounded." Holinshed, speaking of the spectacles exhibited at London, when Philip king of Spain, with Mary his consort, made their public entry in the city, calls them, in the margin of his Chronicle, "the vaine pageants of London" ; and he uses the same epithet twice in the description immediately subsequent ; "Now," says he, "as the king came to London, and as he entered at the drawbridge, [on London Bridge,] there was a vaine great spectacle, with two images representing two giants, the one named Corinens, and the other Gog-magog, holding betweene them certeine Latin verses, which, for the vaine ostentation of flatterye, I overpasse." He then adds : "From the bridge they passed to the conduit in Gratious Street, which was finely painted ; and, among other things," there exhibited, "were the Nine Worthies ; of these King Henry VIII. was one. He was painted in harnesse, having in one hand a sword, and in the other hand a booke, whereupon was written Verbum Dei. He was also delivering, as it were, the same booke to his sonne King Edward VI. who was painted in a corner by him." [1]

The Nine Worthies appear to have been favourite characters, and were often exhibited in the pageants ; those mentioned in the preceding passage were probably nothing more than images of wood or pasteboard. These august personages were not, however, always degraded in this manner, but, on the contrary, they were frequently personified by human beings suitably habited, and sometimes mounted on horseback. They also occasionally harangued the spectators as they passed in the procession.

CHESTER PAGEANTS.—The same species of shows, but probably not upon so extensive a scale, were exhibited in other cities and large towns throughout

[1] Holinshed, vol. iii. pp. 1091, 1120, etc.

the kingdom. I have now before me an ordinance for the mayor, aldermen, and common councilmen of the city of Chester, to provide yearly for the setting of the watch, on the eve of the festival of Saint John the Baptist, a pageant, which is expressly said to be "according to ancient custome," consisting of four giants, one unicorn, one dromedary, one luce, one camel, one ass, one dragon, six hobby-horses, and sixteen naked boys. This ordinance is dated April 26th, 1564.[1] In another MS. of the same library, it is said, "A.D. 1599, Henry Hardware, esq. the mayor, was a godly and zealous man"; he caused "the gyauntes in the midsomer show to be broken," and not to goe; "the devil in his feathers," alluding perhaps to some fantastic representation not mentioned in the former ordinance, "he put awaye, and the cuppes and cannes, and the dragon and the naked boys." In a more modern hand it is added, "And he caused a man in complete armour to go in their stead. He also caused the bull-ring to be taken up," etc. But in the year 1601, John Ratclyffe, beer-brewer, being mayor, "sett out the giaunts and midsommer show, as of oulde it was wont to be kept."[2] In the time of the Commonwealth this spectacle was discontinued, and the giants, with the beasts, were destroyed. At the restoration of Charles II. it was agreed by the citizens to replace the pageant as usual, on the eve of the festival of St John the Baptist, in 1661; and as the following computation of the charges for the different parts of the show are exceedingly curious, I shall lay them before the reader without any further apology. We are told that "all things were to be made new, by reason the ould modells were all broken." The computist then proceeds: "For finding all the materials, with the workmanship of the four great giants, all to be made new, as neere as may be lyke as they were before, at five pounds a giant the least that can be, and four men to carry them at two shillings and six pence each." The materials for the composition of these monsters are afterwards specified to be "hoops of various magnitudes, and other productions of the cooper, deal boards, nails, pasteboard, scaleboard paper of various sorts, with buckram, size cloth, and old sheets for their bodies, sleeves, and shirts, which were to be coloured." One pair of the "olde sheets" were provided to cover the "father and mother giants." Another article specifies "three yards of buckram for the mother's and daughter's hoods"; which seems to prove that three of these stupendous pasteboard personages were the representatives of females. There were "also tinsille, tinfoil, gold and silver leaf, and colours of different kinds, with glue and paste in abundance." Respecting the last article, a very ridiculous entry occurs in the bill of charges, it runs thus: "For arsnick to put into the paste to save the giants from being eaten by the rats, one shilling and fourpence." But to go on with the estimate. "For the new making the city mount, called the maior's mount, as auntiently it was, and for hreing of bays for the same, and a man to carry it, three pounds six shillings and eight pence." The bays mentioned in this and the succeeding article was hung round the bottom of the frame, and extended to the ground, or

---

[1] No. 1968, f. 576.   [2] Harl. MS. 2125.

near it, to conceal the bearers. "For making anew the merchant mount, as it aunciently was, with a ship to turn round, the hiring of the bays, and five men to carry it, four pounds." The ship and new dressing it, is charged at five shillings; it was probably made with pasteboard, which seems to have been a principal article in the manufacturing of both the moveable mountains; it was turned by means of a swivel attached to an iron handle underneath the frame. In the bill of charges for "the merchant's mount," is an entry of twenty pence paid to a joyner for cutting the pasteboard into several images. "For making anew the elephant and castell, and a Cupid," with his bow and arrows, "suitable to it," the castle was covered with tinfoil, and the Cupid with skins, so as to appear to be naked, "and also for two men to carry them, one pound sixteen shillings and eight-pence. For making anew the four beastes called the unicorne, the antelop, the flower-de-luce, and the camell, one pound sixteen shillings and fourpence apiece, and for eight men to carry them, sixteen shillings. For four hobby-horses, six shillings and eight-pence apiece; and for four boys to carry them, four shillings. For hance-staves, garlands, and balls, for the attendants upon the mayor and sheriffs, one pound nineteen shillings. For makinge anew the dragon, and for six naked boys to beat at it, one pound sixteen shillings. For six morris-dancers, with a pipe and tabret, twenty shillings."

The sports exhibited on occasions of solemnity did not terminate with the pageants and processions; the evening was generally concluded with festivity and diversions of various kinds to please the populace. These amusements are well described in a few lines by an early dramatic poet, whose name is not known; his performance is entitled *A pleasant and stately Morall of the Three Lordes of London*, black letter, no date:[1]

> " ——Let nothing that's magnifical,
> Or that may tend to London's graceful state,
> Be unperformed, as showes and solemne feasts,
> Watches in armour, triumphes, cresset lights,
> Bonefires, belles, and peales of ordinaunce
> And pleasure. See that plaies be published,
> Mai-games and maskes, with mirth and minstrelsie,
> Pageants and school-feastes, beares and puppet-plaies."

The "cresset light" was a large lanthorn placed upon a long pole, and carried upon men's shoulders. There is extant a copy of a letter from Henry VII. to the mayor and aldermen of London, commanding them to make bonfires, and to show other marks of rejoicing in the city, when the contract was ratified for the marriage of his daughter Mary with the prince of Castile.[2]

PUBLIC SHOWS IN THE SIXTEENTH CENTURY.—These motley displays of pomp and absurdity were highly relished by the nobility, and repeatedly exhibited by them, on extraordinary occasions. For want of more rational entertainments, they maintained for ages their popularity, and do not appear to

[1] Garrick's Collection of Old Plays. [2] Cotton MS. *Titus*, B. i.

have lost the smallest portion of their attraction by the frequency of representation. Shows of this kind were never more fashionable than in the sixteenth century, when they were generally encouraged by persons of the highest rank, and exhibited with very little essential variation; and especially during the reign of Henry VIII. His daughter Elizabeth appears to have been equally pleased with this species of pageantry; and therefore it was constantly provided for her amusement by the nobility whom she visited from time to time, in her progresses or excursions to various parts of the kingdom.[1] I shall simply give the outlines of a succession of entertainments contrived to divert her when she visited the Earl of Leicester at Kenelworth Castle, and this shall serve as a specimen for the rest.

QUEEN ELIZABETH AT KENELWORTH.—Her majesty came thither on Saturday, the ninth of July 1575;[2] she was met near the castle by a fictitious Sibyl, who promised peace and prosperity to the country during her reign. Over the first gate of the castle there stood six gigantic figures with trumpets, real trumpeters being stationed behind them, who sounded as the queen approached. "By this dumb show," says my author, "it was meant that in the daies of King Arthur, men were of that stature; so that the castle of Kenelworth should seem still to be kept by King Arthur's heirs and their servants." Laneham says these figures were eight feet high. Upon her majesty entering the gateway, the porter, in the character of Hercules, made an oration and presented to her the keys. Being come into the base court, a lady "came all over the pool, being so conveyed, that it seemed she had gone upon the water; she was attended by two water nymphs, and calling herself the Lady of the Lake, she addressed her majesty with a speech prepared for the purpose." The queen then proceeded to the inner court, and passed the bridge, which was railled on both sides, and the tops of the posts were adorned with "sundry presents and gifts," as of wine, corn, fruits, fishes, fowls, instruments of music, and weapons of war. Laneham calls the adorned posts "well-proportioned pillars turned": he tells us there were fourteen of them, seven on each side of the bridge; on the first pair were birds of various kinds alive in cages, said to be the presents of the god Silvanus; on the next pair were different sorts of fruits in silver bowls, the gift of the goddess Pomona; on the third pair were different kinds of grain in silver bowls, the gift of Ceres; on the fourth, in silvered pots, were red and white wine with clusters of grapes in a silver bowl, the gift of Bacchus; on the fifth were fishes of various kinds in trays, the donation of Neptune; on the sixth were weapons of war, the gift of Mars; and on the seventh, various musical instruments, the presents of Apollo. The meaning of these emblematical decorations was explained in a Latin speech delivered by the author of it. Then an excellent band of music began to play

[1] The reader may find accounts of most of these excursions in a work entitled *The Progresses of Queen Elizabeth*, in two volumes 4to, published by Mr Nichols.

[2] This account is chiefly taken from a small pamphlet called *Princely Pleasures at Kenelworth Castle*. *Progresses*, vol. i.

as her majesty entered the inner court, where she alighted from her horse, and went upstairs to the apartments prepared for her.

On Sunday evening she was entertained with a grand display of fireworks, as well in the air as upon the water.

On Monday, after a great hunting, she was met on her return by Gascoigne the poet, so disguised as to represent a savage man, who paid her many high-flown compliments in a kind of dialogue between himself and an echo.

On Tuesday she was diverted with music, dancing, and an interlude upon the water.

On Wednesday was another grand hunting.

On Thursday she was amused with a grand bear-beating, to which were added tumbling and fire-works. Bear-beating and bull-beating were fashionable at this period, and considered as proper pastimes for the amusement of ladies of the highest rank. Elizabeth, though a woman, possessed a masculine mind, and preferred, or affected to prefer, the exercises of the chace and other recreations pursued by men, rather than those usually appropriated to her sex.

On Friday, the weather being unfavourable, there were no open shows.

On Saturday there was dancing within the castle, and a country brideale, with running at the quintain in the castle yard, and a pantomimical show called "the Old Coventry Play of Hock Thursday," performed by persons who came from Coventry for that purpose. In the evening a regular play was acted, succeeded by a banquet and a masque.

On the Sunday there was no public spectacle.

On the Monday there was a hunting in the afternoon, and, on the queen's return, she was entertained with another show upon the water, in which appeared a person in the character of Arion, riding upon a dolphin twenty-four feet in length; and he sung an admirable song, accompanied with music performed by six musicians concealed in the belly of the fish. Her majesty, it appears, was much pleased with this exhibition. The person who entertained her majesty in the character of Arion is said to have been Harry Goldingham, of whom the following anecdote is related: "There was a spectacle presented to Queen Elizabeth upon the water, and among others, Harry Goldingham was to represent Arion upon the back of a dolphin; but finding his voice to be very hoarse and unpleasant when he came to perform his part, he tears off his disguise, and swears that he was none of Arion, not he, but even honest Harry Goldingham; which blunt discovery pleased the queen better than if it had gone thorough in the right way. Yet he could order his voice to an instrument exceedingly well."[1]

On Tuesday the Coventry play was repeated, because the queen had not seen the whole of it on Saturday.

On Wednesday, the twentieth of the same month, she departed from Kenel-

[1] Harl. MSS. 6395, entitled *Merry Passages and Jests*, art. 221.

worth. Various other pastimes were prepared upon this occasion ; but, for want of time and opportunity, they could not be performed.

*THE MASTER OF THE REVELS.—From very early days there was an official of the English court termed the Master of the Revels. This was a permanent office quite distinct from the one who had temporary control over all Christmas or Epiphany merriment. It was his duty to superintend and provide for plays, interludes, and every variety of entertainment, apart from field sports, for the king's court. It was stated in 1660 that "the allowance of Playes, the ordering of Players and Playmakers, and the Permission for Erecting of Playhouses, Hath time out of minde, wherof the memory of man is not to the Contrary belonged to the Master of his Majesties Office of the Revells." In 1544 Henry VIII. appointed, by letters patent, Sir Thomas Cawardin, Knight, to this office, with an annual fee of £10, and powers to appoint a deputy. Queen Elizabeth made a like grant, in 1579, to Edmond Tilney, Esquire ; King James in 1603 to George Buck, Esquire, in 1613 to Sir John Ashley, and in 1622 to Ben. Jonson ; and Charles I., in 1629, jointly to Henry Herbert, Knight, and Simon Thelwall, Esquire. Sir Henry Herbert and Mr Thelwall at the Restoration claimed to exercise their office. This was resisted by playwrights and others, with the result that various interesting documents and statements were produced in support of their claims. In these it was stated that the office originated in the days of the Saxons ; that "mountebanks, lotteries, clockwork motions, ordinary motions, extra motions, dancing horses and mares, ropedancers, and slights of hand" all required licenses from the Master of the Revels, as well as "all Comedies, Tragedies, Poems, Ballads, half-sides, drolleries, and all billes relating to jokes." Moreover, Edward Hayward, gentleman, as deputy to Sir Henry Herbert, claimed to enjoy "all ancient privileges at Court, the ordering of maskes in the Innes of Law, halls, houses of great personages, and societies, all Balls, Dancing schooles, and musick, except his Majesty's and the priviledges of the Corporation touching freemen, if it extend soe farre ; Pageantry and other publique tryumphes, the rurall feasts called Wakes, where there is constant revelling and musick, Cockpitts, fencing and fencing schooles, nocturnal feasts, and banquettings in publique houses when attended with minstrelsy, singing, and Dancing, together with the ordering of all mommeries, fictions, Disguises, scenes, and masking attire, all which (in the judgment of an able Lawyer) are within the verge and comprehension of the Master of the Revells Patent from the words *Jocorum, Revelorum, et Mascorum.*"

*The words of the original patent gave jurisdiction throughout the whole kingdom of England, and Mr Hayward's claim for a very liberal interpretation was apparently granted. On July 23rd, 1663, Mr Hayward, in conjunction with Mr Poyntz, instructed Edward Thomas, one of the messengers belonging to his Majesties office of the Revels, to proceed to Bristol, with a view to the approaching fairs, and to acquaint the mayor with the king's grant to them, and the Lord Chamberlain's mandate, "touching musick, cockfightings, maskings,

d

prizes, stage-players, tumblers, vaulters, dancers on the ropes, such as act, sett forth, shew or present any play, shew, motion, feats of activity, or sights whatsoever."[1] Thomas was given power to grant temporary licenses to persons from Wales or remote parts, who seldom or never came to London, but others were to be required to take out licenses at the London office. Any presuming to act or exhibit unlicensed, were to be taken into custody, and kept until bound with good security to appear within ten days at the London office under penalty of £20. In 1668, Charles II. appointed Alexander Stafford, gentleman, Master of the Revels.

*Various interesting particulars relative to the Master of the Revels can be gleaned from the State Papers of the Public Record Office. There are full accounts extant of the expenditure of Richard Gibson, Master of the Revels, from 1509 to 1522, which show the extravagant character of the mummings and disguisings at the court of the young king.[2] Crimson, purple, blue, and yellow velvet; cloth of gold of Venice; blue, green, white, black, yellow, and crimson satin; blue, crimson, and yellow sarcenet; brabant cloth; crimson copper tinsel of Bruges; cotton cloth; white fustian; gray furs; and ostrich feathers were all used in the attiring of a single year. In February 1511, revels were held on a most costly scale in the house of Black Friars, Ludgate, and in White Hall, Westminster. On New Year's Day and Epiphany 1512, Gibson had the ordering of a pageant called "Dangerus Fortress." In the following year the pageant was called "The Rydie Mount," which was planted with broom to signify Plantaganet, and with red and white roses. At the foot were six lords, above them six minstrels, and at the entrance two armed men. It was drawn by two "mighty woord wossys or wyld men," and after the descent of the lords, the mount opened and showed six ladies. The six "lords" were the king, Mr Brandon, Earl of Essex, Sir Henry Guildford, Mr Nevell, and Mr Thomas Chene. The disguisings of Twelfth Night, 1514, cost the then great total of £404, 6s. 9d. The Twelfth Night revel at Greenwich, in 1516, as ordered by Gibson, was called "The Gardyn de Esperans." In 1520, a mummery was held at Greenwich on New Year's Eve; Gibson had to prepare dresses for fourteen persons. On January 5th, 1521, the king went "in meskellyng apparell" by water to visit the Cardinal with nineteen gentlemen. There were maskings on Shrove Monday and Shrove Tuesday, 1521, at Greenwich, in which the king took part; and he also played his share in several maskings both at Greenwich and York Place in the following year.

*Queen Elizabeth's expenditure on revels, early in her reign, outrivalled the extravagance of her father. From the first Christmas after her accession down to April 1567, the provisions and payments made by the Master of the Revels reached the then gigantic total of £4588, 1s. 10d.[3] Towards the end of the

---

[1] A Collection of Ancient Documents respecting the Office of Master of the Revels (Halliwell), 1870, *passim*.
[2] These are given with much detail in *Letters and Papers, Hen. VIII.*, vol. ii. pp. 1490-1518.
[3] *Dom. State Papers, Elizabeth*, vol. i. 47.

reign the expenses under this head were but small. In May 1594 Edmund Tilney, Master of the Revels, received a warrant of £311, 2s. 2d. for wares delivered and works done in the office of the revels, and for three years' wages of the officers.[1] In January 1597 £200 was assigned to the Master for wares and works, and three years' officers' wages; and also £66, 6s. 8d. yearly as composition for defraying the charges of the office for plays only, according to a rate of a late composition.[2]

*In 1603 Sir George Buck succeeded to the Mastership of the Revels. On July 10th, 1615, Sir George wrote to the Lord Chamberlain, saying that the King had been pleased, at the Queen's intercession on behalf of Samuel Danyell, to appoint a company of youths to perform comedies and tragedies at Bristol, under the name of the Youths of Her Majesty's Royal Chamber of Bristol; he had consented to it, without prejudice to the rights of his office; but he reminded the Chamberlain that he had received no wages for two years, and begged for payment of the arrears.[3]

*Sir Henry Herbert, the next Master of the Revels, got into rather serious trouble in the summer of 1674, almost immediately after his appointment, by licensing the poet Middleton's play *A Game at Chess*, which was a thinly-veiled political attack on Spain, that gave great umbrage to the Spanish ambassador.[4] Sir Henry Herbert was confirmed in his office on the accession of Charles I.

*In 1631 the churchwardens and constables of Blackfriars, on behalf of the whole parish, petitioned Bishop Laud to revive an order made by the Council and the Corporation in June 1600, limiting the playhouses to one each side of the Thames, and an order of 1619 suppressing the house in Blackfriars. They tabulated their reasons, which were briefly as follows: (1) hindrance to shop-keepers from great recourse to the plays, especially of coaches, their goods being broken and beaten off their stalls; (2) coaches so numerous in an afternoon that the inhabitants could not take in their beer or coals; (3) the passage through Ludgate and to the water was stopped; (4) if any fire occurred it could not be quenched; (5) baptisms and burials often disturbed; and (6) persons of honour and quality resident in the parish are restrained by the coaches from ingress and egress.[5]

*In May 1633, some strolling players visited Banbury. The mayor and justices, suspecting them to be wandering rogues, if not more dangerous persons, called on them for their license, they produced a patent which they pretended to be granted by the crown, and also a commission from the Master of the Revels. Believing these papers to be forgeries, or wrongly obtained, they arrested the six men, examined them, and committed them to prison, till the council's pleasure should be signified. The patent and commission and examinations were forwarded to London. The company had been acting, as they alleged, at Leicester, Market Bosworth, Stratford, Meriden, and Solihull, and at Sir Thomas Lucy's, and Sir William Spencer's.[6]

---

[1] *Dom. State Papers, Elizabeth*, vol. ccxlviii. 120. [2] *Ibid.* vol. cclxii. 18. [3] *Ibid. James I.*, vol. ii. 12; vol. lxxxi. 12. [4] *Ibid. James I.*, vol. clxxi. 64. [5] *Ibid. Charles I.*, ccv. 32. [6] *Ibid. Charles I.*, ccxxxviii. 32.

*Sir Henry Herbert received £200, as Master of the Revels, in October 1660, together with a warrant to advance him yearly such sums as might be needful for his office.[1] The official immediately under the master was termed the Yeoman of the Revels; his salary was usually £50 a year. In May 1661, one John Tredeskyn was brought before Sir Henry Herbert charged with showing " severall strainge cretures " without authority from the office of the revels ; but in the following month he obtained a royal warrant to continue as before to show to all who wish it his " rare and ingenious collection of rarities in art and nature," which had been for many years exhibited by him and his father before him. In July of the same year an order was made for the suppression of all stage players, tumblers, rope dancers, and showmen unless approved and authorised by the Master of the Revels, as some persons had obtained recently commissions from the king, acted plays and exhibited shows full of scandal, and abused their commissions by selling or lending them.

*George Jolly obtained a license from the revel office on January 1st, 1663, to raise a company of players for acting tragedies, comedies, pastorals, and interludes, throughout England, provided they outstayed not forty days in one place, and acted nothing offensive, nor in the time of divine worship, nor at prohibited seasons. At the same time general orders were issued that " what company soever, either stage players, musicians, mountebanks, or such as go about with monsters and strange sights," as had no authority confirmed by the Master of the Revels, should have their commissions taken from them and sent to the office.[3] In July of that year the king empowered the mayor and sheriff and magistrates of Norwich, as he understood that the meaner sort of people were diverted from their work through the frequency of lotteries, puppet-shows, etc., to determine the length of stay of such shows in the city notwithstanding any licenses from the revel office.[4]

ROPE-DANCING, TUTORED ANIMALS, AND PUPPET-SHOWS.—Great delight was taken in seeing men and animals perform such feats as appeared to be entirely contrary to their nature ; as, men and monkeys dancing upon ropes, or walking upon wires ; dogs dancing minuets, pigs arranging letters so as to form words at their master's command ; hares beating drums, or birds firing off cannons. These exhibitions, for all of them have in reality been brought to public view, are ridiculed by the *Spectator*, in a paper dated the 3rd of April 1711. The author pretends that he received the following letter from a showman who resided near Charing-Cross.

" Honoured Sir,—Having heard that this nation is a great encourager of ingenuity, I have brought with me a rope-dancer that was caught in one of the woods belonging to the great Mogul. He is by birth a monkey, but swings upon a rope, takes a pipe of tobacco, and drinks a glass of ale, like any reason-

---

[1] *Dom. State Papers, Charles II.*, vol. xvii. 2.
[3] *Ibid.* lxvii. 2.
[2] *Ibid.* xxxix. 110.
[4] *Ibid.* xxvi. 61.

able creature.[1] He gives great satisfaction to the quality; and if they will make a subscription for him, I will send for a brother of his out of Holland, that is a very good tumbler; and also for another of the same family whom I design for my merry-andrew, as being an excellent mimic, and the greatest droll in the country where he now is. I hope to have this entertainment in readiness for the next winter; and doubt not but it will please more than the opera or the puppet-show. I will not say that a monkey is a better man than some of the opera heroes; but certainly he is a better representative of a man than any artificial composition of wood and wire."

The latter part of this sarcasm relates to a feigned dispute for seniority between Powel, a puppet-showman, who exhibited his wooden heroes under the little piazza in Covent Garden, and the managers of the Italian opera; which is mentioned in a preceding paper[2] to this effect: "The opera at the Haymarket, and that under the little piazza of Covent Garden, are at present the two leading diversions of the town; Powel professing in his advertisements to set up Whittington and his Cat against Rinaldo and Armida."—After some observations, which are not immediately to the present purpose, the author proceeds: "I observe that Powel and the undertakers of the opera had both of them the same thought, and I think much about the same time, of introducing animals on their several stages, though indeed with different success. The sparrows and chaffinches at the Haymarket fly as yet very irregularly over the stage, and instead of perching on the trees, and performing their parts, these young actors either get into the galleries, or put out the candles; whereas Powel has so well disciplined his pig, that in the first scene he and Punch dance a minuet together. I am informed that Powel resolves to excel his adversaries in their own way, and introduce larks into his opera of Susanna, or Innocence betrayed; which will be exhibited next week with a pair of new elders."

From the same source of information, in a subsequent paper,[3] we may find a catalogue of the most popular spectacles exhibited in London at the commencement of the last century. Our author has introduced a projector, who produces a scheme for an opera entitled *The Expedition of Alexander the Great*; and proposes to bring in "all the remarkable shows about the town among the scenes and decorations of his piece"; which is described in the following manner: "This Expedition of Alexander opens with his consulting the Oracle at Delphos; in which the Dumb Conjurer, who has been visited by so many persons of quality of late years, is to be introduced as telling his fortune; at the same time Clench of Barnet[4] is represented in another corner of the temple, as ringing the bells of Delphos for joy of his arrival. The Tent of Darius is to be

---

[1] There actually was such a monkey exhibited at that time near Charing Cross, but in the bills which were given to the public he is called a Wild Hairy Man, and they tell us he performed all that the *Spectator* relates concerning him; but this subject is treated more fully in the body of the work.

[2] *Spectator*, vol. i. No. 14.   [3] *Ibid.* vol. i. No. 31, dated Thursday, April 5, 1711.

[4] A man famous at that time for imitating a variety of musical instruments with his voice, and, among others, the bells.

peopled by the ingenious Mrs Salmon, where Alexander is to fall in love with a piece of waxwork that represents the beautiful Statira. When Alexander comes to that country in which, Quintus Curtius tells us, the dogs were so exceedingly fierce, that they would not loose their hold, though they were cut to pieces limb by limb, and that they would hang upon their prey by their teeth when they had nothing but a mouth left, there is to be a scene of Hockley in the Hole, in which are to be represented all the diversions of that place, the Bull-Baiting only excepted, which cannot possibly be exhibited in the theatre by reason of the lowness of the roof. The several Woods in Asia, which Alexander must be supposed to pass through, will give the audience a sight of Monkies dancing upon ropes, with many other pleasantries of that ludicrous species. At the same time, if there chance to be any strange animals in town, whether birds or beasts, they may be either let loose among the woods, or driven across the stage by some of the country people of Asia. In the last Great Battle, Pinkethman is to personate king Porus upon an Elephant, and is to be encountered by Powel, representing Alexander the Great upon a Dromedary, which, nevertheless, he is desired to call by the name of Bucephalus. On the close of this great Decisive Battle, when the two Kings are thoroughly reconciled, to show the mutual friend-ship and good correspondence that reigns between them, they both of them go together to a puppet-show, in which the ingenious Mr Powel junior may have an opportunity of displaying his whole art of machinery for the diversion of the two monarchs." It is further added, that, "after the reconciliation of these two kings, they might invite one another to dinner, and either of them entertain his guest with the German artist, Mr Pinkethman's Heathen Gods, or any of the like Diversions which shall then chance to be in vogue."

The projector acknowledged the thought was not originally his own, but that he had taken the hint from "several Performances he had seen upon our stage; in one of which there was a Raree Show, in another a Ladder Dance, and in others a posture or a moving picture with many curiosities of the like nature."

MINSTRELSY, BELL-RINGING, ETC.—The people of this country in all ages delighted in secular music, songs, and theatrical performances;[1] which is abundantly evident from the great rewards they gave to the bards, the scalds, the gleemen, and the minstrels, who were successively the favourites of the opulent, and the idols of the vulgar. The continual encouragement given to these professors of music, poetry, and pantomime, in process of time swelled their numbers beyond all reasonable proportion, inflamed their pride, increased their avarice, and corrupted their manners; so that at length they lost the favour they had so long enjoyed among the higher classes of society; and, the dona-tions of the populace not being sufficient for their support, they fell away from affluence to poverty, and wandered about the country in a contemptible condition,

---

[1] "To pass over griefe," says an author of our own, "the Italians sleepe, the English go to playes, the Spaniards lament, and the Irish bowl," etc. Fynes Moryson's *Itinerary*, in 1617, part iii. book i. cap. 3.

dependent upon the casual rewards they might occasionally pick up at church-ales, wakes, and fairs.

Hentzner, who wrote at the conclusion of the sixteenth century, says, "the English excel in dancing and music, for they are active and lively." A little further on he adds, "they are vastly fond of great noises that fill the ear, such as the firing of cannon, beating of drums, and the ringing of bells; so that it is common for a number of them that have got a glass in their heads to get up into some belfry and ring the bells for hours together for the sake of exercise."[1] Polydore Vergil mentions another remarkable singularity belonging to the English, who celebrated the festival of Christmas with plays, masques, and magnificent spectacles, together with games at dice and dancing, which, he tells us, was as ancient as the year 1170, and not customary with other nations;[2] and with respect to the Christmas prince, or lord of the misrule, he was, as the same author informs us, a personage almost peculiar to this country.[3]

BAITING OF ANIMALS.—It were well if these singularities were the only vulnerable parts of the national character of our ancestors; but it must be confessed that there are other pastimes which equally attracted their attention, and manifested a great degree of barbarism, which will admit of no just defence. Sir Richard Steele, reprobating the inhumanity of throwing at cocks, makes these pertinent observations: "Some French writers have represented this diversion of the common people much to our disadvantage, and imputed it to a natural fierceness and cruelty of temper, as they do some other entertainments peculiar to our nation; I mean those elegant diversions of bull-baiting, and prize-fighting, with the like ingenious recreations of the bear-garden. I wish I knew how to answer this reproach which is cast upon us, and excuse the death of so many innocent cocks, bulls, dogs, and bears, as have been set together by the ears, or died an untimely death, only to make us sport."[4]

PASTIMES FORMERLY ON SUNDAYS.—I know not of any objection that can have more weight in the condemnation of these national barbarisms, than the time usually appropriated for the exhibition of them; which, it seems, was the after part of the Sunday. The same portion of time also was allotted for the performance of plays, called, in the writings of the sixteenth and seventeenth centuries, "vaine playes and interludes";[5] to which are added, "dice and card-playing, dancing, and other idle pastimes." Stephen Gosson, a very zealous, if not a very correct writer, declaiming vehemently against plays and players, says of the latter, "because they are permitted to play every Sunday, they make four or five Sundayes at leaste every weeke."[6] Nor is he less severe upon those who frequented such amusements: "To celebrate the Sabbath," says he, "they go to the theatres, and there keepe a general market of bawdrie; by

---

[1] Hentzner's *Itinerary*, pp. 88, 89.   [2] *Hist. Angl.* lib. xiii.   [3] *De Rerum Invent.* lib. v. cap. 2.
[4] *Tatler*, No. 134, dated Thursday, Feb. 16, 1709.
[5] See a pamphlet written by John Northbrooke, published in the reign of Queen Elizabeth, without date.
[6] *School of Abuse*, published 1579.

which means," as he afterwards expresses himself, "they make the theatre a place of assignation, and meet for worse purposes than merely seeing the play." A contemporary writer, endeavouring to prove the impropriety of an established form of prayer for the church service, among other arguments, uses the following: "He," meaning the minister, "posteth it over as fast as he can galloppe; for, eyther, he hath two places to serve; or else there are some games to be playde in the afternoon, as lying for the whetstone, heathenishe dauncing for the ring, a beare or a bull to be baited, or else a jackanapes to ride on horsebacke, or an interlude to be plaide; and, if no place else can be gotten, this interlude must be playde in the church. We speak not of ringing after mattins is done."[1] To what has been said, I shall add the following verses, which made their appearance rather earlier than either of the foregoing publications; and they describe, with much accuracy I doubt not, the manner of spending the Sunday afternoons according to the usage of that time: but it is proper previously to observe, that such amusements on holidays were by no means peculiar to the young gallants of this country, but equally practised upon the continent.

> "Now, when their dinner once is done, and that they well have fed,
> To play they go; to casting of the stone, to runne, or shoote;
> To tosse the light and windy ball aloft with hand or foote;
> Some others trie their skill in gonnes; some wrastell all the day;
> And some to schooles of fence do goe, to gaze upon the play;
> Another sort there is, that doe not love abroad to roame,
> But, for to passe their time at cardes, or tables, still at home."[2]

ROYAL INTERFERENCE WITH SUNDAY PASTIMES.—Citations to this purpose might be made from infinity of pamphlets, written professedly against the profanation of the Sabbath: it was certainly an evil that called loudly for redress; and the pens of various writers, moral and religious, as well of the clergy as the laity, have been employed for that purpose. There are some few treatises on this subject that do honour to their authors; but far the larger part of them are of a different description, consisting of vehement and abusive declamations, wherein the zeal of the writers is too frequently permitted to run at random, without the least restraint from reason and moderation, and, what is still worse, without that strict adherence to the truth which the seriousness of the subject necessarily required. It must be granted, however, that the continued remonstrances from the grave and religious parts of the community were not without effect. In the twenty-second year of the reign of Elizabeth, the magistrates of the city of London obtained from the queen an edict, " that all heathenish playes and interludes should be banished upon Sabbath days";[3] but this restriction, I apprehend, was confined to the jurisdiction of the lord mayor; for, it is certain that such amusements were publicly exhibited in other districts, and especially

---

[1] *Admonition to Parliament*, by Tho. Cartwright, published A.D. 1572.

[2] *The Pope's Kingdom*, book iv. translated from the Latin of Tho. Neogeorgus, by Barnabe Googe, and dedicated to Queen Elizabeth, A.D. 1570.

[3] John Field, in his *Declaration of God's Judgment at Paris Garden*, published A.D. 1603, fol. 9.

at the Paris Garden in Southwark, a place where these sort of sports were usually exhibited; and where three years afterwards a prodigious concourse of people being assembled together on a Sunday afternoon, to "see plays and a bear-baiting, the whole theatre gave way and fell to the ground; by which accident many of the spectators were killed, and more hurt." This lamentable misfortune was considered as a judgment from God, and occasioned a general prohibition of all public pastimes on the Sabbath-day. The wise successor of Elizabeth, on the other hand, thought that the restrictions on the public sports were too generally and too strictly applied, and especially in the country places; he therefore published on the 24th of May 1618 the following declaration: "Whereas we did justly, in our progresse through Lancashire, rebuke some puritanes and precise people, in prohibiting and unlawfully punishing of our good people for using their lawfull recreations and honest exercises on Sundayes and other holy dayes, after the afternoone sermon or service: It is our will, that after the end of divine service, our good people be not disturbed, letted, or discouraged, from any lawful recreation, such as dauncing, either for men or women; archery for men, leaping, vaulting, or any other such harmless recreation; nor for having of May-games, Whitson-ales, and morris-daunces, and the setting up of May-poles, and other sports therewith used; so as the same be had in due and convenient time, without impediment or neglect of divine service. But withall, we doe here account still as prohibited, all unlawfull games to be used upon Sundayes onely, as beare and bull-baitings, interludes, and, at all times in the meaner sort of people by law prohibited, bowling." This proclamation was renewed by Charles I. in the eighth year of his reign; which occasioned many serious complaints from the puritanical party; but, three years afterwards, a pamphlet was published which defended the principles of the declaration; wherein the author, who was a high churchman, endeavours to fine away the objections of its opponents. In one part he says, "those recreations are the meetest to be used, which give the best refreshment to the bodie, and leave the least impression in the minde. In this respect, shooting, leaping, pitching the barre, stool-ball, and the like, are rather to be chosen than diceing or carding." This publication was immediately answered by the other party, who certainly had the best end of the argument, and were not sparing in their severity, but wounded the ordinance itself through the sides of its defender. The more precise writers objected not only to the profanation of the Sabbath, but to the celebration of most of the established festivals and holidays, as we find from the following verses of Neogeorgus:

> "Their feastes, and all their holydayes they keep throughout the yeare,
> Are full of vile idolatry, and heathen like appeare.
> I shew not here their daunces yet with filthy gestures mad,
> Nor other wanton sports that on the holydayes are had.
> In some place solemne sights and showes, and pageants faire are play'd
> With sundry sorts of maskers brave, in strange attire arrai'd."

INTRODUCTION

DICE AND CARDS.—The Saxons and the Danes, as we have observed already,[1] were much addicted to gaming; and the same destructive propensity was equally prevalent among the Normans. The evil consequences arising from the indulgence of this pernicious pleasure have in all ages called loudly for reprehension, and demanded at last the more powerful interference of the legislature. The vice of gambling, however, is by no means peculiar to the people of this country: its influence is universally diffused among mankind; and in most nations the same strong measures that have been adopted here are found to be absolutely necessary to prevent its extension beyond the limits of subordination. Dice, and those games of chance dependent upon them, have been most generally decried; and cards, in latter times, are added to them as proper companions. Cards, when compared with dice, are indeed of modern invention, and originally, I doubt not, were productive only of innocent amusement; they were, however, soon converted into instruments of gambling equally dangerous as the dice themselves, and more enticing from the variety of changements they admit of, and the pleasing mixture of chance with skill, which often gives the tyro an advantage over the more experienced player; that is, supposing fair play on both sides; but woeful experience has convinced many that this is not always the case.

REGULATION OF GAMES FOR MONEY, BY RICHARD CŒUR DE LION, ETC.— Towards the close of the twelfth century, we meet with a very curious edict relative to gaming, and which shows how generally it even prevailed among the lower classes of the people at that period. This edict was established for the regulation of the Christian army under the command of Richard I. of England and Philip of France, during the crusade in 1190: It prohibits any person in the army beneath the degree of a knight from playing at any sort of game for money: knights and clergymen might play for money, but no one of them was permitted to lose more than twenty shillings in one whole day and night, under the penalty of one hundred shillings, to be paid to the archbishops in the army; the two monarchs had the privilege of playing for what they pleased; but their attendants were restricted to the sum of twenty shillings; and, if they exceeded, they were to be whipped naked through the army for three days.[2]

STATUTES AGAINST DICE, CARDS, BALL-PLAY, ETC.—The decrees established by the council held at Worcester, in the twenty-fourth year of Henry III., prohibited the clergy from playing at dice, or at cards: but neither the one nor the other of these games are mentioned in the succeeding penal statutes, before the twelfth year of Richard II., when diceing is particularised, and expressly forbidden; though perhaps they were both of them included under the general title of games of chance, and dishonest games, mentioned in the proclamation of Edward III. which, with other pastimes therein specified, were generally practised to the great detriment of military exercises, and of archery in particular.

---

[1] See p. xx. [2] Benedict. Abbas, Vit. Ric. I. edit. à Hearne, tom. ii. p. 610.

In the eleventh year of Henry VII. cards are first mentioned among the games prohibited by the law;[1] and at that time they seem to have been very generally used; for, the edict expressly forbids the practice of card-playing to apprentices, excepting the duration of the Christmas holidays, and then only in their masters' houses.[2] We learn from Stow, that these holidays extended "from All-Hallows evening to the day after Candlemasday, when," says the historian, "there was, among other sports, playing at cards for counters, nailes, and points in every house, more for pastime than for gain."[3] The recreations prohibited by proclamation in the reign of Edward III., exclusive of the games of chance, are thus specified; throwing of stones,[4] wood, or iron; playing at hand-ball, foot-ball, club-ball, and cambucam, which I take to have been a species of goff, and probably received its name from the crooked bat with which it was played. These games, as before observed, were not forbidden from any particular evil tendency in themselves, but because they engrossed too much of the leisure and attention of the populace, and diverted their minds from the pursuits of a more martial nature. I should not forget to add, that " bull-baiting and cock-fighting " are included with " other dishonest games as trivial and useless." In[5] the reign of Edward IV. we find coits, closh or claish, kayles or nine-pins, half-bowl, hand-in and hand-out, with quick-borde, classed among the unlawful amusements;[6] which list was considerably augmented in the succeeding reigns, and especially in the eighteenth year of Henry VIII., when bowling, loggating, playing at tennis, dice, cards and tables, or back-gammon, were included.[7]

In the preamble to the Parliamentary Statutes as early as the sixth year of Edward III., there is a clause prohibiting of boys or others from playing at barres, or snatch-hood, or any other improper games, in the king's palace at Westminster during the sitting of the parliament; neither might they, by striking, or otherwise, prevent any one from passing peaceably about his business.

ARCHERY SUCCEEDED BY BOWLING.—The general decay of those manly and spirited exercises, which formerly were practised in the vicinity of the metropolis, has not arisen from any want of inclination in the people, but from the want of places proper for the purpose; such as in times past had been allotted to them are now covered with buildings, or shut up by enclosures, so that, if it were not for skittles, dutch-pins, four-corners, and the like pastimes, they would have no amusements for the exercise of the body; and these amusements are only to be met with in places belonging to common drinking-houses, for which reason their play is seldom productive of much benefit, but more frequently becomes the

---

[1] An. 11, Hen. VII. cap. 2.

[2] No householder might permit the games prohibited by the statute to be practised in their houses, excepting on the holidays, as before specified, under the penalty of six shillings and eight-pence for every offence.

[3] *Survey of London*, p. 79.   [4] *Pilam manualem, pedinam, et bacculoream, et ad cambucam*, etc.

[5] Rot. Claus. 39 Ed. III. m. 23.

[6] The magistrates are commanded to seize upon the said tables, dice, cards, boules, closhes, tennice-balls, etc., and to burn them.   [7] An. 17 Edw. II. cap. 3.

prelude to drunkenness. This evil has been increasing for a long series of years; and honest Stow laments the retrenchments of the grounds appropriated for martial pastimes which had begun to take place in his day. "Why," says he, "should I speak of the ancient exercises of the long bow, by the citizens of this city, now almost clean left off and forsaken? I over-pass it; for, by the means of closeing in of common grounds, our archers, for want of room to shoot abroad, creep into bowling-alleys and ordinarie diceing-houses neer home, where they have room enough to hazard their money at unlawful games."[1] He also tells us, that "Northumberland house, in the parish of St Katherine Coleman, belonging to Henry Percy, Earl of Northumberland, in the thirty-third year of Henry the Sixth; but of late, being deserted by that noble family, the gardens were converted into bowling-alleys, and the other parts of the estate into diceing-houses. But bowling-alleys and houses for the exercise of diceing and other unlawful games are at this time so greatly increased in the other parts of the city and its suburbs, that this parent spot," or, as he afterwards calls it, "the ancient and only patron of misrule, is forsaken of its gamesters." And here we may add the following remark from an author somewhat more ancient than Stow:[2] "common bowling-alleyes are privy mothes that eat up the credit of many idle citizens, whose gaynes at home are not able to weigh downe theyr losses abroad; whose shoppes are so farre from maintaining their play, that theyr wives and children cry out for bread, and go to bedde supperlesse ofte in the yeere." In another place, his reflections are more general, and he exclaims, "Oh, what a wonderful change is this! our wreastling at armies is turned to wallowing in ladies' laps, our courage to cowardice, our running to royot, our bowes into bowls, and our darts into dishes."

MODERN GAMBLING.—The evils complained of by these writers were then in their infancy; they have in the present day (1801) attained to a gigantic stature; and we may add to them E.O. tables, as also other tables for gambling distinguished by the appellation of Rouge et Noir, Pharo-banks, and many more fashionable novelties, equally as detrimental to morality, and as equally destructive to the fortunes of those who pursue them, as any of the recreations of the former times. Even horse-racing, which anciently was considered as a liberal sport, and proper for the amusement of a gentleman, has been of late years degraded into a dangerous species of gambling, by no means the less deserving of censure, because it is fashionable and countenanced by persons of the highest rank and fortune. The good old Scotch poet little dreamed of such an innovation, when he lamented that horse-racing was falling into disrepute through the prevalency of games of chance. His words are these:

> "Halking, hunting, and swift horse running
> Are changit all in wrangus, wynning;
> There is no play but cartes and dyce," etc.[3]

---

[1] *Survey of London*, p. 85.   [2] Stephen Gosson, in *The School of Abuse*, 1579.
[3] An old anonymous poem "of Covetice," cited by Warton, *History of Poetry*, vol. ii. p. 316.

*The warmth with which dice-playing and every form of gaming is condemned in the writings of the Fathers and the later expounders of Christianity is a sufficient proof of its prevalence throughout Europe. With the introduction of cards in the fourteenth century, the flame of gambling burnt with renewed ardour, and provoked fresh remonstrances from the guardians of religion. In England gambling attained to an extraordinary pitch in the reign of Henry VIII., the king being himself an unscrupulous gamester; and the practice flourished under the highest auspices during the reign of Elizabeth and James I. Sir Miles Partridge threw dice with Henry VIII. for the great Jesus bells in "the tower of St Paul's, London, and won them; but the ropes afterwards catched about his neck, for in Edward the Sixth's days he was hanged for some criminal offences."[1]

*Modern club gaming in England is said to date from 1777 or 1778. In a pamphlet as to gambling by an M.P., published in 1784, it is stated that thirty years before there was but one gaming club in the metropolis, and the stakes very low, namely crowns or half-crowns, but at that date the clubs were numerous, and the fashion of high stakes generally prevalent.[2]

*Roulette or Roly Poly tables, so called from the balls used in them, were introduced into England about 1739, and were first set up at Tunbridge Wells.

*The first English lottery named in history was drawn 1569. It consisted of 400,000 lots at ten shillings each, and was drawn at the west door of the Cathedral Church of St Paul's. The prizes were in plate, and the profits to go to the repairing of the havens or ports of the kingdom. Another state lottery was held in 1612, in favour of the plantation of English colonists in Virginia; the chief prize, "4000 crowns in fair plate," was won by Thomas Sharplys, a London tailor. In 1680 a lottery was granted to supply the metropolis with water, and a few years later the Government resorted to a huge lottery scheme to find the war funds which resulted in the capture of Namur. From 1709 until 1824 lottery bills were in the programme of every session, the prizes being generally paid in terminable annuities. This state gambling led to an appalling amount of vice and misery as well as direct fraud. The last public lottery in Great Britain was drawn in October 1826.

LADIES' PASTIMES—NEEDLE-WORK.—It now remains to say a few words in a general way respecting the diversions of the English ladies. In the early ages, our fair countrywomen employed a large portion of their time in needlework and embroidery; and their acquirements in these elegant accomplishments most probably afforded them little leisure for the pursuits of trifling and useless amusements; but, though we are not acquainted with the nature of their recreations, there is no reason to suppose that they were unbecoming in themselves, or indulged beyond the bounds of reason or decorum. I have already, on a former occasion, particularly noticed the skilfulness of the Saxon and Norman ladies in handling the needle, embroidering, and working in tapestry; and that their per-

[1] Harl. Misc.   [2] Steinmetz *Gaming Table* (1870) i. ch. vi.

formances were not only held in very high estimation at home, but were equally prised upon the continent, where none were produced that could be placed in competition with them.[1]

DANCING AND CHESS PLAY.—Dancing was certainly an ancient and favourite pastime with the women of this country : the maidens even in a state of servitude claimed, as it were by established privilege, the license to indulge themselves in this exercise on holidays and public festivals ; when it was usually performed in the presence of their masters and mistresses.

In the middle ages, dice, chess, and afterwards tables, and cards, with other sedentary games of chance and skill, were reckoned among the female amusements ; and the ladies also frequently joined with the men in such pastimes, as we find it expressly declared in the metrical romance of *Ipomydom.* The passage alluded to runs thus :

> "When they had dyned, as I you saye,
> Lordes and ladyes yede to to playe ;
> Some to tables, and some to chesse,
> With other gamys more or lesse." [2]

In another poem, by Gower,[3] a lover asks his mistress, when she is tired of "dancing and caroling," if she was willing to "play at chesse, or on the dyes to cast a chaunce." Forrest, speaking in praise of Catharine of Arragon, first wife of Henry VIII., says, that when she was young,

> "With stoole and with needyl she was not to seeke,
> And other practiseings for ladyes meete ;
> To pastyme at tables, tick tack or gleeke,
> Cardis and dyce"—etc.[4]

LADIES' RECREATIONS IN THE FOURTEENTH CENTURY.—The English ladies did not always confine themselves to domestic pastimes, they sometimes participated with the other sex in diversions of a more masculine nature ; and engaged with them in the sports of the field. These violent exercises seem to have been rather unfashionable among them in the seventeenth century ; for Burton, in his *Anatomy of Melancholy,* speaks of their pastimes as much better suited to the modesty and softness of the sex. "The women," says he, "instead of laborious studies, have curious needle-works, cutworks, spinning, bone-lace making, with other pretty devices to adorn houses, cushions, carpets, stool-seats," etc.[5] Not but some of these masculine females have occasionally made their appearance : and at the commencement of the last century, it should seem that they were more commonly seen than in Burton's time, which gave occasion for the following satirical paper in one of the *Spectators,*[6] written

---

[1] In the *Manners and Customs of the English* ; the *Chronicle of England* ; and more particularly in the *View of the Dresses of the English,* vol. i. p. 73, vol. ii. p. 140, etc.

[2] Harl. MS. 2252.   [3] *Confessio Amantis.*   [4] Warton's *History of English Poetry,* vol. iii. p. 311.

[5] Part ii. sect. 2, cap. 4.   [6] No. 55, A.D. 1711.

by Addison: " I have," says he, "very frequently the opportunity of seeing a rural Andromache, who came up to town last winter, and is one of the greatest foxhunters in the country; she talks of hounds and horses, and makes nothing of leaping over a six-bar gate. If a man tells her a waggish story, she gives him a push with her hand in jest, and calls him an impudent dog; and, if her servant neglects his business, threatens to kick him out of the house. I have heard her in her wrath call a substantial tradesman a lousie cur; and I remember one day when she could not think of the name of a person, she described him, in a large company of men and ladies, by the fellow with the broad shoulders."

THE AUTHOR'S [JOSEPH STRUTT] LABOURS—CHARACTER OF THE ENGRAVINGS.—Having laid before my readers a general view of the sports and pastimes of our ancestors, I shall proceed to arrange them under their proper heads, and allot to each of them a separate elucidation. The task in truth is extremely difficult; and many omissions, as well as many errors, must of necessity occur in the prosecution of it; but none, I hope, of any great magnitude, nor more than candour will overlook, especially when it is recollected, that in a variety of instances, I have been constrained to proceed without any guide, and explore, as it were, the recesses of a trackless wilderness. I must also entreat the reader to excuse the frequent quotations which he will meet with, which in general I have given verbatim; and this I have done for his satisfaction, as well as my own, judging it much fairer to stand upon the authority of others than to arrogate to myself the least degree of penetration to which I have no claim.

It is necessary to add, that the engravings, which constitute an essential part of this work, are not the produce of modern invention, neither do they contain a single figure that has not its proper authority. Most of the originals are exceedingly ancient, and all the copies are faithfully made without the least unnecessary deviation. As specimens of the art of design they have nothing to recommend them to the modern eye, but as portraitures of the manners and usages of our ancestors, in times remote, they are exceedingly valuable, because they not only elucidate many obsolete customs, but lead to the explanation of several obscurities in the history of former ages.

January 1801.

SPORTS AND PASTIMES OF THE PEOPLE OF ENGLAND

BOOK I

RURAL EXERCISES PRACTISED BY PERSONS OF RANK

CHAPTER I

State of Hunting among the Britons—The Saxons expert in Hunting—The Danes also—The Saxons subsequently—The Normans—Their tyrannical Proceedings—Hunting and Hawking after the Conquest—Laws relating to Hunting —Hunting and Hawking followed by the Clergy—The Manner in which the dignified Clergy in the Middle Ages pursued these Pastimes—The English Ladies fond of these Sports—Privileges of the Citizens of London to Hunt —Private Privileges for Hunting—Two Treatises on Hunting considered—Names of Beasts to be hunted—Wolves —Wild Boars—Fox and Badger—Wild Cat and Marten—Otter—Dogs for Hunting—Royal Hunting—Hare Coursing—Terms used in Hunting—Times when to Hunt—Later Hunting Treatises.

HUNTING AMONG THE BRITONS.—Dio Nicæus, an ancient author, speaking of the inhabitants of the northern parts of this island, tells us, they were a fierce and barbarous people, who tilled no ground, but lived upon the depredations they committed in the southern districts, or upon the food they procured by hunting. Strabo also says, that the dogs bred in Britain were highly esteemed upon the continent, on account of their excellent qualities for hunting; and these qualities, he seems to hint, were natural to them, and not the effect of tutorage by their foreign masters. The information derived from the above-cited authors does not amount to a proof that the practice of hunting was familiar with the Britons collectively; yet it certainly affords much fair argument in the support of such an opinion; for it is hardly reasonable to suppose that the pursuit of game should have been confined to the uncultivated northern freebooters, and totally neglected by the more civilised inhabitants of the southern parts of the island. We are well assured that venison constituted a great portion of their food, and as they had in their possession such dogs as were naturally prone to the chase, there can be little doubt that they would exercise them for the purpose of procuring their favourite diet; besides, they kept large herds of cattle, and flocks of sheep, both of which required protection from the wolves, and other ferocious animals, that infested the woods and coverts, and must frequently have rendered hunting an act of absolute necessity.

A

We do not find, that, during the establishment of the Romans in Britain, there were any restrictive laws promulgated respecting the killing of game. It appears to have been an established maxim, in the early jurisprudence of that people, to invest the right of such things as had no master with those who were the first possessors. Wild beasts, birds, and fishes, became the property of those who first could take them. It is most probable that the Britons were left at liberty to exercise their ancient privileges; for, had any severity been exerted to prevent the destruction of game, such laws would hardly have been passed over without the slightest notice being taken of them by the ancient historians.

HUNTING AMONG THE SAXONS.—The Germans, and other northern nations, were much more strongly attached to the sports of the field than the Romans, and accordingly they restricted the natural rights which the people claimed of hunting. The ancient privileges were gradually withdrawn from them, and appropriated by the chiefs and leaders to themselves; at last they became the sole prerogative of the crown, and were thence extended to the various ranks and dignities of the state at the royal pleasure.

As early as the ninth century, and probably long before that period, hunting constituted an essential part of the education of a young nobleman. Asser assures us, that Alfred the great, before he was twelve years of age, "was a most expert and active hunter, and excelled in all the branches of that most noble art, to which he applied with incessant labour and amazing success." It is certain that, whenever a temporary peace gave leisure for relaxation, hunting was one of the most favoured pastimes followed by the nobility and persons of opulence at that period. It is no wonder, therefore, that dogs proper for the sport should be held in the highest estimation. When Athelstan, the grandson of Alfred, had obtained a signal victory at Brunan-burgh over Constantine king of Wales, he imposed upon him a yearly tribute of gold, silver, and cattle; to which was also added a certain number of "hawks, and sharp-scented dogs, fit for hunting of wild beasts." His successor, Edgar, remitted the pecuniary payment on condition of receiving annually the skins of three hundred wolves. We do not find, indeed, that the hawks and the hounds were included in this new stipulation; but it does not seem reason-able that Edgar, who, like his predecessor, was extremely fond of the sports of the field, should have given up that part of the tribute.

*By the laws of King Ethelred hunting was prohibited on the Sunday's festival; an enactment that was renewed by King Cnut. Hunting was con-sidered so unsuitable a pastime for the clergy that Archbishop Theodore assigned a year's penance for anyone in minor orders that indulged in it, two years for a deacon, and three years for a priest. Archbishop Egbert, of York, improved on this by assigning seven years of penance for the like offence on an episcopal offender. King Edgar's canons forbade a priest to hunt, hawk, or dice, but to study books as becometh his order.[1]

---

[1] *Ancient Laws and Institutes of England* (1840), *passim.*

Hunting.

HUNTING AMONG THE DANES.—The Danes deriving their origin from the same source as the Saxons, differed little from them in their manners and habitudes, and perhaps not at all in their amusements; the propensity to hunting, however, was equally common to both. When Cnut the Dane had obtained possession of the throne of England, he imposed several restrictions upon the pursuit of game, which were not only very severe, but seem to have been altogether unprecedented; and these may be deemed a sufficient proof of his strong attachment to his favourite pastime, for, in other respects, his edicts breathed an appearance of mildness and regard for the comforts of the people.[1]

HUNTING DURING THE RESTORATION OF THE SAXONS.—After the expulsion of the Danes, and during the short restoration of the Saxon monarchy, the sports of the field still maintained their ground. Edward the Confessor, whose disposition seems rather to have been suited to the cloister than to the throne, would join in no other secular amusements; but he took the greatest delight, says William of Malmsbury, "to follow a pack of swift hounds in pursuit of game, and to cheer them with his voice." He was equally pleased with hawking, and every day, after divine service, he spent his time in one or other of these favourite pastimes. Harold, who succeeded him, was so fond of his hawk and his hounds, that he rarely travelled without them. He is so represented upon the famous tapestry of Bayeux, with his hounds by his side and a hawk upon his hand, when brought before William duke of Normandy.[2] Travelling thus accompanied, was not a singular trait in the character of a nobleman at this period.

The representation in the centre of the first plate of a Saxon chieftain, attended by his huntsman and a couple of hounds, pursuing the wild swine in a forest, is taken from a painting of the ninth century in the Cotton Library.[3]

At the top of the same plate is a representation of the manner of attacking the wild boar, from a manuscript written about the commencement of the fourteenth century, in the possession of Mr Francis Douce; whilst the unearthing of a fox, at the bottom of the plate, is from a manuscript in the Royal Library,[4] written about the same time as the latter.

HUNTING AMONG THE NORMANS OPPRESSIVELY EXERCISED.—During the tyrannical government of William the Norman, and his two sons who succeeded him, the restrictions concerning the killing of game were by no means meliorated. The privileges of hunting in the royal forests were confined to the king and his favourites; and, to render these receptacles for the beasts of the chase more capacious, or to make new ones, whole villages were depopulated, and places of divine worship overthrown; not the least regard being

---

[1] *Cnut allowed every freeman to hunt in wood and field on his own lands; but the laws pertaining to the royal forests were terribly severe. For a first offence a freeman lost his liberty, and a villain his right hand; for a second offence the common punishment was death.

[2] Montfaucon, *Monarch. Fran.*, and Ducarel's *Anglo-Norman Antiquities.*

[3] Tiberius, B. v.

[4] No. 2, B. vii.

paid to the miseries of the suffering inhabitants, or the cause of religion.[1] These despotic proceedings were not confined to royalty, as may be proved from good authority. I need not mention the New Forest, in Hampshire, made by the elder William, or the park at Woodstock in Oxfordshire, seven miles in circumference, and walled round with stone by Henry his son. This park, Stowe tells us, was the first made in England. The royal example was first followed by Henry earl of Warwick, who made a park at Wedgenoke, near Warwick, to preserve his deer and other animals for hunting; after this the practice of park-making became general among persons of opulence.

This subject is delineated, with great force of colouring, by John of Salisbury, a writer of the twelfth century, when the severity of the game laws was somewhat abated. " In our time," says the author, " hunting and hawking are esteemed the most honourable employments, and most excellent virtues, by our nobility; and they think it the height of worldly felicity to spend the whole of their time in these diversions; accordingly they prepare for them with more solicitude, expense, and parade, than they do for war; and pursue the wild beasts with greater fury than they do the enemies of their country. By constantly following this way of life, they lose much of their humanity, and become as savage, nearly, as the very brutes they hunt." He then proceeds in this manner: " Husbandmen, with their harmless herds and flocks, are driven from their well cultivated fields, their meadows, and their pastures, that wild beasts may range in them without interruption." He adds, addressing himself to his unfortunate countrymen, " If one of these great and merciless hunters shall pass by your habitation, bring forth hastily all the refreshment you have in your house, or that you can readily buy, or borrow from your neighbour; that you may not be involved in ruin, or even accused of treason."[2] If this picture of Norman tyranny be correct, it exhibits a melancholy view of the sufferings to which the lower classes of the people were exposed; in short, it appears that these haughty Nimrods considered the murder of a man as a crime of less magnitude than the killing of a single beast appointed for the chase.

HUNTING AND HAWKING AFTER THE CONQUEST. — King John was particularly attached to the sports of the field; and his partiality for fine horses, hounds, and hawks, is evident, from his frequently receiving such animals, by way of payment, instead of money, for the renewal of grants, fines, and forfeitures, belonging to the crown.[3]

In the reign of Edward I. this favourite amusement was reduced to a perfect science, and regular rules established for its practice; these rules were afterwards extended by the master of the game belonging to king Henry IV. and drawn up for the use of his son, Henry prince of Wales. Both these

---

[1] * Domesday Survey proves that this oft repeated statement as to the New Forest, and the overthrow of churches by the Conqueror, requires considerable qualification. See Round's introduction to the Hampshire Domesday, *Victoria County Histories, Hants,* vol. i.

[2] *De Nugis Cuiralium,* lib. i. cap. 4.   [3] Blount's *Ancient Tenures,* p. 135.

tracts are preserved, and we shall have occasion to speak a little fuller concerning them in the course of this chapter.

Edward III. took so much delight in hunting, that even at the time he was engaged in war with France, and resident in that country, he had with him in his army sixty couple of stag hounds, and as many hare hounds,[1] and every day he amused himself with hunting or hawking.

It also appears that many of the great lords in the English army had their hounds and their hawks, as well as the king; to this may be added, from the same author, that is, Froissart, who was himself a witness to the fact, that Gaston earl of Foix, a foreign nobleman contemporary with king Edward, kept upwards of six hundred dogs in his castle for the purpose of hunting. He had four greyhounds called by the romantic names of Tristram, Hector, Brute, and Roland.[2]

*James I. preferred the amusement of hunting to hawking or shooting. It is said of this monarch that he divided his time betwixt his standish, his bottle, and his hunting; the last had his fair weather, the two former his dull and cloudy.[3] In "The King's Christian Duties," which James wrote for his son, he says: "I cannot omit hare hunting, namely with running hounds, which is the most honourable and noblest thereof; for it is a thievish form of hunting to shoot with guns or bows, and greyhound hunting (coursing) is not so martial a game." James enclosed the park of Theobalds with a brick wall ten miles in extent, the deer in which were valued at £1000. Neither age nor illness deterred him from his favourite amusement; in 1619, when only able to be carried in a chair or litter, he came to Theobalds, and would have the deer mustered before him; and in 1624, contrary to the order of his physicians, he left Royston to see some hawks fly at Newmarket.[4]

It would be an endless, as well as a needless task, to quote all the passages that occur in the poetical and prose writings of the last three centuries, to prove that this favourite pastime lost nothing of its relish in more modern times; on the contrary, it seems to have been more generally practised. Sir Thomas More, who wrote in the reign of Henry VIII., describing the state of manhood, makes a young gallant to say,

> Man-hod I am, therefore I me delyght
> To hunt and hawke, to nourishe up and fede
> The greyhounde to the course, the hawke to th' flight,
> And to bestryde a good and lusty stede.[5]

These pursuits are said by later writers to have been destructive to the fortunes of many inconsiderate young heirs, who, desirous of emulating the state of their superiors, have kept their horses, hounds, and hawks, and flourished away for a short time, in a style that their income was inadequate to support.

LAWS RELATING TO HUNTING.—Laws for punishing such as hunted, or

---

[1] " Fort chiens et chiens de levries," Froissart, *Chron.* vol. i. cap. 210. [2] Froissart, vol. iv.
[3] Wellwood's *Memoirs*, p. 35. [4] *Victoria County Histories, Hertfordshire*, i. 347-8.
[5] Sir Thomas More's *Poems.* See also Watson's *History of English Poetry*, 4to vol. iii. p. 101.

destroyed the game, in the royal forests, and other precincts belonging to the crown, were, as we have just hinted above, established with unprecedented severity by Cnut, the Dane, when he ascended the throne of England.

The severity of the game laws was rather increased, than abated, under the governance of the first four Norman monarchs. Henry II. is said to have relaxed their efficacy; rather, I presume, by not commanding them to be enforced with rigour, than by causing them to be abrogated; for they seem to have virtually existed in the reign of king John; and occasioned the clause in the Forest Charter, insisting that no man should forfeit his life, or his limbs, for killing the king's deer;—but, if he was taken in the fact of stealing venison belonging to the king, he should be subjected to a heavy fine; and, in default of payment, be imprisoned for one year and one day; and after the expiration of that time, find surety for his good behaviour, or be banished the land.[1] This charter was afterwards confirmed by his son Henry III. and the succeeding monarchs.

HUNTING BY THE CLERGY.—Another clause in the same charter grants to an archbishop, bishop, earl, or baron, when travelling through the royal forests, at the king's command, the privilege to kill one deer or two in the sight of the forester, if he was at hand; if not, they were commanded to cause a horn to be sounded, that it might not appear as if they had intended to steal the game.

It is evident that this privilege was afterwards construed into a permission for the personages named therein to hunt in the royal chases; but the words of the charter are not to that amount, and ought, says Spelman, to be taken literally as they stand in the translation: they could not however, at any rate, adds he, mean, "that the ecclesiastics are to hunt the deer themselves, for they suppose them to be no hunters, as the earls and barons might be; and therefore it is not said, that he who claims the venison shall blow the horn, but only that he shall cause it to be sounded.[2]

The propensity of the clergy to follow the secular pastimes, and especially those of hunting and hawking, is frequently reprobated by the poets and moralists of the former times. Chaucer makes the monks much better skilled in riding and hunting, than in divinity. The same poet, afterwards, in the "Ploughman's Tale," takes occasion to accuse the monks of pride, because they rode on coursers like knights, having their hawks and hounds with them. In the same tale he severely reproaches the priests for their dissolute manners, saying that many of them thought more upon hunting with their dogs, and blowing the horn, than of the service they owed to God.[3]

The prevalence of these excesses occasioned the restrictions, contained in an edict established in the thirteenth year of Richard II., which prohibits any priest, or other clerk, not possessed of a benefice to the yearly amount of ten

---

[1] Carta de Foresta, cap. II.

[2] Spelman's *Answer to the Apology for Archbishop Abbot.*

[3] *Canterbury Tales* by Chaucer. Numerous quotations might be made from other writers in addition to those above; but they are sufficient for my purpose.

pounds, from keeping a greyhound, or any other dog for the purpose of hunting; neither might they use ferrits, hayes, nets, hare-pipes, cords, or other engines to take or destroy the deer, hares, or rabbits, under the penalty of one year's imprisonment.[1] The dignified clergy were not affected by this statute, but retained their ancient privileges, which appear to have been very extensive. By the game law of Cnut the Dane they were permitted to hunt in the forests belonging to the crown; and these prerogatives were not abrogated by the Normans. Henry II., displeased at the power and ambition of the ecclesiastics, endeavoured to render these grants of none effect; not by publicly annulling them, but by putting in force the canon law, which strictly forbade the clergy to spend their time in hunting and hawking; and for this purpose, having obtained permission from Hugo Pertroleonis, the Pope's legate, he caused a law to be made, authorising him to convene the offenders before the secular judges, and there to punish them.[2] The establishment of this edict was probably more to show his power, than really to restrain them from hunting.

HUNTING AND HAWKING IN THE MIDDLE AGES BY BISHOPS, &c.—The bishops and abbots of the middle ages hunted with great state, having a large train of retainers and servants; and some of them are recorded for their skill in this fashionable pursuit. Walter, bishop of Rochester, who lived in the thirteenth century, was an excellent hunter, and so fond of the sport, that at the age of fourscore he made hunting his sole employment, to the total neglect of the duties of his office.[3] In the succeeding century an abbot of Leicester surpassed all the sportsmen of the time in the art of hare hunting;[4] and even when these dignitaries were travelling from place to place, upon affairs of business, they usually had both hounds and hawks in their train. Fitzstephen assures us that Thomas à Becket, being sent as ambassador from Henry II. to the court of France, assumed the state of a secular potentate; and took with him dogs and hawks of various sorts, such as were used by kings and princes.[5]

The clergy of rank, at all times, had the privilege of hunting in their own parks and inclosures; and therefore, that they might not be prevented from following this favourite pastime, they took care to have such receptacles for game belonging to their houses. At the time of the Reformation, the See of Norwich, only, was in the possession of no less than thirteen parks, well stocked with deer and other animals for the chase.[6] At the end of a book of Homilies in MS., in the Cotton Library,[7] written about the reign of Henry VI., is a poem containing instructions to priests in general, and requiring them, among other things, not to engage in "hawkynge, huntynge, and dawnsynge."

HUNTING AND HAWKING BY LADIES.—The ladies often accompanied the gentlemen in hunting parties; upon these occasions it was usual to draw the game into a small compass by means of inclosures, and temporary stands were

[1] Stat. 13 Rich. II.
[2] An. 21 Hen. II. A.D. 1157. *Vide* Spelman's *Answer to the Apology for Archbishop Abbot.*
[3] P. Blensens. epist. lvi. p. 81.   [4] Knyghton, *apud Decem Script.* p. 263.
[5] Stephanid. vit. S. Thom.   [6] *Vide* Spelman, *ut supra.*   [7] Claudius, A. 2.

made for them to be spectators of the sport; though in many instances they joined in it, and shot at the animals as they passed by them, with arrows. Agreeable to these manners, which custom reconciled to the fair sex, most of the heroines of romance are said to be fond of the sports of the field. In an old poem entitled the " Squyer of lowe degre," [1] the king of Hungary promises his daughter that in the morning she shall go with him on a hunting party, arrayed most gorgeously, and riding in a chariot covered with red velvet, drawn by

> Jennettes of Spayne that ben so white,
> Trapped to the ground with velvet bright.

In the field, says he, the game shall be inclosed with nets, and you placed at a stand so conveniently that the harts and the hinds shall come close to you—

> Ye shall be set at such a tryst,
> That hert and hynde shall come to your fyst.

He then commends the music of the bugle-horn—

> To here the bugles there yblow
> With theyr bugles in that place,
> And seven score raches at his rechase.

He also assures her that she should have—

> A lese of herhounds with her to strake.

The harehound, or greyhound, was considered as a very valuable present in former times, and especially among the ladies, with whom it appears to have been a peculiar favourite; and therefore in another metrical romance, probably more ancient than the former, called " Sir Eglamore," [2] a princess tells the knight that if he was inclined to hunt, she would, as an especial mark of her favour, give him an excellent greyhound, so swift that no deer could escape from his pursuit—

> Syr yf you be on huntynge founde,
> I shall you gyve a good greyhounde
>   That is dunne as a doo :
> For as I am trewe gentylwoman,
> There was never deer that he at ran,
>   That myght yscape him fro.

It is evident, however, that the ladies had hunting parties by themselves. An illustration in a manuscript of the early part of the fourteenth century reproduced on the second plate depicts them in the open fields winding the horn, rousing the game, and pursuing it, without any other assistance. [3] We may also observe, that, upon these occasions, the female Nimrods dispensed with the method of riding best suited to the modesty of the sex, and sat astride on the saddle like the men; but this indecorous custom, I trust, was never general, nor of long continuance, even with the heroines who were most delighted with these

---

[1] Garrick's Collection of Old Plays, K. vol. ix.
[2] Garrick's Collec. K. vol. x.
[3] Royal Library, 2 B. vii.

Hunting.

masculine exercises. An author of the seventeenth century speaks of another fashion, adopted by the fair huntresses of the town of Bury in Suffolk. "The Bury ladies," says he, "that used hawking and hunting, were once in a great vaine of wearing breeches," which it seems gave rise to many severe and ludicrous sarcasms. The only argument in favour of this habit, was decency in case of an accident. But it was observed that such accidents ought to be prevented, in a manner more consistent with the delicacy of the sex, that is, by refraining from those dangerous recreations.[1]

The hunting dresses, as they appeared at the commencement of the fifteenth century, are given from a manuscript of that time in the Harleian Collection,[2] at the top of the second plate.

Queen Elizabeth was extremely fond of the chase, and the nobility who entertained her in her different progresses, made large hunting parties, which she usually joined when the weather was favourable. She very frequently indulged herself in following of the hounds, and hunted the red and fallow deer, the hare, and the otter. "Her majesty," says a courtier, writing to Sir Robert Sidney, "is well and excellently disposed to hunting, for every second day she is on horseback and continues the sport long."[3] At this time her majesty had just entered the seventy-seventh year of her age, and she was then at her palace at Outlands. Often, when she was not disposed to hunt herself, she was entertained with the sight of the pastime. At Cowdrey, in Sussex, the seat of Lord Montecute, A.D. 1591, one day after dinner her grace saw from a turret, "sixteen bucks all having fayre lawe, pulled downe with greyhounds in a laund or lawn."[4]

*At the close of the eighteenth century Hertfordshire knew a distinguished lady huntress who rivalled Queen Elizabeth in her keenness for the chase at an advanced age. In 1793 Lady Salisbury, a most daring rider and sportswoman, became the active mistress of the Hertfordshire hounds, which were called during her reign the Hatfield hounds. It was not until Lady Salisbury was seventy-eight years of age that she gave up the mistresship and ceased to follow the foxhounds; even then she said that she thought she was good enough to hunt with the harriers.[5]

PRIVILEGES OF THE CITIZENS OF LONDON TO HUNT AND HAWK.—The citizens of London were permitted to hunt and hawk in certain districts. And one of the clauses, in the royal charter granted to them by Henry I., runs to this purport: "The citizens of London may have chases, and hunt as well, and as fully, as their ancestors have had; that is to say, in the Chiltre, in Middlesex, and Surry."[6] Hence we find, that these privileges were of ancient standing. They were also confirmed by the succeeding charters. Fitzstephen, who wrote towards the close of the reign of Henry II., says, that the Londoners delight

---

[1] MS. Harl. 6395. *Merry Passages and Jeasts*, art. 345. * It is said that Anne of Bohemia, consort of Richard II., was the first to introduce the side-saddle into England; but ladies usually rode like men for at least two more centuries, and peasant-women until comparatively recent times. [2] No. 4431.
[3] Rowland Whyte to Sir Robert Sidney, dated September 12, A.D. 1600. [4] Nichols's *Progresses*, vol. ii.
[5] *Vict. Co. Histories, Hertfordshire*, i. 349. [6] Maitland's *Hist. London*, book i. chap. 6.

themselves with hawks and hounds, for they have the liberty of hunting in Middlesex, Hertfordshire, all Chilton, and in Kent to the waters of Grey,[1] which differs somewhat from the statement in the charter. These exercises were not much followed by the citizens of London at the close of the sixteenth century, not for want of taste for the amusement, says Stow, but for leisure to pursue it.[2] Strype, however, so late as the reign of George I., reckons among the modern amusements of the Londoners, " Riding on horseback and hunting with my Lord Mayor's hounds, when the common-hunt goes out."

This common-hunt of the citizens is ridiculed in an old ballad called the " London Customs," published in D'Urfey's Collection,[3] I shall select the three following stanzas only.

> Next once a year into Essex a hunting they go ;
> To see 'em pass along, O 'tis a most pretty shew :
> Through Cheapside and Fenchurch-street, and so to Aldgate pump,
> Each man with 's spurs in 's horses sides, and his back-sword cross his rump.
>
> My lord he takes a staff in hand to beat the bushes o'er ;
> I must confess it was a work he ne'er had done before.
> A creature bounceth from a bush, which made them all to laugh ;
> My lord, he cried, a hare a hare, but it prov'd an Essex calf.
>
> And when they had done their sport, they came to London where they dwell,
> Their faces all so torn and scratch'd, their wives scarce knew them well ;
> For 'twas a very great mercy, so many 'scap'd alive,
> For of twenty saddles carried out, they brought again but five.

Privileges to hunt in certain districts, were frequently granted to individuals either from favour, or as a reward for their services. Richard I. gave to Henry de Grey, of Codnor, the manor of Turroe, in Essex, with permission to hunt the hare and the fox, in any lands belonging to the crown, excepting only the king's own demesne parks ; and this special mark of the royal favour was confirmed by his brother John, when he succeeded to the throne.[4]

Others obtained grants of land, on condition of their paying an annual tribute in horses, hawks, and hounds. And here I cannot help noticing a curious tenure, by which Bertram de Criol held the manor of Setene, or Seaton, in Kent, from Edward I. ; he was to provide a man, called *veltarius*, or huntsman,[5] to lead three greyhounds when the king went into Gascony, so long as a pair of shoes, valued at fourpence, should last him.[6]

TWO EARLY TREATISES ON HUNTING.—The earliest known English treatise on hunting dates from early in the fourteenth century ; it was originally written

---

[1] Stephanides *Descript. London.* [2] Stow's *Survey of London*, vol. i. p. 157.
[3] *Pills to Purge Melancholy*, 1719, vol. iv. p. 42. [4] Blount's *Ancient Tenures.*
[5] Or *vautrarius*, which Blount derives from the French *vaultre*, a mongrel hound, and supposes the name to signify an inferior huntsman ; and this opinion I have adopted.
[6] E. c. An. 34 Edward I. No. 37. Richard Rockesley held the same land by the same tenure, in the second year of Edward II. Blount, *ut supra.*

in French, by William Twici, or Twety, grand huntsman to king Edward II.[1] There is an English version of this, nearly coeval with the original in the Cotton collection, but in that copy the name of John Gyfford is joined to that of Twety, and both of them are said to be "maisters of the game" to king Edward, and to have composed this treatise upon "the crafte of huntynge."[2] In the same volume of the Cotton collection is a treatise written by the Master of the Game to Henry IV. for the use of prince Henry his son; it is little more than an enlargement of the former tract.[3] The Book of St Albans, so called because it was printed there, contains the first treatise upon the subject of hunting that ever appeared from the press. It is however evidently compiled from the two tracts above mentioned, notwithstanding the legendary authority of Sir Tristram, quoted in the beginning. The Book of St Albans is said to have been written by Juliana Barnes, or Berners, the sister of lord Berners, and prioress of the nunnery of Sopewell, about the year 1481, and was printed soon afterwards. This book contains two other tracts, the one on hawking, and the other on heraldry. It has been reprinted several times, and under different titles, with some additions and amendments, but the general information is the same.[4]

NAMES OF BEASTS OF SPORT.—Twici introduces the subject with a kind of poetical prologue, in which he gives us the names of the animals to be pursued; and these are divided into three classes.

The first class contains four, which, we are informed, may be properly called beasts for hunting; namely, the hare, the hart, the wolf, and the wild boar.

The second class contains the names of the beasts of the chase, and they are five; that is to say, the buck, the doe, the fox, the martin, and the roe.

In the third class we find three, that are said to afford "greate dysporte" in the pursuit, and they are denominated, the grey or badger, the wild-cat, and the otter.

Most of the books upon hunting agree in the number and names of the first class; but respecting the second and third they are not so clear. The beasts of the chase in some are more multifarious, and divided into two classes: the first called beasts of sweet flight, are the buck, the doe, the bear, the reindeer, the elk ,and the spytard, which was the name for a hart one hundred years old. In the second class, are placed the fulimart, the fitchat or fitch, the cat,

---

[1] Entitled "Art de Venerie le quel Maistre Guillame Twici venour le Roy dangleterre fist en son temps per aprandre Autres." See Warton's *Hist. Eng. Poetry*, vol. ii. p. 221.

[2] Cotton MSS. Vespasian, B. xii.

[3] *There is a copy on paper of this treatise among the Harl. MSS. (No. 5086), where it is entitled *The Book of Venerye callyd the Maistre of Game.* No. 6824 of the same collection contains the prologue and first six chapters of this work, written on vellum.

[4] *There was, however, no such prioress of Sopewell nunnery, and the story of "Dam Julyano Barnes" being a sister of Lord Berners was an invention of Chauncy in his *Hist. of Herts* (1700). This compilation was first printed in 1486 under the title "The Boke of St Albans," and the next edition was by Wynken de Worde in 1496. There were about fifteen editions, under various titles, issued in the sixteenth century. See Blades' edition and introduction, printed by Elliot Stock in 1881.

the grey, the fox, the weasel, the martin, the squirrel, the white rat, the otter, the stoat, and the pole-cat ; and these are said to be beasts of stinking flight.

Wolves.—The reader may possibly be surprised, when he casts his eye over the foregoing list of animals for hunting, at seeing the names of several that do not exist at this time in England, and especially of the wolf, because he will readily recollect the story so commonly told of their destruction during the reign of Edgar. It is generally admitted that Edgar gave up the fine of gold and silver imposed by his uncle Athelstan, upon Constantine the king of Wales, and claimed in its stead the annual production of three hundred wolves' skins ; because, say the historians, the extensive woodlands and coverts, abounding at that time in Britain, afforded shelter for the wolves, which were exceedingly numerous, and especially in the districts bordering upon Wales. By this prudent expedient, add they, in less than four years the whole island was cleared from these ferocious animals, without putting his subjects to the least expense ; but, if this record be taken in its full latitude, and the supposition established that the wolves were totally exterminated in Britain during the reign of Edgar, more will certainly be admitted than is consistent with the truth, as certain documents clearly prove.

The words of William of Malmsbury relative to wolves in Edgar's time are to this purport. " He, Edgar, imposed a tribute upon the king of Wales exacting yearly three hundred wolves. This tribute continued to be paid for three years, but ceased upon the fourth, because *nullum se ulterius posse invenire professus* ; it was said that he could not find any more " ;[1] that is, in Wales, for it can hardly be supposed that he was permitted to hunt them out of his own dominions.

As respects the existence of wolves in Great Britain afterwards, and till a very much later period, it appears that in the forty-third year of Edward III. Thomas Engaine held lands in Pytchley, in the county of Northampton, by service of finding at his own cost certain dogs for the destruction of wolves, foxes, etc. in the counties of Northampton, Rutland, Oxford, Essex, and Buckingham. As late as the eleventh year of Henry VI. (1433) Sir Robert Plumpton held one bovate of land, in the county of Nottingham, called Wolf hunt land, by service of winding a horn, and chasing or frighting the wolves in the forest of Shirewood.

*It seems most probable that wolves became extinct in England during the reign of Henry VII., or at all events they were exceedingly rare after that reign. The Lancashire forests of Blackburnshire and Bowland, the wilder parts of the Derbyshire Peak, and the wolds of Yorkshire were among the last retreats of the wolf. It has been confidently stated that entries of payments for the destruction of wolves in the account books of certain parishes of the East Riding, presumably of the sixteenth or seventeenth century date, are still extant,[2] but this appears to be an error. Wolves were common in Scotland in

---

[1] *Hist. Reg. Angl.* lib. ii. cap. 8.   [2] Blaine's *Encyclop. Rural Sports* (1858), p. 105.

the seventeenth century, and they lingered on in exceptional cases until about the middle of the eighteenth century; the last recorded instance of one being killed was in 1743. The packs of Irish wolves were extirpated in 1710, but the last one was not killed in Ireland until 1770.[1]

*The wolves of England in historic times were probably more often trapped than hunted. The family of Wolfhunt who held land of the king in Peak forest by the service of taking the wolves, adopted other means than hunting to keep them down. An inquiry as to the rights of the foresters of the Peak was held in 1285. John le Wolfhonte and Thomas Folejambe then held a bovate of land, which was formerly one serjeanty assigned for taking the forest wolves. They stated that twice each year, namely, in March and September, they had to go through the midst of the forest to place pitch to take the wolves[2] in the places they frequented, because at those seasons of the year the wolves were not able to smell disturbed soil as at others. In dry summers they also went at the feast of St Barnabas (June 11th), when the wolves had whelps, to take and destroy them; and then they had with them a servant to carry their traps (*ingenia*), and they carried an axe and a spear, with a cutlass or hunting knife attached to their girdle, but neither bow nor arrows. They had also with them a mastiff, not lawed, and trained for this work.[3]

*WILD BOARS.—The wild boar is one of the oldest and most renowned of the animals of the British forests. It appears on ancient British coins, and was figured in various works of art pertaining to the later Celtic period.[4] The wild boar graces more than one piece of sculpture of the time of the Roman occupation, and two altars have been found in the north of England dedicated to the god Sylvanus by grateful hunters who had succeeded in killing enormous boars.[5] The story of Edward the Confessor rewarding the huntsman Nigell for slaying a fierce wild boar in the royal forest of Bernwood, Bucks, by granting him an estate and the custody of that forest has often been told. The hunting of the wild boar was assiduously followed up by the Norman conquerors. The wild boar not infrequently occurs in their ecclesiastical sculpture, as on the tympana of church doorways at Hognaston, Parwich, and Ashford, Derbyshire; Little Longford, Wilts; and St Nicholas', Ipswich.[6]

*Holinshed states that Henry I. was specially devoted to boar hunting, which he describes as "a very dangerous exercise." The boar was one of the badges of Edward III., and was specially adopted by Richard III. The manor of Blechesdon, Oxfordshire, was held by the service of presenting the king with a boar spear when he came to hunt at Cornbury or Woodstock. The use of

---

[1] Harting's *Extinct British Animals*, pp. 115-205; *Notes and Queries*, Ser. VI. iii.

[2] *Ad ponendam pegas ad lupos capiendos.*

[3] *Journal of Derbyshire Archæological Society*, xv. 82.

[4] Evans' *British Coins*, pls. vi., viii., xi., xii., xiii.; Stephen's *Literature of the Kymry*, p. 250; *Horæ Ferales*, pl. xiv.

[5] Wright's *Celt, Roman, and Saxon*, pp. 207, 267.

[6] *Romilly Allan's *Christian Symbolism*, passim.

boar spears in Norfolk in the middle of the fifteenth century is twice named in the " Paston Letters,"

*A full inventory of the arms and armour pertaining to Henry VIII., at Westminster, the Tower, and Greenwich, at the close of his reign, enumerates no fewer than 550 "bore-speres." Of this number, 291 had "asshen staves trymed with crymesym velvet and fringed with redde silke," 162 were knotted and leathered, and 97 had "asshen staves trymed with lether." Two others were "graven and gilt." At Greenwich there was also "a bore-spere hedde of Morish worke." Many of these weapons were doubtless for parade and possibly for warlike use if the necessity arose ; but those that were simply knotted and leathered (to secure a firmer grip) were probably genuine and serviceable boar spears. In the same inventory are vast numbers of Moorish pikes, bills, halberds, partisans, and javelins.[1] The chief distinction between the boar spear and other spears was its broad head and the cross-bar just below the head to prevent the weapon entering too deeply. It is not generally remembered that the javelin, as its name implies (*jabali*, a wild boar), was originally a boar spear of a light character, that could be thrown as a dart.

*References to wild boars might be almost indefinitely extended, for they overran the whole country for many centuries, and were afterwards hunted in all the great forests of England. As forests lessened in extent the wild swine decreased in numbers, but there are abundant proofs of their thriving in Durham, Lancashire, Staffordshire, and Wiltshire in the sixteenth century. James I. hunted the wild boar at Windsor in 1617.[2] They were still wild at Chartley, Staffordshire, in 1683. Charles II.'s reign is the latest time at which this animal is known to have been found in England in a really wild state. Various vain efforts were made to reintroduce them into England during the nineteenth century.[3]

*The best account of the old English hunting of the wild boar is given in George Turbervile's liberally illustrated " Noble Art of Venerie or Hunting," which was first printed in 1575 and reproduced in 1611. He says, in chapter forty-nine, that the boar ought not to be counted among the beasts of venery chaseable with hounds, as he is the proper prey of a mastiff or such like dogs, for as much as he is a heavy beast and of great force, and will not lightly flee nor make chase before hounds. He thinks it a great pity to hunt the boar with a good kennel of hounds, as " he is the only beast which can dispatch a hound at one blow, for though other beasts do bite, snatch, teare, or rend your houndes, yet there is hope of remedie if they be well attended ; but if a Bore do once strike your hounde, and light betweene the foure quarters of him, you shall hardly see him escape ; and there withall this subtilitie he hath, that if he be run with a good kenell of hounds, which he perceiveth holde in rounde and followe him harde, he will flee into the strongest thicket that he can finde, to the end he may kill them at leisure one after another, the which I have seene by experience

[1] *Archæologia*, li. 219-280.
[2] *Court and Times of James I.*, ii. 34.
[3] Harting's *Extinct British Animals*, 77-114.

oftentimes. And amongst others I saw once a Bore chased and hunted with fiftie good hounds at the least, and when he saw that they were all in full crie, and helde in round togethers, he turned heade afore them, and thrust amiddest the thickest of them. In such sorte that he slew sometimes sixe or seaven (in manner) with twinkling of an eye; and of the fiftie houndes there went not twelve sounde and alive to their masters' houses." Turbervile then proceeds to show how the boar may properly be hunted and killed with either the sword or the boar spear. The boar was to be followed up by relays of dogs until brought to bay, and then the huntsmen were to ride in upon all at once, having cast round the place where he was, "and it shall be hard if they give him not one scratch with a sword or some wound with a boar-spear." He recommends the hanging of bells on the boar-hounds necks, as a preventative to the boar striking them.

*Foxes.—In Turbervile's book, the hunting of the fox and badger are described together. Both were then hunted or rather drawn with terriers, and Turbervile remarks—"as touching foxes, I account small pastime of hunting of them, especially within the ground; for as soone as they perceyve the Terryers, if they yearne hard and ge neare unto them, they will bolte and come out streygthwaies, unlesse it be when the bitch hathe yong Cubbes: then they will not forsake their yong ones though they die for it." When a fox was hunted "above grounde," after the earths had been stopped, the hounds of the chase thus employed are described as greyhounds, showing that the fox was usually coursed by sight and not followed by scent.

*The keeping of public packs of hounds did not obtain in England until about the close of the seventeenth century, and these packs hunted the stag, the fox, and the hare, indiscriminately. One of the first packs of hounds kept solely for fox hunting was the Hertfordshire; it was started in 1725 with Mr John Calvert as the first master, the kennels being at Cheshunt and Redbourne.[1] The first real steady pack of foxhounds in the West of England was that hunted by Mr Thomas Fownes, of Stapleton, Dorset, which was started in 1730.[2]

*Wild Cats and Martins.—The wild cat is named by Turbervile, in 1575, in connection with the martin, as vermin which used to be commonly hunted in England. At that time they were not hunted designedly, but if a hound chanced to cross a wild cat he would hunt it as soon as any chase—"and they make a noble crye for the time that they stand up. At last when they may no more they will take a tre, and therein seeke to beguile the hounds. But if the hounds hold into them, and will not so give it over, then they leape from one tree to another, and make great shift for their lives, with no lesse pastime to the huntsmen." The wild cat is now extinct in England as well as in the southern counties of Scotland. Probably the last wild cat killed in England was that shot by Lord Ravensworth at Eslington, Northumberland, in 1853. That beautiful animal, the

[1] *Vict. Co. Histories, Hertfordshire*, i. 349.   [2] Blaine's *Encyclop. of Rural Sports*, p. 383.

martin, once so common in England's forests, is now rapidly disappearing. It is supposed to still linger in the Somersetshire and Devonshire confines of Exmoor.[1] Mr Harting, writing in 1883, says that the martin still holds its own in the mountainous parts of Cumberland and Westmoreland, where it is occasionally hunted with foxhounds.[2]

*The Rev. H. A. Macpherson, writing in 1901, says that "the marten continues to preserve a precarious footing among the mountain tops in the centre and west of Cumberland. . . . As long as these animals were fairly numerous they used to be hunted by the dalesmen, and many a spirited chase has been described to me by venerable sportsmen." The last wild cat of this county was killed on Great Mell Fell early in the nineteenth century.[3] The martin has become extinct in Derbyshire and Staffordshire within the last fifty years.[4]

*OTTERS.—The directions given for hunting the otter in the earliest known treatises and books correspond so closely to the customs still observed in that sport, which has never died out in England, that it would be superfluous to reproduce them. Otter-hunting was especially popular in the days of James I. In November 1604 a commission was issued by John Parry, master of the Herts otter hounds, to take dogs up the rivers for the king's diversions; millers were at the same time ordered to stop their watercourses during the hunting. In 1607 the king made a grant of hounds and beagles, spaniels, and mongrels to Henry Mynours, master of the otter hounds at Theobalds, for his majesty's disport.[5]

*DOGS OF THE CHASE.—General Pitt-Rivers, in his recent series of painstaking excavations at Rushmore, Rotherley, etc., has established the fact that a great variety of dogs were known and domesticated in Romano-British days, from the mastiff and greyhound down to small terriers and lapdogs.[6]

In the manuscripts before mentioned we find the following names for the dogs employed in the sports of the field; that is to say, raches, or hounds; running hounds, or harriers, to chase hares; and greyhounds, which were favourite dogs with the sportsmen; alauntes, or bull-dogs, these were chiefly used for hunting the boar; the mastiff is also said to be "a good hounde" for hunting the wild boar; the spaniel was of use in hawking; "hys crafte," says the author, "is for the perdrich or partridge, and the quaile; and, when taught to couch, he is very serviceable to the fowlers, who take those birds with nets." There must, I presume, have been a vast number of other kinds of dogs known in England at this period; these, however, are all that the early writers, upon the subject of hunting, have thought proper to enumerate.

*The following is the amusing list given by Dam Julyano in 1406:—

[1] I several times saw specimens in the "fifties" and "sixties" of last century that had been shot by the keepers of Sir Thomas Acland and Mr Knight on the Somersetshire side of Exmoor; I once saw one wild in the Horner Woods, below Cloutsham, I think in the year 1860, when it had been disturbed by the "tufters" of the Devon and Somerset staghounds.—J. CHARLES COX.

[2] Harting's *Sport* and *Natural History*, ibid. 27-29.

[3] *Vict. Co. Histories, Cumberland*, i. 219-220.

[4] *Ibid. Derbyshire*, vol. i.

[5] *Ibid. Hertfordshire*, i. 347.

[6] *Excavations*, i. 174, ii. 223-4, iii. 235, iv. 124, 128, 131, 133.

" Thyse be the names of houndes. Fyrste there is a Grehoun ; a Bastard ; a Mengrell ; a Mastif ; a Lemor ; a Spanyel ; Raches ; Kenettys ; Teroures ; Butchers houndes ; Dunghyll dogges ; Tryndeltaylles ; and pryckeryd currys ; and smalle ladye's popees that bere awaye the flees and dyvers small sawtes."

ROYAL HUNTING.—Several methods of hunting were practised by the sportsmen of this kingdom, as well on horseback as on foot. Sometimes this exercise took place in the open country ; sometimes in woods and thickets ; and sometimes in parks, chases, and forests, where the game was usually enclosed with a haye or fence-work of netting, supported by posts driven into the ground for that purpose. The manner of hunting at large needs no description ; but, as the method of killing game within the enclosures is now totally laid aside, it may not be amiss to give the reader some idea how it was performed, and particularly when the king with the nobility were present at the sport. All the preparations and ceremonies necessary upon the occasion are set down at large in the manuscript made for the use of Prince Henry, mentioned before ; the substance of which is as follows.

When the king should think proper to hunt the hart in the parks or forests, either with bows or greyhounds, the master of the game, and the park-keeper, or the forester, being made acquainted with his pleasure, was to see that everything be provided necessary for the purpose. It was the duty of the sheriff of the county, wherein the hunting was to be performed, to furnish fit stabling for the king's horses, and carts to take away the dead game. The hunters and officers under the forester, with their assistants, were commanded to erect a sufficient number of temporary buildings[1] for the reception of the royal family and their train ; and, if I understand my author clearly, these buildings were directed to be covered with green boughs,[2] to answer the double purpose of shading the company and the hounds from the heat of the sun, and to protect them from any inconveniency in case of foul weather. Early in the morning, upon the day appointed for the sport, the master of the game, with the officers deputed by him, was to see that the greyhounds were properly placed, and the person nominated to blow the horn, whose office was to watch what kind of game was turned out, and, by the manner of winding his horn, signify the same to the company, that they might be prepared for its reception upon its quitting the cover. Proper persons were then to be appointed, at different parts of the enclosure, to keep the populace at due distance. The yeomen of the king's bow, and the grooms of his tutored greyhounds, had in charge to secure the king's standing, and prevent any noise being made to disturb the game before the arrival of his majesty. When the royal family and the nobility were conducted to the places appointed for their reception, the master of the game, or his lieutenant, sounded three long mootes, or blasts with the horn, for the uncoupling of the hart hounds. The game was then driven from the cover, and turned by the huntsmen and the

---

[1] They are called "trists" or "trestes" in the MS. and might possibly be temporary stages.
[2] The passage runs thus in the MS.: " the fewtrerers ought to make fayre logges of grene boughes at their trestes," etc.

B

hounds so as to pass by the stands belonging to the king and queen, and such of the nobility as were permitted to have a share in the pastime ; who might either shoot at them with their bows, or pursue them with the greyhounds at their pleasure. We are then informed that the game which the king, the queen, or the prince or princesses slew with their own bows, or particularly commanded to be let run, was not liable to any claim by the huntsmen or their attendants ; but of all the rest that was killed they had certain parts assigned to them by the master of the game, according to the ancient custom.

This arrangement was for a royal hunting, but similar preparations were made upon like occasions for the sport of the great barons and dignified clergy. Their tenants sometimes held lands of them by the service of finding men to enclose the grounds, and drive the deer to the stands whenever it pleased their lords to hunt them.[1]

*In the first edition of Turbervile's " Noble Art of Venerie," issued in 1575, there is a woodcut representing Queen Elizabeth being entertained in the midst of a forest scene. In the second edition, issued in 1611, the same woodcut was used, but Elizabeth was ingeniously changed into James I., and the Queen's two maids of honour into pages in waiting. These two cuts are given side by side on plate three.

*HUNTING — COURSING. — Turbervile states, at the end of his volume, that he could find nothing in the foreign works that he had translated relative to coursing with greyhounds, but that in England they set great store by the pastime of coursing with greyhounds " at Deare, Hare, Foxe, or such like, even of themselves, when there are neyther hounds hunting, nor other means to help them." He sets forth that in coursing deer (especially red deer) the greyhounds were divided into three leashes, Teasers, Sidelaies, and Backsets, which were set at the deer in turn. In coursing hares, a quaint method of procedure is laid down in detail. Thus, " Let him which found the Hare go towards and say *Up pusse up*, untill she ryse out of her forme." . . . " When you go to course eyther Hare or Deare or to Hunt any chace, it is a forfayture (amongst us here in England) to name eyther Beare, Ape, Monkie, or Hedgehogge ; and he which nameth any of those shoulde be payd with a slippe upon the Buttockes in the field before he go any furder." Turbervile's last words in his treatise of 250 pages on hunting are warmly in favour of coursing with greyhounds—" which is doubtlesse a noble pastime, and as mete for Nobility and Gentleman as any of the other kinds of Venerie before declared : Especially the course at the Hare which is a sport continually in sight, and made without any great travaile : so that recreation is therein to be found without immeasurable toyle and payne : whereas in hunting with hounds, although the pastime be great, yet many times the toyle and paine is also exceeding great : And then it may be called eyther a painful pastime, or a pleasant payne."

[1] See Blount's *Ancient Tenures*.

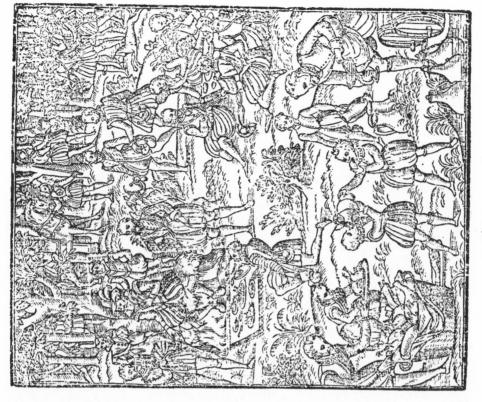

Turbervile. 1611.

Turbervile. 1575.

*There were coursing matches in the old days, for Turbervile states that if it was "a solemn assembly" for coursing, that expert judges stationed themselves on surrounding hills to judge which dog did best. It was in Elizabeth's reign that certain "laws of the Leash or Coursing" were drawn up to regulate hare coursing matches, which were allowed and subscribed by Thomas, Duke of Norfolk.[1]

HUNTING TERMS.—There was a peculiar kind of language invented by the sportsmen of the middle ages, which it was necessary for every lover of the chase to be acquainted with.

When beasts went together in companies, there was said to be a pride of lions ; a lepe of leopards ; an herd of harts, of bucks, and of all sorts of deer ; a bevy of roes ; a sloth of boars ; a singular of boars ; a sownder of wild swine ; a dryft of tame swine ; a route of wolves ; a harras of horses ; a rag of colts ; a stud of mares ; a pace of asses ; a baren of mules ; a team of oxen ; a drove of kine ; a flock of sheep ; a tribe of goats ; a sculk of foxes ; a cete of badgers ; a richness of martins ; a fesynes of ferrets ; a huske or a down of hares ; a nest of rabbits ; a clowder of cats, and a kyndyll of young cats ; a shrewdness of apes ; and a labour of moles.

And also, of animals when they retired to rest ; a hart was said to be harbored, a buck lodged, a roebuck bedded, a hare formed, a rabbit set, etc.

Two greyhounds were called a brace, three a leash, but two spaniels or harriers were called a couple. We have also a mute of hounds for a number, a kenel of raches, a litter of whelps, and a cowardice of curs.

It is well worthy of notice, that this sort of phraseology was not confined to birds and beasts, and other parts of the brute creation, but it was extended to the various ranks and professions of men, as the specimens, which I cannot help adding, will sufficiently demonstrate ; the application of some of them, will, I trust, be thought apt enough :—

A state of princes ; a skulk of friars ; a skulk of thieves ; an observance of hermits ; a lying of pardoners ; a subtiltie of serjeants ; an untruth of sompners ; a multiplying of husbands ; an incredibility of cuckolds ; a safeguard of porters ; a stalk of foresters ; a blast of hunters ; a draught of butlers ; a temperance of cooks ; a melody of harpers ; a poverty of pipers ; a drunkenship of coblers ; a disguising of taylors ; a wandering of tinkers ; a malepertness of pedlars ; a fighting of beggars ; a rayful (that is, a netful) of knaves ; a blush of boys ; a bevy of ladies ; a nonpatience of wives ; a gagle of women ; a gagle of geese ; a superfluity of nuns ; and a herd of harlots. Similar terms were applied to inanimate things, as a caste of bread, a cluster of grapes, a cluster of nuts, etc.

SEASONS FOR HUNTING.—As to "the seasons for alle sortes of venery," the ancient books upon hunting seem to be agreed.

The "time of grace" begins at Midsummer, and lasteth to Holyrood-day. The fox may be hunted from the Nativity to the Annunciation of our Lady ;

---

[1] Badminton Library : *Coursing*, pp. 4-6.

the roebuck from Easter to Michaelmas; the roe from Michaelmas to Candlemas; the hare from Michaelmas to Midsummer; the wolf as the fox; and the boar from the Nativity to the Purification of our Lady.

*The seasons are thus expressed in the rhymes of Dam Julyans, as printed in 1486:—

"The Tyme of Grece beginnyth at mydsomer day,
And tyll Hol' Roode day lastyth as I you say.
The seson of the fox fro the Nativyty,
Tyll the annunciacion of owre lady free.
Seson of the Robucke at Ester shall begynne,
And tyll Mychelmas lastith nigh or she blynne.
The seson of the Roo begynnyth at Michelmas,
And hit shall endure and last untill Candilmas.
At Michelmas begynnyth huntyng of the hare,
And lastith till mydsomer, ther will no man hit spare.
The seson of the Wolfe is in iche cuntre
As the seson of the fox and evermore shall be.
The seson of the boore is from the Nativyte,
Till the purification of owre lady so fre.
For at the Nativyte of owre lady swete,
He may fynde Where he goth under his feete,
Booth in Wodys and feldis, corne and oder frute,
When he after foode makyth any sute.
Crabbys and acornys and nottis ther they grow,
Hawys and heeppes and other thynges ynow.
That till the Purification lastys as ye se,
And makyth the Boore in seson to be.
For whyle that frute may last,
His time is never past."

*LATER HUNTING TREATISES.—The seventeenth century supplied two works of some celebrity on the sport of hunting. The first of these was by that industrious and prolific writer Gervase Markam, who had edited an edition of The Boke of St Albans in 1596. In 1615 appeared the first issue of his "Country Contentments," in which hunting holds a foremost place. He died in 1636. Before the end of the century, this work had passed through fifteen editions. The second was "The Gentleman's Recreation," compiled by a literary hack named Richard Blome, and first issued in folio in 1686. The chief value of the latter production lies in the plates, which aptly illustrate the sporting costume of our forefathers towards the end of the seventeenth century.

*In the next century books and essays on hunting multiplied; the one memorable production being Beckford's charming and scholarly work, first printed in 1781, entitled "Thoughts upon Hunting."

*The classic work that tells the tale of English hunting since the days of Beckford is the Duke of Beaufort's volume of the Badminton Library, which has deservedly run through so many editions. The story for each county is being treated of in the respective volumes of the Victoria County Histories now in course of publication.

CHAPTER II

Hawking practised by the Nobility—Its Origin not well known—A favourite Amusement with the Saxons—Romantic Story relative to Hawking — Grand Falconer of France, his State and Privileges — Edward III. partial to Hawking—Saxon Hawking—Ladies fond of Hawking—Its Decline—Caparison of a Hawk—Treatises concerning Hawking—Laws respecting Hawks—Their great Value—The different Species of Hawks, and their Appropriation—Terms used in Hawking—Fowling and Fishing—The Stalking Horse—Lowbelling.

HAWKING BY THE NOBILITY.—Hawking, or the art of training and flying of hawks, for the purpose of catching other birds, is very frequently called falconry, and the person who had the care of the hawks is denominated the falconer. The sport is generally placed at the head of those amusements that can only be practised in the country, and probably it obtained this precedency from its being a pastime so generally followed by the nobility, not in this country only, but also upon the continent. Persons of high rank rarely appeared without their dogs and their hawks; the latter they carried with them when they journeyed from one country to another, and sometimes even when they went to battle, and would not part with them to procure their own liberty when taken prisoners. Sometimes they formed part of the train of an ecclesiastic. These birds were considered as ensigns of nobility; and no action could be reckoned more dishonourable to a man of rank than to give up his hawk.[1] The ancient English illuminators have uniformly distinguished the portrait of king Stephen by giving him a hawk upon his hand, to signify, I presume, by that symbol, that he was nobly, though not royally born.[2]

Sebastian Brant, a native of Germany, the author of a work entitled "Stultifera Navis," the Ship of Fools, published towards the conclusion of the fifteenth century, accuses his countrymen of bringing their hawks and hounds into the churches, and interrupting the divine service; which indecency he severely reprobates and with the greatest justice. The passage is thus translated by Alexander Barclay:[3]

Into the church then comes another sotte,
Withouten devotion, jetting up and down,
Or to be seene, and showe his garded cote.
Another on his fiste a sparhawke or fawcone,
Or else a cokow ; wasting so his shone ;
Before the aulter he to and fro doth wander,
With even as great devotion as doth a gander.
In comes another, his houndes at his tayle,
With lynes and leases, and other like baggage ;
His dogges barke, so that withouten fayle,
The whole church is troubled by their outrage.

[1] *Memoirs des Inscrip.* tom. ix. p. 542.   [2] See Struth's *Regal and Ecclesiastical Antiquities of England.*
[3] Printed by Pynson A. D. 1508.

ORIGIN OF HAWKING.—I cannot trace the origin of hawking to an earlier period than the middle of the fourth century. Julius Firmicus, who lived about that time, is the first Latin author that speaks of falconers, and the art of teaching one species of birds to fly after and catch others.[1] Pliny is thought to have attributed a sport of this kind to the inhabitants of a certain district in Thrace, but his words are too obscure for much dependence to be placed upon them.[2] An English writer, upon what authority I know not, says, that hawking was first invented and practised by Frederic Barbarossa, when he besieged Rome.[3] It appears, however, to be very certain that this amusement was discovered abroad, where it became fashionable, some time before it was known in this country : the period of its introduction cannot be clearly determined ; but, about the middle of the eighth century, Boniface, archbishop of Mons, who was himself a native of England, presented to Ethelbert, king of Kent, one hawk and two falcons ; and a king of the Mercians requested the same Boniface to send to him two falcons that had been trained to kill cranes.[4] In the succeeding century, the sport was very highly esteemed by the Anglo-Saxon nobility ; and the training and flying of hawks became one of the essentials in the education of a young man of rank. Alfred the Great is commended for his early proficiency in this, as well as in other fashionable amusements ;[5] he is even said to have written a treatise upon the subject of hawking, but there is no such work at present in existence, that can with any degree of certainty be attributed to him. The pastime of hawking must, no doubt, at this period, have been very generally followed, to call for the prohibition inserted in a charter granted to the Abbey of Abingdon, by Kenulph, king of the Mercians ; which restrains all persons carrying hawks or fellows trespassing upon the lands belonging to the monastery.[6] This amusement continued to be a fashionable one to the end of the Saxon æra. Byrhtric, a Saxon nobleman, who died towards the end of the tenth century, among other valuable articles, left by will, to earl Ælfric, two hawks, and all his hedge-hounds, which were, I suppose, spaniels, for the purpose of flushing the game.[7] We have already seen that Edward the Confessor was highly pleased with the sports of the field, allotting the whole of his leisure time to hunting or hawking.

ROMANTIC STORY RELATIVE TO HAWKING.—The monkish writers, after the conquest, not readily accounting for the first coming of the Danes, or for the cruelties that they committed in this country, have assigned several causes ; and among others, the following story is related, which if it might be depended upon, would prove that the pastime of hawking was practised by the nobility of Denmark at a very early period ; such a supposition has at least probability on its side, even if it should not be thought to derive much strength from the authority of this narrative.

---

[1] Lib. v. cap. 8.   [2] Pliny *Nat. Hist.* lib. x. cap. 8.   [3] Peacham's *Complete Gentleman*, p. 183.
[4] See Warton's *Hist. Eng. Poet.* vol. ii. p. 405.   [5] See p. 3. sec. iii.
[6] This charter was granted A.D. 821. Dugdale's *Monasticon*, vol. i. p. 100.
[7] See the whole of the curious will in Lambarde's *Perambulation of Kent*, p. 540.

A Danish chieftain, of high rank, some say of royal blood, named Lothbroc, amusing himself with his hawk near sea, upon the western coasts of Denmark, the bird, in pursuit of her game, fell into the water; Lothbroc, anxious for her safety, got into a little boat that was near at hand, and rowed from the shore to take her up, but before he could return to the land, a sudden storm arose, and he was driven out to sea. After suffering great hardship, during a voyage of infinite peril, he reached the coast of Norfolk, and landed at a port called Rodham: he was immediately seized by the inhabitants, and sent to the court of Edmund, king of the East Angles; when that monarch was made acquainted with the occasion of his coming, he received him very favourably, and soon became particularly attached to him, on account of his great skill in the training and flying of hawks. The partiality which Edmund manifested for this unfortunate stranger, excited the jealousy of Beoric, the king's falconer, who took an opportunity of murdering the Dane, whilst he was exercising of his birds in the midst of a wood, and secreted the body: which was soon afterwards discovered by the vigilance of a favourite spaniel. Beoric was apprehended, and, it seems, convicted of the murder; for he was condemned to be put into an open boat (some say the very boat in which the Danish chieftain came to England) without oars, mast, or rudder, and in that condition abandoned to the mercy of the ocean. It so chanced, that the boat was wafted to the very point of land that Lothbroc came from; and Beoric, escaped from the danger of the waves, was apprehended by the Danes, and taken before two of the chieftains of the country, named Hinguar and Hubba; who were both of them the sons of Lothbroc. The crafty falconer soon learned this circumstance, and, in order to acquire their favour, made them acquainted with the murder of their father, which he affirmed was executed at the command of king Edmund, and that he himself had suffered the hardship at sea, from which he had been delivered by reaching the shore, because he had the courage to oppose the king's order, and endeavoured to save the life of the Danish nobleman. Incited by this abominable falsehood to revenge the murder of their father, by force of arms, they invaded the kingdom of the East Angles, pillaged the country, and having taken the king prisoner, caused him to be tied to a stake, and shot to death with arrows.

This narration bears upon the face of it the genuine marks of a legendary tale. Lidgate, a monk of Saint Edmund's Bury, has given it a place, with the addition of several miraculous circumstances, in his poetical life of king Edmund, who was the tutelar saint of the abbey to which he belonged.[1] On the other hand, every one who is acquainted with the history of the Anglo-Saxons must know, that the Danish pirates had infested the coasts of England, and committed many dreadful depredations, long before the time assigned for the above event; and the success of the first parties encouraged others to make the like attempts.

GRAND FALCONER OF FRANCE.—Hawking is often mentioned, says a

---

[1] Lidgate presented this poem to King Henry VI. when that monarch held his court at Bury. The presentation MS. is yet extant in the Harleian Library, No. 2278.

modern author, in the capitularies of the eighth and ninth centuries. The grand fauconnier of France was an officer of great eminence; his annual salary was four thousand florins; he was attended by fifty gentlemen, and fifty assistant falconers; he was allowed to keep three hundred hawks, he licensed every vender of hawks in France, and received a tax upon every bird sold in that kingdom, and even within the verge of the court; and the king never rode out upon any occasion of consequence without this officer attending upon him.[1]

In Doomsday-book a hawk's airy[2] is returned among the most valuable articles of property; which proves the high estimation these birds were held in at the commencement of the Norman government; and probably some establishment, like that above mentioned, was made for the royal falconer in England.

FONDNESS OF EDWARD III. &c. FOR HAWKING.—Edward III., according to Froissart, had with him in his army when he invaded France, thirty falconers on horseback, who had charge of his hawks;[3] and every day he either hunted, or went to the river for the purpose of hawking, as his fancy inclined him. From the frequent mention that is made of hawking by the water-side, not only by the historians, but also by the romance writers of the middle ages, I suppose that the pursuit of water-fowls afforded the most diversion. The author last quoted, speaking of the earl of Flanders, says, he was always at the river, where his falconer cast off one falcon after the heron, and the earl another. In the poetical romance of the "Squire of low Degree," the king of Hungary promises his daughter, that, at her return from hunting, she should hawk by the river-side, with gos hawk, gentle falcon, and other well-tutored birds; so also Chaucer, in the rhime of sir Thopas, says that he could hunt the wild deer,

> And ryde on haukynge by the ryver,
> With grey gos hawke in hande.

On the fourth plate is a representation of a Saxon nobleman and his falconer, with their hawks, upon the bank of a river, waiting for the rising of the game. The delineation is from a Saxon manuscript written at the close of the ninth century, or at the commencement of the tenth; in the Cotton Library.[4] Another drawing upon the same subject, with a little variation, occurs in a Saxon manuscript, somewhat more modern.[5] The two other engravings on the same plate are from drawings in a manuscript written early in the fourteenth century, preserved in the Royal Library.[6] We see a party of both sexes hawking by the water side; the falconer is frightening the fowls to make them rise, and the hawk is in the act of seizing upon one of them.

We may also here notice, that the ladies not only accompanied the gentlemen in pursuit of this diversion, but often practised it by themselves; and, if we

---

[1] Warton's *Hist. of English Poetry*, vol. ii. p. 406.   [2] *Aira Accipitris.*
[3] *Trente fauconniers à cheval, chargez d'oiseaux.* Froissart's Chron. vol. i. cap. 210.
[4] Tiberius, C. vi.   [5] Julius, A. vi.   [6] Marked 2 B. vii.

Hawking.

may believe a contemporary writer,[1] in the thirteenth century, they even excelled the men in knowledge and exercise of the art of falconry, which reason, he very ungallantly produces, in proof that the pastime was frivolous and effeminate. Hawking was forbidden to the clergy by the canons of the church; but the prohibition was by no means sufficient to restrain them from the pursuit of this favourite and fashionable amusement. On which account, as well as for hunting, they were severely lashed by the poets and moralists; and, indeed, the one was rarely spoken of without the other being included; for those who delighted in hawking were generally proficients in hunting also.

DECLINE OF HAWKING.—The practice of hawking declined, from the moment the musket was brought to perfection, which pointing out a method more ready and more certain of procuring game, and, at the same time, affording an equal degree of air and exercise, the immense expense of training, and maintaining of hawks became altogether unnecessary; it was therefore no wonder that the assistance of the gun superseded that of the bird; or that the art of hawking, when rendered useless, should be laid aside. Its fall was very rapid. Hentzner, who wrote his "Itinerary" in 1598, assures us that hawking was the general sport of the English nobility; at the same time, most of the best treatises upon this subject were written. At the commencement of the seventeenth century, it seems to have been in the zenith of its glory. At the close of the same century, the sport was rarely practised, and a few years afterwards hardly known.

* The great Civil War brought the use of the musket and hence of the fowling piece much more into fashion, to the still further decay of hawking. Charles II. did his best to revive it from a characteristic reason; "of all the diversions of the chase," said a contemporary, "the king likes none but hawking, because it is the most convenient for the ladies."[2] In *The Compleat Sportsman* by Giles Jacob, published in 1718, the author excuses himself for taking no notice of this sport for the following excellent reasons:—"The diversion of hawking, by reason of the trouble and expence in keeping and breeding the hawk, and the difficulty in the management of her in the field, is in a great measure disused: especially since sportsmen are arrived to such a perfection in shooting, and so much improved in the making of dogs, which facilitates the pleasures in taking all sorts of game."[3] The Earl of Oxford, who died in 1791, made strenuous efforts to revive falconry; and at the opening of the nineteenth century it was supported with some spirit on different estates in Yorkshire and Norfolk.

* The most recent treatise on hawking, published in 1892, says :—" Falconry has never for a single hour been extinct in Great Britain; and there are probably at the present time more hawks in training, well and ably trained too, both by

---

[1] Johan. Sarisburiensis, lib. i. cap. 4.

[2] *Memoirs of Count Grammont*, ii. 279.

[3] Shooting with guns became a recognised and customary sport in the second half of the seventeenth century, Brome's *Gentleman's Recreation* (1686), and Fairfax's *Compleat Sportsman* (1689) have chapters on Shooting and Shooting Flying.

amateurs and professionals, than ever there were since the beginning of the century." [1]

CAPARISON OF A HAWK.—When the hawk was not flying at her game, she was usually hood-winked, with a cap or hood provided for that purpose, and fitted to her head; and this hood was worn abroad, as well as at home. All hawks taken upon "the fist," the term used for carrying them upon the hand, had straps of leather called jesses, put about their legs. The jesses were made sufficiently long for the knots to appear between the middle and the little fingers of the hand that held them, so that the lunes, or small thongs of leather, might be fastened to them with two tyrrits, or rings; and the lunes were loosely wound round the little finger. It appears that sometimes the jesses were of silk. Lastly, their legs were adorned with bells, fastened with rings of leather, each leg having one; and the leathers, to which the bells were attached, were denominated bewits; and to the bewits was added the creance, or long thread, by which the bird in tutoring, was drawn back, after she had been permitted to fly; and this was called the reclaiming of the hawk. The bewits, we are informed, were useful to keep the hawk from "winding when she bated," that is, when she fluttered her wings to fly after her game.

Respecting the bells, it is particularly recommended that they should not be too heavy, to impede the flight of the bird; and that they should be of equal weight, sonorous, shrill, and musical; not both of one sound, but the one a semitone below the other; and they ought not to be broken, especially in the sounding part, because, in that case, the sound emitted would be dull and unpleasing. There is, says the Book of St Albans, great choice of sparrow-hawk bells, and they are cheap enough; but for gos-hawk bells, those made at Milan are called the best; and, indeed, they are excellent; for they are commonly sounded with silver, and charged for accordingly. But we have good bells brought from Dordreght (Dort), which are well paired, and produce a very shrill, but pleasant sound.

I am told, that silver being mixed with the metal when the bells are cast, adds much to the sweetness of the tone; and hence probably the allusion of Shakespear, when he says,

How silver sweet sound lovers' tongues by night.

I cannot help adding in this place a passage from an old play, written by Thomas Heywood; wherein one of the characters, speaking of a hawk flying, says

Her bels, Sir Francis, had not both one waight,
Nor was one semitune above the other.
Mei thinkes these Millane bels do sound too full,
And spoile the mounting of your hawke. [2]

So much for the birds themselves; but the person who carried the hawk

---

[1] Badminton Library: *Falconry*, by Hon. G. Lascelles. For the literature of this subject, see Harting's *Bibliotheca Accipitraria*.

[2] "A Woman killed with Kindness," third edition, 1617. Garrick's Coll. E. vol. iv.

was also to be provided with gloves for that purpose, to prevent their talons from hurting his hand. In the inventories of apparel belonging to king Henry VIII., such articles frequently occur; at Hampton Court, in the jewel house, were seven hawkes' gloves embroidered.[1]

EARLY TREATISES ON HAWKING.—We have a poetical fragment, written in old Norman French, as early as the thirteenth century, containing some general observations respecting the management of hawks, which the author informs us he found in a book made for, or by, the good king Edward.[2] Wanley, in his catalogue of the Harleian manuscripts, suspects there is some mistake in the name; and that this fragment is really part of a treatise upon hawking, which he tells us was written by king Alfred; but I rather think the author is correct in this particular; for another manuscript[3] in English, and about a century more modern, treating upon the same subject, has the following indication at the close, "Here endith the booke of haukyng, after Prince Edwarde, kynge of Englande."

*The manuscript treatises named under Hunting, as well as "The Boke of St Albans" (1486), all begin with description of hawking. In 1575 George Turbervile, a Dorsetshire gentleman, published the first separate English treatise on the subject entitled "The Booke of Faulconrie or Hawking; for the onely delight and pleasure of all Noblemen and Gentlemen." It is, in the main, a compilation from Italian and French sources, and covers upwards of 370 pages. It is divided into three parts, the first gives a description of all kinds of hawks; the second deals with "The reclayming, imping, mewing, and fleyng both the fielde and river of the same haukes"; whilst the third part, which is far the longest, is solely concerned with the diseases of the hawks. In 1615 Symon Latham wrote and printed "Falconry, or the Faulcon's Luere and Cure," considered by experts to be a good and practical work, even for those who now may desire to follow up this ancient sport; a fourth edition appeared in 1158. This was followed by an original work by Edmund Bert, issued in 1619 under the title, "An Approved Treatise of Hawkes and Hawking," divided into three books.[4] The author was a gentleman of Essex. When hawking on the Sussex downs for just five weeks with "an intermewed goshawke," he killed in that time, "with that one hawke foure score and odd partridges, five pheasants, seven rayles, and foure hares." For one of his goshawks he was once offered £40, and subsequently completed a sale for £30.

In the last quoted Harley manuscript, we find not only the general rules relative to hawking, but an account of the diseases incident to the birds themselves, and the medicines proper to be administered to them upon such occasions. I shall only mention the following superstitious ceremonies: after a hawk has been ill, and is sufficiently recovered to pursue the game, the owner has this admonition given to him; "On the morrow tyde, when thou goest oute to haukyng, say, In

[1] MS. Harl. 1419. [2] MS. Harl. 978. [3] MS. Harl. 2340. [4] Reprinted by Quaritch in 1891.

the name of the Lord, the birds of heaven shall be beneath thy feet: also, if he be hurt by the heron, say, The Lion of the tribe of Judah, the root of David, has conquered; Hallelujah; and if he be bitte of any man, say, He that the wicked man doth bind, the Lord at his coming shall set free." These sentences, I suppose, were considered as charms, but how far they operated, I shall leave the reader to judge.

LAWS RESPECTING HAWKING.—No persons but such as were of the highest rank were permitted under the Norman government to keep hawks, as appears from a clause inserted in the Forest Charter: this charter king John was compelled to sign; and by it the privilege was given to every free man to have airies of hawks, sparrow-hawks, falcons, eagles, and herons in his own woods.[1] In the thirty-fourth year of the reign of Edward III. a statute was made, by which a person finding a falcon, tercelet, laner, laneret, or any other species of hawk, that had been lost by its owner, was commanded to carry the same to the sheriff of the county wherein it was found; the duty of the sheriff was to cause a proclamation to be made in all the principal towns of the county, that he had such a hawk in his custody, and that the nobleman to whom it belonged, or his falconer, might ascertain the same to be his property, and have it restored to him, he first paying the costs that had been incurred by the sheriff; and, if in the space of four months no claimant appeared, it became the property of the finder, if he was a person of rank, upon his paying the costs to the sheriff; on the contrary, if he was an unqualified man, the hawk belonged to the sheriff: but the person who found it was to be rewarded for his trouble. If the person who found the hawk concealed the same from the owner or his falconer, he was liable upon discovery to pay the price of the bird to the owner, and to suffer two years' imprisonment; and if he was unable to pay the fine, his imprisonment was extended to a longer term.[2] In the thirty-seventh year of the same monarch this act was confirmed, with additional severity; and the stealing and concealing of a hawk, was made felony.[3] In the same reign the bishop of Ely excommunicated certain persons for stealing a hawk that was sitting upon her perch in the cloisters of Bermondsey, in Southwark; but this piece of sacrilege was committed during divine service in the choir, and the hawk was the property of the bishop.[4]

In the reign of Henry VII. a restrictive act was established, prohibiting any man from bearing a hawk bred in England, called a nyesse,[5] a gos-hawk, a tassel, a laner, a laneret, or a falcon, upon pain of forfeiting the same to the king, but that he should use such hawks as were brought from abroad;[6] what good purpose this ordinance was to promote, I am at a loss to say. The laws respecting these birds were frequently varied in the succeeding times, and the alterations seem, in some instances, to have been exceedingly capricious.

---

[1] Carta de Forresta, cap. xi.   [2] Rot. Parl. 34 Ed. III.   [3] *Ibid.* 37 Ed. III.
[4] A. D. 1337.   Regist. Adami Orleton. Epis. Wint. fol. 56.
[5] A hawk was called a nyesse, or an eyesse, from her having watery eyes.   [6] Stat. xi. Hen. VII.

As the hawk was a bird so highly esteemed by the nobility of England, there will be no wonder if we find the royal edicts established for the preservation of their eggs ; accordingly, in the eleventh year of Henry VII. it was decreed, that if any person was convicted of taking from the nests, or destroying the eggs of a falcon, a gos-hawk, a laner, or a swan, he should suffer imprisonment for one year and one day, and be liable to a fine at the king's pleasure ; one half of which belonged to the crown, and the other half to the owner of the ground whereon the eggs were found ; and, if a man destroyed the same sort of eggs upon his own ground, he was equally subject to the penalty.[1]   This act was somewhat meliorated in the reign of Elizabeth, and the imprisonment reduced to three months : but then the offender was obligated to find security for his good behaviour for seven years, or remain in prison until he did.

VALUE OF HAWKS.—The severity of the above-mentioned laws may probably excite the surprise of such of my readers, as are not informed how highly this kind of birds was formerly appreciated.   At the commencement of the seventeenth century, we find, that a gos-hawk and a tassel-hawk were sold for one hundred marks, which was a large sum in those days.   Such as were properly trained and exercised were esteemed presents worthy the acceptance of a king or an emperor.   In the eighth year of the reign of Edward III. the king of Scotland sent him a falcon gentle as a present, which he not only most graciously received, but rewarded the falconer who brought it with the donation of forty shillings ; a proof how highly the bird was valued.[2]   It is further said, that in the reign of James I. Sir Thomas Monson gave one thousand pounds for a cast of hawks.

DIFFERENT SPECIES OF HAWKS.—The books of hawking assign to the different ranks of persons the sort of hawks proper to be used by them : and they are placed in the following order :—

The eagle, the vulture, and the merloun, for an emperor.
The ger-faulcon, and the tercel of the ger-faulcon, for a king.
The faulcon gentle, and the tercel gentle, for a prince.
The faulcon of the rock, for a duke.
The faulcon peregrine, for an earl.
The bastard, for a baron.
The sacre, and the sacret, for a knight.
The laner, and the laneret, for an esquire.
The marlyon, for a lady.
The hobby, for a young man.
The gos-hawk, for a yeoman.
The tercel, for a poor man.
The sparrow-hawk, for a priest.
The musket, for a holy water clerk.
The kesterel, for a knave or servant.

---

[1] Stat. xi. Hen. VII.   [2] MS. Cott. Nero, C. viii. p. 275.

This list includes, I presume, the greater part, if not all, of the names appertaining to the birds used in hawking. The Mews at Charing-cross, Westminster, is so called, from the word mew, which in the falconers' language, is the name of a place wherein the hawks are put at the moulting time, when they cast their feathers. The king's hawks were kept at this place as early as the year 1377, an. 1 Richard II.; but A.D. 1537, the 27th year of Henry VIII., it was converted into stables for that monarch's horses, and the hawks were removed.[1]

*The conversion of this building, in which the king's hawks were kept while they *mewed* or moulted, into a stable, gave an entirely new general signification to the word *mews*.

TERMS USED IN HAWKING.—As in hunting, so in hawking, the sportsmen had their peculiar impressions, and therefore the tyro in the art of falconry is recommended to learn the following arrangement of terms as they were to be applied to the different kinds of birds assembled in companies. A sege of herons, and of bitterns; an herd of swans, of cranes, and of curlews; a dopping of sheldrakes; a spring of teels; a covert of cootes; a gaggle of geese; a badelynge of ducks; a sord or sute of mallards; a muster of peacocks; a nye of pheasants; a bevy of quails; a covey of partridges; a congregation of plovers; a flight of doves; a dule of turtles; a walk of snipes; a fall of wood-cocks; a brood of hens; a building of rooks; a murmuration of starlings; an exaltation of larks; a flight of swallows; a host of sparrows; a watch of nightingales; and a charm of goldfinches.

FOWLING AND FISHING — THE STALKING HORSE — LOWBELLING. — The arts of Fowling and Fishing are usually added to the more modern treatises upon hunting and hawking. I shall select a few observations that occur respecting the former; but with regard to the latter, I have not met with any particulars sufficiently deviating from the present methods of taking fish to claim a place in this work.

Fowling, says Burton, may be performed with guns, lime-twigs, nets, glades, gins, strings, baits, pit-falls, pipe-calls, stalking horses, setting dogs, and decoy ducks; or with chaff-nets for smaller birds[2]; there may also be added bows and arrows, which answered the purpose of guns before they were invented and brought to perfection.

The Stalking Horse, originally, was a horse trained for the purpose and covered with trappings, so as to conceal the sportsman from the game he intended to shoot at. It was particularly useful to the archer, by affording him an opportunity of approaching the birds unseen by them, so near that his arrows might easily reach them; but as this method was frequently inconvenient, and often impracticable, the fowler had recourse to art, and caused a canvas figure to be stuffed, and painted like a horse grazing, but sufficiently light, that it might be moved at pleasure with one hand. These deceptions were also made in the

---

[1] Stow's *Survey of London*.   [2] Burton's *Anatomy of Melancholy*, book v. chap. 8, edit. Lond. 1660.

form of oxen, cows, and stags, either for variety, or for conveniency sake. In the inventories of the wardrobes, belonging to king Henry VIII., we frequently find the allowance of certain quantities of stuff for the purpose of making " stalking coats, and stalking hose for the use of his majesty." [1]

There is also another method of fowling, which, says my author, for I will give it nearly in his own words, is performed with nets, and in the night time; and the darker the night the better.—" This sport we call in England, most commonly bird-batting, and some call it lowbelling; and the use of it is to go with a great light of cressets, or rags of linen dipped in tallow, which will make a good light; and you must have a pan or plate made like a lanthorn, to carry your light in, which must have a great socket to hold the light, and carry it before you, on your breast, with a bell in your other hand, and of a great bigness, made in the manner of a cow-bell, but still larger; and you must ring it always after one order.—If you carry the bell, you must have two companions with nets, one on each side of you; and what with the bell, and what with the light, the birds will be so amazed, that when you come near them, they will turn up their white bellies: your companions shall then lay their nets quietly upon them, and take them. But you must continue to ring the bell; for, if the sound shall cease, the other birds, if there be any more near at hand, will rise up and fly away."—" This is," continues the author, " an excellent method to catch larks, woodcocks, partridges, and all other land birds." [2]

The pipe-call, mentioned by Burton, is noticed under a different denomination by Chaucer; " Lo," says he, " the birde is begyled with the merry voice of the foulers' whistel, when it is closed in your nette,"—alluding to the deceptive art of the bird-catchers in his time. [3]

I shall just observe, that there are twelve prints, published by John Overton, upon the popular subjects of hunting, hawking, and fishing, etc., engraved by Hollar, from designs by Francis Barlow, which perfectly exemplify the manner in which those pastimes were practised, somewhat more than a century back.

[1] MS. Harl. 2284.   [2] *Jewel for Gentrie*, Lond. 1614.   [3] *Testament of Love*, book ii.

CHAPTER III

Horse-racing known to the Saxons—Races in Smithfield, and why—Races, at what Seasons practised—The Chester Races—Stamford Races—Value of Running-horses—Highly prized by the Poets, etc.—Horse-racing commended as a liberal Pastime—Charles II. and other monarchs encouragers of Horse-racing—Races on Coleshill-heath—Corporation Races and later.

HORSE-RACING KNOWN TO THE SAXONS.—It was requisite in former times for a man of fashion to understand the nature and properties of horses, and to ride well; or, using the words of an old romance writer, "to runne horses and to approve them."[1] In proportion to the establishment of this maxim, swift running-horses of course rose into estimation; and we know that in the ninth century they were considered as presents well worthy the acceptance of kings and princes.

When Hugh, the head of the house of the Capets, afterwards monarchs of France, solicited the hand of Edelswitha, the sister of Athelstan, he sent to that prince, among other valuable presents, several running-horses,[2] with their saddles and their bridles, the latter being embellished with bits of yellow gold. It is hence concluded, and indeed with much appearance of truth, that horse-racing was known and practised by the Anglo-Saxons, but most probably confined to persons of rank and opulence, and practised only for amusement sake.

RACES IN SMITHFIELD.—The first indication of a sport of this kind occurs in the description of London, written by Fitzstephen, who lived in the reign of Henry II. He tells us, that horses were usually exposed for sale in West Smithfield; and, in order to prove the excellency of the most valuable hackneys and charging steeds, they were matched against each other; his words are to this effect,[3] "When a race is to be run by this sort of horses, and perhaps by others, which also in their kind are strong and fleet, a shout is immediately raised, and the common horses are ordered to withdraw out of the way. Three jockeys, or sometimes only two, as the match is made, prepare themselves for the contest; such as being used to ride know how to manage their horses with judgment: the grand point is, to prevent a competitor from getting before them. The horses, on their part, are not without emulation: they tremble and are impatient, and are continually in motion: at last the signal once given, they strike, devour the course, hurrying along with unremitting velocity. The jockeys, inspired with the thoughts of applause and the hopes of victory,

---

[1] *Knight of the Swan*, Garrick's Collect. K. vol. x.

[2] *Equos cursores.* Malmsb. de Gest. Reg. Angl. lib. ii. cap. 6.

[3] I have followed the translation published by Mr White, of Fleet-street, A.D. 1772. See Stow's *Survey of London*, republished with additions by Strype.

32

clap spurs to their willing horses, brandish their whips, and cheer them with their cries."

HORSE-RACING SEASONS.—In the middle ages there were certain seasons of the year when the nobility indulged themselves in running their horses and especially in the Easter and Whitsuntide holidays. In the old metrical romance of "Sir Bevis of Southampton,"[1] it is said,

> In somer at Whitsontyde,
> Whan knightes most on horsebacke ride ;
> A cours, let they make on a daye,
> Steedes, and Palfraye, for to assaye
> Whiche horse, that best may ren,
> Three myles the cours was then,
> Who that might ryde him shoulde
> Have forty pounds of redy golde.

Commenius in his vocabulary, entitled "Orbis Sensualium Pictus," published towards the conclusion of the sixteenth century, indeed says, "At this day, tilting, or the quintain is used, where a ring is struck with a truncheon, instead of horse-races, which," adds he, "are grown out of use."

A writer of the seventeenth century[2] tells us, that horse-racing, which had formerly been practised at Eastertide, "was then put down, as being contrary to the holiness of the season"; but for this prohibition I have no further authority."

CHESTER RACES.—It is certain, that horse-races were held upon various holidays, at different parts of the kingdom, and in preference to other pastimes. "It had been customary," says a Chester antiquary,[3] "time out of mind, upon Shrove Tuesday, for the company of saddlers belonging to the city of Chester, to present to the drapers a wooden ball, embellished with flowers, and placed upon the point of a lance ; this ceremony was performed in the presence of the mayor, at the cross in the 'Rodhee,' or Roody, an open place near the city ; but this year" (1540), continues he, "the ball was changed into a bell of silver, valued at three shillings and sixpence, or more, to be given to him who shall run the best, and the farthest on horseback, before them upon the same day."[4] These bells were afterwards denominated Saint George's bells ; and we are told that in the last year of James I. John Brereton, inn-keeper, mayor of Chester, first caused the horses entered for this race, then called Saint George's race, to start from the point, beyond the new tower : and appointed them to run five times round the Roody : "and he," says my author,[5] "who won the last course or trayne, received the bell, of a good value, of eight or ten pounds, or thereabout, and to have it forever ; which moneyes were collected of the citizens, to a sum for that purpose."[6] By the author's having added, that the winner at this race was to have the bell, and have it for ever, is implied, that it had formerly been

---

[1] *Syr Bevys of Hampton*, black letter, without date, printed by Wm. Copland. Garrick's Collect. K. vol. ix.
[2] Bourne *Antiq. Vulgares*, chap. xxiv.
[3] Probably the elder Randel Holme of Chester, one of the city heralds. MS. Harl. 2150. fol. 235.
[4] That is Shrove Tuesday.   [5] Probably the younger Randel Holme.   [6] MS. Harl. 2125.

C

used as a temporary mark of honour, by the successful horseman, and afterwards returned to the corporation; this alteration was made April 23, A.D. 1624.

Here we see the commencement of a regular horse-race, but whether the courses were in immediate succession, or at different intervals, is not perfectly clear; we find not, however, the least indication of distance posts, weighing the riders, loading them with weights, and many other niceties that are observed in the present day. The Chester races were instituted merely for amusement, but now such prodigious sums are usually dependent upon the event of a horse-race, that these apparently trivial matters, are become indispensably necessary. Forty-six years afterwards,[1] according to the same writer, the sheriffs of Chester "would have no calves-head feast, but put the charge of it into a piece of plate, to be run for on that day, Shrove Tuesday; and the high-sheriff borrowed a Barbary horse of sir Thomas Middleton, which won him the plate; and being master of the race, he would not suffer the horses of master Massey, of Puddington, and of sir Philip Egerton, of Oulton, to run, because they came the day after the time prefixed for the horses to be brought, and kept in the city; which thing caused all the gentry to relinquish our races ever since."

*Two small silver racing bells, belonging to the corporation of Carlisle, of globular form, were exhibited before the Royal Archæological Institute in 1879. The largest, which is $2\frac{1}{4}$ inches in diameter, is gilt, and thus inscribed—" The sweftes hors thes bel to tak for mi lade Daker sake." The other bears date 1599, with initials H. B. M. C., that is, Henry Baines, Mayor of Carlisle.[2]

STAMFORD RACES.—Races something similar to those above mentioned, are described by Butcher,[3] as practised in the vicinity of the town of Stamford, in Lincolnshire. "A concourse," says he, "of noblemen and gentlemen meet together, in mirth, peace, and amity, for the exercise of their swift running-horses, every Thursday in March. The prize they run for is a silver and gilt cup, with a cover, to the value of seven or eight pounds, provided by the care of the alderman for the time being; but the money is raised out of the interest of a stock formerly made up by the nobility and gentry, which are neighbours, and well-wishers to the town."

VALUE OF RUNNING-HORSES. — Running-horses are frequently mentioned in the registers of the royal expenditures. It is notorious, that king John was so fond of swift horses and dogs for the chase, that he received many of his fines in the one or the other; but at the same time it does not appear that he used the horses for any purposes of pleasure, beyond the pursuits of hunting, hawking, and such like sports of the field.

In the reign of Edward III. the running-horses purchased for the king's service, were generally estimated at twenty marks, or thirteen pounds, six shillings, and eightpence each; but some few of them were prized as high as

---

[1] A.D. 1665. and 5 Charles II.
[2] *The Archæological Journal*, xxxvi. 383, where these bells are figured.
[3] In his *Survey of the Town of Stamford*, first printed A.D. 1646, chap. 10.

twenty-five marks.[1]   I met with an entry, dated the ninth year of this king's reign, which states, that the king of Navarre sent him as a present two running-horses, which I presume were very valuable, because he gave the person who brought them no less than one hundred shillings for his reward.[2]

RUNNING-HORSES OF THE HEROES OF ROMANCE.—If we appeal to the poets, we shall find, that swift running-horses were greatly esteemed by the heroes who figure in their romances; and rated at prodigious prices; for instance, in an ancient poem,[3] which celebrates the warlike actions of Richard I., it is said, that in the camp of the emperor, as he is called, of Cyprus,

> Too stedes fownde kinge Richarde,
> Thatt oon Favell, thatt other Lyard :
> Yn this worlde, they hadde no pere ;
> Dromedary, neither destrere,[4]
> Stede, rabyte, ne cammele,
> Goeth none so swyfte without fayle
> For a thousand pownd of golde,
> Ne sholde the one be solde.

And though the rhymist may be thought to have claimed the poetical licence for exaggeration, respecting the value of these two famous steeds, the statement plainly indicates that in his time there were horses very highly prized on account of their swiftness.   We do not find indeed, that they were kept for the purpose of racing only, as horses are in the present day ; but rather, as I before observed, for hunting and other purposes of a similar nature ; and also to be used by heralds and messengers in cases of urgency.

Race-horses were prized on account of their breed, in the time of Elizabeth, as appears from the following observations in one of Bishop Hall's Satires.—

> ————dost thou prize
> Thy brute beasts worth by their dams qualities?
> Say'st thou this colt shall prove a swift pac'd steed,
> Onely because a Jennet did him breed?
> Or say'st thou this same horse shall win the prize,
> Because his dam was swiftest Trunchefice
> Or Runcevall his syre ; himself a gallaway?
> While like a tireling jade, he lags half away.[5]

HORSE-RACING, A LIBERAL PASTIME.—Two centuries back horse-racing was considered as a liberal pastime, practised for pleasure rather that profit, without the least idea of reducing it to a system of gambling.   It is ranked with hunting and hawking, and opposed to dice and card playing by an old Scotch poet, who laments that the latter had in great measure superseded the former.[6] One of the puritanical writers[7] in the reign of Elizabeth, though he is very severe against cards, dice, vain plays, interludes, and other idle pastimes, allows

---

[1] MS. Cot. Nero, C. viii. fol. 219.   [2] *Ibid.*
[3] MS. Harl. 4690, written early in the fourteenth century.   [4] A French word, signifying a large powerful horse.
[5] Lib. iv. f. 3.   Edit. 1599.   [6] *Poem of Covetice*, quoted by Warton.   *Hist. English Poetry*, vol. ii. p. 316.
[7] John Northbrooke.

of horse-racing as "yielding good exercise," which he certainly would not have done, had it been in the least degree obnoxious to the censure which at present it so justly claims.

Burton,[1] who wrote at the decline of the seventeenth century, says sarcastically, " Horse-races are desports of great men, and good in themselves, though many gentlemen by such means gallop quite out of their fortunes"; which may be considered as a plain indication, that they had begun to be productive of mischief at the time he wrote : and fifty years afterwards, they were the occasion of a new and destructive species of gambling.   The following lines are from a ballad in D'Urfey's collection of songs : it is called " New Market," which place was then famous for the exhibition of horse-races.

> Let cullies that lose at a race
> Go venture at hazard to win,
> Or he that is bubbl'd at dice
> Recover at cocking again ;
> Let jades that are founder'd be bought,
> Let jockeys play crimp to make sport.—
> ———Another makes racing a trade,
> And dreams of his projects to come ;
> And many a crimp match has made,
> By bubbing another man's groom.[2]

ROYAL PATRONS OF HORSE-RACING—RACES ON COLESHILL HEATH, &C.—From what has been said, it seems clear enough, that this pastime was originally practised in England for the sake of the exercise, or by way of emulation, and, generally speaking, the owners of the horses were the riders.   These contests, however, attracted the notice of the populace, and drew great crowds of people together to behold them ; which induced the inhabitants of many towns and cities to affix certain times for the performance of such sports, and prizes were appointed as rewards for the successful candidates.   The prize was usually a silver cup or some other piece of plate, about eight or ten pounds value.

In the reign of James I. public races (as distinguished from private matches between gentlemen) were established in many parts of the kingdom, such as Gathorty, Yorkshire ; Croydon, Surrey, and on Enfield Chase.   It is said that the discipline and modes of preparing the horses upon such occasions, were much the same as are practised in the present day.   The races were then called bell courses, because, as we have seen above, the prize was a silver bell.

At the latter end of the reign of Charles I. races were held in Hyde Park, and at Newmarket.   After the Restoration, horse-racing was revived and much encouraged by Charles II. who frequently honoured this pastime with his presence ; and, for his own amusement, when he resided at Windsor, appointed races to be made in Datchet mead.   At Newmarket, where it is said he entered horses and run them in his name, he established a house for his better accommo-

---

[1] *Anatomy of Melancholy*, part ii. sec. 2, chap. 4, edit. 1660.
[2] *Pills to purge Melancholy*, fourth edit. 1719, vol. ii. p. 53.

dation ; and he also occasionally visited other places where horse-races were instituted. I met with the following doggerel verses in a metrical Itinerary, written at the close of the seventeenth century. The author,[1] for he hardly deserves the name of poet, speaking of Burford Downs, makes these remarks :

> Next for the glory of the place,
> Here has been rode many a race,—
> —King Charles the Second I saw here ;
> But I've forgotten in what year.
> The duke of Monmouth here also,
> Made his horse to swete and blow ;
> Lovelace, Pembrook, and other gallants
> Have been ventring here their talents,
> And Nicholas Bainton on black Sloven,
> Got silver plate by labor and drudging, &c.

At this time it seems, that the bells were converted into cups, or bowls, or some other pieces of plate, which were usually valued at one hundred guineas each ; and upon these trophies of victory the exploits and pedigree of the successful horses were most commonly engraved. William III. was also a patroniser of this pastime, and established an academy for riding, and his queen not only continued the bounty of her predecessors, but added several plates to the former donations.

*Queen Anne not only continued this practice, but kept a racing stud and ran horses in her own name. At York, in 1712 the Queen's grey gelding, Pepper, ran for the Royal Gold Cup, value £100 ; and Mustard, described as a nutmeg-grey horse, another of the Queen's stud, ran for the same stake in the following year. On Friday, July 30th, 1714, the Queen's bay horse Star won a plate of £40 on the York course. On the following Monday, during a race for a gold cup with a sweepstake of sixteen guineas, an express arrived with the news of her majesty's death. The nobility and gentry left the course and attended the Archbishop of York and the Lord Mayor of York, who proclaimed the accession of George I.[2] Towards the close of his reign George I. discontinued the plates and gave in lieu one hundred guineas.

In one of the Spectators, we meet with the following advertisement, extracted, as we are told, from a paper called the Post Boy:[3] "On the ninth of October next will be run for on Coleshill Heath, in Warwickshire, a plate of six guineas value, three heats, by any horse, mare, or gelding, that hath not won above the value of five pounds : the winning horse to be sold for ten pounds, to carry ten stone weight if fourteen hands high : if above, or under, to carry or be allowed weight for inches, and to be entered on Friday the fifth, at the Swan, in Coleshill, by six in the evening. Also a plate of less value, to be run for by asses"; which, though by no means so noble a sport as the other, was, I doubt not, productive of the most mirth.

---

[1] Probably Matthew Thomas Baskervile, whose name appears at the end ; it was written about the year 1690. MS. Harl. 4716.

[2] Badminton Library, *Racing*, p. 24.   [3] Dated Sept. 11, A.D. 1711. *Spectator*, vol. iii. No. 173.

* CORPORATION PLATES.—It was the custom of several of our more important corporations to support horse-racing by presenting money or money's worth. Horse-racing on Harleston Heath, near Northampton, was established early in the seventeenth century. In 1632 the corporation of Northampton covenanted to make an annual gift of a silver-gilt covered cup of the value of £16, 13s. 4d. The Chamberlain's accounts for the seventeenth and beginning of the eighteenth centuries always contain an entry for this payment, generally characterised as "the horse-race plate," and sometimes as "the Harleston race cup." In the reign, however, of George II., the Duke of Marlborough made good his claim to Harleston Heath against the Corporation, and those races ceased. At certain times the Northampton corporation also supported the town races held on their common fields. The earliest entry to this effect is curiously enough in the time of the Commonwealth. In 1658, "at the desire of the Country Gentlemen," two plates were provided, one of the value of £30 and the other of £14.[1]

* In 1727 John Chency printed "an historical list of all the horse-matches run, and all Plates and Prizes run for in England and Wales (of the value of Ten Pounds or upwards.)" This list shows that there were no fewer than one hundred and twelve cities and towns in England and five in Wales where horse-races were held. To this work succeeded Weatherby's well-known "Racing Calendar."

[1] Dr Cox's *Records of the Borough of Northampton*, ii. 539-541.

BOOK II

RURAL EXERCISES GENERALLY PRACTISED

CHAPTER I

The English famous for their Skill in Archery—The Use of the Bow known to the Saxons and the Danes—Form of the Saxon Bow, &c.—Norman Archery—The Ladies fond of Archery—Observations relative to the Cross-Bow—Its Form, and the Manner in which it was used—Bows ordered to be kept—The Decay of Archery, and why—Ordinances in its Favour—The Fraternity of St George established—Henry VIII. an Archer—The Price of Bows—Equipment for Archery—Directions for its Practice—The Marks to shoot at—The Length of the Bow and Arrows—Extraordinary Performances of the Archers—The modern Archers inferior to the ancient in long Shooting—The Duke of Shoreditch, why so called—Grand Procession of the London Archers—Archery a royal Sport—A good Archer, why called Arthur—Archery at Buxton—Elizabethan Archers—Archery in the Civil War—Sir William Wood—The Artillery Company—The Toxophilites.

SKILL OF THE ENGLISH IN ARCHERY.—Among the arts that have been carried to a high degree of perfection in this kingdom, there is no one more conspicuous than that of Archery. Our ancestors used the bow for a double purpose : in time of war, it was a dreadful instrument of destruction ; and in peace it became an object of amusement. It will be needless to insist upon the skill of the English archers, or to dilate upon their wonderful performances in the field of battle. The victories they obtained over their enemies are many and glorious ; they are their best eulogiums, and stand upon record in the histories of this country for the perusal, and for the admiration of posterity. I shall therefore consider this subject in a general point of view, and confine myself, in the main, to such parts of it as relate to amusement only.

* Though the use of the bow for the projection of darts or arrows shows some advance on the rudest forms of savage life, there can be no doubt that it was in common use throughout the British Isles for many centuries before the advent of the Romans. Vast numbers of flint arrow heads have been found throughout England, particularly on the wolds of Yorkshire and the moors of Derbyshire.[1]

THE BOW KNOWN TO THE ANGLO-SAXONS AND DANES.—The Anglo-Saxons, and the Danes, were certainly well acquainted with the use of the bow ; a knowledge they derived at an early period from their progenitors. The Scandinavian scalds, speaking in praise of the heroes of their country, frequently add to the rest of their acquirements a superiority of skill in handling of the bow.[2] Offrid, son of Edwin, king of Northumberland, was killed by an arrow in a battle which was fought near Hatfield, Yorkshire, about the year 633. Polydore

---

[1] Evans' *Ancient Stone Implements of Great Britain*, chap. xvi.
[2] Olaii Worm. *Lit. Run.* p. 129. Barthol. p. 420. Pontoppman's *Hist. Norway*, p. 248.

Virgil says that a great number of archers were placed in the right wing of King Alfred's army. Edmund, king of the East Angles, was shot to death with arrows by the Danes.

FORM OF THE SAXON BOW.—Representations of the bow occur frequently in the Saxon manuscripts ; and from one of them in the Cotton Library, written about the tenth century,[1] I have selected two archers, who are figured on the fifth plate. The one accompanied by his dog, is in search of the wild deer ; the other has no companion, but is depicted in the act of shooting at a bird ; and from the adornment of his girdle, appears to have been no bad marksman. The first represents Esau going to seek venison for his father, and the second, Ishmael, after his expulsion from the house of Abraham, and residing in the desert.

This plate also contains a Saxon bow and arrow on a larger scale, taken from the same manuscript. The bow is curiously ornamented, having the head and tail of a serpent carved at the ends ; and was, probably, such a one as was used by the nobility. In all these bows we may observe one thing remarkable, that is, the string not being made fast to the extremities, but permitted to play at some distance from them. How far this might be more or less advantageous than the present method, I shall not presume to determine.

*NORMAN ARCHERY.—Contrary to the assertions of Speed and certain later historians, the bow was in well-established use in England at the period of the Norman Conquest, though apparently at that time used by them but little in warfare. There is only one English archer represented on the historic Bayeux embroidery, whilst the credit of William's victory was mainly due to the archers of Louviers and Evreux.[2] Of the Conqueror it was recorded, as of Ulysses, that no man could bend his bow. The Normans speedily popularised the general use of a weapon, with which they were such adepts, throughout England, both for the chase and amusement, as well as for military purposes. Under Henry II. the use of the bow contributed materially to the conquest of Ireland. Fitzstephen, who *baliste*, in that reign, states that the London skaters moved faster than *telum* wrote which seems to prove that the cross-bow was also in common use at that period.

In the ages of chivalry the usage of the bow was considered as an essential part of the education of a young man who wished to make a figure in life. The heroes of romance are therefore usually praised for their skill in archery ; and Chaucer, with propriety, says of sir Thopas, " He was a good archere."

ARCHERY PRACTISED BY LADIES.—The ladies were also fond of this amusement, and by a previous representation on the second plate, from an original drawing in a manuscript of the fourteenth century, we see it practised by one who has shot at a deer, and wounded it with great adroitness ; and in another previous engraving (plate five) the hunting equipments of the female archers about the middle of the fifteenth century are represented.

---

[1] Cott. MSS., Claud. B. iv.　　　　　[2] Freeman's *Norman Conquest*, iii. ch. 15.

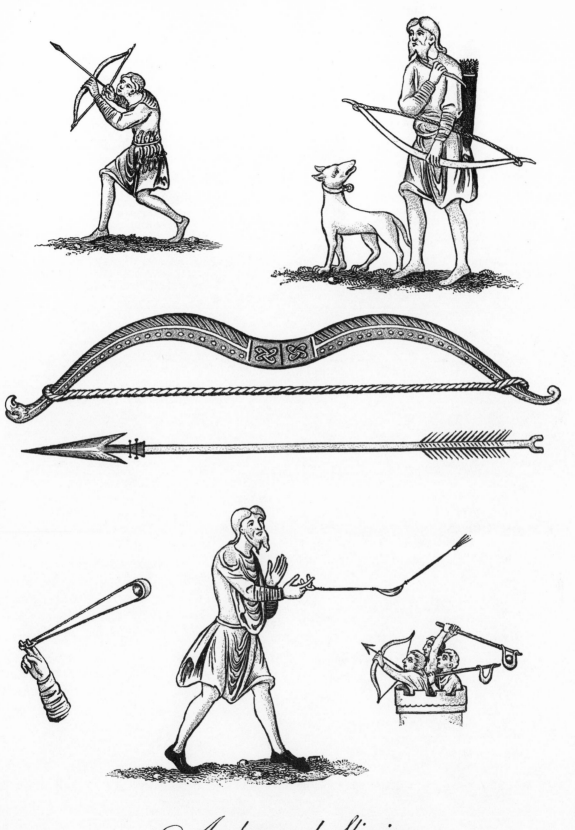

Archery and Slinging.

It was usual, when the ladies exercised the bow, for the beasts to be confined by large inclosures, surrounded by the hunters, and driven in succession from the covers to the stands, where the fair sportswomen were placed ; so that they might readily shoot at them, without the trouble and fatigue of rousing and pursuing them.[1] It is said of Margaret, the daughter of Henry VII., that when she was on her way towards Scotland, a hunting party was made for her amusement in Alnwick Park, where she killed a buck with an arrow.[2] It is not specified whether the long-bow or the cross-bow was used by the princess upon this occasion ; we are certain that the ladies occasionally shot with both, for when queen Elizabeth visited lord Montecute at Cowdrey, in Sussex, on the Monday, August 17, 1591, " Her highness tooke horse, and rode into the park, at eight o'clock in the morning, where was a delicate bowre prepared, under the which were her highness musicians placed ; and a cross-bow, by a nymph, with a sweet song, was delivered into her hands, to shoote at the deere ; about some thirty in number were put into a paddock, of which number she killed three or four, and the Countess of Kildare one."[3]

THE CROSS-BOW.—The arbalist, or cross-bow, which was much shorter than the long-bow, fastened upon a stock, and discharged by the means of a catch or trigger, which probably gave rise to the lock on the modern musket. Bayle, explaining the difference between testimony and argument, uses this simile, " Testimony is like the shot of a long-bow, which owes its efficacy to the force of the shooter ; argument is like the shot of a cross-bow, equally forcible, whether discharged by a dwarf or a giant."

I cannot pretend to determine at what period the cross-bow was first brought into this country, but I believe not long before the commencement of the thirteenth century ; at least, I have never met with any representation of such an engine prior to that period. On the continent its appearance might be somewhat earlier. Our historians assure us that Richard I. was wounded by an arrow from a bow of this kind, while he was reconnoitring the walls of the castle of Chalezun ; which wound was the occasion of his death. William Brito seems to attribute the introduction of the cross-bow to this monarch, who, he says, first showed it to the French.[4]

In the twenty-third year of the reign of Edward I. the Earl of Warwick had in his army a number of soldiers called *ballistarii*, and this word is translated cross-bow men by our chronological writers, but certainly it may with equal propriety be rendered slingers, or casters of stones, who frequently formed a part of the Anglo-Norman armies.[5]

* In 1341 an order was issued by Edward III. to the sheriffs of most of the English counties to supply five hundred white bows and five hundred bundles of arrows, ready for the war against France. In the two following years like

---

[1] See book i. ch. i.
[3] Nichols's *Progresses*, vol. ii.
[5] See *Manners and Customs of the English*, vol. i.

[2] Leland's *Collect.* vol. iv. p. 278.
[4] Camden's *Remains*.

orders were repeated, save that the sheriff of Gloucestershire was instructed to provide five hundred painted bows as well as five hundred white or unpainted, the latter being sixpence cheaper than the former. The painting of these long-bows was intended either to make them smarter for military use, or to increase their duration.[1]

From this period we hear but little concerning the cross-bows, as military weapons, until the battle of Cressy in 1346; at which time they were used by a large body of Genoese soldiers, who were particularly expert in the management of these weapons, and assisted the French upon that memorable occasion; but their efforts were ineffectual when opposed to the archery of the English. Previous to the commencement of the battle there fell a sharp shower of rain, which wetted the strings of the cross-bows; and, we are told, in great measure prevented the archers from doing their usual execution;[2] but the strings of the long-bows used by the Englishmen do not appear to have been damaged in the least by the rain; this might arise from their being made with different materials; or more probably, from their being kept with the bows, in the bow-cases, during the continuance of the shower; for every man had a case of canvass, or of some such material, to draw over his bow when he had done using of it.[3]

In the succeeding annals the cross-bow is continually spoken of as a weapon of war. In 1347, the year after the celebrated victory was obtained at Cressy, Charles, carl of Blois, at the siege of le Roche de Rien, had no less than two thousand cross-bowmen in his army. The cross-bow was used by the English soldiery chiefly at sieges of fortified places, and on shipboard, in battles upon the sea. But the great fame acquired by our countrymen in archery, was derived from their practice with the long-bow: and to this instrument they gave the preference.

FORM AND USE OF THE CROSS-BOW.—The reader may see the manner in which the cross-bow was formerly used for fowling purposes upon the sixth plate. The representation given at the bottom is taken from a manuscript of the fourteenth century in the Royal Library.[4]

In the centre is an illustration, from a painting on another manuscript in the Royal Library, much more modern.[5] We find here exhibited a school for practice; and the manner in which the archers shot at the butts, or dead marks, a pastime frequently alluded to by the authors of the fifteenth and sixteenth centuries.

At the end of the reign of Henry VII. the cross-bow was forbidden by law to be used by any man, except by the King's license, unless he was a lord or had two hundred marks in land. To still further favour the use of the long-bow it was at the same time provided that no custom should be paid on good bow-

[1] *Archæologia*, vii. 48.

[2] Serres, and also most of our own historians. Froissart praises the skill of the Genoese cross-bowmen upon another occasion, saying, "They shot so surely, that lightly they myst not of their level." Vol. iv. chap. 38. fol. 47. English translation [by Lord Berners], and in several other places.

[3] Ascham's *Toxophilus*. [4] 2 B. vii. [5] 19 C. viii. dated 1496.

Archery.

staves brought into the realm.[1] In 1514 a much more severe statute was passed, whereby any one keeping a cross-bow in his house, unless he had land to the yearly value of three hundred marks, was to forfeit; and the great penalty of £10 was imposed for every time a cross-bow was used for shooting.[2] This Act was renewed and further strengthened in 1533.[3] This severe fine might probably produce a temporary reformation; which certainly was not of long continuance, for cross-bows were commonly used again in the succeeding reigns. Hentzner tells us, that in the year 1598, he saw in the armory of the Tower of London, cross-bows, and bows and arrows: of which, says he, to this day, the English make great use in their exercises. Stow speaks of a large close, called the Tazell, let in his time to the cross-bow makers, wherein, he says, they used to shoot for games at the popinjay, which, Maitland tells us, was an artificial parrot.[4]

BOWS AND ARROWS ORDERED TO BE KEPT.—To return to the long-bow: As far back as the thirteenth century, every person not having a greater annual revenue in land than one hundred pence, was obliged to have in his possession a bow and arrows, with other arms offensive and defensive; and all such as had no possessions, but could afford to purchase arms, were commanded to have a bow with sharp arrows, if they dwelt without the royal forests, and a bow with round-headed arrows, if they resided within the forests. The words of the statute are, "arcs e setes hors de forestes, e dedenz forestes arcs e pilets."[5] The word *pilet* I believe is derived from the Latin, *pila*, a ball; and I suppose these arrows were used to prevent the owners from killing the king's deer. The round-headed arrows were also called bolts, and also used with the cross-bow; hence the old adage, "A fool's bolt is soon shot," where the retort of an ignorant man is compared to the blunted arrow of an unskilful archer, shot off hastily, and without any aim. The proverb is thus versified by John Heywood,

> A fooles bolte is soone shot, and fleeth oftymes fer
> But the fooles bolte, and the marke, cum few times ner.[6]

It was also ordained by the forementioned statute that proper officers should be appointed to see that these weapons were kept in good order, and ready for immediate service.

DECAY OF ARCHERY.—Notwithstanding the manifest advantages accruing to the nation from the practice of archery, it seems to have been much neglected even at a time when the glory of the English archers was in its zenith, I mean in the reign of Edward III.; which occasioned that monarch to send a letter of complaint upon this subject to the sheriffs of London, declaring that the skill in shooting with arrows was almost totally laid aside, for the pursuit of various useless and unlawful games. He therefore commanded them to prevent such idle practices within the city and liberties of London; and to see that the leisure

---

[1] Stat. 19 Hen. VII. caps. 2 and 4.
[2] Stat. 6 Hen. VIII. cap. 13.   [3] Stat. 25 Hen. VIII. cap. 17.   [4] *History of London*, book ii. p. 482.
[5] The Statute of Winchester, 13 Edw. I. cap. vi.   [6] Heywood's *Epigrams and Proverbs*, 1566. No. 13.

time upon holidays was spent in recreations with bows and arrows. In the thirty-ninth year of this reign, A.D. 1349, the penalty incurred by the offenders was imprisonment at the king's pleasure ; the words of the letter are, " arcubus et sagittis vel pilettis aut boltis," with bow and arrows, or piles or bolts. The same command was repeated in the twelfth year of the reign of Richard II.; but probably its good effects were merely temporary. And in the fifth year of Edward IV. an ordinance was made, commanding every Englishman and Irishman dwelling in England, to have a long-bow of his own height ; the act directs, that butts should be made in every township, at which the inhabitants were to shoot at up and down, upon all feast days, under the penalty of one halfpenny for every time they omitted to perform this exercise. This in the poetical legends is called "shooting about."

*Suitable wood for bows became so scarce in England, owing mainly to the long continued wars with France, that in 1436 Nicholas Hisham, merchant of York, had license to sail to Prussia with four ships in quest of wood for bows and spears. In 1472 it was enacted that all merchant strangers sending goods to England in any vessel or ship of Venice, or of any other city, town, or country whence bow-staves have been imported, were to send four bow-staves for every ton of merchandise thus imported.[1]

In the sixteenth century we meet with frequent complaints respecting the disuse of the long-bow, and especially in the vicinity of London. Stow informs us, "that before his time it had been customary at Bartholomew tide, for the lord mayor, with the sheriffs and aldermen, to go into the fields at Finsbury, where the citizens were assembled, and shoot at the standard, with broad and flight arrows, for games." This exercise was continued for several days ; but at the period in which our author lived it was practised only one afternoon, three or four days after the festival of Saint Bartholomew.[2]

The same writer attributes the decay of archery among the Londoners to the enclosures made near the metropolis, by which means the citizens were deprived of room sufficient or proper for the purpose; and his observations appear to have been justly founded, for a few years posterior to his death, a commission was granted by James I., in 1612, to many persons of quality; in which were recited and established the good statutes, ordinances, and proclamations, that had been previously made at different times in favour of archery. This commission extended to the prevention of enclosures in the grounds formerly used for the practice of the bow.

The commissioners were also impowered to survey the lands adjoining to the city of London, its suburbs, and within two miles circuit ; and to reduce them to the same state and order for the use of the archers, as they stood at the beginning of the reign of Henry VIII.; and where they found any encroachments, to cause the banks to be thrown down, the ditches filled up, and the open

---

[1] *Archæologia*, li. 232.   [2] Stow's *Survey of London*, by Strype, vol. ii. p. 257. Stow died A.D. 1605.

spaces to be made level. Charles I. confirmed this commission, or granted another to the same purpose.

ORDINANCES IN FAVOUR OF ARCHERY.—CROSS-BOWS, &c.— In the reign of Henry VIII. three several acts were made for promoting the practice of shooting with the long-bow; one, as we have already seen, prohibited the use of cross-bows and hand-guns: another was occasioned by a complaint from the bowyers, the fletchers, or arrow-makers, the stringers, and the arrow-head-makers, stating that many unlawful games were practised in the open fields, to the detriment of the public morals, and great decay of archery. Those games were therefore strictly prohibited by parliament; and a third act followed, which obliged every man, being the king's subject, to exercise himself in shooting with the long-bow; and also to keep a bow with arrows continually in his house. From this obligation were excepted such as were sixty years old, or by lameness or by any other reasonable impediment claimed an exemption; and also all ecclesiastics, the justices of the two benches, or of the assizes, and the barons of the exchequer. Fathers and guardians were also commanded to teach the male children the use of the long-bow, and to have at all times bows provided for them as soon as they arrived at the age of seven years; and masters were ordered to find bows for their apprentices, and to compel them to learn to shoot with them upon holidays, and at every other convenient time. By virtue of the same act, every man who kept a cross-bow in his house was liable to a penalty of ten pounds.

Soon afterwards, that is, in the twenty-ninth year of the same king's reign, the use of cross-bows under certain restrictions was permitted, a patent being then granted by him to sir Christopher Morris, master of his ordinance, Anthony Knevyt and Peter Mewtas, gentlemen of his privy chamber, for them to be overseers of the science of artillery, by which was meant long-bows, cross-bows, and hand-guns. Others were appointed to be masters and rulers of the same science, with power to them and their successors, to establish a perpetual corporation, called the Fraternity of Saint George, and to admit such persons as they found to be eligible. The members of this society were also permitted, for pastime sake, to practise shooting at all sorts of marks and butts, and at the game of the popinjay, and other games, as at fowls and the like, in the city and suburbs of London, as well as in any other convenient places. There is the following remarkable proviso in this charter; " In case any person should be wounded, or slain in these sports, with an arrow shot by one or other of the archers, he that shot the arrow was not to be sued or molested, if he had, immediately before the discharge of the weapon, cried out, 'fast,' the signal usually given upon such occasions." [1]

*HENRY VIII. AN ARCHER.— Henry VIII. not only took the greatest interest in promoting archery, but was himself a remarkable expert in the use of

---

[1] Stow's *Survey*, by Strype, vol. i. p. 250.

the bow. His prowess before Francis at the Field of the Cloth of Gold has often been recorded, when if we are to give credit to the loyal chroniclers, "he repeatedly shot into the centre of the white, though the marks were erected at the extraordinary distance of twelve score yards apart." Cavendish, the historian of Cardinal Wolsey, when he bore the news of Wolsey's death to the king at Hampton Court, in 1530, "found him shooting at the rounds in the park, on the backside of the garden. And perceiving him occupied in shooting, thought it not my duty to trouble him. . . . 'I will,' quoth he, 'make an end of my game, and then I will talk with you,' and so departed to his mark, whereat the game was ended. Then the king delivered his bow unto the yeoman of his bows, and went his way inward to the palace, when I followed."

*The privy purse expenses of Henry VIII. prove his great attachment to archery when in the prime of life. The following occur in the years 1530-1 :—
" To Scawesby, for bows, arrows, shafts, broad-heads, bracer, and shooting-glove for Lady Anne . . . . . . 23s. 4d.
Four bows for Lady Anne . . . . . . 13s. 4d.
To Pynnery for his well shooting . . . . . 7s. 6d.
To Byrde, yeoman of the King's bows, for making the rounds at Totehill 17s. 4d.
To George Coton, for 6 shots lost by the King to him at Totehill, at 6s. 8d. the shot.
To George Gifford, for money won of the King at Totehil at shooting 12s. 6d.
To George Coton, that he won of the King at the roundes on April 30th £3.
To the three Cotons, for three sets which the King lost to them in Greenwich Park £20, and for one upshot won of the King . . 6s. 8d.
To Thomas Harte, for making a pair of new butts, rounds, and pricks 51s. 2d.
To Guilliam for pelletts for the stone bow . . . . 5s. 4d.
To my lord of Rocheford, won from the King at the pricks and by betting £16.
To Antony Kingston, for 8 shots of 3 angels a shot which he won of Thos. Cary shooting on the King's side . . . . £9.
To William Browne, won by him and others of the King and his match at the pricks and by bets in Eltham Park . . . £132 15 0.
To Browne the merchant, for money won of the King at shooting . £22, 10s.
To Henry Byrde, for making pricks at Antyll and Grafton . . 6s. 8d." [1]

*Latimer enforced his royal patron's keenness for archery from the pulpit, when preaching before the king, and received £5 from the privy purse for his pains.

" The art of shooting hath been in times past much esteemed in this realme ; it is a gift of God, that he hath gyven us to excell all other nations withal—It hath been Goddes instrumente whereby he hath gyven victories agayneste our enemyes. But now we have taken up horynge in townes insteade of shutynge

[1] Add. MSS. 20, 030.

in the fyldes. A wondrous thynge that so excellente a gyft of God shoulde be so lyttle esteemed. I desire you, my lordes, even as you love honoure, and glorye of God, and intende to remove his indignacion, let there be sente furth some proclimacion—some sharpe proclimacion, to the justices of peace, for they do not theyr dutye—Justices now be no justices, there be manye good actes made for thys matter already. Charge them upon their allegiance, that this singular benefit of God may be practised; and that it be not turned into bollying, and glossying, and horing, within the townes; for they be negligente in executyng there lawes of shootynge. In my tyme, my poore father was as diligent to teach me to shoote, as to learne any other thynge, and so I thynke other menne dyd thyr children. He taught me howe to drawe, how to laye my bodye in my bowe, and not to draw wyth strength of armes, as other nacions do, but wyth strength of bodye. I had my bowes bought me according to my age and strength; as I increased in them, so my bowes were made bigger; for men shall never shute well excepte they be brought up in it. It is a goodly arte, a holesome kind of exercise, and much commended in phisike. Marcilius Sicinus, in hys boke *de triplica vita* (it is a greate while sins I red him nowe) but I remember he commendeth thys kynde of exercise, an sayth, that it wrestleth agaynst many kyndes of diseases. In the reverence of God, let it be continued. Let a proclimacion go furth, charging the justices of peace, that they see such actes and statutes kept, as were made for thys purpose."

*In the great inventory of arms and armour at Westminster, the Tower, and Greenwich, taken in 1547, the long-bows at the Tower numbered 3060, with " 13,050 sheife of livery arrowes "; at Westminster were " twoo Longe Bowes of Ewghe to shote stones "; and at Greenwich eighty four long bows of various kinds. There were also at the Tower eight boxes containing eighty gross of bow-strings.[1]

PRICES ORDAINED FOR BOWS.—In the reign of Edward IV. an ordinance was established, which compelled the bowyers of London to sell the best bow-staves at three shillings and fourpence each; which was confirmed in the third year of Henry VII., and in the thirty-third year of his son Henry VIII.; but these acts were repealed in the third year of queen Mary, and the following prices were settled by the parliament: for a bow made of the best foreign yew, six shillings and eightpence; for an inferior sort, three shillings and fourpence; and for one made of English yew, two shillings.[2]

*Sir Thomas Elyot's delightful book " The Governour," first issued in 1531, contains the earliest printed account of English archery; chapter xxvii. is devoted to the praise of the long-bow. It was not, however, until 1545 that a whole treatise was published on this subject.

*In that year Ascham's treatise, entitled " Toxophilus, the Schole of Shoot-inge, conteyned in two bookes," was first published. It was " newlye perused "

---

[1] *Archæologia*, li. 231-2, 264.   [2] Maitland's *London*, book v.

and reprinted in 1571 ; and again in 1589 and in 1591. There have been numerous later reprints.

EQUIPMENT FOR ARCHERY.—Ascham informs us, that it was necessary for the archer to have a bracer, or close sleeve, to lace upon the left arm ; it was also proper for this bracer to be made with materials sufficiently rigid to prevent any folds which might impede the bow-string when loosed from the hand ; to this was to be added a shooting-glove, for the protection of the fingers. The bow, he tells us, ought to be made with well-seasoned wood, and formed with great exactness, tapering from the middle towards each end. Bows were sometimes made of Brazil, of elm, of ash, and of several other woods ; but eugh, or yew, had the sanction, from general experience, of superiority. Respecting the bow-string, the author was not decided which to prefer ; those made with good hemp, according to the common usage of the time in which he lived, or those manufactured with flax, or silk ; he therefore thinks the choice ought to be left to the string-maker. There are, he tells us, three essential parts in the composition of the arrow, that is to say, the stele or wand, the feathers, and the head. The stele was not always made with the same species of wood, but varied as occasion required, to suit the different manners of shooting practised by the archers ; he commends sound ash for military arrows, and preferred it to asp, which in his day was generally used for the arrows belonging to the army ; but for pastime, he thought that none were better than those made of oak, hardbeam, or birch ; but after all, says he, in this point I hold it best to trust to the recommendation of an honest fletcher. The feathers from the wing of a goose, and especially of a grey-goose, he thought were preferable to any others for the pluming of an arrow. Thus in the popular ballad of Chevy Chace, an English archer aimed his arrow at sir Hugh Mountgomerye, with such skill, that it hit him on the breast, and the poet elegantly says,

> The grey-goose-winge that was thereon
> In his hearts blood was wett.

The more ancient ballad upon this subject, given in the first volume of the Reliques of Ancient Poetry, reads, the "swane-feathers."

There was, it seems, but little difference between the two wings of one bird ; but, according to the opinion of the best arrow-makers, the second feather was best in some cases and the pinion in others. It was necessary for an archer to have several arrows of one flight (I presume Ascham means of one shape, length, and weight), plumed with feathers from different wings, to suit the diversity of the winds. We are not from these directions to conclude, that the goose alone afforded the plumage for the arrows ; the feathers of many other birds were used for the same purpose, and are mentioned in the metrical romances of the middle ages. An old ballad of Robin Hood says, that he and his followers had an hundred bows furnished with strings, and an hundred sheafs of goose arrows, with bright burnished heads ; every arrow was an ell long, adorned with peacocks' feathers, and bound at the notching with white silk.[1]

> With them they had an hundred bowes,
> The stringes were well ydight ;
> An hundred shefe of arrows good
> With hedes burnish'd full bryght ;
> And every arrowe an ell longe,
> With peacocke well ydight,
> And nocked they were with white silk,
> It was a semely syght.

And Chaucer, in his description of the "squyers yeoman," says,

> And he was clad in cote and hode of grene,
> A shefe of pecocke arrowes bryght and shene ;
> Under his belt he bare ful thriftely
> Well coude he dresse his tackle yomanly ;
> His arrowes drouped not with fethers lowe,
> And in hande he bare a myghty bowe.[2]

The adornment of these arrows with peacocks' feathers is not to be considered as a mere poetical flourish, for we have sufficient testimony, that such plumage was actually used.[3]

But, returning to our author, he informs us, that the English arrows had forked heads and broad-heads, yet he thought, that round pointed heads resembling a bodkin were the best. The notch, or small hollow part at the bottom of the arrow, made for the reception of the bow-string, was varied as occasion required, or at the will of the archer, being sometimes deep and narrow, and sometimes broad and not deep.

DIRECTIONS FOR ARCHERY.—Having thus furnished the archer with his necessary accoutrements, Ascham proceeds to instruct him how they ought to be managed ; but first of all he recommends a graceful attitude. He should stand, says another writer, fairly, and upright with his body, his left foot at a convenient distance before his right ; holding the bow by the middle, with his left arm stretched out, and with the three first fingers and the thumb of the right hand upon the lower part of the arrow affixed to the string of the bow.[4] In the second place, a proper attention was to be paid to the nocking, that is, the application of the notch at the bottom of the arrow to the bow-string ; we are told that the notch of the arrow should rest between the fore-finger and the middle finger of the right hand.[5] Thirdly, our attention is directed to the proper manner of drawing the bow-string : in ancient times, says Ascham, the right hand was brought to the right pap ; but at present it is elevated to the right ear, and the latter method he prefers to the former. The shaft of the arrow below the feathers, ought to be rested upon the knuckle of the fore-finger

---

[1] *Geste of Robyn Hode.* Garrick's Collect. K. vol. x.   [2] Prologue to Canterbury Tales.
[3] *Lib. Compotis Garderobe,* 4 Ed. II. page 53, is this entry, *Pro duodecim flecchiis cum pennis de pavone emptis pro rege,* de 12 den. ; that is, For twelve arrows plumed with peacocks' feathers, bought for the king, twelve pence. MS. Cott. Lib. Nero, C. viii.   [4] *Country Contentments,* 1615, chap. viii. p. 107.   [5] *Ibid.*

D

of the left hand; the arrow was to be drawn to the head, and not held too long in that situation, but neatly and smartly discharged, without any hanging upon the string. Among the requisites necessary to constitute a good archer, are a clear sight, steadily directed to the mark; and proper judgment, to determine the distance of the ground; he ought also to know how to take the advantage of a side wind, and to be well acquainted with what compass his arrows would require in their flight: courage is also an indispensable requisite, for whoever, says our author, shoots with the least trepidation, he is sure to shoot badly. One great fault in particular he complains of, which young archers generally fall into, and that is, the direction of the eye to the end of the arrow, rather than to the mark; to obviate this evil habit he advises such, as were so accustomed, to shoot in the dark, by night, at lights set up at a proper distance for that purpose. He then concludes with observing, that "bad tutorage" was rarely amended in grown-up persons; and therefore he held it essentially necessary, that great attention should be paid to the teaching an archer properly, while he was young; "for children," says he, "if sufficient pains are taken with them at the onset, may much more easily be taught to shoot well, than men," because the latter have frequently more trouble to unlearn their bad habits, than was primitively requisite to learn them good ones.[1]

MARKS FOR SHOOTING.—The marks usually shot at by the archers for pastime, were, "butts, prickes, and roavers." The butt, we are told, was a level mark, and required a strong arrow, with a very broad feather; the pricke was a "mark of compass," but certain in its distance; and to this mark strong swift arrows, of one flight, with a middling sized feather, were best suited; the roaver was a mark of uncertain length; it was therefore proper for the archer to have various kinds of arrows, of different weights, to be used according to the different changements made in the distance of the ground.

The Cornish men are spoken of as good archers, and shot their arrows to a great length; they are also, says Carew, "well skilled in near shooting, and in well aimed shooting;—the butts made them perfect in the one, and the roaving in the other, for the prickes, the first corrupters of archery, through too much preciseness, were formerly scarcely known, and little practised."[2] Other marks are occasionally mentioned, as the standard, the target, hazel wands, rose garlands, and the popinjay, which, we are told, was an artificial parrot. I have not met with such a mark in any manuscript delineation; but, in the presentment on plate six, the reader will find a cock substituted for the parrot, and the archer has discharged his arrow very skilfully. I am by no means certain, whether the draughtsman designed to represent an artificial, or a living cock: the manner of its being placed on the post, may favour the first idea; but the mouth being open, and the elevation of the head, as if in the last gasp of life, will justify the latter. It is taken from a MS. written early in the fourteenth century, preserved in the Royal Library.[3]

[1] *Country Contentments.*   [2] *Survey of Cornwall*, by Richard Carew, 1602, B. i. p. 73.   [3] 2 B. vii.

LENGTH OF BOWS AND ARROWS.—The length of the bow is not clearly ascertained; those used by the soldiery appear, in the manuscript drawings, to have been as tall, at least, as the bearers; agreeable to an ordinance made in the fifth year of Edward IV. commanding every man to have a bow his own height; and they might, upon the average, be something short of six feet long. The arrows used by the English archers at the memorable battle of Agincourt, were a full yard in length. Carew, in his survey of Cornwall, says, "The Cornish archers for long shooting, used arrows a cloth yard long." The old and more modern ballads of Chevy Chace speak of the arrow as being the length of a cloth yard, but some of these poetical legends extend it an ell.

Hall mentions a company of archers, who met king Henry VIII. at Shooter's Hill, on a May-day morning, where they discharged their bows in his presence, and the arrows made a loud whistling in their flight, "by crafte of the heade."[1] The strangeness of the noise, we are informed, surprised his Majesty, though at the same time he was much pleased with the contrivance. A modern author, the Hon. Daines Barrington, assures us, this sound was occasioned by holes being made in the arrow heads, and that such weapons were used upon military occasions, and especially as signals;[2] but not, I presume, before the time mentioned by the historian; for had not those arrows been newly introduced, there is no reason why the king, who was well acquainted with every branch of archery, should have been surprised at the sound they made, or pleased at the sight of them.

FEATS IN ARCHERY.—If the metrical romances and ballads of the former ages may be depended upon, the strength of our English archers in drawing of the bow, and their skill in directing the arrow to its mark, were justly the objects of admiration.

The reader, I trust, will pardon the insertion of the following extracts from two old poetical legends, which convey, at least, some idea of the practice of archery in times anterior to our own; the first is a ballad in eight fyttes or parts, entitled, " A mery Geste of Robyn Hode."[3] According to the story, the king [4] thought proper to pay Robin Hood a visit, disguised in the habit of an abbot: and the outlaw, by way of entertaining his guest, proposed a shooting match. Two wands were then set up, but at so great a distance from each other, that,

> By fyfty space our kyng sayde
> The markes were to longe.—
> On every syde a rose garlande,
> The shot under the lyne.
> Whoso faileth of the rose garland, said Robyn,
> His takyll he shal tyne;[5]

---

[1] An. 7 Hen. VIII. fol. 56. [2] *Archæologia*, vol. vii. p. 58.

[3] Black letter, without date. Imprinted at London upon the Three Crane Wharfe, by William Copland. Garrick's Collect. Old Plays, K. vol. x.

[4] King Edward IV., I presume, is meant by the poet, for in one of the lines we read " Edward our comely kynge." Anachronisms of this kind were common enough in the old ballads.

[5] That is, he shall lose it, or rather, it shall be forfeited.

And yelde it to his maister,
Be it never so fine.—
Twyse Robyn shot about,
And ever he cleved the wande.—

And so did Gilbert, Little John, and Scathelocke, his companions; but,

At the last shot, that Robyn shot,
For all his frendes fore,
Yet he fayled of the garland,
Three fyngers and more—

of course his "takill" was forfeited, which he presented to the king, saying,

Syr abbot, I deliver thee myne arowe.

The second poem is also of the ballad kind, and apparently as old as the former,[1] wherein Adam Bell, Clym of the Cloughe, and William Cloudesle, are introduced to shoot before the king. The butts, or dead marks set up by the king's archers, were censured by Cloudesle, saying,

I hold hym never no good archer,
That shoteth at buttes so wide—

and having procured two "hasell roddes," he set them up at the distance of twenty score paces from each other; his first attempt in shooting at them, contrary to the expectation of the king, was successful, for it is said,

Cloudesle with a bearyng arowe
Clave the wand in two.

The king, being much surprised at the performance, told him he was the best archer he ever saw. Cloudesle then proposed to show him a more extraordinary proof of his skill, and tied his eldest son, a child only seven years old, to a stake, and placed an apple upon his head. When he bound his son he charged him not to move, and turned his face from him, that he might not be intimidated by seeing the arrow directed towards him: six score paces were measured from the stake, and Cloudesle went to the end of the measurement; he first entreated the spectators to be silent,

And then drew out a fayre brode arowe;
Hys bow was great and longe,
He set that arrowe in his bowe
That was both styffe and stronge.

Then Cloudesle cleft the apple in two,
As many a man myght se,
Over Gods forbode, sayde the kynge,
That thou sholde shote at me.

---

[1] Black letter, without date, and printed also by Copland in Lothbury. Its title is, The Names of the Three Archers; the whole ballad, with some small variations, is in the Reliques of Ancient Poetry, vol. i. p. 154, etc. This copy is bound up in the same volume of the Garrick Collection of Old Plays with the Geste of Robyn Hode.

SUPERIORITY OF ANCIENT BOWMEN.—If we were to judge of the merits of the ancient bowmen from the practice of archery as it is exercised in the present day, these poetical eulogiums would appear to be entirely fictitious. There are no such distances now assigned for the marks as are mentioned before, nor such precision, even at short lengths, in the direction of the arrows. By an act established An. 33 Hen. VIII., no person who had reached the age of twenty-four years, might shoot at any mark at less than two hundred and twenty yards distance.[1] I believe few, if any, of the modern archers, in shooting at a mark, exceed the distance of eighty or a hundred yards, or, in long shooting, reach four hundred yards. I have seen the gentlemen who practise archery in the vicinity of London, repeatedly shoot from end to end, and not touch the target with an arrow ; and for the space of several hours, without lodging one in the circle of gold, about six inches diameter in the centre of the target : this, indeed, is so seldom done, that one is led to think, when it happens, it is rather the effect of chance than of skill : which proves what Ascham has asserted, that an archer should be well taught early in life, and confirm the good teaching by continual practice afterwards. We may also recollect, that archery is now followed for amusement only, and is to be commended as a manly and gentleman-like exercise.

I remember about four or five years back,[2] at a meeting of the society of archers, in their ground near Bedford Square, the Turkish ambassador paid them a visit ; and complained that the enclosure was by no means sufficiently extensive for a long shot : he therefore went into the adjacent fields to show his dexterity ; where I saw him shoot several arrows more than double the length of the archery ground, and his longest shot fell upwards of four hundred and eighty yards from his standing. The bow he used was much shorter than those belonging to the English archers ; and his arrows were of the bolt kind, with round heads made of wood. This distance rather exceeds the length our rhymist has given to the wands set up by Cloudesle and his companions, but then we are to recollect they shot with vast precision to that distance, which the ambassador did not, he had no mark, and his arrows fell exceedingly wide of each other.[3]

Carew, speaking of the Cornish archers three centuries back, says, " For long shooting, their shaft was a cloth yard in length. and their prickes twenty-four score paces, equal to four hundred and eighty yards ; and for strength, they would pierce any ordinary armour "; he then adds, "and one Robert Arundell, whom I well knew, could shoot twelve score paces with his right hand, with his left, and from behind his head." [4]

*Very few archers, with strong bows and light arrows, can now cover more than three hundred yards. To attain this range a bow of at least sixty-two pounds must not only be used but mastered.[5]

---

[1] *Archæologia*, vol. i. p. 58.   [2] [Mr Strutt wrote this in 1800.]
[3] *This incident occurred in 1795, in the presence of several gentlemen of the Toxophilite Society. The archer was not the Turkish Ambassador, but his secretary, Mahmoud Effendi, a man of great muscular strength. He used a Turkish bow, which owed its length of cast to the elasticity of the horn of which it was composed.
[4] *Survey of Cornwall*, 1602.   [5] Butt's *Theory and Practice of Archery* (1887), 137-8.

THE DUKE OF SHOREDITCH.—Henry VIII., having appointed a great match of archery at Windsor, a citizen of London, named Barlow, an inhabitant of Shoreditch, joined the archers, and surpassed them all in skill; the king was so much pleased with his performance, that he jocosely gave him the title of " Duke of Shoreditch " ; and this title the captain of the London archers retained for a considerable time afterwards. In 1583, in the reign of Elizabeth, a grand shooting match was held in London, and the captain of the archers assuming his title of Duke of Shoreditch, summoned a suit of nominal nobility, under the titles of marquis of Barlo, of Clerkenwell, of Islington, of Hoxton, of Shackle-well, and earl of Pancrass, etc., and these meeting together at the appointed time, with their different companies, proceeded in a pompous march from Merchant Taylors Hall, consisting of three thousand archers, sumptuously apparelled ; every man had a long-bow, and four arrows. With the marquis of Barlo and the marquis of Clerkenwell were " Hunters who wound their horns." [1] Nine hundred and forty-two of the archers had chains of gold about their necks. This splendid company was guarded by four thousand whifflers and billmen, besides pages and footmen. They passed through Broad-street, the residence of their captain, and thence into Moorfields, by Finsbury, and so on to Smithfield, where, having performed several evolutions, they shot at a target for honour. [2]

ROYAL SPORT—A GOOD ARCHER WHY CALLED ARTHUR.—Kings and princes have been celebrated for their skill in archery, and among those of our own country may be placed king Henry VII., who in his youth was partial to this exercise, and therefore it is said of him in an old poem, written in praise of the princess Elizabeth, afterwards queen to Henry VII. [3]

> See where he shoteth at the butts,
> And with hym are lordes three ;
> He weareth a gowne of velvette blacke,
> And it is coted above the knee.

He also amused himself with the bow after he had obtained the crown, as we find from an account of his expenditures, [4] where the following memorandums occur : " Lost to my lord Morging at buttes, six shillings and eightpence : " and again, " Paid to sir Edward Boroughe thirteen shillings and fourpence, which the kynge lost at buttes with his cross-bowe." Both the sons of king Henry followed his example, and were excellent archers ; and especially the eldest, prince Arthur, who used frequently to visit the society of London bowmen at Mile-end, where they usually met, and practised with them. From his expert-ness in handling of the bow, every good shooter was called by his name. The captain also of the fraternity was honoured with the title of Prince Arthur, and

---

[1] Stow's *Survey*, by Strype, vol. i. p. 250.   [2] Strype's *London*, vol. i. p. 250.
[3] MS. Harl. 3653, fol. 96.
[4] An. 7 et 9 Hen. VII. MS. in the Remembrancer's Office. See also Appendix to Henry's *Hist. Brit.* vol. vi.

the other archers were styled his knights.[1]   The title of Prince Arthur seems to have been superseded by the creation of the " Duke of Shoreditch."

After the death of prince Arthur, his brother Henry continued to honour the meeting at Mile-end with his presence.   His exceeding fondness for archery has already been described.   Hall says that at the time of his accession Henry VIII. " shotte as strong and as greate a lengthe as any of his garde."

*ARCHERY AT BUXTON.—In Elizabeth's reign archery was warmly recommended as a healthy pastime.   Of all the exercises that Dr Jones, the Buxton physician in Elizabethan days, recommended to his patients, archery was the favourite.   "Shootinge at Garden Buttes too them whome it agreeth and pleaseth, in place of Noblest exercyse standeth, and that rather wythe Longe bowe, than with Tyller, Stone bowe, or Cross bowe.   Albeeit, to them that otherwyse cannot, by reason of greefe, feeblenesse, or lacke of use, they may bee allowed.   This practise of all other the manlyest leaveth no part of the body unexercised, the breaste, backe, reynes, wast, and armes, withdrawing the thyghes and legges with running or going."[2]

*ELIZABETHAN ARCHERS.—The county musters of the first year of Elizabeth prove that the country at large was then exceedingly well furnished with duly equipped archers.   The return for Derbyshire, made on March 9th, 1559, shows that that comparatively small county put into the field, as "able footemen," 292 archers as against 918 billmen.[3]   During this reign, however, archery was slowly but surely made to give way to musketry.   From the muster certificate of Derbyshire, in November 1587, it appears that out of 400 foot pressed for immediate service, 160 were "for shot," 160 were billmen, and 80 archers ; whilst out of 1300 able men selected for further service, only 200 were "for bowes."[4]   It therefore follows that the proportion of archers had been reduced in thirty years from a third to a fifth.

*In some counties the change in these thirty years was greater than in Derbyshire.   In 1587-8, out of 1170 men under training in Lancashire, 700 bore light muskets and but 80 bows ; whilst in Cheshire, out of a total of 2189, there were only 80 archers.[5]   Within a few years after the Armada, the old national weapon of the long-bow became nearly extinct.   Nevertheless it lingered longer in England than on the continent; a foreigner visiting the Tower in 1598, expressed his surprise at finding bows in the arsenals.   In the more remote counties, an archer's equipment lingered on, as the armour of the parish soldier occasionally supplied for the musters, not only to the end of Elizabeth's reign, but even into that of the first two Stuarts.

*ARCHERY IN THE CIVIL WAR.—It has usually been said that the last instance of the serious use of bows in Great Britain, and that to a very partial extent, was in the guerilla warfare carried on against Cromwell in remote parts of the Scottish Highlands.   The Derbyshire records, however, supply an

---

[1] *Archæologia*, vol. vii.   [2] *The Benefit of the Auncient Bathes of Buckstones*, 1572.
[3] Cox's *Three Centuries of Derbyshire Annals*, i. 130-145.   [4] *Ibid*. ii. 151.   [5] Scott's *British Army*, ii. 96.

English instance; one James Wintone was "wounded in ye righte hande by an arowe," in a skirmish at Hathersage in 1647, as alleged in his claim for a pension. This was clearly a bow used by the Royalists, for Wintone appealed to the Parliamentarians for a pension. It is scarcely reasonable to suppose that this wounding by an arrow in the Peak district was a solitary instance of the use of the bow; probably many of the country gentlemen's houses were defended with these weapons.[1]

*REVIVAL AT THE RESTORATION.—No sooner was the Restoration of the monarchy accomplished than a determined effort was made, particularly in London, to restore England's fame in archery.

*On March 21st, 1661, four hundred archers made "a splendid and glorious show" in Hyde Park, with Sir Gilbert Talbot as their colonel, and Sir Edward Hungerford their lieutenant-colonel. "Several of the Archers Shot near Twenty score yards within the compass of a Hat with their Crossbows; and many of them, to the amazement of the Spectators hit the mark; there were likewise three Showers of Whistling Arrows. So great was the delight, and so pleasing the Exercise, that three Regiments of Foot laid down their Arms to come and see it." In 1675, three hundred and fifty richly-habited archers marched through the city to compliment Sir Robert Vyner, the Lord Mayor, who entertained them at dinner. In the following year upwards of a thousand archers were reviewed by the king at Tuttlefields. The archers marched from London to Hampton Court in July 1681, when the king watched them shooting for £30 worth of plate at eight score yards. A manuscript postscript to the copy of the *Bowman's Glory* in the British Museum names a march through the city of a thousand archers on April 21st, 1682, to Tuttlefields, where the king again watched their manœuvres, including the "Three Showers of Whistling Arrows."[2]

*A dull poem, published in 1676, makes the following appeal in favour of the revival of archery as a pastime :—

> "Forsake your lov'd Olympian games awhile,
> With which the tedious minutes you beguile,
> Wave quoits and nine-pins, those bear-garden sports,
> And follow shooting, often used at courts."[3]

*SIR WILLIAM WOOD.—"Sir" William Wood, the famous archer, and author of *The Bowman's Glory*, who died in 1691, at the age of 82, had the following epitaph erected to his memory on the south side of the church of St James, Clerkenwell; his title was a jocular suffix, like that of the Duke of Shoreditch :—

> "Sir William Wood lies very near this stone
> In's time of archery excelled by none;
> Few were his equalls, and this noble art
> Hath suffer'd now in the most tender part.

---

[1] Cox's *Derbyshire Annals*, i. 160.
[2] *The Bowman's Glory, or Archery Revived*, by William Wood, Marshal to the Regiment of Archers, 1682.
[3] *Archerye Revived*, by Robert Shotterel and Thomas D'Urfey.

Long did he live the honour of the bow,
And his long life to that alone did owe ;
But how can art secure, or what can save
Extreme old age from an appointed grave ?
Surviving archers much his loss lament,
And in respect bestow'd this monument,
Where whistling arrows did his worth proclaim,
And eternize his memory and name." [1]

*Wood was buried with archers' honours, three flights of whistling arrows being discharged over his grave.

*In 1696, Elizabeth Shakerley, a widow lady, left by her will thirty-five pounds to be distributed in prizes to the Artillery Company.

*The Artillery Company originally confined to archers, as founded by Henry VIII. and patronised by successive monarchs, were wont to practise in Finsbury Fields, and hence were commonly known as the Finsbury Archers. There are a variety of printed tracts and manuscripts extant relative to the archers' marks in these fields, which were used by them for upwards of two centuries. The earliest of these was printed and sold at the sign of the Swan in Grub Street, by T. Sergeant, in 1594. The full title is :—"Ayme for Finsburie Archers, or an alphabeticall table of the names of every marke within the same fields, with their true (or due) distances, both by the map and dimensuration of the line, published for the ease of the skillfull and behoofe of the younge beginners in the famed exercise of Archerie." [2]

*No point of archery, from a military or sporting point of view, was more important than keeping the length. On this account roving or ranging across the fields, and shooting at marks of varying and unascertained distances was much preferred, in old-time archery, to pricking or shooting at a given mark from a fixed and known distance. With one of the last editions of the Finsbury Archers, issued in 1738, a plan was given of these fields with all the marks entered by name. [3] These marks were originally 164 in number, and they varied in length from 73 yards to 265 yards. When Mr Barrington contributed his paper on Archery to the Society of Antiquaries in 1783, the fields from Peerless-pool to the Rosemary-branch and for a considerable distance northward were studded with roving marks. At that period, however, there were only twenty-one of the original marks standing, but the Artillery Company still claimed access to them and tried to insist on their maintenance and repair.

*In 1782, the Artillery Company marched, on Accession Day, to Baumer Fields, where they found the gate of a large field, wherein stood one of their stone marks, locked and chained and guarded by four men. The Company however forced the gate and marched across. In 1786 they marched to Finsbury Fields " to view their several stone marks " and removed several obstructions. In the same year, on August 17th, the Company on its march came to a

---

[1] *Archæologia*, vii. 50.   [2] For the bibliography of Archery, see *Notes and Queries*, Ser. v. vols. 9 and 10.
[3] Reproduced in the *Gentleman's Magazine* for 1832, p. 209.

piece of ground lately enclosed with a brick wall by the proprietors of a white-lead mill, " between the marks of Bob Peak and the Levant." The work of demolition began, but the Company was induced to desist on one of the partners of the mill assuring the commanding officer of the battalion of their ignorance of the Company's rights in these fields and their willingness to enter into any reasonable terms of accommodation. " One of the archer's division was then ordered to shoot an arrow over the said inclosure, as an assertion of the Company's right ; which having been done, the battalion proceeded on its march to several of the other marks." [1] But bricks and mortar eventually gained the day along the whole line, and all the Finsbury marks have disappeared for more than a century.

*THE TOXOPHILITES.—In 1780 Sir Aston Lever and Mr Waring founded a society called the Toxophilites, who met regularly at Leicester House and shot at butts erected in the gardens. From that date onwards, with varying degrees of enthusiasm, shooting at targets with the long bow has been an accepted pastime for ladies and gentlemen. A special impetus was given to archery associations in 1844.

[1] Highmore's *Hist. of the Artillery Company*, pp. 366, 396, 399.

CHAPTER II

Slinging of Stones an Ancient Art—Known to the Saxons—And the Normans—How practised of late Years—Throwing of Weights and Stones with the Hand—By the Londoners—Casting of the Bar and Hammer—Of Spears—Of Quoits—Swinging of Dumb Bells—Foot Races—The Game of Base—Wrestling much practised formerly—Prizes for—How performed—Sir Thomas Parkyns—Hippas—Swimming—Sliding—Skating—Rowing—Sailing.

SLINGING OF STONES.—The art of slinging, or casting of stones with a sling, is of high antiquity, and probably antecedent to that of archery, though not so generally known nor so universally practised. The tribe of Benjamin among the Israelites is celebrated in holy writ for the excellency of its slingers. In the time of the judges there were seven hundred Benjamites who all of them used their left hands, and in the figurative language of the Scripture it is said, they " could sling stones at an hair-breadth and not miss," [1] that is, with exceedingly great precision. Again we are told, that when David fled to Ziklag, he was joined by a party of valiant men of the tribe of Benjamin, who could use both the right and the left in slinging of stones and shooting arrows out of a bow.[2] David himself was also an excellent marksman, as the destruction of Goliath by the means of his sling sufficiently testifies. It was, perhaps, an instrument much used by the shepherds in ancient times, to protect their flocks from the attacks of ferocious animals : if so, we shall not wonder that David, who kept his father's sheep, was so expert in the management of this weapon.[3]

*SLINGING BY THE ANGLO-SAXONS.—The later Assyrian sculptures frequently show soldiers armed with the sling, and the Persians, as we gather from Xenophon, were expert slingers. Sling bullets of lead, stone, and hard-baked clay or terra-cotta were used by the Romans ; their slingers were an important light-armed division of their armies ; they appear on the Trajan column. Sling stones have been found, occasionally in considerable numbers, at Romano-British stations ; but there are also good reasons for knowing that the archaic tribes of the British Isles were well acquainted with the use of the sling long before the arrival of the Romans. Stones for this purpose have been found in early barrows and entrenchments, both in England and Ireland.[4] The sling and its deadly effects are frequently alluded to in the Irish annals.

Our Anglo-Saxon ancestors were skilful in the management of the sling ; its form is preserved in several of their paintings, and the manner in which it was used by them, as far back as the eighth century, may be seen on plate five, from

[1] Judges, chap. xx. ver. 16.   [2] 1 Chron. chap. xii. ver. 2.   [3] 1 Samuel, chaps. xvii. and xviii.
[4] *Journal of the Brit. Arch. Assoc.*, xx. 73-80 ; *Notes and Queries*, Ser. 1, vi. 17, 377 ; Evans' *Ancient Stone Implements of Great Britain*, chap. xviii.

a manuscript of that age in the Cotton Library.[1] It is there represented with one of the ends unloosened from the hand and the stone discharged. In the original the figure is throwing the stone at a bird upon the wing, which is represented at some distance from him.

In other instances we see it depicted with both the ends held in the hand, the figure being placed in the action of taking his aim, and a bird is generally the object of his exertion, as in another drawing on the same plate from a parchment roll in the Royal Library, containing a genealogical account of the kings of England to the time of Henry III.[2]

Sometimes the sling is attached to a staff or truncheon, about three or four feet in length, wielded with both hands, and charged with a stone of no small magnitude. These staff-slings, known by the Romans as *fustibalus*, appear to have been chiefly used in besieging of cities, and on board of ships in engagements by sea. The representation of two such slings on plate five is taken from a drawing supposed to have been made by Matthew Paris, in a MS. at Bennet' College, Cambridge.[3]

SLINGING BY THE ANGLO-NORMANS.—We have sufficient testimony to prove that men armed with slings formed a part of the Anglo-Norman soldiery,[4] and the word balistarii, used by our early historians, may, I doubt not, be more properly rendered slingers than cross-bowmen; though indeed, upon the introduction of the cross-bow, these men might take the place of the slingers. In fact the cross-bow itself was modified to the purpose of discharging of stones, and for that reason was also called a stone-bow, so that the appellation *Balistarius* and *Arcubalistarius* were both of them latterly applied to the same person. At the battle of Hastings slingers formed part of both the armies; from this period until the close of the fourteenth century they formed an important element in every military expedition. They also continued to be used for fowling purposes, and doubtless often for mere pastime. The sling, however, was not entirely superseded by the bow at the commencement of the fifteenth century, as the following verses plainly indicate : they occur in a manuscript poem in the Cotton Library,[5] entitled, " Knyghthode and Batayle," written about that time, which professedly treats upon the duties and exercises necessary to constitute a good soldier.

Use eek the cast of stone, with slynge or honde :
It falleth ofte, yf other shot there none is,
Men harneysed in steel may not withstonde,
The multitude and mighty cast of stonys ;
And stonys in effecte, are every where,
And slynges are not noyous for to beare.

By the two last lines the poet means to say, that stones are every where readily procured, and that the slings are by no means cumbersome to the

---

[1] Claudius, B. iv. [2] 14. B. v. [3] C. v. 16.
[4] *Manners and Customs of the English*, vol. I. [5] Titus A. xxiii. part I, fol. 8.

bearers, which were cogent reasons for retaining them as military weapons; neither does he confine their use to any body or rank of soldiers, but indiscriminately recommends the acquirement of skill in the casting of stones, to every individual who followed the profession of a warrior.

*In the metrical tale of *King Edward and the Shepherd* (fourteenth century), the countryman exclaims—

> "I have slyngs smort and good";

and proudly declares—

> "The best archer of ilk one
> I durst meet him with a stone,
>   And gif him lefe to shoot.
> There is no bow that shall laste
> To draw to my slyng's cast."

In Barclay's *Eclogues*, issued in 1508, a shepherd states that—

> "I can dance the rage; I can both pipe and sing
> If I were mery; I can both hurl and sling."

Leland in his *Itinerary*, when describing the isle of Portland in 1536, states —"The people be good there in slyngging of stonys, and use it for defence of the isle."

MODERN MODES OF SLINGING.—I remember in my youth to have seen several persons expert in slinging of stones, which they performed with thongs of leather, or, wanting those, with garters; and sometimes they used a stick of ash or hazel, a yard or better in length, and about an inch in diameter; it was split at the top so as to make an opening wide enough to receive the stone, which was confined by the re-action of the stick on both sides, but not strong enough to resist the impulse of the slinger. It required much practice to handle this instrument with any great degree of certainty, for if the stone in the act of throwing quitted the sling either sooner or later than it ought to do, the desired effect was sure to fail. Those who could use it properly, cast stones to a considerable distance and with much precision. In the present day (1800) the use of all these engines seems to be totally discontinued.

THROWING WITH THE HAND.—Throwing of heavy weights and stones with the hand was much practised in former times, and as this pastime required great strength and muscular exertion, it was a very proper exercise for military men. The Greeks, according to Homer, at the time of the siege of Troy, amused themselves with casting of the discus, which appears to have been a round flat plate of metal of considerable magnitude and very heavy.[1] "The discus of the ancients," says Dr Johnson, in his dictionary, "is sometimes called in English quoit, not improperly. The game of quoits is a game of skill; the discus was only a trial of strength, as among us to throw the hammer."

[1] *Iliad*, book xxiii.

THROWING BY THE LONDONERS.—In the twelfth century we are assured, that among the amusements practised by the young Londoners on holidays, was casting of stones,[1] darts, and other missive weapons. Bars of wood and iron were afterwards used for the same purpose, and the attention of the populace was so much engaged by this kind of exercise, that they neglected in great measure the practice of archery, which occasioned an edict to be passed in the thirty-ninth year of Edward III. prohibiting the pastimes of throwing of stones, wood, and iron, and recommending the use of the long-bow upon all convenient opportunities.[2]

CASTING OF THE BAR AND HAMMER.—Casting of the bar is frequently mentioned by the romance writers as one part of a hero's education, and a poet of the sixteenth century thinks it highly commendable for kings and princes, by way of exercise, to throw " the stone, the barre, or the plummet." Henry VIII., after his accession to the throne, according to Hall and Holinshead, retained " the casting of the barre " among his favourite amusements. The sledge hammer was also used for the same purpose as the bar and the stone ; and among the rustics, if Barclay be correct, an axletree.

An early instance of throwing the stone occurs in a manuscript of the thirteenth century ; it is reproduced at the top of plate sixty-two.[3]

*Throughout the reign of Henry VIII., encouraged by royal example, gentlemen were eager to take part in pedestrian as well as equestrian exercises. Sir William Forest, in his *Poesye of Princelye Practice*, holds that a gentleman should—

> " In featis of maistries bestowe some diligence
> Too ryde, runne, lepe, or caste by violence
> Stone, barre, or plummett, or such other thinge
> It not refuseth any prince or kynge."

*Elyot's *Governour* names "labouryng with poyses made of ledde, and lifting and throwing the heavy stone or barre." At the commencement of the seventeenth century, these pastimes seem to have lost their relish among the higher classes of the people, and for this reason Peacham, in his *Complete Gentleman*, speaks of throwing the hammer as an exercise proper for soldiers in camp, or for the amusement of the prince's guard, but not so well " beseeming nobility."

*Hammer throwing, as a modern athletic sport, follows the form that has come to us from over the Border. The weight of the hammer is the same as that of the weight in weight-putting, namely, sixteen pounds.

THROWING OF SPEARS.—Throwing of darts and javelins being properly a military exercise, was not prohibited by the act above mentioned. In 1529 Erasmus, writing to Cochloeus, said that the king outstripped every one in throwing the dart. Chafrins, ambassador of Charles V., wrote in 1532 that Anne Boleyn had presented Henry with certain darts of Biscayan fashion richly ornamented.[4] It was sometimes practised as a mere trial of strength, when the attempt was to throw beyond a certain boundary, or to exceed a competitor in

---

[1] Fitzstephen's *Description of London.*   [2] Rot. claus. Memb. 23.
[3] Roy. Lib. 10 E. iv. f. 96.   [4] *Archæologia*, li. 239.

distance ; and of skill, when the spear was cast at a quintain, or any other determined mark. The pastime is frequently mentioned by the writers of the middle ages. Charles VI. of France and the lords of his court, after a grand entertainment, were amused with "Wrastling, and casting of the bar, and the dart, by Frenchmen and the Gascoyns."[1]

QUOITS.—The game of quoits, or coits, as an amusement, is superior to any of the foregoing pastimes ; the exertion required is more moderate, because this exercise does not depend so much upon superior strength as upon superior skill. The quoit seems evidently to have derived its origin from the ancient discus, and with us in the present day it is a circular plate of iron perforated in the middle, not always of one size, but larger or smaller to suit the strength or conveniency of the several candidates. It is further to be observed, that quoits are not only made of different magnitudes to suit the poise of the players, but sometimes the marks are placed at extravagant distances, so as to require great strength to throw the quoit home ; this, however, is contrary to the general rule, and depends upon the caprice of the parties engaged in the contest.

*An interesting reference to quoit-playing early in the fifteenth century has recently come to light. When the evidence was taken as to alleged miracles at the tomb of Bishop Osmund of Salisbury, before a papal commission, for the purpose of procuring his canonisation, four witnesses testified to the marvellous recovery of Cristina Cerlee, a girl of nine years of age, on St Mark's Day, 1409 ; the child was struck by accident by a quoit on the head so severely that the brain was exposed and she was taken up for dead and lay lifeless for an hour and a half. Richard Wodewell, carpenter, stated that he was playing quoits with his companions at Laverstock when he overthrew an iron quoit weighing a pound, and it struck Cristina who was seated on the ground twelve feet beyond the mark. Others picked her up saying she was killed, and he at once ran to the church of Salisbury for refuge, and there prayed to God, the Blessed Virgin and Bishop Osmund, at the bishop's tomb for the child's life. Cristina recovered, and made an offering of the quoit at the tomb.[2]

*Quoits was one of those games prohibited in the reigns of Edward III. and Richard II. in favour of archery. Ascham, in his *Toxophilus* (1545), says that "quoiting be too vile for scholars." It seems always to have been, as at present, a game chiefly popular among the working-classes, although it admits of much skill, dexterity, and judgment.

To play at this game, an iron pin, called a hob, is driven into the ground, within a few inches of the top ; and at the distance of eighteen, twenty, or more yards, for the distance is optional, a second pin of iron is also made fast in a similar manner ; two or more persons, as four, six, eight, or more at pleasure, who divided into two equal parties are to contend for the victory, stand at one

---

[1] Froissart, Lord Berners' translation, vol. iv. chao. 149, fol. 184.

[2] *Canonization of St Osmund* (Wilts Record Soc. 1902), pp. viii., 64-6. The depositions speak of a "*massa ferrea*" being thrown by Wodewell, but in Harding's Register (p. 25) it is described as a "coyte."

of the iron marks and throw an equal number of quoits to the other, and the nearest of them to the hob are reckoned towards the game. But the determination is discriminately made : for instance, if a quoit belonging to A lies nearest to the hob, and a quoit belonging to B the second, A can claim but one towards the game, though all his other quoits lie nearer to the mark than all the other quoits of B; because one quoit of B being the second nearest to the hob, cuts out, as it is called, all behind it : if no such quoit had interfered, then A would have reckoned all his as one each. Having cast all their quoits, the candidates walk to the opposite side, and determine the state of the play, then taking their stand there, throw their quoits back again and continue to do so alternately as long as the game remains undecided.

Formerly in the country, the rustics not having the round perforated quoits to play with, used horse-shoes, and in many places the quoit itself, to this day, is called a shoe.

DUMB BELLS.—John Northbroke, in a treatise against Diceing, Dancing, etc. written in the time of queen Elizabeth, advises young men, by way of amusement, to "labour with poises of lead or other metal"; this notable pastime, I apprehend, bore some resemblance to the Skiomachia ($\Sigma\kappa\iota o\mu\alpha\chi\iota\alpha$) or fighting with a man's own shadow, mentioned in one of the *Spectators* :[1] "It consisted," says the author, "in brandishing of two sticks, grasped in each hand and loaden with plugs of lead at either end;—this pastime opens the chest, exercises the limbs, and gives a man all the pleasure of boxing without the blows." It is sometimes practised in the present day, and called "ringing of the dumb bells."

*The use of dumb-bells, and of the bar-bell which is but a two-handed dumb-bell, still forms one of the most important elements of modern gymnastics.

*The origin of the term is somewhat curious. Dumb-bells take their name by analogy, as was pointed out in *Notes and Queries* in 1861, "from a machine used for exercise, consisting of a rough, heavy, wooden flywheel with a rope passing through and round a spindle . . . and set in motion like a church bell."[2] This statement, however, does not sufficiently explain the transference of such a name to the short bar and rounded lead or iron ends of a hand dumb-bell. This difficulty was explained by the late Chancellor Ferguson in a paper read before the Archæological Institute in 1895, wherein a dumb-bell apparatus, now at Lord Sackville's seat at Knowle, was described and illustrated.[3] The roller round which the rope winds and unwinds has four iron arms, each of which has a leaden poise or ball at the end, just like the end of an ordinary hand dumb-bell. This Knowle example is fixed in an attic and the rope passed through to a gallery beneath. Anyone pulling the rope would get much the same exercise as in pulling a bell rope in a church tower, but without annoying his neighbours by the noise. There used to be a similar apparatus at New College, Oxford. The date of such contrivances for exercise cannot be older than the opening of

---

[1] Vol. ii. No. 115. (A.D. 1711.)   [2] *Notes and Queries*, Ser. II., xii. 45.
[3] *Archæological Journal*, lii. 95-6.

the seventeenth century when the practice of change-ringing in England first began. Change-ringing became fashionable among gentlemen in the reign of Charles II., and the healthiness of the exercise was much vaunted.[1]

FOOT-RACING.—There is no kind of exercise that has more uniformly met the approbation of authors in general than running. In the middle ages, foot-racing was considered as an essential part of a young man's education, especially if he was the son of a man of rank, and brought up to a military profession.

It is needless, I doubt not, to assert the antiquity of this pastime, because it will readily occur to every one, that variety of occasions continually present themselves, which call forth the exertions of running even in childhood; and when more than one person are stimulated by the same object, a competition naturally takes place among them to obtain it. Originally, perhaps, foot-races had no other incitement than emulation, or at best the prospect of some small reward: but in process of time the rewards were magnified, and contests of this kind were instituted as public amusements; the ground marked out for that purpose, and judges appointed to decide upon the fairness of the race, to ascertain the winner, and to bestow the reward.

*In Sir Thomas Elyot's *Governour*, "rennyng" is named as "bothe a goode exercise and a laudable solace;" he defends the custom of running races by references to such heroes of classical antiquity as Achilles, Alexander, and Epaminondas. Both private matches and public competitions are mentioned by Shakespeare. Falstaff says to Poins: "I could give a thousand pounds I could run as fast as thou canst." In the third part of Henry VI. occur the lines—

> "Forspent with toil, as runners with a race,
> I lay me down a little while to breathe."

Running was one of the exercises commended to his son by James I.

*After the Restoration, every form of sport was resumed with vigour. Pepys' *Diary* contains many references to foot races. On August 10th, 1660, Pepys went "With Mr Moore and Creed to Hide Park by coach, and saw a fine footrace three times round the Park between an Irishman and Crew, that was once my Lord Claypoole's footman." On July 30th, 1663, he writes: "The town talk this day is of nothing but the great foot-race run this day on Banstead Downes, between Lee, the Duke of Richmond's footman, and a tiler, a famous runner. And Lee hath beat him; though the king and Duke of York, and all men almost, did bet three or four to one upon the tiler's head." Occasionally noblemen performed feats of this description. Pepys records the

---

[1] Chancellor Ferguson also contributed *Notes about Dumb Bells*, as an appendix to his former paper, to the *Archæological Journal* of the next year (lii. 19-25). Mr Albert Hartshorne contributed to that paper a brief description and sketch of what he terms "a complete and ancient example of a dumb-bell" in the belfry of Bradbourne church, Derbyshire. This is, however, in reality a mere windlass for bell raising such as can be found in scores of old belfries. Having visited every Derbyshire belfry, and hundreds of others, I have no doubt on the matter, and agree in this respect with our best bell expert, Dr Raven. When first learning bell ringing the practice always was and still obtains of simply tying back the clapper, and so producing dumb bells.—J. C. C.

E

remarkable performance, for a wager before the king, of Lords Castlehaven and Arran, when they ran down and killed a buck in St James' park. He also praised the extraordinary nimbleness of the Duke of Monmouth, of whom Macaulay says that he " won foot-races in his boots against fleet runners in shoes." The *Luttrell Papers* mention that in 1690 " Mr Peregrine Bertie, son to the late Earl of Lindsey, upon a wager, ran the Mall in St James' Park eleven times in less than an hour."

*Philip Kinder, in his MS. *History of Derbyshire*, written about the middle of the seventeenth century, says of the natives of that shire : " Theire exercise for a greate part is ye Gymnopaidia or naked boy, an ould recreation among ye Greeks, and this in foote-races. You shall have in a winter's day, ye earth crusted over wth ice, two Antagonists starke naked runn a foote-race for 2 or 3 miles, wth many hundred spectators, and ye betts very smale." [1]

*Any attempt to deal with foot-racing in the eighteenth century would require a whole treatise, and would for the most part be a record of foolish contests for extravagant wagers. It will suffice to quote a paragraph from the first chapter of the standard work on modern English athletics. " The annals of the eighteenth century are full of accounts of wagers for the performance of athletic feats, both sublime as well as ridiculous. The majority of the genuine athletic performances are those of professional pedestrians, amateurs only figuring occasionally in these wagers, and often in preposterous ones. Luttrell's *Diary* tells us of a wager made by a German of sixty-four years old, to walk 300 miles in Hyde Park in six days, which he did within the time and a mile over. In 1780, the *Gentleman's Magazine* tells us that a man of seventy-five years ran four miles and a half round Queen Square in 58 minutes. Eight years later a young gentleman, with a jockey booted and spurred on his back, ran a match against an elderly fat man (of the name of Bullock) running without a rider. The more extraordinary the wager the more excitement it often caused amongst the public. A fish-hawker is reported to have run for a wager seven miles, from Hyde Park Corner to Brentford, with 56 lbs. weight of fish on his head, in 45 minutes ! Another man trundled a coach-wheel eight miles in an hour round a platform erected in St Giles' Fields. Another extraordinary match was one between a man on stilts against a man on foot, the former receiving twenty yards start in a hundred and twenty yards. What is more astounding is that the man upon the stilts won the match." [2]

Foot-races are not now (1800) much encouraged by persons of fortune, and seldom happen but for the purpose of betting, and the racers are generally paid for their performance. In many instances the distance does not exceed one hundred yards. At fairs, wakes, and upon many other occasions where many people are assembled together, this species of amusement is sometimes promoted, but most frequently the contest is confined to the younger part of the concourse.

[1] Bodleian, Ashm, MSS. 788.

[2] Badminton Library: *Athletics*, by Montague Shearman. This is the best book to consult as to the remarkable revival of foot-racing, both amateur and professional, during the nineteenth century.

*Foot-racing in connection with wedding festivities was a very old custom in the north of England, and still lingers in some parts of north Yorkshire. In that charming book, *Forty Years in a Moorland Parish*, by the late Canon Atkinson, incumbent of Danby-in-Cleveland, published in 1891, occur the following passages :—

" The most typical Dales Wedding I ever remember having witnessed was nearly forty years ago, and on Martinmas Day. But I should not have spoken of the event in the singular number; for there were, in point of fact, four weddings all to be solemnised coincidently. . . . After the ceremony was over, great was the scramble among the small boys for the coppers, which it was and is customary for the newly-married man, or his best man, to scatter the moment the chancel door is left. And then an adjournment to the field adjoining the churchyard was made, and there was a series of races, all on foot, to be run for the ribbons which were the gift of the several brides; and as some of them gave more than one, the races were multiplied accordingly. Time was, and not so very long before the commencement of my incumbency here, when these races were ridden on horseback; and, at an earlier period still, the race was a 'steeple-chase' across country—the goal being the house whence the bride had come, and to which the wedding cavalcade was to return for the usual festivities. More than once, too, I have known, when the bride in some way incurred the suspicion of niggardness, through not complying with the recognised usage of supplying one ribbon at least to be run for, the 'stithy was fired upon her,' *i.e.* a charge of powder was rammed into a hole in the anvil (much after the shot in a mine), and fired in derision; well pronounced, if the loudness of the report counted for anything, as the wedding party passed on the journey home from the church. The direct converse of this, was the firing of guns as the party passed the residences of friends and well wishers. . . . The races still linger on, and only a week or two since the bride gave two 'ribbons to be run for'; and a few years ago one young chap, fleet of foot, and with as much inclination for 'laiking' (playing) as for sticking to work—some folk said more—was quoted as the fortunate winner of almost enough to start an itinerant haberdasher in trade."[1]

BASE, OR PRISONERS' BARS.—There is a rustic game called Base or Bars, and sometimes written Bays,[2] and in some places Prisoners' Bars; and as the success of this pastime depends upon the agility of the candidates and their skill in running, I think it may properly enough be introduced here. It was much practised in former times, and some vestiges of the game are still remaining in

---

[1] Pp. 205-7. Shortly after Canon Atkinson published this book, one of my oldest parishioners in Barton-le-Street (of which I was rector 1886-1894) told me that he had seen a stark naked race of young men over the moors from Danby-in-Cleveland churchyard at the conclusion of a wedding at which Canon Atkinson officiated in the year 1851. Needless to say the sport did not begin till after the parson had left. I had some most interesting correspondence with the Canon on this subject, and was able to convince him by the evidence of several that this occasional stripping for a race after a wedding was only abandoned soon after he entered on his incumbency.—J. C. C.

[2] Johnson's Dictionary, word *Base*.

many parts of the kingdom. The first mention of this sport that I have met with occurs in the Proclamations at the head of the parliamentary proceedings, early in the reign of Edward III., where it is spoken of as a childish amusement, and prohibited to be played in the avenues of the palace at Westminster,[1] during the sessions of Parliament, because of the interruption it occasioned to the members and others in passing to and fro as their business required. It is also spoken of by Shakespear as a game practised by the boys:

> He with two striplings, lads more like to run
> The country base, than to commit such slaughter,
> Made good the passage.[2]

It was, however, most assuredly played by the men, and especially in Cheshire and other adjoining counties, where formerly it seems to have been in high repute.

The performance of this pastime requires two parties of equal number, each of them having a base or home, as it is usually called, to themselves, at the distance of about twenty or thirty yards. The players then on either side taking hold of hands, extend themselves in length, and opposite to each other, as far as they conveniently can, always remembering that one of them must touch the base; when any one of them quits the hand of his fellow and runs into the field, which is called giving the chase, he is immediately followed by one of his opponents; he again is followed by a second from the former side, and he by a second opponent; and so on alternately, until as many are out as choose to run, every one pursuing the man he first followed, and no other; and if he overtake him near enough to touch him, his party claims one toward their game, and both return home. They then run forth again and again in like manner, until the number is completed that decides the victory; this number is optional, and I am told rarely exceeds twenty. It is to be observed, that every person on either side who touches another during the chase, claims one for his party, and when many are out, it frequently happens that many are touched.

About 1770, I saw a grand match at base played in the fields behind Montague House, now the British Museum, by twelve gentlemen of Cheshire against twelve of Derbyshire, for a considerable sum of money, which afforded much entertainment to the spectators. In Essex they play this game with the addition of two prisons, which are stakes driven into the ground, parallel with the home boundaries, and about thirty yards from them; and every person who is touched on either side in the chase, is sent to one or other of these prisons, where he must remain till the conclusion of the game, if not delivered previously by one of his associates, and this can only be accomplished by touching him, which is a difficult task, requiring the performance of the most skilful players, because the prison belonging to either party is always much nearer to the base of their opponents than to their own; and if the person sent to relieve his confederate be touched by an antagonist before he reaches him, he also becomes

---

[1] " Nul enfaunt ne autres ne jue—à barres." Rot. Parl. MS. Harl. 7057.   [2] Cymbeline.

a prisoner, and stands in equal need of deliverance. The addition of the prisons occasions a considerable degree of variety in the pastime, and is frequently productive of much pleasantry.

WRESTLING.—The art of wrestling, which in the present day is chiefly confined to the lower classes of the people, was, however, highly esteemed by the ancients, and made a very considerable figure among the Olympic games. In the ages of chivalry, to wrestle well was accounted one of the accomplishments which a hero ought to possess.

Wrestling is a kind of exercise that, from its nature, is likely to have been practised by every nation, and especially by those the least civilised. It was probably well known in this country long before the introduction of foreign manners. The inhabitants of Cornwall and Devon have, we are well assured, from time immemorial, been celebrated for their expertness in this pastime, and are universally said to be the best wrestlers in the kingdom. To give a Cornish hug is a proverbial expression. The Cornish, says Fuller, are masters of the art of wrestling, so that if the Olympian games were now in fashion, they would come away with the victory. Their hug is a cunning close with their fellow-combatants, the fruits whereof is his fair fall or foil at the least.[1] They learned the art at an early period of life, for you shall hardly find, says Carew, an assembly of boys in Devon and Cornwall, where the most untowardly among them will not as readily give you a muster (or trial) of this exercise as you are prone to require it.[2]

*The entirely different systems of wrestling developed in different parts of the kingdom is a slight but genuine proof of the great variety of nationalities and tribes that were involved in the making of England. Owing to difficulties of locomotion, these different methods held their own in their respective districts until comparatively modern days. The styles of Cornwall and Devon are usually reckoned together, though they differed in at least one important particular, namely, that the latter sanctioned kicking and tripping, whilst the former confined themselves almost entirely to hugging. The style of Cumberland and Westmoreland was the next most famous. Thirdly, there was the more general practice of "loose" wrestling, in which Norfolk and Bedfordshire were for a long time pre-eminent ; this style differed much in different localities.[3]

The citizens of London, in times past, were expert in the art of wrestling, and annually upon St James's day they were accustomed to make a public trial of their skill. In the sixth year of Henry III. they held their anniversary meeting for this purpose near the hospital of St Matilda, at St Giles's-in-the-Fields, where they were met by the inhabitants of the city and suburbs of Westminster, and a ram was appointed for the prize ; the Londoners were victorious, having greatly excelled their antagonists, which produced a challenge from the conquered party, to renew the contest upon the Lammas day following at West-

---

[1] Worthies of England in Cornwall, p. 197. [2] Survey of Cornwall, 1602, p. 75.
[3] Armstrong's Wrestling (Badminton Library), passim.

minster : the citizens of London readily consented, and met them accordingly, but in the midst of the diversion, the bailiff of Westminster and his associates took occasion to quarrel with the Londoners, a battle ensued, and many of the latter were severely wounded in making their retreat to the city. This unjustifiable petulance of the bailiff gave rise to a more serious tumult, and it was several days before the peace could be restored.[1] Stow informs us, that in the thirty-first year of Henry VI. A.D. 1453, at a wrestling match near Clerkenwell, another tumult was excited against the lord mayor, but he does not say upon what occasion it arose.

In the old time, says Stow, wrestling was more used than it has been of later years.[2] In the month of August, about the feast of St Bartholomew, adds this very accurate historian, there were divers days spent in wrestling ; the lord mayor, aldermen, and sheriffs, being present in a large tent pitched for that purpose near Clerkenwell ;[3] upon this occasion the officers of the city, namely, the sheriffs, serjeants, and yeomen, the porters of the king's beam or weighing-house, and others of the city, gave a general challenge to such of the inhabitants of the suburbs as thought themselves expert in this exercise ; but of late years, continues he, the wrestling is only practised on the afternoon of St Bartholomew's day.[4] The latter ceremony is thus described by a foreign writer, who was an eye-witness to the performance : " When," says he, " the mayor goes out of the precincts of the city, a sceptre,[5] a sword, and a cap, are borne before him, and he is followed by the principal aldermen in scarlet gowns with golden chains ; himself and they on horseback. Upon their arrival at a place appointed for that purpose, where a tent is pitched for their reception, the mob begin to wrestle before them two at a time." He adds a circumstance not recorded by the historian : " After this is over, a parcel of live rabbits are turned loose among the crowd, which are pursued by a number of boys, who endeavour to catch them with all the noise they can make." [6]

PRIZES FOR WRESTLING.—The reward proposed for the best wrestlers in the contest between the Londoners and the inhabitants of Westminster, as mentioned above, was a ram. Anciently this animal was the prize most usually given upon such occasions, and therefore in the rhyme of sir Thopas, Chaucer says of the Knight,

> Of wrastling was there none his pere,
> Where any Ram shulde stonde.

And again, in his character of the miller,

> ————for over al ther he cam,
> At wrastlyng he wolde have away the Ram.

Other rewards, no doubt, were sometimes proposed, as we may see upon the eighth plate, where two men are wrestling for a cock : the original drawing, from a manuscript in the Royal Library,[7] is certainly more ancient than the time

---

[1] Matthew Paris. *Hist. Ang.* sub an. 1222.　　　　　　[2] *Survey of London*, pp. 78, 85.
[3] The margin says, " at Skinner's Well."　　　　　　　[4] *Survey of London*, p. 85.
[5] I presume he means the mace.　　[6] Hentzner's *Itinerary*, p. 36.　　[7] 2 B. viii.

of Chaucer. This is clearly an example of "loose" wrestling, when the hold was got with the open hand, grasping either the body or tunic of the opponent, or, as in this case, of a sort of scarf put on for the purpose.

In later times the prizes were not only much varied, but were occasionally of higher value. If we may believe the author of the old poem, entitled " A mery Geste of Robyn Hode," there were several prizes put up at once. The poet, speaking of a knight who was going to Robin Hood, says,[1]

> ———Unto Bernisdale,
> As he went, by a bridge was a wrastling,
> And there taryed was he,
> And there was all the best yemen,
> Of all the west countrey.
> A full fayre game there was set up ;
> A white bull, up ypyght ;
> A great courser with sadle and brydle,
> With gold burnished full bryght :
> A payre of gloves, a red gold ringe,
> A pipe of wine, good faye :
> What man bereth him best, ywis,
> The prize shall bear away.

A humorous description is given in one of the Spectators of a country wake : the author there mentions "a ring of wrestlers ; the squire," says he, " of the parish always treats the whole company, every year, with a hogshead of ale, and proposes a beaver hat, as a recompence to him who gives the most falls."[2]

WRESTLING, HOW PERFORMED.—The manner in which this pastime was exhibited in the western parts of England, at the distance of two centuries, is thus described by Carew, an author then living. " The beholders then cast, or form themselves into a ring, in the empty space whereof the two champions step forth, stripped into their dublets and hosen, and untrussed, that they may so the better command the use of their lymmes ; and first shaking hands, in token of friendship, they fall presently to the effect of anger ; for each striveth how to take hold of the other with his best advantage, and to bear his adverse party downe ; wherein, whosoever overthroweth his mate, in such sort, as that either his backe, or the one shoulder, and contrary heele do touch the ground, is accounted to give the fall. If he be only endangered, and makes a narrow escape, it is called a foyle."

He then adds, " This pastime also hath his laws, for instance ; of taking hold above the girdle—wearing a girdle to take hold by—playing three pulls for trial of the mastery, the fall giver to be exempted from playing again with the taker, but bound to answer his successor. Silver prizes, for this and other activities, were wont to be carried about, by certain circumferanci, or set up at bride ales ; but time, or their abuse," perhaps I might add both, " hath now worn them out of use."[3]

---

[1] Second fit, or part, Garrick's Collect. Old Plays, K. vol. x.   [2] Vol. ii. No. 191, published 1711.
[3] *Survey of Cornwall* (1602), p. 75.

*SIR THOMAS PARKYNS.—Towards the end of the seventeenth century wrestling was much declining in importance and respectability; but it received a considerable impetus from the strenuous support of a Nottinghamshire squire of education and position. Sir Thomas Parkyns, Bart., of Bunny Park, Nottingham, was the author of a curious work entitled, "The Inn-Play, or the Cornish - Hugg Wrestler. Digested in a Method which teacheth to break all Holds, and throw most Falls Mathematically. Easie to be understood by all Gentlemen, etc., and of great Use to such who understand the Small Sword in Fencing. And by all Tradesmen and Handicrafts that have competent knowledge of the Use of the Stilliards, Bor, Crove - Iron, or Lever, with their Hypomochlions, Fulcimen or Baits." A corrected second edition, from which this title is taken, was issued in 1714. Sir Thomas begins his "prefatory introduction" with an epigram from Martial, which gives him occasion to speak of his classical education under the famed Dr Busby, of Westminster School, where he learnt that wrestling was one of the five great Olympian sports. When he went to Trinity College, Cambridge, he noted, as a spectator of wrestling contests, the vast difference between "the Norfolk Out-Players and the Cornish Huggers," and that the latter could throw the other when they pleased. The use and application of mathematics he learnt when an undergraduate, from his tutor Dr Bathurst, but more especially from Sir Isaac Newton, who, seeing his inclination, invited him to his public lectures, "though I was Fellow Commoner, and seldom if ever any such were called to them." From Cambridge Sir Thomas proceeded to Gray's Inn, and there learnt fencing and vaulting, and also wrestling from Mr Cornish, who was his "Inn-Play Wrestling Master." He committed to writing the great variety of holds that he was taught. Out-Play wrestling is compared to French Fencing, and is the prettier to look at, but "Inn-Play soon decidethe who is the better gamester by an indisputable fall." "If wrestling," says Sir Thomas, "was more practic'd by Gentlemen, few or none would be killed by the sword in rencounters, but a severe fall or two, a black face or the like, would allay their fury and heat for that time, nay perhaps till quite forgotten." He backs up his preference for Cornish wrestling by the quaint suggestion that it commended itself to the other sex. "For the most part our country rings for wrestlings, at wakes and other festivals, consist of a small party of young women, who come not thither to choose a coward, but the daring, healthy and robust persons. . . . I ne'er could hear that the women approved of the Norfolk Out-Play, the rending and tearing of waistcoats, kicking and breaking of shins, and rendering them so tender they could not endure to be rub'd, but that their inclinations were the strongest for the Bedfordshire Inn-Play, and for such as approve themselves to be good on the Cornish Close Hugg."

*This enthusiastic champion of wrestling established annual matches in his own park, the prize being a hat of the value of twenty-two shillings. These

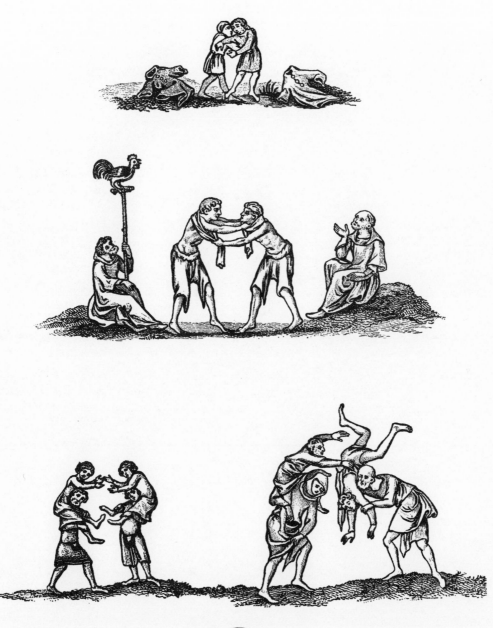

Wrestling.

were continued for more than half a century after his death ; they were finally abandoned about 1810. It is recorded of him that he never knew a day's illness until the time of his death, which occurred on March 29th, 1741. In addition to being a skilled athlete, Sir Thomas was of much repute as a man of probity and learning, and was on the commission of the peace for the counties of Nottingham and Leicester. He had his monument erected in the chancel of Bunny church in his lifetime, whereon his fame as a wrestler is set forth, and his effigy rudely carved, with arms extended, in the first position of Cornish-hug.[1]

*During the nineteenth century wrestling revived from time to time, but the rowdyism and roguery, so often associated with the matches, have for the most part kept this sport in deserved disrepute.

HIPPAS.—The Greeks had a pastime called Hippas, which, we are told, was one person riding upon the shoulders of another, as upon a horse ;[2] a sport of this kind was in practice with us at the commencement of the fourteenth century, but generally performed by two competitors who struggled one with the other, and he who pulled his opponent from the shoulders of his carrier was the victor.

The representations of this curious pastime on plate seven are taken from different manuscripts ; one in the Royal Library,[3] and the other in the Bodleian Library at Oxford, dated 1344.[4]

This seems to bear more analogy to wrestling than to any other sport, for which reason I have given it a place in the present chapter.

SWIMMING.—Swimming is an exercise of great antiquity ; and, no doubt, familiar to the inhabitants of this country at all times. The heroes of the middle ages are sometimes praised for their skill in swimming : it is said of Olaf Fryggeson, a king of Norway, that he had no equal in his art.[5] Peacham, describing the requisites for a complete gentleman, mentions swimming as one ; and particularly recommends it to such as were inclined to follow a military profession. In this he seems to have followed an old poetical writer,[6] who speaks in this manner :—

> To swymme, is eke to lerne in sommer leson.
> Men fynde not a bridge, so often as a flood,
> Swymmyng to voyde ; and chase an hoste wil eson.
> Eke after rayne the rivers goeth wood,[7]
> That every man in t'host can swymme, is good :
> Knyght, squyer, footman, cook, and cosynere.
> And grome, and page, in swymmyng is to lere.

Meaning thereby, that the art of swimming ought to be learned by every class

[1] Thorston's *Nottinghamshire*, i. 93 ; Chambers' *Book of Days*, i. 435-7. It is not a little remarkable that the Badminton account of wrestling omits all reference to Sir Thomas Parkyns, and to his book which passed through so many editions.

[2] Pollux, lib. ix. cap. 7.   [3] 2 B. vii.   [4] Bod. 264.
[5] Pontoppidan's *Hist. of Norway*, p. 148.   [6] MS. Cott. Titus, A. xxiii.
[7] Wood, or wode, signifies wild or mad ; and here, that the rain makes the rivers swell and overpass their bounds.

of persons belonging to an army : and, perhaps, it may not be improper to add, by every other person also.

Swimming and diving are mentioned by the author of the Visions of Pierce Ploughman [1] in the following manner :—

> Take two strong men and in Temese [2] cast them,
> And both naked as a needle, ther non sikerer [3] than other ;
> The one hath cunnynge and can swymme and dyve,
> The other is lewd of that laboure, lerned never to swym,
> Which trowest of these two in Temese is most in dred,
> He that never dived ne nought of swymmyng,
> Or the swymmer that is safe if he himself lyke ?

*The first printed book in the world published on swimming was issued in 1538 ; it is in Latin, and was written by N. Wynman, professor of languages at Ingoldstadt. The first treatise published in England was that by Everard Digby in 1587 ; it is in Latin, and styled *De Arte Natandi*. The numerous illustrations are most quaint. *The Compleat Swimmer*, by William Pearcey Gent, was issued in 1658 ; it is a sad bit of plagiarism, being a literal and unacknowledged translation of Digby's work. Monsieur Thévenot's *Art of Swimming with advice for Bathers* was issued in 1696, and translated into English in 1699 ; it has forty small copperplate cuts showing the different postures. None of these works say anything about the history of swimming in England.

Boys in the country usually learn to swim with bundles of bull-rushes, and with corks where the rushes cannot readily be procured ; particularly in the neighbourhood of London, where we are told, two centuries back, there were men who could teach the art of swimming well, and, says the author, " for commoditie of river and water for that purpose, there is no where better." [4]

I am sorry to add, that swimming is by no means so generally practised with us in the present day as it used to be in former times. We have several treatises on the art of swimming and diving, and in the Encyclopædia Britannica are many excellent directions relating to it, under the article Swimming. [5]

SLIDING.—Sliding upon the ice appears to have been a very favourite pastime among the youth of this country in former times ; at present the use of skates is so generally diffused throughout the kingdom, that sliding is but little practised, except by children, and such as cannot afford to purchase them.

Sliding is one of the diversions ascribed to young men of London by Fitzstephen, and, as far as one can judge from his description of the sport, it differed not in the performance from the method used by the boys of our own

---

[1] Edit. 1550, p. 13.   [2] The river Thames.

[3] Sikerer, surer, safer ; that is, neither the one nor the other should have any extraneous assistance, but each should depend entirely upon his own exertions to escape from the water.

[4] History of all the Schools and Colleges in and about London, printed A.D. 1615

[5] *It is almost unnecessary to state that the art and pastime of swimming underwent a remarkable revival during the nineteenth century. There can be but little doubt that the proportion of the English population who can swim is now (1903) far higher than it has ever been before. It is greatly encouraged in schools.

time: but he adds another kind of pastime upon the ice that is not now in practice; his words are to this effect, "Others make a seat of ice as large as a millstone, and having placed one of their companions upon it, they draw him along, when it sometimes happens that moving on slippery places they all fall down headlong." Instead of these seats of ice, among the moderns, sledges are used, which being extended from a centre, by the means of a strong rope, those who are seated in them are moved round with great velocity, and form an extensive circle. Sledges of this kind were set upon the Thames during the hard frost, in the year 1716, as the following couplet in a song written upon that occasion[1] plainly proves:

> While the rabble in sledges run giddily round,
> And nought but a circle of folly is found.

SKATING.—Skating is by no means a recent pastime, and probably the invention proceeded rather from necessity than the desire of amusement.

The wooden skates shod with iron or steel, which are bound about the feet and ancles like the talares of the Greeks and Romans, were most probably brought into England from the Low Countries, where they are said to have originated, and where it is well known they are almost universally used by persons of both sexes when the season permits. The word itself is a proof that this pastime came to us from Holland, for skate is not an old English word, but is borrowed from the Dutch *schaats*. In Hoole's translation of the Vocabulary by Comenius, called Orbis Sensualium Pictus (1658) the skates are called scrick-shoes from the German, and in the print at the head of the section, in that work, they are represented longer than those of the present day, and the irons are turned up much higher in the front.

*Some antiquaries are of opinion that there was skating in England even in prehistoric times, the earliest skates being those made from bones. In January 1874 "two British skates" of bone, found at Blackfriars, on the old bed of the Fleet river, were exhibited before the British Archæological Association. In the following month two bone skates, one polished and one in process of manufacture, found in the city of London, were exhibited before the same association. Mr Loftus Brock also exhibited in June of the same year "a fine bone skate about a foot long with a flat polished surface, of prehistoric date," which had been found in Bucklersbury, on the site of the ancient church of St Benet Sherchog.[2]

*In 1841 Mr Roach Smith exhibited to the Society of Antiquaries a bone skate which had been found in boggy ground in Moorfields, near Finsbury Circus. He considered that it was one of those described as used in the twelfth century on this very site.[3] Fitzstephen, the chronicler of London in the time of Henry

---

[1] In D'Urfey's Collection of Songs, 1719, vol. iii. p. 4.

[2] Journal of the Arch. Assoc., xxx. pp. 72, 91, 338. Ancient bone skates or runners are exhibited at the Guildhall Museum as well as at the British Museum. [3] *Archæologia*, xxix. 397.

II., says—"When that great moor which washed Moorfields, at the north wall of the city, is frozen over, great companies of young men go to sport upon the ice, and bind to their shoes bones, as the legs of some beasts; and hold stakes in their hands, headed with sharp iron, which sometimes they stick against the ice; and these men go on with speed, as doth a bird in the air, or darts shot from some warlike engine. Sometimes two men set themselves at a distance, and run one against another, as it were at tilt, with these stakes; wherewith one or both parties are thrown down, not without some hurt to their bodies; and after their fall, by reason of their violent motion, are carried a good distance one from another; and wheresoever the ice doth touch their heads, it rubs off the skin and lays it bare; and if one fall upon his leg or arm, it is usually broken; but young men, being greedy of honour and desirous of victory, do thus exercise themselves in counterfeit battles that they may bear the brunt more strongly when they come to it in good earnest."

*The two great diarists of the Restoration period, Evelyn and Pepys, both record skating feats that they witnessed on December 1st, 1662, when this revived exercise on metal skates had been reintroduced frem Holland.

*Evelyn says:—"Having seen the strange and wonderful dexterity of the sliders on the new canal in St James's Park, performed before their Maties by divers gentlemen, and others with Scheetes after the manner of the Hollanders, with what swiftnesse they passe, how suddainely they stop in full carriere upon the ice, I went home by water, but not without exceeding difficulties, the Thames being frozen, greate flakes of ice incompassing our boate." Pepys' entry is as follows:—"St James's Park, Dec. 1, 1662. Over the Park, where I first in my life, it being a great frost, did see people sliding with their skeates, which is a very pretty art."

*Little is recorded of the development of skating in England in the eighteenth century, but illustrations of fairs held on the frozen Thames in 1716 and in 1740 prove that it was popular at both those dates. The first English "Treatise on Skating, Founded on certain Principles deduced from many Years Experience" was printed in 1772. The author was Robert Jones, Lieutenant of Artillery; it was dedicated to Lord Spencer Hamilton as an expert on the ice. The writer expresses a strong preference for English rather than Dutch skates, but acknowledges that the latter are better for travelling. In England skating was only "an exercise and diversion," whereas in Holland it was a "business and necessity."

*Roller skates are not the novelty that they are usually supposed to be. Joseph Merlin, a native of Liège, who came to England with the Spanish ambassador in 1760, invented a pair of skates that ran on wheels. But his exhibition of them was not a success. Gliding about in them at a masquerade at Carlisle House, Soho Square, he ran into a valuable mirror worth £500, which he completely shattered in addition to wounding himself severely.[1] A

---

[1] *Notes and Queries*, Ser. V., vi. 36.

patent for wheel skates was taken out in 1819; and the old tennis court in Windmill Street was turned into a rink for roller skating in the year 1823.[1]

Some modern writers have asserted, that "the metropolis of Scotland has produced more instances of elegant skaters than perhaps any other country whatever, and the institution of a skating-club, about forty years ago, has contributed not a little to the improvement of this amusement.[2] I have, however, seen, some years back, when the Serpentine river in Hyde Park was frozen over, four gentlemen there dance, if I may be allowed the expression, a double minuet in skates, with as much ease, and I think more elegance, than in a ball room; others again, by turning and winding with much adroitness, have readily in succession described upon the ice the form of all the letters in the alphabet.

*During the nineteenth century the development of English skating has been most remarkable.[3]

ROWING.—I shall not pretend to investigate the antiquity of boat-rowing. This art was certainly well understood by the primitive inhabitants of Britain, who frequently committed themselves to the mercy of the sea in open boats, constructed with wicker work, and covered with leather.[4] The Saxons were also expert in the management of the oar, and thought it by no means derogatory for a nobleman of the highest rank to row or steer a boat with dexterity and judgment. Kolson, a northern hero, boasting of his qualifications, declares, that "he was expert in handling the oar."[5] The reader may possibly call to his recollection the popular story related by our historians concerning Edgar, surnamed the Peaceable, who they tell us was conveyed in great state along the river Dee, from his palace in the city of West Chester, to the church of St John, and back again: the oars were managed by eight kings, and himself, the ninth, sat at the stern of the barge and held the helm.[6] This frolic, for I cannot consider it in any other light, appears to be well attested, and is the earliest record of a pastime of the kind.

The boat-quintain and tilting at each other upon the water, which were introduced by the Normans as amusements for the summer season,[7] could not be performed without the assistance of the oars, and probably much of the success of the champion depended upon the skilfulness of those who managed the boat. If we refer to two engravings[8] whereon both these sports are represented, we shall see that the rowers are seated contrary to the usual method, and face the head of the vessel instead of the stern.

The institution of the water pageantry at London upon the lord mayor's day, was of an essential service to the professed watermen, who plied about the bridge; and gave occasion to the introduction of many pleasure boats, which in

---

[1] *Notes and Queries*, Ser. V., v. 309.
[2] Ency. Brit. art. Skating.   [3] Badminton Library: *Skating*, by Messrs Heathcote, Tebbutt, and Witham.
[4] Cæsar Bell, Gall. lib. v. cap. 12.   [5] Bartholin, p. 420.   [6] Will. Malms. Mat. West. in the reign of Edgar.
[7] Fitzstephen's *Description of London*. Stow's *Survey*.   [8] See book iii. chap. i. sec. v.

the modern times have been greatly increased. The first procession to Westminster by water was made A.D. 1453, by John Norman, then lord mayor, for which he was highly commended by the watermen.

When tilting at the quintain and justing one against another in boats upon the water were discontinued in this country, rowing matches were substituted, and are become exceedingly popular: we may see them frequently exhibited upon the Thames during the summer season; and as these contests, which depend upon skill as well as upon strength, are rarely productive of any thing further than mere pastime, they are in my opinion deservedly encouraged. When a rowing-match takes place near London, if the weather be fine, it is astonishing to see what crowds of people assemble themselves upon the banks of the Thames as spectators, and the river itself is nearly covered with wherries, pleasure boats, and barges, decorated with flags and streamers, and sometimes accompanied with bands of music. This pastime, though very ancient, and frequently practised upon solemn occasions by the Greeks and the Romans, does not seem to have attracted the notice of our countrymen in former times.

It may be thought unnecessary for me to mention the well-known annual legacy of Thomas Dogget, a comedian of some celebrity at the commencement of the eighteenth century, which provides three prizes to be claimed by three young watermen, on condition they prove victorious in rowing from the Old Swan Stairs near London Bridge, to the White Swan at Chelsea. The contest takes place upon the first of August; the number of competitors upon this occasion is restricted to six, who must not have been out of their times beyond twelve months. Every man rows singly in his boat, and his exertions are made against the tide; he who first obtains his landing at Chelsea receives the prize of honour, which is a waterman's coat, ornamented with a large badge of silver, and therefore the match is usually called "Rowing for the Coat and Badge." The second and the third candidates have small pecuniary rewards, but the other three get nothing for their trouble.

Of late years (1800) the proprietor of Vauxhall Gardens, and Astley the rider, give each of them in the course of the summer a new wherry, to be rowed for by a certain number of watermen, two of which are allowed to row in one boat; and these contests are extended to two or three heats or trials before the successful candidates are determined.

SAILING.—Another popular amusement upon the water is sailing, and many persons have pleasure boats for this purpose; I do not mean the open boats which are usually let out for hire by the boat-builders for the purpose of sailing, but vessels of much greater magnitude, that are covered with a deck, and able with skilful management to weather a rough storm; many large bets are frequently dependent upon the swiftness of these boats, and the contest is sometimes determined at sea.

A society, generally known by the appellation of the Cumberland Society, consisting of gentlemen partial to this pastime, give yearly a silver cup to be sailed for in the vicinity of London. The boats usually start from the bridge at Blackfriars, go up the Thames to Putney, and return to Vauxhall, where a vessel is moored at a distance from the stairs, and the sailing boat that first passes this mark upon her return obtains the victory.[1]

[1] It would require two volumes to record the progress in rowing and sailing, as amusements, since the days of Strutt, or to expand their earlier history, so that it is thought better to leave his remarks exactly as they stood when first issued.

CHAPTER III

Hand-ball an ancient Game—Used by the Saxons—And by the Schoolboys of London—Ball Play in France—Hand Tennis or Fives—Fives in Church and Churchyard—Tennis—Tennis Courts erected—Tennis fashionable in England—Killed by a Tennis Ball—London Tennis Courts in 1615—Origin of Tennis Courts—Tennis in Monasteries—Rackets—Lawn Tennis—Balloon-ball—Hurling—Hockey—Camp-ball—Football—Golf—Cricket —Cricket on Horseback—Trap-ball and Knur and Spell.

HAND-BALL.—The ball has given origin to many popular pastimes, and I have appropriated this chapter to such of them as are or have been usually practised in the fields and other open places. The most ancient amusement of this kind, is distinguished with us by the name of hand-ball, and is, if Homer may be accredited, coeval at least with the destruction of Troy. Herodotus attributes the invention of the ball to the Lydians; succeeding writers have affirmed, that a female of distinction named Anagalla, a native of Corcyra, was the first who made a ball for the purpose of pastime, which she presented to Nausica, the daughter of Alcinous, king of Phœacia, and at the same time taught her how to use it; this piece of history is partly derived from Homer, who introduces the princess of Corcyra with her maidens, amusing themselves at hand-ball:

> O'er the green mead the sporting virgins play,
> Their shining veils unbound, along the skies,
> Tost and retost, the ball incessant flies.

Homer has restricted this pastime to the young maidens of Corcyra, at least he has not mentioned its being practised by the men; in times posterior to the poet, the game of hand-ball was indiscriminately played by both sexes.

ANGLO-SAXON BALL PLAY.—It is altogether uncertain at what period the ball was brought into England: the author of a manuscript in Trinity College, Oxford, written in the fourteenth century, and containing the life of Saint Cuthbert,[1] says of him, that when he was young, "he pleyde atte balle with the children that his fellowes were." On what authority this information is established I cannot tell. The venerable Bede, who also wrote the life of that saint, makes no mention of ball play, but tells us he excelled in jumping, running, wrestling, and such exercises as required great muscular exertion, and among them, indeed, it is highly probable that of the ball might be included.

LONDON BALL PLAY.—Fitzstephen, who wrote in the thirteenth century, speaking of the London school-boys, says, "Annually upon Shrove Tuesday, they go into the fields immediately after dinner, and play at the celebrated

---

[1] No. lvii.

80

Games with the Ball.

game of ball;[1] every party of boys carrying their own ball"; for it does not appear that those belonging to one school contended with those of another, but that the youth of each school diverted themselves apart. Some difficulty has been stated by those who have translated this passage, respecting the nature of the game at ball here mentioned. Stow, considering it as a kind of goff or bandy-ball, has, without the least sanction from the Latin, added the word bastion,[2] meaning a bat or cudgel; others again have taken it for foot-ball,[3] which pastime, though probably known at the time, does not seem to be a very proper one for children: and indeed, as there is not any just authority to support an argument on either side, I see no reason why it should not be rendered hand-ball.[4]

BALL PLAY IN FRANCE.—The game of hand-ball is called by the French palm play,[5] because, says St Foix, a modern author, originally "this exercise consisted in receiving the ball and driving it back again with the palm of the hand. In former times they played with the naked hand, then with a glove, which in some instances was lined; afterwards they bound cords and tendons round their hands to make the ball rebound more forcibly, and hence the racket derived its origin."[6] During the reign of Charles V. palm play, which may properly enough be denominated hand-tennis, was exceedingly fashionable in France, being played by the nobility for large sums of money; and when they had lost all that they had about them, they would sometimes pledge a part of their wearing apparel rather than give up the pursuit of the game. The duke of Burgundy, according to an old historian,[7] having lost sixty franks at palm play with the duke of Bourbon, Messire William de Lyon, and Messire Guy de la Trimouille, and not having money enough to pay them, gave his girdle as a pledge for the remainder; and shortly afterwards he left the same girdle with the comte D'Eu for eighty franks, which he also lost at tennis.

*HAND-TENNIS OR FIVES.—At the top of plate eight is the reproduction of a supposed game at ball-play between a man and woman from an illuminated Hours of the fourteenth century; but on referring to the original[8] it is doubtful whether this is any game at all; the figures are on opposite pages, and the ball appears to be an accidental blemish on the vellum! Another picture, however, on the same plate, is of much interest. It is at the foot of a fourteenth-century copy of the romance called *Histoire de Lancelot, ou S. Graal.*[9] To the left is a player about to strike the ball with his right hand, whilst behind him stands another player apparently suggesting how he should make his stroke. To the right, on the opposite page, separated by an upright ornament—of which the

---

[1] "Lusum pilæ celebrem." Stephanides de ludis.

[2] "The scholars of each school have their ball or bastion in their hands." *Survey of London.*

[3] Lord Lyttelton, *History of Henry the Second,* vol. iii. p. 275; and [Dr Pegge] the translator of Fitzstephen in 1772.

[4] By the word *celebrem* Fitzstephen might advert to the antiquity of the pastime.

[5] *Jeu de paume,* and in Latin *pila palmaria.*   [6] *Essais Historiques sur Paris,* vol. i. p. 160.

[7] Laboureur, sub an. 1368.   [8] Roy. Lib. 20 D. iv. f. 207.   [9] Harl. MSS. 6563, f. 95.

F

designer apparently took advantage to indicate an intervening line—stand two more players, with open hands or palms uplifted ready to receive and return the ball.

*In a fifteenth-century beautifully illuminated copy of Valerius Maximus there is a picture of a game of hand-tennis or fives; each of the two players wears a white glove on the right hand.[1] This is reproduced in the centre of plate nine.

*Hand-tennis still continues to be played, though under a different name, and probably a different modification of the game; it is now called fives, which denomination perhaps it might receive from having five competitors on each side, as the succeeding passage seems to indicate. In 1591, when queen Elizabeth was entertained at Elvetham in Hampshire, by the earl of Hertford, "after dinner, about three o'clock, ten of his lordship's servants, all Somersetshire men, in a square greene court before her majesties windowe, did hang up lines, squaring out the forme of a tennis-court, and making a cross line in the middle; in this square they (being stript out of their dublets) played five to five with hand-ball at bord and cord as they tearme it, to the great liking of her highness."[2]

*Edicts against ball-playing in St Paul's of the time of Elizabeth are often cited, but the desecration of the great church by such games is of far older date. In 1385 Robert Braybrooke, bishop of London, denounced the custom both within and without his cathedral church:—*Necnon ad pilam infra et extra ecclesiam ludunt.*[3]

*The custom of playing fives in churchyards continued in many a country district until quite recent years, notably in Somersetshire and Staffordshire. Ball-playing in such a place no doubt prevailed because the church tower often afforded so suitable a wall for fives. It was usually practised on the north side, because there were generally no graves on that side, and the sport created less scandal. A painted line for the game still remains on some of our church towers, but a string-course of suitable elevation more usually sufficed. Fives used to be played at Eton between the buttresses on the north wall of the college chapel, and the "pepper box" peculiar to Eton fives courts had its origin in a natural angle in one of these buttresses. Notices against ball play on church walls may be seen in various parts of Italy. In the Basque district, on both sides of the Pyrenees, church walls are still openly used for the *jeu de paume.*

*TENNIS.—Tennis, though essentially a French game in its origin, soon became domesticated in England. Here as on the Continent it was originally played in unenclosed spaces, but its great popularity caused it to be adopted as a good means of recreation and exercise in towns. Hence came about the use of spaces surrounded by walls, and the introduction of rackets made boundaries desirable. Eventually this led to special buildings for the purpose and roofed-in tennis courts.

---

[1] Harl. MSS. 4375, f. 151. Two men are playing chess in a cloister at the back of the court.
[2] Nichols' *Progresses of Q. Eliz.* vol. ii. p. 19.   [3] Wilkins' *Concilia*, iii. 194.

Glove Fives.

Golf.

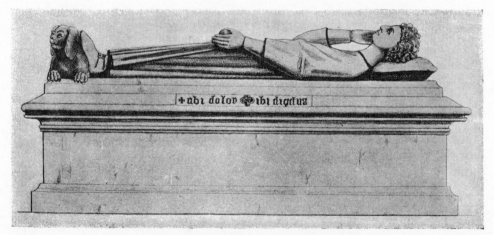

Stanley Effigy at Elford.

*As to the origin of the name, though the best authorities consider the term to be of French extraction, there is still much dispute. The suggestion, originally made in 1617, that the word comes from *tenez*, a term used by the player as a warning to receive the ball, *tenez le jeu*, is still accepted by some. Others consider that the passage just quoted as to the game played before queen Elizabeth, when the players were five to five in hand-ball, is the origin not only of the name Fives, but that the aggregate number of ten may well have given its name to Tenes, Tennes, Teneis, Tenice, Tennice, Tenys, Tynes, Tenyse, Tenice, Tennies, or Tennis, for the game is found spelt in all these varieties.[1]

*In 1365 the earliest restrictive Act prohibiting various sports in favour of archery was passed; the first game named is that of hand-ball. This was renewed in 1388, when it took the form of sumptuary or class legislation, laying down that servants and labourers were to find their only pastime in bows and arrows, and prohibiting their playing tennis, foot-ball, etc. In 1410 this latter statute was re-enacted and confirmed, delinquents on conviction being liable to imprisonment for six days.

*The antiquity of the racket in this country is shown by a passage in Chaucer's *Troylus and Cryseyde* (*circa* 1380), where Troylus says:

> But canstow playen racket, to and fro,
> Nettle in, dokke out, now this, now that, Pandare?

This evidently alludes to the hitting of a ball with a racket backwards and forwards, and to the curing of a nettle-sting by a dock leaf, in protest to the kind of inconstancy suggested to Troylus by Pandarus. Much the same words are also used in the first book of Chaucer's *Testament of Love*.

*Probably the first English mention of the word tennis occurs in Gower's ballad to Henry IV. (*circa* 1400):—

> Of the tennis to winne or lese a chace
> May no life wete or that the bal be ronne,
> Al stant in God what thing men shal purchase,
> Th' ende is in hym or that it be begonne.

*In the beginning of the reign of Henry V. occurred a remarkable incident in connection with the royal game of tennis, immortalised by Shakespeare. Holinshed, who was the dramatist's favourite chronicler, relates that:

"Whilest in the Lente season the Kyng laye at Kenilworth, there came to him from Charles, Dolphin of Fraunce, the Frenche King's eldest sonne, certayne Ambassadours, that broughte with them a barrell of Paris balles, which they presented to hym for a token from their maister, whiche presente was taken in verie ill parte, as sent in scorne, to signifie that it was more mete for the King to passe the tyme with suche childish exercise, than to attempte anye worthy exployte: wherefore the Kyng wrote to hym, that ere ought long, hee woulde sende to hym some London balles, that should breake and batter downe the roofes of his houses about hys eares."

---

[1] Marshall's *Annals of Tennis*, 53. In the 6th Series of *Notes and Queries* there are long and frequent references to the etymology of Tennis, in which Professor Skeat and other learned men took part.

*Caxton, in the continuation of Higden's *Polycronicon* (1482), calls these *pilas Parisianes* "tenyse balles," as the name by which Englishmen would most readily recognise them. Hall, in his *Chronicle* (1545) describes them as "a tunne of tennis balles."

*The passage in Shakespeare's *Henry V.* (Act i. sc. 2) is that in which the French ambassador brings the young king "a tun of treasure" from the Dauphin, and Henry asks:

> What treasure, uncle?
>   *Exeter.*   Tennis balls, my liege.
>   *K. Henry.* We are glad the Dauphin is so pleasant with us ;
> His present and your pains we thank you for :
> When we have match'd our rackets to these balls,
> We will, in France, by God's grace, play a set
> Shall strike his father's crown into the hazard.
> Tell him he hath made a match with such a wrangler
> That all the courts of France will be disturb'd
> With chases.

*In Drayton's poem *The Battaile of Agincourt*, the king's answer is thus given :—

> . . . I'll send him Balls and Rackets if I live,
> That thy such Racket shall in Paris see,
> When over lyne with Bandies I shall drive,
> As that before the Set be fully done,
> France may (perhaps) into the Hazard runne.

This passage is cited by Mr Marshall as offering one of the first examples of the double sense of racket meaning *hubbub*, as well as a tennis bat, and also as showing the early use of the word bandy in the game.

*About the same period a rude sort of tennis, in spite of statutory prohibition, was practised out of doors by the working classes. In 1447, the bishop, and dean and chapter of Exeter complained to the mayor that ungodly young people of the commonalty were in the habit, during divine service, of playing at unlawful games in the cloister, such "as the toppe, penny prykke, and most atte tenys," by which the walls were defiled and the glass windows broke.[1] In some towns, such as Lydd, Kent, the laws against games were sought to be enforced. In 1456-8, 1462-3, and 1477-8, proclamations were made in that town forbidding tennis and dice-playing, and exhorting the youth to turn to bow and arrows and other manlier recreations.[2]

*Towards the end of the reign of Henry VI. begin a number of curious entries in the accounts of the Ironmongers' Company relative to tennis balls. The earliest of these is of the year 1459 :—

"ix daie of March Anno xxxvij (Hen. VI.)—And at the tyme of the accompt ther was delyvèd to the seid wardeyns for ballis lixs. ijd."

An entry *temp.* Edward IV. records the receipt of £4 for "teneis balles" from Robert Tooke. The trade was vigorous, for in another year of the same

---

[1] *Shillingford's Letters* (Camd. Soc. 1871), p. 101.
[2] Hist. MSS. Reports, v. pp. 516, 521, 523, 526.

reign the wardens sold 47 gross of tennis balls to Thomas Tooke at 20d. the gross. The entries as to the sale of these balls continue up to 1535. Their sale by this company led to the singular supposition that the balls were made of iron;[1] but Mr Marshall has shown that there are strong probabilities that the Ironmongers' Company owned a tennis court in Fenchurch Street, for which they made balls so well that they were in demand with players in other courts.

*KILLED BY A TENNIS BALL.—The foolish suggestion that tennis balls used to be made of iron has been used by some to account for the death of the youthful son of John Stanley in the fifteenth century. But an ordinary tennis ball striking a child, when in full play, on the temple might readily have a fatal result. In the beautiful village church of Elford, five miles from Lichfield, is a small monumental effigy, indicating by its attitude, after a pathetic fashion, the cause of death. The boy, who has curly hair and is clad in a long tunic reaching to his ankles, holds in his left hand a ball, whilst the right hand is raised to the head, the fingers evidently pointing to the seat of injury behind the right ear. On the monument is inscribed—*Ubi dolor, ibi digitus.* The date of this memorial is about the year 1460. It is said to represent the grandson and heir of Sir John Stanley, first cousin of Thomas, first Lord Stanley, who died in 1474, and whose fine alabaster effigy is close to that of the lad slain by a tennis ball.[2] This effigy is shown on plate nine.

*TENNIS FASHIONABLE IN ENGLAND.—The journals of the Proceedings of the Court of Common Council of the City of London show that the injunctions against games (headed by tennis) played by labourers, servants, or apprentices, were enforced by severe penalties during the reign of Edward IV., at the very time when nobles, gentlefolk, and the wealthier burgesses were free to use the tennis courts, and when one of the most prominent of the city companies was largely adding to its revenue by the manufacture and sale of tennis balls!

*The game was also forbidden to the common folk by legislation of Henry VII. and Henry VIII., though both those monarchs were fond of tennis, and lost both balls and money at the pastime, as their accounts show. They played in courts at Woodstock, Wycombe, Sheen, Greenwich, Richmond, Blackfriars, and Whitehall or Westminster. There was also a court at Windsor in the time of Henry VII. It was standing in 1607, though roofless, and is shown in John Norden's MS. account of Windsor Castle, as lying within the walls, on the eastern side, just below the keep.[3] A later drawing of Hollar, among the Ashmolean MSS., shows that the Windsor tennis court was still standing in 1672.

*It was in this court, probably at that time roofed, as it is called a room, that on January 31st, 1516, the king of Castile played tennis with the marquis of Dorset, Henry VII. looking on. This match is noteworthy as showing that

---

[1] *Notes and Queries*, Series IV. ii. 178; v. 263, 436.

[2] The reproduction of this effigy is taken from plate viii. of Edward Richardson's *Monumental Effigies of Elford Church* (1852).   [3] Harl. MSS. 3749.

the hand was still in use by English players. The king of Castile used a racket, and as the marquis played with the bare hand, he gave him fifteen.[1]

Mr Marshall gives numerous interesting references and extracts relative to Henry VIII.'s devotion to the royal game.[2]

*Pages might readily be filled as to the popularity and general use of tennis by the noblemen and gentlefolk of the reign of Elizabeth. It must suffice to give one anecdote that yields a vivid picture of court manners even in the presence of the virgin queen. In a letter from Thomas Randolphe to Sir Nicholas Throckmorton, dated March 31st, 1565, at Edinburgh, occurs the following passage :—"I have it from this nobleman's mouthe that latlye the Duke [of Norfolk] and my L. of L[eicester] were playinge at tennes, the Q. beholdinge of them, and my L. Rob. being verie hotte and swetinge, tooke the Q. napken owte of her hande and wyped his face, wch the Duke seinge saide that he was to sawcie and swhore y^t he wolde laye his racket upon his face. Hereupon rose a great troble and the Q. offendid sore wth the Duke. Thys tale is tolde by the Earle Atholl the same daye that Fowler came to thys towne w^t hys M^ties license."[3]

*The privilege of keeping tennis courts in Elizabeth's reign was eagerly sought, and in 1597 one Thomas Bedingfield applied for an exclusive license to keep houses in London and Westminster for tennis, bowling, cards, dice, and backgammon. The application, which was apparently granted, represented that the number of such houses was very great, but that they were often kept by disorderly persons, so that the honest sort would not resort thither ; and further that it would not only be well to restrict the number, but to prohibit any play on the forenoon of any Sabbath day and during evening and morning prayers on holy days, to forbid all swearing and blasphemy, and to suffer none to play save noblemen, gentlemen, and merchants, or such as shall be entered in the Book of Subsidies at £10 in land or goods."[4]

*The demanding a money qualification from the tennis player is to some extent paralleled by the dress test of the keeper of the court alluded to by Prince Henry in his speech to Poins :—

"What a disgrace is it to me to remember thy name! or to know thy name to-morrow! or to take note how many pair of silk stockings thou hast, viz. these, and those that were the peach-colour'd ones! or to bear the inventory of thy shirts, as, one for superfluity, and one other for use! But that the tennis-court keeper knows better than I ; for it is a low ebb of linen with thee when thou keepest not racket there."[5]

*The tennis ball of this period was stuffed with hair, to which the dramatists of Elizabethan and Stuart days make many satirical allusions. Thus in *The Gentle Craft*, of 1600, occurs the phrase—"He'll shave it off, and stuffe tenice balls with it."

---

[1] Cott. MSS. Vesp. C. xii. fol. 281.   [2] *Annals of Tennis*, 63-68.   [3] State Papers, Scotland, x. No. 31d.
[4] Dom. State Papers, Eliz. ccxliii. 58.   [5] *Henry IV*. Part ii. Act ii. sc. 2.

*James I. commended tennis, with certain other games, to be used in moderation, and not as a craft, to his son Henry.[1] The young prince became a great adept at tennis by assiduous practice in the Whitehall court, and there are records of various quarrels in which he took part when engaged in this game.

*Gervase Markham, in 1615, describes tennis as "a pastime in close or open courts, striking little round balls to or fro, either with the palm of the hand or with racket."[2]

*Charles I., when duke of York, began to play tennis; the sum of £20 was paid to John Webb, "Master of His Majesty's Tennis plays," for his attendance in teaching the young duke to play tennis, and providing him with balls and rackets for the year ending Michaelmas, 1610.[3]

*A list of the London tennis courts, in 1615, in a book kept by the clerk of the works at Petworth, and cited by Mr Marshall, shows that there were then fourteen courts in the metropolis, whose dimensions are given, in addition to one at St James'. Whitehall had two, one covered and one uncovered; the rest were all roofed. The largest was at Essex House, which was 84 ft. long by 22 ft. broad, and 21 ft. high; the smallest was "Powles chaine tennis courte," which was 55 ft. long by 16 ft. broad, and 17 ft. high.

*The game was fashionable both at Oxford and Cambridge in the seventeenth century.

*In a rare book, published in 1641, entitled *The True Effigies of our Most Illustrious Sovereigne Lord King Charles, Queene Mary, with the rest of the Royal Progenie*, a most interesting portrait of the Duke of York (James II.) is given on p. 7. The young prince is represented holding a short-handled racket in his right hand, in a tennis court with a gallery full of spectators; it is evidently intended for the uncovered court of Whitehall. A reproduction of this portrait is given on plate nine.

*In July 1649 a warrant was issued by the Council of State to John Hooke, keeper of the St. James' tennis court, to deliver up the key to Colonel Pride to enable him therein to quarter his soldiers.[4]

*Charles Hoole, in 1659, translated, from the High Dutch and Latin, J. A. Komensky's *Orbis Sensualium Pictus*. Plate cxxxiii. gives a rude representation of a smaller tennis court, termed "Ludus Pilæ or Tennis Play." The remarks of the brief letterpress refer to the like numbers on the plate. Numbers 4 and 5 refer to the game of wind-ball played outside. "In a Tennis-Court 1 they play with a ball 2 which one throweth and another taketh and sendith it back with a Racket 3; and that is the sport of Noblemen to stir their body."

*After the Restoration, Charles II. frequently used the court at Hampton Court, and had a new one built at Whitehall. Pepys states that the new court was built so badly that it fell down in June 1663. The great diarist has several

---

[1] *His Majesties Instructions to his dearest Sonne, Henry the Prince* (1603), p. 120.
[2] *Country Contentments*, bk. i. p. 109.   [3] Devon's *Issues of the Exchequer*, p. 116.
[4] *Cal. of State Papers*, 1649-50, p. 542.

other allusions to play in this court when re-erected. In December 1663 he watched the king and Sir Arthur Slingsby play against Lord Suffolk and Lord Chesterfield, and admired the royal play; but in the following month, when watching the royal game, he remarks: "To see how the King's play was extolled, without any cause at all, was a loathsome sight, though sometimes indeed he did play very well, and deserved to be commended; but such open flattery is beastly."

*A curious book of fiction appeared in 1701, written by Gatien de Courtilz de Sandras, styled *Mémoires de M. le Marquis de Montbrun*, most of the scene of which is laid in England. This French adventurer is described as visiting England to replenish his purse, when he took with him one of the best tennis-markers of Paris disguised as his valet. By concealing at first his own skill and introducing the marker as his partner, and no more skilled than himself, Montbrun succeeded in winning a vast sum from his chief antagonist, the "Comte de Nortampton." The novel has a good many illustrations, and plate 20 represents the marquis and his valet playing a deliberately clumsy game in a London tennis court, to delude Nortampton, who is concealed behind a thick wire-netting on the left and disguised in female attire, though recognised by the accomplices. Mr Marshall, in reproducing this plate, says that "the court is evidently one of the kind called Quarré and uncovered. The mode of erecting nets above the walls on every side to prevent balls from flying over is clearly shown. The *cord* (as usual then) has no net attached to it, but only a sort of fringe. The marker stands at a door, nearly in the middle of the length of the court; but including that door, there are only three gallery-divisions on that side of the line, while there are four on the other side. Running along the end-wall, on the service side, is a very peculiarly built thickening of the wall, seeming to be a sort of horizontal, but flat-topped tambour, and containing a *petit trou* in the fore-hand corner." [1]

*ORIGIN OF TENNIS COURTS.—It has been more than once suggested that the origin of the tennis court is to be found in the cloister court or garth. The cloister roofs were supposed to be the first *pent-houses;* a buttress the origin of the *tambour;* and the *grille* a development of the opening through which strangers spoke to the inmates. We do not at all believe this; those who advance the theory apparently forget that domestic houses and other buildings, besides those of monastic foundations, of the period when tennis courts were developing, were usually built round an open quadrangular space which had usually cloisters or alleys to give access to the various rooms. It is quite possible, nay probable, to suppose that some of the eccentricities of the tennis-court arrangement arose from their being copied from some secular courtyard where the game had previously been played—in the same way as an Eton fives-court imitates a chapel buttress. Although it is not in the least likely that its construction was imitated from a conventual cloister, some of those who object to the theory go quite astray in their strenuous objections. Mr

---

[1] *Annals of Tennis*, 93, 94.

THE HIGH BORNE PRINCE IAMES DVKE OF YORKE.
borne October = the 13. 1633.

M. Merian. J.

Marshall, when gainsaying it, writes:—"No one possessed of the smallest knowledge of monastic institutions will for a moment believe the statement. That a game should be played, openly, within the walls or cloisters of an abbey or monastery, would be entirely opposed to every rule of such a fraternity. . . . It would show a ludicrous ignorance of monastic institutions to place the smallest confidence in this alleged origin of the game."[1]

*TENNIS IN MONASTERIES.—Now it so happens that clear proof can be given of the not infrequent playing of this very game in the cloister court of the religious houses of at all events one order. In the original twelfth-century statutes of the Premonstratensian or White Canons, who had so many important houses in England, it was laid down that twice a week the brethren might find recreation in some honest exercise.[2] The time for this varied, but was usually after Nones (three o'clock service) and ceased with the first bell for Vespers. In course of time this somewhat vaguely worded order got so abused in the houses that were laxly conducted, that the General Chapter of 1559 interfered. It was stated that it had come to their knowledge that the very cloisters and their roofs were used for hand tennis (*ludo palmario*), and all exercises in such sacred places (for one wall of the cloister court was always formed by the nave wall of the conventual church) or in the cemeteries were strictly prohibited. The important General Chapter of 1639, in their revision and interpretation of the statutes, laid down, in comment on the recreation rule, the wise principle that man, however religiously he lived, was still man, and that therefore it was not prudent to deny him honest and moderate relaxation, which might prove of service to his soul as well as his body. They adopted, however, this precautionary measure, namely, that in houses where ball-play (*lusus pili*) was allowed, it was only to be permitted in some secluded place to which no secular person could gain access.[3]

*In the edition of *Britannia Illustrata*, published in 1720, a bird's-eye view of Hampton Court shows the tennis court as restored by William III.

*The Hanoverian dynasty were not specially addicted to tennis, but Frederick, prince of Wales, who died in March 1751, is said, by Horace Walpole, to have been a victim to the game. "An imposthume had broken, which, on his body being opened, the physicians were of opinion had not been occasioned by the fall, but from the blow of a tennis ball three years before."[4] During the latter half of the eighteenth century the game lost much of its popular character and became still more the amusement of the wealthy. The *Sporting Magazine* of September 1793 shows, however, that the outdoor form of this sport was in full vigour:—"Field tennis threatens ere long to bowl out cricket. The former game is now patronised by Sir Peter Burrel; the latter has for some time back been given up by Sir Horace Mann."

*Throughout the nineteenth century, especially towards its close, there

[1] *Tennis, Rackets, Fives* (All England Series, 1890), p. 9.
[2] Norbert's Statutes, Dist. i. cap. viii.
[3] Holstein's *Codex Regularum* (1759), v. 206, 207.
[4] *Memoirs of George II.* vii. 61, 62.

was a marked revival of tennis in England, though it is almost extinct on the Continent. Mr Marshall's account of tennis, in the All England Series, published in 1890, enumerates thirty-one courts in England, nineteen of which were attached to private houses. Mr Heathcote in the Badminton Library volume, the fourth edition of which was published in 1897, increases the list to thirty-four. Nevertheless, there can be no doubt that, though somewhat on the increase, the number of English courts at the opening of the twentieth century is considerably behind those in constant use at the beginning of either the seventeenth or eighteenth century. The enthusiasts say of this sport that it is not only the game for kings but the king of games.

*RACKETS.—There is not much history attached to the game of rackets apart from tennis. It originated in the tennis courts, as has been shown by Mr Marshall, who has drawn attention to a print at the British Museum, inscribed: "Fives Played at the Tennis Court, Leicester Fields. Printed by Carrington Bowles, 1788." The players are represented as using tennis rackets and playing against only one wall of the tennis court, on which is chalked out a certain area within which the balls had to be driven. Mr Marshall has thus clearly defined the sequence of the game:—"First came fives, played with the hand against any available wall. Then came bat-fives, in which a wooden instrument, roughly imitated from the tennis racket, was employed. That was a good game; and it is still played in many places, and notably at some of our great schools, Rugby, Westminster, Cheltenham, and others. Not content with the wooden bat, players acquainted with the tennis racket seem to have adopted that instrument about 1749, or a little earlier . . . so it continued to be played until 1788, the date of the print mentioned above, which the players still called the game fives."[1]

*With the introduction of the racket, the change in the name gradually followed. It used to be popular in the prisons of the Fleet and King's Bench, and afterwards in the gardens of some of the great London taverns. A special form of the real game became localised at Harrow about 1822. With its later history we are not here concerned, nor with the various developments of the present game of fives, which is essentially a pastime for boys.

*LAWN TENNIS.—Of the widespread pastime of lawn tennis, which assumed definite shape in 1874, it need only be remarked in these pages that it can lay claim to a long pedigree, though suspended in its action for a considerable period. The earlier notices of tennis establish the fact that the royal game was originally played in the open air.

*THE WIND-BALL OR BALLOON.—The wind-ball or leathern ball filled with air, after the fashion of the later form of football, but struck with the hand or fist, is as old as the time of the Romans, by whom it was termed *follis*. Gervase Markham, in 1615, couples the "Baloone" with tennis as good sports either for health or action. He describes it as "a strong and moving sport in the open

---

[1] *Tennis, Rackets, Fives* (All England Series, 1890), by Julian Marshall, pp. 43, 44.

fields, with a great ball of double leather fill'd with winde, and driven to and fro with the strength of a man's arme arm'd in a bracer of wood." [1]

*In the 1659 English edition of Komensky's *Orbis Sensualium Pictus*, this game is depicted as being played outside a tennis court, and is thus described, the numerals being references to the picture :—" A Winde-ball 4 being filled with air by means of a Ventie is tossed to and fro with the fist 5 in the open air." [2]

*Doctor Jones, the Buxton physician of Elizabethan fame, did not disdain to recommend his patients to play at ball. "The wind baule, or yarne ball, betwene three or foure shall not bee inutile to be used in a place convenient, eache keeping their limite. For tossinge wherein may bee a very profitable exercise, bycause at all tymes they keepe not the lyke force in striking, so that shalbee constrayned to use more violent stretching with swifter moving at one time than another, which will make the exercise more nymble, and deliver both of hand and whole body: therefore encreasing of heat through swift moving in all partes the sooner." [3]

HURLING, HOCKEY, CAMP-BALL.—Hurling is an ancient exercise, and seems originally to have been a species of the hand-ball; it was played by the Romans with a ball called harpastum, a word probably derived from harpago, to snatch or take by violence. The contending parties endeavoured to force the ball one from the other, and they who could retain it long enough to cast it beyond an appointed boundary were the conquerors. The inhabitants of the western counties of England have long been famous for their skill in the practice of this pastime. There were two methods of hurling in Cornwall, at the commencement of the seventeenth century, and both are particularly described by Carew, a contemporary writer,[4] whose words are these: "Hurling taketh his denomination from throwing of the ball, and is of two sorts; in the east parts of Cornwall to goales, and in the west to the country. For hurling to goales there are fifteen, twenty, or thirty players, more or less, chosen out on each side, who strip themselves to their slightest apparell and then join hands in ranke one against another; out of these rankes they match themselves by payres, one embracing another, and so passe away, every of which couple are especially to watch one another during the play; after this they pitch two bushes in the ground, some eight or ten feet asunder, and directly against them, ten or twelve score paces off, other twain in like distance, which they term goales, where some indifferent person throweth up a ball, the which whosoever can catch and carry through his adversaries goale, hath wonne the game; but herein consisteth one of Hercules his labours, for he that is once possessed of the ball, hath his contrary mate waiting at inches and assaying to lay hold upon him, the other thrusteth him in the breast with his closed fist to keep him off, which they call *butting*." According to the laws of the game, "they must hurle man to man, and not two set upon one man at

[1] *Country Contentments*, bk. i. p. 109.   [2] Pl. cxxxiii.
[3] *The Benefit of the Ancient Bathes of Buckstones*, 1572.   [4] *Survey of Cornwall*, 1602, bk. i. p. 73.

once. The hurler against the ball must not *but* nor *handfast* under the girdle, he who hath the ball must *but* only in the other's breast, and deale no fore ball, that is, he may not throw it to any of his mates standing nearer to the goale than himself." In hurling to the country, "two or three, or more parishes agree to hurl against two or three other parishes. The matches are usually made by gentlemen, and their goales are either those gentlemen's houses, or some towns or villages three or four miles asunder, of which either side maketh choice after the nearnesse of their dwellings; when they meet there is neyther comparing of numbers nor matching of men, but a silver ball is cast up, and that company which can catch and carry it by force or slight to the place assigned, gaineth the ball and the victory. Such as see where the ball is played give notice, crying 'ware east,' 'ware west,' as the same is carried. The hurlers take their next way over hilles, dales, hedges, ditches; yea, and thorow bushes, briars, mires, plashes, and rivers whatsoever, so as you shall sometimes see twenty or thirty lie tugging together in the water, scrambling and scratching for the ball."

About the year 1775, the hurling to the goales was frequently played by parties of Irishmen, in the fields at the back of the British Museum, but they used a kind of bat to take up the ball and to strike it from them; this instrument was flat on both sides, and broad and curving at the lower end. I have been greatly amused to see with what facility those who were skilful in the pastime would catch up the ball upon the bat, and often run with it for a considerable time, tossing it occasionally from the bat and recovering it again, till such time as they found a proper opportunity of driving it back amongst their companions, who generally followed and were ready to receive it. In other respects, I do not recollect that the game differed materially from the description above given. The bat for hurling was known and probably used in England more than two centuries ago, for it is mentioned in a book published in the reign of Queen Elizabeth,[1] and is there called "a clubbe" or "hurle batte."

*Mr Strutt's paragraph as to the Irish bat hurling at once suggests hockey. In Chambers's *Information for the People* it is stated that, "shinty in Scotland, hockey in England, and hurling in Ireland appear to be very much the same out-of-door sport."[2] In a recent brief essay on the history of hockey, an enthusiastic writer states that "the game existed in Ireland two thousand years ago, though possibly in a form that would not be recognised by the modern player, and its trail may be found here and there, across the story of social England from quite early days."[3] The earliest known use of the word occurs in certain local statutes enacted by the town of Galway in the year 1527, when, amongst prohibited games is named—"The horlinge of the litill balle with hockie stickes or staves."[4] Hockey is described in Murray's *Dictionary* as equivalent to bandy or shinty.

---

[1] *Philogamus*, black letter, without date.
[2] Edit. 1842, vol. ii. p. 543.
[3] Mr H. F. Prevost Battersby, in *Football, Hockey, Lacrosse* (The Sports Library), p. 80.
[4] *Hist. MSS. Com.* 10th Report, app. v. p. 402.

The game, which was for a long time during last century chiefly confined to the ice, has of late years experienced a remarkable revival among both sexes.

*All games with ball have a tendency to change and mingle with others, and vary much in different districts, as well as at different periods. Hence it is difficult to keep their nomenclature accurate and distinct. The true Cornish hurling, and a like game in other parts of England, seems to have consisted in the hurling or hand-throwing of a comparatively small ball. An interesting, but unfortunately brief, reference to this western game as a sport between counties occurs as early as 1648 : "The Counties of Devon and Cornwall are, on Monday next, to meet at a hurling, a sport they have with a ball."[1]

*This form of western hurling was very similar to the camp-ball (from A.S. *camp*, a combat) of the eastern counties, which was distinct from football, termed "kicking-camp." In Mr Albert Way's notes to the *Promptorium Parvulorum* (Camden Society), it is stated that "camping-land appropriated to this game occurs, in several instances, in authorities of the fifteenth century." Camp-ball prevailed in many parts of Norfolk, Suffolk, and Essex in the seventeenth and eighteenth centuries. It is thus described by Major Moor in 1823 :—

"Goals were pitched 150 to 200 yards apart, formed of the thrown-off clothes of the competitors. Each party has two goals, 10 or 15 yards apart. The parties, 10 to 15 a side, stand in a line facing their own goals and each other, at 10 yards distance, midway between the goals and nearest that of their adversaries. An indifferent spectator throws up the ball—the size of a cricket ball—midway between the confronted players, whose object is to seize and convey it between their own goals. The shock of the first onset to catch the falling ball is very great, and the player who seizes it speeds home pursued by his opponents, through whom he has to make his way, aided by the jostlings of his own side. If caught and held, he throws the ball—but must in no case give it—to a comrade, who, if it be not arrested in its course, or be jostled away by his eager foes, catches it and hurries home, winning the notch or snotch if he continues to carry—not throw—it between the goals. A holder of the ball caught with it in his possession loses a snotch. At the loss of each of these the game recommences, after a breathing time. Seven or nine snotches are the game, and these it will sometimes take two or three hours to win. At times a large football was used, and the game was then called 'kicking camp'; and if played with shoes on was termed 'savage camp.'"[2]

*The same correspondent of *Notes and Queries*, who cited this account in 1892, stated that the game seemed to have died away owing to numerous and fatal accidents that happened to players. "Two men were killed at a grand match at Euston, Suffolk, about the close of last century."

FOOTBALL.—Football is so called because the ball is driven about with the feet instead of the hands. It was formerly much in vogue among the common people of England, though of late years it seems to have fallen into disrepute,

---

[1] *Hamilton's Papers* (Camden Soc.), p. 171.   [2] *Notes and Queries*, Ser. VIII. ii. 214.

and is but little practised. I cannot pretend to determine at what period the game of football originated; it does not, however, to the best of my recollection, appear among the popular exercises before the reign of Edward III., and then, in 1349, it was prohibited by a public edict; not, perhaps, from any particular objection to the sport in itself, but because it co-operated, with other favourite amusements, to impede the progress of archery.

When a match at football is made, two parties, each containing an equal number of competitors, take the field, and stand between two goals, placed at the distance of eighty or an hundred yards the one from the other. The goal is usually made with two sticks driven into the ground, about two or three feet apart. The ball, which is commonly made of a blown bladder, and cased with leather, is delivered in the midst of the ground, and the object of each party is to drive it through the goal of their antagonists, which being achieved the game is won. The abilities of the performers are best displayed in attacking and defending the goals; and hence the pastime was more frequently called a goal at football than a game at football. When the exercise becomes exceeding violent, the players kick each other's shins without the least ceremony, and some of them are overthrown at the hazard of their limbs.

Barclay in his fifth eclogue [1] has these lines:

> The sturdie plowmen lustie, strong and bold,
> Overcometh the winter with driving the foote-ball,
> Forgetting labour and many a grievous fall.

And a more modern poet, Waller:

> As when a sort of lusty shepherds try
> Their force at foot-ball; care of victory
> Makes them salute so rudely breast to breast,
> That their encounter seems too rough for jest.

The danger attending this pastime occasioned King James I. to say, " From this court I debarre all rough and violent exercises, as the foot-ball, meeter for lameing than making able the users thereof." [2]

The rustic boys made use of a blown bladder without the covering of leather by way of football, putting peas and horse beans withinside, which occasioned a rattling as it was kicked about.

> —And nowe in the winter, when men kill the fat swine,
> They get the bladder and blow it great and thin,
> With many beans and peason put within:
> It ratleth, soundeth, and shineth clere and fayre,
> While it is throwen and caste up in the ayre,
> Eche one contendeth and hath a great delite
> With foote and with hande the bladder for to smite;
> If it fall to grounde, they lifte it up agayne,
> And this waye to labour they count it no payne. [3]

" It had been the custom," says a Chester antiquary, [4] " time out of mind,

---

[1] *Ship of Fools*, 1508.   [2] *Basilicon Doron*, bk. iii.   [3] Barclay, *ut supra*.
[4] I rather think the elder Randel Holmes, one of the city heralds, MS. Harl. 2150, fol. 23.

for the shoemakers yearly on the Shrove Tuesday, to deliver to the drapers, in the presence of the mayor of Chester, at the cross on the Rodehee,[1] one ball of leather called a foote-ball, of the value of three shillings and fourpence or above, to play at from thence to the Common Hall of the said city; which practice was productive of much inconvenience, and therefore this year (1540), by consent of the parties concerned, the ball was changed into six glayves of silver of the like value, as a reward for the best runner that day upon the aforesaid Rodehee."

In an old comedy, the *Blind Beggar of Bethnal Green*, by John Day,[2] one of the characters speaks thus of himself: "I am Tom Stroud of Hurling, I'll play a gole at camp-ball, or wrassel a fall a the hip or the hin turn." Camp-ball, I conceive, is only another denomination for foot-ball, and is so called, because it was played to the greatest advantage in an open country. The term may probably be a contraction of the word campaign.

*It has been thought well to give the whole of the passage originally published by Joseph Strutt in 1801, relative to football, as it not only gives an account of the game as played at the end of the eighteenth century, but also points with emphasis to the marvellous growth and popularity achieved by football in the course of a hundred years.

*Mr Strutt conceived that camp-ball was but another name for football; his partial error in that respect has already been pointed out, yet he might have claimed a good and early authority for such a mistake. In the *Promptorium Parvulorum* occurs this definition: "*Campan*, or playar at foott balle, *pediluson*; *campyon*, or champion." It is also obvious that Rugby football owes a good deal to the old camp-ball proper, which was a hand game.

*The legends connected with English football point to a very early use of the game. The Shrovetide game at Chester is said to have been in commemoration of the barbarous kicking about of the head of a captured Dane; whilst the Derby game is supposed to have been a memorial of a local victory over the Romans.

*Ball play, apparently football, was so popular in London in the time of Edward II. that a proclamation was issued in 1314 forbidding the hustling of over-large balls (*rageries de grosses pelotes*) within the city under pain of imprisonment.

*There is a curious instance of a fatal football accident caused by a religious of the Gilbertine order in the time of Edward II. During a game William de Spalding, canon of the Gilbertine house of Shouldham, Norfolk, when in the act of kicking the ball was run against by a lay friend of his, who was also called William. The canon was carrying a sheathed knife in his girdle, but in the collision the layman wounded himself on the knife so severely that he died within six days. The canon was instantly suspended from all clerical duty; but on appealing to the pope, dispensation to resume his work was granted him,

---

[1] An open place near the city.   [2] Acted A.D. 1659.

as it was shown that no blame attached to him, and that he deeply regretted the death of his friend.[1]

*In 1349 football and other games were forbidden by Edward III. in favour of archery. It was again forbidden by statute under Richard II. in 1389, which statute was re-enacted in 1401. These statutes had, however, but partial and temporary success. Football came again under the ban of the law in the sixteenth century, both under Henry VIII. and Elizabeth. There seems, however, to have been reasonable excuse for these repressive measures, judging from the violence with which it was played.

*Mr Montague Shearman cites various official records as to serious or fatal results from football of the sixteenth century;[2] and these might be materially increased by reference to coroners' rolls.

*After the dissolution of the monasteries, when Sir Roger Townsend was pulling down the tower of Coxford Priory, Norfolk, to build himself a goodly house, the steeple came down with a crash and fell upon a house near by, "breaking it down and slaying one Mr Seller, that lay lame in it of a broken leg gotten at foot-ball."[3]

*Sir Thomas Elyot, in his charming little work entitled *The Boke named the Governour*, first published in 1531, says of football that it "is nothyng but beastely fury and extreme violence, whereof procedeth hurte, and consequently rancour and malice do remayne with thym that be wounded, wherfore it is to be put in perpetuall silence."[4]

*In Stubbes' *Anatomie of Abuses* (1583) football is described as "a develishe pastime . . . and hereof groweth envy, rancour, and malice, and sometimes brawling, murther, homicide, and great effusion of blood, as experience daily teacheth."

*And yet there must have been gentler forms of this exercise. The married women and spinsters of Inverness used to have a Shrovetide match of football; and a writer in *Notes and Queries* for 1892 cites the following lines as to matron and girls playing from Sir Philip Sidney's *Dialogue between Two Shepherds :—*

> A time there is for all, my mother often says,
> When she, with skirts tucked very high,
> With girls at football plays.

*One of the chief objections to football in the early part of the seventeenth century naturally arose from the habit of playing it in the streets of towns instead of the open country. In Hone's *Table-Book* the following passage is cited from Davenant's description of London in 1634 :—

" I would now make a safe retreat, but that methinks I am stopped by one of your heroic games called football; which I conceive (under your favour) not very conveniently civil in the streets, especially in such irregular and narrow

---

[1] *Cal. of Papal Letters*, ii. 214. [2] *Football* (Badminton Library, 1844), 7, 8.
[3] Spelman's *History of Sacrilege*, 1632, edit. 1853, p. 251. [4] Edit. 1546, p. 32b.

roads as Crooked Lane. Yet it argues your courage, much like your military pastime of throwing at cocks, since you have long allowed these two valiant exercises in the streets."

*This extract seems to show that the numerous town bye-laws against football were but seldom enforced. A century earlier than this football had been singled out for special honour by the town of Galway, but to be played outside the walls; the local statutes of 1527 forbad, in favour of archery, every other kind of sport and pastime "onely the great foote balle."[1]

*Football seems to have been well established at Cambridge in the time of Charles II. In the second register book of Magdalen College occurs the following entry of 1679, relative to abuses connected with Michaelmas football:—

*" That no schollers give or receive at any time any treat or collation upon account of ye football play, on or about Michaelmas Day, further then Colledge beere or ale in ye open hall to quench their thirsts. And particularly that that most vile custom of drinking and spending money—Sophisters and Freshmen together—upon ye account of making or not making a speech at that football time be utterly left off and extinguished."[2]

*Pepys and other well-known authorities give evidence of much football play in the latter half of the seventeenth century. It is alluded to in the *Spectator*, as a game played on village greens, but save in a few traditionary towns at certain dates—usually Shrovetide—football seems to have gradually died out during the eighteenth century, and to have remained quiescent during the first half of the nineteenth century. The revival began in our great public schools.

*Derby and Kingston were among the most noteworthy places for Shrovetide town football; the game was vigorously and furiously played in both these towns well into the nineteenth century. At Dorking efforts are still made to maintain the annual street game.

GOLF.—There are many games played with the ball that require the assistance of a club or bat, and probably the most ancient among them is the pastime now distinguished by the name of golf.[3] In the northern parts of the kingdom golf is much practised. It requires much room to perform this game with propriety, and therefore I presume it is rarely seen at present in the vicinity of the metropolis. It answers to a rustic pastime of the Romans which they played with a ball of leather stuffed with feathers, called *paganica*, because it was used by the common people: the golf-ball is composed of the same materials to this day: I have been told it is sometimes, though rarely, stuffed with cotton. In the reign of Edward III. the Latin name *cambuca*[4] was applied to this pastime, and it derived the denomination, no doubt, from the crooked

---

[1] *Hist. MSS. Com.* 10th Report, App. v. 402.   [2] *Ibid.* 5th Report, 483.

[3] Spelt *goff* throughout in the original edition, which is undoubtedly the right pronunciation. See *Notes and Queries*, Ser. viii. vols. 4, 5, and 6.

[4] *Cambuta vel cambuca. Baculus incurvatus*, a crooked club or staff: the word *cambuca* was also used for the *virga episcoparum*, or episcopal crosier, because it was curved at the top. Du Cange, *Glossary*, in voce *cambuta*.

G

club or bat with which it was played; the bat was also called a bandy, from its being bent, and hence the game itself is frequently written in English bandy ball. At the bottom of plate eight are two figures engaged at bandy-ball, showing the form of the bandy, as it was used early in the fourteenth century, from a MS. book of prayers beautifully illuminated, in the possession of Mr Francis Douce.

Golf, according to the present modification of the game, is performed with a bat, not much unlike the bandy: the handle of this instrument is straight, and usually made of ash, about four feet and a half in length; the curvature is affixed to the bottom, faced with horn and backed with lead; the ball is a little one, but exceedingly hard, being made with leather, and, as before observed, stuffed with feathers. There are generally two players, who have each of them his bat and ball. The game consists in driving the ball into certain holes made in the ground; he who achieves it the soonest, or in the fewest number of strokes, obtains the victory. The golf-lengths, or the spaces between the first and last holes, are sometimes extended to the distance of two or three miles; the number of intervening holes appears to be optional, but the balls must be struck into the holes, and not beyond them; when four persons play, two of them are sometimes partners, and have but one ball, which they strike alternately, but every man has his own bandy.

It should seem that golf was a fashionable game among the nobility at the commencement of the seventeenth century, and it was one of the exercises with which prince Henry, eldest son to James I., occasionally amused himself, as we learn from the following anecdote recorded by a person who was present:[1] "At another time playing at goff, a play not unlike to pale-maille, whilst his school-master stood talking with another, and marked not his highness warning him to stand farther off, the prince thinking he had gone aside, lifted up his goff-club to strike the ball; mean tyme one standing by said to him, "beware that you hit not Master Newton": wherewith he drawing back his hand, said, "Had I done so, I had but paid my debts.""

*In addition to the early drawing given on plate eight, another one has been reproduced at the bottom of plate eleven. In this drawing of fourteenth-century date, which has been named as illustrating golf, two men are standing with the ends of their knobbed clubs, which they hold in both hands, crossed on the ground; but this illustration seems to point to some form of bandy-ball or hockey rather than golf.[2] A third illustration, at the top of plate nine, taken from a series of miniatures in a Book of Hours, *circa* 1500, undoubtedly refers to golf as then played; the figure down on his knees is "holing."[3]

*The definition of the word given in Murray's *New Dictionary* is admirable :—

"A game of considerable antiquity in Scotland, in which a small hard ball

---

[1] An anonymous author, Harl. MSS. 6391.

[2] Roy. Lib. 10 E. iv. fol. 95. [3] Add. MSS. 24,098, fol. 27.

Various Games.

is struck with various clubs into a series of small cylindrical holes made at intervals, usually of a hundred yards or more, on the surface of a moor, field, etc. The aim is to drive the ball into any one hole, or into all the holes successively, with the fewest possible strokes. Commonly two persons or two couples (a 'foursome') play against each other."

*The same work cites authorities for "golf," 1457; "gouff," 1491; "goiff," 1538; "golf," 1575; and "goff," 1615 and 1669. The origin of the word is obscure.

*Golf is essentially the national pastime of Scotland, and has been so for more than four centuries. The first known notice of the game by its proper name is of the year 1457, when the lords and barons, spiritual and temporal, of the kingdom ruled that football and golf were to be utterly cried down and not to be used, lest they should interfere with the due following of archery.

*Golf-playing on Sunday was frequently punished by the local authorities of Edinburgh and other Scotch towns in the sixteenth and seventeenth centuries.

*It was a royal as well as a popular game before the time of England's James I. In 1503, nine shillings were paid for the royal club and balls when the king played golf with the earl of Bothwell. The clubs at that time cost one shilling, and the feather-stuffed balls of leather were four shillings the dozen. In 1603 James I. appointed one William Mayne "clubmaker to his Hienes all the days of his lyftime." Montrose, who played at the Leith and St Andrews Links, was a golf expert; evidently in his days those who could afford it used a variety of clubs, for he was the purchaser of a set of six.[1] Charles I. was a player; the story of his breaking off a match at Leith, when news of the outbreak of the Irish rebellion reached him, is well known.

*Charles's son, James II., when duke of York, was a frequent player, and made use of a "fore-cadie" to run in front and mark the ball down. It was probably through the duke, and the royal family generally, that the game became known in England. In *Westminster Drollery*, published in London in 1671, occurs the couplet :—

> At Goff and at Football, and when we have done
> These innocent sports we'll laugh and lie down.

*The game was first formally established at Blackheath, so far as England was concerned. Some think that it was begun there as early as the time of James I. A club was certainly in existence there some time prior to 1745. A club that was formed at Pau in the "fifties" was one of the chief causes of establishing the game in various parts of England, such as Westward Ho and Wimbledon. English officers and gentlemen who had wintered at Pau, and found that golf was congenial to mature years, became anxious to see it established in their own country. Of late years golf has spread with extraordinary rapidity to almost every part of England.

*Much more might be recorded of the early history and development of

---

[1] Napier's *Memoirs of Montrose*, 1856.

golf in Scotland, but that would not be in accord with a work on the "sports and pastimes of the people of England."[1]

*CRICKET.—The exact origin of cricket is somewhat difficult to determine, but there is no doubt whatever that it is a game essentially and exclusively English in its rise and development. As early as the middle of the thirteenth century a game of ball was played with a crooked or clubbed stick called *cryc*. In the Wardrobe Accounts of Edward I. for 1300 the sum of 100s. is entered towards the expenses incurred by John Luk, tutor and chaplain of the young prince (Edward II.), in playing at *Creag'* and other games. *Cricce*, Anglo-Saxon for a crooked stick, is the probable origin of the name; but if this be the case the shape of the stick or club changed and became for the most part straight. Club-ball, as distinguished from cambuc or goff, seems to have been of the nature of cricket, and was played for some time with a comparatively straight club or bat. A Bodleian MS. of the year 1344 shows a woman in the act of throwing a ball to a man who elevates his bat to give it a back-hand stroke.[2] This is shown at the top of plate twelve. In the original drawing there are several figures of both sexes at a little distance behind the bowler, apparently waiting to catch or stop the ball when returned by the batsman. An earlier drawing of the end of the reign of Henry III., in the centre of the same plate, of two figures one with a ball and straight bat, and the other with hands outstretched for a catch,[3] can scarcely be considered a forerunner of cricket, as the player possessed of the bat himself holds the ball which he is about to strike. A third drawing, of the fourteenth century (plate eleven), gives two players, one of them holding a large ball in the left hand, and a straight bat or club in the right, whilst the other is grasping a plucked-up stump or wicket in a bat-like attitude.[4]

*There is an interesting reference to this early form of cricket about 1420. John Combe of Quidhampton was one of the witnesses examined by the commissioners appointed by the pope to inquire into the alleged miracles at the tomb of Bishop Osmund, of Salisbury, when a petition had been presented for that prelate's canonisation. Combe testified that, ten years before, his neighbours were playing at ball with great clubs (*ludentes ad pilam cum baculis magnis*) in the village of Bemerton, when they quarrelled over the game. The witness interposed and tried to make peace, when one of the players struck him with his club, breaking his head and right shoulder, so that he lay sick and unable to hear or to see or to move head or arm for more than three months. Eventually he was healed by making an offering of his head and shoulders in wax, marked with wounds similar to his own, at the tomb of the bishop, accompanied by prayers.[5]

*But in none of these early drawings, or in any mention of club-ball, is there any reference to that essential of cricket, the stumps or wicket at which the ball

[1] *Historical Gossip about Golf and Golfers*, Edinburgh, 1863; *Golf, an Ancient and Royal Game*, R. and R. Clark, Edinburgh, 1875; *Golf* (Badminton Library, 1898), historical chapter by Andrew Lang.
[2] Bodl. 264.   [3] Roy. Lib. 14 B. v.   [4] *Ibid.* 10 E. iv. fol. 94b.
[5] *The Canonisation of St Osmund* (Wilts Record Soc. 1902), pp. xiv. 71.

Bat and Ball.

is aimed. This is to be found in another old game which went by the name of stool-ball.

Stool-ball is frequently mentioned by the writers of the three last centuries, but without any proper definition of the game. I (Mr Strutt) have been informed that a pastime called stool-ball is practised to this day in the northern parts of England, which consists simply in setting a stool upon the ground, and one of the players takes his place before it, while his antagonist, standing at a distance, tosses a ball with the intention of striking the stool, and this it is the business of the former to prevent by beating it away with the hand, reckoning one to the game for every stroke of the ball; if, on the contrary, it should be missed by the hand and touch the stool, the players change places; the conquerer at this game is he who strikes the ball most times before it touches the stool. I believe the same also happens if the person who threw the ball can catch and retain it when driven back, before it reaches the ground.

*From this description it is fairly obvious that a combination of stool-ball with club-ball, a bat being substituted for the hand, produced the origin of the game now known as cricket.

*The pastime of "handyn and handout" named in the prohibitory statute of 17 Edward IV., is supposed by some to refer to cricket.

*The oldest known mention of the game by its modern name goes back to the time of Edward VI. In the "Constitution Book" of Guildford, there is record of a dispute of the year 1598 as to the enclosure of an acre of common land near the town. John Derrick, a county coroner, deposed that he knew it fifty years ago or more when it lay waste. "When he was a scholler in the free school of Guildeford he and severell of his fellowes did run and play there at crickett and other plaies."

*Cotgrave, in his French-English Dictionary of 1611, translates the French *crosse*, "a crosier, or bishop's staffe, also a cricket staffe, or the crooked staffe wherewith boies play at cricket." Edward Phillips, the poet Milton's nephew, in a work called *The Mysteries of Love and Eloquence* published in 1685, exclaims—"Would my eyes had been beat out of my head with a cricket-ball the day before I saw thee!" Several other references to the word and the game of seventeenth-century writers might be given, but when the eighteenth century is entered they become numerous.

*In the Cambro-British doggerel of D'Urfey, in 1719, occurs the stanza :—

> Hur was the prettiest fellow
> At football or at cricket,
> At hunting-chase, or prison-base,
> Cot's plut, how hur could nick it.

Pope wrote in the *Dunciad*—

> The Judge to dance his brother Serjeants call,
> The Senators at cricket urge the ball.

Lord Chesterfield, in 1740, told his son that—"if you have a right ambition you will desire to excell all boys of your age at cricket." Horace Walpole, Gray, and others allude to its being played early in the century at Eton, and there is a strikingly vivid description of the game in a poem in the *Gentleman's Magazine* for October 1756, where it is described as "An Exercise at Merchant Taylors' School." It ends with a moral:

> Yes, all in public and in private strive
> To keep the ball of action still alive;
> And just to all, when each his ground has run,
> Death tips the wicket, and the game is done.

*A writer in the same magazine for September 1743 abuses the extravagant use of the game, which was evidently by that time exceedingly popular, and is disgusted to find that "noblemen, gentlemen, and clergymen" were then, as now, in the habit of playing with their social inferiors. The moralist also considered that the game was responsible for propagating a sad spirit of idleness. He was on safer ground when finding fault with the heavy stakes, even for £500 or £1000, which "advertisements of the game most impudently recite." However much betting may have increased in England of late years, there is no doubt whatever that the habit in connection with cricket has much decreased as compared with that which was prevalent in the eighteenth and earlier part of the nineteenth centuries.[1]

*Kent was one of the earliest counties where the game throve under the lead of Lord John Sackville. In 1746 a match was played on the Artillery Ground, London, by Kent against All England, eleven a side, when the latter won by two wickets. A newspaper advertisement announced a match on the same ground on July 24th, 1749, between five of the Addington Club and an All England five. The advertisement gave the names of the players, and thus concluded: "*N.B.*—The last match, which was play'd on Monday the 10th instant, was won by All England, notwithstanding it was eight to one on Addington in the playing."

*Hambledon, in Hampshire, was the special home of cricket; its club long maintained great efficiency and popularity, and it is to Hambledon that the honour belongs of being the first to promote regular laws for the guidance of the game. These rules were drawn up by a committee of noblemen and gentlemen who met at the "Star and Garter" in Pall Mall in the year 1774. Among those present were the duke of Dorset, Lord Tankerville, and Sir Horace Mann. The distance between the stumps was the same as at present; the crease was cut in the turf, not painted; the stumps were twenty-two inches in height; and there was only one bail, six inches in length. Just about this time the epic poet of the sport, James Love, comedian, put forth a shilling quarto, dedicated to the Richmond Club. The poem opens with an exhortation to Britain to leave "puny Billiards" and all meaner sports, and only to cultivate cricket:—

> Hail Cricket, glorious, manly, British game,
> First of all sports, be first alike in fame!

---

[1] For an interesting account of betting at cricket see Pycroft's *Cricket Field*, ch. vi.

*The bat of those days has been described as "similar to an old-fashioned dinner-knife, curved at the back, and sweeping in the form of a volute at the front and end. With such a bat, the system must have been all for hitting; it would be barely possible to block; and when the practice of bowling length balls was introduced, which gave the bowler so great an advantage in the game, it became absolutely necessary to change the form of the bat, in order that the striker might be able to keep pace with the improvement. It was therefore made straight in the pod; in consequence of which, a total revolution, it may be said a reformation too, ensued in the style of play . . . the system of stopping or blocking was adopted."[1] A picture by Francis Hayman, R.A. (who exhibited between 1769 and 1772), belonging to the M.C.C., shows the almost cudgel shape of the bat in a country cricket match; the wicket is very low with only two stumps; a lad in the foreground is scoring "notches" on a stick.

*Among the satirical prints of the British Museum[2] is one published on January 1st, 1778, from a picture painted in 1770, which bears witness to the early attention paid to this game by the fair sex, and also pourtrays with exactness the shape of the bat. It is entitled "Miss Wicket and Miss Trigger," and is a mezzotint engraving showing a meadow near a farmhouse, where two young women appear. Below are the lines—

> Miss Trigger you see is an excellent shot,
> And forty-five notches Miss Wicket's just got.

*Miss Wicket is represented leaning on a cricket-bat, wearing a dress trimmed with ribbons, and red shoes. A little girl catches a ball in the foreground. The stumps of the wicket are but two, and forked at the top to carry a transverse stick or bail.

*The exact shape of the bat is also shown in the picture of "A Young Cricketer," of about the same date, ascribed to Gainsborough, which belongs to the M.C.C.

*The ball in Miss Wicket's picture has heavy cross seams; but a silver ball, over a hundred years old, which was used as a snuff-box by the Vine Club, Sevenoaks, is marked with seams like those now in use.

*That central parliament of cricket, the Marylebone Club, came into existence on the dissolution of the old White Conduit Club in 1787. One Thomas Lord, a cricket enthusiast, with the aid of some members of the dissolved association, made a ground on the site of what is now Dorset Square. This was the first "Lord's." After a move to North Bank, Thomas Lord finally pitched his camp, in the year 1814, on the present famous ground.

*This is not the place in which to chronicle the general run of cricket eccentricities, but early instances of attempts to play the game on horseback may perhaps be recorded.

---

[1] Nyren's *Cricketer's Guide*, 4th edit. (1846), pp. 93, 94.
[2] Stephen's *Catalogue*, iv. 728.

*CRICKET ON HORSEBACK. — The advertisement columns of the *Kentish Gazette* of 29th April 1794, contain the following :—

"Cricketing on Horseback. — A very singular game of cricket will be played on Tuesday, the 6th of May, in Linsted Park, between the Gentlemen of the Hill and the Gentlemen of the Dale, for one guinea a man. The whole to be performed on horseback. To begin at nine o'clock, and the game to be played out. A good ordinary on the ground by John Hogben."

*In Lilywhite's *Score Sheets* it is stated that, in or about 1800, Sir Horace Mann caused a cricket match to be played on ponies at Harrietsham.[1]

*TRAP-BALL, AND KNUR AND SPELL. — The game of trap-ball, or trap-bat-and-ball, which can be traced back to at least the beginning of the fourteenth century (see Plate 13[2]), afterwards developed into the northern game of knur and spell. In the first quarter of the nineteenth century this game was a favourite one amongst adults in several of our northern counties, particularly in Hallamshire. The knur, or ball, used in the game, was made of various hard materials. It was sometimes carved by hand out of a hard wood, such as holly, or engine-turned out of lignum-vitæ; in the pottery districts it was commonly made of white Wedgewood material, and usually called a "pottie"; whilst in its most scientific form the knur was made out of stag-horn and weighted with lead. The spell, or trap, was of varying design, sometimes assuming the shoe form, which could commonly be obtained in toy shops in the middle of the last century and later; but ingenuity devised a spring spell, which, being set and detached by means of a toothed click, could be regulated so as to always raise the knur to the same height, thus greatly increasing the certainty of the player hitting it. The third implement required for this game is the trip-stick used for striking the ball. It differs much from the old form of short bat, and consists of two parts, the stick and the pomel. The former is made of ash or lance wood, so as to combine stiffness and elasticity, and for a two-handed player is about four feet in length. The widened end, or pomel, is made of any hard heavy wood that will not easily split. The main point of the game is the distance to which the player can strike the knur; a first-rate hand is said to have been able to send a loaded ball as far as sixteen score yards.[3]

---

[1] On the general question of the early history of cricket, see Nyren's *Cricketer's Guide*; Blaine's *Rural Sports*, 133-136; Badminton Library *Cricket*, history of the game by Andrew Lang; *Notes and Queries*, Ser. ii. and v. etc.

[2] Bodl. MS.   [3] *Reliquary*, Ser. I. vi. 233-236.

BOOK III

PASTIMES USUALLY EXERCISED IN TOWNS AND CITIES, OR PLACES ADJOINING TO THEM

CHAPTER I

Tournament a general Name for several Exercises—The Quintain an ancient Military Exercise—Various Kinds of the Quintain—Derivation of the Term—The Water Quintain—Running at the Quintain practised by the Citizens of London; and why—The Manner in which it was performed—Exhibited for the Pastime of Queen Elizabeth— Tilting at a Water Butt—The Human Quintain—Exercises probably derived from it—Running at the Ring— Difference between the Tournaments and the Jousts—Origin of the Tournament—The Troy Game; the Bohordicum or Cane Game—Derivation of Tournament; How the Exercise was performed—Lists and Barriers—When the Tournament was first practised—When first in England—Its Laws and Ordinances—Pages, and Perquisites of the Kings at Arms, etc.—Preliminaries of the Tournament—Lists for Ordeal Combats—Respect paid to the Ladies— Jousts less honourable than Tournaments—The Round Table—Nature of the Jousts—Made in Honour of the Fair Sex—Great Splendour of these Pastimes; The Nobility partial to them—Toys for initiating their Children in them —Boat Jousts, or Tilting on the Water—Challenges to all comers.

TOURNAMENT.—Every kind of military combat made in conformity to certain rules, and practised by the knights and their esquires for diversion or gallantry, was anciently called a tournament; yet these amusements frequently differed materially from each other, and have been distinguished accordingly by various denominations in the modern times. They may, however, I think, be all of them included under the four following heads: tilting and combating at the quintain, tilting at the ring, tournaments, and jousts.

All these, and especially the two last, were favourite pastimes with the nobility of the middle ages. The progress and decline of tournaments in this country has already been mentioned in a general way;[1] I shall in this place be a little more particular with respect to the nature and distinction of these celebrated diversions.

THE QUINTAIN.—Tilting or combating at the quintain is certainly a military exercise of high antiquity, and antecedent, I doubt not, to the jousts and tournaments. The quintain, originally, was nothing more than the trunk of a tree or post set up for the practice of the tyros in chivalry.[2] Afterward a staff or spear was fixed in the earth, and a shield being hung upon it, was the mark to strike at: the dexterity of the performer consisted in smiting the shield in such a manner as to break the ligatures and bear it to the ground. In process of time this diversion was improved, and instead of the staff and the shield, the resemblance of a human figure carved in wood was introduced. To render the

---

[1] In the Introduction. [2] Vegetius, *De re militari*, lib. i. cap. xi. et xiv.

appearance of this figure more formidable, it was generally made in the likeness of a Turk or a Saracen armed at all points,[1] bearing a shield upon his left arm, and brandishing a club or a sabre with his right. Hence this exercise was called by the Italians, "running at the armed man, or at the Saracen." The quintain thus fashioned was placed upon a pivot, and so contrived as to move round with facility. In running at this figure it was necessary for the horseman to direct his lance with great adroitness, and make his stroke upon the forehead between the eyes or upon the nose; for if he struck wide of those parts, especially upon the shield, the quintain turned about with much velocity, and, in case he was not exceedingly careful, would give him a severe blow upon the back with the wooden sabre held in the right hand, which was considered as highly disgraceful to the performer, while it excited the laughter and ridicule of the spectators.[2] When many were engaged in running at the Saracen, the conqueror was declared from the number of strokes he had made, and the value of them; for instance, if he struck the image upon the top of the nose between the eyes, it was reckoned for three; if below the eyes, upon the nose, for two; if under the nose to the point of the chin, for one; all other strokes were not counted; but whoever struck upon the shield and turned the quintain round, was not permitted to run again upon the same day, but forfeited his courses as a punishment for his unskilfulness.[3]

VARIOUS QUINTAINS.—The quintain in its original state was not confined to the exercise of young warriors on horseback: it was an object of practice for them on foot, in order to acquire strength and skill in assaulting an enemy with their swords, spears, and battle-axes. I met with a manuscript in the Royal Library,[4] written early in the fourteenth century, entitled "Les Etablissmentz des Chevalerie," wherein the author, who appears to have been a man scientifically skilled in the military tactics of his time, strongly recommends a constant and attentive attack of the *pel* (from the Latin *palus*), for so he calls the post-quintain. The pel, he tells us, ought to be six feet in height above the ground, and so firmly fixed therein as not to be moved by the strokes that were laid upon it. The practitioner was then to assail the pel, armed with sword and shield in the same manner as he would an adversary, aiming his blows as if at the head, the face, the arms, the legs, the thighs, and the sides; taking care at all times to keep himself so completely covered with his shield, as not to give any advantage supposing he had a real enemy to cope with: so far my author; and prefixed to the treatise is a neat little painting representing the *pel*, with a young soldier performing his exercise, which is copied on plate thirteen. Immediately opposite is the quintain in the form of a Saracen, from Pluvinel.

An English poet who has taken up the subject of chivalry under the title of

---

[1] Menestrier, *Traité des Tournois, Joustes, etc.*, p. 264.
[2] Menestrier, *ut supra*; Du Cange, *Glossary*, in voce *quintana*; Pluvinel, *Sur l'exercise de monter à cheval*, part iii. p. 177. [3] Menestrier, p. 112, et Pluvinel *ut supra*. [4] 20 B. xi.

The Quintain.

"Knighthood and Battle,"[1] describes the attack of the pel in the following curious manner :—

> Of fight, the disciplyne, and exercise
> Was this. To have a pale or pile upright
> Of mannys hight, thus writeth olde and wise ;
> Therewith a bacheler, or a yong knyght,
> Shal first be taught to stonde and lerne to fight.—
> And fanne of doubil wight, tak him his shelde
> Of doubil wight, a mace of tre to welde.
>
> This fanne and mace whiche either doubil wight,
> Of shelde, and swayed in conflicte, or bataile,
> Shal exercise as well swordmen, as knyghtes.
> And noe man, as they sayn, is seyn prevaile,
> In field, or in castell, thoughe he assayle,
> That with the pile, nathe firste grete exercise,
> Thus writeth Werrouris olde and wyse.
>
> Have eche his pile or pale upfixed fast,
> And as it were uppon his mortal foe ;
> With mightyness and weapon most be cast
> To fight stronge, that he ne skape hym fro.
> On hym with shield, and sword avised so,
> That thou be cloos, and preste thy foe to smyte,
> Lest of thyne own dethe thou be to wite.
>
> Empeche[2] his head, his face, have at his gorge,
> Beare at the breste, or sperne him one the side.
> With myghte knyghtly poost,[3] ene as Seynt George
> Lepe o thy foe ; looke if he dare abide :
> Will he not flee ? wounde him ; make woundis wide,
> Hew of his honde, his legge, his theyhs, his armys,
> It is the Turk, though he be sleyn noon harm is.

Both the treatises commend the use of arms of double weight upon these occasions, in order to acquire strength, and give the warrior greater facility in wielding the weapons of the ordinary size ; to which the poet adds,

> And sixty pounds of weight 'tis good to bear.

The lines just now quoted evidently allude to the quintain in the form of a Turk or Saracen, which, I presume, was sometimes used upon this occasion. The pel was also set up as a mark to cast at with spears, as the same poet informs us :—

> A dart of more wight then is mester,[4]
> Take hym in honde and teche him it to stere ;
> And cast it at the pile as at his foo,
> So that it conte and right uppon him go.

And likewise for the practice of archery :—

> Set hert and eye uppon the pile or pale,
> Shoot nyghe or onne ; and if so be thou ride
> On horse, is eck the bowis bigge up hale,
> Smyte in the face, or breste, or back or side,
> Compelle to fle, or falle, yf that he bide.

---

[1] *Knyghthode and Batayle*, MS. Cott. Titus A. xxiii. fols. 6 and 7. This curious poem, written early in the fifteenth century, appears to be a translation of a former treatise, or rather a paraphrase upon it.

[2] From the French *empêcher*, to hinder or withstand, here used for attack.

[3] Power, strength.   [4] Than is required, that is in time of real action.

*Shakespeare, in *As You Like It*, says :

> My better parts
> Are all thrown down, and that which here stands up
> Is but a quintain, a mere lifeless block.

DERIVATION OF QUINTAIN.—This exercise is said to have received the name of quintain from Quinctus or Quintas the inventor,[1] but who he was, or when he lived, is not ascertained. The game itself, I doubt not, is of remote origin, and especially the exercise of the pel, or post quintain, which is spoken of at large by Vegetius; and from him the substance of what the two authors above quoted have said upon the subject is evidently taken. He tells us that this species of mock combat was in common use among the Romans, who caused the young military men to practise at it twice in the day, at morning and at noon; he also adds that they used clubs and javelins, heavier than common, and fought at the pel as if they were opposing an adversary, etc.[2]

In the code of laws established by the emperor Justinian, the quintain is mentioned as a well-known sport; and permitted to be continued, upon condition that it should be performed with pointless spears, contrary to the ancient usage, which it seems required them to have heads or points.

THE WATER QUINTAIN.—To the best of my recollection, Fitzstephen is the first of our writers who speaks of an exercise of this kind, which he tells us was usually practised by the young Londoners upon the water during the Easter holidays. A pole or mast, he says, is fixed in the midst of the Thames, with a shield strongly attached to it; and a boat being previously placed at some distance, is driven swiftly towards it by the force of oars and the violence of the tide, having a young man standing in the prow, who holds a lance in his hand with which he is to strike the shield; and if he be dexterous enough to break the lance against it and retain his place, his most sanguine wishes are satisfied; on the contrary, if the lance be not broken, he is sure to be thrown into the water, and the vessel goes away without him, but at the same time two other boats are stationed near to the shield, and furnished with many young persons who are in readiness to rescue the champion from danger. It appears to have been a very popular pastime; for the bridge, the wharfs, and the houses near the river were crowded with people on this occasion, who come, says the author, to see the sports and make themselves merry.[3] A representation of the water quintain, taken from a manuscript of the fourteenth century in the Royal Library, is given upon plate fourteen, where a square piece of board is substituted for the shield.[4]

RUNNING AT THE QUINTAIN PRACTISED BY THE LONDONERS; AND WHY.— Matthew Paris mentions the quintain by name, but he speaks of it in a cursory manner as a well-known pastime, and probably would have said nothing about

---

[1] A quincto auctore nomen habebat, vide Joan Meursi, de Ludis Græcorum, in tit. Κονταξ Κυντανος. *But this is probably an error. The *Century Dictionary* gives—" *Quintana*, a street in a camp between the fifth and sixth maniples, where were the market and forum of the camp, and, it is supposed, the place of martial exercise, etc., whence the Middle Latin use *quintana*, a quintain."

[2] Vegetius, *De re militari*, lib. i. cap. xi. et xiv.   [3] Stephanides, *Descrip. Lond.*   [4] 2 B. vii.

Quintain.

it, had not the following circumstance given him the occasion. In the thirty-eighth year of the reign of Henry III., A.D. 1254, the young Londoners, who, he tells us, were expert horsemen, assembled together to run at the quintain, and set up a peacock as a reward for the best performer. The king then keeping his court at Westminster, some of his domestics came into the city to see the pastime, where they behaved in a very disorderly manner, and treated the Londoners with much insolence, calling them cowardly knaves and rascally clowns, which the Londoners resented by beating them soundly; the king, however, was incensed at the indignity put upon his servants, and not taking into consideration the provocation on their parts, fined the city one thousand marks.[1] Some have thought these fellows were sent thither purposely to promote a quarrel, it being known that the king was angry with the citizens of London for refusing to join in the crusade.[2]

We may here observe, that the rules of chivalry, at this time, would not admit of any person, under the rank of an esquire, to enter the lists as a combatant at the jousts and tournaments; for which reason the burgesses and yeomen had recourse to the exercise of the quintain, which was not prohibited to any class of the people; but, as the performers were generally young men whose finances would not at all times admit of much expense, the quintain was frequently nothing better than a stake fixed into the ground, with a flat piece of board made fast to the upper part of it, as a substitute for the shield that had been used in times remote; and such as could not procure horses, contented themselves with running at this mark on foot. On plate thirteen we see a representation of a lad mounted on a wooden horse with four wheels, drawn by two of his comrades, tilting at the immoveable quintain; it is taken from a MS. in the Bodleian Library at Oxford, dated 1344.[3] Others, again, made use of a moveable quintain, which was also very simply constructed; consisting only of a cross-bar turning upon a pivot, with a broad part to strike against on one side, and a bag of earth or sand depending from the other: there was a double advantage in these kind of quintains, they were cheap and easily to be procured. Their form, at an early period in the fourteenth century, is illustrated on plates thirteen and fourteen, from the same manuscript. Both these quintains are marked, I know not why, with the figure of a horseshoe.

MANNER OF EXERCISING WITH THE QUINTAIN.—But to return: Stow, in his *Survey of London*, having related the above-mentioned disturbance from Matthew Paris, goes on as follows: "This exercise of running at the quintain was practised in London, as well in the summer as in the winter, but especially at the feast of Christmas. I have seen," continues my author, "a quintain set upon Cornhill by Leadenhall, where the attendants of the lords of merry disports have run and made great pastime; for he that hit not the board end of the quintain was laughed to scorn, and he that hit it full, if he rode not the faster, had a sound blow upon his neck with a bag full of sand hanged on the other

[1] Matthew Paris, *Hist. Angl.* sub. an 1253.   [2] Strype's *Stow*, etc.   [3] Bod. 264.

end."[1] But the form of the modern quintain is more fully described by Dr Plott, in his *History of Oxfordshire*:[2] "They first set a post perpendicularly into the ground, and then place a slender piece of timber on the top of it on a spindle, with a board nailed to it on one end, and a bag of sand hanging at the other; against this board they anciently rode with spears. Now I saw it at Deddington in this county, only with strong staves, which violently bringing about the bag of sand, if they make not good speed away, it strikes them in the neck or shoulders, and sometimes knocks them off their horses; the great design of this sport being to try the agility both of horse and man, and to break the board. It is now," he adds, "only in request at marriages, and set up in the way for young men to ride at as they carry home the bride; he that breaks the board being counted the best man."

*A writer in *Notes and Queries* in 1866 mentions a quintain as then standing at Offham Green, near Maidstone, supposed to be of Elizabethan date. "The cross-piece and weight at one end turned readily upon its pivot."[3]

THE QUINTAIN, A PASTIME BEFORE QUEEN ELIZABETH. — Among other sports exhibited for the amusement of queen Elizabeth, during her residence at Kenilworth Castle, in Warwickshire, then the seat of the earl of Leicester, who entertained her majesty there for several days, A.D. 1575, there was, says Laneham, "a solemn country bridal; when in the castle was set up a comely quintane for feats at armes, where, in a great company of young men and lasses, the bridegroom had the first course at the quintane, and broke his spear "très hardiment" (very boldly, or with much courage). But his mare in his manage did a little stumble, that much ado had his manhood to sit in his saddle. But after the bridegroom had made his course, ran the rest of the band, awhile in some order, but soon after tag and rag, cut and long tail; where the speciality of the sport was to see how some for his slackness had a good bob with the bag, and some for his haste to topple downright, and come tumbling to the post; some striving so much at the first setting out, that it seemed a question between man and beast, whether the race should be performed on horseback or on foot; and some put forth with spurs, would run his race byas, among the thickest of the throng, that down they came together hand over head. Another while he directed his course to the quintane, his judgment would carry him to a mare among the people; another would run and miss the quintane with his staff, and hit the board with his head."[4] This whimsical description may possibly be somewhat exaggerated, but no doubt the inexpertness of the riders subjected them to many laughable accidents.

*The use of the quintain survived in many parts of rural England in the eighteenth century, particularly as a wedding sport. The following passage from Baker's *History of Northamptonshire* records its late use in that county:— "The quintain consisted of a high upright post, at the top of which was placed

---

[1] *Survey of London.*   [2] First published in 1677.
[3] *Notes and Queries*, Ser. III. x. 312.   [4] Laneham in *Queen Elizabeth's Progresses*, by Mr Nichols, vol. i. p. 249.

The Quintain.

a cross piece on a swivel, broad at one end and pierced full of holes, and a bag of sand suspended at the other. The mode of running at the quintain was by an horseman full speed and striking at the broad part with all his force; if he missed his aim he was derided for his want of dexterity; if he struck it and the horse slackened pace, which frequently happened through force of the shock, he received a violent blow on the neck from the bag of sand which swung round from the opposite end; but if he succeeded in breaking the board he was hailed the hero of the day. The last and indeed only instance of this sport which I have met with in this county was in 1722, on the marriage of two servants at Brington, when it was announced in the *Northampton Mercury* that a quintain was to be erected on the green at Kingsthorp, 'and the reward of the horseman that splinters the board is to be a fine garland as a crown of victory, which is to be borne before him to the wedding house, and another is to be put round the neck of his steed; the victor is to have the honour of dancing with the bride, and to sit on her right hand at supper.'"[1]

TILTING AT A WATER BUTT.—At the bottom of plate thirteen is a picture, from a MS. in the Bodleian Library, dated 1343, of three boys tilting jointly at a tub full of water, which is to be struck in such a manner as not to throw it over them. I presume they are learners only, and that therefore they are depicted without their clothes; they undressed themselves, I apprehend, in order to save their garments from being wetted in case the attempt should prove unsuccessful.

This farcical pastime, according to Menestrier, was practised occasionally in Italy, where, he says, a large bucket filled with water is set up, against which they tilt their lances; and if the stroke be not made with great dexterity, the bucket is overset and the lanceman thoroughly drenched with the contents.[2]

THE HUMAN QUINTAIN.—I shall here say a few words concerning the human quintain, which has escaped the notice of most of the writers upon this subject; it is, however, very certain that the military men in the middle ages would sometimes practise with their lances at a man completely armed; whose business it was to act upon the defensive, and parry their blows with his shield. A representation of this exercise occurs upon plate fourteen, taken from the same Bodleian manuscript, dated 1344.

This representation is justified by the concurrent testimony of an ancient author, cited by Du Cange, who introduces one knight saying to another, "I do not by any means esteem you sufficiently valiant (si bons chevalier) for me to take a lance and just with you; therefore I desire you to retire some distance from me, and then run at me with all your force, and I will be your quintain."[3] The satirist Hall, who wrote in the time of Elizabeth, evidently alludes to a custom of this kind, in a satire[4] first printed in 1599, when he was twenty-five years of age. He says:

> Pawne thou no glove for challenge of the deed,
> Nor make thy quintaine other's armed head.

[1] Baker's *Northamptonshire*, i. 40.   [2] *Traité de Tournois*, 1669, p. 347.
[3] Le Roman de Giron le courtois.   Du Cange, Gloss. in voce *quintana*.   [4] Lib. iv. Sat. 3.

EXERCISES PROBABLY DERIVED FROM THE QUINTAIN.—The living quintain, according to the representation just given, is seated upon a stool with three legs without any support behind; and the business, I presume, of the tilter, was to overthrow him; while, on his part, he was to turn the stroke of the pole or lance on one side with his shield, and by doing so with adroitness occasion the fall of his adversary.

Something of a similar kind of exercise, though practised in a different way, appears on plate fifteen, where a man seated, holds up one of his feet, opposed to the foot of another man, who, standing upon one leg, endeavours to thrust him backwards; and again where his opponent is seated in a swing and drawn back by a third person, so that the rope being left at liberty in the swing, the man, of course, descended with great force, and striking the foot of his antagonist with much violence, no doubt very frequently overthrew him. The two last sports were probably never exhibited by military men, but by rustics and others in imitation of the human quintain. The contest between the two figures at the bottom of the same plate seems to depend upon the breaking of the stick which both of them hold, or is a struggle to overthrow each other.

At the top of plate sixteen, taken from a manuscript book of prayers of the fourteenth century, in the possession of Mr Douce, is a representation of two men or boys with a pole or headless spear, who grasp it at either end, and are contending which shall dispossess the other of his hold. This feat the single figure on the same plate, from the Oxford MS. of 1344, seems to have achieved, and is bearing away the pole in triumph.

RUNNING AT THE RING.—Tilting, or, as it is most commonly called, running at the ring, was also a fashionable pastime in former days; the ring is evidently derived from the quintain, and indeed the sport itself is frequently called running or tilting at the quintain. With the Italians, says Du Cange, *quintana* sometimes signifies a ring, hence the Florentines say, "*correr alla quintana*," which with us is called running at the ring: the learned author produces several quotations to the same purpose.[1] Commenius also, in his vocabulary,[2] says, "At this day tilting at the quintain is used where a hoop or ring is struck with a lance." Hence it is clear that the ring was put in the place of the quintain. The excellency of the pastime was to ride at full speed, and thrust the point of the lance through the ring, which was supported in a case or sheath, by the means of two springs, but might be readily drawn out by the force of the stroke, and remain upon the top of the lance. The form of the ring, with the sheath, and the manner in which it was attached to the upright supporter, taken from Pluvinel, are given upon plate sixteen, and also the method of performing the exercise. The letter A indicates the ring detached from the sheath; B represents the sheath with the ring inserted and attached to the upright post, in which there are several holes to raise or lower the ring to suit the conveniency of the performer. At the commencement of the seventeenth century, the

---

[1] *Glossary*, in voce *quintana*.　　　　[2] *Orbis Sensualium Pictus*, by Hoole, 1658.

Tilting at the Ring &c.

pastime of running at the ring was reduced to a science. Pluvinel, who treats this subject at large, says, the length of the course was measured, and marked out according to the properties of the horses that were to run: for one of the swiftest kind, one hundred paces from the starting-place to the ring, and thirty paces beyond it, to stop him, were deemed necessary; but for such horses as had been trained to the exercise, and were more regular in their movements, eighty paces to the ring, and twenty beyond it, were thought to be sufficient. The ring, says the same author, ought to be placed with much precision, somewhat higher than the left eyebrow of the practitioner, when sitting upon his horse; because it was necessary for him to stoop a little in running towards it.[1]

In tilting at the ring, three courses were allowed to each candidate; and he who thrust the point of his lance through it the oftenest, or, in case no such thing was done, struck it the most frequently, was the victor; but if it so happened, that none of them did either the one or the other, or that they were equally successful, the courses were to be repeated until the superiority of one put an end to the contest.[2]

DIFFERENCE BETWEEN TOURNAMENTS AND JOUSTS.—Tournaments and jousts, though often confounded with each other, differed materially. The tournament was a conflict with many knights, divided into parties and engaged at the same time. The joust was a separate trial of skill, when only one man was opposed to another. The latter was frequently included in the former, but not without many exceptions; for the joust, according to the laws of chivalry, might be made exclusive of the tournament.[3]

In the romantic ages, both these diversions were held in the highest esteem, being sanctioned by the countenance and example of the nobility, and prohibited to all below the rank of an esquire; but at the same time the jousts were considered as less honourable than the tournaments; for the knight who had paid his fees and been admitted to the latter, had a right to engage in the former without any further demand, but he who had paid the fees for jousting only, was by no means exempted from the fees belonging to the tournament, as will be found in the laws relative to the lance, sword, and helmet, a little further on.

ORIGIN OF THE TOURNAMENT.—It is an opinion generally received, that the tournament originated from a childish pastime practised by the Roman youths called Ludus Troiæ (the Troy game), said to have been so named because it was derived from the Trojans, and first brought into Italy by Ascanius, the son of Æneas. Virgil has given a description of this pastime, according to the manner, I presume, in which it was practised at Rome. If he be accurate, it seems to have been nothing more than a variety of evolutions performed on horseback. The poet tells us that the youth were each of them armed with two little cornel spears, headed with iron.

Cornea bina ferunt præfixa hastilia ferro.—*Æneid*, lib. v. l. 556.

[1] *Art de monter à cheval*, part iii. p. 156. [2] Menestrier, *Traité de Tournois*, p. 112.
[3] Du Cange, *Glossary*, in voce *justa*.

H

Having passed in review before their parents, upon a signal given, they divided themselves into three distinct companies; and each company consisted of twelve champions exclusive of its appropriate leader, when, according to Trapp's translation, which, if not so poetical, is more literal than Dryden's, the tutor of Ascanius, and overseer of the sports,

> Epityden, from far
> Loud with a shout, and with his sounding lash
> The signal gave : they equally divide,
> The three commanders open their brigades
> In sep'rate bodies : straight recall'd they wheel
> Their course, and onward bear their hostile darts.
> Then diff'rent traverses on various grounds,
> And diff'rent counter traverses they form ;
> Orbs within orbs alternately involve,
> And raise th' effigy of a fight in arms,
> Now show their backs in flight—now furious turn
> Their darts ;—now all in peace together ride.

Under the domination of the first emperors, these games were publicly practised by the young nobility in the circus at Rome.[1]

The same kind of sports, or others bearing close resemblance to them, were established in this kingdom in the twelfth century, and probably at a much earlier period. Fitzstephen, an author then living, informs us, "that every Sunday in Lent, immediately after dinner, it was customary for great crowds of young Londoners mounted on war horses, well trained, to perform the necessary turnings and evolutions, to ride into the fields in distinct bands, armed with shields and headless lances; where they exhibited the representation of battles, and went through a variety of warlike exercises : at the same time many of the young noblemen who had not received the honour of knighthood, came from the king's court, and from the houses of the great barons, to make trial of their skill in arms ; the hope of victory animating their minds. The youth being divided into opposite companies, encountered one another : in one place they fled, and others pursued, without being able to overtake them ; in another place one of the bands overtook and overturned the other." According to Virgil, the Roman youth presented their lances towards their opponents in a menacing position, but without striking with them. The young Londoners in all probability went further, and actually tilted one against the other. At any rate, the frequent practice of this exercise must have taught them, insensibly as it were, to become excellent horsemen.

THE TROY GAME.—I am clearly of opinion, that the jousts and tournaments arose by slow degrees from the exercises appointed for the instruction of the military tyros in using their arms, but which of the two had the pre-eminence in point of antiquity cannot easily be determined; we know that both of them were in existence at the time the Troy game was practised by the citizens of London, and also that they were not permitted to be exercised in this kingdom.

---

[1] Tacitus, *Annal.* lib. xi.

In the middle ages, when the tournaments were in their splendour, the Troy game was still continued, though in a state of improvement, and distinguished by a different denomination it was then called in Latin *behordicum*, and in French *bohourt* or *behourt*, and was a kind of lance game, in which the young nobility exercised themselves, to acquire address in handling of their arms, and to prove their strength.

TOURNAMENTS.—Our word tournament, or tournoyement, which signifies to turn or wheel about in a circular manner,[1] comes from the French word *tournoy*. I am led to adopt the opinion of Fauchet,[2] who thinks it came from the practice of the knights running *par tour*, that is, by turns, at the quintain, and wheeling about successively in a circle to repeat their course ; but, says he, in process of time they improved upon this pastime, and to make it more respectable ran one at another, which certainly bore a much greater similitude to a real engagement, especially when they were divided into large parties, and meeting together combated with clubs or maces, beating each other soundly, without any favour or paying the least respect to rank or dignity. In one of these encounters, Robert, earl of Cleremont, son of Saint Louis, and head of the house of Bourbon, was so severely bruised by the blows he received from his antagonist, that he was never well afterwards. This, says Fauchet, was possibly the cause of the ordinance, that the kings and princes should not afterwards enter the lists as combatants at these tournaments ; which law, indeed, continues he, has been ill observed by the succeeding kings, and in our time by Henry II., who, unfortunately for France, was killed at the jousts he made in honour of his daughter's marriage. It was, in fact, very common for some of the combatants to be beat or thrown from their horses, trampled upon and killed upon the spot, or hurt most grievously. Indeed, a tournament at this period was rarely finished without some disastrous accident ; and it was an established law, that if any one of the combatants killed or wounded another, he should be indemnified ; which made them less careful respecting the consequences, especially when any advantage gave them an opportunity of securing the conquest. Tournaments were consequently interdicted by the ecclesiastical decrees.

The following quotation from an ancient manuscript romance, in the Harleian Collection, entitled *Ipomydon*,[3] plainly indicates the performance of the tournament in an open field ; and also, that great numbers of the combatants were engaged at one time, promiscuously encountering with each other ; we learn, moreover, that the champion who remained unhorsed at the conclusion of the sports, besides the honour he attained, sometimes received a pecuniary reward.

> The kyng his sonne a knyght gan make,
> And many another for his sake ;
> Justes were cryed ladyes to see,
> Thedyr came lordes grete plente.
> Tournementis atyred in the felde,
> A thousand armed with spere and shelde ;

---

[1] Cotgrave. [2] *Origines des Chevaliers*, etc., p. 9. [3] No. 2252, fol. 61.

Knyghtis began togedre to ryde,
Some were unhorsyd on every side,
Ipomydom that daye was victorius,
And there he gaff many a cours ;
For there was none that he mette,
But he hys spere on hym woulde sette :
Then after within a lytell stounde,[1]
Horse and man both went to grounde.
The Heraudes [2] gaff the child the gree,[3]
A thousand pound he had to fee ;
Mynstrellys had giftes of golde
And fourty dayes this fest was holde.

In some instances the champions depended upon their military skill and horse-manship, and frequently upon their bodily strength ; but at all times it was highly disgraceful to be unhorsed, by whatever exertion it might be effected.

Thomas of Walsingham tells us,[4] that when Edward I. returned from Palestine to England, and was on his passage through Savoy, the earl of Chabloun invited him to a tournament,[5] in which himself and many other knights were engaged. The king with his followers, although fatigued by the length of their journey, accepted the challenge. On the day appointed both parties met, and, being armed with swords, the engagement commenced ; the earl singled out the king, and on his approach, throwing away his sword, cast his arms about the neck of the monarch, and used his utmost endeavour to pull him from his horse. Edward, on the other hand, finding the earl would not quit his hold, put spurs to his horse, and drew him from his saddle hanging upon his neck, and then shaking him violently, threw him to the ground. The earl having recovered himself and being remounted, attacked the king a second time, but finding his hand "too heavy," he gave up the contest, and acknowledged him to be the conqueror. The knights of the earl's party were angry when they saw their leader drawn from his horse, and run upon the English with so much violence, that the pastime assumed the tumultuous appearance of a real battle ; the English on their side repelled force by force ; and had not the resigna-tion of the earl put an end to the conflict, in all probability the consequences would have been very serious.

LISTS AND BARRIERS.—It was a considerable time after the establishment of jousts and tournaments, before the combatants thought of making either lists or barriers ; they contented themselves, says Menestrier,[6] with being stationed at four angles of an open place, whence they run in parties one against another. There were cords stretched before the different companies, previous to the commencement of the tournaments, as we learn from the following passage in an old English romance, among the Harleian manuscripts :[7] "All these thinges donne thei were embatailed eche ageynste the othir, and the corde drawen

---

[1] A small space of time.
[2] Heralds, whose office it was to superintend the ceremonious parts of the tournaments.
[3] Reward. 　　　　[4] *Hist. Angl.* fol. 3, A.D. 1274.
[5] *Ludum militarum (qui vulgo torneamentum dicitur). Ibid.*
[6] *Traité de Tournois.* 　　　　[7] No. 326.

before eche partie, and whan the tyme was, the cordes were cutt, and the trumpettes blew up for every man to do his devoir, *duty*. And for to assertayne the more of the tourney, there was on eche side a stake, and at eache stake two kyngs of armes, with penne, and inke, and paper, to write the names of all them that were yolden, for they shold no more tournay." As these pastimes were accompanied with much danger, they invented in France the double lists, where the knights might run from one side to the other, without coming in contact, except with their lances; other nations followed the example of the French, and the usage of lists and barriers soon became universal.

WHEN THE TOURNAMENT WAS FIRST PRACTISED.—It is impossible to ascertain the precise period when tournaments first made their appearance; nor is it less difficult to determine by whom they were invented. Peacham, on the authority of Nicetas, tells us, that the emperor Emanuel Comminus, at the siege of Constantinople, invented tilts and tournaments;[1] but this is certainly a mistake. The French and the Germans both claim the honour. The historian, Nithard, mentions a military game, frequently exhibited in Germany, before the emperor Louis, and his brother Charles the Bald, about the year 842, which bears great resemblance to the tournament; for he speaks of many knights of different nations, divided into parties equal in number, and running at each other with great velocity, as though they were in battle.[2] Most of the German writers, however, make the emperor Henry I., surnamed L'oiseleur, who died in 936, the institutor of these pastimes; but others attribute their origin to another Henry, at least a century posterior. The French, on their side, quote an ancient history,[3] which asserts, that Geoffrey, lord of Previlli in Anjou, who was slain at Gaunt in 1066, was the inventor of the tournament.

THE TOURNAMENT IN ENGLAND.—It seems to be certain that tournaments were held in France and Normandy before the conquest, and, according to our own writers, they were not permitted to be practised in this country for upwards of sixty years posterior to that event. The manner of performing the tournament, as then used, says Lambarde, "not being at the tilt, as I think, but at random and in the open field, was accounted so dangerous to the persons having to do therein, that sundry popes forbad it by decree; and the kings of this realm before king Stephen would not suffer it to be frequented within their land, so that such as for exercise of this feat of arms were desirous to prove themselves, were driven to pass over the seas, and to perform it in some different place in a foreign country."[4] This author's statement of the fact is perfectly correct. In the troublesome reign of king Stephen, the rigour of the laws was much relaxed, and tournaments, among other splendid species of dissipation, were permitted to be exercised; they were, however, again suppressed by Henry II.; and therefore it was, I presume, that the young king Henry, son of Henry II., went every third year, as Matthew Paris assures us he did, over the seas, and expended

---

[1] *Complete Gentleman*, p. 178.
[2] See more upon this subject in the *Encyclopédie François*, art. "Tournoi."
[3] *Chronique de Tours*.
[4] *Perambulation of Kent*, p. 492.

vast sums of money "in conflictibus Gallicis," or French combats, meaning tournaments.[1] But Richard I. having, as it is said, observed that the French practising frequently in the tournaments, were more expert in the use of their arms than the English, permitted his own knights to establish the like martial sports in his dominions; but at the same time he imposed a tax, according to their quality, upon such as engaged in them. An earl was subjected to the fine of twenty marks for his privilege to enter the field as a combatant; a baron, ten; a knight having a landed estate, four; and a knight without such possession, two; but all foreigners were particularly excluded.

*The holding of tournaments was restricted by Richard to five places or districts, namely between (1) Salisbury and Wilton, (2) Warwick and Kenilworth, (3) Stamford and Warmington,[2] (4) Brackley and Mixbury, and (5) Tickhill and Blyth. To these must be added Smithfield for the use of the citizens of London on Saturdays. Frequent endeavours were made in the thirteenth and fourteenth centuries to hold tournaments elsewhere, but they were always proclaimed, save when they were held under royal license. The act also specifies that the peace should not be broken thereby, nor justice hindered, nor damage done to the royal forests.[3]

How long these imposts continued to be collected does not appear; but tournaments were occasionally exhibited with the utmost display of magnificence in the succeeding reigns, being not only sanctioned by royal authority, but frequently instituted at the royal command, until the conclusion of the sixteenth century. From that period they declined rapidly, and fifty years afterwards were entirely out of practice.

LAWS AND ORDINANCES OF JOUSTS AND TOURNAMENTS.—All military men, says Fauchet,[4] who bore the title of knights or esquires, were not indiscriminately received at these tournaments: there were certain laws to which those who presented themselves became subject, and which they swore to obey before they were permitted to enter the lists.

In one of the Harleian manuscripts,[5] I met with the following ordinance for the conducting of the jousts and tournaments according to the ancient establishment. It is preceded by a proclamation that was to be previously made, which is couched in these terms: Be it known, lords, knights, and esquires, ladies, and gentlewomen; you are hereby acquainted, that a superb achievement at arms, and a grand and noble tournament will be held in the parade[6] of Clarencieux, king-at-arms, on the part of the most noble baron, lord of T. C.B., and on the part of the most noble baron, the lord of C. B.D., in the parade of

---

[1] *Hist. Angl.* A.D. 1179.

[2] "Stamford and Wallingford" is mistakenly given in Godwin's *Archæologist's Hand-Book* and elsewhere. Wallingford, Berks, is absurdly remote from Stamford; Warmington is but a little distance from Stamford, on the main road to Oundle.

[3] Harl. MS. 69. "The Booke of Certaine Triumphs," which opens with an account of the "Just-Roiall" at the marriage of Richard, duke of York, son of Edward IV.

[4] *Origines des Chevaliers*, etc.   [5] No. 69.

[6] *Marche*, part of the lists, I presume, or portion of ground appropriated to the tournament.

Norroy, king-at-arms. The regulations that follow are these: The two barons on whose parts the tournament is undertaken, shall be at their lodges (pavilions) two days before the commencement of the sports, when each of them shall cause his arms to be attached[1] to his pavilion, and set up his banner in the front of his parade; and all those who wish to be admitted as combatants on either side, must in like manner set up their arms and banners before the parades allotted to them. Upon the evening of the same day they shall show themselves in their stations, and expose their helmets to view at the windows of their pavilions; and then "they may depart to make merry, dance, and live well." On the morrow the champions shall be at their parades by the hour of ten in the morning, to await the commands of the lord of the parade, and the governor, who are the speakers of the tournament; at this meeting the prizes of honour shall be determined.

In the document before us, it is said, that he who shall best resist the strokes of his adversary, and return them with most adroitness on the party of Clarencieux, shall receive a very rich sword, and he who shall perform in like manner the best on the part of Norroy, shall be rewarded with an helmet equally valuable.

On the morning of the day appointed for the tournament, the arms, banners, and helmets of all the combatants shall be exposed at their stations, and the speakers present at the place of combat by ten of the clock, where they shall examine the arms and approve or reject them at their pleasure; the examination being finished, and the arms returned to the owners, the baron who is the challenger shall then cause his banner to be placed at the beginning of the parade, and the blazon of his arms to be nailed to the roof of the pavilion:[2] his example is to be followed by the baron on the opposite side, and all the knights of either party who are not in their stations before the nailing up of the arms, shall forfeit their privileges, and not be permitted to tourney.

The kings-at-arms and the heralds are then commanded by the speakers to go from pavilion to pavilion, crying aloud, "To achievement, knights and esquires, to achievement";[3] being the notice, I presume, for them to arm themselves; and soon afterwards the company of heralds shall repeat the former ceremony, having the same authority, saying, "Come forth, knights and esquires, come forth":[4] and when the two barons have taken their places in the lists, each of them facing his own parade, the champions on both parties shall arrange themselves, every one by the side of his banner; and then two cords shall be stretched between them, and remain in that position until it shall please the speakers to command the commencement of the sports. The combatants shall each of them be armed with a pointless sword having the edges rebated,

---

[1] *Feront clouer leurs armes,* literally nail them; the clouage or nail money, as we shall see afterwards, was the perquisite of the heralds.

[2] "*Mettra sa banier, au commencement dedits bastons et clouera la blason de ses armes, à lautre vout.*" The passage is by no means clear; I have therefore given the words of the original.

[3] *A l'aschevier, chevaliers,* etc.   [4] *Hors chevaliers,* etc.

and with a baston, or truncheon, hanging from their saddles, and they may use either the one or the other so long as the speakers shall give them permission, by repeating the sentence, "Laisseir les aler," Let them go on. After they have sufficiently performed their exercises, the speakers are to call to the heralds, and order them to "ployer vos baniers," fold up the banners, which is the signal for the conclusion of the tournament. The banners being rolled up, the knights and the esquires are permitted to return to their dwellings.

PAGES AND PERQUISITES OF THE KINGS-AT-ARMS, ETC.—Every knight or esquire performing in the tournament was permitted to have one page, armed, within the lists, but without a truncheon or any other defensive weapon, to wait upon him and give him his sword, or truncheon, as occasion might require ; and also in case of any accident happening to his armour, to amend the same. In after times, three servitors were allowed for this purpose.

The laws of the tournament permitted any one of the combatants to unhelm himself at pleasure, if he was incommoded by the heat ; none being suffered to assault him in any way, until he had replaced his helmet at the command of the speakers.

The kings-at-arms, and the heralds who proclaimed the tournament, had the privilege of wearing the blazon of arms of those by whom the sport was instituted ; besides which they were entitled to six ells of scarlet cloth as their fee, and had all their expenses defrayed during the continuation of the tournament : by the law of arms they had a right to the helmet of every knight when he made his first essay at the tournament, which became their perquisite as soon as the sports were concluded ; they also claimed every one of them six crowns as nail money, for affixing the blazon of arms to the pavilions. The kings-at-arms held the banners of the two chief barons on the day of the tournament, and the other heralds the banners of their confederates according to their rank.

PRELIMINARIES OF THE TOURNAMENT.—An illumination to a manuscript romance in the Royal Library,[1] entitled *St Graal,* written in the thirteenth century, represents the manner in which the two chief barons anciently entered the lists at the commencement of a tournament. The king-at-arms standing in the midst of the ground holds both the banners, and the instruments of the minstrels are ornamented with the blazonry of the arms (plate seventeen). The action of the two combatants, who have not yet received their weapons, seems to be that of appealing to heaven in proof of their having no charm to protect them, and no inclination to make use of any unlawful means to secure the conquest ; which I believe was a ceremony usually practised upon such occasions.

In the reign of Henry V. a statute was enacted by the parliament, containing the following regulations relative to the tournaments, which regulations were said to have been established at the request of all the nobility of England.[2] The act prohibits any combatant from entering the lists with more than three esquires to bear his arms, and wait upon him for that day. In another clause it

[1] No. 14, E. iii.　　　　　[2] Harl. MS. 69.

Tournament.

is said, If any of the great lords, or others, keep a public table, they shall not be allowed any additional esquires, excepting those who carve for them. It further specifies, that no knight or esquire, who was appointed to attend in the lists as a servitor, should wear a sword or a dagger, or carry a truncheon, or any other weapon excepting a large sword used in the tournament; and that all the combatants who bore lances, should be armed with breastplates, thigh-pieces, shoulder-pieces, and bascinets, without any other kind of armour. No earl, baron, or knight might presume to infringe upon the regulations of this statute, under the forfeiture of his horse and his arms, and the pain of imprisonment for a certain space of time, at the pleasure of the governors of the tournament. Another clause, which probably refers to such as were not combatants for the day, runs thus: No one except the great lords, that is to say, earls or barons, shall be armed otherwise than above expressed; nor bear a sword, pointed knife, mace, or other weapon, except the sword for the tournament. In case of transgression, he forfeited his horse, and was obnoxious to imprisonment for one year. If an esquire transgressed the law in any point, he not only lost his horse and his arms, but was sent to prison for three years. But if the knights or esquires in the above cases were possessed of lands, and appeared in arms for the service of their lords, it seems they might recover their horses. The "Roys des harnoys," kings-at-arms, the heralds, and the minstrels, were commanded not to wear any kind of sharp weapons, but to have the swords without points which belonged to them. Those who came as spectators on horseback were strictly forbidden to be armed with any kind of armour, or to bear any offensive weapons, under the penalty that was appointed to the esquires; and no boy or man on foot, coming for the same purpose, might appear with a sword, dagger, cudgel, or lance; they were to be punished with one year's imprisonment in case of disobedience to the statute.

LISTS FOR ORDEAL COMBATS. — The lists for the tilts and tournaments resembled those, I doubt not, appointed for the ordeal combats, which, according to the rules established by Thomas, duke of Gloucester, uncle to Richard II., were as follows: "The king shall find the field to fight in, and the lists shall be made and devised by the constable; and it is to be observed, that the list must be sixty paces long and forty paces broad, set up in good order, and the ground within hard, stable, and level, without any great stones or other impediments; also that the lists must be made with one door to the east, and another to the west, and strongly barred about with good bars seven feet high or more, so that a horse may not be able to leap over them." [1]

RESPECT PAID TO LADIES IN THE TOURNAMENT.—After the conclusion of the tournament, the combatants, as we have seen above, returned to their dwellings; but in the evening they met again in some place appropriated for the purpose, where they were joined by the ladies, and others of the nobility who had been spectators of the sports; and the time, we are told, was passed in

---

[1] Cotton MS. Nero D. vi. and Harl. MS. 69, *ut supra*.

feasting, dancing, singing, and making merry. But, "after the noble supper and dancing," according to the ancient ordinance above quoted, the speakers of the tournament called together the heralds appointed on both parties, and demanded from them, alternately, the names of those who had best performed upon the opposite sides; the double list of names was then presented to the ladies who had been present at the pastime, and the decision was referred to them respecting the awardment of the prizes;[1] who selected one name for each party, and, as a peculiar mark of their esteem, the favourite champions received the rewards of their merits from the hands of two young virgins of quality. The statutes and ordinances for jousts and tournaments made by John Tiptoft, earl of Worcester, at the command of Edward IV., in the sixth year of his reign, conclude thus: "Reserving always to the queenes highness and the ladyes there present, the attribution and gift of the prize after the manner and forme accustomed."[2]

Neither was this the only deference that was paid to the fair sex by the laws of the tournament, for we are told, that if a knight conducted himself with any impropriety, or transgressed the ordinances of the sport, he was excluded from the lists with a sound beating, which was liberally bestowed upon him by the other knights with their truncheons, to punish his temerity, and to teach him to respect the honour of the ladies and the rights of chivalry; the unfortunate culprit had no other resource in such case for escaping without mischief, but by supplicating the mercy of the fair sex, and humbly intreating them to interpose their authority on his behalf, because the suspension of his punishment depended entirely upon their intercession.

JOUSTS INFERIOR TO TOURNAMENTS.—The joust or lance-game, in Latin *justa*, and in French *jouste*, which some derive from *jocare*, because it was a sort of sportive combat, undertaken for pastime only, differed materially, as before observed, from the tournament, the former being often included in the latter, and usually took place when the grand tournamental conflict was finished. But at the same time it was perfectly consistent with the rules of chivalry, for the jousts to be held separately; it was, however, considered as a pastime inferior to the tournament, for which reason a knight, who had paid his fees for permission to joust, was not thereby exempted from the fees of the tournament; but, on the contrary, if he had discharged his duties at the tournament, he was privileged to joust without being liable to any further demand. This distinction seems to have arisen from the weapons used, the sword being appropriated to the tournament, and the lance to the joust, and so it is stated in an old document cited by Du Cange.[3] "When," says this author, "a nobleman makes his first appearance in the tournament, his helmet is claimed by the heralds, notwithstanding his having jousted before, because the lance cannot give the freedom of the sword, which the sword can do of the lance; for it is to be observed, that

---

[1] "Avec une grêle de coups." *Encyclop. Fran.* in voce *tournoi.*
[2] Harl. MS. 69.   [3] *Glossary*, in voce *justa.*

he who has paid his helmet at the tournament is freed from the payment of a second helmet at the joust; but the helmet paid at jousting does not exclude the claim of the heralds when a knight first enters the lists at the tournament."

THE ROUND TABLE.—The joust, as a military pastime, is mentioned by William of Malmsbury, and said to have been practised in the reign of king Stephen.[1] During the government of Henry III. the joust assumed a different appellation, and was also called the Round Table game.[2] This name was derived from a fraternity of knights who frequently jousted with each other, and accustomed themselves to eat together in one apartment, and, in order to set aside all distinction of rank or quality, seated themselves at a circular table, where every place was equally honourable. Athenæus, cited by Du Cange,[3] says, the knights sat round the table, bearing their shields at their backs: I suppose for safety sake. Our historians attribute the institution of the round table to Arthur, the son of Uter Pendragon, a celebrated British hero, whose achievements are so disguised with legendary wonders, that it has been doubted if such a person ever existed in reality.

In the eighth year of the reign of Edward I., Roger de Mortimer,[4] a nobleman of great opulence, established a round table at Kenilworth, for the encouragement of military pastimes; where one hundred knights, with as many ladies, were entertained at his expense. The fame of this institution occasioned, we are told, a great influx of foreigners, who came either to initiate themselves, or make some public proof of their prowess. About seventy years afterwards Edward III. erected a splendid table of the same kind at Windsor, but upon a more extensive scale. It contained the area of a circle two hundred feet in diameter; and the weekly expense for the maintenance of this table, when it was first established, amounted to one hundred pounds; which, afterwards, was reduced to twenty pounds, on account of the large sums of money required for the prosecution of the war with France. This receptacle for military men gave continual occasion for the exercise of arms, and afforded to the young nobility an opportunity of learning, by the way of pastime, all the requisites of a soldier. The example of king Edward was followed by Philip of Valois, king of France, who also instituted a round table at his court, and by that means drew thither many German and Italian knights who were coming to England.[5] The contest between the two monarchs seems to have had the effect of destroying the establishment of the round table in both kingdoms, for after this period we hear no more concerning it. In England the round table was succeeded by the Order of the Garter, the ceremonial parts of which order are retained to this day, but the spirit of the institution ill accords with the present manners.

---

[1] "Pugnæ facere quod justam vocant." *Hist. Novellæ*, fol. 106, sub an. 1142.

[2] Matthew Paris properly distinguishes it from the tournament. "Non hastiludio, quod torneamentum dicitur, sed —ludo militari, qui mensa rotunda dicitur." *Hist. Angl.* sub an. 1252.

[3] *Glossary*, in voce *Mensa Rotunda*.

[4] Rogerus de Mortuo Mari. Tho. Walsingham, *Hist. Angl.* sub an. 1280, fol. 8.

[5] Tho. Walsingham, *Hist. Angl.* sub an. 1344, fol. 154.

NATURE OF THE JOUSTS.—The cessation of the round table occasioned little or no alteration respecting the jousts which had been practised by the knights belonging to it; they continued to be fashionable throughout the annals of chivalry, and latterly superseded the tournaments, which is by no means surprising, when we recollect that the one was a confused engagement of many knights together, and the other a succession of combats between two only at one time, which gave them all an equal opportunity of showing individually their dexterity and attracting the general notice.

In the jousts the combatants most commonly used spears without heads of iron; and the excellency of the performance consisted in striking the opponent upon the front of his helmet, so as to beat him backwards from his horse or break the spear. Froissart[1] mentions a trick used by Reynaud de Roy, at a tilting match between him and John de Holland: he fastened his helmet so slightly upon his head that it gave way, and was beaten off by every stroke that was made upon the vizor with the lance of John of Holland, and of course the shock he received was not so great as it would have been, had he made the helmet fast to the cuirass; this artifice was objected to by the English on the part of Holland; but John of Gaunt, duke of Lancaster, who was present, permitted Roye to use his pleasure; though he at the same time declared, that for his part, he should prefer a contrary practice, and have his helmet fastened as strongly as possible. And again the same historian, speaking of a jousting between Thomas Harpingham and Sir John de Barres, says, "As me thought the usage was thanne, their helmes wer tied but with a lace, to the entente the spere should take no hold"; by which it seems the trick became more common afterwards.[2]

On plate eighteen is a representation of the joust, taken from a manuscript in the Royal Library,[3] of the thirteenth, or early in the fourteenth century, where two knights appear in the action of tilting at each other with the blunted spears.

This delineation was made before the introduction of the barrier, which was a boarded railing erected in the midst of the lists, but open at both ends, and between four and five feet in height. In performing the jousts, the two combatants rode on separate sides of the barrier, and were thereby prevented from running their horses upon each other.

*This dividing of the lists was at first done by having a long cloth (*toile*) suspended on a rope along the centre of the ground. The riders stationed themselves one at each side and end of this *toile*, which was called in English the tilt.[4] The first time the tilt is mentioned in the chronicles of Froissart and Monstrelet is on the occasion of some jousting at Dijon in 1443; it was not introduced until the beginning of the fifteenth century. At Dijon on this

---

[1] Vol. iii. chap. lix.
[2] Froissart, vol. iii. chap. cxxxiii. fol. 148, Lord Berners' translation. [3] No. 14, E. iii.
[4] This word in its original signification tarries with us in the term "waggon-*tilt*," which means a canvas cover.

occasion the cloth and cord, or tilt, was six feet high. This form of tilt or division was soon, however, found to be ineffective and occasionally dangerous, and gave way generally, by the middle of the fifteenth century, to a wooden partition. The rules for tilting, or jousting over the tilt, were, according to Viscount Dillon, to this effect : [1]—

Breaking a spear between the saddle and the fastening of the helmet to the breast	1 point
Breaking a spear above this place	2 points
Breaking a spear so as to unhorse the opponent or unarm him, so that he could not run the next course	3 points

But—

Breaking a spear on the saddle forfeited	1 point
Striking the tilt once forfeited	2 points
Striking the tilt twice forfeited	3 points

*The striking of a horse or an opponent on the back, or after he was disarmed, or striking the tilt thrice, disqualified the offender from further contention.

*In Henry VIII.'s reign this tilting was frequently practised. The grand tilting of the king and chief nobles is splendidly pourtrayed on the Tournament Roll of the Heralds' College.

*Tilting, notwithstanding all precautions, was a dangerous sport. On the occasion of king Francis' marriage at Paris in February 1515, the duke of Suffolk wrote to Henry VIII. that many had been hurt at the tilting, and one in the throat like to die.[2] At the Field of the Cloth of Gold in 1520, where both Henry and Francis distinguished themselves, a Frenchman died of a blow he had received on the previous day.

*There were permanent tilt-yards in the sixteenth century at Westminster, Hampton Court, and Greenwich. The tilt is marked on old maps of Westminster; it was on the site of the Horse Guards Parade, and the guardroom there is still known as the Tilt Guard. In the Tower collection are several fine examples of the tilt lance. The largest is that attributed to Charles Brandon, duke of Suffolk; its total length is 14 ft. 4 in., and the girth just in front of the grip is $27\frac{1}{2}$ in.; it is hollow and weighs 20 lbs. Six other examples average twelve feet in length.

JOUSTS PECULIARLY IN HONOUR OF THE LADIES.—We have seen that the privilege of distributing the prizes and remitting the punishment of offenders was, by the laws of the tournament, invested with the fair sex, but at the jousts their authority was much more extensive. In the days of chivalry the jousts were usually made in honour of the ladies, who presided as judges paramount over the sports, and their determinations were in all cases decisive; hence in the spirit of romance, arose the necessity for every "true knight" to have a favourite fair one, who was not only esteemed by him as the paragon of beauty and of virtue, but supplied the place of a tutelar saint, to whom he paid his

[1] *Archæological Journal*, v. 296-321, "Tilting in Tudor Times."   [2] Calig. D. vi. fol. 165.

vows and addressed himself in the day of peril; or it seems to have been an established doctrine, that love made valour perfect, and incited the heroes to undertake great enterprises. "Oh that my lady saw me!" said one of them as he was mounting a breach at the head of his troops and driving the enemy before him. The French writer St Foix, who mentions this,[1] says in another place, "It is astonishing that no author has remarked the origin of this devotion in the manners of the Germans, our ancestors, as drawn by Tacitus, who," he tells us, "attributed somewhat of divinity to the fair sex."[2] Sometimes it seems the knights were armed and unarmed by the ladies; but this, I presume, was a peculiar mark of their favour, and only used upon particular occasions, as, for instance, when the heroes undertook an achievement on their behalf, or combating in defence of their beauty or their honour.[3]

GREAT SPLENDOUR OF THESE SPORTS ATTRACTIVE TO THE NOBILITY.—At the celebration of these pastimes, the lists were superbly decorated, and surrounded by the pavilions belonging to the champions, ornamented with their arms, banners, and banerolls. The scaffolds for the reception of the nobility of both sexes who came as spectators, and those especially appointed for the royal family, were hung with tapestry and embroideries of gold and silver. Every person, upon such occasions, appeared to the greatest advantage, decked in sumptuous array, and every part of the field presented to the eye a rich display of magnificence. We may also add the splendid appearance of the knights engaged in the sports; themselves and their horses were most gorgeously arrayed, and their esquires and pages, together with the minstrels and heralds who superintended the ceremonies, were all of them clothed in costly and glittering apparel. Such a show of pomp, where wealth, beauty, and grandeur were concentred, as it were, in one focus, must altogether have formed a wonderful spectacle, and made a strong impression on the mind, which was not a little heightened by the cries of the heralds, the clangour of the trumpets, the clashing of the arms, the rushing together of the combatants, and the shouts of the beholders; and hence the popularity of these exhibitions may be easily accounted for.

The tournament and the joust, and especially the latter, afforded to those who were engaged in them an opportunity of appearing before the ladies to the greatest advantage; they might at once display their taste and opulence by the costliness and elegancy of their apparel, and their prowess as soldiers; therefore these pastimes became fashionable among the nobility; and it was probably for the same reason that they were prohibited to the commoners.

TOYS FOR INITIATING CHILDREN IN THESE SPORTS.—Persons of rank were taught in their childhood to relish such exercises as were of a martial

---

[1] Essais Hist. sur Paris, vol. iii. p. 263.　　　　　[2] Ibid. vol. i. p. 327.

[3] As the ladies, say some modern authors, were l'âme, the soul of the jousts, it was proper that they should be therein distinguished by some peculiar homage; and accordingly, at the termination of a joust with lances, the last course was made in honour of the sex, and called the lance of the ladies. The same deference was paid to them in single combats with the sword, the axe, and the dagger.

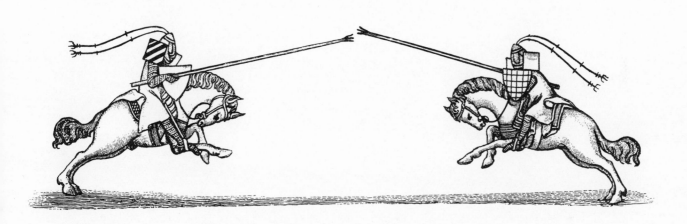

Justs.

nature, and the very toys that were put into their hands as playthings were calculated to bias the mind in their favour. These toy figures could be readily separated from the horses, and were so contrived as to be thrown backwards by a smart blow upon the top of the shield or the front of his helmet, and replaced again with much ease; two such toys were requisite, and by the concussion of the spears and shields, if dexterously managed, one or both of the men were cast to the ground. These toys, as we may see on plate sixteen, from a curious engraving on wood by Hans Burgmair, which makes one of a series of prints representing the history and achievements of the emperor Maximilian the First, were pushed by the hand upon a table towards each other.

BOAT JOUSTS, OR TILTING ON THE WATER.—It has been previously observed, that all persons below the rank of an esquire were excluded from the jousts and the tournaments; but the celebration of these pastimes attracted the common mind in a very powerful manner, and led to the institution of sports, that bore at least some resemblance to them : tilting at the quintain was generally practised at a very early period,[1] and jousting upon the ice by the young Londoners. The early inclination to join in such kind of pastimes is strongly indicated by the two boys represented upon the top of plate eighteen : the place of the horse is supplied by a long switch, and that of a lance by another. The original delineation occurs in a beautiful MS. book of prayers, written in the fourteenth century, in the possession of Mr Douce. Here we may also add the boat jousts, or tilting upon the water. The representation of a pastime of this kind is given at the bottom of the same plate, from a manuscript of the fourteenth century in the Royal Library.[2]

The conqueror at these jousts was the champion who could dexterously turn aside the blow of his antagonist with his shield, and at the same time strike him with his lance in such a manner as to overthrow him into the river, himself remaining unmoved from his station; and perhaps not a little depended upon the skill of the rowers. When queen Elizabeth visited Sandwich in 1573, she was entertained with a tilting upon the water, "where certain wallounds that could well swym had prepared two boates, and in the middle of each boate was placed a borde, upon which borde there stood a man, and so they met together, with either of them a staff and a shield of wood ; and one of them did overthrowe another, at which the queene had good sport."[3] The same kind of laughable pastime was practised at London, as we learn from Stow. "I have seen," says he, "in the summer season, upon the river of Thames, some rowed in wherries, with staves in their hands flat at the fore end, running one against another, and for the most part one or both of them were overthrown and well ducked."

CHALLENGES TO ALL COMERS.—I shall now conclude this long chapter with the two following extracts from a manuscript in the Harleian Collection.[4] Six gentlemen challenged "all commers at the just roial, to runne in osting harnies

---

[1] See sect. vii. p. 118. [2] No. 1, B. vii. [3] Nichols' *Progresses*, vol. i. p. 56. [4] No. 69.

along a tilte, and to strike thirteen strokes with swordes, in honour of the marriage of Richard duke of York[1] with the Lady Anne, daughter to the duke of Norfolk."

When Henry VII. created his second son Henry prince of Wales, four gentlemen offered their service upon the occasion. First, they made a declaration that they do not undertake this enterprise in any manner of presumption, but only "for the laude and honour of the feaste, the pleasure of the ladyes, and their owne learning, and exercise of deedes of armes, and to ensewe the ancient laudable customs."

They then promised to be ready at Westminster on a given day, the twenty-fourth of November, to keep the jousts in a place appointed for that purpose by the king. To be there by "eleven of the clock before noone to answer all gentlemen commers, and to runne with every commer one after another, six courses ensewingly; and to continue that daye as long as it shal like the kynges grace, and to tilt with such speares as he shall ordeyn, of the which speares, the commers shall have the choise; but if the said six courses by every one of the commers shall be performed, and the day not spent in pleasure and sport according to the effect of these articles, it shall then be lawful for the said commers to begin six other courses, and so continue one after another as long as it shall be at the king's pleasure. If it shall happen to any gentleman that his horse fayleth him, or himself be unarmed in such wise as he cannot conveniently accomplish the whole courses, then it shall be lawful for his felowe to finish up the courses."

Again, they promise upon a second day, the twenty-ninth of November, to be in readiness to mount their horses at the same place and hour as before, to tourney with four other gentlemen, with such swordes as the king shall ordain, until eighteen strokes be given by one of them to the other; and add that it shall be lawful to strike all manner of ways, the foyne only excepted, and the commers shall have their choice of the swords. Here it may be observed, that to foyne, is to thrust, as in fencing, which was exceedingly dangerous when the swords were pointed. The author of a MS. poem, in the Cotton Collection,[2] frequently referred to in the course of this work, entitled *Knyghthode and Batayle*, says, in fighting with an enemy, "to foyne is better than to smyte," and afterwards two inches, "entre foyned," hurteth more than a broader wound with the edge of a sword.

"Whosoever," continues the Harleian manuscript, "shall certifye and give knowledge of his name and of his comming to one of the three kings of arms, whether it be to the jousts or at the tourney, he shall be first answered, the states always reserved which shall have the prehemience. If any one of the said commers shall think the swordes or spears be too easy for him, the said four gentlemen will be redye to answer him or them after their owne minde, the king's licence obteyned in that behalf."

---

[1] Son to king Edward IV., who lost his life with his brother Edward in the Tower. [2] Titus, A. xxiii. part i. fol. 7.

The gentlemen then entreat the king to sign the articles with his own hand, as sufficient licence for the heralds to publish the same in such places as might be thought requisite. The king accepted their offer, and granted their petition; at the same time he promised to reward the best performer at the jousts royal with a ring of gold set with a ruby; and the best performer at the tournament with another golden ring set with a diamond, equal in value to the former.

Upon some particular occasions the strokes with the sword were performed on foot, and so were the combats with the axes; the champions having, generally, a barrier of wood breast-high between them.

CHAPTER II

Ancient Plays—Miracle Plays, Dramas from Scripture, etc. continued several days—The Coventry Play—Mysteries described—How enlivened—The "Pageant" or Stage—Cornish Miracle Plays—Moralities described—Secular Plays—Interludes—Chaucer's Definition of the Tragedies of his Time—Plays on Holy Days—Royal Companies of Players—The Puritans—Court Plays—Play in honour of the Princess Mary's Marriage—The Play of Hock-Tuesday—Decline of Secular Plays—Sir Miles Stapleton and Yorkshire Players—Origin of Puppet Plays—Nature of the Performances—Giants and other Puppet Characters—Puppet Plays superseded by Pantomimes—The modern Puppet-show Man—Moving Pictures described.

ANCIENT PLAYS.—It is not my design to enter deeply upon the origin and progress of scenic exhibitions in England: this subject has already been so ably discussed, that very little new matter can be found to excite the public attention: I shall, therefore, be as brief as possible, and confine myself chiefly to the lower species of comic pastimes, many of which may justly claim the sanction of high antiquity.

MIRACLE PLAYS, DRAMAS FROM SCRIPTURE, ETC. CONTINUED SEVERAL DAYS. —The theatrical exhibitions in London, in the twelfth century, were called Miracles, because they consisted of sacred plays, or representations of the miracles wrought by the holy confessors, and the sufferings by which the perseverance of the martyrs was manifested.[1] Such subjects were certainly very properly chosen, because the church was usually the theatre wherein these pious dramas were performed, and the actors were the ecclesiastics or their scholars.[2] The first play of this kind specified by name, is that of St Katherine, *Ludus de St Katharine*. According to Matthew Paris, it was written by Geoffrey, a Norman, afterwards abbot of St Albans: he was sent over into England by abbot Richard, to take upon him the direction of the school belonging to that monastery, but coming too late, he went to Dunstable and taught there, where he caused his play to be performed about the year 1110, and borrowed from the sacrist of St Albans some of the choir copes of the abbey, to adorn the actors.

*In the first half of the twelfth century three Latin plays were composed by Hilarius, an Englishman of French education; they deal respectively with the stories of Daniel, Lazarus, and St Nicholas. The earliest known manuscript that gives any sequence of Scriptural plays dates from the same century, and pertains to Tours, in France. In this series occurs the first mention of a stage

---

[1] Fitzstephen's *Description of London*.

[2] *Dr A. W. Ward, in his *English Dramatic Literature* (1899), vol. i. chap. i, has pointed out how the dramatic illustration of the liturgy of the Church, such as the Office of the Shepherds after the *Te Deum* on Christmas Day, or the use of the Sepulchre in Holy Week, gradually developed into the popular mystery plays.

See, too, the opening chapter of *The English Religious Drama*, by K. L. Bates, 1893.

erected outside the church door. From that date the plays which had originated in the quire, and hence transferred to the nave of the church, took up their position in the churchyard. In the thirteenth century various bishops protested against the use of churchyards as consecrated places for the miracle plays with their somewhat coarse associations, and priests were often forbidden to take part in them. Nevertheless, down to Reformation days, these dramas were usually written by the clergy and controlled by them, whilst the actors were frequently drawn from the ranks of the minor orders of the ministry and from the friars. Particularly was this the case with the parish clerks, like Chaucer's "Joly Absolon," of whom the poet says :—

> Sometimes to show his lightness and maistrie,
> He plaieth Herod on a scaffold hie.

According to the Wife of Bath's prologue in the *Canterbury Tales*, the miracle plays of Chaucer's days were exhibited during the season of Lent, and sometimes a sequel of Scripture histories was carried on for several days. In the reign of Richard II. (1391) the parish clerks of London put forth a play at Skinners Wells, near Smithfield, which continued three days; the king, queen, and many of the nobility, being present at the performance.[1] In the succeeding reign, 10 Henry IV. A.D. 1409, another play was acted by them at the same place, and lasted eight days; this drama began with the creation of the world, and contained the greater part of the history of the Old and New Testament. It does not appear to have been honoured with the royal presence, but was well attended by most of the nobility and gentry of the realm.

*Although Gregory IX. prohibited in strong terms the exhibition of dramatic spectacles in consecrated places, and secured their prohibition by the Council of Treves in 1227, the first year of his papacy, the Church almost inadvertently gave a great impetus to religious pageantry and plays at the hands of one of his immediate successors. Pope Urban IV. instituted the festival of Corpus Christi in 1263, and its general use was established by the Council of Vienne in 1311. The peculiar honour paid to this new festival by the trading gilds and corporations of our English towns and cities led to their seizing on the occasion of the great Corpus Christi procession as the appropriate time for the setting forth of the miracle plays with much pageantry.

*Chester claims by tradition to have been the first, *circa* 1270, to start its cycle of Corpus Christi plays. In the fourteenth and fifteenth centuries it is known that religious plays were performed at Bassingbourne, Bath, Bethersden, Beverley, Cambridge, Coventry, Heybridge, Kendal, Lancaster, Leeds, Lincoln, London, Morebath, Newcastle-on-Tyne, Northampton, Norwich, Oxford, Preston, Reading, Shrewsbury, Sleaford, Tewkesbury, Tintinhull, Winchester, Worcester, Woodkirk near Wakefield, Wymondham, and York. Such a list as this proves how thoroughly these religious plays had taken hold of the English

---

[1] Stow's *Survey of London*, p. 76.

people, especially as the names given are probably not a tithe of those whose definite performances of this character were regularly enacted. At several of these places, not only in villages of Somersetshire, Cambridgeshire, Kent or Essex, but in small towns such as Reading and Tewkesbury, the churchwardens' accounts are charged with the expenses of the performance. This points to the probability that, where there were no flourishing trading gilds to support them, these performances were carried on under a certain amount of clerical direction.

THE COVENTRY PLAY.—The best known of these mysteries is that entitled Corpus Christi, or *Ludus Coventrie*, the Coventry Play; transcripts of this play, nearly if not altogether coeval with the time of its representation, are yet in existence; one in particular is preserved in the Cotton Library.[1] The prologue to this curious drama is delivered by three persons, who speak alternately, and are called vexillators; it contains the argument of the several pageants, or acts, that constitute the piece, and they amount to no less than forty; and every one of these acts consists of a detached subject from the Holy Writ, beginning with the creation of the universe and concluding with the last judgment. In the first pageant, or act, the Deity is represented seated on His throne by Himself, delivering a speech of forty lines beginning thus:

Ego sum de Alpha et Omega principium et finis.

My name is knowyn God and Kynge,
My worke for to make now wyl I wende,
In myself restyth my reyneynge,
It hath no gynnyg ne non ende.

The angels then enter, singing from the *Te Deum*, "To Thee all angels cry aloud, the heavens and all the powers therein; To Thee Cherubin and Seraphin continually do cry, Holy, holy, holy Lord God of Sabaoth." Lucifer next makes his appearance, and desires to know if the hymn they sang was in honour of God or in honour of him? The good angels readily reply, in honour of God; the evil angels incline to worship Lucifer, and he presumes to seat himself in the throne of the Deity, who commands him to depart from heaven to hell, which dreadful sentence he is compelled to obey, and with his wicked associates descends to the lower regions. I have given a much fuller account of this curious mystery in the third volume of the *Manners and Customs of the English People*, with long extracts, and from several others nearly equal in antiquity, to which the reader is referred. This play was acted by the Friars Minors, or Mendicant Friars, of Coventry; and commenced on Corpus Christi day, whence it received its title.[2]

[1] *Vesp. D.* viii.

[2] *It is thought best to leave Strutt's brief account of the Coventry Play and his subsequent reference to the two plays of St Paul and St Mary Magdalene just as they were issued in 1801. To attempt to deal with this great subject in a page or two would be altogether vain, for so much has come to light during the nineteenth century about these miracle plays, and they have been subjected to so much critical scholarship. In addition to Miss Bates's admirable *English Religious Drama*, already cited, Hone's *Ancient Mysteries Described*, Pollard's *English Miracle Plays*, and Wright's *Early Mysteries* may be named. A large number of the original cycles of plays of Chester, Coventry, Woodkirk, and York are extant, and many have been separately edited. There is a good bibliography at the end of Miss Bates's book.

MYSTERIES DESCRIBED.—The mysteries often consisted of single subjects, and made but one performance. In the Bodleian Library at Oxford [1] I met with two mysteries that to the best of my knowledge have not been mentioned: the subject of one is the conversion of Saint Paul, and of the other the casting out of the devils from Mary Magdalene; they are both very old and imperfect, especially the latter, which seems to want several leaves. The first is entitled *Saulus;* and after a short prologue the stage direction follows, "Here outeyth Saul, goodly besene in the best wyse lyke an adventrous knyth, thus sayynge:

> Most dowtyd man, I am lyvynge upon the grounde
> Goodly besene with many a ryche harlement;
> My pere on lyve I trow ys nott yfound
> Thorow the world, fro the oryent to the occydent."

The interlocutors, besides the poet who speaks the prologue, and Saul, are Caiaphas, Ananias, first and second soldiers, the "Stabularyus," or hostler, the servant, and Belial.

MYSTERIES, HOW ENLIVENED.—Notwithstanding the seriousness of the subjects that constituted these mysteries, it seems clear that they were not exhibited without a portion of pantomimical fun to make them palatable to the vulgar taste; and indeed the length and the dulness of the speeches required some such assistance to enliven them, and keep the spectators in good humour; and this may be the reason why the mysteries are in general much shorter than the modern plays. Beelzebub seems to have been the principal comic actor, assisted by his merry troop of under-devils, who, with variety of noises, strange gestures, and contortions of the body, excited the laughter of the populace. [2]

*In towns such as York, Chester, and Coventry, where the cycle of plays was divided into a number of pageants or acts that extended over several days, great care was taken that the scenes should be divided amongst those gilds or companies who could most readily furnish the desired "properties." Thus the shipwrights were called upon to build up Noah's ark, the plasterers to represent the creation of the earth, the goldsmiths to have charge of the Adoration of the Magi, the vintners the turning of water into wine, and the bakers the Last Supper.

*THE "PAGEANT" OR STAGE.—The term *pageant* was originally applied in England to the movable platform that served as a stage, and hence to the play exhibited upon it. The original pageant was a wooden structure of two stories on wheels, the lower of which was the "green room," and the upper the stage proper. Archdeacon Rogers, who died in 1595, and who saw the Whitsuntide

---

[1] Digby, 113.

[2] *Dr Ward, in his discussion of the literary features of these mystery plays (*English Dramatic Literature*, vol. i. pp. 63, 64), has some admirable remarks on the homeliness and vigour of their style, from which the following sentence may be quoted:—"It certainly would not have occurred either to author or audience that the former were dishonouring the sacred narrative by patching it with rude lappets of their own invention; or that a bit of buffoonery introduced into a religious play implied irreverence towards its holy theme, any more than a grotesque head disfigured the columns in a church of which it diversified the ornamentation."

plays performed at Chester in the previous year, gives a clear description of these stages and the method of procedure :—

"The maner of these playes were, every company had his pagiant, wch pagiante were a high scafold with 2 roomes, a higher and a lower, upon 4 wheeles. In the lower they apparelled themselves, and in the higher roome they played, beinge all open on the tope, that all behoulders might heare and see them. The places where they played them was in every streete. They began first at the Abay gates, and when the first pagiante was played, it was wheeled to the highe crosse before the Mayor, and so to every streete, and soe every streete had a pagiante playing before them at one time, till all the pagiantes for the day appointed were played, and when one pagiant was neere ended, worde was brought from streete to streete, that soe they might come in place thereof, exceedinge orderly."[1]

CORNISH MIRACLE PLAYS.—In Cornwall the miracle plays were differently represented : they were not performed in the churches, nor under any kind of cover, but in the open air, as we learn from Carew, whose words upon this subject are as follow : "The guary-miracle, in English, a miracle play, is a kind of interlude compiled in Cornish out of some scripture history, with that grossness which accompanied the Romanes vetus comedia. For representing it, they raise an earthen amphitheatre in some open field, having the diameter of his enclined plain some forty or fifty feet. The country people flock from all sides many miles of, to hear and see it, for they have therein devils and devices to delight as well the eye as the eare. The players conne not their parts without booke, but are prompted by one called the ordinary, who followeth at their backs with the book in his hand, and telleth them what to say."[2] In the Harleian Library is preserved a miracle play of this kind in the Cornish language, written by William Gordon, A.D. 1611, accompanied with an English translation by John Keygwyn, A.D. 1693. It begins with the creation and ends with Noah's flood. Noah himself concludes the play, with an address to the spectators, desiring them to "come to-morrow betimes" to see another play on the redemption of man ; and then speaking to the musicians, says, "Musicians, play to us, that we may dance together as is the manner of the sport." This species of amusement continued to be exhibited in Cornwall long after the abolition of the miracles and moralities in the other parts of the kingdom, and when the establishment of regular plays had taken place.[3]

MORALITIES DESCRIBED.—When the mysteries ceased to be played, the subjects for the drama were not taken from historical facts, but consisted of moral reasonings in praise of virtue and condemnation of vice, on which account they were called Moralities ; and these performances requiring some degree of

[1] See Wright's *Introd. to Chester Plays*, xix. xx.
[2] *Survey of Cornwall*, Lond. 1602, p. 71.
[3] *Three of these Cornish miracle plays, in the native Cymric dialect, were edited and translated by Mr Edward Norris, in two volumes, in 1859, under the title, *The Ancient Cornish Drama*. He considers their date to be fifteenth century, but the language used shows their origin to belong to a period earlier than the fourteenth.

invention, laid the foundation for our modern comedies and tragedies. The dialogues were carried on by allegorical characters, such as Good Doctrine, Charity, Faith, Prudence, Discretion, Death, and the like, and their discourses were of a serious and exceedingly dull cast; but the province of making the spectators merry, descended from the Devil in the mystery, to Vice or Iniquity of the morality, who usually personified some bad quality incident to human nature, as Pride, or Lust, or any other evil propensity. Alluding to the mimicry of this motley character, Jonson, in Epig. 159, has these lines :—

> But the old Vice
> Acts old Iniquity, and in the fit
> Of mimicry gets th' opinion of a wit.

In the *Staple of Newes*, acted in 1625, it is said, "Iniquity came in like Hokos-pokos in a jugler's jerkin, with false skirts like the knave of clubs"; and afterward, "Here is never a fiend to carry him, the Vice, away; besides, he has never a wooden dagger : I'd not give a rush for a Vice that has not a wooden dagger to snap at every one he meetes": in another part, the Vice is described, "in his long coat, shaking his wooden dagger." Hence it appears this character had a dress peculiar to himself. Philip Stubs, in his *Anatomie of Abuses*, printed A.D. 1595, says, "You must go to the playhouse if you will learne to play the Vice, to sweare, teare, and blaspheme both heaven and hell": and again, "Who can call him a wise man, who playeth the part of a Foole or a Vice?" I remember to have seen a stage direction for the Vice, to lay about him lustily with a great pole, and tumble the characters one over the other with great noise and riot, "for dysport sake." Even when regular tragedies and comedies were introduced upon the stage, we may trace the descendants of this facetious Iniquity in the clowns and the fools which so frequently disgraced them. The great master of human nature, in compliance with the false taste of the age in which he lived, has admitted this motley character into the most serious parts of one of his best tragedies. The propensity to laugh at the expense of good sense and propriety, is well ridiculed in the "Intermeane" at the end of the first act of the *Staple of Newes*, by Jonson, and again in the prelude to the *Careless Shepherdess*, a pastoral tragi-comedy by Thomas Goffe, in 1656, where several characters are introduced upon the stage as spectators, waiting for the commencement of the performance. One of them says :—

> Why, I would have a fool in every act,
> Be't comedy or tragedy : I've laugh'd
> Until I cr'yd again, to see what faces
> The rogue will make. Oh! it does me good
> To see him hold out's chin, hang down his hands,
> And twirle his bawble. There is nere a part
> About him but breaks jests. I heard a fellow
> Once on the stage, cry doodle doodle dooe
> Beyond compare; I'de give th' other shilling
> To see him act the Changling once again.

To this another character replies :—

And so would I ; his part has all the wit,
For none speakes, carps, and quibbles besides him ;
I'd rather see him leap, or laugh, or cry,
Than hear the gravest speech in all the play ;
I never saw Rheade peeping through the curtain,
But ravishing joy entered into my heart.

A boy then comes upon the stage, and the first speaker inquires for the Fool ; but being told he is not to perform that night, he says :—

Well, since there will be nere a fool i' th' play,
I'll have my money again ; the comedy
Will be as tedious to me as a sermon.

SECULAR PLAYS.—The plays mentioned in the preceding pages, and especially the miracles and mysteries, differed greatly from the secular plays and interludes which were acted by strolling companies, composed of minstrels, jugglers, tumblers, dancers, bourdours or jesters, and other performers properly qualified for the different parts of the entertainment, which admitted of a variety of exhibitions. These pastimes are of higher antiquity than the ecclesiastical plays ; and they were much relished not only by the vulgar part of the people, but also by the nobility. The courts of the kings of England, and the castles of the great earls and barons, were crowded with the performers of the secular plays, where they were well received and handsomely rewarded.

INTERLUDES.—The interludes, which, I presume, formed a material part of the performances exhibited by the secular players, were certainly of a jocular nature, consisting probably of facetious or satirical dialogues, calculated to promote mirth, and therefore they are censured by Matthew Paris[1] as "vain pastimes." Something of this kind was the representation made before king Henry VIII. at Greenwich, in 1528, thus related by Hall : "Two persons plaied a dialogue, the effect whereof was, whether riches were better than love ; and, when they could not agree upon a conclusion, each called in thre knightes all armed ; thre of them woulde have entered the gate of the arche in the middle of the chambre, and the other thre resisted ; and sodenly betweene the six knightes, out of the arche fell downe a bar all gilte, at the which bar the six knightes fought a fair battail, and then they departed, and so went out of the place ; then came in an olde man with a silver berd, and he concluded that love and riches bothe be necessarie for princes, that is to say, by love to be obeyed and served, and with riches to rewarde his lovers and frendes ; and with this conclusion the dialogue ended." We hereby find, that these dialogues were not only a part of the entertainment, but also ingeniously made the vehicles for the introduction of other sports. Sometimes they were of a satirical nature ; and, when occasion required, they took another turn, and became the agents of flattery and adulation : both these purposes were answered by the following dialogue, taken from the author just now quoted : "On Sonday at night the fifteenth of June, 1523, in the great halle at Wyndsore," the emperor Maximilian

---

[1] *Vitæ Abbatum*, p. 6.

and Henry VIII. being present, "was a disguisiyng or play; the effect of it was, that there was a proud horse which would not be tamed nor bridled; but Amitie sent Prudence and Policie which tamed him, and Force and Puissance brideled him. This horse was meant by the Frenche kyng, and Amitie by the kynge of England, and the emperor and the other persons were their counsail and power."

TRAGEDIES IN CHAUCER'S TIME.—Comedies were not known, nor tragedies according to the modern acceptation of the word in Chaucer's time; for what he calls tragedies, are simply tales of persons who have fallen from a state of prosperity, or worldly grandeur, to great adversity; as he himself tells us in the following lines :—

> Tragedy is to tel a certayne story,
> As olde bokes maken memory,
> Of them that stode in great prosperite,
> And be fallen out of hye degre
> Into misery and ended wretchedly.[1]

*PLAYS ON HOLY DAYS.—A short poem in the Harleian Collection, *temp*. Henry VI., which is a quaint amalgam of English and Latin, shows that the performance of plays, even on God's holidays, was then frequent. The author says :—

> Ingland goith to noughte, *plus fecit homo viciosus*,
> To lust man is brought, *nimis est homo deliciosus*;
> Goddis halidays *non observantur honeste*,
> For unthryfty pleyis *in eis regnant manifeste*.[2]

*The households of Henry VI. and of Edward IV. included twelve minstrels who were permanently engaged; possibly they occasionally played interludes. A sumptuary law of 1464 exempted "players in their enterludes" from its enactments. In the Rolls of Winchester College for 1466 is the entry of a payment of 4s. to *iiij interludentibus et J. Meke cithariste*. The Household Book of the duke of Norfolk, from 1483 to 1501, contains entries of payments to the players of the duke of Gloucester (afterwards Richard III.), and to the players of Cocksale, Chelmsford, and Lavenham.[3]

*ROYAL COMPANIES OF PLAYERS.—Dramatic performances were frequent throughout England in the reign of Henry VII. The king had two distinct sets of actors, namely the "players of interludes," and the "players of the chapel," who performed set pieces at Christmas-tide; each of the former received a salary of five marks yearly. The king's household books from 1492 to 1509 show that the players of the duke of Buckingham and of the earls of Oxford and Northumberland performed at court; and that separate companies of players were attached to London, Coventry, Wycombe, Mile-End, Wimborne Minster, and Kingston.[4]

*On the accession of Henry VIII. every form of court amusement was at

---

[1] Prologue to the Monk's Tale, which consists of seventeen short stories or tragedies, of which, he tells us, he had an hundred in his cell.   [2] There were two copies, Nos. 536 and 941.

[3] Collier's *Hist. of Dramatic Poetry*, i. 34-37.   [4] Collier's *Hist. of Dramatic Poetry*, i. 43-64.

once placed on a more costly and extensive footing. He retained "the King's old players," but added a new company of "the King's players"; the children of the chapel were converted at particular seasons into a company of comedians; and masks and revels of every kind were fostered on extravagant lines. On the death of Henry VIII. there was a considerable reduction in the establishment of both musicians and players; only four of the latter were retained by Protector Somerset. The number of "Players of Enterludes" sustained by royalty, was raised to eight under queen Mary.

*In the first year of Elizabeth, the performance of plays and interludes was forbidden unless licensed by mayors of towns, or lords lieutenant, or two justices of counties. In June 1559, Sir Robert Dudley (afterwards earl Leicester), wrote to the earl of Shrewsbury, as lord president of the North, asking that his company of "plaiers of interludes," already licensed to perform in divers shires, might have his sanction to play in Yorkshire. Between July 1567 and March 1568 "seven plays and one tragedy" were performed before the queen. There is abundance of evidence of the frequency of play-acting throughout the kingdom during Elizabeth's reign. The companies of actors belonging to the nobility did not disdain to perform in the open air by daylight in towns, when suitable buildings could not be found. Towards the latter part of this reign there was much discord between the Court and the City of London on the subject of plays, particularly as to Sunday acting. In 1591 the lord mayor and aldermen addressed themselves to the archbishop of Canterbury, representing the evils produced by the number of players and playing houses within the city, and requesting his help towards reforming and banishing the same.

*THE PURITANS.—Considerable use was at the same time made by the Puritans of the printing press as an engine against players. One of the earliest and the fiercest of these publications was a treatise issued in 1579 by John Northbrooke, "Minister and Preacher of the Worde of God" against "Dicing, Dancing, Vaine Plaies or Enterludes, with other idle pastimes, commonly used on the Sabbath day." The section against players comes first, and occupies more than half of the book. The writer in his list of persons "to be rejected and cast out of this Commonwealth" places "Enterlude plaiers" between Thieves and Cutpurses. He names separately the "histrioners which play upon Scaffoldes and Stages Enterludes and Comedies or otherwise with gestures, etc.," and those who acted in places specially constructed for them with theatre and curtain. He complains that "Many can tary at a vayne Playe two or three houres, when as they will not abide scarce one houre at a Sermon. They will runne to everie Plaie, but scarce will come to a preached Sermon."

COURT PLAYS.—There was another species of entertainment which differed materially from any of the pastimes mentioned in the preceding pages, I mean the ludi, or plays exhibited at court in the Christmas holidays: we trace them as far back as the reign of Edward III. The preparations made for them at that time are mentioned without the least indication of novelty, which admits of the

Mummeries.

supposition that they were still more ancient. From the numeration of the dresses appropriated in 1348 to one of these plays, which consisted of various kinds of disguisements, they seem to have merited rather the denomination of mummeries than of theatrical divertisements.[1] The king then kept his Christmas at his castle at Guildford; the dresses are said to be *ad faciendum ludos domini regis*, and consisted of eighty tunics of buckram of various colours; forty-two visors of different similitudes, namely, fourteen of faces of women, fourteen of faces of men, and fourteen heads of angels made with silver; twenty-eight crests; fourteen mantles embroidered with heads of dragons; fourteen white tunics wrought with the heads and wings of peacocks; fourteen with the heads of swans with wings; fourteen tunics painted with the eyes of peacocks; fourteen tunics of English linen painted; and fourteen other tunics embroidered with stars of gold.[2] How far these plays were enlivened by dialogues, or interlocutory eloquence is not known; but probably they partook more of the feats of pantomime than of colloquial excellency, and were better calculated to amuse the sight than to instruct the mind.

The magnificent pageants and disguisings frequently exhibited at court in the succeeding times, and especially in the reign of Henry VIII., no doubt originated from the ludi above mentioned. These mummeries, as a modern writer justly observes, were destitute of character and humour, their chief aim being to surprise the spectators "by the ridiculous and exaggerated oddity of the visors, and by the singularity and splendour of the dresses; every thing was out of nature and propriety. Frequently the masque was attended with an exhibition of gorgeous machinery, resembling the wonders of a modern pantomime."[3]

The reader may form some judgment of the appearance the actors made upon these occasions, from the masquerade figures at the top and bottom of plate nineteen, which are taken from a beautiful manuscript in the Bodleian written and illuminated in the reign of Edward III.[4]

The performance seems to have consisted chiefly in dancing, and the mummers are usually attended by the minstrels playing upon different kinds of musical instruments.

These pageants were frequently movable and drawn upon wheels. In honour of the marriage of Arthur, prince of Wales, with Catherine of Spain, there were three pageants exhibited in Westminster Hall, which succeeded each other, and were all of them drawn upon wheels: the first was a castle with ladies; the second a ship in full sail, that cast anchor near the castle; and the third a mountain with several armed knights upon it, who stormed the castle, and obliged the ladies to surrender. The show ended in a dance, and the pageantry disappeared.[5]

---

[1] Wardrobe Roll of Edward III.   [2] Warton's *Hist. Eng. Poet.* vol. i. p. 238.

[3] Warton, vol. iii. p. 156. See also Henry's *Hist. Brit.* vol. vi. book vi. chap. 7.

[4] No. 264. This MS. was completed in the year 1343.

[5] Harl. MS. 69, p. 31.

PLAY IN HONOUR OF THE PRINCESS MARY.—In the tenth year of the same king's reign, in honour of his sister the princess Mary's marriage with the king of France, there was exhibited in the great hall at Greenwich, "a rock full of al maner of stones very artificially made, and on the top stood five trees: the first was an olive tree, on which hanged a shield of the armes of the church of Rome; the second was a pyne aple tree,[1] with the arms of the emperor; the third was a rosyer,[2] with the armes of England; the fourth a braunche of lylies, bearing the armes of France; and the fifth a pomegranet tree, bearing the armes of Spayn; in token that all these five potentates were joined together in one league against the enemies of Christe's fayth: in and upon the middes of the rock satte a fayre lady, richly appareyled, with a dolphin in her lap. In this rock were ladies and gentlemen appareled, in crimosyn sattyn, covered over with floures of purple satyn, embroudered with wrethes of gold knit together with golden laces, and on every floure a hart of gold moving. The ladies' tyer[3] was after the fashion of Inde, with kerchiefes of pleasaunce[4] hached with fyne gold, and set with letters of Greeke in gold of bullion, and the edges of their kerchiefes were garnished with hanging perle. These gentlemen and ladyes sate on the neyther part of the rock, and out of a cave in the same rock came ten knightes armed at all poyntes, and faughte together a fayre tournay. And when they were severed and departed, the disguysers dissended from the rock and daunced a great space, and sodeynly the rock moved and receaved the disguysers and imediately closed agayn. Then entred a person called report, appareled in crymosyn satin full of tongues, sitting on a flying horse with wynges and feete of gold called Pegasus; this person in Frenche declared the meaning of the rocks, the trees, and the tourney."[5]

PLAY OF HOCK-TUESDAY.—Among the pastimes exhibited for the entertainment of queen Elizabeth during her stay at Kenilworth Castle, Warwickshire, was a kind of historical play, or old storial show, performed by certain persons who came for that purpose from Coventry. It was also called the old Coventry play of Hock-Tuesday, but must not be confounded with the *Ludus de Corpus Christi*, or Coventry Mystery, mentioned before, to which it did not bear the least analogy. The subject of the Hock-Tuesday show was the massacre of the Danes, a memorable event in the English history, on St Brice's night, November 13, 1002, which was expressed "in action and in rhimes." It is said to have been annually acted in the town of Coventry, according to ancient custom; but that it was suppressed soon after the Reformation, at the instance of some of their preachers, whose good intention the towns-people did not deny, but complained of their severity; urging in behalf of the show, that it was "without ill example of manners, papistry, or any superstition."[6] The rhimes originally belonging to the play, I presume, were omitted upon the above-

---

[1] Pine-apple. [2] A rose tree. [3] Head-dress.
[4] Pleasaunce was a fine thin species of gauze, which was striped with gold. [5] Hall, *ut sup.* fol. 59.
[6] Laneham's account of the sports at Kenilworth Castle, in Nichols' *Progresses of Queen Elizabeth*, vol. i. p. 22.

mentioned occasion; for it appears to have been performed without any recitation in mere dumb show, and consisted of hot skirmishes and furious encounters between the English and the Danish forces: first by the launce knights on horseback, armed with spears and shields, who being many of them dismounted, fought with swords and targets. Then followed two "host of foot men," one after the other, first marching in ranks, then, turning about in a warlike manner, they changed their form from ranks into squadrons, then into triangles, then into rings, and then "winding out again they joined in battle; twice the Danes had the better, but at the last conflict they were beaten down, overcome, and many of them led captive for triumph by our English women." Her majesty was much pleased with this performance, "whereat," says my author, "she laughed well," and rewarded the actors with two bucks, and five marks in money; and with this munificence they were highly satisfied.[1]

DECLINE OF SECULAR PLAYS.—The secular plays, as we have seen, consisted of a medley of different performances, calculated chiefly to promote mirth without any view to instruction; but soon after the production of regular plays, when proper theatres were established, the motley exhibitions of the strolling actors were, as a rule, only relished by the vulgar; the law set her face against them, the performers were stigmatised with the names of rogues and vagabonds, and access was usually denied them at the houses of the opulent.

*Certain companies, however, continued to move about the country, as has been shown in the Introduction in the account given of the licensing by the Master of the Revels.

*Moreover, in many a place there were local companies formed to visit the houses of the gentlefolk of the immediate district at Christmas and other festive seasons. Such companies could not properly be termed either amateurs or professionals. They were not amateurs, for they received largesse from their patrons; they were not professionals, for at ordinary seasons they followed their usual town or country occupations.

*SIR MILES STAPLETON AND YORKSHIRE PLAYERS.—After the Restoration such local companies came greatly into favour in certain districts. The extracts recently published from the Household Books of Sir Miles Stapleton, of Carlton, Yorkshire, afford various interesting particulars of this character.[2]

*Sir Miles was ever ready to encourage local or itinerant players and musicians to entertain the household at Carlton. In Easter week, 1661, he gave to Joseph Robinson and the Selby players 10s. "for playing the play called Musidorus." *Mucedorus and Amadine* was a comedy frequently acted at the Globe and at Whitehall; it was first published in 1598, and had passed through eleven editions by 1668. The gaieties of Christmas-tide 1662, were duly observed by the newly-made baronet at Carlton. The following entries

[1] Laneham, *ut supra*, p. 24.
[2] See papers of Rev. Dr Cox in *Ancestor*, Nos. 2 and 3, 1902.

in his accounts show that he did his best to make it a bright season for his neighbours :—

	£ s. d.
It. Given to two fidlers of Selbye that was here one day in Christmas when I had invited some neighbours to diner	oo o2 oo
It. Given to Bartle Fular and his boy who was here fidling two days in Christmas when I invited some neighbours and tenants to diner . . .	oo o3 oo
It. Given to Will. Peares and the rest of our neighbours of Carleton when they played their play in the house on Tuesday, December the 30th, 1662, the play is called the gentle craft	oo 10 oo
It. Given to some mumers y^t came in Christmas.	oo oo o6
It. Given to Nicholas Daniell and the rest of the players y^t came from about Beedall when they played their two playes here on Friday night, January the 23rd, 1662-3 one of the playes was the tragadye of Baitman and the other was called the courageous generall	o1 oo oo

The Gentle Craft or the Shoemaker's Holiday was a play by Thomas Deaker, first printed in 1638. *The Tragedy of Bateman* was probably another name for *The Fair Maid of Bristol*, by John Day, first played before the king and given at Hampton in 1605. *The Courageous General* was probably *The General*, a tragi-comedy by James Shirley; Pepys saw it acted in 1669 and was pleased with it.

*The accounts for 1664 contain various entries relative to entertainments. The following are all of this year :—

	£ s. d.
It. Given then to Marmaduke Grainge and his son and daughter Pearson and their boy for playing on the musicke that time when wee were all merry together at Will Lodge	oo o7 oo
It. Given to a trumpeter y^t came and sounded his trumpett . . .	oo o1 oo
It. Given to a poore fidler y^t came in Christmas and was here two or three dayes &c.	oo o2 o6
It. Given to Pocklington players y^t played the shepherdes play . . .	oo o5 oo
It. Given to Rickall players y^t played the play here called wilye beguilee in Christmas	oo 10 oo
It. Given to Nickolas Daniell and the players that came from about Beedall January the 19th, 1664 (5) for playing two playes here, the one called the two constant lovers, and the other called a maidens head well lost . .	o1 o1 oo
It. Given to Selbye musicke y^t came beging March the 11th . . .	oo oo o6

*The cultivation of the dramatic art at this period in the small towns and large villages of Yorkshire is not a little remarkable. The actors were no mere country mummers, for the plays chosen were all ones of some repute. *The Shepherd's Holiday* was a pastoral tragi-comedy which had been presented before their Majesties at Whitehall by the queen's servants in 1635; the author was Joseph Rutter, a dependant of the family of Lord Dorset, and a playwright of some experience. *Wily Beguiled* was "a pleasant comedy," of which there are four editions extant between 1606 and 1638. *The Two Constant Lovers* was probably another name for *The Constant Maid*, by James Shirley, first published in 1640. *A Maiden-head Well Lost* was a comedy by that well-known early dramatist, Thomas Heywood; it was first acted at the Cockpit, Drury Lane, in 1633.

The following is a later entry of expenditure in the like direction :—

1668

It. Given to Beedale players when they acted here January 11th Sir John Dauncy and his company and Sir Tho. Yarbrough and his being here y^t night and the play is called a girl worth gold . . . . . $£$ $s.$ $d.$ 00 15 00

But the frequent bands of professional strolling players undoubtedly diminished most rapidly in numbers as permanent theatres multiplied. The tragitour now became a mere juggler, and played a few paltry tricks occasionally, assisted by the jester, transformed into a modern jack-pudding. It is highly probable, that necessity suggested to him the idea of supplying the place of his human confederates by automaton figures made of wood, which, by means of wires properly attached to them, were moved about, and performed many of the actions peculiar to mankind; and, with the assistance of speeches made for them behind the scenery, produced that species of drama commonly distinguished by the appellation of a droll, or a puppet-play; wherein a facetious performer, well known by the name of Punchinello, supplied the place of the Vice, or mirth-maker, a favourite character in the moralities. In modern days this celebrated actor, who has something to say to the greater part of his auditory, is called plain Punch. In the moralities, the Devil usually carried away the Iniquity, or Evil, at the conclusion of the drama; and, in compliance with the old custom, Punch, the genuine descendant of the Iniquity, is constantly taken from the stage by the Devil at the end of the puppet-show. Ben Jonson, by way of burlesque, in the comedy entitled *The Devil is an Asse*, reverses the ancient usage, and makes the Iniquity run away with the Fiend, saying—

The Divell was wont to carry away the Evill,
But now the Evill out-carries the Divell.—Act v. scene 6.

The first appearance of a company of wooden actors excited, no doubt, the admiration of the populace, and the novelty of such an exhibition was probably productive of much advantage to the inventor. I cannot pretend to determine the time that puppet-plays were first exhibited in England. I rather think this species of entertainment originated upon the Continent. Cervantes has made Don Quixote a spectator at a puppet-show, and the knight's behaviour upon this occasion is described with great humour. The puppets were originally called motions: we find them mentioned in *Gammer Gurton's Needle*, which is supposed to have been written in 1517; and there the master of the puppet-show seems to have been considered as no better than an idle vagrant. One of the characters says, he will go "and travel with young Goose, the motion-man, for a puppet-player."

ORIGIN OF PUPPET-PLAYS.—Previous to the invention of puppets, or rather to the incorporating of them into companies, there were automatons that performed variety of motions. The jack of the clock-house, often mentioned by the writers of the sixteenth century, was also an automaton, that either struck the hours upon the bell in their proper rotation, or signified by its gestures that the clock was about to strike. In a humorous pamphlet called *Lanthorn and Candle, or the Bellman's Second Walk*, published at London, 1605, it is said, "The Jacke of the Clocke-house goes upon screws, and his office is to do nothing but strike"; and in an old play still more early, "He shakes his heade and throws his arms about like the Jacke of the Clocke-house."

*There are also references to these Jacks in Shakespeare's plays of *Richard II.* and *Richard III*. The figure was at one time a fairly common adjunct of the larger church clocks of the fifteenth and seventeenth centuries. There are two Jacks o' the Clock still to be seen in neighbouring Suffolk churches. At Southwold the figure clad in armour has been removed from the tower window and placed over the screen at the east end of the north aisle. Jack strikes a bell suspended before him with a battle-axe, and it is customary to make him ring just before the beginning of service. At Blythburgh, the Jack has also been removed from the tower to the body of the church; in this case the somewhat mutilated figure, which is about four feet high, is also clad in plate armour, but with the addition of a flowing beard.[1]

NATURE OF PERFORMANCES BY PUPPETS.—From such figures as these originated the more modern heroes of the puppet-show. The puppet-shows usually made their appearance at great fairs, and especially at those in the vicinity of the metropolis; they still (1801) continue to be exhibited in Smithfield at Bartholomew-tide, though with very little traces of their former greatness; indeed, of late years, they have become unpopular, and are frequented only by children. It is, however, certain, that the puppet-shows attracted the notice of the public at the commencement of the last century, and rivalled in some degree the more pompous exhibitions of the larger theatres.[2] Powel, a famous puppet-show man, is mentioned in one of the early papers of the *Spectator*,[3] and his performances are humorously contrasted with those of the Opera House. At the same time there was another motion-master, who also appears to have been of some celebrity, named Crawley; I have before me two bills of his exhibition, one for Bartholomew Fair, and the other for Southwark Fair. These are preserved in a miscellaneous collection of advertisements and title-pages among the Harleian MSS.[4] The first of these bills runs thus: "At Crawley's Booth, over against the Crown Tavern in Smithfield, during the time of Bartholomew Fair, will be presented a little opera, called the Old Creation of the World, yet newly revived; with the addition of Noah's Flood; also several fountains playing water during the time of the play.—The last scene does

---

[1] In vol. xxv. of the *Journal of Brit. Arch. Assoc.* there is an article on this subject.
[2] See the Introduction.   [3] No. xiv. vol. i. first published in 1711.   [4] No. 5931.

present Noah and his family coming out of the Ark, with all the beasts two and two, and all the fowls of the air seen in a prospect sitting upon trees; likewise over the ark is seen the Sun rising in a most glorious manner: moreover, a multitude of Angels will be seen in a double rank, which presents a double prospect, one for the sun, the other for a palace, where will be seen six Angels ringing of bells.—Likewise Machines descend from above, double and treble, with Dives rising out of Hell, and Lazarus seen in Abraham's bosom, besides several figures dancing jiggs, sarabands, and country dances, to the admiration of the spectators; with the merry conceits of squire Punch and Sir John Spendall." This curious medley was, we are told, "completed by an Entertainment of singing, and dancing with several naked swords, performed by a Child of eight years of age." In the second bill, we find the addition of "the Ball of little Dogs"; it is also added, that these celebrated performers had danced before the queen (Anne) and most of the quality of England, and amazed everybody.[1]

GIANTS AND OTHER PUPPET CHARACTERS.—The subjects of the puppet-dramas were formerly taken from some well-known and popular stories, with the introduction of knights and giants; hence the following speech in the *Humorous Lovers*, a comedy, printed in 1617: "They had like to have frighted me with a man dressed up like a gyant in a puppet-show." In my memory, these shows consisted of a wretched display of wooden figures, barbarously formed and decorated, without the least degree of taste or propriety; the wires that communicated the motion to them appeared at the tops of their heads, and the manner in which they were made to move, evinced the ignorance and inattention of the managers; the dialogues were mere jumbles of absurdity and nonsense, intermixed with low immoral discourses passing between Punch and the fiddler, for the orchestra rarely admitted of more than one minstrel; and these flashes of merriment were made offensive to decency by the actions of the puppet. In the reign of James II. there was a noted merry-andrew named Philips. "This man," says Granger, "was some time fiddler to a puppet-show; in which capacity he held many a dialogue with Punch, in much the same strain as he did afterwards with the mountebank doctor, his master upon the stage. This zany, being regularly educated, had confessedly the advantage of his brethren."[2]

PUPPET-PLAYS SUPERSEDED BY PANTOMIMES.—The introduction, or rather the revival of pantomimes, which indeed have long disgraced the superior theatres, proved the utter undoing of the puppet-show men; in fact, all the absurdities of the puppet-show, except the discourses, are retained in the pantomimes, the difference consisting principally in the substitution of living puppets for wooden ones; but it must be confessed, though nothing be added to the rationality of the performances, great pains is taken to supply the defect, by fascinating the eyes and the ears; and certainly the brilliancy of the dresses and scenery, the skilful management of the machinery, and the excellence of the

---

[1] *See H. Morley's *Memoirs of Bartholomew's Fair*, first issued in 1859. [2] *Biogr. Hist.* vol. iv. p. 350.

K

music, in the pantomimes, are great improvements upon the humble attempts of the vagrant motion-master.

THE MODERN PUPPET-SHOW MAN.*—In April 1751 the tragedy of "Jane Shore" was advertised for representation at "Punch's Theatre in James Street in the Haymarket," by puppets. Italian Fantoccini were exhibited in the same place, better known as Hickford's Rooms, in 1770. There was another like exhibition at No. 22 Piccadilly, in 1780, on an elaborate scale, when comic operas, harlequinades, and other pieces were represented by puppets. It was a fashionable entertainment, for the tickets were 5s. and 2s. 6d. "The room," say the advertisements, "is neatly fitted up, kept warm, and will be illuminated with wax."[1]

In the present day (1801) the puppet-show man travels about the streets when the weather will permit, and carries his motions, with the theatre itself, upon his back! The exhibition takes place in the open air; and the precarious income of the miserable itinerant depends entirely on the voluntary contributions of the spectators, which, as far as one may judge from the square appearance he usually makes, is very trifling.

MOVING PICTURES.—Another species of scenic exhibition with moving figures, bearing some distant analogy to the puppets, appeared at the commencement of the eighteenth century. Such a show is thus described in the reign of queen Anne, by the manager of a show exhibited at the great house in the Strand, over against the Globe Tavern, near Hungerford Market; the best places at 1s., and the others at 6d. each: "To be seen, the greatest Piece of Curiosity that ever arrived in England, being made by a famous engineer from the camp before Lisle, who, with great labour and industry, has collected into a moving picture the following figures: first, it doth represent the confederate camp, and the army lying intrenched before the town; secondly, the convoys and the mules with prince Eugene's baggage; thirdly, the English forces commanded by the duke of Marlborough; likewise, several vessels, laden with provisions for the army, which are so artificially done as to seem to drive the water before them. The city and the citadel are very fine, with all its outworks, ravelins, hornworks, counter-scarps, half-moons, and palisados; the French horse marching out at one gate, and the confederate army marching in at the other; the prince's travelling coach with two generals in it, one saluting the company as it passes by; then a trumpeter sounds a call as he rides, at the noise whereof a sleeping centinel starts, and lifts up his head, but, not being espied, lies down to sleep again; besides abundance more admirable curiosities too tedious to be inserted here." He then modestly adds, "In short the whole piece is so contrived by art, that it seems to be life and nature." These figures, I presume, were flat, painted images moving upon a flat surface, like those frequently seen upon the tops of clocks, where a carpenter's shop, or a stone-mason's yard, are by no means unusually represented. A juggler named Flockton, some few years back,

---

[1] *Notes and Queries*, Ser. III. v. 52.

had an exhibition of this kind, which he called a grand piece of clock-work. In this machine the combination of many different motions, and tolerably well contrived, were at one time presented to the eye.

Pinkethman's Pantheon, mentioned in the *Spectator*, was, I presume, an exhibition something similar to that above described, and probably the heathen deities were manufactured from pasteboard, and seated in rows one above the other upon clouds of the same material; at least I have seen them so fabricated, and so represented, about 1760, at a show in the country, which was contrived in such a manner, that the whole group descended and ascended with a slow motion to the sound of music.

CHAPTER III

The British Bards—The Northern Scalds—The Anglo-Saxon Gleemen—The Nature of their Performances—A Royal Player with three Darts—Bravery of a Minstrel in the Conqueror's Army—Other Performances by Gleemen—The Harp an Instrument of Music much used by the Saxons—Harpers at Durham—The Norman Minstrels, and their different Denominations and Professions—Troubadours—Jestours—Tales and Manners of the Jesters—Further Illustration of their Practices—Patronage, Privileges, and Excesses of the Minstrels—A Guild of Minstrels—Abuses and Decline of Minstrelsy—Minstrels were Satirists and Flatterers—Anecdotes of offending Minstrels, Women Minstrels—The Dress of the Minstrels—The King of the Minstrels, why so called—Rewards given to Minstrels—Payments to Minstrels—Durham Minstrels and Players—Minstrels at Parish Festivals.

THE BRITISH BARDS.—The Britons were passionately fond of vocal and instrumental music : for this reason, the bards, who exhibited in one person the musician and the poet, were held in the highest estimation among them. "These bards," says an early historian, "celebrated the noble actions of illustrious persons in heroic poems which they sang to the sweet sounds of the lyre ;[1] and to this testimony we may add another of equal authority : "The British bards are excellent and melodious poets, and sing their poems, in which they praise some, and censure others, to the music of an instrument resembling a lyre."[2] Their songs and their music are said, by the same writer, to have been so exceedingly affecting, that "sometimes when two armies are standing in order of battle, with their swords drawn, and their lances extended upon the point of engaging in a most furious conflict, the poets have stepped in between them, and by their soft and fascinating songs calmed the fury of the warriors, and prevented the bloodshed. Thus, even among barbarians," adds the author, "rage gave way to wisdom, and Mars submitted to the Muses."

THE NORTHERN SCALDS.—The scalds[3] were the poets and the musicians of the ancient northern nations ; they resembled the bards of the Britons, and were held in equal veneration by their countrymen. The scalds were considered as necessary appendages to royalty, and even the inferior chieftains had their poets to record their actions and indulge their vanity.

THE ANGLO-SAXON GLEEMEN.—Upon the establishment of the Saxons in Britain, these poetical musicians were their chief favourites ; the courts of the kings and the residences of the opulent afforded them a constant asylum ; their persons were protected, and admission granted to them without the least restraint. In the Anglo-Saxon language they were distinguished by two appellations ; the one equivalent to the modern term of gleemen or merry-makers, and the other harpers, derived from the harp, an instrument on which

---

[1] Ammianus Marcell. lib. xv. cap. 9. [2] Diodorus Siculus, lib. v. cap. 31.
[3] Bartholin, *De causis contemp. a Danis Mortis*, lib. i. cap. 2, et Wormii, *Lit. Run.* ad finim.

Saxon Glecmen.

they usually played. The appellation of harper was long retained by the English rhymists. The gleemen added mimicry, and other means of promoting mirth to their profession, as well as dancing and tumbling, with sleights of hand, and variety of deceptions to amuse the spectators: it was therefore necessary for them to associate themselves into companies, by which means they were enabled to diversify their performances, and render many of them more surprising through the assistance of their confederates. In Edgar's oration to Dunstan, the mimi, or minstrels, are said to sing and dance; and, in the canons made in that king's reign, A.D. 960 (Can. 58), it is ordered that no priest shall in any wise act the gleeman with himself or with other men, but be, as becomes his order, wise and reverend.[1]

NATURE OF THE PERFORMANCES BY THE GLEEMEN.—Representations of some of these pastimes are met with occasionally in early manuscripts; and where they do occur, we uniformly find that the illuminators, being totally ignorant of ancient customs and the habits of foreign nations, have not paid the least regard to propriety in the depicting of either, but substituted those of their own time, and by this means they have, without design on their part, become the communicators of much valuable information. The following observations upon two very early paintings will, I doubt not, in great measure confirm the truth of this assertion.

On plate twenty are two persons dancing to the music of the horn and the trumpet, and it does not appear to be a common dance in which they are engaged; on the contrary, their attitudes are such as must have rendered it very difficult to perform. On the same plate is a curious specimen of a performer's art.

We here see a man throwing three balls and three knives alternately into the air, and catching them one by one as they fall, but returning them again in a regular rotation. To give the greater appearance of difficulty to this feat, it is accompanied with the music of an instrument resembling the modern violin. It is necessary to add, that these two figures, as well as those dancing, previously exhibited, form a part only of two larger paintings, which, in their original state, are placed as frontispieces to the Psalms of David; and in both, the artists have represented that monarch seated upon his throne in the act of playing upon the harp or the lyre, and surrounded by the masters of sacred music. In each the king is depicted considerably larger than the other performers, a compliment usually paid to saints and dignified persons; which absurdity has been frequently practised by the more modern painters. The inferior figures form a sort of border to the sides and bottom of the royal portrait. In addition to the four figures in the middle of the Plate, and exclusive of the king, there are four more, all of them instrumental performers; one playing upon the horn, another upon the trumpet, and the other two upon a kind of tabor or drum, which, however, is beaten with a single drum-stick: the manuscript in which this illumination is

---

[1] *Ancient Laws and Institutes*, p. 400.

preserved, was written as early as the eighth century, and is in the Cotton Collection at the British Museum.[1] The second painting, which is more modern than the former by full two centuries, contains four figures besides the royal psalmist; the two not engraved are musicians: the one is blowing a long trumpet supported by a staff he holds in his left hand, and the other is winding a crooked horn.[2] In a short prologue, immediately preceding the psalms, we read as follows: *David, filius Jesse, in regno suo quatuor elegit qui psalmos fecerunt, id est Asaph, Æman, Æthan, et Idithun;* which may be thus translated literally, " David, the son of Jesse, in his reign elected four persons who composed psalms, that is to say, Asaph, Æman, Æthan, and Idithun." In the painting these four names are separately appropriated, one to each of the four persons there represented; the player upon the violin is called Idithun, and Æthan is tossing up the knives and the balls.

I have been thus particular in describing these curious delineations, because I think they throw much light upon the profession of the Anglo-Saxon gleeman, and prove that his exhibitions were diversified at a very early period; for the reader, I doubt not, will readily agree with me, that dancing and sleights of hand were better calculated for secular pastimes than for accompaniments to the solemn performances of sacred psalmody. The honest illuminators having no ideas, as I before observed, of foreign or ancient manners, saw not the absurdity of making the Jewish monarch a president over a company of Saxon gleemen; they had heard, no doubt, that these persons whose names they found recorded in the book of Psalms, were poets and musicians; and therefore naturally concluded that they were gleemen, because they knew no others who performed in that double capacity but the gleemen: they knew also that these facetious artists were greatly venerated by persons of the highest rank, and their company requested by kings and princes, who richly rewarded them for the exercise of their talents, and for this reason, conceived that they were proper companions for the royal psalmist.

A ROYAL PLAYER WITH THREE DARTS.—The sleight of casting up a certain number of sharp instruments into the air, and catching them alternately in their fall, though part of the gleeman's profession, was not entirely confined to this practice. It is said of Olaf Fryggeson, one of the ancient kings of Norway, that he could play with three darts at once, tossing them in the air, and always kept two up while the third was down in his hand.[3] Our Saxon joculator, however, has the advantage of the monarch by adding the three balls, which of course must have made the trick more difficult to be performed.

BRAVERY OF A MINSTREL IN THE CONQUEROR'S ARMY.—The celebrated minstrel or juggler Taillefer, who came into England with William the Norman, was a warrior as well as a musician. He was present at the battle of Hastings, and appeared at the head of the Conqueror's army, singing the songs of Charlemagne and of Roland; but previous to the commencement of the action, he

---

[1] Vespasian, A. i.   [2] Tiberius, C. vi.   [3] Pontoppidan, *Hist. Norway*, p. 148.

advanced on horseback towards the army of the English, and, casting his spear three times into the air, he caught it as often by the iron head; and the fourth time he threw it among his enemies, one of whom he wounded in the body : he then drew his sword, which he also tossed into the air as many times as he had done his spear, and caught it with such dexterity, that those who saw him attributed his manœuvres to the power of enchantment. After he had performed these feats he galloped among the English soldiers, thereby giving the Normans the signal of battle; and in the action it appears he lost his life.[1]

OTHER PERFORMANCES BY GLEEMEN.—One part of the gleeman's profession, as early as the tenth century, was, teaching animals to dance, to tumble, and to put themselves into variety of attitudes, at the command of their masters.

Upon plate twenty-five we see the copy of a curious though rude delineation, being little more than an outline, which exhibits a specimen of this pastime. The principal joculator appears in the front, holding a knotted switch in one hand, and a line attached to a bear in the other; the animal is lying down in obedience to his command; and behind them are two more figures, the one playing upon two flutes or flageolets, and elevating his left leg while he stands upon his right, supported by a staff that passes under his armpit; the other dancing, in an attitude exceedingly ludicrous. This performance takes place upon an eminence resembling a stage made with earth; and in the original a vast concourse are standing round it in a semicircle as spectators of the sport, but they are so exceedingly ill drawn, and withal so indistinct, that I did not think it worth the pains to copy them. The dancing, if I may so call it, of the flute player, is repeated twice in the same manuscript. I have thence selected two other figures and placed them upon plate twenty.

Here we see a youth playing upon a harp with only four strings, and apparently singing at the same time, while an elderly man is performing the part of a buffoon or posture master, holding up one of his legs, and hopping upon the other to the music. Both these drawings occur in a MS. psalter in the Harleian Collection,[2] written in Latin, and apparently about the middle of the tenth century. It contains many drawings, all of them exceedingly rude, and most of them merely outlines. We shall have occasion farther on to speak more largely concerning all these kinds of diversions.

THE HARP USED BY THE SAXONS.—The bards and the scalds most assuredly used the harp to accompany their songs and modulate their voices. The Saxon gleemen and joculators followed their example, and are frequently called harpers for that reason; but, at the same time, it is equally certain, that they were well acquainted with several other instruments of music, as the violin, or something very similar to it; pipes or flutes of various kinds; horns and trumpets; to which may be added the tabor, or drum. The harp, indeed, was the most

---

[1] Wace, *Hist. de tut les Reys de Brittaigne*, continued by Geoffrai Gaimer, MS. in the Royal Library, marked 13 A. xxi.

*See Freeman's *Norman Conquest*, iii. 478; v. 582.　　　　[2] No. 603.

popular, and frequently exercised by persons who did not follow the profession of gleemen. We learn from Bede, an unquestionable authority, that, as early as the seventh century, it was customary at convivial meetings to hand a harp from one person to another, and every one who partook of the festivity played upon it in his turn, singing a song to the music for merriment sake.[1] The historian adds, that Cædmon, not being acquainted with such sort of songs, gat up when he saw the harp brought near him, and went home; the king adds the reason, namely, that he arose for shame, not being able to comply with the general practice. Probably this was not the practice when the professional harper was present, whose province it was to amuse the company.

*HARPERS AT DURHAM.—The Account Rolls of the abbey of Durham for the fourteenth century yield frequent reference to the harp and harpers. The prior had a harper attached to his great establishment; a harp was bought in 1335 for Thomas the harper at a cost of 3s.; in 1330 an itinerant harper received 12d.; in 1357 William, a blind harper, received 2s. at Christmas; and in 1360 a Welsh harper obtained 3s. 4d. In 1362 a harper belonging to the bishop of Norwich visited the abbey at the feast of the translation of St Cuthbert, and was rewarded with 5s.; he was an actor or jester as well as a harper, for he is termed *histrio harper*.[2]

THE NORMAN MINSTRELS.—Soon after the Conquest, these itinerant musicians lost the ancient Saxon appellation of gleemen, and were called ministraulx, in English minstrels, a term well known in Normandy some time before. As the minstrel's art consisted of several branches, the professors were distinguished by different denominations, as, "rimours, chanterres, conteours, jougleours or jongleurs, jestours, lecours, and troubadours or trouvers"; in modern language, rhymers, singers, story-tellers, jugglers, relaters of heroic actions, buffoons, and poets; but all of them were included under the general name of minstrel. In the Latin, *ministerellus*, or *ministrallus*, is also called *mimus, mimicus, histrio, joculator, versificator, cantor*, and *scurra*. An eminent French antiquary says of the minstrels, that some of them themselves composed the subjects they sang or related, as the trouvers and the conteurs; and some of them used the compositions of others, as the jugleours and the chanteurs. He farther remarks, that the trouvers may be said to have embellished their productions with rhyme, while the conteurs related their histories in prose; the jugleours, who in the middle ages were famous for playing upon the vielle accompanied the songs of the trouvers. The vielle was a stringed instrument, sounded by the turning of a wheel within it, resembling that which we frequently see about the streets played by the Savoyards, vulgarly called a hurdy-gurdy.[3]

---

[1] Bede's *Eccles. Hist.* lib. iv. cap. 24.

[2] Fowler's *Durham Account Rolls*, 3 vols. (1898-1900), *passim*.

[3] *A reward of 6s. 8d. was given to a *rotour* or player on a rotour on St Cuthbert's Day 1395, at Durham. It is described as "a sort of fiddle"; it was probably the same as the vielle described in the next paragraph. *Durham Account Rolls*, iii. 599, 955.

A man playing on a lute and his wife singing were awarded 2s. at Christmas 1361, by the prior of Durham. *Ibid.* i. 127.

These jugleours were also assisted by the chanteurs; and this union of talents rendered the compositions more harmonious and more pleasing to the auditory, and increased their rewards, so that they readily joined each other, and travelled together in large parties.[1] It is, however, very certain, that the poet, the songster, and the musician, were frequently united in the same person.

TROUBADOURS.—The Norman rhymers appear to have been the genuine descendants of the ancient Scandinavian scalds; they were well known in the northern part of France long before the appearance of the provincial poets called troubadours, and trouvers, that is, finders, probably from the fertility of their invention. The troubadours brought with them into the north a new species of language called the Roman language, which in the eleventh and twelfth centuries was commonly used in the southern provinces of France, and there esteemed as the most perfect of any in Europe. It evidently originated from the Latin, and was the parent of the French tongue; and in this language their songs and their poems were composed.[2] These poets were much admired and courted, being, as a very judicious modern writer[3] says, the delight of the brave and the favourites of the fair; because they celebrated the achievements of the one and the beauties of the other. Even princes became troubadours, and wrote poems in the provincial dialect; among others, a monarch of our own country certainly composed verses of this kind. The reader will, I doubt not, readily recollect the common story of Richard I., who, being closely confined in a castle belonging to the duke of Austria, was discovered by his favourite minstrel Blondel, a celebrated troubadour, through the means of a poem composed by the poet, in conjunction with his royal master. The story is thus related in a very ancient French author, quoted by Claude Fauchet: Blondel, seeing that his lord did not return, though it was reported that he had passed the sea from Syria, thought that he was taken by his enemies, and probably very evilly entreated; he therefore determined to find him, and for this purpose travelled through many countries without success: at last he came to a small town, near which was a castle belonging to the duke of Austria; and, having learned from his host that there was a prisoner in the castle who had been confined for upwards of a year, he went thither, and cultivated an acquaintance with the keepers; for a minstrel, says the author, can easily make acquaintance. However, he could not obtain a sight of the prisoner, nor learn his quality; he therefore placed himself near to a window belonging to the tower wherein he was shut up, and sang a few verses of a song which had been composed conjointly by him and his patron. The king, hearing the first part of the song, repeated the second; which convinced the poet that the prisoner was no other than Richard himself. Hastening therefore into England, he acquainted the barons with his adventure, and they, by means of a large sum of money, procured the liberty of the monarch.[4]

[1] Fauchet, *Origine de la Langue et Poësie Françoise*, 1581, liv. i. chap. viii. fol. 72.
[2] Le Grand, *Fables, ou Contes des 12. 13. Siècles*, tom. v. [3] Henry's *Hist. Brit.* vol. viii. sect. 3. chap. v. p. 502.
[4] Fauchet, *Des anciens Poëts François*, liv. ii. chap. vii. p. 92; and see Walpole, *Royal and Noble Authors*, vol. i. p. 6.

JESTOURS.—The conteurs and the jestours, who are also called dissours, and seggers, or sayers, and, in the Latin of that time, *fabulatores* and *narratores*, were literally, in English, tale-tellers, who recited either their own compositions or those of others, consisting of popular tales and romances, for the entertainment of public companies, on occasions of joy and festivity. Gower, a writer contemporary with Chaucer, describing the coronation of a Roman emperor, says,

> When every ministrell had playde,
> And every dissour had sayde,
> Which was most pleasaunt in his ear.[1]

In a manuscript collection of old stories, in the Harleian Library, we read of a king who kept a tale-teller on purpose to lull him to sleep every night; but some untoward accident having prevented him from taking his repose so readily as usual, he desired the fabulator to tell him longer stories; who obeyed, and began one upon a more extensive scale, and fell asleep himself in the midst of it.

TALES AND MANNERS OF THE JESTOURS.—The jestours, or, as the word is often written in the old English dialect, gesters, were the relaters of the gestes, that is, the actions of famous persons, whether fabulous or real; and these stories were of two kinds, the one to excite pity, and the other to move laughter, as we learn from Chaucer:[2]

> And jestours that tellen tales,
> Both of wepying and of game.

The tales of game, as the poet expresses himself, were short jocular stories calculated to promote merriment, in which the reciters paid little respect to the claims of propriety, or even of common decency. The tales of game, however, were much more popular than those of weeping, and probably for the very reason that ought to have operated the most powerfully for their suppression. The jestours, or jesters, whose powers were chiefly employed in the hours of conviviality, finding by experience that lessons of instruction were much less seasonable at such times than idle tales productive of mirth and laughter, accommodated their narrations to the general taste of the times, regardless of the mischiefs they occasioned by vitiating the morals of their hearers; hence it is, that the author of the *Vision of Pierce the Ploughman* calls them contemptibly "japers, and juglers, and janglers of gests."[3] He describes them also as haunters of taverns and common ale-houses, amusing the lower classes of the people with "myrth of minstrelsy and losels tales," loose vulgar tales, and calls them tale-tellers and "tutelers in ydell," tutors of idleness, occasioning their auditory, "for love of tales, in tavernes to drink," where they learned from them to jangle and to jape, instead of attending to their more serious duties; he therefore makes one to say,

> I can not parfitly my pater noster as the priest it singeth,
> But I can ryms of Roben Hode, and Randol erl of Chester
> But of our Lord or our Lady I lerne nothing at all:
> I am occupied every daye, holy daye, and other,
> With idle tales at the ale.—

---

[1] *Confessio Amantis*, lib. viii.   [2] The thirde boke of Fame.   [3] Edition of 1550.

He then blames the opulent for rewarding these "devils dissours," as he calls them, and adds,

He is worse than Judas that giveth a japer silver.[1]

The japers, I apprehend, were the same as the bourdours, or rybauders, an inferior class of minstrels, and properly called jesters in the modern acceptation of the word; whose wit, like that of the merry-andrews of the present day, consisted in low obscenity, accompanied with ludicrous gesticulation. They sometimes, however, found admission into the houses of the opulent. Knighton indeed mentions one of these japers who was a favourite in the English court, and could obtain any grant from the king "*a burdando*," that is, by jesting. They are well described by the poet:

As japers and janglers, Judas chyldren,
Fayneth them fantasies, and fooles them maketh.

It was a very common and a very favourite amusement, so late as the sixteenth century, to hear the recital of verses and moral speeches, learned for that purpose, by a set of men who obtained their livelihood thereby, and who, without ceremony, intruded themselves, not only into taverns and other places of public resort, but also into the houses of the nobility.

FURTHER ILLUSTRATION OF THEIR PRACTICES.—The different talents of the minstrels are sarcastically described by an ancient French poet;[2] who, supposing a company of them assembled in the hall of an opulent nobleman, says, the count caused it to be made known to them, that he would give his best new scarlet robe to the minstrel who should occasion the most merriment, either by ridiculous words or by actions. This proposal occasioned them to strive with each other; some of them imitated the imbecility of drunkards, others the actions of fools; some sang, others piped; some talked nonsense, and some made scurrilous jests; those who understood the juggler's art played upon the vielle; others of them depended on the narration of quaint fables, which were productive of much laughter.

PATRONAGE, PRIVILEGES, AND EXCESSES OF THE MINSTRELS.—There is great reason to conclude that the professors of music were more generally encouraged, and of course more numerous in this country, subsequent to the Norman conquest, than they had been under the government of the Saxons. We are told, that the courts of princes swarmed with poets and minstrels. The earls also and great barons, who in their castles emulated the pomp and state of royalty, had their poets and minstrels: they formed part of their household establishment; and, exclusive of their wages, were provided with board, lodging, and clothing by their patrons, and frequently travelled with them when they went from home.

These minstrels, as well as those belonging to the court, were permitted to perform in the rich monasteries, and in the mansions of the nobility, which they frequently visited in large parties, and especially upon occasions of festivity. They entered the castles without the least ceremony, rarely waiting for any

---

[1] A reward.   [2] *Fabliaux et Contes*, edit. Par. tom. ii. p. 161.

previous invitation, and there exhibited their performances for the entertainment of the lord of the mansion and his guests. They were, it seems, admitted without any difficulty, and handsomely rewarded for the exertion of their talents.

It was no uncommon thing with the itinerant minstrels to find admission into the houses of the opulent. The Saxon and the Danish gleemen followed the armies in the time of war, and had access to both the camps without the least molestation. The popular story of king Alfred, recorded by William of Malmsbury and other writers, may be mentioned in proof of this assertion. He, it is said, assumed the character of a gleeman,[1] and entered the Danish camp, where he made such observations as were of infinite service. This stratagem was afterwards repeated by Aulaff, the Dane, who was equally successful. He assumed, says the historian, the profession of the mimic, "who by this species of art makes a daily gain;" and then adds, "being commanded to depart, he took with him the reward for his song."[2]

The extensive privileges enjoyed by the minstrels, and the long continuance of the public favour, inflated their pride and made them insolent; they even went so far as to claim their reward by a prescriptive right, and settled its amount according to the estimation they had formed of their own abilities, and the opulence of the noblemen into whose houses they thought proper to intrude. The large gratuities collected by these artists not only occasioned great numbers to join their fraternity, but also induced many idle and dissipated persons to assume the characters of minstrels, to the disgrace of the profession. These evils became at last so notorious, that in the reign of king Edward II. it was thought necessary to restrain them by a public edict, which sufficiently explains the nature of the grievance. It states, that many indolent persons, under the colour of minstrelsy, intruded themselves into the residences of the wealthy, where they had both meat and drink, but were not contented without the addition of large gifts from the householder. To restrain this abuse, the mandate ordains, that no person should resort to the houses of prelates, earls, or barons, to eat, or to drink, who was not a professed minstrel; nor more than three or four minstrels of honour at most in one day, meaning, I presume, the king's minstrels and those retained by the nobility, except they came by invitation from the lord of the house.

Thus we read in the old romance of Launfel,

> They had menstrelles of moche honours,
> Fydelers, sytolyrs, and trompoters.

The edict also prohibits a professed minstrel from going to the house of any person below the dignity of a baron, unless invited by the master; and, in that case, it commands him to be contented with meat and drink, and such reward as the housekeeper willingly offered, without presuming to ask for anything. For the first offence the minstrel lost his minstrelsy, and for the second

---

[1] Malmsb. lib. ii. cap. 4.　　　　　[2] *Hist.* lib. ii. cap. 6.

he was obliged to forswear his profession, and was never to appear again as a minstrel.[1] This edict is dated from Langley, an. 9 Edward II. A.D. 1315.

A GILD OF MINSTRELS.—In little more than a century afterwards, the same grievances became again the subject of complaint; and in the ninth year of Edward IV. (1469) it was stated, that certain rude husbandmen and artificers of various trades had assumed the title and livery of the king's minstrels, and, under that colour and pretence, had collected money in divers parts of the kingdom, and committed other disorders; the king therefore granted to Walter Haliday, marshal, and to seven others, his own minstrels, named by him, a charter, by which he created, or rather restored, a fraternity, or perpetual gild, such as the king understood the brothers and sisters of the fraternity of minstrels to have possessed in former time. This fraternity was to be governed by a marshal appointed for life, the same office as that anciently possessed by the king of the minstrels, and two wardens, who were empowered to admit members into the gild, and to regulate and govern, and to punish, when necessary, all such as exercised the profession of minstrels throughout the kingdom.[2]

*This gild was attached to the cathedral church of St Paul's for its religious functions. The minstrels of Chester, who had already several charter privileges, were exempted from the operations of the general charter of 1469. There was also a famous gild of minstrels at Beverley. The ordinances of gilds of minstrels at York and Canterbury are still extant.[3]

ABUSES AND DECLINE OF MINSTRELSY.—It does not appear that much good was effected by the foregoing institution or general gild; it neither corrected the abuses practised by the fraternity, nor retrieved their reputation, which declined apace from this period. Under queen Elizabeth, the minstrels had lost the protection of the opulent; and their credit was sunk so low in the public estimation, that, by a statute in the thirty-ninth year of her reign against vagrants, they were included among the rogues, vagabonds, and sturdy beggars, and subjected to the like punishments. This edict also affected all fencers, bearwards, common players of interludes (with the exception of such players as belonged to great personages, or had obtained licences from town or country authorities), as well as minstrels wandering abroad, jugglers, tinkers, and pedlars; and seems to have given the death's wound to the profession of the minstrels, who had so long enjoyed the public favour, and basked in the sunshine of prosperity. The name, however, remained, and was applied to itinerant fiddlers and other musicians, whose low estate is thus described by Putenham, in his *Arte of English Poesie*, printed in 1589:[4] "Ballads and small popular musickes sung by these cantabanqui upon benches and barrels heads, where they have none other audience than boyes or countrye fellowes that passe by them in the streete, or else by blind harpers, or such like taverne minstrels that give a fit of mirth for a groat; and their matters being for the most part stories of old time, as the

---

[1] App. to Leland's *Collect.* vol. vi. p. 36.   [2] Patent Rolls of Edw. IV. pt. i. m. 17.
[3] *Jusseraud's *English Wayfaring Life*, 205-6; Lambert's *Two Thousand Years of Gild Life*, 132-137.
[4] Book ii. chap. 9.

tale of Sir Topas, Bevis of Southampton, Guy of Warwick, Adam Bell and Clymme of the Clough, and such other old romances or historical rhimes, made purposely for the recreation of the common people at Christmas dinners and bride ales, and in tavernes and alehouses, and such other places of base resort." Bishop Hall, the satirist, adverts to the poor plight of the minstrels at this time, in the last two lines of the following couplet :—

> Much better than a Paris-garden beare,
> Or prating puppet on a theatre,
> Or Mimoes whistling to his tabouret,
> Selling a laughter for a cold meales meat.[1]

It is necessary, however, to observe, that public and private bands of musicians were called minstrels for a considerable time after this period, and without the least indication of disgrace; but then the appellation seems to have been confined to the instrumental performers, and such of them as were placed upon a regular establishment: the musicians of the city of London, for instance, were called indifferently waits and minstrels.[2]

We hear of the itinerant musicians again in an ordinance from Oliver Cromwell, dated 1656, during his protectorship, which prohibits "all persons commonly called fidlers, or minstrells," from "playing, fidling, and making music, in any inn, alehouse, or tavern"; and also from "proffering themselves, or desireing, or intreating any one to hear them play, or make music in the places aforesaid." The only vestige of these musical vagrants now remaining, is to be found in the blind fiddlers wandering about the country, and the ballad singers, who frequently accompany their ditties with instrumental music, especially the fiddle, vulgarly called a crowd, and the guitar. And here we may observe, that the name of fiddlers was applied to the minstrels as early at least as the four-teenth century: it occurs in the *Vision of Pierce the Ploughman*,[3] where we read, "not to fare as a fydeler, or a frier, to seke feastes." It is also used, but not sarcastically, in the poem of Launfel.

MINSTRELS WERE SATIRISTS AND FLATTERERS.—The British bards employed their musical talents in the praise of heroic virtue, or in the censure of vice, apparently without any great expectation of reward on the one hand, or fear of punishment on the other. The Scandinavian scalds celebrated the valiant actions of their countrymen in appropriate verses; and sometimes accompanied the warriors to the field of battle, that they might behold their exploits and describe them with more accuracy. The gleemen of the Saxons imitated their pre-decessors, and attached themselves to the persons of princes and chieftains, and retained their favour by continual adulation. The minstrels of the Normans trod in the same steps, but seem to have been more venal, and ready at all times to flatter or to satirise, as best suited their interest, without paying much regard to justice on either side.

ANECDOTES OF OFFENDING MINSTRELS.—It is said of William Longchamp,

---

[1] Lib. iv. sat. i. [2] Stow's *Survey of London*, pp. 84, 85 Pass. xi.

bishop of Ely, chancellor and justiciary of England, who was also the Pope's legate, and a great favourite of Richard I., that he kept a number of poets in his pay, to make songs and poems in his praise; and also, that with great gifts he allured many of the best singers and minstrels from the Continent, to sing those songs in the public streets of the principal cities in England.[1]

It was, on the other hand, a very dangerous employment to censure the characters of great personages, or hold their actions up to ridicule; for, though the satirist might be secure at the moment, he was uncertain that fortune would not one day or another put him into the power of his adversary, which was the case with Luke de Barra, a celebrated Norman minstrel; who, in his songs having made very free with the character of Henry I. of England, by some untoward accident fell into the hands of the irritated monarch. He condemned him to have his eyes pulled out: and, when the earl of Flanders, who was present, pleaded warmly in his favour, the king replied: "This man, being a wit, a poet, and a minstrel, composed many indecent songs against me, and sung them openly to the great entertainment of mine enemies; and, since it has pleased God to deliver him into my hands, I will punish him, to deter others from the like petulance." The cruel sentence was executed, and the miserable satirist died soon after with the wounds he had received in struggling with the executioner.[2]

Again, in the reign of king Edward II., at the solemnisation of the feast of Pentecost in the great hall at Westminster, when that prince was seated at dinner in royal state, and attended by the peers of the realm, a woman habited like a minstrel, riding upon a great horse trapped in the minstrel fashion, entered the hall, and, going round the several tables, imitated the gestures of a mimic,[3] and at length mounted the steps to the royal table, upon which she deposited a letter; and, having so done, she turned her horse, and saluting all the company, retired. The letter was found to contain some very severe reflections upon the conduct of the monarch, which greatly angered him; and the actress, being arrested by his command, discovered the author of the letter, who acknowledged the offence and was pardoned; but the door-keeper, being reprimanded on account of her admission, excused himself, by declaring it had never been customary to prevent the entry of minstrels and persons in disguisements, upon the supposition that they came for the entertainment of his majesty. This woman had probably assumed the habit of a man, and a female was chosen on this occasion, according to the opinion of Dr Percy,[4] because, upon detection, her sex might plead for her, and disarm the king's resentment. It is, however, certain that at this time, and long before it, there were women who practised the minstrel's art, or at least some branches of it. We read of the glee-maidens, or

[1] Benedict. Abbas, sub an. 1190. Hoveden writes thus: "*Cantores et joculatores de illo canerent in plateis; ut jam dicebatur ubique quod non erat talis in orbe*"; declaring everywhere that his equal was not in the world. *Hist.* p. 103.

[2] Orderic. Vitalis, *Eccles. Hist.* pp. 880, 881.

[3] Walsingham, *Hist. Anglæ.* sub an. 1317, p. 85.

[4] Essay upon Ancient Minstrels, in *Reliques of Ancient Poetry.*

female minstrels, in the Saxon records; and I believe that their province in general was to dance and to tumble, whence they acquired the name of tomble-steres, from the Saxon zumbian, to dance or tumble, and saylours, from salio, to leap or dance, in the time of Chaucer, who uses both these denominations.[1]

THE DRESS OF THE MINSTRELS.—It is very clear, that the minstrels wore a peculiar kind of dress by which they might readily be distinguished: the woman above mentioned· is expressly said to have been habited like a mimic or a minstrel, and by that means obtained admission without the least difficulty to the royal presence. I remember also a story recorded in a manuscript, written about the reign of Edward III., of a young man of family, who came to a feast, where many of the nobility were present, in a vesture called a coat hardy, cut short in the German fashion, and resembling the dress of a minstrel. The oddity of his habit attracted the notice of the company, and especially of an elderly knight, to whom he was well known, who thus addressed him: "Where, my friend, is your fiddle, your ribible, or such-like instrument belonging to a minstrel?" "Sir," replied the young man, "I have no crafte nor science in using such instruments." "Then," returned the knight, "you are much to blame; for, if you choose to debase yourself and your family by appearing in the garb of a minstrel, it is fitting you should be able to perform his duty."[2] On a column in Saint Mary's church at Beverley in Yorkshire is the following inscription: "This pyllor made the maynstrels"; its capital is decorated with small figures of men in short coats painted blue, with red stockings and yellow girdles and stocks. The instruments they bear are a crowth (fiddle), a guitar, a treble and base flute, and a side drum and tabor. The date is early sixteenth century. The minstrels retained in noblemen's families wore their lords' livery; and those appertaining to the royal household did the same. The edict of Edward IV. against the pretended minstrels, mentioned above, expressly says, that they assumed the name, and the livery or dress, of the king's own minstrels. The queen had also minstrels in her service, who probably wore a livery different from those of the king for distinction sake. The following lines, which are somewhat to the purpose, occur in an old historical poem, in the Harleian Collection: they relate to Sir Edward Stanley, who is highly praised by the author for his great skill in playing upon all kinds of instruments :—

> He stood before the kinge, doubtless this was true,
> In a fayre gowne of cloth of gold, and of tilshewe,
> Lyke no common mynstrel, to shew taverne mirth,
> But lyke a noble man, both of lands, and of birth.[3]

And again, in the history of John Newchombe, the famous clothier of Newbury, usually called Jack of Newbury, it is said, "They had not sitten long, but in comes a noise of musicians in tawnie coats; who, putting off their caps, asked if they would have any music?"

[1] The first in the "Pardoner's Tale," and the last in the "Romance of the Rose."
[2] Harl. MS. 1764.   [3] Harl. MS. 541.

THE KING OF THE MINSTRELS.—The king's minstrel, frequently in Latin called *joculator regis*, or the king's juggler, was an officer of rank in the courts of the Norman monarchs. He had the privilege of accompanying his master when he journeyed, and of being near his person; and probably was the regulator of the royal sports, and appointed the other minstrels belonging to the household; for which reason, I presume, he was also called the king, or chief of the minstrels. At what time this title was first conferred on him does not appear: we meet with it, however, in an account of the public expenditures made in the fifth year of Edward I.; at which time, the king of the minstrels, whose name was Robert, received his master's pay for military services.[1] The same name, with the same title annexed to it, occurs again in a similar record, dated the fourth year of Edward II.; when he, in company with various other minstrels, exhibited before the king and his court, then held in the city of York; and received forty marks, to be by him distributed among the fraternity.[2]

The title of royalty was not confined to the king's chief minstrel: it was also bestowed upon the regent of other companies of musicians, as we find in a charter granted by John of Gaunt, duke of Lancaster, to the minstrels of Tutbury in Staffordshire. This document he addresses, under his seal, at the castle of Tutbury, August 24, in the fourth year of Richard II., to *nostre bene ame le roy des ministraulx*, his well beloved the king of the minstrels; and concedes to him full power and commission to oblige the minstrels belonging to the honour of Tutbury to perform their services and minstrelsies in the same manner that they had been accustomed to be done in ancient times.[3] In a ballad intituled "The marriage of Robin Hood and Clorinda the Queen of Tutbury Feast,"[4] written probably after the disgrace of the minstrels, this officer is called the king of the fidlers. The poet supposes himself to have been present at the wedding, and witness of the facts he relates; and therefore he speaks thus:—

> This battle was fought near to Titbury town,
> When the bagpipes baited the bull.
> I am king of the fidlers, and swear 'tis a truth,
> And I call him that doubts it a gull.

Claude Fauchet, a French author of eminence, before quoted, speaking concerning the title of king, formerly given to many officers belonging to the court, makes these observations: "I am well assured, the word king signifies comptroller, or head, as the chief heralds are called kings at arms, because it belonged solely to them to regulate the ceremonies of the justs and tournaments." He then applies this reasoning to the Roy des Ribaulx, an officer in the ancient court of France;[5] and says, his charge was to clear the palace of

---

[1] MS. Cott. Vespasianus, C. xvi.

[2] "*Regi Roberto, et aliis ministrallis diversis, facientibus ministralsias suas coram rege et aliis magnatibus, de dono ipsius regis, per manus dicti regis Roberti, recipientis denarios ad participandum inter eosdem, apud Eboracum 20 die Feb. 40 marc.*" MS. Cott. Nero, C. viii.

[3] Dugd. *Monast.* vol. i. fol. 355.   [4] *Collection of Old Ballads*, London, 1723.

[5] Chaucer, in the *Romance of the Rose*, where the title *Roy des Ribaulx* occurs in the original, translates it "king of harlotes."

L

indolent and disorderly persons, who followed the court, and had no business there ; and had his title as king of vagabonds, because he was the examiner and corrector of dissolute persons.[1] In like manner, I presume, in this country, the king of the minstrels was the governor and director of the fraternity over which he presided. The title was dropped in the reign of Edward IV., and that of marshal became its substitute.

REWARDS GIVEN TO MINSTRELS.—In the middle ages, the courts of princes, and the residences of the opulent, were crowded with minstrels ; and such large sums of money were expended for their maintenance, that the public treasuries were often drained. Matilda, queen to Henry I., is said to have lavished the greater part of her revenue upon poets and minstrels, and oppressed her tenants to procure more.[2] She was, however, by no means singular in so doing, as the invectives of the monks sufficiently demonstrate. These selfish professors of religion grudged every act of munificence that was not applied to themselves, or their monasteries ; and could not behold the good fortune of the minstrels without expressing their indignation ; which they often did in terms of scurrilous abuse, calling them janglers, mimics, buffoons, monsters of men, and contemptible scoffers. They also severely censured the nobility for patronising and rewarding such a shameless set of sordid flatterers, and the populace for frequenting their exhibitions, and being delighted with their performances, which diverted them from more serious pursuits, and corrupted their morals.[3] On the other hand, the minstrels appear to have been ready enough to give them ample occasion for censure ; and, indeed, I apprehend that their own immorality and insolence contributed more to their downfall than all the defamatory declamations of their opponents. The ecclesiastics were mightily pleased with the conduct of the emperor Henry III., because, at his marriage with Agnes of Poictou, he disappointed the poor minstrels who had assembled in great multitudes on the occasion, giving them neither food nor rewards, but "sent them away," says a monkish author, "with empty purses, and hearts full of sorrow."[4] But to go on.

The rewards given to the minstrels did not always consist in money, but frequently in rich mantles and embroidered vestments : they received, says Fauchet, great presents from the nobility, who would sometimes give them even the robes with which they were clothed. It was a common custom in the middle ages to give vestments of different kinds to the minstrels. In an ancient poem, cited by Fauchet, called "La Robe Vermeille," or, The Red Robe, the wife of a vavaser, that is, one who, holding of a superior lord, has tenants under him, reproaches her husband for accepting a robe. "Such gifts," says she, "belong to jugglers, and other singing men, who receive garments from the nobility, because it is their trade :

---

[1] *Origines des Dignitez et Magistrats de France*, fol. 43.   [2] Will. Malmsb. p. 93, col. I.

[3] Johan. Sarisburiensis, *De Nugis Curial.* lib. i. cap. 8 ; lib. iii. cap. 7. Matt. Paris, in *Vit. Hen. III.* sub an. 1251, etc.

[4] "*Infinitum histrionum et joculatorum multitudinem, sine cibo et muneribus, vacuam et mœrentum abire permisit.*" Chron. Virtziburg.

> S'appartient à ces jorgleours,
> Et à ces autres chanteours,
> Quils ayent de ces chevaliers,
> Les robes car c'est lor mestier." [1]

These garments the jugglers failed not to take with them to other courts, in order to excite a similar liberality. Another artifice they often used, which was, to make the heroes of their poems exceedingly bountiful to the minstrels, who appear to have been introduced for that purpose : thus, in the metrical romance of Ipomedon, where the poet speaks of the knight's marriage, he says :—

> Ipomydon gaff, in that stound,
> To mynstrelles five hundred pound. [2]

The author of *Pierce the Ploughman*, who lived in the reign of Edward III., gives the following general description of the different performances of the minstrels, and of their rewards, at that period :—

> I am mynstrell, quoth that man ; my name is Activa Vita ;
> All Idle iche hate, for All Active is my name ;
> A wafirer [3] well ye wyt ; and serve many lordes,
> And few robes I get, or faire furred gownes.
> Could I lye, to do men laugh ; then lachen [4] I should
> Nother mantill, nor money, amonges lords minstrels :
> And, for I can neither taber, ne trumpe, ne tell no gestes,
> Fartin ne fislen, at feastes, ne harpen ;
> Jape, ne juggle, ne gentilly pype,
> Ne neither saylen ne saute, [5] ne singe to the gytterne,
> I have no good giftes to please the great lordes.

And, if we refer to history, we shall find that the poets are not incorrect in their statement. Gaston, earl of Foix, whose munificence is much commended by Froissart, lived in a style of splendour little inferior to that of royalty. The historian, speaking of a grand entertainment given by this nobleman, which he had an opportunity of seeing, says, " Ther wer many mynstrells, as well of his own, as of straungers ; and each of them dyd their devoyre, in their faculties. [6] The same day the earl of Foix gave to the heraulds and minstrelles the som of five hundred frankes ; and gave to the duke of Tourayn's minstrelles gownes of cloth of gold, furred with ermyne, valued at two hundred frankes." [7]

Respecting the pecuniary rewards of the minstrels, we have, among others, the following accounts. At the marriage of Elizabeth, daughter of Edward I. to John, earl of Holland, every king's minstrel received forty shillings. [8] In the fourth of Edward I[1]. Perrot de la Laund, minstrel to Lord Hugh de Nevill, received twenty shillings for performing his minstrelsy before the king. [9] In the same year, Janino la Cheveretter, who is called Le Tregettour, [10] was paid at one

---

[1] *Origine de la Langue et Poësie Françoise*, lib. i. cap. 4. [2] Harl. MS. 2252.
[3] A confectioner. [4] Lack, or want.
[5] Dance, nor jump. Pass. xiv. [6] Duty in their several stations.
[7] Lord Berners' *Froissart*, vol. iv. cap. 41. [8] Anstis, *Ord. Gart.* vol. ii. p. 303.
[9] *Liber de Computis Garderobæ*, MS. Cott. Lib. Nero, C. viii. fol. 82.

[10] *Cheveretter*, or bagpiper ; from chevre, a bagpipe, and tregettor, or juggler, a sleight of hand player. *Ibid.* See more on this subject in the next chapter relating to the joculator.

time forty shillings, and at another twenty, for the same service; and John le Mendlesham, the servant of Robert le Foll, twenty shillings;[1] the same sum was also given to John le Boteller, the servant of Perrot Duzedeys, for his performances; and, again, Perrot Duzedeys, Roger the Trumpeter, and Janino le Nakerer, all of them king's minstrels, received from the king sixty shillings for the like service.

PAYMENTS TO MINSTRELS.—In the eighth year of Edward III. licence was granted to Barbor the bagpiper to visit the schools for minstrels in parts beyond the seas,[2] with thirty shillings to bear his expenses. Licence was also granted to Morlan the bagpiper to visit the minstrels' schools; and forty shillings for his expenses. A little lower we find a present of five shillings made by the king to a minstrel, for performing his minstrelsy before the image of the Blessed Virgin.[3] In the eleventh year of the same reign, John de Hoglard, minstrel to John de Pulteney, was paid forty shillings for exhibiting before the king at Hatfield, and at London; and to Roger the Trumpeter, and to the minstrels his associates, performing at the feast for the queen's delivery, held at Hatfield, ten pounds. The permanent salary of the royal minstrels of Edward III. was $7\frac{1}{2}$d. a day.[4]

*Henry V., in 1415, engaged eighteen minstrels to follow him to Guyenne at a wage of 12d. a day each for three months.[5] Henry VI., as has been already stated, retained twelve minstrels among his household servants. Two of the court minstrels of Edward IV. obtained grants of ten marks yearly.

In the ninth year of Henry VII. "Pudesay the piper in bagpipes," received six shillings and eight pence from the king, for his performance.[6] In the fourteenth year of his reign, five pounds were paid to three stryng-mynstrels for wages, but the time is not specified; in a subsequent entry, however, we find that fifteen shillings were given to "a stryng-mynstrel, for one moneth's wages"; also to a "straunge taberer, in reward, sixty-six shillings and eight pence."[7]

*MINSTRELS AND PLAYERS AT DURHAM.—The *Durham Account Rolls* yield much information as to minstrels. In 1278 a minstrel of Newcastle-on-Tyne obtained 2s. from the prior of Durham. In 1336 a band of minstrels were rewarded with 20s. A trumpeter and a minstrel received 5s. on the festival of St Cuthbert 1369, and on the like occasion in 1374 twelve minstrels received 20s. 8d. March 20th was the original festival of St Cuthbert, but his transla-tion on September 14th was considered the greater festival; at the former of these, in 1375, the minstrels received 13s. 4d., and at the latter 20s. In the

---

[1] Another entry specifies twenty shillings paid to Robert le Foll to buy himself *boclarium*, a buckler, to play, *aa ludendum*, before the king. *Liber de Computis Garderobæ*, MS. Cott. Lib. Nero, C. viii. f. 85.

[2] *Scolas ministrallis in partibus trans mare. Ibid.* f. 276.

[3] *Facienti ministralsiam suam coram imagine Beatæ Mariæ in Veltam, rege presente*, 5 sol. *Ibid.* f. 277.

[4] *Issue Roll of Tho. de Brantingham*, pp. 54-57.

[5] Rymer's *Fœdera*, ix. 260.

[6] MS. in the Remembrancer's Office. See the extract in Henry's *British History*, vol. vi. Appendix No. V.

[7] From another MS. in the same office. *Ibid.*

same year three minstrels of the earl of March obtained 6s. 8d.; one of the king's minstrels, who came with Lord Neville, 5s.; four minstrels of the prince of Wales, on the feast of the Exaltation of the Cross, 13s. 4d.; a minstrel on St Matthew's day, 20d.; two minstrels at Easter, 2s.; and a certain minstrel who played before the prior in his chamber, 18d. Earl Percy's minstrels visited the abbey in 1376, at Christmas, and received 6s. 8d. A minstrel accompanied by a dancer performed before the prior in his chamber in 1382; they received 6s. 8d. for their pains. In the year 1394 duly rewarded visits were paid to the abbey by the minstrels of Earl Percy, of the duke of Lancaster, of Lord Neville, of the duke of York, and of the earl of Kent, as well as by a royal trumpeter. Various minstrel entries occur in the fifteenth century. The last reference in these Durham Rolls is at an interesting date in ecclesiastical history. March 3, 1555, was the day that " the proclamation and bonefyres war made for receyving of the Pope in this realm agayn," when three pottles of wine were drunk in the dean's chamber, and two gallons of ale in the garth, in addition to the wine and ale consumed by the servants. Four pence was paid for a tar barrel, and eight pence "for two mynstralles."

*All these payments just cited are entered under the head of minstrels (*ministralli*); but there are an almost equal number entered under the head or title of players (*histriones*), which extend in date from 1301 to 1360. There probably was but slight difference between the two, and the use of the varied terms mainly depended on the fashion of the time or the caprice of the scribe. Nevertheless, although the actor might be also a musician or juggler, the phrase *histrio* seems to convey more definite notion of a play actor than that of *ministrallus*, and the former word is possibly usually entered in these accounts when the strolling band of entertainers were capable of representing certain set pieces. This would doubtless be the case when particular companies visited the abbey. In 1334, the king's players received 40s. when the king was returning from Newcastle; and in the following year the players of the king of Scotland obtained 5s. from the prior. The king's players at Christmas 1343 were rewarded with 10s. At Christmas 1352, one William Pyper and other players received 6s. At St Cuthbert's feast in March 1353, two players of the lord bishop together with two players of the earl of Northampton obtained 6s. 8d. The two players of the bishop, who were probably merely harpers or genuine minstrels, received 3s. 4d. at Easter in the same year.[1]

*MINSTRELS AT PARISH FESTIVALS.—The hiring of minstrels for parish festivals at the end of the fifteenth and beginning of the sixteenth century is testified by various churchwardens' accounts, such as those of St Mary's, Reading. The parish accounts of Yatton, Somerset, show that the wardens paid with considerable regularity for a minstrel or minstrels at Whitsuntide. The first entry is for the year 1521, when 12d. was "payd to a mynnystrelle." In 1531 the "mynestrell att Wytsonday" received 2s. 8d.; in 1532, 6s.; and

---

[1] Fowler's *Durham Account Rolls*, 3 vols. (1898-1900), *passim*.

in 1533, 8s. 4d. Occasionally as much as ten shillings is entered for the Whitsuntide minstrel, as though only one; but in these larger payments, the entry probably means that the money was given to the head minstrel. In 1536 two minstrels were paid 6s., and the same number in 1540 received 6s. 9d. Three were given 13s. 8d. in 1543. The last minstrel entry of these accounts is under the year 1559, when ten shillings was their fee.[1] It is clear that this minstrelsy had no connection with music in church, but was rather for the festivities of the Whitsun Ale.

[1] Bishop Hobhouse's *Churchwarden Accounts* (Somerset Record Society, vol. iv.).

CHAPTER IV

The Joculator—His different Denominations and extraordinary Deceptions—His Performances ascribed to Magic—Asiatic Jugglers—Remarkable Story from Froissart—Tricks of the Jugglers ascribed to the Agency of the Devil; but more reasonably accounted for—John Rykell, a celebrated Tregetour—Their various Performances—Privileges of the Joculators at Paris—The King's Joculator an Officer of Rank—The great Disrepute of modern Jugglers.

THE JOCULATOR.—The *joculator*, or the jugglour of the Normans, was frequently included under the collective appellation of minstrel. His profession originally was very comprehensive, and included the practice of all the arts attributed to the minstrel; and some of the jugglers were excellent tumblers. Joinville, in the *Life of St Louis and Charpentier*, quotes an old author, who speaks of a joculator, *qui sciebat tombare*.[1] He was called a gleeman in the Saxon era, and answers to the juggler of the more modern times. In the fourteenth century he was also denominated a *tregetour*, or *tragetour*, at which time he appears to have been separated from the musical poets, who exercised the first branches of the gleeman's art, and are more generally considered as minstrels.

DIFFERENT DENOMINATIONS OF THE JOCULATOR, AND HIS EXTRAORDINARY DECEPTIONS.—The name of tregetours was chiefly, if not entirely, appropriated to those artists who, by sleight of hand, with the assistance of machinery of various kinds, deceived the eyes of the spectators, and produced such illusions as were usually supposed to be the effect of enchantment; for which reason they were frequently ranked with magicians, sorcerers, and witches; and, indeed, the feats they performed, according to the descriptions given of them, abundantly prove that they were no contemptible practitioners in the arts of deception. Chaucer, who, no doubt, had frequently an opportunity of seeing the tricks exhibited by the tregetours in his time, says, "There I sawe playenge jogelours, magyciens, trageteours, phetonysses, charmeresses, olde witches, and sorceresses," etc.[2] He speaks of them in a style that may well excite astonishment: "There are," says he, "sciences by which men can delude the eye with divers appearances, such as the subtil tregetours perform at feasts. In a large hall they will produce water with boats rowed up and down upon it." In the library of Sir Hans Sloane, at the British Museum, is a MS[3] which contains "an experiment to make the appearance of a flode of water to come into a house." The directions are, to steep a thread in the liquor produced from snakes' eggs bruised, and to hang it up over a basin of water in the place where

---

[1] Supplement to Du Cange.

[2] Chaucer, *House of Fame*, book iii. [3] No. 1315.

the trick is to be performed. The tregetours, no doubt, had recourse to a surer method. Chaucer goes on to say, "Sometimes they will bring in the similitude of a grim lion, or make flowers spring up as in a meadow; sometimes they cause a vine to flourish, bearing white and red grapes; or show a castle built with stone; and when they please, they cause the whole to disappear." He then speaks of "a learned clerk," who, for the amusement of his friend, showed to him "forests full of wild deer, where he saw an hundred of them slain, some with hounds and some with arrows; the hunting being finished, a company of falconers appeared upon the banks of a fair river, where the birds pursued the herons, and slew them. He then saw knights justing upon a plain"; and, by way of conclusion, "the resemblance of his beloved lady dancing; which occasioned him to dance also." But, when "the maister that this magike wrought thought fit, he clapped his hands together, and all was gone in an instante."[1] Again, in another part of his works, the same poet says :—

> There saw I Coll Tregetour,
> Upon a table of sycamour,
> Play an uncouthe thynge to tell ;
> I sawe hym cary a wynde-mell
> Under a walnote shale.[2]

THE JOCULATORS' PERFORMANCES ASCRIBED TO MAGIC.—Chaucer attributes these illusions to the practice of natural magic. Thus the Squire, in his Tale, says :—

> An appearance made by some magyke,
> As jogglours playen at their festes grete.

And again, in the third book of the *House of Fame* :—

> And clerkes eke which conne well
> All this magyke naturell.

Meaning, I suppose, an artful combination of different powers of nature in a manner not generally understood; and therefore he makes the Devil say to the Sompner in the Friar's Tale, "I can take any shape that pleases me; of a man, of an ape, or of an angel; and it is no wonder, a lousy juggler can deceive you; and I can assure you my skill is superior to his." I need not say, that a greater latitude was assigned to what the poet calls natural magic in his days, than will be granted in the present time.

ASIATIC JUGGLERS.—Sir John Mandeville, who wrote about the same period as Chaucer, speaks thus of a similar exhibition performed before the Great Chan : "And then comen jogulours, and enchauntours, that doen many marvaylles"; for they make, says he, the appearance of the sun and the moon in the air; and then they make the night so dark, that nothing can be seen; and again they restore the daylight, with the sun shining brightly; then they "bringen-in daunces, of the fairest damsels of the world, and the richest arrayed"; afterwards they make other damsels to come in, bringing cups of gold, full of the milk of

---

[1] Frankeleyn's Tale.   [2] *House of Fame*, book iii.

divers animals, and give drink to the lords and ladies; and then "they make knyghts jousten in armes fulle lustily," who run together, and in the encounter break their spears so rudely, that the splinters fly all about the hall.[1] They also bring in a hunting of the hart and of the boar, with hounds running at them open-mouthed; and many other things they do by the craft of their enchantments, that are "marvellous to see." In another part he says, "And be it done by craft, or by nicromancy, I wot not."[2]

REMARKABLE STORY FROM FROISSART.—The foregoing passages bring to my recollection a curious piece of history related by Froissart, which extends the practice of these deceptions far beyond the knowledge of the modern jugglers. When, says that author, the duke of Anjou and the earl of Savoy were lying with their army before the city of Naples, there was "an enchaunter, a conning man in nigromancy, in the Marches of Naples." This man promised to the duke of Anjou, that he would put him in possession of the castle of Leufe, at that time besieged by him. The duke was desirous of knowing by what means this could be effected; and the magician said, "I shall, by enchauntment, make the ayre so thicke, that they within the castell will think there is a great brydge over the sea, large enough for ten men a-breast to come to them; and when they see this brydge, they will readily yeilde themselves to your mercy, least they should be taken perforce." And may not my men, said the duke, pass over this bridge in reality? To this question the juggler artfully replied, "I dare not, syr, assure you that; for, if any one of the men that passeth on the brydge shall make the sign of the cross upon him, all shall go to noughte, and they that be upon it shall fall into the sea." The earl of Savoy was not present at this conference; but being afterwards made acquainted with it, he said to the duke, "I know well it is the same enchaunter, by whom the queene of Naples and syr Othes of Bresugeth were taken in this castle; for he caused, by his crafte, the sea to seeme so high, that they within were sore abashed, and wend all to have died; but no confidence," continued he, "ought to be placed in a fellow of this kind, who has already betrayed the queen for hire; and now, for the sake of another reward, is willing to give up the man whose bounty he has received." The earl then commanded the enchanter to be brought before him; when he boasted that, by the power of his art, he had caused the castle to be delivered to Sir Charles de la Paye, who was then in possession of it; and concluded his speech with these words: "Syr, I am the man of the world that syr Charles reputeth most, and is most in fear of." "By my fayth," replied the earl of Savoy, "ye say well; and I will that syr Charles shall know that he hath great wrong to feare you: but I shall assure hym of you, for ye shal never do more enchauntments to deceyve hym, nor yet any other." So saying, he ordered him to be beheaded; and the sentence was instantly put into execution before the door of the earl's tent. "Thus," adds our author, "ended the mayster enchantour: and so he was payed hys wages according to his desertes."[3]

---

[1] Mandeville's *Travels*, p. 285.   [2] *Ibid.*   [3] Froissart's *Chronicle*, vol. iii. chap. 392, fol. 272.

TRICKS OF THE JUGGLERS ASCRIBED TO INFERNAL AGENCY ; BUT MORE REASON-ABLY ACCOUNTED FOR.—Our learned monarch James I. was perfectly convinced that these, and other inferior feats exhibited by the tregetours, could only be per-formed by the agency of the Devil, " who," says he, " will learne them many juglarie tricks, at cardes and dice, to deceive men's senses thereby, and such innumerable false practiques, which are proved by over-many in this age."[1] It is not, how-ever, very easy to reconcile with common sense the knowledge the king pre-tended to have had of the intercourse between Satan and his scholars the con-jurers ; unless his majesty had been, what nobody, I trust, suspects him to have been, one of the fraternity. But, notwithstanding the high authority of a crowned head in favour of Beelzebub, it is the opinion of some modern writers, that the tricks of the jugglers may be accounted for upon much more reasonable, as well as more natural, principles. These artists were greatly encouraged in the middle ages ; they travelled in large companies, and carried with them, no doubt, such machinery as was necessary for the performance of their deceptions ; and we are all well aware, that very surprising things may be exhibited through the medium of a proper apparatus, and with the assistance of expert confederates. A magic lanthorn will produce appearances almost as wonderful as some of those described by Sir John Mandeville, to persons totally ignorant of the existence and nature of such a machine. The principles of natural philosophy were very little known in those dark ages ; and, for that reason, the spectators were more readily deceived. In our own times we have had several exhibitions that excited much astonishment ; such as an image of wax, suspended by a ribband in the middle of a large room, which answered questions in various languages ; an automaton chess-player, that few professors of the game could beat ;[2] and men ascending the air with-out the assistance of wings : yet these phenomena are considered as puerile, now the secrets upon which their performance depends have been divulged. But, returning to the tregetour, we shall find that he often performed his feats upon a scaffold erected for that purpose ; and probably, says a late ingenious writer,[3] received his name from the *trebuchet*, or trap-door, because he frequently made use of such insidious machines in the displayment of his operations. Chaucer has told us, that Coll the tregetour exhibited upon a table ; and other authors speak of "juggling upon the boardes," which clearly indicates the use of a stage or temporary scaffold. Now, let us only add the machinery proper for the occasion, and all the wonders specified in the foregoing passages may be reduced to mere pantomimical deceptions, assisted by sleight of hand, and the whole readily accounted for without any reference to supernatural agency.

JOHN RYKELL, A CELEBRATED TREGETOUR.—In the fourteenth century, the tregetours seem to have been in the zenith of their glory ; from that period they gradually declined in the popular esteem ; their performances were more confined,

---

[1] *Dæmonologie.*

[2] See *The Conjuror Unveiled*, a small pamphlet translated from the French ; which gives a full account of these curious pieces of mechanism, and of several others equally surprising.

[3] Mr. Tyrwhitt, in his edition of Chaucer's *Canterbury Tales*, vol. iii. p. 299.

and of course became less consequential. Lydgate, in one of his poems,[1] introduces Death speaking to a famous tregetour belonging to the court of king Henry V. in this manner :—

> Maister John Rykell, sometime tregitour
>   Of noble Henry kinge of Englonde,
> And of France the mighty conqueror ;
>   For all the sleightes, and turnyng of thyne honde,
>   Thou must come nere this dance, I understonde ;
> Nought may avail all thy conclusions,
>   For Dethe shortly, nother on see nor land,
> Is not desceyved by no illusions.

To this summons the sorrowful juggler replies :—

> What may availe mankynde naturale ?
>   Not any crafte schevid by apparance,
> Or course of steres above celestial,
>   Or of heavens all the influence,
>   Ageynst Deth to stonde at defence.
> Lygarde-de-mayne now helpith me right noughte :
>   Farewell, my craft and all such sapience ;
> For Deth hath mo masteries than I have wroughte.

In "The Disobedient Child," an old morality, or interlude, written by Thomas Ingeland in the reign of queen Elizabeth, a servant, describing the sports at his master's wedding, says :—

> What juggling was there upon the boardes !
>   What thrusting of knyves through many a nose !
> What bearynge of formes ! what holdinge of swordes !
>   What puttynge of botkyns throughe legge and hose ! [2]

These tricks approximate nearly to those of the modern jugglers, who have knives so constructed, that, when they are applied to the legs, the arms, and other parts of the human figure, they have the appearance of being thrust through them ; the bearing of the forms, or seats, I suppose, was the balancing of them ; and the holding of swords, the flourishing them about in the sword-dance ; which the reader will find described in the succeeding chapter.

VARIOUS PERFORMANCES OF THE JOCULATORS.—Originally, as we have before observed, the profession of the joculator included all the arts attributed to the minstrels ; and accordingly his performance was called his minstrelsy in the reign of Edward II., and even after he had obtained the appellation of a tregetour.[3] We are well assured, that playing upon the vielle and the harp, and singing of songs, verses, and poems taken from popular stories ; together with dancing, tumbling, and other feats of agility, formed a principal part of the joculator's occupation at the commencement of the thirteenth century ; and

---

[1] "The Daunce of Macabre," translated, or rather paraphrased, from the French. In this Daunce, Death is represented addressing himself to persons of all ranks and ages. MS. Harl. No. 116.

[2] Garrick's *Collection of Old Plays*, K. vol. ii.

[3] "Janino le tregettor, facienti ministralsiam suam coram rege," etc.; that is, to Janino the tregetour, for performing his minstrelsy before the king, in his chamber near the priory of Swineshead, twenty shillings. *Lib. Comput. Garderobæ*, an. 4 Edw. II. fol. 86, MS. Cott. Nero, C. viii.

probably so they might in the days of Chaucer. Another part of the juggler's profession, and which constituted a prominent feature in his character, was teaching bears, apes, monkeys, dogs, and various other animals, to tumble, dance, and counterfeit the actions of men; but we shall have occasion to enlarge upon this subject a few pages farther on.

In a book of customs, says St Foix,[1] made in the reign of Saint Louis, for the regulation of the duties to be paid upon the little chatelet at the entrance into Paris, we read, that a merchant, who brought apes to sell, should pay four deniers; but, if an ape belonged to a joculator, this man, by causing the animal to dance in the presence of the toll-man, was privileged to pass duty-free, with all the apparatus necessary for his performances: hence came the proverb, "Pay in money; the ape pays in gambols." Another article specifies that the joculator might escape the payment of the toll by singing a couplet of a song before the collector of the duty.

Comenius, I take it, has given us a proper view of the juggler's exhibition, as it was displayed a century and a half back, in a short chapter entitled Prestigiæ, or Sleights.[2] It consists of four divertisements, including the joculator's own performances; and the other three are tumbling and jumping through a hoop; the grotesque dances of the clown, or mimic, who, it is said, appeared with a mark upon his face; and dancing upon the tight rope. The print at the head of his chapter is made agreeably to the English custom, and differs a little from the original description. In the latter it is said, "The juggler sheweth sleights out of a purse." In the print there is no purse represented; but the artist is practising with cups and balls in the manner they are used at present. The tumbler is walking upon his hands. The rope-dancing is performed by a woman holding a balancing pole; and on the same rope a man, probably "clown to the rope," is represented hanging by one leg with his head downwards. In modern times, the juggler has united songs and puppet-plays to his show.

PRIVILEGES OF THE JOCULATORS AT PARIS—THE KING'S JOCULATOR.—The *ioculator regis*, or king's juggler, was anciently an officer of note in the royal household; and we find, from Domesday Book (under Gloucestershire) that Berdic, who held that office in the reign of the Conqueror, was a man of property.[3] In the succeeding century, or soon afterwards, the title of rex juglatorum, or king of the jugglers, was conferred upon the chief performer of the company, and the rest, I presume, were under his control. The king's juggler continued to have an establishment in the royal household till the time of Henry VIII.;[4] and in his reign the office and title seem to have been discontinued.

GREAT DISREPUTE OF MODERN JUGGLERS.—The profession of the juggler,

---

[1] *Essais Hist. sur Paris*, vol. ii. p. 39.   [2] *Orbis Sensualium Pictus*, by Hoole, 1658; chap. 132.
[3] " *Glowecesterscire. Berdic, joculator regis, habet iij villas, et ibi v car.; nil redd.*"
[4] *Essay on Ancient Minstrels*, prefixed to Bishop Percy's *Reliques of Ancient Poetry*, vol. i. p. xciii.

with that of the minstrel, had fallen so low in the public estimation at the close of the reign of queen Elizabeth, that the performers were ranked, by the moral writers of the time, not only with "ruffians, blasphemers, thieves, and vaga-bonds"; but also with "Heretics, Jews, Pagans, and sorcerers";[1] and, indeed, at an earlier period they were treated with but little more respect, as appears from the following lines in Barclay's Eclogues :—

> Jugglers and pipers, bourders and flatterers,
> Baudes and janglers, and cursed adouteres.[2]

In another passage, he speaks of a disguised juggler, and a vile jester or bourder;[3] by the word disguised he refers, perhaps, to the clown, or mimic; who, as Comenius has just informed us, danced "disguised with a vizard." In more modern times, by way of derision, the juggler was called a hocus-pocus,[4] a term applicable to a pick-pocket, or a common cheat.

[1] A Treatise against Dicing, Dauncing, vaine Playes, or Enterludes, etc., by John Northbrooke, 1579.

[2] Egloge the third, at the end of Brant's *Ship of Fools*, by Barclay, printed A.D. 1508.

[3] *Mirrour of Good Manners*, translated from the Latin by Barclay.

[4] Or hokos-pokos, as by Ben Jonson, in *The Staple of Newes* (1625). This is the earliest mention I have found of this term. It occurs again in the *Seven Champions*, by John Kirk, acted in 1663 : "My mother could juggle as well as any hocus-pocus in the world."

*Murray's *Dictionary* says that this term as the appellation of a juggler, and apparently as the assumed name of a particular conjurer, appears early in the seventeenth century, and was derived from the sham Latin formula employed by him. Ady's *Candle in Dark* (1655) is cited :—"I will speak of one man . . . that went about in king James his time . . . who called himself The Kings Majesties most excellent Hocus Pocus, and so was called, because that at the playing of every Trick, he used to say *Hocus pocus, toutus taloutus, vade celeriter jubeo*, a dark composure of words, to blinde the eyes of the beholders, to make his Trick pass the more currantly without discovery." Tillotson (Sermon xxvi.) in 1742 is responsible for the highly improbable and irreverent suggestion that *Hocus-pocus* is a corruption of *Hoc est Corpus* of the Mass. *Hocus* apparently is responsible for originating the later word *hoax*, that is to play a trick upon any one.

CHAPTER V

Dancing, Tumbling, and Balancing, part of the Joculator's Profession—Performed by Women—Dancing connected with Tumbling—Antiquity of Tumbling—Various Dances described—The Gleemen's Dances—Exemplification of Gleemen's Dances—The Sword Dance—Rope-Dancing and wonderful Performances on the Rope—Rope-Dancing from the Battlements of St Paul's—Rope-Dancing from St Paul's Steeple—Rope-Dancing from All Saints' Church, Hertford—Rope-Dancing from All Saints, Derby—A Dutchman's Feats on St Paul's Weathercock—Jacob Hall the Rope-Dancer—Modern celebrated Rope-Dancing—Rope-Dancing at Sadler's Wells—Fool's Dance—Morris Dance—Egg Dance—Ladder Dance—Jocular Dances—Wire-Dancing—Ballette Dances—Leaping and Vaulting—Balancing—Remarkable Feats—The Posture-Master's Tricks—The Mountebank—Domestic Dancing—The Pavone—Antiquity of Dancing—The Carole Dance.

JOCULATORS' DANCING.—Dancing, tumbling, and balancing, with variety of other exercises requiring skill and agility, were originally included in the performances exhibited by the gleemen and the minstrels; and they remained attached to the profession of the joculator after he was separated from those who only retained the first branches of the minstrel's art, that is to say, poetry and music.

WOMEN DANCERS AND TUMBLERS.—The joculators were sometimes excellent tumblers; yet, generally speaking, I believe that vaulting, tumbling, and balancing were not executed by the chieftain of the gleeman's company, but by some of his confederates; and very often this part of the show was performed by females, who were called glee-maidens by the Saxons, and tumbling women, tomblesteres, and tombesteres, in Chaucer. The same poet, in the " Romance of the Rose," calls them *saylours* or dancers, from the Latin word *salio*. They are also denominated *sauters*, from *saut* in French, to leap. Hence, in *Pierce Ploughman*, one says, " I can neither saylen ne saute." They are likewise called tymbesteres, players upon the tymbrel, which they also balanced occasionally, as we shall find a little farther on. It is almost needless to add, that the ancient usage of introducing females for the performances of these difficult specimens of art and agility has been successively continued to the present day.

DANCING CONNECTED WITH TUMBLING.—Dancing, in former times, was closely connected with those feats of activity now called vaulting and tumbling; and such exertions often formed part of the dances that were publicly exhibited by the gleemen and the minstrels; for which reason, the Anglo-Saxon writers frequently used the terms of leaping and tumbling for dancing. Both the phrases occur in the Saxon versions of St Mark's Gospel, where it is said of the daughter of Herodias, that she vaulted or tumbled, instead of danced, before king Herod.[1] In a translation of the seventh century, in the Cotton Library,[2] it

---

[1] St Mark, chap. vi. ver. 22.　　　　　　　　　　　　[2] Nero, D. iv.

Dancing.

says, she jumped, or leaped, and pleased Herod. In another Saxon version of the eleventh century, in the Royal Library,[1] she tumbled, and it pleased Herod. A third reads, Herodias' daughter tumbled there, etc.[2] These interpretations of the sacred text might easily arise from a misconception of the translators, who, supposing that no common dancing could have attracted the attention of the monarch so potently, or extorted from him the promise of a reward so extensive as that they found stated in the record, therefore referred the performance to some wonderful displayments of activity, resembling those themselves might have seen exhibited by the glee-maidens, on occasions of solemnity, in the courts of Saxon potentates. We may also observe, that the like explication of the passage was not only received in the Saxon versions of the Gospel, but continued in those of much more modern date; and, agreeably to the same idea, many of the illuminators, in depicting this part of the holy history, have represented the damsel in the action of tumbling, or, at least, of walking upon her hands. Mr Brand, in his edition of Bourne's *Vulgar Antiquities*, has quoted one in old English that reads thus : "When the daughter of Herodyas was in comyn, and had tomblyde and pleside Harowde." I have before me a MS. of the Harleian Collection,[3] in French, in the thirteenth century, written by some ecclesiastic, which relates to the church fasts and festivals. Speaking of the death of John Baptist, and finding this tumbling damsel to have been the cause, the pious author treats her with much contempt, as though she had been one of the dancing girls belonging to a company of jugglers, who in his time, it seems, were not considered as paragons of virtue any more than they are in the present day. He says of her, "Bien saveit treschier e tumber"; which may be rendered, "She was well skilled in tumbling and cheating tricks." And thus we find her in two examples given in the middle of plate twenty-one. The first, where her servant stands by her side, is taken from a series of Scripture histories,[3] written and illuminated at the beginning of the thirteenth century; and the second from a book of prayers more modern than the former by almost one hundred and fifty years.[4]

ANTIQUITY OF TUMBLING.—The exhibition of dancing, connected with leaping and tumbling, for the entertainment of princes and noblemen on occasions of festivity, is of high antiquity. Homer mentions two dancing tumblers, who stood upon their heads,[5] and moved about to the measure of a song, for the diversion of Menelaüs and his courtiers, at the celebration of his daughter's nuptials. It seems that the astonishment excited by the difficulty of such performances, obviated the absurdity, and rendered them agreeable to persons of rank and affluence. The Saxon princes encouraged the dancers and tumblers; and the courts of the Norman monarchs were crowded with them : we have, indeed, but few of their exertions particularised; for the monks, through whose medium the histories of the middle ages have generally been conveyed to us,

---

[1] No. 1, A. xiv.   [2] No. 2253, fol. 45.
[3] Harl. MSS. No. 1527.   [4] Roy. Lib. 2, B. vii.   [5] *Odyssey*, lib. iv. 18.

were their professed enemies: it is certain, however, notwithstanding the censure promulgated in their disfavour, that they stood their ground, and were not only well received, but even retained, in the houses of the opulent. No doubt they frequently descended to the lowest kinds of buffoonery. We read, for instance, of a tumbler in the reign of Edward II. who rode before his majesty, and frequently fell from his horse in such a manner, that the king was highly diverted, and laughed exceedingly, and rewarded the performer with the sum of twenty shillings, which at that period was a very considerable donation.[1] A like reward of twenty shillings was given, by order of Henry VIII., to a strange tumbler, that is, I suppose, an itinerant who had no particular establishment; a like sum to a tumbler who performed before him at Lord Bath's; and a similar reward to the "tabouretts and a tumbler," probably of the household.[2] It should seem that these artists were really famous mirth-makers; for one of them had the address to excite the merriment of the solemn queen Mary. "After her majesty," observes Strype, "had reviewed the royal pensioners in Greenwich Park, there came a tumbler, and played many pretty feats, the queen and cardinal Pole looking on; whereat she was observed to laugh heartily."[3]

VARIOUS DANCES.—Among the pastimes exhibited for the amusement of queen Elizabeth at Kenilworth castle, there were shown, as Laneham says, before her highness, surprising feats of agility, by an Italian, "in goings, turnings, tumblings, castings, hops, jumps, leaps, skips, springs, gambauds, somersaults, caprettings, and flights, forward, backward, sideways, downward, upward, and with sundry windings, gyrings, and circumflections," which he performed with so much ease and lightness, that words are not adequate to the description; "insomuch that I," says Laneham, "began to doubt whether he was a man or a spirit"; and afterwards, "As for this fellow, I cannot tell what to make of him; save that I may guess his back to be metalled like a lamprey, that has no bone, but a line like a lute-string."[4] So lately as the reign of queen Anne, this species of performance continued to be fashionable; and in one of the *Tatlers* we meet with the following passage: "I went on Friday last to the Opera; and was surprised to find a thin house at so noble an entertainment, 'till I heard that the tumbler was not to make his appearance that night."[5]

Three ancient specimens of the tumbler's art are given upon plate twenty-two. The first is a woman bending herself backwards, from a MS. of the thirteenth century, in the Cotton Library;[6] the second a man performing the same feat, but in a more extraordinary manner;[7] and the third represents a girl turning over upon her hands, her feats being enlivened with music.[8] The last two MSS. are of the fourteenth century.

THE GLEEMEN'S DANCES.—It is not by any means my intention to insinuate,

---

[1] Roll of Expenses, Edward II., in the possession of Thomas Astle, Esq.
[2] From a MS. in the Remembrancer's Office, an. 13 Hen. VIII.
[3] *Eccles. Mem.* vol. iii. p. 312.
[4] Laneham's Letter, in Mr. Nichols' *Progresses of Queen Elizabeth*, pp. 16, 17.
[5] No. 115, dated Jan. 3, 1709.
[6] Domitian, A. 2.
[7] Sloane MSS. No. 335.
[8] Bodleian MSS. No. 264.

Tumbling.

from what has been said in the foregoing pages, that there were no dances performed by the Saxon gleemen and their assistants but such as consisted of vaulting and tumbling.

EXEMPLIFICATION OF GLEEMEN'S DANCES.—We have already noticed a dance represented on plate twenty, from a painting of the tenth century, the most ancient of the kind that I have met with. The crouching attitudes of the two dancers, point out great difficulty in the part they are performing, but do not convey the least indication of vaulting or tumbling. Attitudes somewhat similar I have seen occur in some of the steps of a modern hornpipe. Again, on plate twenty-one, we find a young man dancing singly to the music of two flutes and a lyre; and the action attempted to be expressed by the artist is rather that of ease and elegancy of motion than of leaping, or contorting of the body in a violent manner. It is evident that this delineation, which is from a Latin and Saxon MS. of the ninth century, in the Cotton Library,[1] was intended for the representation of part of the gleeman's exhibition; for the designer has crowded into the margin a number of heads and parts of figures, necessarily incomplete from want of room, who appear as spectators; but these are much confused, and in some places obliterated, so that they could not have been copied with any tolerable effect. The dance on the top of plate twenty-five, from a MS. of the ninth century, in which the musician bears a part, I take to be of the burlesque kind, and intended to excite laughter by the absurdity of the gestures practised by the performers; but that at the bottom of the same Plate, from a MS. of the fourteenth century, in the Royal Library,[2] has more appearance of elegance. This dance is executed by a female; and probably the perfection of the dance consisted in approaching and receding from the bear with great agility, so as to prevent his seizing upon her, and occasioning any interruption to the performance, which the animal, on the other hand, appears to be exceedingly desirous of effecting, being unmuzzled for the purpose, and irritated by the scourge of the juggler.

THE SWORD-DANCE.—There is a dance which was probably in great repute among the Anglo-Saxons, because it was derived from their ancestors the ancient Germans; it is called the sword-dance; and the performance is thus described by Tacitus:[3] "One public diversion was constantly exhibited at all their meetings; young men, who, by frequent exercise, have attained to great perfection in that pastime, strip themselves, and dance among the points of swords and spears with most wonderful agility, and even with the most elegant and graceful motions. They do not perform this dance for hire, but for the entertainment of the spectators, esteeming their applause a sufficient reward."[4] This dance continues to be practised in the northern parts of England about Christmas time, when, says Mr Brand, "the fool-plough goes about; a pageant that consists of a

---

[1] Cleopatra, C. viii.   [2] No. 2, B. viii.   [3] Tacit. *De Morib. Germ.* cap. 24.

[4] The reader may find a more particular account of the various motions and figures formed by the dancers, from Olaüs Magnus, in Mr Brand's notes upon the 14th chapter of Bourne's *Vulgar Antiquities*, p. 175.

M

number of sword-dancers dragging a plough, with music." The writer then tells us that he had seen this dance performed very frequently, with little or no variation from the ancient method, excepting only that the dancers of the present day, when they have formed their swords into a figure, lay them upon the ground, and dance round them.[1]

I have not been fortunate enough to meet with any delineation that accords with the foregoing descriptions of the sword-dance; but in a Latin manuscript of Prudentius with Saxon notes, written in the ninth century, and now in the Cotton Library,[2] a military dance of a different kind occurs. It is exceedingly curious, and has not, that I recollect, been mentioned by any of our writers. The drawing is copied upon plate twenty-one. It represents two men, equipped in martial habits, and each of them armed with a sword and a shield, engaged in a combat; the performance is enlivened by the sound of a horn; the musician acts in a double capacity, and is, together with a female assistant, dancing round them to the cadence of the music; and probably the actions of the combatants were also regulated by the same measure.

Early in the last century, and, I doubt not, long before that period, a species of sword-dance, usually performed by young women, constituted a part of the juggler's exhibition at Bartholomew fair. I have before me two bills of the shows there presented some time in the reign of queen Anne. The one speaks of "dancing with several naked swords, performed by a child of eight years of age," which, the showman assures us, had given "satisfaction to all persons." The other, put forth, it seems, by one who belonged to Sadler's Wells, promises the company, that they shall see "a young woman dance with the swords, and upon a ladder, surpassing all her sex." Both these bills were printed in the reign of queen Anne: the first belonged to a showman named Crawley; and the second to James Miles, from Sadler's Wells, who calls his theatre a music booth, and the exhibition consisted chiefly of dancing. The originals are in the Harleian Library.[3] About thirty years back (c. 1770) I remember to have seen at Flockton's, a much noted but very clumsy juggler, a girl about eighteen or twenty years of age, who came upon the stage with four naked swords, two in each hand; when the music played, she turned round with great swiftness, and formed a great variety of figures with the swords, holding them over her head, down by her sides, behind her, and occasionally she thrust them in her bosom. The dance generally continued about ten or twelve minutes; and when it was finished, she stopped suddenly, without appearing to be in the least giddy from the constant reiteration of the same motion.

THE ROPE-DANCE.—This species of amusement is certainly very ancient. Terence, in the prologue to *Hecyra*, complains that the attention of the public was drawn from his play, by the exhibitions of a rope-dancer.

---

[1] *The sword-dance still survives at Christmastide in some parts of Northumberland, Yorkshire, and the north Midlands. See *Dancing* (Badminton Library), 175, 176.   [2] Cleopatra, C. viii.

[3] No. 5931.

We are well assured that dancing upon the rope constituted a part of the entertainment presented to the public by the minstrels and joculators, and we can trace it as far back as the thirteenth century; but whether the dancers at that time exhibited upon the slack or tight rope, or upon both, cannot easily be ascertained; and we are equally in the dark respecting the extent of their abilities; but, if we may judge from the existing specimens of other feats of agility performed by them or their companions, we may fairly conclude that they were by no means contemptible artists.

When Isabel of Bavaria, queen to Charles VI. of France, made her public entry into Paris, among other extraordinary exhibitions prepared for her reception was the following, recorded by Froissart, who was himself a witness to the fact: "There was a mayster[1] came out of Geane; he had tied a corde upon the hyghest house on the brydge of Saynt Michell over all the houses, and the other ende was tyed to the hyghest tower of our Ladye's churche; and, as the quene passed by, and was in the great streat called Our Ladye's strete; bycause it was late, this sayd mayster, wyth two brinnynge candelles in hys handes, issued out of a littel stage that he had made on the heyght of our Lady's tower, synginge as he went upon the cord all alonge the great strete, so that all that sawe him hadde marvayle how it might be; and he bore still in hys handes the two brinnynge candelles, so that he myght be well sene all over Parys, and two myles without the city. He was such a tombler, that his lightnesse was greatly praised. He gave them many proofs of his skill, so that his agility and all his performances were highly esteemed." The manner in which this extraordinary feat was carried into execution is not so clear as might be wished. The translation justifies the idea of his walking down the rope; but the words of Froissart seem to imply that he seated himself upon the cord and came sliding down, and then the trick will bear a close resemblance to those that follow. But St Foix, on the authority of another historian, says, he descended dancing upon the cord; and, passing between the curtains of blue taffety, ornamented with large fleurs-de-lis of gold, which covered the bridge, he placed a crown upon the head of Isabel, and then remounted upon the cord.[2]

ROPE-DANCING FROM THE BATTLEMENTS OF ST PAUL'S.—A performance much resembling the foregoing was exhibited before king Edward VI. at the time he passed in procession through the city of London, on Friday, the nineteenth of February 1546, previous to his coronation. "When the king," says the author, "was advanced almost to St George's church,[3] in Paul's churchyard, there was a rope as great as the cable of a ship stretched in length from the battlements of Paul's steeple, with a great anchor at one end, fastened a little before the dean of Paul's house-gate; and, when his majesty approached near the same, there came a man, a stranger, being a native of Arragon, lying on the rope with his head forward, casting his arms and legs abroad, running

---

[1] Vol. iv. chap. 38.   [2] *Essais sur Paris*, vol. ii. p. 42.
[3] It should be St Gregory's church, which stood on the south side of St Paul's nearly opposite to the Dean's Gateway.

on his breast on the rope from the battlements to the ground, as if it had been an arrow out of a bow, and stayed on the ground. Then he came to his majesty, and kissed his foot; and so, after certain words to his highness, he departed from him again, and went upwards upon the rope till he came over the midst of the churchyard; where he, having a rope about him, played certain mysteries on the rope, as tumbling, and casting one leg from another. Then took he the rope, and tied it to the cable, and tied himself by the right leg a little space beneath the wrist of the foot, and hung by one leg a certain space, and after recovered himself again with the said rope and unknit the knot, and came down again. Which stayed his majesty, with all the train, a good space of time." [1]

Rope-Dancing from St Paul's Steeple.—This trick was repeated, though probably by another performer, in the reign of queen Mary; for, according to Holinshed, among the various shows prepared for the reception of Philip, king of Spain, was one of a man who "came downe upon a rope, tied to the battlement of Saint Paule's church, with his head before, neither staieing himself with hand or foot; which," adds the author, "shortlie after cost him his life." [2]

Rope-Dancing from All Saints' Church, Hertford.—A similar exploit was put in practice, about fifty years back (1750), in different parts of this kingdom. I received the following account of the manner in which it was carried into execution at Hertford from a friend of mine,[3] who assisted the exhibitor in adjusting his apparatus, and saw his performance several times. A rope was stretched from the top of the tower of All Saints' church, and brought obliquely to the ground about fourscore yards from the bottom of the tower, where, being drawn over two strong pieces of wood nailed across each other, it was made fast to a stake driven into the earth; two or three feather-beds were then placed upon the cross timbers, to receive the performer when he descended, and to break his fall. He was also provided with a flat board having a groove in the midst of it, which he attached to his breast; and when he intended to exhibit, he laid himself upon the top of the rope, with his head downwards, and adjusted the groove to the rope, his legs being held by a person appointed for that purpose, until such time as he had properly balanced himself. He was then liberated, and descended with incredible swiftness from the top of the tower to the feather-beds, which prevented his reaching the ground. This man had lost one of his legs, and its place was supplied by a wooden leg, which was furnished on this occasion with a quantity of lead sufficient to counterpoise the weight of the other. He performed this three times in the same day: the first time, he descended without holding anything in his hands; the second time, he blew a trumpet; and the third, he held a pistol in each hand, which he discharged as he came down.

---

[1] *Archæologia*, vol. vii.

[2] Holinshed's *Chron.* vol. iii. p. 1121.

[3] Mr John Carrington of Bacon's, near Hertford.

*ROPE FEATS AT ALL SAINTS, DERBY. — The lofty tower of All Saints, Derby, has been the scene of several of these queer feats. "There are characters," wrote Hutton, the old historian of Derby, "who had rather amuse the world at the hazard of their lives, for a slender and precarious pittance, than follow an honest calling for an easy subsistence. A small figure of a man, seemingly composed of spirit and gristle, appeared in October, to entertain the town by sliding down a rope. One end of this was to be fixed at the top of All Saints steeple, and the other at the bottom of St Michael's, an horizontal distance of 150 yards which formed an inclined plane extremely steep. A breastplate of wood, with a groove to fit the rope, and his own equilibrium were to be his security while sliding down upon his belly, with his arms and legs extended. He could not be more than six or seven seconds in this airy journey, in which he fired a pistol and blew a trumpet. The velocity with which he flew raised a fire by friction, and a bold stream of smoke followed him. He performed this wonderful exploit three successive days, in each of which he descended twice and marched up once; the latter took him more than an hour, in which he exhibited many surprising achievements, as sitting unconcerned with his arms folded, lying across the rope on his back, then his belly, his hams, blowing the trumpet, swinging round, hanging by the chin, the hand, the heels, the toe, etc. The rope being too long for art to tighten, he might be said to have danced upon the slack. Though he succeeded at Derby, yet, in exhibiting soon after at Shrewsbury, he fell and lost his life."

*He was buried in the churchyard of St Mary's, Shrewsbury, in 1740, and over his remains was placed a tombstone bearing the following epitaph :—

> Let this small monument record the name
> Of Cadman, and to future times proclaim
> How, by an attempt to fly from this high spire,
> Across the Sabrine stream, he did acquire
> His fatal end. 'Twas not for want of skill,
> Or courage to perform the task, he fell;
> No, no, a faulty cord being drawn too tight
> Hurried his soul on high to take her flight,
> Which bid the body here beneath, good-night.

Hogarth immortalised Cadman in one of his most popular pictures.

*To return to Derby, we find that, in 1734, a second "flyer" visited the town. He was much older than the first performer, and less in stature. "His coat," we are told, "was in deshabille; no waistcoat; his shirt and his shoes the worse for wear; his hat, worth threepence exclusive of the band, which was pack-thread bleached white by the weather; and a black string supplied the place of buttons to his waistband. He wisely considered if his performances did not exceed the others he might as well stay at home—if he had one. His rope, therefore, from the same steeple, extended to the bottom of St Mary's-gate, more than twice the former length. He was to draw a wheelbarrow after him, in which was a boy of thirteen. After this surprising performance, an ass was to fly down, armed as before, with a breastplate, and at each foot a lump of lead about half a hundred. The man, the barrow, and its contents arrived safe at the end of their journey. When the vast multitude turned their eyes towards the ass, which had been braying several days at the top of the steeple for food, but, like many a lofty courtier for a place, brayed in vain; the slackness of the rope, and the great weight of the animal and his apparatus, made it seem, at setting off, as if he were falling perpendicularly. The appearance was tremendous!! About twenty yards before he reached the gates of the County Hall, the rope broke. From the velocity acquired by the descent, he bore down all before him. A whole multitude was overwhelmed; nothing was heard but dreadful cries; nor seen, but confusion. Legs and arms went to destruction. In this dire calamity, the ass, which maimed others, was unhurt himself, having a pavement of soft bodies to roll over. No lives were lost. As the rope broke near the top, it brought down both chimneys and people at the other end of the street. This dreadful catastrophe put a period to the art of flying. It prevented the operator from making the intended collection; and he sneaked out of Derby as poor as he sneaked in."

A DUTCHMAN'S FEATS ON ST PAUL'S WEATHERCOCK.—To the foregoing extraordinary exhibitions we may add another equally dangerous, but executed without the assistance of a rope. It was performed in the presence of queen Mary in her passage through London to Westminster, the day before her coronation, in 1553, and is thus described by Holinshed: "When she came to Saint Paule's churchyard against the school, master Heywood sat in a pageant under a vine, and made to her an oration in Latin; and then there was one Peter, a Dutchman, that stoode upon the weathercocke of Saint Paul's steeple, holding a streamer in his hands of five yards long, and waving thereof. He sometimes stood on one foot, and shook the other, and then he kneeled on his knees, to the great marvell of all the people. He had made two scaffolds under him: one above the cross, having torches and streamers set upon it, and another over the ball of the cross, likewise set with streamers and torches, which could not burn, the wind was so great." The historian informs us, that "Peter had sixteene pounds, thirteene shillings, and foure pence, given to him by the citie for his costs and paines, and for all his stuffe." [1]

JACOB HALL THE ROPE-DANCER.—In the reign of Charles II. there was a famous rope-dancer named Jacob Hall, whose portrait is still in existence. [2] The open-hearted Duchess of Cleveland is said to have been so partial to this man, that he rivalled the king himself in her affections, and received a salary from her grace.

MODERN CELEBRATED ROPE-DANCING.—Soon after the accession of James II. to the throne, a Dutch woman made her appearance in this country; and "when," says a modern author, "she first danced and vaulted upon the rope in London, the spectators beheld her with a pleasure mixed with pain, as she

[1] Holinshed's *Chron.* vol. iii. p. 1091.   [2] Granger, *Biog. Hist.* vol. iv. p. 349.

seemed every moment in danger of breaking her neck." This woman was afterwards exceeded by Signora Violante, who not only exhibited many feats which required more strength and agility of body than she was mistress of, but had also a stronger head, as she performed at a much greater distance from the ground than any of her predecessors. Signor Violante was no less excellent as a rope-dancer. The spectators were astonished, in the reign of George II., at seeing the famous Turk dance upon the rope, balance himself on a slack wire without a poise, and toss up oranges alternately with his hands; but this admiration was considerably abated when one of the oranges happened to fall, and appeared by the sound to be a ball of painted lead. Signor and Signora Spinacuta were not inferior to the Turk. "The former danced on the rope (in 1768) at the Little Theatre in the Haymarket, with two boys tied to his feet. But what is still more extraordinary, a monkey has lately performed there, both as a rope-dancer and an equilibrist, such tricks as no man was thought equal to before the Turk appeared in England."[1]

ROPE-DANCING AT SADLER'S WELLS, ETC.—During the eighteenth century, Sadler's Wells was a famous nursery for tumblers, balance-masters, and dancers upon the rope and upon the wire. These exhibitions have of late years lost much of their popularity: the tight-rope dancing, indeed, is still (1800) continued there by Richer, a justly celebrated performer. This man certainly displays more ease and elegance of action, and much greater agility, upon the rope, than any other dancer that I ever saw: his exertions at all times excite the astonishment, while they command the applause of the spectators.

I shall only observe, that the earliest representation of rope-dancing which I have met with occurs in a little print affixed to one of the chapters of the vocabulary of Comenius, translated by Hoole;[2] where a woman is depicted dancing upon the tight-rope, and holding a balance charged with lead at both ends, according to the common usage of the present day; and behind her we see a man, with his hand downwards, and hanging upon the same rope by one of his legs. This feat, with others of a similar kind, are more usually performed upon the slack-rope, which at the same time is put into motion; the performer frequently hanging by one foot, or by both his hands, or in a variety of different manners and attitudes; or by laying himself along upon the rope, holding it with his hands and feet, the latter being crossed, and turning round with incredible swiftness, which is called roasting the pig.

FOOL'S DANCE.—The fool's dance, or a dance performed by persons equipped in the dresses appropriated to the fools, is very ancient, and originally, I apprehend, formed a part of the pageant belonging to the festival of fools. This festival was a religious mummery, usually held at Christmas time; and consisted of various ceremonials and mockeries. A vestige of the fool's dance, preserved in a MS. in the Bodleian Library,[3] written and illuminated in the

---

[1] Granger, vol. iv. pp. 352, 353.

[2] *Orbis Sensualium Pictus*, A.D. 1658.

[3] No. 964.

reign of king Edward III. and completed in 1344, is copied upon the middle of plate nineteen.

In this representation of the dance, it seems conducted with some degree of regularity; and is assisted by the music of the regals and the bagpipes. The dress of the musicians resembles that of the dancers, and corresponds exactly with the habit of the court fool at that period.[1] I make no doubt, the morris-dance, which afterwards became exceedingly popular in this country, originated from the fool's dance; and thence we trace the bells which characterised the morris-dancers. Antiquaries are agreed that the word is derived from Morisco, which in the Spanish language signifies a Moor.[2] The dance was brought in to England from Spain about the beginning of the sixteenth century.

MORRIS-DANCE. — The morris-dance was sometimes performed by itself, but was much more frequently joined to older pageants, and especially to those appropriated for the celebration of the May-games. On these occasions, the Hobby-horse, or a Dragon, with Robin Hood, the maid Marian, and other characters, supposed to have been the companions of that famous outlaw, made a part of the dance. In latter times, the morris was frequently introduced upon the stage. Stephen Gosson, who wrote about 1579, in a little tract entitled *Playes Confuted*, speaks of "dauncing of gigges, galiardes, and morisces, with hobbi-horses," as stage performances.

The garments of the morris-dancers, as we observed before, were adorned with bells, which were not placed there merely for the sake of ornament, but were to be sounded as they danced. These bells were of unequal sizes, and differently denominated, as the fore bell, the second bell, the treble, the tenor or great bell, and mention is also made of double bells. In the third year of queen Elizabeth, two dozen of morris-bells were estimated at one shilling.[3] The principal dancer in the morris was more superbly habited than his companions, as appears from a passage in an old play, *The Blind Beggar of Bednal Green*, by John Day, 1659, wherein it is said of one of the characters, " He wants no cloths, for he hath a cloak laid on with gold lace, and an embroidered jerkin; and thus he is marching hither like the foreman of a morris."

I do not find that the morris-dancers were confined to any particular number. A modern writer speaks of a set of morris-dancers who went about the country, consisting of ten men who danced, besides the maid Marian, and one who played upon the pipe and tabor.

The hobby-horse, which seems latterly to have been almost inseparable from the morris-dance, was a compound figure; the resemblance of the head and

---

[1] Mr Douce was of opinion, that the dance set forth above by Mr Strutt, from the Bodleian MS., did not form a part of the festival of fools.

[2] In the same way *morris*-pike, a constantly mentioned weapon in the sixteenth century, meant a Spanish or Moorish pike.

*The churchwardens' accounts of a considerable variety of parishes—indeed the majority of those which are extant of the sixteenth century—show the almost universal custom of morris-dances and Robin Hood sports on May Day throughout England at that period.

[3] *Archæologia*, vol. i. p. 15. See also the *Witch of Edmonton*, a tragi-comedy, by William Rowley, printed in 1658.

tail of a horse, with a light wooden frame for the body, was attached to the person who was to perform the double character, covered with trappings reaching to the ground, so as to conceal the feet of the actor, and prevent its being seen that the supposed horse had none. Thus equipped, he was to prance about, imitating the curvetings and motions of a horse, as we may gather from the following speech in an old tragedy called the *Vow-breaker, or Fair Maid of Clifton*, by William Sampson, 1636. "Have I not practised my reines, my carreeres, my prankers, my ambles, my false trotts, my smooth ambles, and Canterbury paces—and shall the mayor put me, besides, the hobby-horse? I have borrowed the fore-horse bells, his plumes, and braveries; nay, I have had the mane new shorn and frizelled.—Am I not going to buy ribbons and toys of sweet Ursula for the Marian—and shall I not play the hobby-horse? Provide thou the dragon, and let me alone for the hobby-horse." And afterwards : "Alas, Sir! I come only to borrow a few ribbandes, bracelets, ear-rings, wyertyers, and silk girdles, and handkerchers, for a morris and a show before the queen—I come to furnish the hobby-horse."

THE EGG-DANCE.—I am not able to ascertain the antiquity of this dance. The indication of such a performance occurs in an old comedy, entitled "The longer thou livest, the more Foole thou art," by William Wager,[1] in the reign of queen Elizabeth, where we meet with these lines :—

> Upon my one foote pretely I can hoppe,
> And daunce it trimley about an egge.

Dancing upon one foot was exhibited by the Saxon gleemen, and probably by the Norman minstrels, but more especially by the women-dancers, who might thence acquire the name of hoppesteres, which is given by Chaucer. A vestige of this denomination is still retained, and applied to dancing, though somewhat contemptuously; for an inferior dancing-meeting is generally called a hop. A representation of the dance on one foot, taken from a manuscript of the tenth century, appears upon the top of plate twenty, where the gleeman is performing to the sound of the harp.

Hopping matches for prizes were occasionally made in the sixteenth century, as we learn from John Heywoode the epigrammatist. In his *Proverbs*, printed in 1566, are the following lines :—

> Where wooers hoppe in and out, long time may bring
> Him that hoppeth best at last to have the ring—
> —I hoppyng without for a ringe of a rushe.

And again, in the *Four P's*, a play by the same author, one of the characters is directed "to hop upon one foot"; and another says :—

> Here were a hopper to hop for the ring.

Hence it appears a ring was usually the prize, and given to him who could hop best, and continue to do so the longest.

---

[1] Garrick's *Collection of Old Plays*, 1 vol. 18mo.

But to return to the egg-dance. This performance was common enough about thirty years back (1770), and was well received at Sadler's Wells; where I saw it exhibited, not by simply hopping round a single egg, but in a manner that much increased the difficulty. A number of eggs, I do not precisely recollect how many, but I believe about twelve or fourteen, were placed at certain distances marked upon the stage; the dancer, taking his stand, was blind-folded, and a hornpipe being played in the orchestra, he went through all the paces and figures of the dance, passing backwards and forwards between the eggs without touching one of them.

THE LADDER-DANCE.—So called, because the performer stands upon a ladder, which he shifts from place to place, and ascends or descends without losing the equilibrium, or permitting it to fall. This dance was practised at Sadler's Wells at the commencement of the eighteenth century, and revived about 1770. It is still (1800) continued there by Dubois, who calls himself the clown of the Wells, and is a very useful actor, as well as an excellent performer upon the tight-rope. In the reign of queen Anne, James Miles, who declared himself to be a performer from Sadler's Wells, kept a music-booth in Bartholomew Fair, where he exhibited nineteen different kinds of dances; among them were a wrestler's dance, vaulting upon the slack-rope, and dancing upon the ladder; the latter, he tells us, as well as the sword-dance, was performed by "a young woman surpassing all her sex."[1]—An Inventory of Playhouse Furniture, quoted in the *Tatler*[2] under the article "Materials for Dancing," specifies masques, castanets, and a ladder of ten rounds. I apprehend the ladder-dance originated from the ancient pastime of walking or dancing upon very high stilts. A specimen of such an exhibition is given on plate twenty-three, from a MS. roll in the Royal Library, written and illuminated in the reign of Henry III.[3] The actor is exercising a double function, that is, of a musician and of a dancer.

JOCULAR DANCES.—In the "Roman de la Rose" we read of a dance, the name of which is not recorded, performed by two young women lightly clothed. The original reads, "Qui estoient en pure cottes, et tresses a menu tresse"; which Chaucer renders, "In kyrtels, and none other wede, and fayre ytressed every tresse." The French intimates that their hair was platted, or braided in small braids. The thin clothing, I suppose, was used then, as it is now upon like occasions, to show their persons to greater advantage. In their dancing they displayed a variety of singular attitudes; the one coming as it were privately to the other, and, when they were near together, in a playsome manner they turned their faces about, so that they seemed continually to kiss each other.

> They threw yfere
> Ther mouthes, so that, through ther play,
> It semed as they kyste alway.

A dance, the merit of which, if I mistake not, consisted in the agility and adroitness of the performer, has been noticed already; it is represented on plate

---

[1] Harl. Lib. 5931.　　　　[2] Vol. i. No. 42.　　　　[3] 14, B. v.

twenty-one, where a woman is dancing, and eluding the pursuit of a bear made angry by the scourge of his master. The various situations of the actress and the disappointment of the animal excited, no doubt, the mirth as well as the applause of the spectators.

Many of the ancient dances were of a jocular kind, and sometimes executed by one person : we have, for instance, an account of a man who danced upon a table before king Edward II. A thirteenth century manuscript in the Royal Library, represented on plate twenty-two, shows a girl dancing upon the shoulders of the joculator, who at the same time is playing upon the bagpipes and appears to be in the action of walking forwards.[1]

*In Philip Kinder's MS. *History of Derbyshire*, written about the middle of the seventeenth century, occurs an interesting passage relative to the then common use of bagpipes as an instrument to promote dancing.[2] He says : "For general inclination and disposition the Peakard and Moorlander are of the same ayre, they are given much to dance after ye bagg-pipes, almost every towne hath a bagg-piper in it." The dances for which bagpipes can possibly be suitable are limited in character ; this old Derbyshire dancing was probably of the hornpipe character.

WIRE-DANCING.—Wire-dancing, at least so much of it as I have seen exhibited, appears to me to be misnamed : it consists rather of various feats of balancing, the actor sitting, standing, lying, or walking, upon the wire, which at the same time is usually swung backwards and forwards ; and this, I am told, is a mere trick, to give the greater air of difficulty to the performance. Instead of dancing, I would call it balancing upon the wire.

BALLET-DANCES.—The grand figure-dances, and ballets of action, as they are called, of the modern times, most probably surpass in splendour the ancient exhibitions of dancing. They first appeared, I believe, at the Opera-house ; but have since been adopted by the two royal theatres, and imitated with less splendour upon the summer stages. These spectacles are too extensive by far in their operations, and too multifarious to be described in a general work like this : suffice it to say, they are pantomimical representations of historical and poetical subjects, expressed by fantastical gestures, aided by superb dresses, elegant music, and beautiful scenery ; and sorry am I to add, they have nearly eclipsed the sober portraitures of real nature, and superseded in the public estimation the less attractive lessons of good sense.[3]

LEAPING AND VAULTING.—There are certain feats of tumbling and vaulting that have no connection with dancing, such as leaping and turning with the heels over the head in the air, termed the somersault, corruptly called a somerset. Mrs Piozzi, speaking of Robert Carr, earl of Somerset, and favourite of James I., says, "and the sommerset, still used by tumblers, taken from him."[4] The

---

[1] 14, E. iii.   [2] *Bodleian, Ashm. MSS. 788.

[3] *For a brief history of the ballet see Grove's *Dancing* (Badminton Library), 360-380.

[4] *Retrospection of Eighteen Hundred Years*, vol. ii. p. 224.

word, however, was in use, and applied by the tumblers to the feat above mentioned, before the birth of Carr. There was also the feat of turning round with great rapidity, alternately bearing upon the hands and feet, denominated the fly-flap. In a satirical pamphlet entitled the *Character of a Quack Doctor*, published at London, 1676, the empiric, boasting of his cures, says, "The Sultan Gilgal, being violently afflicted with a spasmus, came six hundred leagues to meet me in a go-cart: I gave him so speedy an acquittance from his dolor, that the next night he danced a saraband with fly-flaps and somersets," etc. ; but this is evidently conjoining the three for the sake of ridicule. The performance of leaping through barrels without heads, and through hoops, especially the latter, is an exploit of long standing ; it is represented upon plate twenty-three from a fourteenth century MS. Two boys are depicted holding the hoop, and the third preparing to leap through it, having deposited his cloak upon the ground to receive him.

William Stokes, a vaulting master of the seventeenth century, boasted, in a publication called the *Vaulting Master*, etc., printed at Oxford in 1652, that he had reduced "vaulting to a method." In his book are several plates containing different specimens of his practice, which consisted chiefly in leaping over one or more horses, or upon them, sometimes seating himself in the saddle and sometimes standing upon the same. All these feats are now (1800) performed at Astley's, and at the circus in St George's Fields, with many additional acquirements ; and the horses gallop round the ride while the actor is going through his manœuvres : on the contrary, the horses belonging to our vaulter remained at rest during the whole time of his exhibition.

A show bill for Bartholomew Fair, during the reign of queen Anne[1] announces "the wonderful performances of that most celebrated master Simpson, the famous vaulter, who, being lately arrived from Italy, will show the world what vaulting is !" The bill speaks pompously : how far his abilities coincided with the promise, I cannot determine, for none of his exertions are specified.

BALANCING.—Under the head of balancing may be included several of the performances mentioned in the preceding pages, and especially the throwing of three balls and three knives alternately into the air, and catching them as they fall, as represented on plate twenty. This trick, in my memory, commonly constituted a part of the puppet-showman's exhibition ; but I do not recollect to have seen it extended beyond four articles ; for instance, two oranges and two forks ; and the performer, by way of conclusion, caught the oranges upon the forks.

In the *Romance of the Rose* we read of tymbesteres, or balance-mistresses, who, according to the description there given, played upon the tymbres, or timbrels, and occasionally tossing them into the air, caught them again upon one finger. The passage translated by Chaucer, stands thus :—

> There was manye a tymbestere—
> —Couthe her crafte full parfytly :

[1] In a volume of Miscellaneous Papers, Bibl. Harl. 5931.

Dancing Leaping, &c.

The tymbres up full subtelly
They cast, and hent full ofte
Upon a fynger fayre and softe,
That they fayled never mo.

Towards the close of last summer (1799) I saw three itinerant musicians parading the streets of London: one of them turned the winch of an organ which he carried at his back, another blew a reed-pipe, and the third played on a tambourine; the latter imitated the timbesters above mentioned, and frequently during the performance of a tune cast up the instrument into the air three or four feet higher than his head, and caught it, as it returned, upon a single finger; he then whirled it round with an air of triumph, and proceeded in the accompaniment without losing time, or occasioning the least interruption.

REMARKABLE FEATS OF BALANCING.—Plate twenty-four contains some few specimens of the fourteenth century balance-master's art, three of which need no explanation; but one of them at the top and another at the bottom are not so clear.

The first, from a MS. in the Bodleian Library,[1] represents a girl, as the length of the hair seems to indicate, habited like a boy, and kneeling on a large broad board, supported horizontally by two men; before her are three swords, the points inclined to each other, and placed in a triangular form; she is pointing to them with her right hand, and holds in her left a small instrument somewhat resembling a trowel, but I neither know its name nor its use.

The man at the bottom of the Plate, from a drawing in a MS. book of prayers possessed by Mr Douce, is performing a very difficult operation: he has placed one sword upright upon the hilt, and is attempting to do the like with the second; at the same time his attitude is altogether as surprising as the trick itself. Feats similar to the other three I have seen carried into execution, and especially that of balancing a wheel. This was exhibited in 1798 at Sadler's Wells, by a Dutchman, who not only supported a wheel upon his shoulder, but also upon his forehead and his chin; and he afterwards extended the performance to two wheels tied together, with a boy standing upon one of them.

In the middle of the eighteenth century, there was a very celebrated balance-master, named Mattocks, who made his appearance also at the Wells; among other tricks, he used to balance a straw with great adroitness, sometimes on one hand, sometimes on the other; and sometimes he would kick it with his foot to a considerable height, and catch it upon his nose, his chin, or his forehead. His fame was celebrated by a song set to music, entitled "Balance a Straw," which became exceedingly popular. The Dutchman mentioned above performed the same sort of feat with a small peacock's feather, which he blew into the air, and caught it as it fell on different parts of his face in a very surprising manner.

THE POSTURE-MASTER.—The display of his abilities consisted in twisting and contorting his body into strange and unnatural attitudes. This art was, no

---

[1] No. 264.

doubt, practised by the jugglers in former ages; and a singular specimen of it, delineated in the reign of Edward III., is given at the bottom of plate twenty-three.

The performer bends himself backwards, with his head turned up between his hands, so as nearly to touch his feet; and in this situation he hangs by his hams upon a pole, supported by two of his confederates.

The posture-master is frequently mentioned by the writers of the seventeenth and eighteenth centuries; but his tricks are not particularised. The most extraordinary artist of this kind that ever existed, it is said, was Joseph Clark, who, "though a well-made man, and rather gross than thin, exhibited in the most natural manner almost every species of deformity and dislocation; he could dislocate his vertebræ so as to render himself a shocking spectacle; he could also assume all the uncouth faces that he had seen at a Quaker's meeting, at the theatre, or any other public place." To this man a paper in the *Guardian* evidently alludes, wherein it is said: "I remember a very whimsical fellow, commonly known by the name of the posture-master, in Charles the Second's reign, who was the plague of all the tailors about town. He would send for one of them to take measure of him; but would so contrive it as to have a most immoderate rising in one of his shoulders; when his clothes were brought home and tried upon him, the deformity was removed into the other shoulder; upon which the taylor begged pardon for the mistake, and mended it as fast as he could; but, on another trial, found him as straight-shouldered a man as one would desire to see, but a little unfortunate in a hump back. In short, this wandering tumour puzzled all the workmen about town, who found it impossible to accommodate so changeable a customer."[1] He resided in Pall Mall, and died about the beginning of king William's reign. Granger tells us he was dead in the year 1697.[2] There was also a celebrated posture-master, by the name of Higgins, in the reign of queen Anne, who performed between the acts at the theatre royal in the Haymarket, and exhibited "many wonderful postures," as his own bill declares:[3] I know no farther of him. In the present day, the unnatural performances of the posture-masters are not fashionable, but seem to excite disgust rather than admiration in the public mind, and for this reason they are rarely exhibited.

THE MOUNTEBANK.—I may here mention a stage-performer whose show is usually enlivened with mimicry, music, and tumbling; I mean the mountebank. It is uncertain at what period this vagrant dealer in physic made his appearance in England: it is clear, however, that he figured away with much success in this country during the seventeenth and eighteenth centuries; he called to his assistance some of the performances practised by the jugglers; and the bourdour, or merry-andrew, seems to have been his inseparable companion: hence it is said in an old ballad, entitled "Sundry Trades and Callings":—

---

[1] No. 102, July 8, 1713.
[2] *Biog. Hist.* vol. iv. See also *Philos. Trans.* No. 242, for July 1698.
[3] Miscell. Collect. Harl. Lib. No. 5931

Balancing.

A mountebank without his fool
Is in a sorrowful case.

The mountebanks usually preface the vending of their medicines with pompous orations, in which they pay as little regard to truth as to propriety. Shakspeare speaks of these wandering empirics in very disrespectful terms :—

As nimble jugglers that deceive the eye,
Disguised cheaters, prating mountebanks,
And many such like libertines of sin.

In the reign of James II. "Hans Buling, a Dutchman, was well known in London as a mountebank. He was," says Granger,[1] "an odd figure of a man, and extremely fantastical in his dress ; he was attended by a monkey, which he had trained to act the part of a jack-pudding, a part which he had formerly acted himself, and which was more natural to him than that of a professor of physic." The ignorance and the impudence of the mountebanks are ridiculed in the *Spectator*, and especially in that paper which concludes with an anecdote of one who exhibited at Hammersmith.[2] He told his audience that he had been "born and bred there, and, having a special regard for the place of his nativity, he was determined to make a present of five shillings to as many as would accept it : the whole crowd stood agape, and ready to take the doctor at his word ; when, putting his hand into a long bag, as every one was expecting his crown-piece, he drew out a handful of little packets, each of which, he informed the spectators, was constantly sold for five shillings and sixpence, but that he would bate the odd five shillings to every inhabitant of that place. The whole assembly immediately closed with this generous offer, and took off all his physic, after the doctor had made them vouch that there were no foreigners among them, but that they were all Hammersmith men."

DOMESTIC DANCING.—I shall here add a few words more on dancing, and consider it as performed for amusement only. In the middle ages dancing was reckoned among the genteel accomplishments necessary to be acquired by both sexes ; and in the romances of those times, the character of a hero was incomplete unless he danced excellently.[3] The knights and the ladies are often represented dancing together, which in the MS. poem of Launfal, in the Cotton Collection,[4] is called playing :—

The quene yede to the formeste ende,
Betweene Launfal and Gauweyn the hende,[5]
    And after her ladyes bryght ;
To daunce they wente alle yn same,
To see them playe hyt was fayr game,
    A lady and a knyght ;
They had menstrelles of moche honours,
Fydelers, sytolyrs, and trompetors,
    And else hyt were unright.

---

[1] *Biog. Hist.* vol. iv. p. 350.   [2] Vol. viii. No. 572 ; see also vol. vi. No. 444.
[3] See the Introduction.   [4] Caligula, A 2, fol. 53.   [5] Polite, courteous.

The poet then tells us, they continued their amusement great part of a summer's day, that is, from the conclusion of dinner to the approach of night.

THE PAVONE.—Dancing was constantly put in practice among the nobility upon days of festivity, and was countenanced by the example of the court. After the coronation dinner of Richard II., the remainder of the day was spent in the manner described by the foregoing poem; for the king, the prelates, the nobles, the knights, and the rest of the company, danced in Westminster Hall to the music of the minstrels.[1] Sir John Hawkins mentions a dance called pavone, from *pavo*, a peacock, which might have been proper upon such an occasion. "It is," says he, "a grave and majestic dance; the method of dancing it anciently was by gentlemen dressed with caps and swords, by those of the long robe in their gowns, by the peers in their mantles, and by the ladies in gowns with long trains, the motion whereof in dancing resembled that of a peacock."[2] Several of our monarchs are praised for their skill in dancing, and none of them more than Henry VIII., who was peculiarly partial to this fashionable exercise. In his time, and in the reign of his daughter Elizabeth, the English, generally speaking, are said to have been good dancers; and this commendation is not denied to them even by foreign writers. Polydore Virgil praises the English for their skill in dancing,[3] and Hentzner says, "the English excell in danceing."[4]

ANTIQUITY, ETC., OF DANCING.—The example of the nobility was followed by the middling classes of the community; they again were imitated by their inferiors, who spent much of their leisure time in dancing, and especially upon holidays; which is noticed and condemned with great severity by the moral and religious writers, as we may find by turning to the Introduction. Dancing is there called a heathenish practice, and said to have been productive of filthy gestures, for which reason it is ranked with other wanton sports unfit to be exhibited. An old drama without date, but probably written early in the reign of Elizabeth, entitled "A new Interlude and a Mery, of the Nature of the four Elements,[5] accuses the people at large with "loving pryncypally disportes, as daunsynge, syngynge, toys, tryfuls, laughynge, and gestynge; for," adds the author, "connynge they set not by." But Sebastian Brant, in his *Ship of Fooles*, is much more severe upon this subject. I shall give the passage as it is paraphrased by Barclay:—[6]

> The priestes, and clerkes, to daunce have no shame;
> The frere, or monke in his frocke and cowle,
> Must daunce; and the doctor lepeth to play the foole.

He derives the origin of dancing from the Jews, when they worshipped the golden calf:—

> Before this ydoll dauncing, both wife and man
> Despised God; thus dauncing first began.

---

[1] Rym. *Fœd.* tom. vii. p. 160, col. 2.   [2] *Hist. Music*, vol. iii. p. 383.
[3] *Hist. Angl.*   [4] *Itinerary.*   [5] Garrick's *Col.* I. vol. iii.
[6] First printed by Pynson, A.D. 1508.

The damsels of London, as far back as the twelfth century, spent the evenings on holidays in dancing before their masters' doors. Stow laments the abolition of this "open pastime," which he remembered to have seen practised in his youth,[1] and considered it not only as innocent in itself, but also as a preventative to worse deeds "within doors," which he feared would follow the suppression.

*THE CAROLE DANCE.—One of the most important of the dances performed by the "professionals," and also much appreciated as a domestic dance, was the Carole, described by Chaucer in his *Romance of the Rose*. He says of the Parish Clerk :—

> In twenty manners he coude skip and daunce
> After the schole of Oxenforde tho',
> And with his legges casten to and fro.

It was usually danced by men and women alternately, who held each other's hands and moved in a circle. The term originally signified a ring dance accompanied with song, and hence became associated with songs at festive seasons, and was finally applied almost exclusively to the Christmas songs of joy.[2]

*THE CUSHION DANCE.—An old English kissing dance, called the Cushion Dance, was a favourite as early as the sixteenth century, and still lingers, but chiefly among children, and at village fairs. This dance is begun by a single person (either man or woman), who taking a cushion in hand, dances about the room, and at the end of the tune, stops, and sings, "This dance it will no further go." The musician answers, "I pray you, good sir, why say you so?" *Man*— "Because Joan Sanderson will not come too." *Musician*—"She must come too, and she shall come too, and she must come whether she will or no." Then he lays down the cushion before the woman, upon which she kneels, and he kisses her, singing, "Welcome, Joan Sanderson, welcome, welcome." Then she rises, takes up the cushion, and both dance, singing, "Prinkam prankum is a fine dance, and shall we go dance it once again, and again and once again, and shall we go dance it once again?" Then making a stop the *woman* sings as before, "This dance it will no further go." *Musician*—"I pray you, madam, why say you so?" *Woman*—"Because John Sanderson will not come too." *Musician*—"He must come too, and he shall come too, and he must come whether he will or no." And so she lays down the cushion before a man, who kneeling upon it, salutes her, she singing, "Welcome, John Sanderson, welcome, welcome." Then he taking up the cushion, they take hands and dance round, singing as before. And thus they do, until the whole company are taken into the ring, and if there is company enough, make a little ring in its middle, and within that ring set a chair, and lay the cushion in it, and the first man set in it. Then the cushion is laid before the first man, the woman singing, "This dance

---

[1] Stow died A.D. 1605, aged 80. *Survey of London*, by Strype, vol. i. p. 251.

[2] *Grove's *Dancing* (Badminton Library), 131. In Murray's *Dictionary* examples are given of the English use of carol meaning a dance, from 1300 to 1600.

N

it will no further go," and as before, only instead of singing "Come too" they sing "Go fro"; and instead of "Welcome, John Sanderson," they sing "Farewell, John Sanderson, farewell, farewell"; and so they go out one by one as they came in. Note the women are kissed by all the men in the ring at their coming and going out, and likewise the men by all the women.

Tutored Bears.

CHAPTER VI

Animals how tutored by the Jugglers—Tricks performed by Bears—Tricks performed by Apes and Monkeys—Bears in Britain—Tricks by Horses in the thirteenth Century—In queen Anne's Reign—Origin of the Exhibitions at Astley's, the Circus, etc.—Dancing Dogs—The Hare beating a Tabor, and learned Pig—A Dancing Cock—The Deserter Bird—Imitations of Animals—Mummings and Masquerades—Mumming to royal Personages—Partial Imitations of Animals—The Horse in the Morris-dance—Counterfeit Voices of Animals—Animals trained for Baiting—Paris Garden—Bull and Bear-baiting patronised by Royalty—How performed—Bears and Bear-wards—Baiting in queen Anne's time—Recent Bull-baiting—Bull-running at Tutbury and Stamford—Sword-play—The Masters of Defence—Pepys on Prize-play—Public Sword-play—Quarter-staff.

ANIMALS HOW TUTORED BY JUGGLER.—One great part of the joculator's profession was the teaching of bears, apes, horses, dogs, and other animals, to imitate the actions of men, to tumble, to dance, and to perform a variety of tricks, contrary to their nature ; and sometimes he learned himself to counterfeit the gestures and articulations of the brutes. The plates that illustrate this chapter relate to both these modes of diverting the public, and prove the invention of them to be more ancient than is generally supposed. The tutored bear lying down at the command of his master, represented on the top of plate twenty-five, is taken from a manuscript of the tenth century ; and the three dancing bears beneath it are as early as the fourteenth century. I have already had occasion to make mention of these delineations ; and the other two require no explanation.[1]

On plate twenty-six we find a bear standing on its head, and another dancing with a monkey on its back ; the original occurs in a book of prayers in the Harleian Collection,[2] written towards the close of the thirteenth century.

I shall only observe, that there is but one among these six drawings in which the animal is depicted with a muzzle to prevent him from biting. The dancing bears have retained their place to the present time, and they frequently perform in the public streets for the amusement of the multitude ; but the miserable appearance of their masters plainly indicates the scantiness of the contributions they receive on these occasions.

*BEARS IN BRITAIN.—That bears were found in Britain during the eighth century is known from Archbishop Egbert's Penitential, where it is laid down that "if any one shall hit a deer or other animal with an arrow, and it escapes and is found dead three days afterwards, and if a dog, a wolf, a fox, or a bear or any other wild beast hath begun to feed upon it, no Christian shall touch it." Mr Harting is of opinion that the trained bears exhibited by the Anglo-Saxon gleemen were native animals taken young and tamed. The great Caledonian

---

[1] The two in the middle are from the Bodleian MS. 264. [2] No. 6563.

forest was so well supplied with bears that it furnished a considerable supply for the barbarous sports of Rome. It is supposed that bears became extinct in Britain before the tenth century.[1]

TRICKS PERFORMED BY APES AND MONKEYS.—Thomas Cartwright, in his *Admonition to Parliament against the Use of the Common Prayer*, published in 1572, says: "If there be a bear or a bull to be baited in the afternoon, or a jackanapes to ride on horseback, the minister hurries the service over in a shameful manner, in order to be present at the show." We are not, however, hereby to conceive, that these amusements were more sought after or encouraged in England than they were abroad. "Our kings," says St Foix, in his *History of Paris*, "at their coronations, their marriages, and at the baptism of their children, or at the creation of noblemen and knights, kept open court; and the palace was crowded on such occasions with cheats, buffoons, rope-dancers, tale-tellers, jugglers, and pantomimical performers. They call those," says he, "jugglers, who play upon the vielle, and teach apes, bears," and perhaps we may add, dogs, "to dance."[2]

Apes and monkeys seem always to have been favourite actors in the joculator's troop of animals. A specimen of the performance of both, as far back as the fourteenth century, is given on plate twenty-six.[3] Leaping or tumbling over a chain or cord held by the juggler, as we here see it depicted, was a trick well received at Bartholomew Fair in the time of Ben Jonson; and in the prologue to a comedy written by him, which bears that title, in 1614, it is said: "He," meaning the author, "has ne're a sword and buckler man in his fayre; nor a juggler with a well-educated ape to come over the chaine for the king of England, and back again for the prince, and sit still on his haunches for the pope and the king of Spaine." In recent times, and probably in more ancient times also, these facetious mimics of mankind were taught to dance upon the rope, and to perform the part of the balance-masters.

*Evelyn records in his *Diary*, under date September 13th, 1660, that he saw "in Southwark, at St Margaret's Fair, monkeys and apes dance and do other feats of activity on the high-rope; they were gallantly clad *à la monde*, went upright, saluted the company, bowing and pulling off their hats; they saluted one another with as good a grace as if instructed by a dancing-master; they turned heels over head with a basket having eggs in it, without breaking any; also with lighted candles in their hands and on their head, without extinguishing them, and with vessels of water without spilling a drop."

In the reign of queen Anne, there was exhibited at Charing Cross, "a wild hairy man," who, we are told, danced upon the tight-rope "with a balance, true to the music"; he also "walked upon the slack-rope" while it was swinging, and drank a glass of ale; he "pulled off his hat, and paid his respects to the company"; and "smoked tobacco," according to the bill, "as well as any

---

[1] Harting's *Extinct British Animals*, 19.　　　　[2] *Essais Hist. sur Paris*, vol. ii. p. 178.
[3] The tumbling ape is from Bodleian MS. No. 264.

Tutored Animals.

Christian."[1]   But all these feats were afterwards outdone by a brother monkey, mentioned before, who performed many wonderful tricks at the Haymarket Theatre, both as a rope-dancer and an equilibrist.[2]

TRICKS PERFORMED BY HORSES IN THE THIRTEENTH CENTURY. — We are told that, in the thirteenth century, a horse was exhibited by the joculators which danced upon a rope ; and oxen were rendered so docile as to ride upon horses, holding trumpets to their mouths as though they were sounding them.[3]   If we refer to plate twenty-seven we shall find the representation of several surprising tricks performed by horses, far exceeding those displayed in the present day (1800).   At the top is depicted the cruel diversion of baiting a horse with dogs, from a fourteenth century manuscript.[4]

*This wretched sport lingered on until the seventeenth century.   In Evelyn's *Diary*, on August 17th, 1667, occurs the following entry : "There was now a very gallant horse baited to death with dogs ; but he fought them all, so as the fiercest of them could not fasten on him, till the men run him through with their swords.   This wicked and barbarous sport deserved to have been punished in the cruel contrivers to get money, under pretence that the horse had killed a man, which was false.   I would not be persuaded to be a spectator."

In the centre of the plate is a horse dancing upon his hind feet to the music of the pipe and tabor ;[5] and opposite to him is another horse rearing up and attacking the joculator, who opposes him with a small shield and a cudgel.[6] These mock combats, to which the animals were properly trained, were constantly regulated by some kind of musical instrument.   The two performances delineated at the bottom of the plate are more astonishing than those preceding them.

In one instance, the horse is standing upon his hind feet, and beating with his fore feet upon a kind of tabor or drum held by his master ; in the other the animal is exhibiting a similar trick with his hind feet, and supports himself upon his fore feet.   The original drawings, represented by these engravings, are all of them upwards of four hundred and fifty years old ; and at the time in which they were made the joculators were in full possession of the public favour.

Here it is deemed worthy to note, that in the year 1612, at a grand court festival, Mons. Pluvinel, riding-master to Louis XIII. of France, with three other gentlemen, accompanied by six esquires bearing their devices, executed a grand ballette-dance upon managed horses.[7]   Something of the same kind is now done (1800) at Astley's and the Circus ; but at these places the dancing is performed by the horses moving upon their four feet according to the direction of their riders ; and of course it is by no means so surprising as that exhibited by the latter engravings.

TRICKS BY HORSES IN QUEEN ANNE'S REIGN.—Horses are animals exceed-

---

[1] From a Miscellaneous Collection of Papers, Harl. Lib. 5931.   [2] Granger, *Biog. Hist.* vol. iv. p. 353.
[3] *Mem. sur Anc. Cheval*, tom. i. p. 247.   [4] Roy. Lib. No. 2, B. vii.   [5] Roy. Lib. 20 D. iv.
[6] This and the two illustrations at the bottom of the Plate are from Bodleian MSS. No. 264.
[7] Menestrier, *Trait. de Tournois*, p. 218.

ingly susceptible of instruction, and their performances have been extended so far as to bear the appearance of rational discernment. In the Harleian Library[1] is a show-bill, published in the reign of queen Anne, which is thus prefaced: "To be seen, at the Ship upon Great Tower Hill, the finest taught horse in the world." The abilities of the animal are specified as follows: "He fetches and carries like a spaniel dog. If you hide a glove, a handkerchief, a door key, a pewter bason, or so small a thing as a silver two-pence, he will seek about the room till he has found it; and then he will bring it to his master. He will also tell the number of spots on a card, and leap through a hoop; with a variety of other curious performances." And we may, I trust, give full credit to the statement of this advertisement: for a horse equally scientific is to be seen in the present day (1800) at Astley's amphitheatre; this animal is so small, that he and his keeper frequently parade the streets in a hackney coach.

ORIGIN OF HORSE EXHIBITIONS AT ASTLEY'S, THE CIRCUS, ETC.—Riding upon two or three horses at once, with leaping, dancing, and performing various other exertions of agility upon their backs while they are in full speed, is, I believe, a modern species of exhibition, introduced to public notice about forty years back (1760) by a man named Price, who displayed his abilities at Dobney's near Islington; soon afterwards, a competitor by the name of Sampson made his appearance; and he again was succeeded by Astley. The latter established a riding-school near Westminster bridge, and has been a successful candidate for popular favour. These performances originally took place in the open air, and the spectators were exposed to the weather, which frequently proving unfavourable interrupted the show, and sometimes prevented it altogether; to remedy this inconvenience, Astley erected a kind of amphitheatre, completely covered, with a ride in the middle for the displayment of the horsemanship, and a stage in the front, with scenes and other theatrical decorations; to his former divertisements he then added tumbling, dancing, farcical operas, and pantomimes. The success he met with occasioned a rival professor of horsemanship named Hughes, who built another theatre for similar performances not far distant, to which he gave the pompous title of the Royal Circus. Hughes was unfortunate, and died some years back; but the Circus has passed into other hands; and the spectacles exhibited there in the present day (1800) are far more splendid than those of any other of the minor theatres.

DANCING DOGS.—I know no reason why the joculators should not have made the dog one of their principal brute performers; the sagacity of this creature and its docility could not have escaped their notice; and yet the only trick performed by the dog, that occurs in the ancient paintings, is simply that of sitting upon his haunches in an upright position, which he might have been taught to do with very little trouble. Three specimens are given, one on plate twenty-six and two on plate twenty-eight; they are all from the oft-cited Oxford manuscript of 1344.

[1] No. 5938.

Tricks taught to Horses.

Neither do I recollect that dogs are included in the list of animals formerly belonging to the juggler's exhibitions, though, no doubt, they ought to have been; for, in Ben Jonson's play of *Bartholmew Fayre*, first acted in 1614, there is mention made of "dogges that dance the morrice," without any indication of the performance being a novelty.

*Neither Pepys nor Evelyn make any reference to "performing dogs" in their respective diaries; but the performance of a non-professional dog recorded by the former, under September 11th, 1661, is certainly worthy of mention: "To Dr Williams, who did carry me into his garden, where he hath abundance of grapes; and he did show me how a dog that he hath do kill all the cats that come thither to kill his pigeons, and do afterwards bury them; and do it with so much care that they shall be quite covered; that if the tip of the tail hangs out, he will take up the cat again and dig the hole deeper, which is very strange; and he tells me that he do believe he hath killed above 100 cats."

Dancing dogs, in the present day (1800), make their appearance in the public streets of the metropolis; but their masters meet with very little encouragement, except from the lower classes of the people, and from children; and of course the performance is rarely worthy of notice. At the commencement of the last century, a company of dancing dogs was introduced at Southwark Fair by a puppet-showman named Crawley. He called this exhibition "The Ball of Little Dogs"; and states in his bill, that they came from Lovain: he then tells us, that "they performed by their cunning tricks wonders in the world of dancing"; and adds, "you shall see one of them, named marquis of Gaillerdain, whose dexterity is not to be compared; he dances with madame Poncette his mistress and the rest of their company at the sound of instruments, all of them observing so well the cadence, that they amaze every body." At the close of the bill, he declares that the dogs had danced before queen Anne and most of the nobility of England. But many other "cunning tricks," and greatly superior to those practised by Crawley's company, have been performed by dogs some few years ago, at Sadler's Wells, and afterwards at Astley's, to the great amusement and disport of the polite spectators. One of the dogs at Sadler's Wells acted the part of a lady, and was carried by two other dogs; some of them were seated at a table, and waited on by others; and the whole concluded with the attack and storming of a fort, entirely performed by dogs.[1]

THE HARE AND TABOR, AND LEARNED PIG.—It is astonishing what may be effected by constant exertion and continually tormenting even the most timid and untractable animals; for no one would readily believe that a hare could have been sufficiently emboldened to face a large concourse of spectators without expressing its alarm, and beat upon a tambourine in their presence; yet such a performance was put in practice not many years back, and exhibited at Sadler's Wells; and, if I mistake not, in several other places in and about the metropolis.

---

[1] *In Chambers's *Book of Days*, i. 293-295, there is an illustrated account of a wonderfully trained troup of dogs and monkeys that performed in London in 1753, under the name of "Mrs Midnight's Animal Commedians."

Neither is this whimsical spectacle a recent invention. A hare that beat the tabor is mentioned by Jonson, in his comedy of *Bartholmew Fayre*, acted at the commencement of the seventeenth century; and a representation of the same feat, taken from a drawing on a manuscript upwards of four hundred years old, is given on plate twenty-two.[1]

And here I cannot help mentioning a very ridiculous show of a learned pig, which of late days attracted much of the public notice, and at the polite end of the town. This pig, which indeed was a large unwieldy hog, being taught to pick up letters written upon pieces of cards, and to arrange them at command, gave great satisfaction to all who saw him, and filled his tormenter's pocket with money. One would not have thought that a hog had been an animal capable of learning: the fact, however, is another proof of what may be accomplished by assiduity; for the showman assured a friend of mine, that he had lost three very promising brutes in the course of training, and that the phenomenon then exhibited had often given him reason to despair of success. It was first shown in the vicinity of Pall Mall, in 1789, at five shillings each person; the price was afterwards reduced to half a crown; and finally to one shilling.

A DANCING COCK AND THE DESERTER BIRD.—The joculators did not confine themselves to the tutoring of quadrupeds, but extended their practice to birds also; and a curious specimen of their art appears on plate twenty-six, where a cock is represented dancing on stilts to the music of a pipe and tabor.[2]

In the present day (1800), this may probably be considered as a mere effort of the illuminator's fancy, and admit of a doubt whether such a trick was ever displayed in reality; but many are yet living who were witnesses to an exhibition far more surprising, shown at Breslaw's, a celebrated juggler, who performed in Cockspur Street, opposite the Haymarket, about 1775. His prices for admission were five shillings and half a crown. A number of little birds, to the amount, I believe, of twelve or fourteen, being taken from different cages, were placed upon a table in the presence of the spectators; and there they formed themselves into ranks like a company of soldiers: small cones of paper bearing some resemblance to grenadiers' caps were put upon their heads, and diminutive imitations of muskets made with wood, secured under their left wings. Thus equipped, they marched to and fro several times; when a single bird was brought forward, supposed to be a deserter, and set between six of the musketeers, three in a row, who conducted him from the top to the bottom of the table, on the middle of which a small brass cannon charged with a little gunpowder had been previously placed, and the deserter was situated in the front part of the cannon; his guards then divided, three retiring on one side, and three on the other, and he was left standing by himself. Another bird was immediately produced; and, a lighted match being put into one of his claws, he hopped boldly on the other to the tail of the cannon, and, applying the match to the priming, discharged the piece without the least appearance of fear or agitation. The

[1] Harl. MSS. No. 6563.   [2] *Ibid.*

moment the explosion took place, the deserter fell down, and lay, apparently motionless, like a dead bird; but, at the command of his tutor he rose again; and the cages being brought, the feathered soldiers were stripped of their ornaments, and returned into them in perfect order.

IMITATIONS OF ANIMALS.—Among the performances dependent on imitation, that of assuming the forms of different animals, and counterfeiting their gestures, do not seem to have originated with the jugglers; for this absurd practice, if I mistake not, existed long before these comical artists made their appearance, at least in large companies, and in a professional way. There was a sport common among the ancients, which usually took place on the kalends of January, and probably formed a part of the Saturnalia, or feasts of Saturn. It consisted in mummings and disguisements; for the actors took upon themselves the resemblance of wild beasts, or domestic cattle, and wandered about from one place to another; and he, I presume, stood highest in the estimation of his fellows who best supported the character of the brute he imitated. This whimsical amusement was exceedingly popular, and continued to be practised long after the establishment of Christianity; it was, however, much opposed by the clergy, and particularly by Paulinus, bishop of Nola, in the ninth century, who in one of his sermons tells us, that those concerned in it were wont to clothe themselves with skins of cattle, and put upon them the heads of beasts.[1] What effect his preaching may have had at the time, I know not: the custom, however, was not totally suppressed, but may be readily traced from vestiges remaining of it, to the modern times. Dr Johnson, in his *Journey to the Western Islands of Scotland*, says a gentleman informed him, that, at new year's eve, in the hall or castle of the laird, where at festivals there is supposed to be a very numerous company, one man dresses himself in a cow-hide, on which other men beat with sticks; he runs with all this noise round the house, which all the company quits in a counterfeited fright; the door is then shut, and no readmission obtained after their pretended terror, but by the repetition of a verse of poetry, which those acquainted with the custom are provided with.[2] The ancient court games, described in a former chapter, are certainly off-shoots from the Saturnalian disfigurements; and from the same stock we may pertinently derive the succeeding masquings and disguisements of the person frequently practised at certain seasons of the year; and hence also came the modern masquerades. Warton says, that certain court theatrical amusements were called mascarades very anciently in France.[3]

MUMMINGS AND MASQUERADES.—In the middle ages, mummings were very common. Mumm is said to be derived from the Danish word *mumme*, or *momme* in Dutch, and signifies to disguise oneself with a mask: hence a mummer, which is properly defined by Dr Johnson to be a masker, one who performs frolics in a personated dress.

---

[1] Du Cange, *Glossary*, in vocibus *Cervula* et *Kalendæ*.　　[2] See also Bourne's *Vulgar Errors*, edited by Brand, p. 175.
[3] *History of English Poetry*, vol. i. p. 237.

Jugglers and dancers, antics, mummers, mimics.

From the time of Edward III. mummings or disguisings, accompanied with figurative dances, were in vogue at court, of which there were memorable instances in the years 1377 and 1400. In the mansions of the nobility, on occasions of festivity, it also frequently happened that the whole company appeared in borrowed characters; and, full license of speech being granted to every one, the discourses were not always kept within the bounds of decency.[1] These spectacles were exhibited with great splendour in former times and particularly during the reign of Henry VIII.; they have ceased, however, of late years to attract the notice of the opulent; and the regular masquerades which succeeded them, are not supported at present (1800) with that degree of mirthful spirit which, we are told, abounded at their institution; and probably it is for this reason they are declining so rapidly in the public estimation.

The mummeries practised by the lower classes of the people usually took place at the Christmas holidays; and such persons as could not procure masks rubbed their faces over with soot, or painted them; hence Sebastian Brant, in his *Ship of Fools*,[2] alluding to this custom, says :—

> The one hath a visor ugley set on his face,
>   Another hath on a vile counterfaite vesture,
> Or painteth his visage with fume in such case,
>   That what he is, himself is scantily sure.

It appears that many abuses were committed under the sanction of these disguisements; and for this reason an ordinance was established, by which a man was liable to punishment who appeared in the streets of London with "a painted visage."[3] In the third year of the reign of Henry VIII. it was ordained that no persons should appear abroad like mummers, covering their faces with vizors, and in disguised apparel, under pain of imprisonment for three months. The same act enforced the penalty of 20s. against such as kept vizors or masks in their houses for the purpose of mumming.

Bourne, in his *Vulgar Antiquities*,[4] speaks of a kind of mumming practised in the North about Christmas time, which consisted in " changing of clothes between the men and the women, who, when dressed in each other's habits, go," says he, " from one neighbour's house to another, and partake of their Christmas cheer, and make merry with them in disguise, by dancing and singing and such like merriments."

MUMMING TO ROYAL PERSONAGES.—Persons capable of well supporting assumed characters were frequently introduced at public entertainments, and also in the pageants exhibited on occasions of solemnity; sometimes they were the bearers of presents, and sometimes the speakers of panegyrical orations.

[1] *Mem. Anc. Cheval*, tom. ii. p. 68.
[2] Translated by Alexander Barclay, and printed by Pynson in 1508.   [3] Stow's *Survey*, fol. 680.
[4] Chap. xvi.

Animals imitated.

Froissart tells us, that, after the coronation of Isabel of Bavaria, the queen of Charles VI. of France, she had several rich donations brought to her by mummers in different disguisements; one resembling a bear, another an unicorn, others like a company of Moors, and others as Turks or Saracens.[1]

When queen Elizabeth was entertained at Kenilworth castle, various spectacles were contrived for her amusement, and some of them produced without any previous notice, to take her as it were by surprise. It happened about nine o'clock one evening, as her majesty returned from hunting, and was riding by torchlight, there came suddenly out of the wood, by the road-side, a man habited like a savage, covered with ivy, holding in one of his hands an oaken plant torn up by the roots, who placed himself before her, and, after holding some discourse with a counterfeit echo, repeated a poetical oration in her praise, which was well received. This man was Thomas Gascoyne the poet; and the verses he spoke on the occasion were his own composition. The circumstance took place on the 10th of July 1575.[2]

The savage men, or wodehouses, as they are sometimes called, frequently made their appearance in the public shows; they were sometimes clothed entirely with skins, and sometimes they were decorated with oaken leaves, or covered, as above, with ivy.

PARTIAL IMITATIONS OF ANIMALS.—The jugglers and the minstrels, observing how lightly these ridiculous disguisements were relished by the people in general, turned their talents towards the imitating of different animals, and rendered their exhibitions more pleasing by the addition of their new acquirements. On plate twenty-eight are three specimens of their performances, all taken from the fourteenth century Bodleian MS. that has supplied so many of our illustrations. One of them presents to us the resemblance of a stag, and another that of a goat walking erectly on his hind feet. Neither of these fictitious animals have any fore legs; but to the first the deficiency is supplied by a staff, upon which the actor might recline at pleasure; his face is seen through an aperture on the breast; and, I doubt not, a person was chosen to play this part with a face susceptible of much grimace, which he had an opportunity of setting forth to great advantage, with a certainty of commanding the plaudits of his beholders. It was also possible to heighten the whimsical appearance of this disguise by a motion communicated to the head; a trick the man might easily enough perform, by putting one of his arms into the hollow of his neck; and probably the neck was made pliable for that purpose. In the third delineation we find a boy, with a mask resembling the head of a dog, presenting a scroll of parchment to his master. In the original there are two more boys, who are following disguised in a similar manner, and each of them holding a like scroll of parchment. The wit of this performance, I protest, I cannot discover.

COUNTERFEIT VOICES OF ANIMALS.—I have not been able to ascertain how

---

[1] *Chron.* tom. i. iv. chap. 157, Lord Berners' translation.　　　[2] See Nichols' *Progresses*, vol. i.

far the ancient jugglers exerted their abilities in counterfeiting the articulation of animals; but we may reasonably suppose they would not have neglected so essential a requisite to make their imitations perfect.

In the reign of queen Anne, a man whose name was Clench, a native of Barnet, made his appearance at London. He performed at the corner of Bartholomew Lane, behind the Royal Exchange. His price for admittance was one shilling each person. I have his advertisement before me;[1] which states that he "imitated the horses, the huntsmen, and a pack of hounds, a sham doctor, an old woman, a drunken man, the bells, the flute, the double curtell, and the organ with three voices, by his own natural voice, to the greatest perfection." He then professes himself to "be the only man that could ever attain to so great an art." He had, however, a rival, who is noted in one of the papers of the *Spectator*, and called the whistling man. His excellency consisted in counterfeiting the notes of all kinds of singing birds.[2] The same performance was exhibited in great perfection by the bird-tutor associated with Breslaw the juggler, mentioned a few pages back. This man assumed the name of Rosignol,[3] and, after he had quitted Breslaw, appeared on the stage at Covent Garden Theatre, where, in addition to his imitation of the birds, he executed a concerto on a fiddle without strings; that is, he made the notes in a wonderful manner with his voice, and represented the bowing by drawing a small truncheon backwards and forwards over a stringless violin. His performance was received with great applause; and the success he met with produced many competitors, but none of them equalled him: it was, however, discovered, that the sounds were produced by an instrument contrived for the purpose, concealed in the mouth; and then the trick lost all its reputation. Six years ago (1794) I heard a poor rustic, a native of St Alban's, imitate, with great exactness, the whole assemblage of animals belonging to a farm-yard; but especially he excelled in counterfeiting the grunting of swine, the squeaking of pigs, and the quarrelling of two dogs.

ANIMALS TRAINED FOR BAITING.—Training of bulls, bears, horses, and other animals, for the purpose of baiting them with dogs, was certainly practised by the jugglers; and this vicious pastime has the sanction of high antiquity. Fitz-Stephen, who lived in the reign of Henry II., tells us that, in the forenoon of every holiday, during the winter season, the young Londoners were amused with boars opposed to each other in battle, or with bulls and full-grown bears baited by dogs.[4] This author makes no mention of horses; and I believe the baiting of these noble and useful animals was never a general practice: it was, however, no doubt, partially performed; and the manner in which it was carried into execution appears on plate twenty-seven. Asses also were treated with the same inhumanity; but probably the poor beasts did not afford sufficient sport in the tormenting, and therefore were seldom brought forward as the objects of this barbarous diversion.

[1] Miscell. Collect. Harl. Lib. No. 115.　　　[2] Vol. viii. No. 570.　　　[3] Literally, nightingale.
[4] *Description of London.* See also Stow's *Survey*, p. 78.

PARIS GARDEN.—There were several places in the vicinity of the metropolis set apart for the baiting of beasts, and especially the district of Saint Saviour's parish in Southwark, called Paris Garden; which place contained two bear-gardens, said to have been the first that were made near London; and in them, according to Stow, were scaffolds for the spectators to stand upon:[1] and this indulgence, we are told, they paid for in the following manner: "Those who go to Paris Garden, the Bell Savage, or Theatre, to behold bear-baiting, enterludes, or fence-play, must not account of any pleasant spectacle, unless first they pay one pennie at the gate, another at the entrie of the scaffold, and a third for quiet standing."[2] One Sunday afternoon in January 1583, the scaffolds being over-charged with spectators, fell down during the performance; and a great number of persons were killed or maimed by the accident.[3]

BULL AND BEAR-BAITING PATRONISED BY ROYALTY.—Bull and bear-baiting is not encouraged by persons of rank and opulence in the present day (1800); and when practised, which rarely happens, it is attended only by the lowest and most despicable part of the people; which plainly indicates a general refinement of manners and prevalency of humanity among the moderns; on the contrary, this barbarous pastime was highly relished by the nobility in former ages, and countenanced by persons of the most exalted rank, without exception even of the fair sex.

*The office of Master of the Bears used to be held under the Crown, with a salary of 16d. a day. It was his duty to provide bears and dogs and superintend the baiting whenever required. He had authority to issue commissions to his officials to press into the royal service any bears or dogs that seemed suitable. On October 11th, 1561, a patent was issued to Sir Saunders Duncombe "for the sole practice and profit of the fighting and combating of wild and domestic beasts within the realm of England for the space of fourteen years." Prince Arthur had a bear-ward; when he visited the prior of Durham in 1530 with his troop of bears and apes, he received a gratuity of five shillings.[4]

Erasmus, who visited England in the reign of Henry VIII., says, there were "many herds of bears maintained in this country for the purpose of baiting."[5] When queen Mary visited her sister the princess Elizabeth during her confinement at Hatfield House, the next morning, after mass, a grand exhibition of bear-baiting was made for their amusement, with which, it is said, "their highnesses were right well content."[6] Queen Elizabeth, on the 25th of May 1559, soon after her accession to the throne, gave a splendid dinner to the French ambassadors, who afterwards were entertained with the baiting of bulls and bears, and the queen herself stood with the ambassadors looking on the

---

[1] *Survey of London*, ubi supra.　　[2] Lambarde's *Perambulation of Kent*, published A.D. 1570, p. 248.

[3] *This accident produced a pamphlet entitled "A Godly Exhortation by occasion of the late Judgment of God shewed at Paris Garden, 13 January, 1583, upon divers Persons, whereof some were killed and many hurt at a Bear-bating."

[4] *Harting's *Extinct British Animals*, 27, 28. Mr Harting makes a curious blunder over the account roll of Durham Abbey, and imagines that the prior himself kept bears and apes.

[5] *Erasmi Adagia*, p. 361.　　[6] *Life of Sir Thomas Pope*, sect. iii. p. 85.

pastime till six at night. The day following, the same ambassadors went by water to Paris Garden, where they saw another baiting of bulls and of bears;[1] and again, twenty-seven years posterior, queen Elizabeth received the Danish ambassador at Greenwich, who was treated with the sight of a bear and bull-baiting, "tempered," says Holinshed, "with other merry disports";[2] and, for the diversion of the populace, there was a horse with an ape upon his back; which highly pleased them, so that they expressed "their inward-conceived joy and delight with shrill shouts and variety of gestures."[3]

BULL AND BEAR-BAITING, HOW PERFORMED.—The manner in which these sports were exhibited towards the close of the sixteenth century, is thus described by Hentzner,[4] who was present at one of the performances: "There is a place built in the form of a theatre, which serves for baiting of bulls and bears; they are fastened behind, and then worried by great English bull-dogs; but not without risque to the dogs, from the horns of the one and the teeth of the other; and it sometimes happens they are killed on the spot; fresh ones are immediately supplied in the places of those that are wounded or tired. To this entertainment there often follows that of whipping a blinded bear, which is performed by five or six men standing circularly with whips, which they exercise upon him without any mercy, as he cannot escape because of his chain; he defends himself with all his force and skill, throwing down all that come within his reach, and are not active enough to get out of it, and tearing the whips out of their hands, and breaking them." Laneham, speaking of a bear-baiting exhibited before queen Elizabeth in 1575, says: "It was a sport very pleasant to see the bear, with his pink eyes learing after his enemies, approach; the nimbleness and wait of the dog to take his advantage; and the force and experience of the bear again to avoid his assaults: if he were bitten in one place, how he would pinch in another to get free; that if he were taken once, then by what shift with biting, with clawing, with roaring, with tossing, and tumbling, he would work and wind himself from them; and, when he was loose, to shake his ears twice or thrice with the blood and the slaver hanging about his physiognomy." The same writer tells us, that thirteen bears were provided for this occasion, and they were baited with a great sort of ban-dogs.[5] In the foregoing relations, we find no mention made of a ring put into the nose of the bear when he was baited; which certainly was the more modern practice; hence the expression by the duke of Newcastle, in the *Humorous Lovers*, printed in 1617: "I fear the wedlock ring more than the bear does the ring in his nose."

BEARS AND BEAR-WARDS.—When a bear-baiting was about to take place, the same was publicly made known, and the bear-ward previously paraded the streets with his bear, to excite the curiosity of the populace, and induce them to become spectators of the sport. The animal, on these occasions, was usually

---

[1] Nichols' *Progresses*, vol. i. p. 40.   [2] *Chronicle of Eng.* vol. iii. fol. 1552.
[3] Nichols' *Progresses*, vol. ii. p. 228.
[4] *Itinerary*, printed in Latin, A.D. 1598. See Lord Orford's translation, Strawberry Hill, p. 42.
[5] Nichols' *Progresses*, vol. i. fol. 249.

preceded by a minstrel or two, and carried a monkey or baboon upon his back. In the *Humorous Lovers*, the play just now quoted, "Tom of Lincoln" is mentioned as the name of "a famous bear"; and one of the characters pretending to personate a bear-ward, says: "I'll set up my bills, that the gamesters of London, Horsleydown, Southwark, and Newmarket, may come in and bait him here before the ladies; but first, boy, go fetch me a bagpipe; we will walk the streets in triumph, and give the people notice of our sport."

BAITING IN QUEEN ANNE'S TIME.—The two following advertisements,[1] which were published in the reign of queen Anne, may serve as a specimen of the elegant manner in which these pastimes were announced to the public :—

"At the Bear Garden in Hockley in the Hole, near Clerkenwell Green, this present Monday, there is a great match to be fought by two Dogs of Smithfield Bars against two Dogs of Hampstead, at the Reading Bull, for one guinea to be spent; five lets goes out of hand; which goes fairest and farthest in wins all. The famous Bull of fire-works, which pleased the gentry to admiration. Likewise there are two Bear-Dogs to jump three jumps apiece at the Bear, which jumps highest for ten shillings to be spent. Also variety of bull-baiting and bear-baiting; it being a day of general sport by all the old gamesters; and a bull-dog to be drawn up with fire-works. Beginning at three o'clock."

"At William Well's bear-garden in Tuttle-fields, Westminster, this present Monday, there will be a green Bull baited; and twenty Dogs to fight for a collar; and the dog that runs farthest and fairest wins the collar; with other diversions of bull and bear-baiting. Beginning at two of the clock."

*The noise of the bear-gardens, with the shouts and excitement of the spectators, was something prodigious; the term "bear-garden" still applied to a noisy household serves to perpetuate a once popular national pastime.

*RECENT BULL-BAITING.—Bull-baiting lingered with us much longer than bear-baiting, and was a far more universal sport throughout England. Butchers who sold unbaited bull beef were subject in various boroughs to considerable penalties. It used to be supposed that this order was made in consequence of baited beef being more digestible, but the enactments were really intended to promote the continuation of what used to be regarded as a manly sport. After the Restoration this pastime was generally resumed with much zest. Sir Miles Stapleton replaced the ring for bull-baiting and the stone to which it was affixed in the market-place of Bedale, Yorkshire, in 1661.[2]

*Bull-baiting was, however, considered more the sport of the populace than of gentlefolk. It was followed up in the Southwark Bear Garden, but it disgusted not only Evelyn, but even Pepys. The latter was present at a Southwark bull-baiting on August 14th, 1666, when the bull tossed one of the dogs "into the very boxes"; Pepys had the sense to write "it is a very rude and nasty pleasure." Evelyn was at the same place on June 16th, 1670, and wrote:

---

[1] Harl. MSS. No. 15.

[2] The details are given in his *Household Books*: see *Ancestor*, Nos. ii. and iii.

"I went with some friends to the Bear Garden, where was cock-fighting, dog-fighting, and bear and bull-baiting, it being a famous day for all these butcherly sports, or rather barbarous cruelties. The bulls did exceeding well, but the Irish wolf-dog exceeded, which was a tall greyhound, a stately creature indeed, who beat a cruel mastiff. One of the bulls tossed a dog full into a lady's lap, as she sate in one of the boxes at a considerable height from the arena. Two poor dogs were killed, and so all ended with the ape on horseback, and I most heartily weary of the rude and dirty pastime, which I had not seen, I think, in twenty years before."

*In bull-baiting a rope about 15 feet long was fastened to the root of the horns, and the other end secured to an iron ring fixed to a stone or stake driven into the ground. The actual ring for bull-baiting still remains in several places in England, such as Hedon, Colchester, and Brading in the Isle of Wight. Several towns, like Birmingham and Dorchester, retain traces of the sport in their street nomenclature. In 1802 a Bill was introduced into Parliament for the suppression of this barbarous custom, but it was resisted, especially by Mr Windham, as part of a conspiracy of the Jacobins and Methodists to render the people grave and serious, and to uproot constitutional government. Notwithstanding the earnestness of Wilberforce and the eloquence of Sheridan, the Bill was defeated by a majority of thirteen. A worse fate befell a like measure introduced in 1829, which was defeated by 73 votes to 28. But after the great Reform Bill became law the protests of decent folk could no longer be set at naught, and bull-baiting was made illegal in 1835. Nevertheless the sport was still continued, after an illicit fashion, in a few places. It is said that there were bull-baitings at Wirksworth in 1840, at Eccles in 1842, and at West Derby in 1853.[1]

*BULL-RUNNING AT TUTBURY AND STAMFORD.—The bull-running, as practiced at Tutbury and Stamford, and probably in other parts of England in old days, was a very different pastime, for which more could be said as a sport than the worrying of a chained-up brute. The bull-running at Tutbury was first described with any detail by Dr Plot in 1686.[2] A court of minstrels was established at Tutbury by John of Gaunt who held their festival on August 16, the morrow of the feast of the Assumption. At the conclusion of the festivities a bull was given them at the priory gate by the prior of Tutbury. The poor beast had the tip of its horns sawn off, his ears and tail cut off, the body smeared with soap, and the nostrils filled with pepper. The minstrels rushed after the maddened creature, and if any of those of the county of Stafford could succeed in holding him long enough to cut off a piece of his hair before sunset, he became the property of the king of the minstrels, who had that day been elected to his office by a jury who chose the monarch of the year alternately from the minstrels of Staffordshire and Derbyshire. If, on the other hand, the beast escaped from them untaken, or crossed another river into Derbyshire, he

---

[1] *Notes and Queries*, Ser. VI. i 86, 105, 186.   [2] *Natural History of Staffordshire*, 439.

Sword and Buckler.

was returned to the prior. This supplying of the bull was a customary tenure due from the prior. After the dissolution of the monasteries, this tenure devolved upon the earls and afterwards the dukes of Devonshire. Dr Plot considered that John of Gaunt had introduced this custom from Spain in imitation of the bull-fights of that nation. But Dr Pegge, in 1765, pointed out the absurdity of this contention.[1] The duke of Devonshire suppressed this riotous custom in 1788.

*From time immemorial the town of Stamford annually celebrated, on November 13th, a bull-running. The animal, provided by the butchers of the town, was turned into the main street, and thence driven by the crowd on to the bridge over the Welland, whence it was usually precipitated into the water. When the bull swam ashore it was again pursued, and the hunt was carried on till both mob and beast were wearied out. Then the animal was killed and its flesh sold at a low rate. There were many local rules connected with the sport, such as there was to be no iron about the clubs or staves carried by the pursuers. Tradition had it that the custom originated in the days of king John, when William, earl of Warren, saw from his castle two bulls fighting in the meadow below. Some butchers striving to part the brutes, one of them ran into the town causing great uproar. The earl on horseback followed the bull, and so enjoyed the sport that he gave the meadow where the fight began to the butchers of Stamford on the condition of their finding a bull to be run on the anniversary for ever. An attempt was made to stop the sport in 1788, but it survived until 1839, when, in spite of a troop of dragoons and a strong force of metropolitan police, the last bull-running, by the successful introduction of a smuggled-in bull, was accomplished amid fierce excitement. In a later year there was a feeble and last attempt to renew the ancient custom.[2]

SWORD-PLAY.—The sword-dance, or, more properly, a combat with swords and bucklers, regulated by music, was exhibited by the Saxon gleemen. We have spoken on this subject in a former chapter, and resume it here, because the jugglers of the middle ages were famous for their skill in handling the sword.

The combat, represented on the centre of plate twenty-nine, taken from a thirteenth century manuscript,[3] varies, in several respects, from that on plate twenty-one, though both, I presume, are different modifications of the same performance, as well as that on the top of plate twenty-nine,[4] which is carried into execution without the assistance of a minstrel.

These combats bore some resemblance to those performed by the Roman gladiators; for which reason the jugglers were sometimes called gladiators by the early historians. *Mimi, salii, balatrones, emiliani, gladiatores, palestrite— et tota joculatorum copia*, are the titles given them by John of Salisbury.[5] It also appears that they instituted schools for teaching the art of defence in

---

[1] *Archæologia*, ii. 86-91.
[2] There is a good summary of the history of the Stamford bull-running in Chambers's *Book of Days*, ii. 574-576.
[3] Roy. Lib. No. 14, E. iii.　　　　　　　　　　[4] Roy. Lib. No. 20, D. vi.
[5] Johan. Sarisburiensis, *De Nugis Curialium*, lib. i. cap. viii. p. 34.

O

various parts of the kingdom, and especially in the city of London, where the conduct of the masters and their scholars became so outrageous, that it was necessary for the legislature to interfere; and, in the fourteenth year of the reign of Edward I. (1286), an edict was published by royal authority, which prohibited the keeping of such schools, and the public exercise of swords and bucklers.

It is said that many robberies and murders were committed by these gladiators; hence the appellation of swash buckler, a term of reproach, "from swashing," says Fuller, "and making a noise on the buckler, and ruffian, which is the same as a swaggerer. West Smithfield was formerly called Ruffian Hall, where such men usually met, casually or otherwise, to try masteries with sword and buckler; more were frightened than hurt, hurt than killed therewith, it being accounted unmanly to strike beneath the knee. But since that desperate traytor Rowland Yorke first used thrusting with rapiers, swords and bucklers are disused."[1] Jonson, in the induction to his play called *Bartholomew Fair*, speaks of "the sword and buckler age in Smithfield"; and again, in the *Two Angry Women of Abbington*, a comedy by Henry Porter, printed in 1599, we have the following observation: "Sword and buckler fight begins to grow out of use; I am sorry for it; I shall never see good manhood again; if it be once gone, this poking fight of rapier and dagger will come up; then a tall man, that is, a courageous man, and a good sword and buckler man, will be spitted like a cat or a rabbit."

Such exercises had been practised by day and by night, to the great annoyance of the peaceable inhabitants of the city; and by the statute of Edward I. the offenders were subjected to the punishment of imprisonment for forty days; to which was afterwards added a mulct of forty marks.[2] These restrictions certainly admitted of some exceptions; for it is well known that there were seminaries at London, wherein youth were taught the use of arms, held publicly after the institution of this ordinance. "The art of defence and use of weapons," says Stow, "is taught by professed masters";[3] but these most probably were licensed by the city governors, and under their control. The author of a description of the colleges and schools in and about London, which he calls *The Third University of England*, printed in black letter in 1615, says: "In this city," meaning London, "there be manie professors of the science of defence, and very skilful men in teaching the best and most offensive and defensive use of verie many weapons, as of the long-sword, back-sword, rapier and dagger, single rapier, the case of rapiers, the sword and buckler, or targate, the pike, the halberd, the long-staff, and others. Henry VIII. made the professors of this art a company, or corporation, by letters patent, wherein the art is intituled 'The Noble Science of Defence.' The manner of the proceeding of our fencers in their schools is this: first, they which desire to be taught

---

[1] *Worthies of England*, A.D. 1662.
[2] Maitland's *History of London*, book i. chap. xi. [3] *Survey of London*, chap. ii.

at their admission are called scholars, and, as they profit, they take degrees, and proceed to be provosts of defence; and that must be wonne by public trial of their proficiencie and of their skill at certain weapons, which they call prizes, and in the presence and view of many hundreds of people; and, at their next and last prize well and sufficiently performed, they do proceed to be maisters of the science of defence, or maisters of fence, as we commonly call them." The king ordained "that none, but such as have thus orderly proceeded by public act and trial, and have the approbation of the principal masters of their company, may profess or teach this art of defence publicly in any part of England." Stow informs us, that the young Londoners, on holidays, after the evening prayer, were permitted to exercise themselves with their wasters and bucklers before their masters' doors. This pastime, I imagine, is represented by the fourteenth century drawing at the bottom of plate twenty-nine,[1] from whence the annexed engraving is taken, where clubs or bludgeons are substituted for swords.

*THE MASTERS OF DEFENCE.—"The Maisters of the Noble Science of Defence" organised by Henry VIII. in July 1540, were still further consolidated in the reign of Elizabeth. Among the Sloane MSS. of the British Museum is an interesting book compiled in 1575, which contains a record of this Association of Masters, with its rules, notes of prizes played by them, and many other details.[2] The Association consisted first of the "Scholler," or probationer; secondly, the "Free Scholler," which was the junior grade; then the "Provost," or assistant master; and lastly the "Maister." From the masters was chosen the small governing body known as "The Four Ancient Maisters of the Noble Science of Defence." The provosts and masters were licensed by "our soveraigne lady, Elizabeth," to teach in their schools "within this realme of England Irelande and Calleis and the precincts of the same" gentlemen or yeomen who were willing to learn the science of defence, "as playinge with the two hande sworde, the Pike, the bastard sworde, the dagger, the Backe sworde, the sworde and Buckeler, and the staffe, and all other maner of weapons apperteyninge to the same science." The scholar had to play with at least six scholars with the long sword and back sword before he could be a free scholar. Before a free scholar could become a provost he had to play at the two-hand sword, the back-sword, and the staff with all manner of provosts that came on the appointed day; notice being sent to all provosts within threescore miles of the place of play. Amongst other obligations, if successful, the new provost had to be bound over to the four ancient masters not to keep any school within seven miles of any master without license from the governing four. When a provost was minded to take the master's degree, he had to play any masters, who might appear from within forty miles of the appointed place, at the two-hand sword, the bastard sword, the pike, the back-sword, and the rapier and dagger.

---

[1] Bodleian MSS. No. 264.

[2] *These rules are printed in full and many other extracts given in the chapter entitled "Prize-players and prize-fighters," of Mr A. Hutton's valuable book, *The Sword and the Centuries* (1901).

*The notes as to play for these different degrees extend from 1575 to 1591, and show the fierceness of the contests. Gregorye Greene, who played for his scholar's prize at Chelmsford in 1578, contended with eight at two-hand sword and seven at back-sword. Edward Harvye in the same year played for his scholar's prize at the Bull within Bishopsgate (the favourite London place of meeting) with fourteen at two-hand sword and two at sword and buckler. The provost's prizes were played in public, usually at some tavern such as the Bull in Bishopsgate and the Bellesavage at Ludgate. Other places named for the playing for master's prizes were Hampton Court, the Artillery Garden, and Canterbury.

*This Association was at its zenith in Elizabeth's reign; it lingered on in the reign of James I. and Charles I., though after a humble fashion, and expired during the Commonwealth struggle. With the Restoration came in prize-fighting as opposed to the earlier prize-playing with broad or back-sword, the cudgel, and the staff. The play of this kind from Henry VIII. to end of Elizabeth was for the honour and gain of being promoted as teachers in a gild or association of fencers; but with the advent of Charles II., when the two-hand sword and the long rapier had gone out of fashion, came the men who merely fought for money prizes, with the addition of whatever coins might be thrown to them on the stage by the public. The lively pages of Pepys yield several accounts of the fierce prize-fighting with swords.

*PEPYS ON PRIZE-PLAY.—"June 1, 1663.—I with Sir J. Minnes to the Strand Maypole, and there light of his coach, and walked to the New Theatre, which, since the King's players are gone to the Royal one, is this day begun to be employed for the fencers to play prizes at. And here I came and saw the first prize I ever saw in my life: and it was between one Matthews, who did beat at all points, and one Westwicke, who was soundly cut both in the head and legs, that he was all over blood; and other deadly blows did they give and take in very good earnest. They fought at eight weapons, three boutes at each weapon. This being upon a private quarrel, they did it in good earnest, and I felt one of their swords, and found it very little, if at all, blunter on the edge than the common swords are. Strange to see what a deal of money is flung to them both upon the stage between every boute.

"May 27th, 1667.—Abroad, and stopped at Beargarden stairs, there to see a prize fought. But the house so full there was no getting in there, so forced to go through an ale house into the pit where the bears are baited; and upon a stool did see them fight, a butcher and a waterman. The former had the better all along, till by and by the latter dropped his sword out of his hand, and the butcher, whether not seeing his sword dropped I know not, but did give him a cut over the wrist, so that he was disabled to fight any longer. But Lord! to see in a minute the whole stage was full of watermen to revenge the foul play, and the butchers to defend their fellow, though most blamed him; and there they fell to it, knocking down and cutting many on each side. It was pleasant to see, but that I stood in the pit, and feared that in the tumult I might get some hurt. At last the battle broke up, so I away.

"Sept. 1st, 1667.—To the Beargarden where now the yard is full of people, and those most of them seamen, striving by force to get in. I got into the common pit; and there with my cloak about my face, I stood and I saw the prize fought, till one of them, a shoemaker, was so cut in both his wrists that he could not fight any longer, and then they broke off. The sport very good, and various humours to be seen among the rabble that is there.

"April 12th, 1669.—By water to the Beargarden, and there happened to sit by Sir Fretcheville Hollis, who is still full of his vainglorious and profane talk. Here we saw a prize fought between a soldier and a country fellow, one Warrell who promised the least in his looks, and performing the most of valour in his boldness and evenness of mind, and smiles in all he did, that ever I saw; and we were all both deceived and infinitely taken with him. He did soundly beat the soldier, and cut him over the head. Thence back to White Hall, mightily pleased all of us with this sight, and particularly this fellow, as a most extraordinary man for his temper and evenness in fighting."

PUBLIC SWORD-PLAY.—The following show-bill, dated July 13, 1709, contains the common mode of challenging and answering used by the combatants of those days; it is selected from a great number now lying before me;[1] and, being rather curious, I shall transcribe it without making any alteration.

"At the Bear Garden in Hockley in the Hole, near Clerkenwell Green, a trial of skill shall be performed between Two Masters of the noble Science of Defence on Wednesday next, at two of the clock precisely.

"I George Gray, born in the city of Norwich, who have fought in most parts of the West Indies, namely, Jamaica and Barbadoes, and several other parts of the world, in all twenty-five times, and upon a stage, and never yet was worsted, and being now lately come to London, do invite James Harris to meet and exercise at these following weapons, namely, back-sword, sword and dagger, sword and buckler, single falchon, and case of falchons."

"I James Harris, Master of the said noble Science of Defence, who formerly rid in the horse-guards, and hath fought a hundred and ten prizes, and never left a stage to any man, will not fail, God willing, to meet this brave and bold inviter at the time and place appointed; desiring sharp swords, and from him no favour. No person to be upon the stage but the seconds. Vivat Regina!"

With the accession of George I. the taste for these gladiatorial shows began to wane, and their place was ere long taken by pugilism.

QUARTER-STAFF.—In another challenge of the reign of Anne the quarter-staff is added to the list of weapons named on these occasions. Quarter-staff Dr Johnson explains to be "A staff of defence, so called, I believe, from the

---

[1] In a Miscellaneous Collection of Title-pages, Bills, etc., in the Harleian Library, No. 115.

*Mr Hutton, in *The Sword and the Centuries*, gives many other particulars of the prize-fighting heroes of queen Anne's days, such as Donald MacBane and James Figs.

manner of using it; one hand being placed at the middle, and the other equally between the end and the middle."[1]   The quarter-staff was formerly used by the English, and especially in the western parts of the kingdom.   I have seen a small pamphlet of 1625 with this title: "Three to One; being an English-Spanish combat, performed by a western gentleman of Tavystock, in Devonshire, with an English quarter-staff, against three rapiers and poniards, at Sherries in Spain, in the presence of the dukes, condes, marquisses, and other great dons of Spain, being the council of war"; to which is added, "the author of this booke, and actor in this encounter, being R. Peecke."   On the same page there is a rude wooden print, representing the hero with his quarter-staff, in the action of fighting with the three Spanyards, who are armed with long swords and daggers. Caulfield has copied this print in his *Assemblage of Noted Persons.*

*This favourite old English weapon or implement was a stout pole or staff varying from eight to five feet in length, but usually in encounters of a regular length of six and a half feet.   It seems to have been originally a mere walking-staff, like the Swiss alpenstock, and then found useful for defence and offence. In action it was grasped by one hand in the middle, and by the other between the middle and the end.   When attacking, the latter hand shifted from one quarter of the staff to the other, giving the weapon a rapid circular motion, which brought the ends on the adversary at unexpected points.[2]

*In the old *Playe of Robyn Hode* mention is made of his meeting a stout friar with "a quarter-staffe in his hande," and of the blows they exchanged with these weapons.[3]   Bouts at quarter-staff are of frequent occurrence in all ballad histories of Robin Hood.   When Robin encountered Arthur a Bland, the tanner of Nottingham, we are told that—

> Then Robin he unbuckled his belt
>   And laid down his bow so long;
> He took up a staff of another oak graff,
>   That was both stiff and strong.
>
> *   *   *   *   *
>
> "But let me measure," said jolly Robin,
>   "Before we begin our fray;
> For I'll not have mine to be longer than thine,
>   For that will be counted foul play."
>
> "I pass not for length," bold Arthur replied,
>   "My staff is of oak so free;
> Eight foot and a half it will knock down a calf,
>   And I hope it will knock down thee."
>
> Then Robin Hood could no longer forbear,
>   He gave him such a knock,
> Quickly and soon the blood came down,
>   Before it was ten o'clock.
>
> *   *   *   *   *

---

[1] Dictionary, word *Quarter-staff.*   [2] *Century Dictionary.*   [3] Child's *Ballads,* iii. 127.

About and about and about they went,
 Like two wild boars in a chase,
Striving to aim each other to maim
 Leg, arm, or any other place.

And knock for knock they hastily dealt,
 Which held for two hours and more ;
That all the wood rang at every bang
 They plied their work so sore.[1]

[1] Child's *Ballads*, iii. 138.

CHAPTER VII

Ancient Specimens of Bowling—Poem on Bowling—Bowling-greens first made by the English—Bowling-alleys—Long-bowling—Gaming at Bowls—Charles I. and Charles II. fond of Bowls—Supposed Origin of Billiards—Kayles—Closh—Loggats—Nine-pins—Skittles—Dutch-pins—Four-corners—Half-bowl—Nine-holes—Troul in Madame—John Bull—Pitch and Hustle—Cock-fighting—Cock-fighting in nineteenth Century—Throwing at Cocks—Duck-hunting—Squirrel-hunting.

ANCIENT BOWLING—POEM ON BOWLING.—The pastime of bowling, whether practised upon open greens or in bowling-alleys, was probably an invention of the middle ages. I cannot by any means ascertain the time of its introduction; but I have traced it back to the thirteenth century. The earliest representation of a game played with bowls occurs on plate thirty from a manuscript of that century.[1]

Here two small cones are placed upright at a distance from each other; and the business of the players is evidently to bowl at them alternately; the successful candidate being he who could lay his bowl the nearest to the mark. The French, according to Cotgrave, had a similar kind of game, called *carreau*, from a square stone which, says he, "is laid in level with and at the end of a bowling-alley, and in the midst thereof an upright point set as the mark whereat they bowl." At the top of the same plate is a fourteenth century drawing from a beautiful MS. Book of Prayers, in the possession of Mr Douce. It represents two other bowlers; but they have no apparent object to play at, unless the bowl cast by the first may be considered as such by the second, and the game require him to strike it from its place.

Below these we see three persons engaged in the pastime of bowling; and they have a small bowl, or jack, according to the modern practice, which serves them as a mark for the direction of their bowls: the action of the middle figure, whose bowl is supposed to be running towards the jack, will not appear by any means extravagant to such as are accustomed to visit the bowling-greens.

*It is recorded of Lord Brooke, who was killed at the storming of Lichfield, 1643, that "he used to be much resorted to by those of the preciser sort, who had got a powerful hand over him; yet they would allow him Christian libertie for his recreation. But being at bowles one day, and following his cast with much eagernesse, he cryed, 'Rubbe, rubbe, rubbe, rubbe, rubbe.' His chaplain (a very strict mann) runns presently to him; and, in the hearing of diverse, 'O good my Lord, leave that to God—you must leave that to God!' says he."[2]

The following little poem, by William Stroad, which I found in "Justin

---

[1] Roy. Lib. No. 20, E. iv.   [2] L'Estrange's *Anecdotes*, No. 164.

216

Bowling

Pagitt's Memorandum Book" (1633), one of the Harleian manuscripts at the British Museum,[1] expresses happily enough the turns and chances of the game of bowls :—

A PARALLEL BETWIXT BOWLING AND PREFERMENT

Preferment, like a game at boules,
  To feede our hope hath divers play :
Heere quick it runns, there soft it roules ;
  The betters make and shew the way
On upper ground, so great allies
  Doe many *cast* on their desire ;
Some up are thrust and forc'd to rise,
  When those are stopt that would aspire.

Some, whose heate and zeal exceed,
  Thrive well by *rubbs* that curb their haste,
And some that languish in their speed
  Are cherished by some favour's blaste ;
Some rest in other's *cutting out*
  The fame by whom themselves are made ;
Some fetch a *compass* farr about,
  And secretly the marke invade.

Some get by *knocks*, and so advance
  Their fortune by a boysterous aime :
And some, who have the sweetest chance,
  Their en'mies *hit*, and win the game.
The fairest *casts* are those that owe
  No thanks to fortune's giddy sway ;
Such honest men good *bowlers* are
  Whose own true *bias cutts* the way.

In the three delineations just represented, we may observe that the players have only one bowl for each person ; the modern bowlers have usually three or four.

*In 1511, when Henry VIII. confirmed previous laws against illegal games in favour of archery, "bowls" occurs for the first time in the Statute Book. The much severer statute of 1541 forbad every kind of labourer, artisan, apprentice, or servant playing at bowls (among a number of other games) "out of Christmas," and even in Christmas only "in their master's houses or in their master's presence." It was further provided that no manner of persons were to play bowls in open places out of their gardens or orchards, under a penalty of 6s. 8d. Moreover, this curious kind of class legislation enabled any nobleman, or any one possessed of lands worth £100 a year, to obtain a license for bowl playing in his own domain.

*Henry VIII., who was devoted to every form of sport, added bowling-alleys to Whitehall, and his privy purse expenses show that he was in the habit of backing his prowess with bets. On January 29th, 1530, Mr Fitzwilliam, the treasurer, won £4 : 10s. of the king at bowls. On April 19th, 1532, Lord Wiltshire and Lord Rocheford won of the king and Mr Baynton £9 at the same

---

[1] No. 1026, p. 41.

game, and £35 : 5s. a few days later. In the next month Lady Anne lost £12 : 7 : 6 at bowls to the serjeant of the cellar.

BOWLING-GREENS FIRST MADE BY THE ENGLISH.—Bowling-greens are said to have originated in England; and bowling upon them, in my memory (1800), was a very popular amusement. In most country towns of any note they are to be found, and some few are still remaining in the vicinity of the metropolis; but none of them, I believe, are now so generally frequented as they were accustomed to be formerly.[1]

BOWLING-ALLEYS.—The inconveniency to which the open greens for bowling were necessarily obnoxious, suggested, I presume, the idea of making bowling-alleys, which, being covered over, might be used when the weather would not permit the pursuit of the pastime abroad; and therefore they were usually annexed to the residences of the opulent; wherein if the ladies were not themselves performers, they certainly countenanced the pastime by being spectators; hence the king of Hungary, in an old poem entitled "The Squyer of Low Degree" (*circa* 1475), says to his daughter, to amuse you in your garden

> An hundredth knightes, truly tolde,
> Shall play with bowles in alayes colde.

Andrew Borde, in his *Dietarie of Helthe*, describing a nobleman's mansion, supposes it not to be complete without "a bowling-alley."

*Dr John Jones, the physician at Buxton in Elizabethan days, recommended his patients to make use of "bowling in allayes, the weather convenient, and the bowles fitte to such a game, as eyther in playne or longe allayes, or in suche as have crankes with halfe bowles, whiche is the fyner and gentler exercise."[2] The reference to alleys and convenient weather is a reminder that the term "bowling-alley" as then used did not necessarily mean a covered-in place with a boarded floor, and might apply to a hedged-in turfed path or narrow enclosure in a garden. Dr Jones's reference to "crankes" and "halfe bowles" is not quite clear; but probably crank is used in the sense of a twist or bias, and half-bowl to the flattened form of bowl, slightly oblate on one side and prolate on the other. When the bowl ceased to be spherical and assumed this flattened shape, a kind of impetus termed "bias" was given to cause it to run obliquely. The term was used in the sixteenth century; thus Shakespeare in the *Taming of the Shrew* :—

> Well, forward, forward! thus the bowl should run,
> And not unluckily against the bias.

*In the later Elizabethan days bowling-greens were a usual part of the "lay-out" of the larger gardens.

Bowling, according to an author in the seventeenth century, is a pastime

---

[1] *Towards the close of the nineteenth century the revival in bowls was remarkable, and it still continues to grow in favour. There are bowling clubs in most towns, and the old bowling-greens attached to country inns, particularly in Norfolk, are again places of much resort.

[2] *The Benefit of the Auncient Bathes of Buckstones*, 1572.

"in which a man shall find great art in choosing out his ground, and preventing the winding, hanging, and many turning advantages of the same, whether it be in open wilde places, or in close allies; and for his sport, the chusing of the bowle is the greatest cunning; your flat bowles being best for allies, your round byazed bowles for open grounds of advantage, and your round bowles, like a ball, for green swarthes that are plain and level." [1]

*GAMING AT BOWLS.—Charles Cotton's *Compleat Gamester*, first issued in 1674, complains that bowling would be a much more commendable sport than it is, save for "those swarms of Rooks which so pester Bowling-greens, Bares, and Bowling-alleys . . . with cunning, betting, crafty matching, and basely playing booty." He further remarks, with some wit, that "A Bowling-green or Bowling-Ally is a place where three things are thrown away besides the Bowls, viz. Time, Money, and Curses, and the last ten for one. The best sport in it is the Gamesters, and he enjoys it that looks on and betts nothing. It is a School of Wrangling, and worse than the Schools; for here men will wrangle for a hair's breadth, and make a stir where a straw would end the controversie."

*CHARLES I. AND CHARLES II. FOND OF BOWLS.—Charles I. was much attached to the game. He made a bowling-green at Spring Gardens, and during his detention at Holdenby Palace, where the green was in bad order, he was allowed to ride over to Lord Vaux's at Harrowden and Earl Spencer's at Althorp, where there were good bowling-greens.

*Pepys enters in his *Diary*, under date May 1st, 1661—"Up early and baited at Petersfield, in the room which the King lay in lately at his being there. Here very merry, and played with our wives at bowles." Again, on July 26th, 1662, he writes—"This afternoon I went to Westminster . . . and thence to White Hall garden and the Bowling-ally, where lords and ladies are now at bowles, in brave condition."

*The Count de Gramont in his *Memoirs* makes frequent mention of visiting Tunbridge to play bowls, and of the devotion of Charles II. to the game.

SUPPOSED ORIGIN OF BILLIARDS.—On the top of plate thirty-one is the representation of a very curious ancient pastime which seems to bear some analogy to bowling.

Here the bowls, instead of being cast by the hand, are driven with a battoon, or mace, through an arch, towards a mark at a distance from it; and hence, I make no doubt, originated the game of billiards, which formerly was played with a similar kind of arch and a mark called the king, but placed upon the table instead of the ground. The improvement by adding the table answered two good purposes; it precluded the necessity for the player to kneel, or stoop exceedingly, when he struck the bowl and accommodated the game to the limits of a chamber.

KAYLES.—Kayles, written also cayles and keiles, derived from the French word *quilles*, was played with pins, and no doubt gave origin to the modern

[1] *Country Contentments*, 1615.

game of nine-pins; though primitively the kayle-pins do not appear to have been confined to any certain number, as we may observe by referring to plate thirty-one, where the pastime of kayles playing is twice represented. In the one instance there are six pins and in the other eight, and the form of the pins is somewhat different. One of them in both cases is taller than the rest, and this, I presume, was the king-pin; it is placed at the end to the left of the thrower upon the middle of the plate, and between the four upright pins at the bottom.

The arrangement of the kayle-pins differs greatly from that of the nine-pins, the latter being placed upon a square frame in three rows, and the former in one row only. The two delineations here copied, from fourteenth century manuscripts, represent that species of the game called club-kayles, *jeux de quilles à baston*, so denominated from the club or cudgel that was thrown at them.[1]

CLOSH.—The game of cloish, or closh, mentioned frequently in the ancient statutes,[2] seems to have been the same as kayles, or at least exceedingly like it: cloish was played with pins, which were thrown at with a bowl instead of a truncheon, and probably differed only in name from the nine-pins of the present time.

LOGGATS.—Loggats, I make no doubt, was a pastime analogous to kayles and cloish, but played chiefly by boys and rustics, who substituted bones for pins. "Loggats," says Sir Thomas Hanmer, one of the editors of Shakespeare, "is the ancient name of a play or game, which is one of the unlawful games enumerated in the thirty-third statute of Henry VIII.: it is the same which is now called kittle-pins, in which the boys often make use of bones instead of wooden pins, throwing at them with another bone instead of bowling." Hence Shakespeare, in Hamlet, speaks thus: "did these bones cost no more the breeding, but to play at loggats with them?" And this game is evidently referred to in an old play, entitled "The longer thou livest the more Fool thou art," published in the reign of queen Elizabeth,[3] where a dunce boasts of his skill

At skales, and the playing with a sheepes-joynte.

In skales, or kayles, the sheepes-joynte was probably the bone used instead of a bowl.

NINE-PINS—SKITTLES.—The kayle-pins were afterwards called kettle, or kittle-pins; and hence, by an easy corruption, skittle-pins, an appellation well known in the present day. The game of skittles, as it is now played, differs materially from that of nine-pins, though the same number of pins are required in both. In performing the latter, the player stands at a distance settled by mutual consent of the parties concerned, and casts the bowl at the pins: the contest is, to beat them all down in the fewest throws. In playing at skittles, there is a double exertion; one by bowling, and the other by tipping: the first is performed at a given distance, and the second standing close to the frame

---

[1] Roy. Lib. No. 2, B. vii.; Mr Douce's MS.

[2] An. 17 Edw. IV. cap. 3; again 18 and 20 Hen. VIII. etc.; in all which acts this game is prohibited.

[3] Garrick's *Collection*, vol. i. 18.

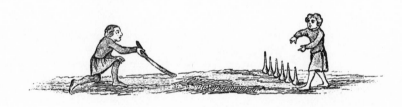

Kayles.

upon which the pins are placed, and throwing the bowl through in the midst of them; in both cases, the number of pins beaten down before the return of the bowl, for it usually passes beyond the frame, are called fair, and reckoned to the account of the player; but those that fall by the coming back of the bowl are said to be foul, and of course not counted. One chalk or score is reckoned for every fair pin; and the game of skittles consists in obtaining thirty-one chalks precisely: less loses, or at least gives the antagonist a chance of winning the game; and more requires the player to go again for nine, which must also be brought exactly, to secure himself.

The preceding quotation from Hanmer intimates that the kittle-pins were sometimes made with bones; and this assertion is strengthened by the language of a dramatic writer, the author of the *Merry Milk-maid of Islington*, in 1680, who makes one of his characters speak thus to another: "I'll cleave you from the skull to the twist, and make nine skittles of thy bones."

DUTCH-PINS.—Dutch-pins is a pastime much resembling skittles; but the pins are taller and slenderer, especially in the middle pin, which is higher than the rest, and called the king-pin. The pins are nine in number, and placed upon a frame in the manner of skittles; and the bowls used by the performers are very large, but made of a light kind of wood. The game consists of thirty-one scores precisely; and every player first stands at a certain distance from the frame, and throws his bowl at the pins, which is improperly enough called bowling; afterwards he approaches the frame and makes his tipp by casting the bowl among the pins, and the score towards the game is determined by the number of them beaten down. If this pin be taken out singly, when the bowl is thrown from a distance, the game is won; this instance excepted, it reckons for no more than the other pins.

FOUR-CORNERS.—Is so called from four large pins which are placed singly at each angle of a square frame. The players stand at a distance, which may be varied by joint consent, and throw at the pins a large heavy bowl, which sometimes weighs six or eight pounds. The excellency of the game consists in beating them down by the fewest casts of the bowl.

HALF-BOWL.—Half-bowl is one of the "new imagined" games prohibited in 1477 in favour of archery,[1] and received its denomination from being played with one half of a sphere of wood. Half-bow is practised to this day (1800) in Hertfordshire, where it is commonly called rolly-polly; and it is best performed upon the floor of a room, especially if it be smooth and level. There are fifteen small pins of a conical form required for this pastime; twelve of which are placed at equal distances upon the circumference of a circle of about two feet and a half diameter; one of the three remaining pins occupies the centre; and the other two are placed without the circle at the back part of it, and parallel with the bowling-place, but so as to be in a line with the middle pin; forming a row of five pins, including two of those upon the circumference. In

---

[1] An. 17 Edw. IV. cap. 3; the prohibition extends also to closh and kayles.

playing this game, the bowl, when delivered, must pass above the pins, and round the end-pin, without the circle, before it beats any of them down; if not, the cast is forfeited: and, owing to the great bias of the bowl, this task is not very readily performed by such as have not made themselves perfect by practice. The middle pin is distinguished by four balls at the top; and, if thrown down, is reckoned for four towards the game; the intermediate pin upon the circle, in the row of five, has three balls, and is reckoned for three; the first pin without the circle has two balls, and is counted for two; and the value of all the others singly is but one. Thirty-one chalks complete the game; which he who first obtains is the conqueror. If this number be exceeded, it is a matter of no consequence: the game is equally won.

NINE-HOLES.—This is mentioned as a boyish game, played at the commencement of the seventeenth century. I have not met with any description of this pastime; but I apprehend it resembled a modern one frequently practised at the outskirts of the metropolis; and said to have been instituted, or more probably revived, about 1780, as a succedaneum for skittles, when the magistrates caused the skittle grounds in and near London to be levelled, and the frames removed. Hence some say the game of nine-holes was called " Bubble the Justice," on the supposition that it could not be set aside by the justices, because no such pastime was named in the prohibitory statutes; others give this denomination to a different game: the name by which it is now most generally known is " Bumble-puppy "; and the vulgarity of the term is well adapted to the company by whom it is usually practised. The game is simply this: nine holes are made in a square board, and disposed in three rows, three holes in each row, all of them at equal distances, about twelve or fourteen inches apart; to every hole is affixed a numeral, from one to nine, so placed as to form fifteen in every row. The board, thus prepared, is fixed horizontally upon the ground, and surrounded on three sides with a gentle acclivity. Every one of the players being furnished with a certain number of small metal balls, stands in his turn, by a mark made upon the ground, about five or six feet from the board; at which he bowls the balls; and according to the value of the figures belonging to the holes into which they roll, his game is reckoned; and he who obtains the highest number is the winner. Doctor Johnson confounds this pastime with that of kayles, and says, " it is a kind of play still retained in Scotland, in which nine holes, ranged in threes, are made in the ground, and an iron bullet rolled in among them." [1]

I have formerly seen a pastime practised by schoolboys, called nine-holes: it was played with marbles, which they bowled at a board, set upright, resembling a bridge, with nine small arches, all of them numbered; if the marble struck against the sides of the arches, it became the property of the boy to whom the board belonged; but, if it went through any one of them, the bowler claimed a number of marbles equal to the number upon the arch it passed through.

[1] Dictionary, word *kayle*.

*TROUL IN MADAME.—A game borrowed from the French, and not unlike our modern bagatelle, only played without a cue or mace, called "Troul in Madame," was popular amongst the well-to-do in Elizabethan times. It was to some extent a precursor of nine-holes. In that curious little work, *The Benefit of the Auncient Bathes of Buckstones*, "by John Jones, Phisition at the King's Mede nigh Darby," published in 1572, occurs the following passage as to the exercise of his patients :—

"The Ladyes, Gentle Women, Wyves, and Maydes maye in one of the Galleries walke : and if the weather bee not aggreeable too theire expectacion, they may have in the ende of a Benche eleven holes made, intoo the which to trowle premmetes, or bowles, of leade, bigge, little, or meane, or also of Copper, Tynne, Woode, eyther vyolent or softe, after their owne discretion, the pastyme *Troule in Madame* is termed.

"Lykewyse, men feeble the same may also practise in another Gallery of the Newe Buyldinges, and this dothe not only strengthen the stomach and upper parts above mydryfe or wast : but also the middle partes beneath the sharp gristle and the extreme partes, as the handes and legges, according to the wayght of the thing trouled, fast, soft, or meane."

JOHN BULL.—This is the name of a modern (1800) pastime, which may be played in the open air, or in a room. A square flat stone, being laid level on the surface of the ground, or let into the floor, is subdivided into sixteen small squares ; in every one of these compartments a number is affixed, beginning from one ; the next in value being five, the next ten ; thence passing on by tens to an hundred, and thence again, by hundreds, to five hundred. These numbers are not placed regularly, but contrasted, so that those of the smallest value are nearest to those of the highest ; and in some instances, as I am informed, the squares for the greater numbers are made much smaller than those for the small ones. On reaching five hundred a mark is made, at an optional distance from the stone, for the players to stand ; who, in succession, throw up one halfpenny or more, and make their score according to the number assigned to the compart-ment in which the halfpenny rests, which must be within the square ; for, if it lies upon one of the lines that divide it from the others, the cast is forfeited, and nothing scored. Two thousand is usually the game ; but this number is extended or diminished at the pleasure of the gamesters.

PITCH AND HUSTLE.—This is a game commonly played in the fields by the lowest classes of the people. It requires two or more antagonists, who pitch or cast an equal number of halfpence at a mark set up at a short distance ; and the owner of the nearest halfpenny claims the privilege to hustle first ; the next nearest halfpenny entitles the owner to a second claim ; and so on to as many as play. When they hustle, all the halfpence pitched at the mark are thrown into a hat held by the player who claims the first chance ; after shaking them together, he turns the hat down upon the ground ; and as many of them as lie with the impression of the head upwards belong to him ; the remainder are then put into the hat a second time, and the second claimant performs the same kind of operation; and so it passes in succession to all the players, or until all the halfpence appear with the heads upwards. Sometimes they are put into the hands of the player, instead of a hat, who shakes them, and casts them up into the air; but in both instances the heads become his property: but if it should so happen, that, after all of them have hustled, there remain some of the half-pence that have not come with the heads uppermost, the first player then hustles again, and the others in succession, until they do come so.

COCK-FIGHTING.—This barbarous pastime, which claims the sanction of high antiquity, was practised at an early period by the Grecians, and probably still more anciently in Asia. It is a very common sport, and of very long standing, in China.[1] It was practised by the Romans:[2] with us, it may be traced back to the twelfth century; at which period we are certain it was in usage, and seems to have been considered as a childish sport. "Every year," says Fitzstephen, "on the morning of Shrove-Tuesday, the school-boys of the city of London[3] bring game cocks to their masters, and in the fore part of the day, till dinner time, they are permitted to amuse themselves with seeing them fight." Probably the same custom prevailed in other cities and great towns. Stow having cited the preceding passage from Fitzstephen, adds, "cocks of the game are yet," that is at the close of the sixteenth century, "cherished by divers men for their pleasures, much money being laid on their heads when they fight in pits, whereof some are costly made for that purpose."[4] The cock-pit was the school, and the master the controller and director of the pastime. This custom, according to Mr. Brand, "was retained in many schools in Scotland within the last century, and perhaps may be still in use there: the schoolmasters claimed the runaway cocks as their perquisites; and these were called fugees, 'corrupt, I suppose,' says he, 'of refugees.'"[5]

In the reign of Edward III. cock-fighting became a fashionable amuse-ment; it was then taken up more seriously than it formerly had been, and the practice extended to grown persons; even at that early period it began to be productive of pernicious consequences, and was therefore prohibited in 1366 by a public proclamation, in which it was ranked with other idle and unlawful pastimes. But notwithstanding it was thus degraded and discountenanced, it still maintained its popularity, and in defiance of all temporary opposition has descended to the modern times. Among the additions made by Henry VIII. to the palace at Whitehall, was a cock-pit;[6] which indicates his relish for the pastime of cock-fighting; and James I. was so partial to this diversion, that he amused himself in seeing it twice a week.[7]

---

[1] *Philos. Transact.* vol. xix. p. 591.

[2] For a full explanation of the manner of cock-fighting among the ancient Greeks and Romans, see a memoir upon that subject by Dr Pegge, *Archæologia*, vol. iii. p. 132.

[3] *Description of London;* temp. Hen. II.

[4] *Survey of London*, p. 76.

[5] Bourne's *Antiq. Vulgares* by Brand, p. 233.

[6] Stow's *Survey of London*, p. 496.

[7] Mons. de la Boderie's *Letters*, vol. i. p. 56.

*Gervaise Martsham issued a tract in 1614, which treats of "The Choice, Ordering, Breeding, and Dyeting of the Fighting Cocke;" he considered that "there is no pleasure more noble, delightsome, or voyd of couzenage and deceipt than this pleasure of cocking."

Exclusive of the royal cock-pit, we are told there was formerly one in Drury Lane, another in Jewin Street, and if the following story be founded on fact, a third in Shoe Lane: "Sir Thomas Jermin, meaning to make himself merry, and gull all the cockers, sent his man to the pit in Shoe Lane, with an hundred pounds and a dunghill cock, neatly cut and trimmed for the battle; the plot being well layd the fellow got another to throw the cock in, and fight him in Sir Thomas Jermin's name, while he betted his hundred pounds against him; the cock was matched, and bearing Sir Thomas's name, had many betts layd upon his head; but after three or four good brushes, he showed a payre of heeles: every one wondered to see a cock belonging to Sir Thomas cry *craven*, and away came the man with his money doubled."[1]

I shall not expatiate upon the nature and extent of this fashionable divertisement; but merely mention a part of it called the Welch main, which seems to be an abuse of the modern times; and as a late judicious author justly says, "a disgrace to us as Englishmen."[2] It consists of a certain or given number of pairs of cocks, suppose sixteen, which fight with each other until one half of them are killed; the sixteen conquerors are pitted a second time in like manner, and half are slain; the eight survivors, a third time; the four, a fourth time; and the remaining two, a fifth time: so that "thirty-one cocks are sure to be inhumanly murdered for the sport and pleasure of the spectators." I am informed that the Welch main usually consists of fourteen pairs of cocks, though sometimes the number might be extended.

In the old illuminated manuscripts we frequently meet with paintings representing cocks fighting; but I do not recollect to have seen in any of them the least indication of artificial spurs; the arming their heels with sharp points of steel is a cruelty, I trust, unknown in former ages to our ancestors. I have been told the artificial spurs are sometimes made with silver.

In addition to what has been said, I shall only observe, that the ancients fought partridges and quails as well as cocks; in like manner as the French do now (1800); how far, if at all, the example has been followed in England, I know not.

*After the fire of 1697, the old cock-pit of Whitehall was turned into the Privy Council room. Treasury Papers of the following century are often, curiously enough, headed "The Cock-pit."

*Pepys has two entries in his *Diary* with reference to cocking; a sport that attracted crowds in the days of "the merry monarch."

"21st December 1663.—To Shoe Lane, to see a cocke-fighting at a new

---

[1] MS. Harl. 6395, written in the reign of James I., and bearing this title: "Merry Passages and Jeasts."
[2] Mr Pegge's "Memoir on Cock-fighting," *Archæol.* vol. iii. p. 132.

P

pit there, a spot I was nere at in my life; but, Lord! to see the strange variety of people, from Parliament man by name Wildes, that was Deputy Governor of the Tower when Robinson was Lord Mayor, to the poorest 'prentices, bakers, brewers, butchers, draymen, and what not; and all these fellows one with another cursing and betting. I soon had enough of it. It is strange to see how people of this poor rank, that look as if they had not bread to put in their mouths, shall bet three or four pounds at a time, and lose it, and yet bet as much the next battle, so that one of them will lose £10 or £20 at a meeting."

*"6th April 1668.—I to the new Cocke-pitt by the king's gate, and there saw the manner of it, and the mixed rabble of people that come thither, and saw two battles of cocks, wherein is no great sport, but only to consider how these creatures, without any provocation, do fight and kill one another, and aim only at one another."

*Although constantly reviled as a singularly cruel and coarse sport by the more refined, cock-fighting or cocking kept a continuous hold on the more sporting natures in England throughout the eighteenth century and in the earlier part of the nineteenth. In 1814, W. Sketchley of Burton-on-Trent published a book called *The Cocker*, which professed to contain every information useful "to the breeders and amateurs of that noble bird the Game Cock," with instruction for those who were attendants on the cock-pit. The names of the leading varieties of cocks then bred in different parts of the kingdom were Piles, Black-reds, Silver black-breasted Ducks, Pirchin Ducks, Dark Greys, Mealy Greys, Blacks, Spangles, Furnaces, Poll Cats, Cuckoos, Gingers, Red Duns, Duns, and Smoky Duns. Sketchley's own favourite breed was the Shropshire Red, a strain that originated in 1785-86 from thirty pairs of cocks that he bought of his "reverend friend," Rev. Mr. Brooks of Shiffnal, Shropshire. One of these cocks fought five mains in one year, twice at Burton-on-Trent, and once at Lichfield, Derby, and Nottingham, "without apparent injury."

*COCK-FIGHTING IN NINETEENTH CENTURY.—Cock-fighting became illegal in 1849. In 1895 *Cocking and its Votaries*, by S. A. T., was issued for private circulation. It is an expensively got-up book, with coloured plates, and its pages make it quite manifest that not a few wealthy men in England still follow up this sport, stealthily but with much zeal—a fact that is as discreditable to the guardians of the law as it is to themselves.

THROWING AT COCKS.—If the opposing of one cock to fight with another may be justly esteemed a national barbarism, what shall be said of a custom more inhuman, which authorised the throwing at them with sticks, and ferociously putting them to a painful and lingering death? I know not at what time this unfortunate animal became the object of such wicked and wanton abuse: the sport, if such a denomination may be given to it, is certainly no recent invention, and perhaps is alluded to by Chaucer, in the Nonnes Priests' Tale, when he says:

> "————There was a cocke,
> For that a priestes' sonne gave hym a knocke,

Upon his legges, when he was yonge and nice,
He made him for to lose his benefice."

The story supposes the cock to have overheard the young man ordering his servant to call him at the cock-crowing; upon which the malicious bird forbore to crow at the usual time, and owing to this artifice the youth was suffered to sleep till the ordination was over.

Throwing at cocks was a very popular diversion, especially among the younger parts of the community. Sir Thomas Moore, who wrote in the sixteenth century, describing the state of childhood, speaks of his skill in casting a cokstele, that is, a stick or cudgel to throw at a cock. It was universally practised upon Shrove-Tuesday. If the poor bird by chance had its legs broken, or was otherwise so lamed as not to be able to stand, the barbarous owners were wont to support it with sticks, in order to prolong the pleasure received from the reiteration of its torment. The magistrates, greatly to their credit, have for some years past put a stop to this wicked custom, and at present (1800) it is nearly, if not entirely, discontinued in every part of the kingdom.

Heath, in his account of the Scilly Islands,[1] speaking of St Mary's, says, "on Shrove-Tuesday each year, after the throwing at cocks is over, the boys of this island have a custom of throwing stones in the evening against the doors of the dwellers' houses; a privilege they claim from time immemorial, and put in practice without control, for finishing the day's sport; the terms demanded by the boys are pancakes or money, to capitulate. Some of the older sort, exceeding the bounds of this whimsical toleration, break the doors and window-shutters, etc. sometimes making a job for the surgeon as well as for the smith, glazier, and carpenter."

In some places it was a common practice to put the cock into an earthen vessel made for the purpose, and to place him in such a position that his head and tail might be exposed to view; the vessel, with the bird in it, was then suspended across the street, about twelve or fourteen feet from the ground, to be thrown at by such as chose to make trial of their skill; twopence was paid for four throws, and he who broke the pot, and delivered the cock from his confinement, had him for a reward. At North Walsham, in Norfolk, about 1760, some wags put an owl into one of these vessels; and having procured the head and tail of a dead cock, they placed them in the same position as if they had appertained to a living one: the deception was successful, and at last, a labouring man belonging to the town, after several fruitless attempts, broke the pot, but missed his prize; for the owl being set at liberty, instantly flew away, to his great astonishment, and left him nothing more than the head and tail of the dead bird, with the potsherds, for his money and his trouble; this ridiculous adventure exposed him to the continual laughter of the town's people, and obliged him to quit the place, to which, I am told, he returned no more.

Duck-Hunting.—This is another barbarous pastime, and for the per-

---

[1] Published in London, 1750.

formance it is necessary to have recourse to a pond of water sufficiently extensive to give the duck plenty of room for making her escape from the dogs when she is closely pursued; which she does by diving as often as any of them come near to her. Duck-hunting was much practised in the neighbourhood of London about thirty or forty years ago; but of late it is gone out of fashion; yet I cannot help thinking, that the deficiency, at present, of places proper for the purpose, has done more towards the abolishment of this sport than any amendment in the nature and inclinations of the populace.

Sometimes the duck is tormented in a different manner, without the assistance of the dogs, by having an owl tied upon her back, and so put into the water, where she frequently dives in order to escape from the burden, and on her return for air, the miserable owl, half drowned, shakes itself, and hooting, frightens the duck; she of course dives again, and replunges the owl into the water; the frequent repetition of this action soon deprives the poor bird of its sensation, and generally ends in its death, if not in that of the duck also.

SQUIRREL-HUNTING.—This is a rustic pastime, and commonly practised at Christmas time and at Midsummer; those who pursue it find plenty of exercise; but nothing can excuse the wantonly tormenting so harmless an animal.

*"At Duffield wakes," says Glover in his history of Derbyshire (1831), "an ancient custom or right is kept up of hunting wild animals in the forest there. This is called the squirrel hunt. The young men of the village assemble in troops on the wakes Monday, some with horns, some with pans, and others with various articles calculated to make a great noise. They then proceed in a body to Kedleston Park, and with shouting and the noise of instruments, frighten the poor little animals until they drop from the trees and are taken by the hunters. After taking several in this manner, the hunters go back to Duffield, release the squirrels, and recommence hunting them again in a similar manner."

*This Derbyshire custom died out in the early fifties, but it survives as a Christmas custom in parts of the New Forest, particularly at Brockenhurst. The hunted squirrels are made into pies, which are said to be more delicate in flavour than rabbits.[1]

---

[1] I talked to various New Forest squirrel hunters in 1900. They are most indignant at the charge of wanton cruelty made against them, saying that, at all events, fox hunters do not eat the foxes they kill.   J. C. C.

BOOK IV

DOMESTIC AMUSEMENTS OF VARIOUS KINDS; AND PASTIMES APPROPRIATED TO PARTICULAR SEASONS

CHAPTER I

Secular Music fashionable—Ballad-singers encouraged by the Populace—Music Houses—Introduction of the Harpsichord—Origin of Vauxhall—Ranelagh—Sadler's Wells—Marybone Gardens—Operas—Oratorios—Bell-ringing—Its Antiquity—Hand-bells—Burlesque Music—Shovel-board—Billiards—French Billiards—Trucks—Mississipi—The Rocks of Scilly—Shove-groat—Swinging—Tetter-totter—Shuttle-cock.

SECULAR MUSIC FASHIONABLE.—The national passion for secular music admitted of little or no abatement by the disgrace and dispersion of the minstrels. Professional musicians, both vocal and instrumental, were afterwards retained at the court, and also in the mansions of the nobility. In the sixteenth century, a knowledge of music was considered as a genteel accomplishment for persons of high rank. Henry VIII. not only sang well, but played upon several sorts of instruments; he also wrote songs, and composed the tunes [1] for them; and his example was followed by several of the nobility, his favourites.

*During Elizabeth's long reign, music was not only fashionable, but held in almost universal esteem. "Tinkers sang catches; milkmaids sang ballads; carters whistled; each trade, and even the beggars, had their special songs; the base-viol hung in the drawing-room for the amusement of waiting visitors; and the lute, cittern, and virginals, for the amusement of waiting customers, were the necessary furniture of the barber's shop. They had music at dinner; music at supper; music at weddings; music at funerals; music at night; music at dawn; music at work; and music at play." [2] Dekker, in the *Gull's Horn Book* of this reign, tells us that it was the customary part of the education of a young gentlewoman "to read and write; to play upon the virginals, lute, and cittern; and to read prick-song at first sight."

An author, who lived in the reign of James I., says, "We have here," that is, in London, "the best musicians in the kingdom, and equal to any in Europe for their skill, either in composing and setting of tunes, or singing, and playing upon any kind of instruments. The musicians have obtained of our sovereign lord the king, his letters patent to become a society and corporation." [3] To which we may add, that the metropolis never abounded more, if so much as at

---

[1] Hall, in the life of that monarch.

[2] *Chappell's *Popular Music of the Olden Time*, i. 98.

[3] A.D. 1604, in the second year of the reign of James I. Treatise on College and Schools in and about London, printed 1615.

present, with excellent musicians, not such only as make a profession of music, but with others who pursue it merely for their amusement; nor must we omit the fair sex; with them the study of music is exceedingly fashionable; and indeed there are few young ladies of family who are not in some degree made acquainted with its rudiments.[1]

PUBLIC BALLAD-SINGERS.—The minstrel being deprived of all his honours, and having lost the protection of the opulent, dwindled into a mere singer of ballads, which sometimes he composed himself, and usually accompanied his voice with the notes of a violin. The subjects of these songs were chiefly taken from popular stories, calculated to attract the notice of the vulgar, and among them the musical poets figured away at wakes, fairs, and church-ales. The ballads multiplied with extraordinary rapidity in the reigns of Elizabeth, James I., and Charles I. Warton speaks of two celebrated trebles; the one called Outroaringe Dick; and the other Wat Wimbas, who occasionally made twenty shillings a day by ballad-singing;[2] which is a strong proof that these itinerants were highly esteemed by the common people.

MUSIC HOUSES.—Towards the close of the seventeenth century, the professed musicians assembled at certain houses in the metropolis, called music houses, where they performed concerts, consisting of vocal and instrumental music, for the entertainment of the public, at the same period there were music booths at Smithfield during the continuance of Bartholomew fair. An author of the time,[3] however, speaks very contemptibly of these music meetings, professing that he "had rather have heard an old barber ring Whittington's bells upon a cittern than all the music the houses afforded."

*INTRODUCTION OF THE HARPSICHORD.—An important event occurred in the musical world of London on October 5th, 1664, namely, the introduction of the harpsichord; it is recorded under that date by both Evelyn and Pepys in their diaries. The graver Evelyn enters:—"To our Society. There was brought a new-invented instrument of music, being a harpsichord with gut-strings, sounding like a concert of viols with an organ, made vocal by a wheel, and a zone of parchment that rubbed horizontally against the strings." The more garrulous Pepys enters, on the same evening:—"To the musique-meeting at the Post-Office, where I was once before. And thither anon came all the Gresham College, and a great deal of noble company; and the new instrument was brought called the Arched Viall, where, being tuned with lute strings, and played on with keys like an organ, a piece of parchment is always kept moving; and the strings, which by the keys are pressed down upon it, are grated in imitation of a bow, by the parchment; and so it is intended to resemble several vialls

---

[1] Some time ago the spinnet was a favourite instrument among the ladies; afterwards the guitar; and now (1800) the harpsichord, or forte-piano.

[2] At Braintree fair in Essex. *Hist. Eng. Poet.* vol. iii. p. 292. *This was a century and a half back, when twenty shillings was a considerable sum. The ancient ballads have frequently this colophon: "Printed by A.B. and are to be sold at the stalls of the ballad-singers." But an ordinance published by Oliver Cromwell against the strolling fiddlers, silenced the ballad-singers, and obliged the sellers to shut up shop. Hawkins, *Hist. Music*, vol. iv. p. 113.

[3] Edward Ward, author of the *London Spy*, part xi. p. 255.

played on with one bow, but so harshly and so basely, that it will never do. But, after three hours' stay, it could not be fixed in tune; and so they were fain to go to some other musique of instrument."

*Nor was Pepys any better pleased with the music he heard three years later, on October 1st, 1667, at Whitehall. "To White Hall; and there in the Boarded Gallery did hear the musick with which the King is presented this night by Monsieur Grebus, the Master of his Musicke; both instrumental—I think twenty-four violins—and vocall, an English song upon Peace. But, God forgive me! I never was so little pleased with a concert of music in my life. The manner of setting of words and repeating them out of order, and that with a number of voices, makes me sick, the whole design of vocall musick being lost by it. Here was great press of people; but I did not see many pleased with it; only the instrumental musick he had brought by practice to play very just."

The music clubs or private meetings for the practice of music, became exceedingly fashionable with people of opulence. Hence, in *The Citizen turned Gentleman*, a comedy by Edw. Ravenscroft, published in 1675, the citizen is told that, in order to appear like a person of consequence, it was necessary for him "to have a music club once a week at his house." The music houses first mentioned were sometimes supported by subscription; and from them originated three places of public entertainment well known in the present day; namely, Vauxhall, Ranelagh, and Sadler's Wells.

ORIGIN OF VAUXHALL.—Spring Gardens, now better known by the name of Vauxhall Gardens, is mentioned in the *Antiquities of Surrey*, by Aubrey, who informs us that Sir Samuel Moreland "built a fine room at Vauxhall (in 1667), the inside all of looking-glass, and fountains very pleasant to behold; which," adds he, "is much visited by strangers. It stands in the middle of the garden, covered with Cornish slate, on the point whereof he placed a punchinello, very well carved, which held a dial; but the winds have demolished it."[1]

*The exact date at which the grounds were first opened to the public is not known; but it is evident that the gardens were public before ever Sir Samuel built his house there. Evelyn names the "New Spring Garden" in 1661, as "a pretty contrived plantation"; whilst Pepys, under date May 27th, 1667, enters:—"Went by water to Fox (*sic*) Hall, and there walked in Spring Gardens; a great deal of company; the weather and gardens pleasant, and cheap going thither; for a man may go to spend what he will or nothing at all; all is one. But to hear the nightingale and other birds, and here fiddles and there a harp, and here a Jew's harp, and there laughing, and there fine people walking is very diverting."

* "The house," says a more modern author, Sir John Hawkins,[2] "seems to have been rebuilt since the time that Sir Samuel Moreland dwelt in it; and, there being a large garden belonging to it, planted with a

---

[1] Vol. i. p. 12.   [2] *Hist. Music*, vol. v. p. 352 (1776).

great number of stately trees, and laid out in shady walks, it obtained the name of Spring Gardens; and, the house being converted into a tavern, or place of entertainment, it was frequented by the votaries of pleasure." This account is perfectly consonant with the following passage in a paper of the *Spectator*,[1] dated May 20, 1712:—"We now arrived at Spring Gardens, which is exquisitely pleasant at this time of the year. When I considered the fragrancy of the walks and bowers, with the choirs of birds that sung upon the trees, and the loose tribe of people that walked underneath their shades, I could not but look upon the place as a kind of Mahometan paradise." In 1730 the house and gardens came into the hands of a gentleman whose name was Jonathan Tyers, who opened it with an advertisement of a *ridotto al fresco*;[2] a term which the people of this country had till then been strangers to. These entertainments were several times repeated in the course of the summer, and numbers resorted to partake of them; which encouraged the proprietor to make his garden a place of musical entertainment for every evening during the summer season: to this end he was at great expense in decorating the gardens with paintings; he engaged an excellent band of musicians, and issued season silver tickets for admission at a guinea each; and receiving great encouragement, he set up an organ in the orchestra; and in a conspicuous part of the gardens erected a fine statue of Handel, the work of Roubiliac, a very famous statuary, to whom we owe several of the best monuments in Westminster Abbey.

*In 1760 a guide to Vauxhall Gardens was issued,[3] dedicated to the Princess Augusta. They are said to be "the first gardens of the kind in England." The season was from the beginning of May till the end of August; they were opened at five o'clock every evening, Sundays excepted. "In that part of the grove which fronts the orchestra a considerable number of tables and benches are placed for the company; and at a small distance from them, fronting the orchestra, is a large pavilion, of the composite order, which particularly attracts the eye by its size, beauty, and ornaments; it was built for his late royal highness, Frederic Prince of Wales, who frequently visited these gardens, and was peculiarly fond of them." The grove is described "as illuminated with about fifteen hundred glass lamps." The fifty pages of the booklet were chiefly taken up with descriptions of Mr Hayman's paintings; but a price list of provisions is appended. Burgundy and Fontiniac was 6s. a bottle; claret, 5s.; champagne, or a quart of arrack, 8s.; old hock, with or without sugar, 5s.; "Rhenish and sugar," or mountain, 7s. 6d.; red port and sherry, 2s.; table beer, a quart mug, 4d.; two pound of ice, 6d.; a dish of ham or beef, 1s.; and an orange or a lemon, 3d.

*Mr Tyers, the proprietor, who had a beautiful house and grounds at Dorking, died in 1767, and so great was the delight he took in this place, that,

---

[1] Vol. v. No. 383.   [2] Or entertainment of music in the open air.
[3] *A Description of Vauxhall Gardens, being a proper companion and guide for all who visit that place. Illustrated with copper plates.* G. Hooper, 1762.

possessing his faculties to the last, he caused himself to be carried into Vauxhall Gardens a few hours before his death to take a last look at them. The gardens were left equally between his four children. The average number of the company used to be about one thousand; but on June 25th, 1781, when the Duke and Duchess of Cumberland supped there, after an annual sailing match for a cup, eleven thousand were present. On July 20th, 1813, a great dinner was held here, in honour of the battle of Vittoria, when the six royal dukes were present; ten, and even fifteen, guineas were given for a dinner ticket.[1] In 1822 they were sold by the Tyers' family to Messrs Bish, Gye, & Hughes for £28,000.

*Fireworks were exhibited here as early as 1780. In 1802 the first balloon ascent was made from the Gardens by Garnerin and two companions. The fashion of the place began to decline in the reign of William IV., but the end did not come until 1855.[2]

RANELAGH.—The success of the Vauxhall Gardens was an encouragement to another of a similar kind. A number of persons purchased the house and gardens of the late Earl of Ranelagh; in 1740 they erected a spacious building of timber, of a circular form, and within it an organ, and an orchestra capable of holding a numerous band of performers. It was opened by a public breakfast in 1742, and for a short time there were morning concerts, but they were soon abandoned for those held in the evening. The entertainment of the auditors during the performance is, either walking round the room, or refreshing themselves with tea and coffee in the recesses thereof, which are conveniently adapted for that purpose. Sir John Hawkins[3] says, "The performance here, as at Vauxhall, is instrumental, intermixed with songs and ballad airs, calculated rather to please the vulgar than gratify those of a better taste."

*Besides the great Rotunda, which had a diameter of 185 feet, there was a lake with a small Venetian pavilion on an island in the centre. An advertisement of August 23d, 1749, states that the admission was one shilling and that the music began at six o'clock; a postscript states that "The Fire-Trees will be Lighted this Evening." The charge for admission was raised on special occasions. On a firework night in 1764, each person paid 2s. 6d., but coffee and tea were included. On June 18th, 1764, a charge was made of 5s.; this payment, however, included not only coffee and tea, but choruses from Handel's "Acis and Galatea" and "The Messiah," together with "a ball with which the whole concludes." The place became specially celebrated for its masquerade balls, the first of which was given on May 24th, 1759, "being the Birth Day of his Royal Highness, George Prince of Wales."[4]

[1] *A Brief Account of the Royal Gardens, Vauxhall.* Published by the Proprietors, 1822.

[2] The best account of Vauxhall and its array of distinguished visitors is in Walford's edition of Thornbury's *Old and New London*, vol. vi. pp. 447-467.

[3] *Hist. of Music*, vol. v. pp. 352-3.

[4] A large coloured print of this ball was issued by Robert Sayn, Fleet Street. There is a copy of it in a collection of Ranelagh views, advertisements, etc., in the British Museum, 840, m., 28.

*Various curious particulars as to social England of the latter half of the eighteenth century can be gleaned from the Ranelagh advertisements at the time when it was the height of fashion to be present. "There will be an armed Guard on Horseback to patrol the roads till all the Company is gone" is a frequent feature of the advertisements from 1760 to 1780. In the colder season "The Amphitheatre and other Rooms are well aired, and particular Care will be taken to have good Fires." "The Company that come by Hyde Park Corner are requested to order their Carriages to keep the Turnpike Road by Pimlico, to prevent the Accidents that must unavoidably happen by going down the Descent of the new Road by the Fire Engine." "The Footway from Buckingham Gate is lately mended and enlarged, so as to make it very safe and easy for chairs." During these years the usual evening admission to the music and fireworks, etc., was 2s. 6d., whilst 1s. was charged to walk in the gardens during the daytime. By the year 1788 a reaction set in, the attendance dropped from thousands to hundreds. A daily paper of April 22nd of that year, stated that—"Ranelagh has been voted a bore with the fashionable circles. The distance from town, the total want of attendance and accommodation, the want of a respectable band of vocal and instrumental music—with a variety of other wants too numerous for description—render this once gay circle the dullest of all dull public amusements." Grand firework nights, with 5s. tickets, and masquerades with guinea tickets did something to restore its fading fortunes as a fashionable resort. The guinea tickets included "an elegant supper served at one o'clock, with champagne, burgundy, claret, etc." The masquerade on April 30th, 1794, was under the patronage of the Prince of Wales; from that date to the end of the century, special nights were frequently under royal patronage. Shortly after the dawn of the nineteenth century Ranelagh Gardens ceased to attract, and the Rotunda and the whole of the premises were taken down in 1805.

SADLER'S WELLS.—We meet with what is said to be "a true account of Sadler's Well," in a pamphlet published by a physician at the close of the seventeenth century. "The water," says he, "of this well, before the Reformation, was very much famed for several extraordinary cures performed thereby, and was thereupon accounted sacred, and called Holy-well. The priests, belonging to the priory of Clerkenwell using to attend there, made the people believe that the virtues of the water proceeded from the efficacy of their prayers; but at the Reformation the well was stopped, upon the supposition that the frequenting of it was altogether superstitious: and so by degrees it grew out of remembrance, and was wholly lost until then found out; when a gentleman named Sadler, who had lately built a new music-house there, and being surveyor of the highways, had employed men to dig gravel in his garden, in the midst whereof they found it stopped up and covered with an arch of stone."[1]

*In the summer of 1700 Sadler's Wells came into high repute. In 1733

[1] A.D. 1683.

the Wells were so fashionable that the Princesses Amelia and Caroline frequented the gardens almost daily during June.

After the decease of Sadler, one Francis Forcer, a musician and composer of songs, became occupier of the wells and music-room ; he was succeeded by his son, who first exhibited there the diversion of rope-dancing and tumbling, which were then performed abroad in the garden.[1] The place was taken afterwards by Mr Rosoman, and the wooden house was replaced in 1765 by a brick building. There is now (1800) a small theatre appropriated to feats of activity, but also furnished with a stage, scenes, and other decorations proper for the representation of dramatic pieces and pantomimes. The diversions of this place are of various kinds, and form upon the whole a succession of performances very similar to those displayed in former ages by the gleemen, the minstrels, and the jugglers.

MARY-BONE GARDENS—ORATORIOS.—To the three preceding places of public entertainment, we may add a fourth, not now indeed in existence, but which about 1770 was held in some degree of estimation, and much frequented ; I mean Mary-bone Gardens ; where, in addition to the music and singing, there were burlettas and fire-works exhibited. The site of these gardens is now covered with buildings.

*This place of resort is named by the gay-hearted Pepys. He records that the Lord Mayor and Aldermen dined there on July 31st, 1667. On May 7th, 1668, he enters in his diary :—"Then we abroad to Marrowbone, and there walked in the garden ; the first time I ever was there, and a pretty place it is." These gardens were formed almost immediately after the Restoration by throwing together a place of public resort called 'The Rose,' and an adjoining bowling-green ; they were on the east side of Marylebone Lane, and the site is partly covered by Manchester Square. In the days of Pope this bowling-green was a place of most fashionable resort. During the last phase of their existence, the Mary-bone Gardens were turned into a regular place of musical and scenic entertainment.

There were also other places of smaller note where singing and music were introduced, but none of them of any long continuance ; for being much frequented by idle and dissolute persons, they were put down by the magistrates.

The success of these musical assemblies, I presume, first suggested the idea of introducing operas upon the stage, which were contrived at once to please the eye and delight the ear ; and this double gratification, generally speaking, was procured at the expense of reason and propriety. Hence, also, we may trace the establishment of oratorios in England. I need not say that this noble species of dramatic music was brought to great perfection by Handel : the oratorios produced by him display in a wonderful manner his powers as a composer of music ; and they continue to be received with that enthusiasm of applause which they most justly deserve. Under this title, oratorios, are included several of his seranatas, as "Acis and Galatea," "Alexander's Feast,"etc.; but generally speaking, the subjects of the oratorios are taken from the Scriptures, and therefore they are permitted to be performed on the Wednesdays and Fridays in Lent when plays are prohibited.

BELL-RINGING.—It has been remarked by foreigners that the English are particularly fond of bell-ringing;[1] and indeed most of our churches have a ring of bells in the steeple, partly appropriated to that purpose. These bells are rung upon most occasions of joy and festivity, and sometimes at funerals, when they are muffled, and especially at the funerals of ringers, with a piece of woollen cloth bound about the clapper, and the sounds then emitted by them are exceedingly unmelodious, and well fitted to inspire the mind with melancholy. Ringing of rounds; that is, sounding every bell in succession, from the least to the greatest, and repeating the operation, produces no variety; on the contrary, the reiteration of the same cadences in a short time becomes tiresome: for which reason the ringing of changes has been introduced, wherein the succession of the bells is shifted continually, and by this means a varied combination of different sounds, exceedingly pleasant to the ear, is readily produced. This improvement in the art of ringing is thought to be peculiar to the people of this country.[2]

*Archbishop Egbert, in 750, ordered that "all priests, at the appointed hours of day and night, do sound the bells of their churches, and then celebrate the sacred offices to God, and instruct the people. These bells (*signa*) were probably hand-bells formed of rivetted sheets of metal, of which various early examples survive. But ere long bells were swinging in church towers in this country. In the beautifully-illuminated Benedictional of St Æthelwold, executed in the tenth century, four bells are represented hung in a lofty open campanile.

*Bells were cast for Abingdon and Canterbury in the tenth century; and we also know there were bells in the towers of the cathedral churches of Exeter and Winchester, and of the minsters of Beverley and Southwell, and doubtless in many other churches prior to the Norman conquest.

*It is supposed that change ringing originated in England and was not practised after any regular fashion until the sixteenth century. The earliest definite promoter of change ringing is said to have been one Fabian Steadman, who was born at Cambridge in 1631. He was a printer by trade, and introduced various peals of five and six bells, printing the numbers on slips of paper. The Society of College Youths, the oldest association of ringers, founded in the sixteenth century, visited Cambridge in 1657, when he presented them with his new and elaborate principle that has ever since been known by his name.[3]

*"The School of Recreation, or the Gentleman's Tutor," first issued in 1684, gives instructions in twelve "most ingenious exercises." One of these is Ringing. The following is the opening paragraph of the forty-five pages that he (the author) devotes to this subject:—"Since the Recreation of Ringing is become so highly esteemed, for its excellent Harmony of Musick it affords the ear, for its Mathematical Invention delighting the Mind, and for the Violence of its

---

[1] See the Introduction. [2] Hawkins' *Hist. of Music*, vol. iv. p. 211. [3] Gatty's *The Bell* (1848) 58-9.

Music

Exercise bringing Health to the Body, causing it to transpire plentifully, and by Sweats dissipate and expel those Fuliginous thick Vapours, which Idleness, Effeminacy, and Delicacy subject men to; I say for these and sundry other Reasons, I was induced to bring this of Ringing into the Company of Exercises in this Treatise, that I might as well recreate you with some health-conducing Pleasure at home, as I have carried you abroad, and there endeavoured to please you in what Pastime your Inclinations may most peculiarly select."

*The author (R. D.) urges his reader to become "enrolled amongst that Honoured Society of Colledge Youths," and "not to let thy frequent coming to the Bell-fire on Week-days for thy Diversion, make thee absent thyself on Sundays from thy Devotion."

HAND-BELLS.—These, which probably first appeared in the religious processions, were afterwards used by the secular musicians, and practised for the sake of pastime. The joculator dancing before the fictitious goat, depicted by the engraving No. 85, has two large hand-bells, and nearly of a size; but in general, they are regularly diminished, from the largest to the least; and ten or twelve of them, rung in rounds or changes by a company of ringers, sometimes one to each bell, but more usually every ringer has two. I have seen a man in London, who I believe is now (1800) living, ring twelve bells at one time; two of them were placed upon his head, he held two in each hand, one was affixed to each of his knees, and two upon each foot; all of which he managed with great adroitness, and performed a vast variety of tunes.

The small bells were not always held in the hand; they were sometimes suspended upon a stand, and struck with hammers, by which means one person could more readily play upon them. An example of this kind, of the fourteenth century, is given on plate thirty-two.[1]

The figure in the original is designed as a representation of King David, and affixed to one of his psalms.

*An earlier instance of five small bells as thus suspended in frame and struck by a single hammer held in one hand occurs in a MS. of the ninth century.[2]

BURLESQUE MUSIC.—The minstrels and joculators seem to have had the knack of converting every kind of amusement into a vehicle for merriment, and among others, that of music has not escaped them. At the bottom of plate thirty-two we see one of these drolls holding a pair of bellows by way of a fiddle, and using the tongs as a substitute for the bow.

This, and such like vagaries, were frequently practised in the succeeding times; and they are neatly ridiculed in one of the papers belonging to the *Spectator*,[3] where the author mentions "a tavern keeper who amused his company with whistling of different tunes, which he performed by applying the edge of a case knife to his lips. Upon laying down the knife he took up a pair of

---

[1] Roy. Lib. 20. B. xi.   [2] Figured on p. 4 of North's *English Bells and Bell Lore* (1888).
[3] Vol. v. No. 570.

clean tobacco pipes, and after having slid the small ends of them over a table in a most melodious trill, he fetched a tune out of them, whistling to them at the same time in concert. In short the tobacco pipes became musical pipes in the hands of our virtuoso, who," says the writer, "confessed ingenuously that he broke such quantities of pipes that he almost broke himself, before he brought this piece of music to any tolerable perfection."[1] This man also "played upon the frying-pan and gridiron, and declared he had layed down the tongs and key because it was unfashionable." I have heard an accompaniment to the violin exceedingly well performed with a rolling-pin and a salt-box, by a celebrated publican named Price, who kept the Green Man, formerly well known by the appellation of the Farthing Pye House, at the top of Portland Row, St. Mary-le-bone. I have also seen a fellow who used to frequent most of the public houses in and about the town, blow up his cheeks with his breath, and beat a tune upon them with his fists, which feat he seemed to perform with great facility. The butchers have a sort of rough music, made with marrow-bones and cleavers, which they usually bring forward at weddings; and in the *Knave in Grain*, a play first acted in 1640,[2] ringing of basons is mentioned. This music, or something like it, I believe, is represented at the bottom of the twenty-third plate.

SHOVEL-BOARD.—Among the domestic pastimes, playing at shovel-board claims a principal place. In former times the residences of the nobility, or the mansions of the opulent, were not thought to be complete without a shovel-board table; and this fashionable piece of furniture was usually stationed in the great hall.[3] The tables for this diversion were sometimes very expensive, owing to the great pains and labour bestowed upon their construction. "It is remarkable," says Dr Plott, in his History of Staffordshire, "that in the hall at Chartley the shuffle-board table, though ten yards one foot and an inch long, is made up of about two hundred and sixty pieces, which are generally about eighteen inches long, some few only excepted, that are scarce a foot, which, being laid on longer boards for support underneath, are so accurately joined and glewed together, that no shuffle-board whatever is freer from rubbs or casting.—There is a joynt also in the shuffle-board at Madeley Manor exquisitely well done."

The length of these tables, if they be perfectly smooth and level, adds to their value in proportion to its increase; but they rarely exceed three feet or three feet and a half in width. At one end of the shovel-board there is a line drawn across parallel with the edge, and about three or four inches from it; at four feet distance from this line another is made, over which it is necessary for the weight to pass when it is thrown by the player, otherwise the go is not reckoned. The players stand at the end of the table, opposite to the two marks above mentioned, each of them having four flat weights of metal, which they shove from them one at a time alternately: and the judgment of the play is, to

---

[1] Vol. v. No. 570. [2] Garrick's Col. Old Plays, G. vol. ii. [3] See the Introduction.

give sufficient impetus to the weight to carry it beyond the mark nearest to the edge of the board, which requires great nicety, for if it be too strongly impelled, so as to fall from the table, and there is nothing to prevent it, into a trough placed underneath for its reception, the throw is not counted; if it hangs over the edge, without falling, three are reckoned towards the player's game; if it lie between the line and the edge without hanging over, it tells for two; if on the line, and not up to it, but over the first line, it counts for one. The game, when two play, is generally eleven; but the number is extended when four or more are jointly concerned. I have seen a shovel-board-table at a low public-house in Benjamin Street, near Clerkenwell Green, which is about three feet in breadth and thirty-nine feet two inches in length, and said to be the longest at this time in London.

*There was no known pastime in which Henry VIII. did not indulge. The privy purse expenses of 1532 show that in January Lord William won £9 of the King at "shovilla bourde," and "My lord of Rocheforde won of the King at shovilla bourde and betting at the game £45." In the following month Lord Rocheford won £41, 12s. 6d. of the King at the same pastime.[1] It must be remembered that these accounts take no notice of the royal wins, only of the losses.

*Shovel-board is now chiefly confined to the decks of passenger vessels, where it is often much used to relieve the tedium of long voyages.

BILLIARDS.—This pastime, which in the present day has superseded the game of shovel-board, and is certainly a more elegant species of amusement, admits of more variety, and requires at least an equal degree of skill in the execution. The modern manner of playing at billiards, and the rules by which the pastime is regulated, are so generally known, that no enlargement upon the subject is necessary. I cannot help thinking it originated from an ancient game played with small bowls upon the ground; or indeed that it was, when first instituted, the same game transferred from the ground to the table.[2]

*The word Billiards is derived from the old French word *billard*, a stick with a curved end, hence a billiard mace or cue. The earliest references given in the Oxford Dictionary are from Spenser's *Mother Hubbard*, 1591, "With all the thriftless games that may be found . . . with dice, with cards, with balliards"; and from Florio's *Trucco*, "a kinde of play with balles upon a table called billiards." Shakespeare, in *Anthony and Cleopatra*, has, "Let it alone, let's to billiards." Cotsgrave, in 1611, defines Billiard, as "a short and thicke trunchion or cudgell : hence the sticke wherewith we touch the ball at billyards."

*It is probably a game of English and not French origin as was at one time maintained; but nothing is really known of it in this country until the end of the sixteenth century. The first printed account of the game in English hitherto noted is that given by Charles Cotton in *The Compleat Gamester*, first published in 1674, where it is said that, "The gentile, cleanly, and most

---

[1] Add MSS. 20,030. [2] See the representation of ground billiards on the thirty-second plate.

ingenious game at Billiards had its first original from Italy, and for the excellency of the recreation is much approved of and plaid by most nations in Europe, especially in England, there being few towns of note therein which hath not a publick billiard table, neither are they wanting in many noble and private families in the country for the recreation of the mind and exercise of the body." Cotton describes the form of the billiard table as oblong, and it had six pockets after the fashion of the present table.[1] The bed of the table was made of oak, covered with fine green cloth, and the cushions were stuffed with "fine flox or cotton." Maces, then called masts, were used, made of lignum vitæ or some other heavy wood and tipped with ivory. The balls were usually ivory, but occasionally wood. The peculiarity of the game of those days, as shown in Cotton's cut, consisted in the use of a small arch of ivory called the *port*, which was placed where the pyramid spot now stands, and of an ivory tapering peg or king placed on a corresponding spot at the other end of the table. There were only two balls used, and the game is five by daylight or seven if odds be given, and three by candle-light or more, according to odds in houses that make a livelihood thereof." The first contest was who should first pass the port, "and herein much pains is taken, and all the art and cunning possible used to do it." The king had to be "touched finely and gently without throwing it down. Breaking the king was subject to a fine of 1s., for the stick 5s., and for the port 10s. Some of the instructions to players given in *The School of Recreation*, 1684, are sufficiently quaint, as may be instanced by citing number five :—

" Be careful that you lay not your hand on the Table when you strike nor let your sleeve drag upon it, if you do it is a loss ; or if you smoke a pipe of Spanish or Virginia, being so wedded to that Fume, that were you sure to smother all the rest of the Company you are insensible of the Indecency, be careful that the ashes fall not on the Table, lest the cloth be burnt which many times falls out : In these two cases, let the mulcts and forfeitures of both, but especially the hinderance the last gives a man in the skilfull managing his game, deter you from the lolling slovenly posture of the first, and the stinking indecency of the latter ; because this Pastime being of a neat and cleanly composition, will not admit any such Irregularities and Indecorums, without an absolute Violation of its Laws and a Punishment attending such unhandsome offences."

*Cotton's *Compleat Gamester* was reprinted in 1676, 1680, 1709, 1721, and 1725. In all these editions, the original account of billiards was simply reproduced *verbatim*.

*FRENCH BILLIARDS.—In the seventh edition of this work, which was issued in 1734, " French Billiards " is described, " so called from their manner of

---

[1] *In Strutt's short account of this game, which we have omitted, the strange mistake is made of saying that, at the beginning of the eighteenth century, the table was square with only three pockets all on one side. This blunder arose from misunderstanding a small illustration on the frontispiece of *The School of Recreation*, first published in 1684, and which is a poor reduced copy of the wood-cut in Cotton's book.

playing the game, which is now only with masts and balls, port and king being now wholly laid aside." The rules show that cues were then permitted; but for many years after this date, only known good players were allowed to use the cue on public tables, the proprietors being alarmed at the risk of damage to the cloth. By the beginning of the nineteenth century cues had come into general use by all good players. The leather tip to the cue, which worked a revolution in play, was invented in 1807, by a French professional player named Mingaud.[1]

*TRUCKS.—*The Compleat Gamester*, of 1674, gives several pages to an account of a game called Trucks. It is described as an Italian game, much used in Spain and Ireland, and not very unlike billiards, "but more boisterous and less gentill." Tables were rarely met with in England, but one was at Tower Hill, though bunglingly composed and irregularly formed. A truck table was at least three feet longer than a billiard table; it had three holes at each end besides the corner holes, and ten holes at each side. The *argolio* was a strong hoop of iron fixed to the table in the place where the *port* stood at billiards. The *sprigg* was another piece of iron, driven into the board at the spot where the *king* stood at billiards. The balls were ivory of the size of tennis balls, "The tacks with which they play are much bigger than billiard sticks, and are headed at each end with iron; the small end is round from the middle, or farther running taperwise, but the great end is flat beneath, though rounding atop; good gamesters play for the most part with the small end." This description of Trucks was repeated in the editions of 1676, 1680, and 1710, but not in the later issues of the eighteenth century.

MISSISSIPI.—Mississipi is played upon a table made in the form of a parallelogram. It much resembles a modern billiard-table, excepting that, instead of pockets, it has a recess at one end, into which the balls may fall; and this recess is faced with a thin board equal in height to the ledge that surrounds the table; and in it are fifteen perforations, or small arches, every one of them surmounted by a number from one to fifteen inclusive, the highest being placed in the middle, and the others intermixed on either side. The players have four or six balls at pleasure. These balls, which are usually made of ivory, and distinguished from each other by their colour, some being red and some white, they cast alternately, one at a time, against the sides of the table, whence acquiring an angular direction, and rolling to the arches, they strike against the intervening parts, or pass by them. In the first instance the cast is of no use; in the second the value of the number affixed to the arches through which they run is placed to the score of the player; and he who first attains one hundred and twenty wins the game. This pastime is included in the statute above mentioned relating to billiards, and the same penalty is imposed upon the publican who keeps a table in his house for the purpose of playing.

---

[1] *Bennett's *Billiards* (4th edit.), p. 9.

Q

THE ROCKS OF SCILLY.—This diversion requires a table oblong in its form, and curved at the top, which is more elevated than the bottom. There is a hollow trunk affixed to one side, which runs nearly the whole length of the table, and is open at both ends. The balls are put in singly at the bottom, and driven through it by the means of a round batoon of wood. When a ball quits the trunk it is impelled by its own gravity towards the lower part of the table, where there are arches similar to those upon the mississipi-table, and numbered in like manner; but it is frequently interrupted in its descent by wires inserted at different distances upon the table, which alter its direction, and often throw it entirely out of the proper track. The game is reckoned in the same manner as at mississipi, and the cast is void if the ball does not enter any of the holes.

SHOVE-GROAT, ETC.—Shove-groat, named also Slyp-groat, and Slide-thrift, are sports occasionally mentioned by the writers of the sixteenth and seventeenth centuries, and probably were analogous to the modern pastime called Justice Jervis, or Jarvis, which is confined to common pot-houses, and only practised by such as frequent the tap-rooms.[1] It requires a parallelogram to be made by chalk, or by lines cut upon the middle of a table, about twelve or fourteen inches in breadth, and three or four feet in length : which is divided, latitudinally, into nine equal partitions, in every one of which is placed a figure, in regular succession from one to nine. Each of the players provides himself with a smooth halfpenny, which he places upon the edge of the table, and striking it with the palm of his hand, drives it towards the marks; and according to the value of the figure affixed to the partition wherein the halfpenny rests, his game is reckoned; which generally is stated at thirty-one, and must be made precisely : if it be exceeded, the player goes again for nine, which must also be brought exactly, or the turn is forfeited; and if the halfpenny rests upon any of the marks that separate the partitions, or overpasses the external boundaries, the go is void. It is also to be observed, that the players toss up to determine who shall go first, which is certainly a great advantage. Some add a tenth partition, with the number ten, to the marks above mentioned; and then they play with four halfpence, which are considered as equivalent to so many cards at cribbage; and the game is counted, in like manner, by fifteens, sequences, pairs, and pairials, according to the numbers appertaining to the partitions occupied by the halfpence.

*This game is nearly akin to shovel-board. It will be remembered that Shakespeare's Falstaff says—

" Quoit him down, Baudolph, like a shove-groat shilling."

SWINGING is a childish sport, in which the performer is seated upon the middle of a long rope, fastened at both ends, a little distance from each other, and the higher above his head the better. The rope we call the Swing, but

---

[1] *Now (1902) better known and occasionally practised as " shove-halfpenny."

formerly it was known by the name of Meritot, or Merry-trotter.[1] This simple pastime was not confined to the children, at least in the last century, but practised by grown persons of both sexes, and especially by the rustics. Hence Gay:

> On two near elms the slacken'd cord I hung,
> Now high, now low, my Blouzalinda swung.

It was also adopted at the watering-places by people of fashion, and the innovation is justly ridiculed in the *Spectator*.[2]

Of late years a machine has been introduced to answer the purpose of the swing,[3] It consists of an axletree, with four or six double arms inserted into it, like the spokes of a large water-wheel; every pair of arms is connected at the extremities by a round rod of iron, of considerable thickness, and upon it a box is suspended, resembling the body of a post-chaise, which turns about and passes readily between the two spokes, in such a manner as to continue upright whatever may be the position of its supporters. These carriages usually contain two or three persons each, and being filled with passengers, if I may be allowed the term, the machine is put into action, when they are successively elevated and depressed by the rotatory motion. This ridiculous method of riding was in vogue for the space of two summers, and was exhibited at several places in the neighbourhood of London; and the places where the machines were erected frequented by persons of both sexes, and by some whose situation in life, one might have thought, would have prevented their appearance in such a mixed, and generally speaking, vulgar company; but the charms of novelty may be pleaded in excuse for many inadvertencies.

TITTER-TOTTER.—To the foregoing we may add another pastime well known with us by the younger part of the community, and called Titter-totter. It consists in simply laying one piece of timber across another, so as to be equipoised; and either end being occupied by a boy or a girl, they raise or depress themselves in turn. This sport was sometimes played by the rustic lads and lasses, as we find from Gay:

> Across the fallen oak the plank I laid,
> And myself pois'd against the tott'ring maid;
> High leap'd the plank, adown Buxoma fell, etc.

*This children's sport is now almost universally known as See-Saw; but the name "Tittermetotter" lingers in Norfolk.

SHUTTLE-COCK is a boyish sport of long standing. It is represented on the thirty-seventh plate, the original of which occurs in Mr Douce's MS. of the fourteenth century.

---

[1] The first occurs in Chaucer; the second in the vocabulary called *Orbis Sensualium Pictus*, as translated by Hoole, chap. cxxxvi. In Latin it is called *Oscillum*, and is described by an old author as a sort of game played with a rope depending from a beam, in which a boy or girl being seated, is driven backwards and forwards. Speght's *Glossary to Chaucer*.

[2] Vol. viii. No. 496; and again No. 492 in the same volume.

[3] *A picture of one is given in a chap-book of a fair, printed in 1778, where it is called an "Up and Down."

"Shuttlecocks" are named by Spenser in *Mother Hubbard*.

It appears to have been a fashionable pastime among grown persons in the reign of James I. In the *Two Maids of Moreclacke*, a comedy printed in 1609, it is said, "To play at shuttle-cock methinks is the game now." And among the anecdotes related of Prince Henry, son to James I., is the following: "His highness playing at shittle-cocke, with one farr taller than himself, and hittyng him by chance with the shittle-cocke upon the forehead, 'This is,' quoth he, 'the encounter of David with Goliath.'"[1]

[1] Harl. MS. 6391.

CHAPTER II

Sedentary Games—Dice-playing—Its Prevalency and bad Effects—Ancient Dice-box—Dicing Games without Tables—Dicing Games within Tables—Backgammon—Its former and present Estimation—Chess—Its Antiquity—The Morals of Chess—Early Chess-play in France and England—The Chess-Board—The Pieces and their Form—The various Games of Chess—Ancient Games similar to Chess—The Philosopher's Game—Draughts, French and Polish—Merelles, or Nine Men's Morris—Boy-Games in Cloisters—Fox and Geese—The Solitary Game—Dominoes—Cards—When Invented—Card-playing in England—Primero and Maw—Ombre—Whist and other Games—Ancient Cards—The Game of Goose—and of the Snake—Cross and Pile.

SEDENTARY GAMES.—This chapter is appropriated to sedentary games, and in treating upon most of them I am under the necessity of confining myself to very narrow limits. To attempt a minute investigation of their properties, to explain the different manners in which they have been played, or to produce all the regulations by which they have been governed, is absolutely incompatible with my present design. Instead, therefore, of following the various writers upon these subjects, whose opinions are rarely in unison, through the multiplicity of their arguments, I shall content myself by selecting such of them as appear to be most cogent, and be exceedingly brief in my own observations.

DICE-PLAY—ITS PREVALENCY AND BAD EFFECTS.—There is not, I believe, any species of amusement more ancient than dice-playing; none has been more universally prevalent, and, generally speaking, none is more pernicious in its consequences. It is the earliest, or at least one of the most early pastimes in use among the Grecians. Dice are said to have been invented, together with chess, by Palamedes, the son of Nauplius, King of Eubœa. Others, agreeing to the time of the invention of dice, attribute it to a Greek soldier named Alea, and therefore say that the game was so denominated. But Herodotus attributes both dice and chess to the Lydians, a people of Asia; in which part of the world, it is most probable, they originated at some very remote but uncertain period. We have already seen that the ancient Germans, even in their state of barbarism, indulged the propensity for gambling with the dice to a degree of madness, not only staking all they were worth, but even their liberty, upon the chance of a throw, and submitted to slavery if fortune declared against them. The Saxons, the Danes, and the Normans, their descendants, were all of them greatly addicted to the same infatuating pastime. One would not, at first sight, imagine that the dice could afford any great variety of amusement, especially if they be abstractedly considered; and yet John of Salisbury, in the twelfth century, speaks of ten different games of dice then in use; but as he has only given us the names, their properties cannot be investigated. He calls it,[1] " The damnable

---

[1] *De Nug. Curialium*, lib. i. cap. 5. * *De alley et usu, et abusu ejus.* The names given are *tessara, calculus, tabula, dardana pugna, tricolus, serio, monarchus, orbiculi, taliorchus,* and *vulpes.*

art of dice-playing." Another author, contemporary with him, says, "The clergymen and bishops are fond of dice-playing."[1]

*It was customary to use a Dice-board in some forms of dice throwing. The board was divided by diagonal lines into ten spaces, and the value of the cast depended not only upon the upper markings of the dice, but upon the particular space into which they fell. One of these Dice-boards is figured on the top of a most beautifully inlaid Elizabethan games table, which was made for Bess of Hardwick, and is still to be seen at Hardwick Hall. It measures 15 inches by $19\frac{1}{2}$. Upon the board, in one of the divisions, are the representations of three dice. On the same table, which is 10 feet in length, there are also inlaid representations of full-sized chess and backgammon boards.[2]

ANCIENT DICE-BOX—ANECDOTE RELATING TO FALSE DICE.—The common method of throwing the dice is with a hollow cylinder of wood, called the dice-box, into which they are put, and thence, being first shaken together, thrown out upon the table; but in one of the prints which occur in the *Vocabulary of Commenius*,[3] we meet with a contrivance for playing with the dice that does not require them to be numbered upon their faces. This curious machine[4] appears on plate thirty-three.

The dice are thrown into the receptacle at the top, whence they fall upon the circular part of the table below, which is divided into six compartments, numbered as the dice usually are; and according to the value of the figures affixed to the compartments into which they fall the throw is estimated. The inner part of the circle, with the apparatus above it, was so constructed as to move round with great rapidity when the dice were put into the funnel.[5] It would thus be analogous to the E O tables of the present day, wherein a ball is used, and the game is determined by the letters E or O being marked upon the compartment into which it falls. The E O tables may have derived their origin from the above contrivance.

Dice-playing has been reprobated by the grave and judicious authors of this country for many centuries back; the legislature set its face against it at a very early period;[6] and in various statutes promulgated for the suppression of unlawful games, from Richard II. to Elizabeth, it is constantly particularised and strictly prohibited.

*In Northbrooke's treatise against dicing, etc., published in 1579, the most unrestrained language is used against dicing, of which the following sentence is but a brief specimen:—"This arte is the mother of lies, of perjuries, of theft, of debate, of injuries, of manslaughter, the verie invention of the Divels of hell." It must, however, be remembered that this strenuous condemnation was directed

---

[1] *Orderic. Vital.* p. 550. [2] *Reliquary,* 1st series, vol. xxiii. 128.
[3] *Orbis Sensualium Pictus,* translated by Hoole, 1658. [4] In Latin, *Pyrgus, Turricula, et Frittillus.*
[5] *In the diary of Count Kilmanseg, who came over to the coronation of George III. in 1760 (published in 1902), is an account of a dicing machine of this description, used by the postilions at a Hanover posting-house, to decide which of them should take the next job.
[6] "Nec ludant ad aleas vel taxillos." Decret. Concil. Vigorn. A.D. 1240, directed to the clergy.

Fox and Geese.

Dice.

Merelles.

Chess.

Chess.

Tables.

Chess Men.

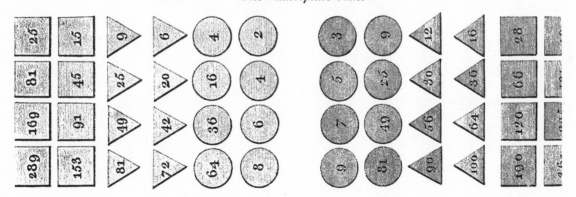

1   2   3   4   5   6

The Philosophers Game.

Reference to the Chess Men.
1. The King.
2. The Queen or Ferce.
3. The Rock.
4. The Alfin.
5. The Knight.
6. The Pawn.

against mere dice-throwing, and not against "tables," by which was implied such a game as backgammon, wherein the dice were thrown within a limited space to direct certain moves. "Playing at tables," says Northbrooke, "is far more tollerable (although in all respects not allowable) than Dice and Cardes are, for that it leaneth partlie to chance, and partlie to industrie of the minde."

Supposing the play to be fair on either side, the chances upon the dice are equal to both parties; and the professed gamblers being well aware of this, will not trust to the determination of fortune, but have recourse to many nefarious arts to circumvent the unwary; hence we hear of loaded dice, and dice of the high cut. The former are dice made heavier on one side than the other by the insertion of a small portion of lead; and the latter may be known by the following anecdote in an anonymous MS. written about the reign of James I., and preserved in the Harleian Collection.[1] "Sir William Herbert, playing at dice with another gentleman, there rose some questions about a cast. Sir William's antagonist declared it was a four and a five; he as positively insisted that it was a five and a six; the other then swore, with a bitter imprecation,[2] that it was as he had said: Sir William then replied, 'Thou art a perjured knave; for give me a sixpence, and if there be a four upon the dice, I will return you a thousand pounds'; at which the other was presently abashed, for indeed the dice were false, and of a high cut, without a four." The dice are usually made of bone or ivory, but sometimes of silver, and probably of other metals. The wife of the unfortunate Arden of Feversham, sent to Mosbie, her paramour, a pair of silver dice, in order to reconcile a disagreement that had subsisted between them, and occasioned his abstaining from her company.[3]

*DICING GAMES WITHOUT "TABLES."—Under the general head of Dicing used to be included two distinct sets of games that were termed "games within the tables" and "games without the tables." The latter were of a purely gambling character; in the *Compleat Gamester*, of 1674, three games of this nature are described. *Inn and Inn* is named as very much used in an ordinary, and could be played by two or three, each having a box in his hand. It was played with four dice, the players depositing sixpences, shillings, or guineas. For an Inn throw nothing was scored, for an Out throw the adversary or adversaries won; for an Inn and Inn throw all was swept by the thrower. An Inn throw was doublets of any sort; an Out throw had no doublets; an Inn and Inn was all doublets, whether of a sort or otherwise. The battle point was fixed beforehand, from twenty shillings to twenty pounds, or on to a thousand; "the battail is not ended till every penny of that money agreed upon for the battail be won."

*PASSAGE was played by two with three dice. The caster threw continually

---

[1] No. 6395, Art. 69.

[2] "As false as dicers' oaths," is a proverbial expression, and used by Shakspeare in Hamlet, act iii. scene 4.

[3] Hollinshed, vol. iii. p. 1062.

till he had thrown doublets under ten, when he was out and lost; or doublets over ten, when he *passed* and won.

*HAZARD was played with two dice, but as many could play it as could stand round the largest round table. Cotton dilates on "main," "chance," "nick," "ames-ace," "deuce-ace," and the like, describing it as "the most bewitching game that is plaid on the dice"; nevertheless he somewhat illogically thus ends his long explanation:—"To conclude, happy is he that having been much inclined to this time-spending, money-wasting Game, hath took up in time, and resolved for the future never to be concerned with it more; but more happy is he that hath never heard the name thereof."

*DICING GAMES WITHIN TABLES.—Of "Games within the Tables" Cotton names seven, of which backgammon is the most important, and has proved the most enduring. *Irish* is described as an ingenious game requiring much skill, and not to be learned without much observation and practice. From the description given it seems to have been much like backgammon, save that it was slower, inasmuch as doublets were not reckoned fourfold. In *Tick-tack* all the men stood on the ace-point, and from thence played forward. If you hit your adversary and neglected the advantage you lost a man. At *Doublets* fifteen men were used. At *Sice-ace* five could play with six men a piece. At *Ketch-dolt* the men were laid down according to the throw from the heap of men without the tables.

*BACKGAMMON.—In Howell's *Letters*, *circa* 1645, occur these words, cited in the Oxford Dictionary:—"Though you have learnt to play at Baggammon, you must not forget Irish, which is a more serious and solid game." Tables was the term always employed for these dice games of mixed chance and skill, until the seventeenth century, when the word backgammon came gradually into general use. The name is apparently derived from back-game or back-play, because the men, under certain circumstances, are hit or taken up and obliged to go back and re-enter the table.

The ancient form of the backgammon-table may be seen at the bottom of plate thirty-four; the original occurs in a beautifully illuminated manuscript of the fourteenth century.[1] The table, as here delineated, is not divided in the middle, but the points, on either side, are contained in a single compartment. If we turn to the thirty-third plate we shall find a table of fifteenth century date. In this the division is fairly made, but the points are not distinguished by different colours, according to the present, and indeed more ancient usage. The writer of the manuscript, from which the latter table is taken, says, "There are many methods of playing at the tables with the dice. The first of these, and the longest, is called the English game, Ludus Anglicorum, which is thus performed: he who sits on the side of the board marked 1—12 has fifteen men (homines) in the part marked 24, and he who sits on the side marked 13—24 has a like number of men in the part 1. They play with three dice, or else with two, allowing always six for a third die. Then he who is seated at 1—12 must bring all his men placed at 24 through the partitions (paginas), from 24 to 19, from 18 to 13, and from 12 to 7, into the division 6—1, and then bear them off; his opponent must do the same from 1 to 7, thence to 12, thence to 18, into the compartment 19—24; and he who first bears off all his men is conqueror." Here we may observe, that the most material circumstances in which the game differed, at this remote period, from the present method of playing it, are, first, in having three dice instead of two, or reckoning a certain number for the third; and secondly, in placing all the men within the antagonist's table, which, if I do not mistake the author, must be put upon his ace-point. But to go on: "There is," says he, "another game upon the tables called *Paume Carie*, which is played with two dice, and requires four players, that is, two on either side; or six, and then three are opposed to three." He then speaks of a third game, called *Ludus Lumbardorum*, the Game of Lombardy, and thus played: he who sits on the side marked 13—24 has his men at 6, and his antagonist has his men at 19"; which is changing the ace point in the English game for the size point: and this alteration probably shortened the game. He then mentions the five following variations by name only; the Imperial game, the Provincial game, the games called Baralie, Mylys, and Faylis.[1]

*The various table games given in the 1674 edition of the *Compleat Gamester* continued to be reprinted in subsequent issues until 1721, when "The Famous Game called *Verqnere*" was placed first among "Games within the Tables." It came from Holland, where they are said to practise it from infancy; the chief feature of it was that "all the table-men are placed on the ace-point, where you set two men at backgammon." The description of Tick-tack is repeated, and that is followed by "The Noble and Courtly Game at Tables called *Grand Trick-track*," played after the same fashion as Tick-tack, but with three other pieces, in addition to the table-men, which were termed markers.

ITS FORMER AND PRESENT ESTIMATION.—At the commencement of the eighteenth century backgammon was a very favourite amusement, and pursued at leisure times by most persons of opulence, and especially by the clergy, which occasioned Dean Swift, when writing to a friend of his in the country, sarcastically to ask the following question: "In what esteem are you with the vicar of the parish; can you play with him at backgammon?" But of late years (1800) this pastime is become unfashionable, and of course it is not often practised. The tables, indeed, are frequently enough to be met with in the country mansions; but upon examination you will generally find the men deficient, the dice lost, or some other cause to render them useless. Backgammon is certainly a diversion by no means fitted for company, which cards are made to accommodate in a more extensive manner; and therefore it is no wonder they have gained the ascendancy.

[1] Roy. Lib. 13 A. xviii.

CHESS—ITS ANTIQUITY.—This noble, or, as it is frequently called, royal pastime, is said, by some authors, to have originated, together with dice-playing, at the siege of Troy; and the invention of both is attributed to Palamedes, the son of Nauplius, king of Eubœa;[1] others make Diomedes, and others again, Ulysses, the inventor of chess.[2] The honour has also been attributed to Ledo and Tyrrheno, two Grecians, and brothers, who being much pressed by hunger, sought to alleviate their bodily sufferings by diverting the mind.[3] None of these stories have any solid foundation for their support; and I am inclined to follow the opinion of Dr Hyde and other learned authors, who readily agree that the pastime is of very remote antiquity, but think it first made its appearance in Asia.

THE MORALS OF CHESS.—John de Vigney wrote a book which he called *The Moralisation of Chess*, wherein he assures us that this game was invented by a philosopher named Xerxes in the reign of Evil Merodach, king of Babylon, and was made known to that monarch in order to engage his attention and correct his manners. "There are three reasons," says de Vigney, "which induced the philosopher to institute this new pastime: the first, to reclaim a wicked king; the second, to prevent idleness; and the third, practically to demonstrate the nature and necessity of nobleness." He then adds, "The game of chess passed from Chaldea into Greece, and thence diffused itself all over Europe." I have followed a MS. copy at the Museum in the Harleian Library.[4] Our countryman Chaucer, on what authority I know not, says it was

—Athalus that made the game
First of the chesse, so was his name.[5]

The Arabians and the Saracens, who are said to be admirable players at chess, have new-modelled the story of de Vigney and adapted it to their own country, changing the name of the philosopher from Xerxes to Sisa.[6]

EARLY CHESS-PLAY IN FRANCE AND ENGLAND.—It is impossible to say when the game of chess was first brought into this kingdom; but we have good reason to suppose it to have been well known here at least a century anterior to the Conquest, and it was then a favourite pastime with persons of the highest rank.

*The Emperor Charlemagne is known to have had much taste for chess, and his chessmen are celebrated. The English scholar Alcuin was on the most intimate terms with the emperor and his family; he visited his native country from 790 to 793, and it is at the least highly probable that he was the first to introduce chess into this country.[7]

---

[1] Palamed. *de Aleatoribus*, cap. 18.

[2] Lepistre Othea, MS. "Ulixes fu un baron de Grece de grant soubtillete, et en temps du siege de Troye il trouva le gieu des esches," etc. Ulysses was a baron of Greece, exceedingly wise, and during the siege of Troy invented the game of chess. Harl. Lib. 4431.

[3] *Ency. Brit.* word Chess.   [4] No. 1275.   [5] Dream of Love.

[6] *Encyclop. Françoise*, in voce Echecs.

[7] *Bird's *Chess History and Reminiscences* (1893), pp. 55-7.

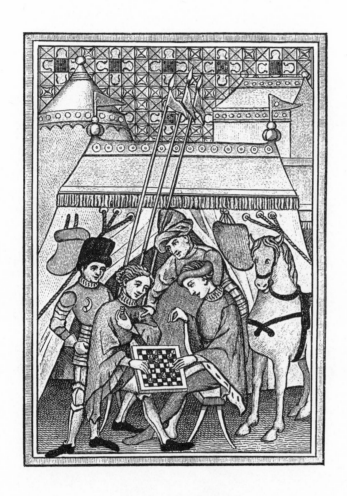

Chess and Tables.

Canute the Dane, who ascended the throne of England A.D. 1017, was partial to this pastime.[1] The following story is told of William, duke of Normandy, afterwards king of England. When a young man, he was invited to the court of the French king, and during his residence there, being one day engaged at chess with the king's eldest son, a dispute arose concerning the play; and William, exasperated at something his antagonist had said, struck him with the chess-board, which obliged him to make a precipitate retreat from France, in order to avoid the consequences of so rash an action.[2] A similar circumstance is said by Leland to have happened in England.[3] John, the youngest son of Henry II., playing at chess one day with Fulco Guarine, a nobleman of Shropshire, a quarrel ensued, and John broke the head of Guarine with the chess-board, who in return struck the prince such a blow that he almost killed him. It seems, however, that Fulco found means of making his peace with King Henry, by whom he was knighted, with three of his brethren, a short time afterwards. John did not so easily forgive the affront; but, on the contrary, showed his resentment long after his accession to the English throne, by keeping him from the possession of Whittington Castle, to which he was the rightful heir.[4] It is also said of this monarch, that he was engaged at chess when the deputies from Rouen came to acquaint him that the city was besieged by Philip, king of France, but he would not hear them out till he had finished the game. In like manner Charles I. was playing at chess when he was told that the final resolution of the Scots was to sell him to the parliament; and he was so little discomposed by the alarming intelligence, that he continued the game with great composure.[5] Several other instances to the same purpose might be produced, but these may suffice; and in truth, I know not what interpretation to put upon such extraordinary conduct; it proves at least that the fascinating powers of this fashionable diversion are very extensive upon the minds of those who pursue it earnestly.

THE CHESS-BOARD.—The number of the pieces and the manner in which they are placed do not appear to have undergone much, if any, variation for several centuries. If the reader will turn to plate thirty-four, he will find the most ancient representation of the pastime that I have met with.[6] On the thirty-third plate he will see two boards with the manner of placing the pieces upon them, taken from a MS. of the thirteenth century, and one of them, a perfect singularity, is of circular form.[7]

---

[1] See the Introduction. [2] See Burton's *Anatomy of Melancholy*. [3] Collect. vol. i. p. 264.
[4] *Ibid*. [5] *Ency. Brit*. word Chess.

[6] This engraving is from a drawing in a beautifully illuminated MS. preserved in the British Museum (Harl. MSS. 4431.) This MS. was written at the close of the fourteenth century, and bears every mark of being the very copy presented to Isabel of Bavaria, the queen of Charies VI. of France. Her portrait, very neatly finished, occurs twice, and that of the king her husband once. The author of this MS. makes Ulysses to be the inventor of chess; and the painting is intended to represent that chieftain engaged with some other Grecian hero who is come to visit and play the game with him, the two by-standers, I presume, are the umpires to decide the matter in case of any dispute.

[7] Cott. MSS. Cleop. B. ix.

In this representation is exhibited the manner of placing the pieces, which are thus called in Latin verse:

Miles et Alphinus, rex, roc, regina, pedinus.

CHESS-PIECES, AND THEIR FORM.—The names of the chess pieces, as they are given in the foregoing manuscript, are these: Rey—Reyne, or Ferce—Roc —Alfin—Chivaler—Poun: that is: 1. The King—2. The Queen, or Ferce[1]— 3. The Rock—4. The Alfin—5. The Knight—6. The Pawn. Their forms are copied on the thirtieth plate.

In more modern times the roc is corruptedly called a rook, but formerly it signified a rock or fortress (now castle); the alfin was denominated by the French *fol*, and with us an archer, and at last a bishop.

THE VARIOUS GAMES OF CHESS.—In a manuscript in the Royal Library,[2] written about the same time as that last mentioned, we find no less than forty-four different names given to so many games of chess, and some of them are played more ways than one, so that on the whole they may be said to amount to fifty-seven;[3] and under every title there are directions for playing the game, but I apprehend they would be of little use to a modern player. I shall, however, give the several denominations as they occur, with an attempt at a translation. If the learned reader should find that I have mistaken the meaning of any of these titles, which is very likely to be the case, he will consider the difficulty I had to encounter, and remember I give the translation with diffidence.

1. Guy de chivaler, *played three ways*—2. De dames—3. De damoyseles— 4. De alfins, *two ways*—5. De anel—6. De covenant—7. De propre confusion, *three ways*—8. Mal assis—9. Cotidian, *two ways*—10. Poynt estraunge, *two ways*—11. Ky perde sey sauve—12. Ky ne doune ces ke il eyme, ne prendrant ke disire—13. Bien trove—14. Beal petit—15. Mieut vaut engyn ke force— 16. Ky est larges est sages—17. Ky doune ganye—18. Ly enginous e ly coveytous—19. Covenaunt fet ley—20. De pres seu joyst ke loyns veyt— 21. Meschief fet hom penser—22. La chace de chivaler—23. La chace de ferce et de chivaler—24. Bien fort—25. Fol si prent—26. Ly envoyns—27. Le seon sey envoye—28. Le veyl conu—29. Le haut enprise—30. De cundut—31. Ky put se prenge—32. La batalie sans array—33. Le tret emble, *two ways*—34. Ly desperes—35. Ly marvelious, *two ways*—36. Ne poun ferce home fet—37. Muse vyleyn—38. De dames et de damoyceles—39. Fol si sey fie, *two ways*—40. Mal veysyn, *two ways*—41. Je mat de ferces—42. Flour de guys—43. La batalie de rokes—44. Double eschec.

1. The knights' game—2. The ladies' game—3. The damsels' game—4. The game of the alfins—5. The ring—6. The agreement—7. Self-confounded —8. Ill placed or bad enough—9. Day by day—10. The foreign point— 11. The loser wins—12. He that gives not what he esteems, shall not take that

---

[1] In Chaucer's *Dream* this piece is called fers and feers.   [2] Roy. Lib. 13 A. xviii.
[3] *Strutt says 55, but reference to the MS. shows that he neglected to note that number 7 was played three ways.

he desires—13. Well found—14. Fair and small—15. Craft surpasses strength —16. He that is bountiful is wise—17. Who gives gains—18. Subtilty and covetousness—19. Agreement makes law—20. He sees his play at hand who sees it at a distance—21. Misfortunes make a man think—22. The chace of the knight—23. The chace of the queen and the knight—24. Very strong—25. He is a fool if he takes—26. The messengers—27. Sent by his own party—28. The old one known—29. The high place taken—30. Perhaps for conduit, managed or conducted—31. Take if you can—32. The battle without arrangement—33. The stolen blow—34. The desperates—35. The wonder—36. A pawn cannot make a queen—37. The clown's lurking place—38. The ladies and the damsels—39. A fool if he trusts—40. Bad neighbour—41. I mate the queen—42. The flower or beauty of the games—43. The battle of the rooks—44. Double chess.

*So great a hold did the game of chess take upon England—a hold that seems to strengthen with every decade of national life—that almost every English writer of repute, from the earliest days, has made reference to this royal pastime, or drawn similes and figures of speech from the chess-board. Such a list includes the names of Chaucer, Lydgate, Gower, Skelton, Sir Philip Sidney, Sir Walter Raleigh, Spenser, Shakespeare, Cowley, Beaumont, Fletcher, Middleton and Dryden.

*The prolific dramatist Thomas Middleton wrote a satirical play called *Game at Chess*, which was first acted at the Globe in 1624. Ignatius Loyola, in the induction, discovers Error asleep, who had seen a strange game of chess in a dream. Loyola expresses a desire to see the game, and the play begins. The dramatis personæ were the chessmen, the white being Protestants and the black Papists. At the conclusion the blacks receive checkmate and are put in a bag. The Spanish Ambassador complained to the authorities that the king of Spain and others were being ridiculed and dishonoured on the stage, with the result that the players were severely reprimanded, the play suppressed, and the author imprisoned. Middleton, however, erelong secured his release by presenting to the king the following rhymed petition :—

> " A harmless game, coyned only for delight,
> Was played betwixt the black house and the white.
> The white house won—yet still the black doth brag,
> They had the power to put me in the bag.
> Use but your royal hand, 'twill set me free :
> 'Tis but removing of a man, that's me." [1]

ANCIENT GAMES SIMILAR TO CHESS.—The ancient pastimes, if more than one be meant, which bear the names of ludus latrunculorum, ludus calculorum, et ludus scrupulorum, have been generally considered as similar to chess, if not precisely the same ; but the authors of the *Encyclopédie Françoise*, assure us they did not bear any resemblance to it, at least in those essential parts of the

---

[1] *Genest's *Hist. of the Stage*, vol. x. pp 11-13.

game which distinguish it from all others; but were played with stones, shells, or counters. The ancients, we are told, used little stones, shells, and nuts, in making their calculations without the assistance of writing. These little stones were called by the Greeks ψηφοι, and calculi or scrupuli by the Romans; and such articles, it is supposed, were employed by them in playing the games above mentioned. This method of reckoning passed from the Greeks to the Romans, but when luxury introduced itself at Rome, the stones and shells were laid aside, and counters made with ivory became their substitutes. If the foregoing observations be well founded, we may justly conclude that the ludus calculorum which Homer mentions as a pastime practised by his heroes, called in Greek πετος or πεσσος, consisted in a certain arrangement and combination of numbers, every piece employed in the game being marked with an appropriate number, and probably might resemble a more modern pastime, which still retains the Greek name of Rithmomachia, from αριθμος, numerus, et μαχι, pugna, expressive of a battle with numbers, said by some to have been invented by Pythagoras,[1] and by others to be more ancient: with us it is called the Philosopher's Game, and seems indeed to have been well calculated for the diversion of soldiers, because it consists, not only in a contention for superiority by the skilful adjustment of the numbers, but in addition, allows the conqueror to triumph and erect his trophy in token of the victory; this part of the game, we are told, requires much judgment to perform with propriety, and if the player fails, his glories are but half achieved.

THE PHILOSOPHER'S GAME.—We have some account of the philosopher's game, but very loosely drawn up, in a manuscript in the Sloan Library[2] at the British Museum. It is called, says the author, "a number fight," because in it men fight and strive together by the art of counting or numbering how one may take his adversary's king and erect a triumph upon the deficiency of his calculations. It is then said, "you may make your triumph as well with your enemy's men taken, as with your own not taken."

The board or table for playing this game is made in the form of a parallelogram just as long again as it is broad; it is divided into eight squares the narrow way, and extended to sixteen the other, and bears the resemblance of two chess-boards fastened together: the chequers in like manner being alternately black and white, and two persons only at one time can properly play the game; to either party is assigned twenty-four soldiers, which constitute his army, (hoste, in the original,) and one of them is called the Pyramis or king: one third of these pieces are circular, which form two rows in the front of the army; one third are triangular, which are placed in the middle; and one third are square, which bring up the rear, and one of these situated in the fifth row is the Pyramis. The men belonging to the two parties are distinguished by being black and white, and every one of them is marked with an appropriate number. There

---

[1] And revived by Claud. Bruxer and others, A.D. 1514, Burton's *Descrip. of Leicestershire*, p. 182.
[2] No. 451.

were sometimes added to these numbers certain signs or algebraic figures, called cossical signings, which increased the intricacy of the game. The army that presents a front of even numbers is called the even host, and the other the odd host. The two armies at the commencement of the play are drawn up in the order represented on plate thirty-three.

It was my wish to have subjoined a general outline of the method of playing the game, but the author is so exceedingly obscure in his phraseology, and negligent in his explanations, that I found it impossible to follow him with the least degree of satisfaction. It is, however, certain, that the great object of each player is to take the king from his opponent, because he who succeeds may make his triumph and erect his trophy.

Burton, speaking of this pastime in his *Anatomy of Melancholy*,[1] calls it the Philosophy Game, and thinks it "not convenient for students"; to which he adds, "the like I say of Dr Fulke's Metromachia, and his Ouronomachia, with the rest of those intricate, astrological, and geometrical fictions, for such as are mathematically given, and other curious games."

*Fulke's *Metromachia eine Suden Geometricus*, was dedicated to the Earl of Leicester, and printed in 1578. It consists of fifty-two pages, and has an elaborate folding plate at the end.

DRAUGHTS.—The pastime of draughts is well known in the present day (1800); and I believe there are now in London as excellent draught-players as ever existed. Draughts, no doubt, is easier to be learnt than chess, because it is not so intricate; for the pieces are of equal value till they become kings, and can only move one way, that is, diagonally; but, like chess, it depends entirely upon skill, and one false move frequently occasions the loss of the game.

*Draughts has a far greater proved antiquity than chess, some of the draughtsmen and part of the board belonging to Queen Hatasu of Egypt, who flourished about 1600 B.C., were discovered in 1887.[2] The game was introduced into Italy from Egypt, and is known in Latin as *ludus latrunculorum*, or the game of the Little Soldiers. The name of draughts is derived from the verb to draw or to move, and was at one time applicable to chess as well as to draughts. The first known work on modern draughts proceeded from Spain in 1547. The earliest French work was that of Pierre Malet, published in 1668. The old French draughts was exactly like English draughts. The Polish game came into fashion in 1727, and in France superseded for the most part the older game; it is played upon a board of a hundred squares with forty men; it never obtained much favour in England, but was occasionally played in London at the beginning of the nineteenth century. Mr J. G. Pohlman brought out an illustrated book on Polish Draughts in 1811.

*There are various casual seventeenth century references to this game as distinct from chess in English writers; but the English school of draught playing did not really begin until Payne brought out the first printed account of it in

---

[1] Part ii. sect. 2, mem. 4.   [2] *They are described in *The Times* of June 22nd, 1887.

the vulgar tongue in 1756. Joshua Sturges first published his standard work in 1800, under the title *Guide to the Game of Draughts, containing* 500 *select games.* In it he reproduced almost all Payne's work, but with considerable amendments and new games. Since that date Sturges's book has been continually reproduced both in England and America.[1]

MERELLES—NINE MEN'S MORRIS.—Merelles, or, as it was formerly called in England, nine men's morris, and also five-penny morris, is a game of some antiquity. Cotgrave describes it as a boyish game, and says it was played here commonly with stones, but in France with pawns, or men, made on purpose, and they were termed merelles; hence the pastime itself received that denomination. It was certainly much used by the shepherds formerly, and continues to be used by them, and other rustics, to the present hour (1800). But it is very far from being confined to the practice of boys and girls. The form of the merelle-table, and the lines upon it, as it appeared in the fourteenth century, is given upon plate thirty-three; and these lines have not since been varied. The black spots at every angle and intersection of the lines are the places for the men to be laid upon. The men are different in form or colour for distinction sake; and from the moving these men backwards or forwards, as though they were dancing a morris, I suppose the pastime received the appellation of nine men's morris; but why it should have been called five-penny morris, I do not know. The manner of playing is briefly this: two persons, having each of them nine pieces, or men, lay them down alternately, one by one, upon the spots; and the business of either party is to prevent his antagonist from placing three of his pieces so as to form a row of three, without the intervention of an opponent piece. If a row be formed, he that made it is at liberty to take up one of his competitor's pieces from any part he thinks most to his own advantage; excepting he has made a row, which must not be touched if he have another piece upon the board that is not a component part of that row. When all the pieces are laid down, they are played backwards and forwards, in any direction that the lines run, but only can move from one spot to another at one time: he that takes off all his antagonist's pieces is the conqueror. The rustics, when they have not materials at hand to make a table, cut the lines in the same form upon the ground, and make a small hole for every dot. They then collect, as abovementioned, stones of different forms or colours for the pieces, and play the game by depositing them in the holes in the same manner that they are set over the dots upon the table. Hence Shakspeare, describing the effects of a wet and stormy season, says:

> The folds stand empty in the drowned field,
> And crows are fatted with the murrain flock,
> The nine men's morris is filled up with mud.

---

[1] *The last revision was published in 1895. The literature of draughts has of late years attained to astonishing proportions; there were twenty-seven distinct works on this one game, issued in England, between 1880 and 1895. This pastime also supports the following periodicals:—*The Draught World, The International Draught Magazine, The Draught Players' Quarterly Review, *and* The Draught Players' Weekly Magazine.

*A correspondent of *Notes and Queries*, in 1875, wrote :—" The game is known in Derbyshire as 'three mans' marriage,' and for this game three men are used, and the board on which the game is played contains nine holes or points. One 'board' on which we played the game was generally a flat stone, upon which, with chalk, we made a square, intersecting it with a horizontal and a vertical line, which produced the nine holes or points. Two played the game, laying their men alternately on any of the points of the board. The object of each player was to get his men 'all in a row,' and the game was won. 'Nine men's marriage' is quite a different affair, and much more elaborate. Each player uses nine men, and the 'board' is three squares one inside the other, and the squares are connected by four lines drawn through the sides of the squares. This board contains twenty-four holes or points. The players in this game lay their men alternately, each taking care that his opponent does not get a row during the placing of the men. When the men have all been dealt the players move a man in turn. Each player tries to get three of his men in a row, at the same time striving to hinder his opponent from making a row. When a player has made a row his three men are married and he may take a man from his opponent. The game 'nine men's marriage' is also called 'tink-track,' because with good play, a player may get five of his men in such a position, that a 'tink-track' is formed, by means of which he can clear the board of the enemy, one by one, in so many moves." [1]

*BOY-GAMES IN CLOISTERS.—In 1892, Mr J. T. Micklethwaite read a most interesting paper before the Archæological Institute " On the Indoor Games of School Boys in the Middle Ages." [2] He was able to prove that certain " cup markings" arranged in squares of nine on the benches of the cloisters of Westminster, Canterbury, Norwich, Salisbury, and Chichester were the work of school boys and others in pre-Reformation times. Other instances have been found in the porches of parochial churches. Some of these stone cut "boards" are for Nine Men's Morris, others for Fox and Geese, and others for a simpler game of In and Out. Mr Micklethwaite's remarks as to the age of these interesting survivals are as follows :—

" For the last three centuries and a half cloisters everywhere in England have been open passages, and there have generally been school-boys about. It is there-fore not unlikely that they should have left behind them such traces as these play-boards. But if they are of later date they would not be found to be distributed in monastic cloisters with respect to the monastic arrangement, and we do find them so. At Westminster Abbey they are only found in the north-west corner, which if the arrangement agreed with that of Durham, as there is reason to believe it did, was the place of the school. At Norwich, where the game boards

---

[1] Other more recent correspondents of *Notes and Queries* have shown that Nine Men's Morris is still played by rustics in Derbyshire, Wilts, Norfolk, and Dorset. It is also in limited use as a parlour game, and was played fairly frequently in the "fifties" and "sixties" of last century under its Shakespeare title. It can now (1902) be obtained at the Army and Navy Stores, as "Morelles, a Game of Skill for Railway Travellers and for Home Amusement."

[2] *Archæol. Journal*, vol. xlix. pp. 319-328. Plans are given of the different " boards."

R

are very many, they are found in every part of the cloister except the north walk, where the monks had their library and studies. At Gloucester the *morris* and *fox and geese* boards are in the north walk and the simpler *in and out* boards in the west walk and none is found in the south, which was the monks' side, or in the east, which was most used by them as a passage way. At Canterbury the play boards are found only in the south walk, which is that against the church, and so according to the usual plan it would be the monks' place. But I think it was not so there, as that walk was the passage between the Archbishop's palace and the quire. We do not really know what the arrangement of the cloister was at Canterbury.

"In the secular cloister of Salisbury the boards are only found in the east walk between the Chapter House door and that towards the Bishop's Palace. I can give no reason for this, unless it be that a school was kept there, which is not unlikely. We know that till comparatively late times school was held in the cloister at Winchester College during the summer.

"As the games themselves did not die out, it is remarkable that all the boards noticed are cut upon stone or wood, which was wrought at the latest before the middle of the sixteenth century, and this is a further confirmation of their antiquity."

*The late Rev. R. S. Baker, rector of Hargrave, Northamptonshire, found a Nine Men's Morris stone in the porch of his church during restoration in 1868. It was recognised by the labouring population as a "Peg Meryll" stone. Sending an account of this to *Land and Water* produced an interesting correspondence, by which he was able to show that the game was at that time played in Essex as "Merelles or Merils"; in Cambridgeshire as "Morels or Murrells"; in Lincolnshire as "Meg Merryleys"; in Norfolk and Cornwall as "Morris or Morrice"; in Leicestershire as "Blind Men's Morris"; and in Oxfordshire as "Ninepenny."[1]

Fox and Geese.—This is a game somewhat resembling that of merelles in the manner the pieces are moved, but in other respects, as well as in the form of the table, it differs materially; the intersection and angles are more numerous, and the dots of course increased, which adds to the number of the moves. It is certainly as old in this country as the thirteenth century.

To play this game there are seventeen pieces, called geese, which are placed as we see them on plate thiry three, and the fox in the middle, distinguished either by his size or difference of colour, as here, for instance, he is black. The business of the game is to shut the fox up, so that he cannot move. All the pieces have the power to move from one spot to another, in the direction of the right lines, but cannot pass over two spots at one time. It is to be observed, that this board is sometimes made with holes bored through it, where the dots are made, and pegs equal to the number of geese put into them, and the fox is distinguished by being larger and taller than the rest. The geese

[1] *Journal of Assoc. Archit. Societies*, vol. xi. pp. 127-131.

are not permitted to take the fox if he stands close to them, but the fox may take a goose, in like case, if the spot behind it be unoccupied, or not guarded by another goose; and if all be taken, or the number so reduced that the fox cannot be blocked, the game is won. The great deficiency of this game is, that the fox must inevitably be blocked if the geese are played by a skilful hand; for which reason, I am told, of late some players have added another fox; but this I have not seen.

THE SOLITARY GAME.—This is so denominated because it is played by one person only. It is said to have been invented by an unfortunate man who was several years kept in solitary confinement at the Bastile in Paris. The board for this pastime is of a circular form, and perforated with holes at half an inch distance from each other, to the amount of fifty or sixty. A certain number of pegs are then fitted to these holes, but not enough to fill them all; and the manner of playing the game is to pass one of the pegs over another into a hole that is unoccupied, taking the peg so passed from the board, and to continue doing so till all the pegs but one are taken away; which is an operation much more difficult to perform than any one could readily imagine who had not made the attempt. It must be remembered that only one peg can be passed over at a time, and that no peg can be put over another, unless it stands close to it without an intervening hole.[1]

DOMINOES.—Dominoes seems to have been little known in England till towards the end of the eighteenth century, when it was imported from France. It consists of twenty-eight small oblong and flat pieces of ivory or bone, and all of the same size and shape. The back of every piece is plain, and sometimes black; the face is white, divided into two parts by a line in the middle, and marked with a double number, or with two different numbers, or with a number and a blank, and one of them is a double blank. The numbers are the same as those upon the dice, from one to six inclusive. When two play, the whole of the pieces are hustled about the table with their faces downwards, and each of them draw seven or nine, according to agreement, and the remaining pieces are undiscovered until the hand is played, which is thus performed: the right of first playing being cut for, he who obtains it lays down one of his pieces, and the other is to match one of the numbers marked upon it with a similar number marked upon a piece of his own, which he lays close to it; the other then matches one of the open numbers in like manner; and thus they continue alternately to lay down their pieces as long as they can be matched; and he who first gets rid of all his pieces wins the game; but if it so happen, as it often does, that neither of them have exhausted their pieces, nor can match the open numbers on the table, they then discover what remains on both sides, and he whose pieces contain the fewest spots obtains the victory. Sometimes four play,

---

[1] *The game of *Solitaire,* re-imported from France, and played with glass marbles on a board with suitable depressions, came again suddenly into fashion in England in the late "fifties" and early "sixties" of the nineteenth century.

in which case they deal out six cards to each, leaving only four upon the table, and then play on in rotation.

*Dominoes is by no means a mere game of chance, and has of late received much attention. In 1879, the special Spanish form of playing dominoes was popularised in England, and is at present (1902) in commoner use than any other form, particularly in City restaurants.[1]

*CARDS—WHEN INVENTED.—So far as English card-playing is concerned, the attempt made by Mr Barrington in the eighteenth century[2] to prove that Edward I. played cards, because an entry, of 1278, in the wardrobe accounts, names his playing at the Four Kings has been upset, and shown to be a form of chess. It is generally admitted that playing cards came to Europe from the East. There have been various more or less plausible suppositions as to the period when they were first used on the continent or in England, but the positive history of cards in Europe does not begin till the year 1393, when three packs of cards (*jeux de cartes*), gilt and coloured, were purchased in Paris of one Jacquemin Gringonneur, painter, for the amusement of King Charles VI., who had lost his reason in the previous year. A French edict relative to games of chance in 1369 makes no reference to cards, but another edict of 1397 prohibits the working people playing cards on working days. Between these two dates it is safe to say that cards became popular in France. By the Synod of Langres, 1404, card-playing was forbidden to the clergy. Early in the fifteenth century card-making and card-painting had become a regular industry in Germany, particularly at Nuremberg.

*CARD-PLAYING IN ENGLAND.—Cards were well known in England in 1463, for by an act of parliament of that year their importation was prohibited, in order, apparently, to protect their home manufacture. A little later in that century there is evidence that they were a common Christmas game. On Christmas Eve, 1484, Margery Paston wrote to her husband to the following effect :—" I sent your eldest sunne to my Lady Morlee to have knolage wat sports were busyd in her hows in Kyrstemesse next folloyng aftyr the decysse of my lord her husbond ; and sche seyd that ther wer non dysgysyngs, ner harpyng, ner lutyng, ner syngyn, ner non lowde dysports, but pleyng at the tabyllys, and schesse, and cards. Sweche dysports sche gave her folkys leve to play and non odyr."[3] The privy purse expenses of Henry VII. show his losses at cards on several occasions.

*When the sixteenth century is reached the references to card-playing in England, and the proofs that it was popular among all classes, are most abundant. Losses at cards occur in Henry VIII. privy purse expenses ; whilst

---

[1] *Dominoes* (1890) forms one of the "Club Series" of games issued by George Bell & Sons. The considerable diversity of play to be found in modern dominoes is indicated by the mere titles of its varieties treated of in these pages :—The Block Game, All Fives or Muggins, All threes, Domino Whist, The Four Game, Sebastopol, Cyprus, Tiddle-a-Wink, The Draw Game, Domino Draw Pool, The Matadore Game, The Bergen Game, and Domino Loo.

[2] *Archæologia*, vol. viii.

Paston Letters, vol. iii. p. 314.

those of his daughter Mary, afterwards Queen, from 1536 to 1544, show that card-playing was her constant habit. A statute of 1541 forbids card-playing by the working-classes. Whole chapters could be filled with the notices of card-playing that occur in the poems and plays of this century. One must suffice. In the comedy of *Gammer Gurton's Needle*, first printed in 1551, old Dame Chat thus invites two of her friends to a game of cards :—

> "What, Diccon? Come nere, ye be no stranger,
> We be fast set a trump, man, hard by the fire ;
> Thou shalt set on the king, if thou come a little nyer.
> Come hither, Dol ; Dol, sit down and play this game,
> And as thou sawest me do, see thou do even the same,
> There is five trumps besides the queen, the hindmost thou shalt find her,
> Take hede of Gim Glover's wife, she hath an eye behind her."

*Minister Northbrooke was most strenuous in his condemnation of card-playing in Elizabeth's reign, stating that—" The plaie at Cardes is an invention of the devill, which he founde out, that he might the easilier bring in idolatrie amongest men : For the Kings and Coate cardes that we use nowe were in olde time the images of idols and false Gods, which since they that woulde seeme Christians have chaunged into Charlemaine, Launcelot, Hector, and suchlike names, because they would not seeme to imitate their idolatrie therein, and yet mainteine the plaie itselfe, the verie invention of Saban the Devill and woulde so disguise this mischiefe under the cloak of suche gaie names." [1]

*The knaves of that date, in English and French packs, were usually known as Lancelot, Hogier, Rolant, and Valery ; the kings bore the names of David, Alexander, Cæsar, and Charlemagne ; and the queens, Rachael, Argine, Pallas, and Judith.

*PRIMERO AND MAW.—Queen Elizabeth was fond of taking a hand at *Primero* which was then the fashionable game of cards. The favourite game of James I. was *Maw* which took the place of Primero during his reign ; it afterwards became popular under the name of Five Cards. In 1643, on the complaint of several poor cardmakers, parliament prohibited all importation of foreign packs. With the restoration of Charles II., card-playing received a great impetus, and their use became almost universal.

*Philip Kinder in his MS. *History of Derbyshire*,[2] written about the middle of the seventeenth century, says of the natives of that shire that "they love ye Cards, and in this they imitate the Spaniard who instade of Kings, Queens and Knaves, they have Kings, Knights and souldiers ; but in all ye rest to ye Ace noe Tradesman, Lawyer, or Divines, signifying y^t all other were but asses to play at Cardes. But this Countrie hath Picts and Spades amongsd ye Minors, and these men at Christmas tyme will carry tenn or twentie pound about them, game freely, and returne home againe all ye yeere after very good husbands."

[1] *Treatise against Diceing, etc.* (1579), f. 54.
[2] Bodleian, Ashm. MSS. 788.

*OMBRE.—Ombre was the particular card game popularised by the court of Charles II., and was the favourite play of his queen, Catherine of Portugal. It is well to remember that the name "Ombre" for the once fashionable card game is a misspelling arising from the non-pronunciation of the h in Spanish; it should be "Hombre," a man, and has no connection with the French "Ombre," a shadow. In this reign the trade of card-making flourished to a remarkable extent, and every kind of eccentricity was used in their illustration both of heraldic and historical character.

*WHIST AND OTHER GAMES.—The first edition of Cotton's *Compleat Gamester*, published in 1674, mentions the following card games :—

(1) Ruff and Honours, otherwise called Slam, described as so well known in England that every child almost of eight years old hath a competent knowledge of it.

(2) Whist, which differed much from the modern game of that name; "it is called Whist from the silence that is to be observed in the play"; "he that can by craft overlook his adversary's game hath a great advantage."

(3) French Ruff, which could be played by either two, four, or six of a-side, dealing to each five a piece.

(4) Gleek, which could be played only by three "neither more nor less." It is styled by Cotton "a noble and delightful game or recreation."

(5) Ombre, described as a Spanish game of several sorts, "but that which is the chief is called Renegado, at which three only can play."

(6) Lanterloo, a round game; two distinct methods of playing are set forth.

(7) Bankafelet, "the cheat lies in securing an ace or any other sure winning card, and if you mark the cards aforehand, so as to know them by the backside, you know how to make your advantage."

(8) Beast, "called by the French *La Bët*," a round game, with five dealt to each player, and the remainder divided into three heaps, called the King, the Play, and the Triolet.

(9) Basset, described as a French game, and "amongst all those on the cards is accounted to be the most courtly, being properly by the understanders of it, thought only fit for Kings and Queens, great princes, noblemen, etc., to play at, by reason of such great losses or advantages, as may possibly be one side or other during time of play." It was very fashionable towards the close of the seventeenth century; it was a round game with a banker, and resembled baccarat.

(10) Bragg is described as "an ingenious and pleasant game in which each gamester is to put down three stakes."

(11) Picquet; the rules given are almost identical with those now in use.

(12) Primero, a Spanish game; though mentioned last by Cotton it is considered the oldest game of cards played in England. It is described as having a close resemblance to Ombre, by which it had been superseded. In

both the spadillo, or ace of spades, was reckoned the best card, but Primero was played with six cards and Ombre with nine.

*Two years later the *Compleat Gamester* was republished. In the 1676 edition there were many changes particularly with reference to cards. The card games not previously mentioned are :—Cribbidge ; All-Fours ; Five-Cards, an Irish game for two, much resembling Maw of James I. reign ; Costly Colours, for two ; Bone-Ace, " trivial and very inconsiderable, but played by ladies and persons of quality, and a licking (round) game for money " ; Putt, " the ordinary rooking game " ; Wit and Reason ; the Art of Memory ; Plain Dealing ; Queen Nazareen ; Penneech ; and Post and Pair. The same list of card games was repeated in several other editions of the *Compleat Gamester* down to 1725.

*Quadrille, which much resembled Ombre with the addition of a fourth player, came into fashion in the first half of the eighteenth century. In 1737 Hoyle's *Treatise on Whist* made its first appearance, and speedily ran through many editions. From that date Whist in its improved shape came rapidly into fashion, and held its own as the essentially English game of English origin throughout the nineteenth century.

ANCIENT CARDS.—The early specimens of playing-cards that have been produced, differ but little in their form from those now used. This form is certainly the most convenient for the purposes assigned to them, and has been most generally adopted. The figures and devices, however, that constitute the different suits of the cards seem anciently to have depended upon the taste and invention of the card-makers and differed much in different countries.

It has been observed, that outlines made upon blocks of wood were stamped upon the cards, and afterwards filled up by the hand ; but, soon after the invention of engraving upon copper, the devices were produced by the graver, and sufficiently finished, so that the impressions did not require any assistance from the pencil. It appears also, that the best artists of the time were employed for this purpose. I am exceedingly happy to have it in my power to lay before my readers a curious specimen of ancient engraved cards (plate thirty-five), in the possession of Mr Douce, with whose permission they are added to this work. I have chosen one from each of the different suits, namely, the King of Columbines, the Queen of Hares, the Knave of Pinks, and the Ace of Roses ; which answered to the spades, the clubs, the diamonds, and the hearts, of the moderns. The annexed engravings are of the same size as the originals. They are nearly square, and, originally, I have no doubt but they were perfectly so.

Upon the other cards belonging to the pack the number of the flowers or animals answered to the pips at present, with the addition of numeral figures corresponding with the devices, that they might be readily distinguished without the trouble of counting them. The originals of these cards, I make no doubt, are the work of Martin Schoen, a well-known and justly celebrated German artist ; and Mr Douce is in possession of part of another set, which evidently appear to be the production of Israel Van Mecken, who was contemporary with Schoen. Mecken outlived Martin Schoen a considerable time; the latter died in 1486, and the former in 1523. The earliest print that I have seen by Mecken with a date is 1480; but he practised the art of engraving some time prior to that period.

A set or pack of cards, but not equally ancient with those above mentioned, were in the possession of Dr Stukeley: the four suits upon them consisted of bells, of hearts, of leaves, and of acorns; by which, the doctor imagined, were represented the four orders of men among us: the bells are such as are usually tied to the legs of the hawks, and denoted the nobility; the hearts were intended for the ecclesiastics; the leaves alluded to the gentry, who possess lands, woods, manors, and parks; the acorns signified the farmers, peasants, woodmen, park-keepers, and hunters. But this definition will, I trust, be generally considered as a mere effusion of fancy. It is remarkable that in these cards there are neither queens nor aces; but the former are supplied by knights, the latter have no substitute. Dr Stukeley's cards were purchased at his sale by Mr Tuttet, and again at his sale by Mr Gough, in whose possession they now remain (1800). The last gentleman has given a full desciption of them in a paper upon the subject of card-playing, in the *Archæologia*.[1] The figured cards, by us denominated court cards, were formerly called coat cards; and originally, I conceive, the name implied coated figures, that is, men and women who wore coats, in contradistinction to the other devices of flowers and animals not of the human species. The pack or set of cards, in the old plays, is continually called a pair of cards; which has suggested the idea that anciently two packs of cards were used, a custom common enough at present in playing at quadrille; one pack being laid by the side of the player who is to deal the next time. But this supposition rests entirely upon the application of the term itself, without any other kind of proof whatever: and seems, indeed, to be entirely overturned by a passage in a very old play entitled *The longer thou livest the more Foole thou art;* in which Idleness desires Moros the clown to look at "his booke," and shows him "a paire of cardes." In a comedy called *A Woman killed with Kindness*, a pair of cards and counters to play with are mentioned.[2]

*The earliest known specimens of the cards engraved on copper are the German ones of circular pattern, with hares, parroquets, pinks, and columbines, as the usual marks of the suits, illustrations of which have just been described. In each suit of such cards there are four coat (or court) cards, namely King, Queen, Squire, and Knave. The marks and names of the suits differed much and still differ in different countries; but from an early date English cards corresponded with those of France, and were distinguished as *cœurs, carreaux, piques, et trefles*, or hearts, diamonds, spades, and clubs. It would be unsatisfactory to attempt, even in two or three pages, to give an account of the great and interesting variety of English playing-cards, and of the moral, political, or

---

[1] Vol. vii. p. 152 *et seq.*   [2] Cf. *pair* of bellows, *pair* of steps, *pair* of organs, etc.

Cards.

historical use to which it was the custom for two or three centuries to apply their pictures.[1]

THE GAME OF GOOSE—AND OF THE SNAKE.—In addition to the pastimes mentioned in the preceding pages, I shall produce two or three more; and they are such as require no skill in the performance, but depend entirely upon chance for the determination of the contest.

We have a childish diversion usually introduced at Christmas time, called the Game of Goose. This game may be played by two persons; but it will readily admit of many more; it originated, I believe, in Germany, and is well calculated to make children ready at reckoning the produce of two given numbers. The table for playing at goose is usually an impression from a copper-plate pasted upon a cartoon about the size of a sheet almanack, and divided into sixty-two small compartments arranged in a spiral form, with a large open space in the midst marked with the number sixty-three; the lesser compartments have singly an appropriate number from one to sixty-two inclusive, beginning at the outmost extremity of the spiral lines. At the commencement of the play, every one of the competitors puts a stake into the space at No. 63. There are also different forfeitures in the course of the game that are added, and the whole belongs to the winner. At No. 5 is a bridge which claims a forfeit at passing; at 19, an alehouse where a forfeit is exacted and to stop two throws; at 30, a fountain where you pay for washing; at 42, a labyrinth which carries you back to 23; at 52, the prison where you must rest until relieved by another casting the same throw; at 58, the grave whence you begin the game again; and at 61, the goblet where you pay for tasting.[2] The game is played with two dice, and every player throws in his turn as he sits at the table: he must have a counter or some other small mark which he can distinguish from the marks of his antagonists, and according to the amount of the two numbers thrown upon the dice he places his mark; that is to say, if he throws a four and a five, which amount to nine, he places his mark at nine upon the table, moving it the next throw as many numbers forward as the dice permit him, and so on until the game be completed, namely, when the number sixty-three is made exactly; all above it the player reckons back, and then throws again in his turn. If the second thrower at the beginning of the game casts the same number as the first, he takes up his piece, and the first player is obliged to begin the game again. If the same thing happens in the middle of the game, the first player goes back to the place the last came from. It is called the game of the goose, because at every fourth and fifth compartment in succession a goose is depicted, and if the cast thrown by the player falls upon a goose, he moves forward double the number of his throw.

We have also the Game of Snake, and the more modern Game of Matri-

---

[1] *See Willshire's *Descriptive Catalogue of Playing and other Cards in the Brit. Museum* (1876); and *Supplement* (1877); also Chatto's *Hist. of Playing Cards* (1848).

[2] See *Des Lust und Spiel Hauses*, published at Buda, 1680.

mony, with others of the like kind; formed upon the same plan as that of the goose, but none of them, according to my opinion, are the least improved by the variations.[1]

CROSS AND PILE.—Cross and pile, or with us heads or tails, is a silly pastime well enough known among the lowest and most vulgar classes of the community, and to whom it is at present very properly confined; formerly, however, it held a higher rank, and was introduced at the court. Edward II. was partial to this and such like frivolous diversions, and spent much of his time in the pursuit of them. In one of his wardrobe rolls we meet with the following entries: " Item, paid to Henry, the king's barber, for money which he lent to the king to play at cross and pile, five shillings. Item, paid to Pires Barnard, usher of the king's chamber, money which he lent the king, and which he lost at cross and pile; to Monsieur Robert Wattewille eightpence."[2]

A halfpenny is generally now used in playing this game; but any other coin with a head impressed on one side will answer the purpose: the reverse of the head being called the tail without respect to the figure upon it, and the same if it was blank. Anciently the English coins were stamped on one side with a cross. One person tosses the halfpenny up and the other calls at pleasure head or tail; if his call lies uppermost when the halfpenny descends and rests upon the ground, he wins; and if on the contrary, of course he loses. Cross and pile is evidently derived from a pastime called Ostrachinda, $O\sigma\tau\rho\alpha\varkappa\iota\nu\delta\alpha$, known in ancient times to the Grecian boys, and practised by them upon various occasions; having procured a shell, it was seared over with pitch on one side for distinction sake, and the other side was left white; a boy tossed up this shell and his antagonist called white or block, $N\upsilon\xi$ et $\eta\mu\epsilon\rho\alpha$, (literally night and day), as he thought proper, and his success was determined by the white or black part of the shell being uppermost.

---

[1] *Varieties of this game, requiring the use of either dice or tee-totum to fix the numbers are continually being put forth.

[2] *Antiq. Repert.*, vol. ii. p. 58.

CHAPTER III

The Lord of Misrule said to be peculiar to the English—A Court Officer—The Master of the King's Revels—The Lord of Misrule and his Conduct reprobated—The King of Christmas—of the Cockneys—A King of Christmas at Norwich—The King of the Bean—Whence originated—Christmastide in Charles I. Reign—The Boy-Bishop—Plough Monday—Shrove Tuesday—Easter Game—Hock-Tide—May-Games—The Lord and Lady of the May —Grand May-Game at Greenwich—Royal May-Game at Shooter's-hill—May Poles—May Milk-Maids—May Festival of the Chimney Sweepers—Whitsun-Games—Lamb Ale—The Vigil of Saint John the Baptist, how kept—Its supposed origin—Setting of the Midsummer Watch—Processions on Saint Clement's and Saint Catherine's day—Wassails—Sheep-shearing and Harvest-home—Wakes—Sunday Festivals—Church Ales— Funds raised by Church Ales—Fairs, and their diversions and abuses—Bonfires—Illuminations—Fireworks— Books on Fireworks—A Fiery Drake or Fiery Kite—London Fireworks—Fireworks on Tower-hill—at Public Gardens, and in Pageants.

THE LORD OF MISRULE PECULIAR TO ENGLAND.—It is said of the English, that formerly they were remarkable for the manner in which they celebrated the festival of Christmas; at which season they admitted variety of sports and pastimes not known, or little practised in other countries.[1] The mock prince, or lord of misrule, whose reign extended through the greater part of the holidays, is particularly remarked by foreign writers, who consider him as a personage rarely to be met with out of England;[2] and, two or three centuries back, perhaps this observation might be consistent with the truth; but I trust we shall upon due examination be ready to conclude, that anciently this frolicksome monarch was well known upon the continent, where he probably received his first honours. In this kingdom his power and his dignities suffered no diminution, but on the contrary were established by royal authority, and continued after they had ceased to exist elsewhere. But even with us his government has been extinct for many years, and his name and his offices are nearly forgotten. In some great families, and also sometimes at court, this officer was called the Abbot of Misrule. Leland says, "This Christmas[3] I saw no disguiseings at court, and right few playes; but there was an abbot of misrule that made much sport, and did right well his office."[4] In Scotland he was called the Abbot of Unreason, and prohibited there in 1555 by the parliament.[5]

THE LORD OF MISRULE A COURT OFFICER.—Holingshed, speaking of Christmas, calls it, "What time there is always one appointed to make sporte at courte called commonly lorde of misrule, whose office is not unknowne to such as have bene brought up in noblemen's houses and among great housekeepers, which use liberal feasting in the season."[6] Again: "At the feast of Christmas," says Stow, "in the king's court wherever he chanced to reside, there was

---

[1] See Introduction.
[2] Polydore Vergil de Rerum Invent. lib. v. cap. 2.
[3] An. 4 Hen. VII. A.D. 1489.
[4] Collect. vol. iii. Append. p. 256.
[5] See Warton's *Hist. Eng. Poetry*, vol. i. p. 381.
[6] *Chron. of Brit.* vol. iii. fol. 1317.

appointed a lord of misrule, or master of merry disports ; the same merry fellow made his appearance at the house of every nobleman and person of distinction, and among the rest the lord mayor of London and the sheriffs had severally of them their lord of misrule, ever contending, without quarrel or offence, who should make the rarest pastimes to delight the beholders ; this pageant potentate began his rule at All-hallow eve, and continued the same till the morrow after the Feast of the Purification ; in which space there were fine and subtle disguisings, masks, and mummeries." [1]

THE MASTER OF THE KING'S REVELS.—In the fifth year of Edward VI., at Christmas time, a gentleman named George Ferrers, who was a lawyer, a poet, and an historian, was appointed by the council to bear this office ; "and he," says Holingshed, "being of better calling than commonly his predecessors had been before, received all his commissions and warrauntes by the name of master of the kinge's pastimes ; which gentleman so well supplied his office, both of shew of sundry sights, and devises of rare invention, and in act of divers interludes, and matters of pastime, played by persons, as not only satisfied the common sorte, but also were verie well liked and allowed by the council, and others of skill in lyke pastimes ; but best by the young king himselfe, as appeared by his princely liberalitie in rewarding that service."

THE LORD OF MISRULE—HIS CONDUCT REPROBATED.—This master of merry disports was not confined to the court, nor to the houses of the opulent, he was also elected in various parishes, where, indeed, his reign seems to have been of shorter date. Philip Stubbs, who lived at the close of the sixteenth century, places this whimsical personage, with his followers, in a very degrading point of view. [2] I shall give the passage in the author's own words, and leave the reader to comment upon them. "First of all, the wilde heades of the parish flocking togither, chuse them a graund captaine of mischiefe, whom they innoble with the title of Lord of Misrule ; and him they crowne with great solemnity, and adopt for their king. This king annoynted chooseth forth twentie, fourty, threescore, or an hundred lustie guttes, like to himself, to waite upon his lordly majesty, and to guarde his noble person. Then every one of these men he investeth with his liveries of greene, yellow, or some other light wanton colour, and as though they were not gawdy ynough, they bedecke themselves with scarffes, ribbons, and laces, hanged all over with gold ringes, pretious stones, and other jewels. This done, they tie aboute either legge twentie or fourtie belles, with riche handkerchiefes in their handes, and sometimes laide acrosse over their shoulders and neckes, borrowed, for the most part, of their pretie mopsies and loving Bessies. Thus all thinges set in order, then have they their hobby horses, their dragons, and other antiques, together with their baudie pipers, and thundring drummers, to strike up the devil's daunce with all. Then march this heathen company towards the church, their pypers pyping, their drummers thundring, their stumpes dauncing, their belles jyngling, their

---

[1] *Survey of London*, p. 79. [2] *Anatomie of Abuses*, first printed, A.D. 1585.

handkerchiefes fluttering aboute their heades like madde men, their hobbie horses and other monsters skirmishing amongst the throng: and in this sorte they go to the church, though the minister be at prayer or preaching, dauncing and singing like devils incarnate, with such a confused noise that no man can heare his owne voyce. Then the foolish people they looke, they stare, they laugh, they fleere, and mount upon the formes and pewes to see these goodly pageants solemnized. Then after this, aboute the church they go againe and againe, and so fourthe into the churche yard, where they have commonly their sommer-halls, their bowers, arbours, and banquetting-houses set up, wherein they feast, banquet, and daunce all that day, and paradventure all that night too; and thus these terrestrial furies spend the sabbath day. Then, for the further innobling of this honourable lurdane, lord I should say, they have certaine papers wherein is painted some babelerie or other of imagerie worke, and these they call my Lord of Misrule's badges or cognizances. These they give to every one that will give them money to maintain them in this their heathenage devilrie, whordom, dronkennesse, pride, and whatnot. And who will not show himself buxome to them and give them money, they shall be mocked and flouted shamefully; yea, and many times carried upon a cowlstaffe, and dived over heade and eares in water, or otherwise most horribly abused. And so assotted are some, that they not only give them money, but weare their badges or cognizances in their hates or cappes openly. Another sorte of fantasticall fooles bring to these helhounds, the Lord of Misrule and his complices, some bread, some good ale, some new cheese, some old cheese, some custardes, some cracknels, some cakes, some flauns, some tartes, some creame, some meat, some one thing, and some another; but if they knewe that as often as they bring any to the maintenance of these execrable pastymes, they offer sacrifice to the Devill and Sathanas, they would refeus and withdrawe their handes, whiche God grant they maie." Hence it should seem the Lord of Misrule was sometimes president over the summer sports. The author has distinguished this pageantry from the May-games, the wakes, and the church-ales, of which, I should otherwise have thought, it might have been a component part.

*As a set-off to the extravagant condemnation of Stubbs, it may be well to state that the old English custom of the Christmas Lord of Misrule, with his twelve days of sovereignty, was maintained and supported by gentle folk of the highest position, who doubtless did their best to suppress the coarser elements. For instance, Richard Evelyn, a most worshipful squire and deputy-lieutenant of the counties of Surrey and Sussex, father of the author of the *Diary*, drew up regulations for appointing and defining the functions of this Christmas official on his Surrey estate at Wotton:—Imprimis, I give free leave to Owen Flood, my trumpeter, gentleman, to be Lord of Misrule of all good orders during the twelve days. And also I give free leave to the said Owen Flood to command all and every person or persons whatsoever, as well servants as others to be at his command whensoever he shall sound his trumpet or music, and to do him good service, as though I were present myself, at their perils. . . . I give full power and authority to his lordship to break up all locks, bolts, bars, doors and latches, and to fling up all doors out of hinges, to come at those who presume to disobey his lordship's commands.　God save the King."

*The various colleges both at Oxford and Cambridge elected a Christmas Lord, or Lord of Misrule, to preside over the sports, plays and pageants of the season.[1]

THE KING OF CHRISTMAS.—The society belonging to Lincoln's Inn had anciently an officer chosen at this season, who was honoured with the title of King of Christmas Day, because he presided in the hall upon that day.　This temporary potentate had a marshal and a steward to attend upon him.　The marshal, in the absence of the monarch, was permitted to assume his state, and upon New Year's Day he sat as king in the hall when the master of the revels, during the time of dining, supplied the marshal's place.　Upon Childermas Day they had another officer, denominated the King of the Cockneys, who also presided on the day of his appointment, and had his inferior officers to wait upon him.[2]

A KING OF CHRISTMAS AT NORWICH.—In the history of Norfolk,[3] mention is made of a pageant exhibited at Norwich upon a Shrove Tuesday, which happened in the month of March, "when one rode through the street, having his horse trapped with tyn foyle and other nyse disgysynges, crowned as King of Christmas, in token that the season should end with the twelve moneths of the year ; and afore hym went yche moneth dysgysyd as the season requiryd."

THE KING OF THE BEAN.—The dignified persons above mentioned were, I presume, upon an equal footing with the King of the Bean, whose reign commenced upon the vigil of the Epiphany, or upon the day itself.[4]　We read that, some time back, "it was a common Christmas gambol in both our universities, and continued," at the commencement of the last century, "to be usual in other places, to give the name of king or queen to that person whose extraordinary good luck it was to hit upon that part of a divided cake which was honoured above the others by having a bean in it."[5]　The reader will readily trace the vestige of this custom, though somewhat differently managed, and without the bean, in the present method of drawing, as it is called, for king and queen upon Twelfth-day.　I will not pretend to say in ancient times, for the title is by no means of recent date, that the election of this monarch, the King of the Bean, depended entirely upon the decision of fortune : the words of an old kalendar belonging to the Romish church[6] seem to favour a contrary opinion ; they are to this effect : On the fifth of January, the vigil of the Epiphany, the Kings of the Bean are created ;[7] and on the sixth the feast of

---

[1] Warton's *Hist. Eng. Poet.* ii. 378-80 ; Wood's *Athenæ,* ii. 239.　　　　[2] Dugdale's *Origines Juridiciales,* fol. 247.

[3] *Blomfield,* vol. ii. p. 3.

[4] *The Christmas Lord of Misrule, elected in November by the fellows of Merton College, Oxford, is termed in the registers *Rex Fabarum,* or *Rex Regni Fabarum.*

[5] Bourne's *Antiq. Vulg.* chap. xvii.

[6] Cited by Mr Brand, notes to Bourne, p. 205.　　　　[7] Reges Fabis creantur.

the kings shall be held, and also of the queen; and let the banqueting be continued for many days. At court, in the eighth year of Edward III., this majestic title was conferred upon one of the king's minstrels, as we find by an entry in a computus so dated, which states that sixty shillings were given by the king, upon the day of the Epiphany, to Regan the trumpeter and his associates, the court minstrels, in the name of King of the Bean.[1]

WHENCE THESE MOCK DIGNITIES WERE DERIVED.—Selden asserts,[2] and in my opinion with great justice, that all these whimsical transpositions of dignity are derived from the ancient Saturnalia, or Feasts of Saturn, when the masters waited upon their servants, who were honoured with mock titles, and permitted to assume the state and deportment of their lords. These fooleries were exceedingly popular, and continued to be practised long after the establishment of Christianity, in defiance of the threatenings and the remonstrances of the clergy, who, finding it impossible to divert the stream of vulgar prejudice, permitted their occasional exercise. The most daringly impious of such practices was the Festival of Fools, in which the most sacred rites and ceremonies of the church were turned into ridicule; but as this festival had happily very little and only short-lived hold on any part of England, it may be passed by.

*An interesting condensed account of England's Christmastide in the days of Charles I. is worth citing:

" It is now Christmas, and not a Cup of drinke must passe without a Caroll, the Beasts, Fowle, and Fish come to a generall execution, and the Corne is ground to dust for the Bakehouse and the Pastry. Cards and Dice purge many a purse, and the Youth show their agility in Shoeing of the Wild Mare.[3] Now good cheere and welcome, and God be with you and I thanke you. And against the new yeare provide for the presents. The Lord of Mis-Rule is no meane man for his time, and the ghests of the High Table must lacke no Wine. The lusty bloods must looke about them like men, and piping and dauncing puts away much melancholy. Stolen Venison is sweet, and a fat Coney is worth money. Pitfalles are now set for small Birdes, and a Woodcocke hangs himselfe in a gynne. A good fire heats all the house, and a full Almesbasket makes the Beggars Prayers. The Masters and the Mummers make the merry sport; but if they lose their money, their Drumme goes dead. Swearers and Swaggerers are sent away to the Alehouse, and unruly Wenches goe in danger of Judgment. Musicians now make their Instruments speake out, and a good song is worth the hearing. In summe, it is a holy time, a duty in Christians, for the remembrance of Christ, and custome among friends, for the maintenance of good fellowship. In briefe, I thus conclude of it, I hold it (Christmas) a memory of

---

[1] In nomine Regis de Fabâ. MS. Cott. Nero, C. viii.   [2] Table Talk, London, 1689, title Christmas.

[3] *" From scattered notices in several old works, I collect that *Shoeing the Wild Mare* was a diversion among our ancestors, more particularly intended for the young, and that the Wild Mare was simply a youth so called, who was allowed a certain start, and who was pursued by his companions with the object of being shoed, if he did not succeed in outstripping them."—Hazlitt's edit. of Brand's *Popular Antiquities*, ii. 332-3.

the Heaven's Love, and the world's peace, the myrth of the honest, and the meeting of the friendly. Farewell."[1]

*THE BOY-BISHOP.—The election and the investment of the Boy-Bishop, a general English custom, was probably derived from the festival of fools. It does not appear at what period this curious ceremony was first established, but apparently it was ancient, at least we can trace it back to the thirteenth century. It had been long established at Salisbury in 1319, when Bishop Roger de Mortival specially regulated its observance.

*On the eve of St Nicholas's Day (December 5th), the most deserving chorister or scholar was appointed the bishop of boys until the end of the day of the Holy Innocents or Childermas (December 28th). The custom seems to have prevailed in all our cathedral churches, in the larger minster and monastic churches to which schools were attached, and in such purely scholastic foundations as those of the colleges of Winchester and Eton. Dean Colet, in his foundation of St Paul's School, desired to perpetuate this custom, as a stimulus to Christian ambition, and expressly orders that the scholars "shall, every Childermas, that is, Innocents' Day, come to Paule's churche, and hear the Childe Byshop's sermon, and after be at hygh masse, and each of them offer a penny to the childe byshop; and with them the maisters and surveyors of the schole."[2] Full episcopal vestments were provided for the Boy-Bishop, and copes for his companions; they occur in a great variety of inventories. At Salisbury, the Boy-Bishop and his fellows completely reversed the usual order of procession. The dean's residentiaries went first, followed by the chaplains, the bishops, and petty prebendaries. The choristers and their bishop came last; they sat in the upper stalls, the residentiaries furnished the incense and book, and the petties were the taper-bearers. The Boy-Bishop gave the benediction. Full Rubrical directions are given in the Sarum *Processional* for the Boy-Bishop during the few days that he held office. There is not the slightest touch of farce or ribaldry.[3] After divine service, the Boy-Bishop and his associates went about to different parts of the town, and visited the religious houses, collecting money. These ceremonies and processions were formally abrogated by proclamation from the king and council, in 1542, the thirty-third year of Henry VIII. The concluding clause of the ordinance runs thus: "Whereas heretofore dyvers and many superstitious and chyldysh observances have been used, and yet to this day are observed and kept in many and sundry places of this realm upon St Nicholas, St Catherines, St Clements, and Holy Innocents, and such like holydaies; children be strangelie decked and apparayled to counterfeit priests, bishops, and women, and so ledde with songs and dances from house to house, blessing the people, and gathering of money; and boyes do singe masse, and preache in the pulpits, with such other unfittinge and inconvenient usages, which tend rather to derysyon than enie true glorie to God, or honor of his

---

[1] Nicholas' *Fantasies*, 1626.   [2] Knight's *Life of Colet*, p. 362.
[3] *Wordsworth's *Salisbury Processional Ceremonies*, 1901.

sayntes."[1] This idle pageantry was revived by his daughter Mary; and in the second year of her reign an edict, dated November 13, 1554, was issued from the Bishop of London to the clergy of his diocese, to have a Boy-Bishop in procession.[2] The year following, "the child bishop, of Paules church, with his company," were admitted into the queen's privy chamber, where he sang before her on Saint Nicholas' Day and upon Holy Innocents' Day.[3] Again the next year, says Strype, "on Saint Nicholas-even, Saint Nicholas, that is, a boy habited like a bishop in pontificalibus,[4] went abroad in most parts of London, singing after the old fashion; and was received with many ignorant but well-disposed people into their houses, and had as much good cheer as ever was wont to be had before."

*On the death of Mary this ancient custom was finally abandoned. The expression in Henry VIII.'s proclamation and elsewhere as to the Boy-Bishop "singing mass" must not be taken too literally; for though he aped much of the offices, the canon of the mass was certainly not sung by him, but only certain parts, such as the prose and offertory at Rouen.

*The elaborate account rolls of the great abbey of Durham for the fourteenth, fifteenth, and sixteenth centuries show that the institution of Boy-Bishop was regularly observed there, year by year, with but few exceptions. It is stated in the hostillar's roll of 1405 that there was no Boy-Bishop that year because of the wars; the insurrection of the Percys had not then come to a close. There was an almery school at Durham in connection with the Infirmary, where the boys were daily fed and taught. The Boy-Bishop seems to have been chosen from these children, and is usually described in the accounts as *Episcopus Elemosinariæ*. He received gratuities from almost all the officers of the abbey, who entered the amount on their different rolls. These sums varied from 20d. to 5s.[5]

*Richard Berde, doctor of laws, by will of May 2nd, 1501, left to the abbey church of the Austin Canons of St James, Northampton, his "mousterdevile hoode, with the lynyng of grene silk, for the cross-bearer on Seynt Nicholas-night." Doubtless the doctor, who had long had a chamber within the precincts, had often in his lifetime lent his parti-coloured hood for the festival of the monastery school.[6]

*PLOUGH MONDAY.—There were three special seasons for the performance of what is termed English folk-drama, and traces of all three survive. They are the Christmas Mumming play, the Plough Monday play, and the Easter or Pace-Egg play. In all three the sword dance was usually introduced. The character of St George, and various forms of his legend, formed part of the Christmas and Easter play, but not of the intermediate one. Plough Monday, the Monday after Twelfth Day, was formerly kept throughout most parts of agricultural England by the ploughmen yoking themselves together and draw-

[1] MS. *Cott. Tiberius*, B. i.
[2] Strype's *Eccl. Mem.* vol. iii. chap. xxxix. p. 310.
[3] *Ibid.* chap. xxxv. p. 202.
[4] *Ibid.* chap. xxxix. p. 310.
[5] *Durham Account Rolls* (Surtees Society), 3 vols., 1898-1900.
[6] Wills of Northampton Probate Court.

S

ing about a plough, accompanied by mummers and music. Their original object was to gather supplies in kind or money for the support of the Plough or Labourers' light in the parish church, and doubtless to use some part of the gathering for their own festivity or for a general Plough-Ale. But after the Reformation, when these special lights and gilds were suppressed, the tribute collected was spent entirely upon themselves. When the ploughboys came to any house of substance in the parish or district, the sword dance was executed, when one of the combatants was usually killed, and revived by a "doctor." Beelzebub or a fool, and one dressed extravagantly as a woman, and usually termed "Bessy," were two other of the characters. At the end of the mumming the money-box was rattled and the music played, and if neither refreshment nor money was forthcoming, the ground in front of the house, whether grass-plot or gravel walk, was roughly ploughed up, and the mummers departed. This last feature used to be vigorously carried out as late as the "forties" in the Peak of Derbyshire.[1] Plough Monday was observed in Huntingdonshire in 1860, where the mummers were termed "Plough-Witchers."[2] A Plough Monday play was acted at Wiverton Hall, Nottinghamshire, in 1893; no plough was brought round, but the mummers' clothes were ornamented with paper ploughs in red and black.[3]

*SHROVE TUESDAY.—Cock-fighting, and throwing at cocks on Shrove Tuesday, have been already mentioned, with other trifling sports which are comprised under their appropriate heads, and need not to be repeated. The day before Lent began used to be a universal holiday given up to a variety of sports.[4]

*EASTER GAMES.—Easter, as has been already stated, was the usual season for an Easter play or mumming, which is still sometimes called the Pace-Egg play, a corruption of *pasche* or passover. The egg was always held to be an apt symbol of the Resurrection, hence Easter eggs and various customs that yet linger connected with them. This Easter play is still occasionally printed,[5] and occasionally acted by village players. The characters are much the same as they probably were in pre-Reformation days, namely, St George, Fool, Slasher, Doctor, Prince of Paradine, King of Egypt, Hector, Beelzebub, and Devil-Doubt. Occasionally the King of Egypt's daughter is introduced in character and not only mentioned. The play doubtless had a crusading origin.

HOCK-TIDE.—The popular holidays of Hock-tide, mentioned by Matthew Paris and other early writers, were kept on the Monday and Tuesday following the second Sunday after Easter Day; and distinguished, according to John Rouse, the Warwickshire historian of the fifteenth century, by various sportive

---

[1] I have a vivid recollection of seeing the Plough Monday mummers with their plough, when a small boy, at Parwich, near Ashborne, in 1847-1848, and being taken in the latter year to see the havoc made by the plough in the small front garden of a well-to-do but niggardly resident.—J. C. C.

[2] *Notes and Queries*, Ser. II. ix. 381.

[3] Mr Ordish on the "English Folk Drama," *Folk Lore Quarterly*, vol. iv. pp. 149-174.

[4] Can it be any survival of Shrove Tuesday cock-throwing that makes this day at the present time (1902), in several English towns, the season for children to begin playing with shuttlecocks in the streets.

[5] I bought copies in Sheffield market-place in 1869 and again in 1878.—J. C. C.

pastimes, in which the towns-people, divided into parties, were accustomed to draw each other with ropes. Spelman is more definite, and tells us, "they consisted in the men and women binding each other, and especially the women the men," and hence it was called Binding-Tuesday.[1] Cowel informs us that it was customary in several manors in Hampshire for "the men to hock the women on the Monday, and the women the men upon the Tuesday; that is, on that day the women in merriment stop the ways with ropes and pull the passengers to them, desiring something to be laid out in pious uses in order to obtain their freedom."[2] Such are the general outlines of this singular institution, and the pens of several able writers have been employed in attempting to investigate its origin.[3] Some think it was held in commemoration of the massacre of the Danes, in the reign of Ethelred the Unready, on Saint Brice's Day;[4] others, that it was in remembrance of the death of Hardicanute, which happened on Tuesday the 8th of June, 1041, by which event the English were delivered from the intolerant government of the Danes: and this opinion appears to be most probable. The binding part of the ceremony might naturally refer to the abject state of slavery in which the wretched Saxons were held by their imperious lords; and the donations for "pious uses," may be considered as tacit acknowledgments of gratitude to heaven for freeing the nation from its bondage. In the churchwarden's accounts for the parish of Lambeth for the years 1515 and 1516, are several entries of hock monies received from the men and the women for the church service. And here we may observe, that the contributions collected by the fair sex exceeded those made by the men.[5]

Hock-day was generally observed as lately as the sixteenth century. We learn from Spelman that it was not totally discontinued in his time. Dr Plott, who makes Monday the principal day, has noticed some vestiges of it at the distance of fifty years, but now it is totally abolished.

*The derivation of the word Hock is still a puzzle to etymologists.[6] The roughly humorous games of this season, when the men extorted payment from the women on the Monday, and the women from the men on the Tuesday, are peculiar to England, whatever may be their historic origin, and were certainly in general use in the fourteenth century, and probably much earlier. The ransom money in olden times was usually handed over to the churchwardens. The large majority of extant parish accounts of pre-Reformation date have entries relative to Hock-tide payments.

MAY-GAMES.—The celebration of the May-games, at which we have only glanced in a former part of the work,[7] will require some enlargement in this chapter. "On the calends or first of May," says Bourne,[8] "commonly called May-day, the juvenile part of both sexes were wont to rise a little after midnight

---

[1] Gloss. under the title Hock-day.   [2] Hist. Hampshire.

[3] See a Memoir by the Rev. Mr Jenne, *Archæologia*, vol. vii. p. 244.

[4] A.D. 1002. But the time of the year does not agree. St Brice's Day is the 13th of November.

[5] Memoir, *ut supra*.   [6] See Oxford Dictionary, *sub. voc.*

[7] Page 223, and Introduction.   [8] *Antiq. Vulgares*, chap. 25.

and walk to some neighbouring wood, accompanied with music and blowing of horns, where they break down branches from the trees, and adorn them with nosegays and crowns of flowers; when this is done, they return with their booty homewards about the rising of the sun, and make their doors and windows to triumph with their flowery spoils; and the after part of the day is chiefly spent in dancing round a tall pole, which is called a May-pole; and being placed in a convenient part of the village, stands there, as it were, consecrated to the Goddess of Flowers, without the least violation being offered to it in the whole circle of the year."

This custom, no doubt, is a relic of one more ancient, practised by the Heathens, who observed the last four days in April, and the first of May, in honour of the goddess Flora. An old Romish calendar, cited by Mr Brand, says, on the 30th of April, the boys go out to seek May-trees, "Maii arbores a pueris exquirunter." Some consider the May-pole as a relic of Druidism; but I cannot find any solid foundation for such an opinion.

It should be observed, that the May-games were not always celebrated upon the first day of the month; and to this we may add the following extract from Stow: "In the month of May the citizens of London of all estates, generally in every parish, and in some instances two or three parishes joining together, had their several mayings, and did fetch their may-poles with divers warlike shows; with good archers, morrice-dancers, and other devices for pastime, all day long; and towards evening they had stage-plays and bonfires in the streets. These great mayings and May-games were made by the governors and masters of the city, together with the triumphant setting up of the great shaft or principal May-pole in Cornhill before the parish church of Saint Andrew,"[1] which was thence called Saint Andrew Undershaft.

No doubt the May-games are of long standing, though the time of their institution cannot be traced. Mention is made of the May-pole at Cornhill, in a poem called the "Chaunce of the Dice," attributed to Chaucer. In the time of Stow, who died in 1605, they were not conducted with so great splendour as they had been formerly, owing to a dangerous riot which took place upon May-day, 1517, in the ninth year of Henry VIII., on which occasion several foreigners were slain, and two of the ringleaders of the disturbance were hanged.

Stow has passed unnoticed the manner in which the May-poles were usually decorated; this deficiency I shall supply from Philip Stubs, a contemporary writer, one who saw these pastimes in a very different point of view, and some may think his invectives are more severe than just; however, I am afraid the conclusion of them, though perhaps much exaggerated, is not altogether without foundation. He writes thus:[2] "Against Maie-day, Whitsunday, or some other time of the year, every parish, towne, or village, assemble themselves, both men, women, and children; and either all together, or dividing themselves into companies, they goe some to the woods and groves, some to the hills and mountaines,

---

[1] *Survey of London*, p. 80.   [2] In his *Anatomie of Abuses*, printed in 1595.

some to one place, some to another, where they spend all the night in pleasant pastimes, and in the morning they return, bringing with them birche boughes and branches of trees to deck their assemblies withal. But their chiefest jewel they bring from thence is the Maie-pole, which they bring home with great veneration, as thus—they have twentie or fourtie yoake of oxen, every oxe having a sweete nosegaie of flowers tied to the tip of his hornes, and these oxen drawe home the May-poale, their stinking idol rather, which they covered all over with flowers and hearbes, bound round with strings from the top to the bottome, and sometimes it was painted with variable colours, having two or three hundred men, women, and children following it with great devotion. And thus equipped it was reared with handkerchiefes and flagges streaming on the top, they strawe the ground round about it, they bind green boughs about it, they set up summer halles, bowers, and arbours hard by it, and then fall they to banquetting and feasting, to leaping and dauncing about it, as the heathen people did at the dedication of their idolls. I have heard it crediblie reported, by men of great gravity, credite, and reputation, that of fourtie, threescore, or an hundred maides going to the wood, there have scarcely the third part of them returned home againe as they went."

In the churchwarden's account for the parish of St Helen's in Abingdon, Berks, dated 1566, the ninth of Elizabeth, is the following article : "Payde for setting up Robin Hoode's bower, eighteenpence ;" that is, a bower for the reception of the fictitious Robin Hood and his company, belonging to the May-day pageant.[1]

THE LORD AND LADY OF THE MAY.—It seems to have been the constant custom, at the celebration of the May-games, to elect a Lord and Lady of the May, who probably presided over the sports. On the thirtieth of May, 1557, in the fourth year of Queen Mary, "was a goodly May-game in Fenchurch Street, with drums, and guns, and pikes ; and with the nine worthies who rode, and each of them made his speech, there was also a morrice dance, and an elephant and castle, and the Lord and Lady of the May appearing to make up the show."[2] We also read that the Lord of the May, and no doubt his Lady also, was decorated with scarfs, ribbands, and other fineries. Hence, in the comedy called *The Knight of the Burning Pestle*, written by Beaumont and Fletcher in 1611, a citizen, addressing himself to the other actors, says, "Let Ralph come out on May-day in the morning, and speak upon a conduit, with all his scarfs about him, and his feathers, and his rings, and his knacks, as Lord of the May." His request is complied with, and Ralph appears upon the stage in the assumed character, where he makes his speech, beginning in this manner :

With gilded staff and crossed scarf the May Lord here I stand.

The citizen is supposed to be a spectator, and Ralph is his apprentice, but permitted by him to play in the piece.

---

[1] *Archæologia*, vol. i. cap. 4, p. 11.
[2] Strype's *Eccles. Mem.* vol. iii. cap. 49, p. 377.

At the commencement of the sixteenth century, or perhaps still earlier, the ancient stories of Robin Hood and his frolicsome companions seem to have been new-modelled, and divided into separate ballads, which much increased their popularity; for this reason it was customary to personify this famous outlaw, with several of his most noted associates, and add them to the pageantry of the May-games. He presided as Lord of the May; and a female, or rather, perhaps, a man habited like a female, called the Maid Marian, his faithful mistress, was the Lady of the May. His companions were distinguished by the title of "Robin Hood's Men," and were also equipped in appropriate dresses; their coats, hoods, and hose were generally green. Henry VIII., in the first year of his reign, one morning, by way of pastime, came suddenly into the chamber where the queen and her ladies were sitting. He was attended by twelve noblemen, all apparelled in short coats of Kentish kendal, with hoods and hosen of the same; each of them had his bow, with arrows, and a sword, and a buckler, "like outlawes, or Robyn Hode's men." The queen, it seems, at first was somewhat afrighted by their appearance, of which she was not the least apprised. This gay troop performed several dances, and then departed.[1]

Bishop Latimer, in a sermon which he preached before king Edward VI., relates the following anecdote, which proves the great popularity of the May pageants. "Coming," says he, "to a certain town on a holiday to preach, I found the church door fast locked. I taryed there half an houre and more, and at last the key was found, and one of the parish comes to me and sayes, Syr, this is a busy day with us, we cannot hear you; it is Robin Hoode's day; the parish are gone abroad to gather for Robin Hood; I pray you let[2] them not. I was fayne, therefore, to give place to Robin Hood. I thought my rochet would have been regarded; but it would not serve, it was faine to give place to Robin Hoode's men."[3] In Garrick's Collection of Old Plays[4] is one entitled "A new Playe of Robyn Hoode, for to be played in the May-games, very pleasaunte and full of Pastyme," printed at London by William Copland, black letter, without date. This playe consists of short dialogues between Robyn Hode, Lytell John, Fryer Tucke, a potter's boy, and the potter. Robyn fights with the friar, who afterwards becomes his chaplain; he also breaks the boy's pots, and commits several other absurdities. The language of the piece is somewhat low, and full of ribaldry.[5]

GRAND MAY-GAME AT GREENWICH.—It has been observed that the May-games were not confined to the first day of the month, neither were they always concluded in one day; on the contrary I have now before me a manuscript,[6] written apparently in the reign of Henry VII., wherein a number of gentlemen, professing themselves to be the servants of the Lady May, promise to be in the

---

[1] Hall, in Vit. Hen. VIII. fol. vi.
[2] Hinder or prevent.
[3] Latimer's Sermons, printed 1589.
[4] K. vol. x.
[5] *On the whole subject of Robin Hood Plays and Ballads, see Child's *Ballads*, iii. pp. 39-333.
[6] Harl. Lib. 69

royal park at Greenwich, day after day, from two o'clock in the afternoon till five, in order to perform the various sports and exercises specified in the agreement; that is to say,

On the 14th day of May they engage to meet at a place appointed by the king, armed with the "harneis[1] thereunto accustomed, to kepe the fielde, and to run with every commer eight courses." Four additional courses were to be granted to any one who desired it, if the time would permit, or the queen was pleased to give them leave; agreeable to the ancient custom by which the ladies presided as arbitrators at the justs.

On the 15th the archers took the field to shoot at "the standard with flight arrows."

On the 16th they held a tournament with "swords rebated to strike with every commer eight strokes," according to the accustomed usage.

On the 18th, for I suppose Sunday intervened, they were to be ready to "wrestle with all commers all manner of ways," according to their pleasure.

On the 19th they were to enter the field, to fight on foot at the barriers, with spears in their hands and swords rebated by their sides, and with spear and sword to defend their barriers: there were to be eight strokes with the spear, two of them "with the foyne," or short thrust, and eight strokes with the sword; "every man to take his best advantage with gript or otherwise."

On the 20th they were to give additional proof of their strength by casting "the barre on foote, and with the arme, bothe heavit and hight." I do not clearly understand this passage, but suppose it means by lifting and casting aloft.

On the 21st they recommenced the exercises, which were to be continued daily, Sundays excepted, through the remaining part of May, and a fortnight in the month of June.

ROYAL MAY-GAME AT SHOOTER'S HILL. — Henry VIII., when young, delighted much in pageantry, and the early part of his reign abounded with gaudy shows; most of them were his own devising, and others contrived for his amusement. Among the latter we may reckon a May-game at Shooter's Hill, which was exhibited by the officers of his guards; they in a body, amounting to two hundred, all of them clothed in green, and headed by their captain, who personated Robin Hood, met the King one morning as he was riding to take the air, accompanied by the queen and a large suite of the nobility of both sexes. The fictitious foresters first amused them with a double discharge of their arrows; and then, their chief approaching the king, invited him to see the manner in which he and his companions lived. The king complied with the request, and the archers, blowing their horns, conducted him and his train into the wood under the hill, where an arbour was made with green boughs, having a hall, a great chamber, and an inner chamber, and the whole was covered with flowers and sweet herbs. When the company had entered the arbour, Robin Hood

---

[1] I suppose the author means tilting armour, for the purpose of justing, here called running of courses.

excused the want of more abundant refreshment, saying to the king, "Sir, we outlaws usually breakfast upon venison, and have no other food to offer you." The king and queen then sat down, and were served with venison and wine; and after the entertainment, with which it seems they were well pleased, they departed, and on their return were met by two ladies riding in a rich open chariot, drawn by five horses. Every horse, according to Hollingshed, had his name upon his head, and upon every horse sat a lady, with her name written. On the first horse, called Lawde, sat Humidity; on the second, named Memeon, sat Lady Vert, or green; on the third, called Pheton, sat Lady Vegitive; on the fourth, called Rimphon, sat Lady Pleasaunce; on the fifth, called Lampace, sat Sweet Odour.[1] Both of the ladies in the chariot were splendidly apparelled; one of them personified the Lady May, and the other Lady Flora, "who," we are told, "saluted the king with divers goodly songs, and so brought him to Greenwich."

We may here just observe that the May-games had attracted the notice of the nobility long before the time of Henry; and agreeable to the custom of the times, no doubt, was the following curious passage in the old romance called *The Death of Arthur*: "Now it befell in the moneth of lusty May, that queene Guenever called unto her the knyghtes of the round table, and gave them warning that, early in the morning, she should ride on maying into the woods and fields beside Westminster." The knights were all of them to be clothed in green, to be well horsed, and every one of them to have a lady behind him, followed by an esquire and two yeomen, etc.[2]

*MAY-POLES.—By an ordinance of the Long Parliament in April, 1644, all May-poles were to be taken down as "a heathenish vanity." The constables and churchwardens were to be fined 5s. weekly until the poles were removed. After the Restoration their use naturally revived. Hall wrote indignantly on the subject, in the bitterest Puritan vein, in a treatise that he called *Funebria Flora, The Downfall of May Games*, published in 1660. At the end he versifies, in "A May Pooles Speech to a Traveller," as follows :—

> "I have a mighty retinue
> The scum of all the raskal crew
> Of fidlers, pedlers, jayle-scapt slaves,
> Of tinkers, turncoats, tospot knaves,
> Of theeves and scape-thrifts many a one,
> With bouncing Besse, and jolly Jone,
> With idle boyes, and journeyman,
> And vagrants that their country run ;
> Yea, hobby-horse doth hither prance,
> Maid Marrian and the morrice dance,
> My summons fetcheth, far and near,
> All that can swagger, roar, and swear,
> All that can dance, and drab, and drink,
> They run to me as to a sink.
> These me for their commander take,
> And I do them my blackguard make.

---

[1] Hall, in Vit. Hen. VIII. an 2, p. vi.   [2] See an account of this book in the Introduction.

The honour of the Sabbath day
My dancing greens have ta'en away,
Let preachers prate till they grow wood,
Where I am they can do no good."

The author states that "most of these May-poles are stollen, yet they give out that the poles are given them." In another place he says:—"If Moses were angry when he saw the people dancing about a golden calf, well may we be angry to see people dancing the morrice about a post in honour of a whore, as you shall see anon."

MAY MILK-MAIDS.—"It is at this time," that is, in May, says the author of one of the papers in the *Spectator*,[1] "we see the brisk young wenches, in the country parishes, dancing round the May-pole. It is likewise on the first day of this month that we see the ruddy milk-maid exerting herself in a most sprightly manner under a pyramid of silver tankards, and like the virgin Tarpeia, oppressed by the costly ornaments which her benefactors lay upon her. These decorations of silver cups, tankards, and salvers, were borrowed for the purpose, and hung round the milk-pails, with the addition of flowers and ribbands, which the maidens carried upon their heads when they went to the houses of their customers, and danced in order to obtain a small gratuity from each of them. In a set of prints called Tempest's *Cryes of London*, there is one called the merry milk-maid's, whose proper name was Kate Smith. She is dancing with the milk-pail, decorated as above mentioned, upon her head.[2] Of late years the plate, with the other decorations, were placed in a pyramidical form, and carried by two chairmen upon a wooden horse. The maidens walked before it, and performed the dance without any incumbrance. I really cannot discover what analogy the silver tankards and salvers can have to the business of the milk-maids. I have seen them act with much more propriety upon this occasion, when in place of these superfluous ornaments they substituted a cow. The animal had her horns gilt, and was nearly covered with ribbands of various colours, formed into bows and roses, and interspersed with green oaken leaves and bunches of flowers.

MAY FESTIVAL OF THE CHIMNEY-SWEEPERS. — The chimney-sweepers of London have also singled out the first of May for their festival; at which time they parade the streets in companies, disguised in various manners. Their dresses are usually decorated with gilt paper, and other mock fineries; they have their shovels and brushes in their hands, which they rattle one upon the other; and to this rough music they jump about in imitation of dancing. Some of the larger companies have a fiddler with them, and a Jack in the Green, as well as a Lord and Lady of the May, who follow the minstrel with great stateliness, and dance as occasion requires. The Jack in the green is a piece of pageantry consisting of a hollow frame of wood or wicker-work, made in the

---

[1] Vol. v. No. 365, first published A.D. 1712.   [2] See Granger's *Biog. Hist.* vol. iv. p. 354.

form of a sugar-loaf, but open at the bottom, and sufficiently large and high to receive a man. The frame is covered with green leaves and bunches of flowers interwoven with each other, so that the man within may be completely concealed, who dances with his companions, and the populace are mightily pleased with the oddity of the moving pyramid.

WHITSUN GAMES.—The Whitsuntide holidays were celebrated by various pastimes commonly practised upon other festivals ; but the Monday after the Whitsun week, at Kidlington in Oxfordshire, a fat lamb was provided, and the maidens of the town, having their thumbs tied behind them, were permitted to run after it, and she who with her mouth took hold of the lamb was declared the Lady of the Lamb, which, being killed and cleaned, but with the skin hanging upon it, was carried on a long pole before the lady and her companions to the green, attended with music, and a morisco dance of men, and another of women. The rest of the day was spent in mirth and merry glee. Next day the lamb, partly baked, partly boiled, and partly roasted, was served up for the lady's feast, where she sat, "majestically at the upper end of the table, and her companions with her," the music playing during the repast, which, being finished, the solemnity ended."[1]

*LAMB-ALE.—Mr G. A. Rowell, in 1886, gave the following interesting and corrected account of this lamb-ale, which was held annually at Kirtlington (not Kidlington), a village about nine miles north of Oxford :[1]

"The name of Kidlington is given for Kirtlington, the two villages being about four miles apart : the story of the maidens catching the lamb with their teeth is doubtless a mere made up tale, and I can only account for its having passed so long without contradiction from its apparent absurdity rendering it unnecessary for those of the neighbourhood. However, a description of the Kirtlington lamb-ale, and how it was conducted, may be interesting and set this question in a proper light. This I hope to do fairly, as my remembrance will go back over seventy years ; and I am kindly assisted by a native, and long resident of the village, an observer, and well qualified to aid in the task.

The lamb-ale was held in a large barn, with a grass field contiguous for dancing, etc. ; this was fitted up with great pains as a refreshment room for company (generally numerous) and was called 'My Lord's Hall.' The lord and lady, being the ruling persons, attending with their mace-bearers, or pages, and other officers. All were gaily and suitably dressed, with a preponderance of light blue and pink, the colours of the Dashwood family, the lady appearing in white only, with light blue or pink ribands on alternate days.

The lamb-ale began on Trinity Monday, when—and on each day at 11 A.M.—the lady was brought in state from her home, and at 9 P.M. was in like manner conducted home again ; the sports were continued during the week, but Monday, Tuesday, and Saturday were the especial days.

The refreshments, as served, were not charged for ; but a plate was after-

[1] Blount's *Ancient Tenures*, p. 49. [2] *Folk Lore Society Journal* (1886), vol. iv. pp. 107-9.

wards handed round for each to give his donation. This seems strikingly to accord with Aubrey's account of the Whitsun-ales of his grandfather's time.

The Morisco dance was not only a principal feature in the lamb-ale, but one for which Kirtlington was noted. No expense was spared in getting up as described in the paper on that subject; and with the liveries of the whitest and ribands of the best, the display of the Dashwood colours was the pride of the parish, and in my early times it was generally understood that the farmers' sons did not decline joining the dancers, but rather prided themselves on being selected as one of them. The simple tabor and pipe was their only music, but by degrees other instruments came into use in the private halls, and dancing on the green, and besides these the surroundings of stalls made up a sort of fair.

On opening the lamb-ale a procession was formed to take the lamb around the town and to the principal houses. It was carried on a man's shoulders or rather on the back of his neck with two legs on each side of it; the lamb being decorated with blue or pink ribands in accordance with the lady's colour of the day.

The great house was first visited, when after a few Morisco dances (as generally supposed) two guineas were given, and thus within the week every farm or other house of importance within the parish was visited. During the week there were various amusements; many hundreds visited the place from all sides, with a very general display of generosity and good will amongst all.

From about sixty or seventy years ago, the lamb used in the lamb-ale has been borrowed and returned; but previous to that time—for how long I cannot say—the lamb was slaughtered within the week, made into pies and distributed —but in what way is uncertain. It would be interesting if some light could be thrown on the lamb-ale. There is much which seems to connect it with the Whitsun-ale of early times; but, from the differences in the days and the possession of the lamb, there seems to be a wide distinction between the festivals.

As the lamb-ale appears to be unique, at least in this part of the country, an examination of the parish-registers might be interesting and throw some light on the subject."

MIDSUMMER EVE FESTIVAL.—On the Vigil of St John the Baptist, commonly called Midsummer Eve, it was usual in most country places, and also in towns and cities, for the inhabitants, both old and young, and of both sexes, to meet together, and make merry by the side of a large fire made in the middle of the street, or in some open and convenient place, over which the young men frequently leaped by way of frolic, and also exercised themselves with various sports and pastimes, more especially with running, wrestling, and dancing. These diversions they continued till midnight, and sometimes till cock-crowing;[1] several of the superstitious ceremonies practised upon this occasion are contained in the following verses, as they are translated by Barnabe Googe from the

[1] Bourne's *Antiq.* vol. ix. chap. 27.

fourth book of *The Popish Kingdome*, written in Latin by Tho. Neogeorgus: the translation was dedicated to queen Elizabeth, and appeared in 1570.

> " Then doth the joyfull feast of John the Baptist take his turne,
> When bonfiers great, with loftie flame, in every towne doe burne:
> And yong men round about with maides doe daunce in every streete,
> With garlands wrought of Mother-wort, or else with Vervaine sweete
> And many other flowres faire, with Violets in their handes
> Whereas they all do fondly thinke, that whosoever stands,
> And thorow the flowres beholds the flame, his eyes shall feele no paine.
> When thus till night they daunced have, they through the fire amaine
> With striving mindes doe run, and all their hearbes they cast therin,
> And then, with wordes devout and prayers, they solemnely begin,
> Desiring God that all their illes may there confounded bee,
> Whereby they thinke through all that yeare, from Agues to be free."

At London, in addition to the bonfires, "on the eve of this saint, as well as upon that of Saint Peter and Saint Paul, every man's door was shaded with green birch, long fennel, Saint John's wort, orpin, white lilies, and the like, ornamented with garlands of beautiful flowers. They, the citizens, had also lamps of glass with oil burning in them all night; and some of them hung out branches of iron, curiously wrought, containing hundreds of lamps lighted at once, which made a very splendid appearance." This information we receive from Stow, who tells us that, in his time, New Fish Street and Thames Street were peculiarly brilliant upon these occasions.

SUPPOSED ORIGIN OF THE MIDSUMMER VIGIL.—The reasons assigned for making bonfires upon the vigil of St John the Baptist in particular are various, for many writers have attempted the investigation of their origin; but unfortunately all their arguments, owing to the want of proper information, are merely hypothetical, and of course cannot be much depended upon. Those who suppose these fires to be a relic of some ancient heathenish superstition engrafted upon the variegated stock of ceremonies belonging to the Romish church, are not, in my opinion, far distant from the truth. The looking through the flowers at the fire, the casting of them finally into it, and the invocation to the Deity, with the effects supposed to be produced by those ceremonies, as mentioned in the preceding poem, are circumstances that seem to strengthen such a conclusion.

According to some of the pious writers of antiquity, they made large fires, which might be seen at a great distance, upon the vigil of this saint, in token that he was said in holy writ to be "a shining light." Others, agreeing with this, add also, these fires were made to drive away the dragons and evil spirits hovering in the air; and one of them gravely says, in some countries they burned bones, which was called a bone-fire; for "the dragons hattyd nothyng mor than the styncke of brenyng bonys." This, says another, habent ex gentilibus, they have from the heathens. The author last cited laments the abuses committed upon these occasions. "This vigil," says he, "ought to be held with cheerfulness and piety, but not with such merriment as is shewn by the profane lovers of this world, who make great fires in the streets, and indulge themselves with filthy and unlawful games, to which they add glotony and drunkenness, and the commission of many other shameful indecencies."[1]

SETTING OF THE MIDSUMMER WATCH.—In former times it was customary in London, and in other great cities, to set the Midsummer watch upon the eve of St John the Baptist; and this was usually performed with great pomp and pageantry.[2] The following short extract from the faithful historian, John Stow, will be sufficient to show the childishness as well as the expensiveness of this idle spectacle. The institution, he assures us, had been appointed, "time out of mind;" and upon this occasion the standing watches "in bright harness." There was also a marching watch, that passed through all the principal streets. In order to furnish this watch with lights, there were appointed seven hundred cressets; the charge for every cresset was two shillings and fourpence; every cresset required two men, the one to bear it, and the other to carry a bag with light to serve it. The cresset was a large lanthorn fixed at the end of a long pole, and carried upon a man's shoulder. The cressets were found partly by the different companies, and partly by the city chamber. Every one of the cresset-bearers was paid for his trouble; he had also given to him, that evening, a strawen hat and a painted badge, besides the donation of his breakfast next morning. The marching watch consisted of two thousand men, most of them being old soldiers of every denomination. They appeared in appropriate habits, with their arms in their hands, and many of them, especially the musicians and the standard-bearers, rode upon great horses. There were also divers pageants and morris-dancers with the constables, one half of which, to the amount of one hundred and twenty, went out on the eve of Saint John, and the other half on the eve of Saint Peter. The constables were dressed in "bright harnesse, some over gilt, and every one had a joinet of scarlet thereupon, and a chain of gold; his henchman following him, and his minstrels before him, and his cresset-light at his side. The mayor himself came after him, well mounted, with his sword-bearer before him, in fair armour on horseback, preceded by the waits, or city minstrels, and the mayor's officers in liveries of worsted, or say jackets party-coloured. The mayor was surrounded by his footmen and torch-bearers, and followed by two henchmen on large horses. The sheriffs' watches came one after the other in like order, but not so numerous; for the mayor had, besides his giant, three pageants; whereas the sheriffs had only two besides their giants, each with their morris-dance and one henchman: their officers were clothed in jackets of worsted, or say party-coloured, but differing from those belonging to the mayor, and from each other: they had also a great number of harnessed men."[3] This old custom of setting the watch in London was maintained until the year 1539, in the 31st year of Henry VIII. when it was discontinued on

[1] MSS. Harl. 2354 and 2391.
[2] The midsummer pageants at Chester are fully described in the Introduction.
[3] *Survey of London*, pp. 84, 85.

account of the expense, and revived in the year 1548, the 2d of Edward VI. and soon after that time it was totally abolished.

On Midsummer eve it was customary annually at Burford, in Oxfordshire, to carry a dragon up and down the town, with mirth and rejoicing; to which they also added the picture [1] of a giant. Dr Plott tells us, this pageantry was continued in his memory, and says it was established, at least the dragon part of the show, in memory of a famous victory obtained near that place, about 750, by Cuthred, king of the west Saxons, over Ethebald, king of Mercia, who lost his standard, surmounted by a golden dragon,[2] in the action.

PROCESSIONS ON ST CLEMENT'S AND ST CATHERINE'S DAYS.—The Anniversary of Saint Clement, and that of Saint Catherine, the first upon the 23rd, and the second upon the 25th, of November, were formerly particularised by religious processions which had been disused after the Reformation, but again established by Queen Mary. In the year she ascended the throne, according to Strype, on the evening of Saint Catherine's Day, her procession was celebrated at London with five hundred great lights, which where carried round Saint Paul's steeple;[3] and again three years afterwards, her image, if I clearly understand my author, was taken about the battlements of the same church with fine singing and many great lights.[4] But the most splendid show of this kind that took placei n Mary's time was the procession on Saint Clement's Day, exhibited in the streets of London; it consisted of sixty priests and clerks in their copes, attended by divers of the inns of court, who went next the priests, preceded by eighty banners and streamers, with the waits or minstrels of the city playing upon different instruments.[5]

WASSAILS.—Wassail, or rather the wassail bowl, which was a bowl of spiced ale, formerly carried about by young women on New-year's eve, who went from door to door in their several parishes singing a few couplets of homely verses composed for the purpose, and presented the liquor to the inhabitants of the house where they called, expecting a small gratuity in return. Selden alludes to this custom in the following comparison: " The Pope, in sending reliques to princes, does as wenches do by their wassails at New-year's tide, they present you with a cup, and you must drink of a slabby stuff; but the meaning is, you must give them monies ten times more than it is worth." The wassail is said to have originated from the words of Rowena, the daughter of Hengist; who, presenting a bowl of wine to Vortigern, the king of the Britons, said, Wæs hæl, or, Health to you, my lord the king; (Ƿæꞃ hæl laꞃoꝃ cẏnninᵹ). If this derivation of the custom should be thought doubtful, I can only say that it has the authority at least of antiquity on its side. The wassails are now (1800) quite obsolete; but it seems that fifty years back, some vestiges of them were remaining in Cornwall; but the time of their performance was changed to twelfth-day.[6]

---

[1] Perhaps it should be image, and resembled those commonly used in other pageants.

[2] *Nat. Hist. Oxford*, p. 343, and Blount's *Ancient Tenures*, p. 154. [3] *Eccl. Memoirs*, vol. iii. chap. xxxix. p. 51.

[4] *Ibid.* p. 309. [5] *Eccl. Memoirs*, iii. 377. [6] Heath's *Cornwall*, 445.

*The custom of carrying round the wassail bowl at Christmastide seems to have long ago disappeared, though the following verse is still (1902) occasionally sung by children when "carolling" in the west of England:

> "Wassail, wassail, all o'er the town,
> Our toast it is white, our ale it is brown;
> Our bowl it is made of the mapling tree,
> With the wassailing bowl we will drink unto thee."

*Wassailing the orchards may possibly survive in the apple-growing districts, but it seems doubtful if it is anything more than boys shouting rhymes round the trees on Twelfth Night. In the "fifties" of the last century, it was not infrequent on the Somersetshire side of Exmoor. A great bowl of cider was placed in one of the biggest trees after dark. When the verses of incantation had been sung, each of the company drank from the bowl, and the remainder was flung up into the tree.[1]

*A correspondent of *Notes and Queries* contributed the following in 1852:

"In this neighbourhood (Chailey, Sussex) the custom of wassailing the orchards still remains. It is called apple-howling. A troop of boys visit the different orchards, and encircling the apple-trees they repeat the following words:

> Stand fast root, bear well top,
> Pray the God send us a good howling crop.
> Every twig, apples big,
> Every bough, apples enow,
> Hats full, caps full,
> Full quarters, sacks full.

They then shout in chorus, one of the boys accompanying them on the cow's horn; during the ceremony they rap the trees with their sticks.[2]

*In Hazlitt's edition of Brand's *Popular Antiquities*, published in 1870, the shouting of the boys in the orchards is said to still prevail in several counties.

SHEEP-SHEARING AND HARVEST-HOME.—There are two feasts annually held among the farmers of this country, which are regularly made in the spring, and at the end of the summer, or the beginning of autumn, but not confined to any particular day. The first is the sheep-shearing, and the second the harvest-home; both of them were celebrated in ancient times with feasting and variety of rustic pastimes; at present (1800), excepting a dinner, or more frequently a supper, at the conclusion of the sheep-shearing and the harvest, we have little remains of the former customs.

The particular manner in which the sheep-shearing was celebrated in old time is not recorded; but respecting the harvest-home we meet with several curious observations. Hentzner, a foreign gentleman, who was in England at the close of the sixteenth century, and wrote an account of what he saw here,

---

[1] I have witnessed this in Luccombe parish on several occasions when a boy.—J. C. C.
[2] *Notes and Queries*, Ser. I. v. 293.

says, "as we were returning to our inn (in or near Windsor), we happened to meet some country people celebrating their harvest-home : their last load of corn they crown with flowers, having besides an image richly dressed, by which, perhaps, they signify Ceres; this they keep moving about, while the men and women, and men and maid-servants, riding through the streets in the cart, shout as loud as they can till they arrive at the barn." Moresin, another foreign writer, also tells us that he saw "in England, the country people bring home," from the harvest field, I presume he means, "a figure made with corn, round which the men and the women were promiscuously singing, and preceded by a piper or a drum."[1] "In the north," says Mr Brand, "not half a century ago, they used everywhere to dress up a figure something similar to that just described, at the end of harvest, which they called a kern-baby, plainly a corruption of corn-baby, as the kern, or churn supper, is of corn-supper."[2]

The harvest-supper in some places is called a mell-supper, and a churn-supper. Mell is plainly derived from the French word mesler, to mingle together, the master and servant promiscuously at the same table.[3] At the mell-supper, Bourne[4] tells us, "the servant and his master are alike, and every thing is done with equal freedom. They sit at the same table, converse freely together, and spend the remaining part of the night in dancing and singing, without any difference or distinction." "There was," continues my author, "a custom among the heathens much like this at the gathering of their harvest, when the servants were indulged with their liberty, and put upon an equality with their masters for a certain time. Probably both of them originated from the Jewish feast of tabernacles."[5]

WAKES.—The wakes, when first instituted in this country, were established upon religious principles, and greatly resembled the agapæ, or love feasts of the early Christians. It seems, however, clear that they derived their origin from some more ancient rites practised in the times of paganism. Hence Pope Gregory, in his letter to Melitus, a British abbot, says, "whereas the people were accustomed to sacrifice many oxen in honour of dæmons, let them celebrate a religious and solemn festival, and not slay the animals, diabolo, to the devil, but to be eaten by themselves, *ad laudem Dei*, to the praise of God."[6] These festivals were primitively held upon the day of the dedication of the church in each district, or the day of the saint whose relics were therein deposited, or to whose honour it was consecrated; for which purpose the people were directed to make booths and tents with the boughs of trees adjoining to the churches,[7] and in them to celebrate the feast with thanksgiving and prayer. In process of time the people assembled on the vigil, or evening preceding the saint's day, and came, says an old author, "to churche with candellys burnyng, and would

---

[1] *Præcedente tibicine aut tympano.* Moresin, *Deprav. Reliq. Orig.* in verbo vacina.
[2] Brand's *Observations* on Bourne's *Vulg. Antiq.* chap. xxxi. p. 303. *As to the occasional later survival of the "kern-baby," or "mell-doll" at harvest celebrations, see the various publications of the Folk-lore Society.
[3] *Ibid.*   [4] *Vulg. Antiq.* ut supra.   [5] *Ibid.*
[6] Bede, *Eccl. Hist.* lib. i. cap. 30.   [7] *Ibid.*

wake, and come toward night to the church in their devocion," [1] agreeable to the requisition contained in one of the canons established by King Edgar, whereby those who came to the wake were ordered to pray devoutly, and not to betake themselves to drunkenness and debauchery. The necessity for this restriction plainly indicates that abuses of this religious institution began to make their appearance as early as the tenth century. The author above cited goes on, "and afterwards the pepul fell to letcherie, and songs, and daunses, with harping and piping, and also to glotony and sinne; and so tourned the holyness to cursydness; wherefore holy faders ordeyned the pepull to leve that waking and to fast the evyn, but it is called vigilia, that is waking, in English, and eveyn, for of eveyn they were wont to come to churche." In proportion as these festivals deviated from the original design of their institution, they became more popular, the conviviality was extended, and not only the inhabitants of the parish to which the church belonged were present at them, but they were joined by others from the neighbouring towns and parishes, who flocked together upon these occasions, and the greater the reputation of the tutelar saint, the greater generally was the promiscuous assembly. The pedlars and hawkers attended to sell their wares, and so by degrees the religious wake was converted into a secular fair, and the time was spent in festive mirth and vulgar amusements.

SUNDAY FESTIVALS.—"In the northern parts of this nation," says Bourne, "the inhabitants of most country villages are wont to observe some Sunday in a more particular manner than the other common Sundays of the year, namely, the Sunday after the day of dedication of their church," that is, the Sunday after the saint's day to whom the church was dedicated. "Then the people deck themselves in their gaudiest clothes, and have open doors and splendid entertainments for the reception and treating of their relations and friends, who visit them on that occasion from each neighbouring town. The morning is spent for the most part at church, though not as that morning was wont to be spent, with the commemoration of the saint or martyr; nor the grateful remembrance of the builder and endower." Being come from church, the remaining part of the day is spent in eating and drinking, and so is a day or two afterwards, together with all sorts of rural pastimes and exercises, such as dancing on the green, wrestling, cudgelling, and the like. "In the northern parts, the Sunday's feasting is almost lost, and they observe only one day for the whole, which among them is called hopping, I suppose from the dancing and other exercises then practised. Here they used to end many quarrels between neighbour and neighbour, and hither came the wives in comely manner, and they which were of the better sort had their mantles carried with them, as well for show as to keep them from the cold at the table. These mantles also many did use at the churches, at the morrow masses, and at other times." [2]

CHURCH-ALES.—The Church-ales, called also Easter-ales, and Whitsun-

---

[1] Homily for the Vigil of St John Baptist. MS. Harl.   [2] *Antiq. Vulg.* chap. 30.

T

ales from their being sometimes held on Easter-Sunday, and on Whit-Sunday, or on some of the holidays that follow them, certainly originated from the wakes. The churchwardens and other chief parish officers, observing the wakes to be more popular than any other holidays, rightly conceived, that by establishing other institutions somewhat similar to them, they might draw together a large company of people, and annually collect from them, such sums of money for the support and repairs of the church, as would be a great easement to the parish rates. By way of enticement to the populace they brewed a certain portion of strong ale, to be ready on the day appointed for the festival, which they sold to them; and most of the better sort, in addition to what they paid for their drink, contributed something towards the collection; but in some instances the inhabitants of one or more parishes were mulcted in a certain sum according to mutual agreement, as we find by an ancient stipulation,[1] couched in the following terms: "The parishioners of Elvaston and those of Okebrook in Derbyshire agree jointly to brew four ales, and every ale of one quarter of malt between this, and the feast of Saint John the Baptist next comming, and every inhabitant of the said town of Okebrook shall be at the several ales; and every husband and his wife shall pay two pence, and every cottager one penny. And the inhabitants of Elvaston shall have and receive all the profits comming of the said ales, to the use and behoof of the church of Elvaston; and the inhabitants of Elvaston shall brew eight ales betwixt this and the feast of Saint John, at which ales the inhabitants of Okebrook shall come and pay as before rehearsed; and if any be away one ale, he is to pay at t'oder ale for both." In Cornwall the church-ales were ordered in a different manner; for there two young men of a parish were annually chosen by their foregoers to be wardens, "who, dividing the task, made collections among the parishioners of whatever provision it pleased them to bestow; this they employed in brewing, baking, and other acates, against Whitsontide, upon which holidaies the neighbours meet at the church-house, and there merely feed on their own victuals, contributing some petty portion to the stock. When the feast is ended, the wardens yield in their accounts to the parishioners; and such money as exceedeth the disbursements, is layed up in store to defray any extraordinary charges arising in the parish."[2]

To what has been said upon this subject, I shall only add the following extract from Philip Stubbs, an author before quoted, who lived in the reign of Queen Elizabeth, whose writings[3] are pointed against the popular vices and immoralities of his time. "In certaine townes," says he, "where drunken Bacchus bears swaie against Christmass and Easter, Whitsunday, or some other time, the churchwardens, for so they call them, of every parish, with the consent of the whole parish, provide half a score or twentie quarters of mault, whereof some they buy of the church stocke, and some is given to them of the

---

[1] Dodsworth's MSS., vol. 148, fol. 97.   [2] Carew's *Survey of Cornwall*, 1602, book i. p. 68.
[3] The *Anatomie of Abuses*, 1595.

parishioners themselves, every one conferring somewhat, according to his ability; which mault being made into very strong ale, or beer, is set to sale, either in the church or in some other place assigned to that purpose. Then, when this nippitatum, this huffe-cappe, as they call it, this nectar of life, is set abroach, well is he that can get the soonest to it, and spends the most at it, for he is counted the godliest man of all the rest, and most in God's favour, because it is spent upon his church forsooth. If all be true which they say, they bestow that money which is got thereby for the repaire of their churches and chappels ; they buy bookes for the service, cupps for the celebration of the sacrament, surplesses for Sir John, and such other necessaries," etc. He then proceeds to speak upon "the manner of keeping wakesses (wakes) in England," in a style similar to that above cited, and says they were "the sources of gluttonie and drunkenness"; and adds, "many spend more at one of these wakesses than in all the whole years besides."

The ingenious researcher into the causes of melancholy on the contrary thinks that these kinds of amusement ought not to be denied to the commonalty.[1] Chaucer, in the Ploughman's Tale, reproves the priests because they were more attentive to the practice of secular pastimes than to the administration of their holy functions, saying they were expert

> "At the wrestlynge and at the wake,
> And chefe chauntours at the nale,
> Markette beaters, and medlyng make,
> Hoppen and houters with heve and hale."

FAIRS.—The church-ales have long been discontinued ; the wakes are still kept up in the northern parts of the kingdom ; but neither they nor the fairs maintain their former importance ; many of both, and most of the latter, have dwindled into mere markets for petty traffic, or else they are confined to the purposes of drinking, or the displayment of vulgar pastimes. These pastimes, or at least such of them as occur to my memory, I shall mention here in a cursory manner, and pass on to the remaining part of this chapter. In a paper belonging to the *Spectator*[2] there is a short description of a country wake. "I found," says the author, "a ring of cudgel-players, who were breaking one another's heads in order to make some impression on their mistresses' hearts." He then came to "a foot-ball match," and afterwards to "a ring of wrestlers." Here he observes, "the squire of the parish always treats the company every year with a hogshead of ale, and proposes a beaver hat as a recompence to him who gives the most falls." The last sport he mentions is pitching the bar. But he might, and with great propriety, have added most of the games in practice among the lower classes of the people that have been specified in the foregoing pages, and perhaps the whistling match recorded in another paper. "The prize," we are told, "was one guinea, to be conferred upon the ablest whistler ; that is, he that could whistle clearest, and go through his tune without laughing, to which at

---

[1] Burton, *Anat. Melancholy*, part ii. sect. 2, cap. 4. [2] Vol. ii. No. 161, first printed 1711.

the same time he was provoked by the antic postures of a merry-andrew, who was to stand upon the stage, and play his tricks in the eye of the performer. There were three competitors; the two first failed, but the third, in defiance of the zany and all his arts, whistled through two tunes with so settled a countenance that he bore away the prize, to the great admiration of the spectators." This paper was written by Addison, who assures us he was present at the performance, which took place at Bath about the year 1708. To this he adds another curious pastime, as a kind of Christmas gambol, which he had seen also; that is, a yawning match for a Cheshire cheese: the sport began about midnight, when the whole company were disposed to be drowsy; and he that yawned the widest, and at the same time most naturally, so as to produce the greatest number of yawns from the spectators, obtained the cheese.

The barbarous and wicked diversion of throwing at cocks usually took place at all the wakes and fairs that were held about Shrovetide, and especially at such of them as were kept on Shrove-Tuesday. Upon the abolition of this inhuman custom, the place of the living birds was supplied by toys made in the shape of cocks, with large and heavy stands of lead, at which the boys, on paying some very trifling sum, were permitted to throw as heretofore; and he who could overturn the toy claimed it as a reward for his adroitness. This innocent pastime never became popular, for the sport derived from the torment of a living creature existed no longer, and its want was not to be compensated by the overthrowing or breaking a motionless representative; therefore the diversion was very soon discontinued.

At present, snuff-boxes, tobacco-boxes, and other trinkets of small value, or else halfpence or gingerbread, placed upon low stands, are thrown at, and sometimes apples and oranges, set up in small heaps; and children are usually enticed to lay out their money for permission to throw at them by the owners, who keep continually bawling, " Knock down one you have them all." A halfpenny is the common price for one throw, and the distance about ten or twelve yards.

The Jingling Match is a diversion common enough at country wakes and fairs. The performance requires a large circle, enclosed with ropes, which is occupied by as many persons as are permitted to play. They rarely exceed nine or ten. All of these, except one of the most active, who is the jingler, have their eyes blinded with handkerchiefs or napkins. The eyes of the jingler are not covered, but he holds a small bell in each hand, which he is obliged to keep ringing incessantly so long as the play continues, which is commonly about twenty minutes, but sometimes it is extended to half an hour. In some places the jingler has also small bells affixed to his knees and elbows. His business is to elude the pursuit of his blinded companions, who follow him, by the sound of the bells, in all directions, and sometimes oblige him to exert his utmost abilities to effect his escape, which must be done within the boundaries of the rope, for the laws of the sport forbid him to pass beyond it. If he be caught in the time allotted for the continuance of the game, the person who caught him claims the prize: if, on the contrary, they are not able to take him, the prize becomes his due.

Hunting the Pig is another favourite rustic pastime. The tail of the animal is previously cut short, and well soaped, and in this condition he is turned out for the populace to run after him; and he who can catch him with one hand, and hold him by the stump of the tail without touching any other part, obtains him for his pains.

Sack Running, that is, men tied up in sacks, every part of them being enclosed except their heads, who are in this manner to make the best of their way to some given distance, where he who first arrives obtains the prize.

Smock Races are commonly performed by the young country wenches, and so called because the prize is a holland smock, or shift, usually decorated with ribbands.[1]

The Wheelbarrow Race requires room, and is performed upon some open green, or in a field free from encumbrances. The candidates are all of them blindfolded, and every one has his wheelbarrow, which he is to drive from the starting-place to a mark set up for that purpose, at some considerable distance. He who first reaches the mark of course is the conqueror. But this task is seldom very readily accomplished; on the contrary, the windings and wanderings of these droll knights-errant, in most cases, produce much merriment.

The Grinning Match is performed by two or more persons endeavouring to exceed each other in the distortion of their features, every one of them having his head thrust through a horse's collar.

Smoking Matches are usually made for tobacco-boxes, or some other trifling prizes, and may be performed two ways: the first is a trial among the candidates who shall smoke a pipe full of tobacco in the shortest time: the second is precisely the reverse; for he of them who can keep the tobacco alight within his pipe, and retain it there the longest, receives the reward.

To these we may add the Hot Hasty-pudding Eaters, who contend for superiority by swallowing the greatest quantity of hot hasty-pudding in the shortest time; so that he whose throat is widest and most callous is sure to be the conqueror.

The evening is commonly concluded with singing for laces and ribbands, which divertisement indiscriminately admits of the exertions of both sexes.

BONFIRES.—It has been customary in this country, from time immemorial, for the people, upon occasions of rejoicing, or by way of expressing their approbation of any public occurrence, to make large bonfires upon the close of the day, to parade the street with great lights, and to illuminate their houses.

---

[1] *In Hazlitt's edition of Brand's *Popular Antiquities* (i. 119), it is stated that :—"The smock race, run by young girls in their chemises only, was formerly used on Ascension Day in the north of England. The sport, not a very delicate one, is described in the *Poetical Miscellanies*, published by Steele, 1714."

These spectacles may be considered as merely appendages to the pageants and pompous shows that usually preceded them; and they seem to have been instituted principally for the diversion of the populace. In the reign of Henry VII. a letter was sent from the king to the lord mayor and aldermen of London, commanding them to cause bonfires to be made, and to manifest other signs of rejoicing, on account of the espousals of his daughter Mary.[1] And within these forty years[2] bonfires continued to be made in London at the city expense, and in certain places at Westminster by order from the court, upon most of the public days of rejoicing; but of late they have been prohibited, and very justly, on account of the mischief occasioned by the squibs and crackers thrown about by the mob who assembled upon these occasions.

In London, and probably in other large cities, bonfires were frequently made in the summer season, not only for rejoicing sake, but to cleanse the air. Hence Stow, writing upon this subject, says, " In the months of June and July, on the vigils of festival days, and on the evenings also of those days after sunset, bonfires were made in the streets. The wealthy citizens placed bread and good drink upon the tables before their doors upon the vigil of the festival; but on the festival evening the same tables were more plentifully furnished with meat and drink, to which not only the neighbours but passengers were also invited to sit and partake, with great hospitality. These were called bonfires, as well of amity among neighbours that, being before at controversie, were, at these times, by the labour of others, reconciled, and made of bitter enemies loving friends; and also for the virtue that a great fire hath to purge the infection of the air."

*Bonfires were in very general use as a token of national rejoicing at the time of the restoration of the monarchy. In the Household Books of Sir Miles Stapleton of Carlton there are entries of village bonfire expenses on his various estates to celebrate the arrival of Charles II. The Northampton Borough Records contain various bonfire entries. The earliest is for the coronation of William of Orange, when 7s. was paid " for halfe c. of faggots." In 1690 12s. 6d. was spent on a bonfire to celebrate the battle of the Boyne; sixty faggots were consumed at the taking of Limerick in October of the following year, whilst the like number, together with a pitch barrel, were burnt on November 5th. On the evening of the Thanksgiving Day for victories in the Spanish Netherlands in 1693, the Northampton account include the following particulars :—

	S.	D.
Pd. John Bradshaw for five score Faggots	10	5
Pd. Thomas Dunckle for 12 c. of woode	12	0
Pd. Wilby for an Oyll Barrell on Thanksgiving night to place on a pole .		0

The taking of Namur, the peace of Ryswick, the coronation of Queen Anne, all Marlborough's victories, the union of England and Scotland, the peace of

---

[1] See the Introduction.   [2] Reckoning from 1800.

Utrecht, the coronation of George II., and "The Defeat of the Rebels" in 1746 were all celebrated by a great bonfire in the market place, round which ale was always drunk at the town's expense. There is no record of a bonfire for the victory of the Nile in 1798, but the Town Hall was illuminated with candles to celebrate the event.[1]

ILLUMINATIONS.—I do not know at what period illuminations were first used as marks of rejoicing. They are mentioned by Stow, in his *Survey of London*, who tells us that lamps of glass, to the amount of several hundreds, were hung upon branches of iron curiously wrought, and placed at the doors of the opulent citizens upon the vigils of Saint John the Baptist, and of Saint Peter and Saint Paul.[2] The historian does not speak of these lights as any novelty, neither is there any reason to conclude that similar illuminations were not made in other great towns and cities as well as in London; so that the custom might have been of long standing, and probably originated from some religious institution. But the lights, for I can hardly call them illuminations, most generally used at this period, were the cressets, or large lanthorns, which were carried in procession about the street. When they were laid aside, the windows of the houses were decorated with lighted candles, or the outsides ornamented with lamps of various colours, and placed in variety of forms; to which may be added, transparent paintings, inscriptions, and variety of other curious and expensive devices, that seem to be almost peculiar to the present age; and certainly the grand illuminations exhibited on the 23d of April 1789, upon the happy occasion of his Majesty's recovery, far surpassed, not only in the number and brilliancy of the lights, but also in the splendour and beauty of the transparencies, every other spectacle of the like kind that has been made in this country, or perhaps in any other.

FIREWORKS.—Fireworks, for pastime, are little spoken of previous to the reign of Elizabeth, and seem to have been of a very trifling nature. We are told, when Ann Bullen was conveyed upon the water from Greenwich to London, previous to her coronation, in 1533, "there went before the lord-mayor's barge, a foyste[3] for a wafter full of ordinance; in which foyste was a great red dragon, continually moving and casting forth wild-fire; and round about the said foyste stood terrible, monstrous, and wilde men, casting of fire, and making a hideous noise." This vessel with the fireworks, I apprehend, was usually exhibited when the lord mayor went upon the water, and especially when he went to Westminster on the lord mayor's day. Hence Morose, in Jonson's comedy of *The Silent Woman*, says to his visitors, who come with drums and trumpets, "Out of my dores, you sonnes of noise and tumult, begot on an ill May-day, or when the gally-foist is afloate to Westminster; a trumpetter could not be conceived till then."[4]

---

[1] Cox's *Northampton Borough Records*, ii. pp. 478-485.

[2] It does not appear that these lamps were made with glass of various colours, according to the present fashion (1800). I rather think this improvement is perfectly modern.

[3] A galley, or small vessel.

[4] Act iv. scene 2.

Among the spectacles prepared for the diversion of Queen Elizabeth at Kenelworth Castle in 1575, there were displays of fireworks, which are thus described by Laneham, who was present.[1] "On the Sunday night," says he, "after a warning piece or two, was a blaze of burning darts flying to and fro, beams of stars coruscant, streams and hail of fire sparks, lightnings of wildfire on the water; and on the land, flight and shot of thunderbolts, all with such continuance, terror, and vehemence, the heavens thundered, the waters surged, and the earth shook." Another author, Gascoyne, speaks thus: "On the Sunday were fireworks showed upon the water, passing under the water a long space; and when all men thought they had been quenched, they would rise and mount out of the water again and burne furiously until they were utterlie consumed."[2] On the Thursday following, according to Laneham, "there was at night a shew of very strange and sundry kinds of fireworks compelled by cunning to fly to and fro, and to mount very high into the air upward, and also to burn unquenchable in the water beneath." And again, sixteen years afterwards, the same queen was entertained by the earl of Hertford at Elvetham in Hampshire, and after supper there was a grand display of fireworks, preceded by "a peale of one hundred chambers, discharged from the Snail Mount"; with "a like peale discharged from the ship Isle, and some great ordinance withal. Then was there a castle of fireworkes of all sorts which played in the fort; answerable to that there was, at the Snail Mount, a globe of all manner of fireworkes, as big as a barrel. When these were spent there were many running rockets upon lines, which passed between the Snail Mount and the castle in the fort. On either side were many fire-wheeles, pikes of pleasure, and balles of wildfire, which burned in the water."

*EARLY BOOKS ON FIREWORKS.—Considerable attention was given in England to the manufacture of fireworks in the sixteenth and seventeenth centuries. *The Arte of Warre*, by Nicholas Machiavell, was first set forth in English, by Peter Whitehouse, in 1560. To this Whitehouse published a supplement in 1562, the concluding part of which deals with "fireworks," but chiefly from a military standpoint, such as "Howe to make certayn fyreworkes to tye to the poinctes of pykes or horsemen-staves." Some of his receipts, however, were equally applicable for peaceful displays. The treatise was reprinted in 1573 and 1588.

*In 1588 Cyprian Lucar translated the *Three Bookes of Colloquies* on the art of gunnery, written by Nicholas Tartaglia in Italian and dedicated to Henry VIII. To the original work Lucar added a considerable appendix, a large portion of which relates to "fireworks," though the term was used by him to denote warlike "Fireworkes which may be shotte out of great Peeces of Artillerie or throne out of men's handes"—or "divers sortes of Fireworkes, which being shotte in a darke night out of a morterpeece . . . will give so great a light that you may discerne by the same light whether or no any

---

[1] Nichols's *Progresses of Elizabeth*, vol. i.   [2] *Princely Pleasures at Kenelworth Castle*, p. 62.

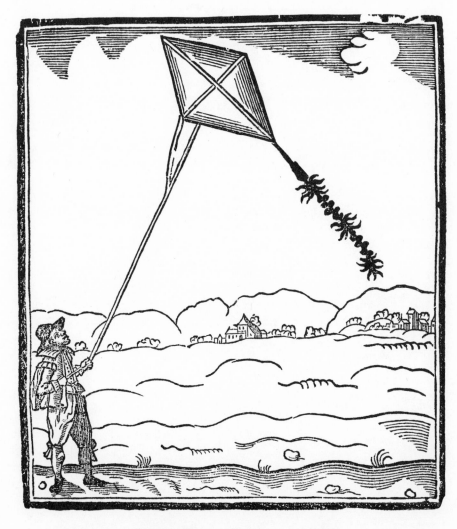

The Fiery Drake or Kite

enemies are in or neare unto that place." But numbers ninety to ninety-three of Lucar's short chapters deal with fireworks that may be used in " triumphes." The last of these chapters is concerned with the making of " Rockettes or Squibbes, which being throne up into the ayre wil cast foorth flames of fire, and in coming downe towards the ground will shew like starres falling from heaven."

*The Gunner, "written by Robert Norton, one of his Majesties Gunners and Engineers," and printed in 1628, shows that considerable advance had been made in the art of artificial fireworks for triumphs and displays. Full directions are given for the making of rockets, coloured fires, serpents, " shewers of gold," elaborate wheels, and set pieces such as castles "with 4 Towers and 4 Curtins and a Cavalaria or domineering Turret in the midst." Chapter seventy-seven deals with " How to make flying Dragons and Rockets that will runne upon a Lyne and returne againe, and of Nocturnall Combates in Fireworkes."

*A " Fier Drake" or Fiery Kite.—In 1634 John Bate put forth the first edition of his *Mysteries of Nature and Art* in four parts, the second of which, covering pages 79 to 116, is entitled " The composing of all manner of Fier-Works for Triumph and Recreation." The numerous illustrations and descriptions show that this art had by that date attained to considerable proportions and displayed much ingenuity. One of the most curious cuts is that which represents a man flying a " Fier Drake," which was a kite with crackers for the tail, reproduced on plate thirty-six. It has usually been stated that kites were not introduced into Europe, or at all events into England, from the East, until early in the eighteenth century; but this picture of a kite proves that it was not only in use but well known early in the seventeenth century. The name kite, taken from the bird, had not however been then given to this flying machine.[1]

Fireworks on Tower Hill, at Public Gardens, and in Pageants.—It was customary, in my memory, for the train of artillery annually to display a grand firework upon Tower Hill on the evening of his Majesty's birthday. This spectacle has been discontinued for several years in compliance with a petition for that purpose made by the inhabitants on account of the inconveniences they sustained thereby.

Fireworks were exhibited at Marybone Gardens while they were kept open for public entertainment; and about five-and-twenty years ago,[2] Torre, a celebrated French artist, was employed there, who, in addition to the usual displayment of fire-wheels, fixed stars, figure pieces, and other curious devices, introduced pantomimical spectacles, which afforded him an opportunity of bringing forward much splendid machinery, with appropriate scenery and stage decoration, whereby he gave an astonishing effect to his performances, and excited the admiration and applause of the spectators. I particularly remember

[1] See "Kite" in next chapter.   [2] Reckoning from 1800.

two, the Forge of Vulcan, and the Descent of Orpheus to Hell in search of his wife Eurydice. The last was particularly splendid : there were several scenes, and one of them supposed to be the Elysian fields, where the flitting backwards and forwards of the spirits was admirably represented by means of a transparent gauze artfully interposed between the actors and the spectators.

Fireworks have for many years been exhibited at Ranelagh Gardens ; they are now (1800) displayed occasionally at Vauxhall ; and, in an inferior style, at Bermondsey Spa.

*The current advertisements of the illuminations and fireworks at Ranelagh Gardens in the eighteenth century are sufficiently curious to warrant the insertion of two of them as specimens. The following is an advertisement at the beginning of the season of 1764 :—

"This Evening at Ranelagh, besides the customary entertainment and a superb Firework in a stile which has been once already honoured with universal applause, will be exhibited a grand transparent view of the following scenes as large as life and under separate arches.

"Poetry, Music, Painting, Architecture—and on a large Obelisk fifty feet high—erected over the Pediment of the great arch at the end of the Canal— three Medalions finely illuminated—the one a crown, the other a plume of feathers, and the third a mitre, alluding to his Majesty, the Prince of Wales, and the Bishop of Osnaburgh with other Prospects, which the Proprietors from the very favourable reception hitherto given to their additional exhibitions, flatter themselves will be equally worthy of public approbation."

*A much more elaborate advertisement, of the same year, appeared in the daily press for the last time of the opening of the Gardens for that season :—

"The music composed by Mr Handel for the grand Firework of 1748 will be performed in the new orchestra lately erected in the Garden which will be elegantly illuminated.

" *The order of firing.*

"First Firing.—1. Eight half-pound Sky-Rockets. 2. Two Tourballoons. 3. Two-air-Balloons. 4. A new piece of three Vertical Wheels with brilliant and white fires intersecting each other. 5. A Pyramid of twenty-one Boxes and Chinese Fires. 6. A Horizontal and vertical Wheel illuminated. Second Firing.—7. Eight half-pound Sky-Rockets. 8. Two Tour-balloons. 9. Two air-Balloons. 10. A regulation Piece of three mutations : first, a brilliant Wheel illuminated ; second, a Sun and Glory ; third, Six Branches representing Ears of Corn. 11. A new Piece with a Vertical Brilliant Wheel and yellow fires in the Centre and eight Turilloni Wheels at the extreme. 12. A regulating piece of three mutations : first, a Brilliant Wheel illuminated ; second, a fixed Sun ; third, a Brilliant Star with eight points. Third Firing.—13. Eight half-pound Sky-Rockets. 14. Two Tour-balloons. 15. Two-air-balloons. 16. A large new piece : first, a large Brilliant Wheel moved by four fires illuminated

Pageantry.

in the centre with tires of various colours; second, a large Brilliant Sun whose rays extend 50 feet. 17. A large horizontal Wheel moved by six fires, with six vertical Wheels and a globe illuminated. 18. A Piece called the Fort, with brilliant Fountains, Roman Candles and Chinese Fires. 19. Twelve Water Rockets. 20. A grand Buffette of three mutations extending across the Canal, consisting of illuminated Wheels, Palm Branches, Fire-Trees of Chinese Fires, and six pont d'argette. 24. Twelve air-balloons."

At the bottom of the thirty-seventh plate is one of the *Green Men* flourishing his fire club, which is taken from Bate's treatise on fireworks issued in 1634. At the top of the same plate is a Wild Man or Woodwose or Wodehouse, a character very common and popular in the pageants of former times. It was in a dress like this, I suppose, that Gascoyne appeared before Queen Elizabeth in 1575, as already narrated. The figure itself is taken from a ballad, in black letter, entitled "The mad, merry pranks of Robin Good Fellow." Bishop Percy, probably with great justice, supposes it to have been one of the stage-disguisements for the representation of this facetious spirit.

CHAPTER IV

Popular manly Pastimes imitated by Children—Horses—Racing and Chacing—Wrestling and other Gymnastic Sports —Marbles and Span-counter—Tops, etc.—The Devil among the Tailors—Even or Odd—Chuck-halfpenny— Duck and Drake—Baste the Bear—Hunt the Slipper, etc.—Sporting with Insects—Kites—Windmills— Bob-cherry — Hoodman-blind — Hot-cockles — Cock-fighting — Anonymous Pastimes — Mock Honours at Boarding-schools—Houses of Cards—Questions and Commands—Handy-dandy—Snap-dragon—Push-pin— Crambo—Lotteries—Creag—Queke-board, and other minor games.

POPULAR MANLY PASTIMES IMITATED BY CHILDREN.—Most of the popular pastimes mentioned in the preceding pages were imitated by the younger part of the community, and in some degree, at least, became the sports of children. Archery, and the use of missive weapons of all kinds, were formerly considered as an essential part of a young man's education; for which reason the bow, the sling, the spear, and other military instruments, were put into his hands at a very early period of his life; he was also encouraged in the pursuit of such sports as promoted muscular strength, or tended to make him acquainted with the duties of a soldier. When the bow and the sling were laid aside in favour of the gun, prudence naturally forbad the putting an instrument of so dangerous a nature into the hands of children; they however provided themselves a substitute for the gun, and used a long hollow tube called a trunk, in which they thrust a small pointed arrow, contrived to fit the cavity with great exactness, and then blowing into the trunk with all their might, the arrow was driven through it and discharged at the other end by the expansion of the compressed air. Sometimes pellets of clay were used instead of the arrows. Dr Johnson in his Dictionary, under the article trunk, has this quotation from Ray: "In a shooting trunk, the longer it is to a certain limit, the swifter and more forcibly the air drives the pellet." The trunks were succeeded by pot-guns made with hollow pieces of elder, or of quills, the pellets being thrust into them by the means of a ramrod. These were also called pop-guns; and perhaps more properly, from the popping noise they made in discharging the pellets. Big bouncing words are compared to pot-gun reports in a comedy called *The Knave in Graine*, printed in 1640.[1]

HORSES.—Most boys are exceedingly delighted with riding, either on horses or in carriages, and also upon men's shoulders, which we have already seen to be a very ancient sport; and I trust there are but few of my readers who have not seen them with a bough or a wand substituted for a horse, and highly pleased in imitating the galloping and prancing of that noble animal. This is an amusement of great antiquity, well known in Greece; and if report speaks truth, some of the greatest men have joined in it, either to relax the

Garrick's Collection, G. vol. ii.

vigour of their own minds for a time, or to delight their children. The Persian ambassadors found Agesilaus, the Lacedemonian monarch, employed in this manner.[1] Socrates also did the same, for which it seems his pupil Alcibiades used to laugh at him.[2] If we turn to the eighteenth plate we shall see two boys, each of them having two wands, the one serves for a horse, and the other for a spear, and thus equipped they are justing together. Again upon the fourteenth plate a boy is mounted upon a wooden horse, drawn by two of his companions, and tilting at the quintain; and here we may remark that the bohourts, the tournaments, and most of the other superior pastimes have been subjected to youthful imitation, and that toys were made on purpose to train up the young nobility in the knowledge and pursuit of military pastimes. Nay, some writers, and not without the support of ancient documents, derive the origin of all these splendid spectacles from the sportive exercises of the Trojan boys.

RACING AND CHACING.—Contending with each other for superiority in racing on foot is natural to children; and this emulation has been productive of many different amusements, among which the following seem to be the most prominent.

Base, or Prisoners' Bars, is described in a preceding part of this work.

Hunt the Fox.—In this game one of the boys is permitted to run out, and having law given to him, that is, being permitted to go to a certain distance from his comrades before they pursue him, their object is to take him if possible before he can return home. We have the following speech from an idle boy in *The longer thou livest the more Fool thou art*, an old comedy, written towards the close of the sixteenth century:[3]

> "And also when we play and hunt the fox,
> I outrun all the boys in the schoole."

Hunt the Hare is the same pastime under a different denomination.

Harry-racket, or Hide and Seek, called also Hoop and Hide; where one party of the boys remain at a station called their home, while the others go out and hide themselves; when they are hid one of them cries hoop, as a signal for those at home to seek after them. If they who are hidden can escape the vigilance of the seekers and get home uncaught, they go out to hide again; but so many of them as are caught, on the contrary, become seekers, and those who caught them have the privilege of hiding themselves.

*There are various references to the common sport of Hide and Seek, usually under the title *All-hid*, in late Elizabethan and Stuart days. It is thus referred to in Decker's *Satiromastix*:—"Our unhandsome-faced poet does play at Bo-peep with your Grace, and cries All-hid, as boys do."

Thread the Tailor's Needle.—In this sport the youth of both sexes

---

[1] Plut. in Apophthegm. Laced. et Ælian. Var. Hist. lib. xii. cap. 15. Val. Max. lib. viii. cap. 8.
[3] Garrick's Collect. I. vol. xviii.

frequently join. As many as choose to play lay hold of hands, and the last in the row runs to the top, where passing under the arms of the two first, the rest follow : the first then becoming the last, repeats the operation, and so on alternately as long as the game continues.

Cat after Mouse; performed indiscriminately by the boys and the girls. All the players but one holding each other's hands form a large circle ; he that is exempted passes round, and striking one of them, immediately runs under the arms of the rest; the person so struck is obliged to pursue him until he be caught, but at the same time he must be careful to pass under the arms of the same players as he did who touched him, or he forfeits his chance and stands out, while he that was pursued claims a place in the circle. When this game is played by an equal number of boys and girls, a boy must touch a girl, and a girl a boy, and when either of them be caught they go into the middle of the ring and salute each other ; hence is derived the name of kiss in the ring.

Barley-brake.—The excellency of this sport seems to have consisted in running well.

*Barley-brake is supposed to have its name from being originally played in a field amid the barley mows or small stacks, one of which was fixed on as the goal, whilst another was the prison or (as usually termed in this pastime) the "hell." In Sir Philip Sidney's *Arcadia*, Herrick's *Hesperides*, and Suckling's poems there are accounts of this game, all of which refer to the "hell." Barley-brake is also several times named in Massinger's plays. The game much resembled a certain form of Prisoners' Base. In the Tragedy of Hoffmann, 1632, the two games are named together as though equivalents :—

"I'll run a little course at Base, or Barley-brake."

Puss in the Corner.—A certain number of boys or girls stand singly at different distances ; suppose we say for instance one at each of the four corners of a room, a fifth is then placed in the middle; the business of those who occupy the corners is to keep changing their positions in a regular succession, and of the out-player, to gain one of the corners vacated by the change before the successor can reach it : if done he retains it, and the loser takes his place in the middle.

Leap Frog.—One boy stoops down with his hands upon his knees and others leap over him, every one of them running forward and stooping in his turn. The game consists in a continued succession of stooping and leaping. It is mentioned by Shakspeare in King Henry the Fifth ; "If I could win a lady at leap-frog, I should quickly leap into a wife" : by Jonson in the comedy of Bartholomew Fair, "A leap-frogge chance now" ; and by several other more modern writers.

WRESTLING AND OTHER GYMNASTIC SPORTS.—To the foregoing pastimes we may add Wrestling, which was particularly practised by the boys in the counties of Cornwall and Devon.   Upon the sixth plate we find two lads contending for mastery at this diversion.

Hopping and standing upon one leg are both of them childish sports, but at the same time very ancient, for they were practised by the Grecian youth ; one they called *akinetinda*,[1] which was a struggle between the competitors who should stand motionless the longest upon the sole of his foot; the other denominated *ascoliasmos*, was dancing or hopping upon one foot,[2] the conqueror being he could hop the most frequently, and continue the performance longer than any of his comrades ; and this pastime is alluded to by the author of the old comedy, *The longer thou livest the more Fool thou art*, wherein a boy boasting of his proficiency in various school games, adds,

> " And I hop a good way upon my one legge."

Among the school-boys in my memory there was a pastime called Hop-Scotch,[3] which was played in this manner : a parallelogram about four or five feet wide, and ten or twelve feet in length, was made upon the ground and divided laterally into eighteen or twenty different compartments, which were called beds ; some of them being larger than others.   The players were each of them provided with a piece of a tile, or any other flat material of the like kind, which they cast by the hand into the different beds in a regular succession, and every time the tile was cast, the player's business was to hop upon one leg after it, and drive it out of the boundaries at the end where he stood to throw it : for, if it passed out at the sides, or rested upon any one of the marks, it was necessary for the cast to be repeated.   The boy who performed the whole of this operation by the fewest casts of the tile was the conqueror.

Skipping.—This amusement is probably very ancient.   It is performed by a rope held by both ends, that is, one end in each hand, and thrown forwards or backwards over the head and under the feet alternately.   Boys often contend for superiority of skill in this game, and he who passes the rope about most times without interruption is the conqueror.   In the hop season, a hop-stem stripped of its leaves is used instead of a rope, and in my opinion it is preferable.

Trundling the hoop is a pastime of uncertain origin, but much in practice at present, and especially in London, where the boys appear with their hoops in the public streets, and are sometimes very troublesome to those who are passing through them.

Swimming, sliding, and of late years skating, may be reckoned among the boys' amusements ; also walking upon stilts, swinging, and the pastime of the meritot and see-saw, or tetter-totter, which have been mentioned already, together with most of the games played with the ball, as well as nine-pins and skittles.

---

[1] Joan. Meursi, de Lud. Græc.   [2] Pollux, lib. ix. cap. 7.
[3] *The second half of the name of this undying game comes from *scotch*, an incised line or scratch.

MARBLES AND SPAN-COUNTER.—Marbles seem to have been used by the boys as substitutes for bowls, and with them they amuse themselves in many different manners. I believe originally nuts, round stones, or any other small things that could be easily bowled along, were used as marbles. Those now played with seem to be of more modern invention. It is said of Augustus when young, that by way of amusement he spent many hours in playing with little Moorish boys with nuts.[1] The author of one of the Tatlers calls it "a game of marbles not unlike our common taw."[2]

Taw, wherein a number of boys put each of them one or two marbles in a ring and shoot at them alternately with other marbles, and he who obtains the most of them by beating them out of the ring is the conqueror.

Nine holes; which consists in bowling of marbles at a wooden bridge with nine arches. There is also another game of marbles where four, five, or six holes, and sometimes more, are made in the ground at a distance from each other; and the business of every one of the players is to bowl a marble by a regular succession into all the holes, which he who completes in the fewest bowls obtains the victory.

Boss out, or boss and span, also called hit or span, wherein one bowls a marble to any distance that he pleases, which serves as a mark for his antagonist to bowl at, whose business it is to hit the marble first bowled, or lay his own near enough to it for him to span the space between them and touch both the marbles; in either case he wins, if not, his marble remains where it lay and becomes a mark for the first player, and so alternately until the game be won.

Span-counter is a pastime similar to the former, but played with counters instead of marbles. I have frequently seen the boys for want of both perform it with stones. This sport is called in French tapper, a word signifying to strike or hit, because if one counter is struck by the other, the game is won.

*The following is a list of the present (1902) best known marble games: —Bounce About, Bounce Eye, Conqueror, Die Shot, Fortifications, Handers, Increase Pound, Knock Out, Long Taw, Picking the Plums, Pyramid, Rising Taw, Spanners, Three Holes, and Tip-Shears.

TOPS, ETC.—THE DEVIL AMONG THE TAILORS.—The top was used in remote times by the Grecian boys. It is mentioned by Suidas, and called in Greek $\tau \rho o \chi o \varsigma$, and in Latin turbo. It was well known at Rome in the days of Virgil,[3] and with us as early at least as the fourteenth century, when its form was the same as it is now, and the manner of using it can admit of but little if any difference. Boys whipping of tops occur in the marginal paintings of the MSS. written at this period.[4] It was probably in use long before.

In a manuscript at the Museum[5] I met with the following anecdote of Prince Henry, the eldest son of James I., and the author assures us it is

---

[1] Sueton., in Vita Aug. cap. 83.
[3] The poet has drawn a simile from this pastime. Æneid, vii. 378.
[4] An example of this is given at the bottom of plate eleven.

[2] No. 112.

[5] Harl. Lib. No. 6391.

perfectly genuine;[1] his words are these: "The first tyme that he the prince went to the towne of Sterling to meete the king, seeing a little without the gate of the towne a stack of corne in proportion not unlike to a topp wherewith he used to play; he said to some that were with him, 'loe there is a goodly topp'; whereupon one of them saying, 'why doe you not play with it then?' he answered, 'sett you it up for me and I will play with it.'"

*In Northbrooke's *Treatise against Dicing, etc.*, printed in 1579, the young are urged to follow Cato's advice, namely, "playe with the Toppe and flee Dice-playing."

We have hitherto been speaking of the whip-top; for the peg-top, I believe, must be ranked among the modern inventions, and probably originated from the tee-totums and whirligigs, which seem all of them to have some reference to the tops, saving only that the usage of the tee-totum may be considered as a kind of petty gambling, it being marked with a certain number of letters: and part of the stake is taken up, or an additional part put down, according as those letters lie uppermost. The author of *Martin Scriblerus* mentions this toy in a whimsical manner: "He found that marbles taught him percussion, and whirligigs the axis and peritrochia, and tops the centrifugal motion." When I was a boy the tee-totum had only four sides, each of them marked with a letter; a T for take all; an H for half, that is of the stake; an N for nothing; and a P for put down, that is, a stake equal to that you put down at first. Toys of this kind are now made with many sides and letters.

There is a childish pastime which may well be inserted here, generally known by the ridiculous appellation of the Devil among the Tailors; it consists of nine small pins placed like skittles in the midst of a circular board, surrounded by a ledge with a small recess on one side, in which a peg-top is set up by means of a string drawn through a crevice in the recess; the top when loosed spins about among the pins and beats some, or all of them, down before its motion ceases; the players at this game spin the top alternately, and he who first beats down the pins to the number of one-and-thirty is the conqueror. This game, I am told, is frequently to be seen at low public-houses, where many idle people resort and play at it for beer and trifling stakes of money.

Even or Odd—Chuck-halfpenny—Duck and Drake.—Even or Odd is another childish game of chance well known to the ancients, and called in Greek Αρτιαζειν, and in Latin *par vel impar*.

The play consists in one person concealing in his hand a number of any small pieces, and another calling even or odd at his pleasure; the pieces are then exposed, and the victory is decided by counting them; if they correspond with the call, the hider loses; if the contrary, of course he wins. The Grecian boys used beans, nuts, almonds, and money; in fact anything that can be easily concealed in the hand will answer the purpose.

Cross and Pile is mentioned some pages back. Here we may add Chuck-

---

[1] Harl. Lib. No. 6391.

U

farthing, played by the boys at the commencement of the last century; it probably bore some analogy to pitch and hustle. There is a letter in the *Spectator* supposed to be from the father of a romp, who, among other complaints of her conduct, says, " I catched her once at eleven years old at chuck-farthing among the boys." [1] I have seen a game thus denominated played with half-pence, every one of the competitors having a like number, either two or four, and a hole being made in the ground with a mark at a given distance for the players to stand, they pitch their halfpence singly in succession towards the hole, and he whose halfpenny lies the nearest to it has the privilege of coming first to a second mark much nearer than the former, and all the halfpence are given to him; these he pitches in a mass towards the hole, and as many of them as remain therein are his due; if any fall short or jump out of it, the second player, that is, he whose halfpenny in pitching lay nearest to the first goer's, takes them and performs in like manner; he is followed by the others so long as any of the half-pence remain.

Duck and Drake, is a very silly pastime, though inferior to few in point of antiquity. It is called in Greek, Εποστρακισμος,[2] and was anciently played with flat shells, which the boys threw into the water, and he whose shell rebounded most frequently from the surface before it finally sunk, was the conqueror. With us a part of a tile, a potsherd, or a flat stone, are often substituted for the shells.

To play at ducks and drakes is a proverbial expression for spending one's substance extravagantly. In the comedy called Green's *Tu Quoque*, one of the characters, speaking of a spendthrift, says, " he has thrown away as much in ducks and drakes as would have bought some five thousand capons."

*In Butler's *Hudibras* occur the lines :

> " What figur'd slates are best to make,
> On watery surface Duck or Drake."

BASTE THE BEAR—HUNT THE SLIPPER, ETC.—Baste, or buffet the bear with hammer and block, are rather appendages to other games than games by themselves, being punishments for failures, that ought to have been avoided; the first is nothing more than a boy couching down, who is laden with the clothes of his comrades and then buffeted by them; the latter takes place when two boys have offended, one of which kneeling down bends his body towards the ground, and he is called the block; the other is named the hammer, and taken up by four of his comrades, one at each arm and one at each leg, and struck against the block as many times as the play requires.

Hunt the Slipper.—In this pastime a number of boys and girls indiscrimin-ately sit down upon the ground in a ring, with one of their companions standing on the outside; a slipper is then produced by those seated in the ring, and passed about from one to the other underneath their clothes as briskly as possibly, so as to prevent the player without from knowing where it is; when

---

[1] Vol. vi. No. 466. [2] Pollux, lib. ix. cap. 7.

Childrens Games.

he can find it, and detain it, the person in whose possession it was, at that time, must change place with him, and the play recommences.

Shuttle-cock has been spoken of in a former chapter; an ancient representation of the game is given upon the thirty-eighth plate.

Sporting with Insects.—On the thirty-eighth plate we see a boy playing with some large insect to which is fastened a string or thread. It is from a manuscript of early fourteenth century date.[1]

This barbarous sport is exceedingly ancient. We find it mentioned by Aristophanes in the comedy of *The Clouds*.[2] It is called in the Greek Μηλολονθη, rendered in the Latin scarabæus, which seems to have been the name of the insect. But the Grecian boys were less cruel in the operation than those of modern times, for they bound the thread about the legs of the beetle, instead of thrusting a pin through its tail, as is the custom of English boys with cockchafers. We are also told that the former frequently amused themselves in the same manner with little birds, substituted for the beetles.[3]

The Kite is a paper machine well known in the present day, which the boys fly into the air and retain by means of a long string. It received its denomination from having originally been made in the shape of a bird called a kite. Paper kites are not restricted to any particular form; they appear in a great diversity of figures, and not unfrequently in the similitude of men and boys. I have been told, that in China the flying of paper kites is a very ancient pastime, and practised much more generally by the children there than it is in England. From that country perhaps it was brought to us, but the time of its introduction is uncertain.

*In the Oxford Dictionary, the earliest references to *Kite*, as applied to the toy from its hovering in the air like the bird, is from Butler's *Hudibras* (1664):

> "As a Boy one night did flie his Tarsel of a Kite,
> The strangest long-wing'd Hawk that flies."

It was evidently well known in England, though not by that name, in 1634, when John Bate gave directions for flying a kite to carry fireworks, "raising it against the wind in an open field." Two lively cuts are given of it (one is reproduced on plate thirty-six), with directions how to make it, but no name is assigned to the ærial machine.[4]

The Paper Windmill, which appears upon the thirty-eighth plate, is taken from a painting which is nearly five hundred years old; though it differs very little in its form from those used by the children at present.

Bob-Cherry.—This is "a play among children," says Johnson, "in which the cherry is hung so as to bob against the mouth," or rather so high as to oblige them to jump in order to catch it in their mouth, for which reason the candidate is often unsuccessful. Hence the point in the passage which Johnson

[1] Roy. Lib. No. 2, B. vii.   [2] Act ii. scene the last.   [3] Pollux, lib. ix. cap. 7.
[4] Bate's *Mysteries of Nature and Art*, pp. 100-102.

quotes from Arbuthnot. "Bob-cherry teaches at once two noble virtues, patience and constancy; the first in adhering to the pursuit of one end, the latter in bearing a disappointment."

At the bottom of the thirty-eighth plate we see a sport of this kind of fourteenth century date, where four persons are playing, but the object they are aiming at is much larger than a cherry, and was probably intended to represent an apple.[1] "It was customary," we are told by Mr Brand, on the eve of All-Hallows, for the young people in the north to dive for apples, or catch at them when stuck at one end of a kind of hanging beam, at the other extremity of which is fixed a lighted candle, and that with their mouths, only having their hands tied behind their back."[2]

HOODMAN BLIND—HOT COCKLES.—*Hoodman Blind*, more commonly called Blind Man's Buff, is where a player is blinded and buffeted by his comrades until he can catch one of them, which done, the person caught is blinded in his stead. This pastime was known to the Grecian youth, and called by them Μυια χαλκι.[3] It is called Hoodman's Blind because the players formerly were blinded with their hoods. In the *Two Angry Women of Abington*, a comedy, this pastime is called the Christmas-sport of Hobman-Blind.

The manner in which Hoodman Blind was anciently performed with us appears from three different representations, given upon the fortieth plate, all from the same Bodleian MS.

The players who are blinded have their hoods reversed upon their heads for that purpose, and the hoods of their companions are separately bound in a knot to buffet them.

*Gay says concerning this pastime:

> "As once I played at Blindman's Buff, it hapt
> About my Eyes the Towel thick was wrapt.
> I miss'd the Swains, and seized on Blouzelind,
> True speaks that antient Proverb, 'Love is blind.'"

Hot Cockles, from the French hautes-coquilles, is a play in which one kneels, and covering his eyes lays his head in another's lap and guesses who struck him. Gay describes this pastime in the following lines:

> "As at Hot Cockles once I laid me down,
> And felt the weighty hand of many a clown,
> Buxoma gave a gentle tap, and I
> Quick rose, and read soft mischief in her eye."

"The Χυτρινδα, of the Grecians," says Arbuthnot, "is certainly not our hot cockles, for that was by pinching, not by striking"; but the description of the chytrinda, as it is given by an ancient writer, bears little or no resemblance to the game of hot cockles, but is similar to another equally well known with us, and called frog in the middle. The chytrinda took place in this manner :—A

---

[1] Roy. Lib. No. 2, B. vii.   [2] Addition to Bourne's *Vulg. Antiq.*   [3] Pollux. lib. ix. cap. 7.

Hoodman blind.

single player, called χοτρα, kotra, and with us the frog, being seated upon the ground, was surrounded by his comrades who pulled or buffeted him until he could catch one of them; which done the person caught took his place, and was buffeted in like manner.[1] I scarcely need to add, that the frog in the middle, as it is played in the present day, does not admit of any material variation. There was another method of playing this game, according to the same author; but it bears no reference to either of those above described. Upon the thirty-ninth plate the reader will find both the pastimes above mentioned, which are also taken from the Bodleian MS.

COCK-FIGHTING.—I have already spoken at large upon cock-fighting, and throwing at cocks. I shall only observe that the latter, especially, was a very common pastime among the boys of this country till within these few years; and at the bottom of the thirty-fourth plate we have the copy of a curious delineation, which I take to represent a boyish triumph.

The hero supposed to have won the cock, or whose cock escaped unhurt from the danger to which he had been exposed, is carried upon a long pole by two of his companions; he holds the bird in his hands, and is followed by a third comrade, who bears a flag emblazoned with a cudgel, the dreadful instrument used upon these occasions. The original painting occurs in the manuscript mentioned in the preceding article.

ANONYMOUS PASTIMES—MOCK HONOURS AT BOARDING SCHOOLS.—Upon the forty-first plate are two representations of a pastime, the name of which is unknown to me; but the purpose of it is readily discovered.

At the top we see a young man seated upon a round pole which may readily turn either way, and immediately beneath him is a vessel nearly filled with water; he holds a taper in each hand, and one of them is lighted, and his business, I presume, is to bring them both together and light the other, being careful at the same time not to lose his balance, for that done, he must inevitably fall into the water. This is from the Bodleian MS.

In the representation in the centre of the same plate, taken from a beautiful fourteenth century book of prayers in the possession of Mr F. Douce, the task assigned to the youth is still more difficult, as well from the manner in which he is seated, as from the nature of the performance, which here he has completed: that is, to reach forward and light the taper held in his hands from that which is affixed to the end of the pole, and at a distance from him.

At the bottom of the plate, also from a drawing in Mr Douce's book of prayers, is a representation of two boys seated upon a form by the side of a water-tub; both of them with their hands fixed below their knees, and one bending backwards in the same position, intending, I presume, to touch the water without immerging his head, or falling into it, and afterward to recover his position.

This trick being done by the one was probably imitated by the other; I speak however from conjecture only. If it be necessary for him who stoops to

[1] Pollux, lib. ix. cap. 7.

take any thing out of the water, the pastime will bear some analogy to the just-mentioned diving for apples.

In some great Boarding Schools for the fair sex, it is customary, upon the introduction of a novice, for the scholars to receive her with much pretended solemnity, and decorate a throne in which she is to be installed, in order to hear a set speech, addressed to her by one of the young ladies in the name of the rest. The throne is wide enough for three persons to sit conveniently, and is made with two stools, having a tub nearly filled with water between them, and the whole is covered by a counterpane or blanket, ornamented with ribands and other trifling fineries, and drawn very tightly over the two stools, upon each of which a lady is seated to keep the blanket from giving way when the new scholar takes her place ; and these are called her maids of honour. The speech consists of high-flown compliments calculated to flatter the vanity of the stranger ; and as soon as it is concluded, the maids of honour rising suddenly together, the counterpane of course gives way, and poor miss is unexpectedly immerged in the water.

HOUSES OF CARDS—QUESTIONS AND COMMANDS—HANDY-DANDY—SNAP-DRAGON—PUSH-PIN—CRAMBO—LOTTERIES.—*Building* of houses *with cards*, and such like materals, is a very common amusement with children, as well as drawing little waggons, carts, and coaches ; and sometimes boys will harness dogs and other animals, and put them to their waggons in imitation of horses. Something of this kind is alluded to by Horace, who writes thus in one of his satires :[1]

"Ædificare cassus, plostello adjungere mures."
To build little houses, and join mice to the diminutive waggons.

Questions and Commands, a childish pastime, which though somewhat different in the modern modification, most probably derived its origin from the basilinda, Βασιλινδα,[2] of the Greeks, in which we are told a king, elected by lot, commanded his comrades what they should perform.

Handy-dandy, a "play," says Johnson, "in which children change hands and places"; this seems clear enough according to the following quotation from Shakspeare (*King Lear*, act iv. sc. 6): "See how yond justice rails upon yond simple thief! hark in thine ear; change places; and handy-dandy which is the justice and which is the thief"; to which is added another from Pope's *Scriblerus*, "neither cross and pile, nor ducks and drakes, are quite so ancient as handy-dandy."

*A truer explanation is that it is a childish play, still (1902) practised, wherein something is placed or shaken in one or other of the hands, and a guess is made as to the hand in which it is retained.

Snap-dragon. This sport is seldom exhibited but in winter, and chiefly at Christmas-time ; it is simply heating of brandy or some other ardent spirit in a dish with raisins ; when the brandy being set on fire, the young folks of both

---

[1] Lib. ii. sat. 3, line 47.   [2] Pollux, lib. ix. cap. 7.

Hot Cockles &c.

sexes standing round it pluck out the raisins, and eat them as hastily as they can, but rarely without burning their hands, or scalding their mouths.

Push-pin is a very silly sport, being nothing more than simply pushing one pin across another.

Crambo is a diversion wherein one gives a word, to which another finds a rhyme; this, with other trifling amusements, is mentioned in a paper belonging to the *Spectator*.[1] "A little superior to these," that is, to persons engaged in cross-purposes, questions, and commands, "are those who can play at crambo, or cap-verses." In this we trace some vestige of a more ancient pastime, much in vogue in the fourteenth and fifteeth centuries, called the A B C of Aristotle; which is strongly recommended by the author, one "Mayster Bennet," not only to children, but also to persons of man's estate, if ignorant of letters. The proem to this curious alliterative alphabet is to the following effect:

"Whoever will be wise and command respect let him learn his letters, and look upon the A B C of Aristotle, against which no argument will hold good: It is proper to be known by clerks and knights, and may serve to amend a mean man, for often the learning of letters may save his life. No good man will take offence at the amendment of evil, therefore let every one read this arrangement and govern himself thereby.

Hearkyn and heare every man and child how that I begynne.

A to amerous, to adventurous ; ne anger the too much.
B to bold, to busy, and board thou not too brode.
C to curtes, to cruel, and care not too sore.
D to dull, to dreadfull, and drynk thou not too oft.
E to ellynge, to excellent ; ne to ernestfull neyther.
F to fierce, ne to familier but frendely of chere.
G to glad, to gloryous, and gealosy thou shalt hate.
H to hasty, to hardy, ne too hevy yn thyne herte.
 I to jettyng, to jangling, and jape not too oft.
K to keeping, to kynd, and ware knaves taches among.
L to lothe, to lovyng, to lyberall of goods.
M to medlurs, to merry but as manner asketh.
N to noyous, to nyce, ne nought to newe fangle.
O to orpyd, to oveyrthwarte, and othes do the hate.
P to preysyng, to prevy, ne peerless with prynces.
Q to queynt, to querelous, but quyene wele thee may.
R to ryetous, to revelyng, ne rage not too moche.
S to strange, ne to stervyng, nor stare not too brode.
T to taylours, ne tayle wyse, for temperance yt hatyth.
V to venemous, to violent, and waste nat too mych.
W to wyld, ne wrathful, and ne too wyse deeme thee.
For fear of a fall.
A measurable meane way is best for us all.   Explicit."[2]

Lotteries, in which toys and other trifling prizes were included to be drawn for by children, were in fashion formerly, but by degrees, and especially since

[1] Vol. vii. No. 504.   [2] Harl. MSS. 1706, 541.

the establishment of the State Lottery, they have been magnified into a dangerous species of gambling, and are very properly suppressed by the legislature. They were in imitation of the State Lotteries, with prizes of money, proportionable to the value of the tickets, and drawn in like manner. These lotteries are called little goes.

CREAG—QUEKE-BOARD, AND OTHER MINOR GAMES.—*Creag* is a game mentioned in a computus dated the twenty-eighth of Edward I., A.D. 1300, and said to have been played by his son Prince Edward.

*It was a form of nine pins.

Queke Borde, with *Hand yn and Hand oute*, are spoken of as new games, and forbidden by a statute made in the seventeenth year of Edward IV.

*The former of this was probably a gambling game with a checker or chess board.

White and Black, and also *Making and Marrying* are prohibited by a public act established in the second and third years of Philip and Mary.

Figgum is said to be a juggler's game in the comedy of *Bartholomew Fayre* by Ben Jonson, acted in 1614; to which is added, "the devil is the author of wicked Figgum." In the same play mention is made of crambe (probably crambo), said to be "another of the devil's games."

Mosel the Pegge, and playing for the hole about the churchyard, are spoken of as boys' games, in a comedy called *The longer thou livest the more Fool thou art*, written in the reign of Queen Elizabeth.

*This may have been the same as *Pegge Morrell*, described on page 258.

Penny-Pricke appears to have been a common game in the fifteenth century, and is reproved by a religious writer of that period.[1]

*The game consisted in throwing at pence, which were placed on pieces of stick called holes, with a piece of iron. It is thus named in 1616:—

> "Their idle hours (I meane all houres beside
> Their hours to eatt, to drinke, drab, sleepe, and ride)
> They spend at shove-board, or at penny-pricke."[2]

Pick-point, Venter-point, Blow-point, and *Gregory*, occur in a description of the children's games in the sixteenth century.[3] Blow-point was probably blowing an arrow through a trunk at certain numbers by way of lottery. To these may be added another pastime, called *Drawing Dun out of the Mire*. Chaucer probably alludes to this pastime in the Manciple's Prologue, where the host seeing the cook asleep, exclaims, "Syr, what dunne is in the mire."

*Brand quotes the following lines from "Humors Ordinaire" (1600):—

> "At shove-groatt, Venter-point, or Bord and Pile,
> At leaping o'er a Midsummer Bone-fier,
> Or at the drawing Dun out of the myer."

[1] Harl. MS. 2391.　　　[2] Scot's *Philomythil.*　　　[3] Harl. MS. 2125.

Games unknown.

*It was a mere Christmas gambol with a great log of wood.[1]

Mottoes, *Similes*, and *Cross Purposes*, are placed among the children's games in a paper belonging to the *Spectator*.[2]   And the *Parson has lost his cloak*, in another, where a supposed correspondent writes thus : " I desire to know if the merry game of the parson has lost his cloak is not much in vogue amongst the ladies this Christmas, because I see they wear hoods of all colours, which I suppose is for that purpose." [3]

[1] *Hazlitt's edit. of Brand's *Popular Antiquities*, iii. 308.   [2] Vol. iii. No. 245.   [3] Vol. iv. 278.

INDEX

INDEX

Darts, 62
Datchet-mead races, 36
David, 59, 149, 237
D'Eu, Count, 81
Deddington, Oxfordshire, 110
Dee River, 77
Deer, 4, 17, 18, 19, 24, 195
Defence, science of, 210-215
Derby, 181, 226
Derbyshire, 12, 13, 16, 39, 55, 66, 68, 95, 97, 208, 228, 257, 274
Derrick, John, 101
Deserter acted, 200
Devonshire, 69, 93, 214, 303
—— Duke of, 209
Dice, l, 2, 86, 245, 246, 247
Digby, Everard, 74
Dijon, 124
Dillon, Viscount, 125
Diomedes, 250
Dio Nicæus, 1
Discus, 61
Doe. See Dee
Dogget's Coat and Badge, 78
Dogs, a ball of little dogs, 145, 199
—— of the Chase, 16, 17, 18
—— performing, 195, 196, 198, 199. See Hounds, etc.
Domino, 259, 260
Dorchester, 208
Dorking, 97, 232
Dorset, 15, 257
—— Duke of, 102
—— Marquis of, 85
Doublets, 248
Douce, Francis, 3
Doves, 30
Draughts, 255, 256
Drawing Dun out of the Mire, 312
Dresses, caparison of a hawk, 26
—— equipment for an archer, 48
—— hunting, 8, 9
—— Minstrels', 158, 159
Drury-lane, 143, 225
Dryden, 253
Dubois, 186
Duck-hunting, 227, 228
—— and Owl, 228
Ducks and Drakes, 306
Duffield, 228
Dumb Bells, 64
Dunghill dogs, 17
Dunstable, 130
Dunstan, St, 149
D'Urfey, 101
Durham, 14, 152, 164, 205, 257, 273
Dutch, 182, 189, 191
Dutch-Pins, 221

Eagles, 28, 29
Easter, 33, 108, 141, 165, 273, 274, 290
Eccles, 208
Edelswitha, 32
Edinburgh, 86, 99
Edgar, 2, 12, 77, 149
Edmund, King of East Angles, 23, 40
Edward the Confessor, 3, 13, 22, 27
—— I., 4, 7, 10, 16, 21, 100, 123, 161, 210, 260, 312
—— II., 11, 95, 100, 156, 159, 161, 171, 176, 187, 266
—— III., 12, 13, 28, 29, 34, 41, 43, 62, 63, 68, 94, 96, 97, 123, 138, 184, 202, 224, 271

Edward IV., 44, 47, 51, 84, 85, 101, 122, 137, 157, 160, 162
—— VI., 101, 179, 268, 278
Edwin, King of Northumberland, 39
Egbert, Archbishop, 2, 195, 236
Egerton, Sir P., 34
Egg dance, 185
Egypt, 255
Elizabeth, xxxix-xlii, 9, 19, 29, 35, 41, 54, 55, 64, 82, 83, 86, 92, 96, 110, 111, 127, 138, 140, 157, 171, 173, 176, 184, 185, 192, 203, 205, 206, 211, 220, 229, 230, 246, 261, 284, 290, 295, 296, 299, 312
—— daughter of Ed. I., 163
Elk, 11
Eltham, Hants, 46
Elvaston, 290
Elvetham, Hants, 82, 296
Ely, Bishop of, 28, 159
Elyot, Sir Thomas, 47, 62, 65, 96
Enfield Chase, 36
Engaine, Thomas, 12
E. O. tables, 246
Epiphany, 270
Erasmus, 62, 205
Esau, 40
Eslington, 15
Essex, 10, 12, 68, 93, 132, 258
Essex House, 87
Ethelbald, King of Mercia, 286
Ethelbert, King of Kent, 22
Ethelred the Unready, 2, 375
Eton, 82, 88, 102
Eubœa, 244, 250
Euston, Suffolk, 93
Evelyn, 76, 196, 197, 199, 207
—— Richard, 269
Even or Odd, 305
Evil Merodac, 250
Evreux, 40
Exeter, 84, 236
Exmoor, 16, 287, 230

Fairs, 291
Falcon, Falconer, Falconry, 21. See Hawking
Fantoccini, 146
Feathers, 48, 49
Fenchurch Street, 10, 85, 277
Fencing, 209-215
Ferguson, Chancellor, 64
Ferrers, George, 268
Ferrets, 7, 19
Festival of Fools, 271
Fiddlers, 158
Figgum, 312
Finsbury Fields, 57
Fireworks, 233, 295-299
Firmicus, Julius, 22
Fishing and Fowling, 30
Fitchat or Fitch, 11
Fitzstephen, 7, 9, 32, 40, 74, 75, 108, 114, 224, xx, xxviii
Five-Cards, 263
Fives, 81
Fletcher, 277
Flight, beasts of sweet and of stinking, 11, 12
Flora, 280
Foix, Earl of, 5, 163
Folejambe, Thomas, 13
Fool's dance, 183, 184
—— plough, 177
Football, 83, 93, 291

Foot racing, 65, 66, 67
—— standing on one, 303
Forcer, Francis, musician, 235
Forest, Sir William, 62
Four Corners, 221
—— Kings, 260
Foursome (Golf), 99
Fowling-piece, 25
Fowling and Fishing, 30
Fownes, Thomas, 15
Fox, 10, 12, 15, 18, 19, 20, 195, 301
—— and Geese, 257, 258
France and French, 5, 7, 11, 24, 27, 32, 41, 42, 44, 63, 81, 82, 83, 123, 140, 153, 205, 216, 223, 225, 250, 256, 259, 260, 264
Frederic Barbarossa, 22
Frederick, Prince of Wales, 89
French Billiards, 240
—— Draughts, 255
—— Ruff, 262
Friar Tuck, 278
Friars, 19
Froissart, 63, 124, 169, 179, 202
Frying-pan music, 238
Fulimart, 11

Gahorty, 36
Galway, 92, 97
Game laws, 2, 3, 28
Gaming, lii - liii, 219, 247, 260, 262
Gardens, Marybone, 29, 235
—— Paris Garden, 215, 216
—— Ranelagh, 231, 233, 295
—— Vauxhall, 78, 231-233, 298
Garnerin, 233
Garter, Order of, 123
Gascony, 10, 63
Gascoygne, Thomas, poet, 203, 299
Gaunt, John of, 124, 161, 208, 209
Geese, 19, 30
Genoese, 42
Gent, William Pearcey, 74
"Gentleman's Recreation, The," 20
Geoffry, a Norman, 130
George I., 10, 37, 213
—— II., 38, 183, 295
—— III., 295
Germans, Germany, 2, 21, 66, 75, 123, 126, 245, 264, 265
Gilbertines, 95
Gilds, xxxii-xxxv
Gleek, 262
Gleemen, 148, 149, 174, 209
Globe Tavern, near Hungerford-market, 146
Gloves, hawks', 27
Gloucester, 258
Gloucestershire, 42
Goats, 19
Goff, game of, 97
Goldfinches, 30
Goliath, 59
Gower, 253
Gray, George, fencer, 213
Gray's Inn, 72
Great Mell Fell, 16
Greeks, 61, 73, 75, 78, 224, 245, 250, 254, 266, 300, 303, 304, 305, 306, 307, 308
Greene, Gregorye, 211
Greenwich, 14, 46, 47, 85, 125, 136, 140, 176, 206, 278, 295
Gregory, Pope, 131, 288

INDEX

INDEX

x

Ref.
790
St927

89436

Reference